KANT'S
TRANSCENDENTAL
METAPHYSICS

Ridgeview Publishing Company Books by Wilfrid Sellars

Philosophical Perspectives: History of Philosophy (1977)

Philosophical Perspectives: Metaphysics and Epistemology (1977)

Naturalism and Ontology (1980)

Pure Pragmatics and Possible Worlds: The Early Essays of Wilfrid Sellars (1980)

The Metaphysics of Epistemology: Lectures by Wilfrid Sellars (1989)

Science, Perception and Reaity (1991)

Science and Metaphysics: Variations on Kantian Themes (1992)

Kant and Pre-Kantian Themes: Lectures by Wilfrid Sellars (2002)

Kant's Transcendental Metaphysics: Sellars' Cassirer Lectures Notes and Other Essays (2002)

Wilfrid Sellars Notre Dame Lectures 1969-1986

KANT'S

TRANSCENDENTAL

METAPHYSICS

Sellars' Cassirer Lectures Notes and Other Essays

Edited and Introduced by

Jeffrey F. Sicha

Ridgeview Publishing Company   Atascadero, California

Copyright © 2002
by Jeffrey F. Sicha
All rights reserved.
No part of this book may be reproduced
or utilized in any form or by any means,
electrical or mechanical, including
photocopying, recording or by any
informational storage or retrieval system,
without written permission from the
copyright owner.

Paper text: ISBN 0-924922-39-7
Cloth (Library edition): ISBN 0-924922-89-3

Published in the United States of America
by Ridgeview Publishing Company
Box 686
Atascadero, California 93423

Printed in the United States of America

To my wife,

Sadie Kendall

CONTENTS

	Page
Acknowledgments	7
Preface	8
Editor's Foreward	12
Contents of Introduction	15
Introduction	19
Bibliography of the introduction	305
Ontology, the A Priori and Kant (OAPK, 119)	307
Some Remarks on Kant's Theory of Experience (KTE, 67)	316
Metaphysics and the Concept of a Person (MP, 68)	333
On Knowing the Better and Doing the Worse (KBDW, 75)	363
Toward a Theory of the Categories (TTC, 77)	378
"...this I or he or it (the thing) which thinks..." (I, 81)	401
Berkeley and Descartes: Reflections on the Theory of Ideas (BD, 95)	428
Kant's Transcendental Idealism (KTI, 98)	474
The Role of Imagination in Kant's Theory of Experience (IKTE, 103)	492
Some Reflections on Perceptual Consciousness (SPRC, 106)	506
On Accepting First Principles (OAFP, 115)	533
Sellars' Cassirer Lectures Notes (CLN, 120)	565
The Philosophical Works of Wilfrid Sellars	565

ACKNOWLEDGMENTS

To *The Journal of Philosophy* for permission to reprint "Some Remarks on Kant's Theory of Experience," *The Journal of Philosophy* 64 (1967): 633-47.

To Yale University Press for permission to reprint "Metaphysics and the Concept of a Person," in *The Logical Way of Doing Things*, edited by Karel Lambert (Yale University Press, 1969): 219-52.

To *International Philosophical Quarterly* for permission to reprint "On Knowing the Better and Doing the Worse," *International Philosophical Quarterly*, 10 (1970): 5-19.

To University of Massachusetts Press for permission to reprint "Towards a Theory of the Categories," in *Experience and Theory*, edited by L. Foster and J.W. Swanson (University of Massachusetts Press, 1970): 55-78.

To The American Philosophical Association for permission to reprint "...this I or he or it (the thing) which thinks," the presidential address, American Philosophical Association (Eastern Division), for 1970, *Proceedings of the American Philosophical Association* 44 (1972): 5-31.

To Ohio State University Press for permission to reprint "Berkeley and Descartes: Reflections on the 'New Way of Ideas'" in *Studies in Perception: Interrelations in the History of Philosophy and Science*, edited by Peter K. Machamer and Robert G. Turnbull (Ohio State University Press, 1977): 259-311.

To University of Ottawa Press for permission to reprint "Kant's Transcendental Idealism" in *Proceedings of the Ottawa Congress on Kant in Anglo-American and Continental Traditions* edited by Pierre LaBerge (University of Ottawa Press, 1976): 165-181.

To Pennsylvania State University Press for permission to reprint "The Role of Imagination in Kant's Theory of Experience," in *Categories: A Colloquium*, edited by Henry W. Johnstone, Jr. (Pennsylvania State University Press, 1978): 231-45.

To Kluwer Academic Publishers for permission to reprint "Some Reflections on Perceptual Consciousness," in *Crosscurrents in Phenomenology (Selected Studies in Phenomenology and Existential Philosophy: No.7)*, edited by R. Bruzina and B. Wilshire (Kluwer Academic Publishers, 1978): 169-185.

PREFACE

In one respect, this volume, now entitled *Kant's Transcendental Metaphysics*, must be accounted a failure. It was intended to contain Sellars' Cassirer Lectures (given in 1979 at Yale University). The central cause of the failure is that Sellars died before finishing these lectures—indeed, even before really beginning the process of re-writing them. What was left to work with is his (handwritten) notes.

When I say "notes," I do mean just that. Apparently, Sellars spoke on many occasions with much less on paper in front of him than his audience would have imagined as they listened to his spoken, complete (and, in many cases, quite complex) sentences. Some paragraphs, particularly in the beginning of the Cassirer Lecture notes, consist of no more than a phrase stating the topic of the paragraph and a (sometimes not very readable) diagram. Sellars used his diagrams, not only as aids in explaining his views, but as guides for himself in delivering the paper.

So, no volume can contain Sellars' Cassirer Lectures: he never wrote them. Perhaps, that should have been that. But I did promise Wilfrid to get the lectures out. It is true, of course, that when I made that promise both he and I thought that *he* would be writing them. I was in a position, once he had died without doing the writing, to consider myself absolved from my promise. Yes—well, on the other hand, there did seem to be good reason to persevere.

Sellars was quite happy with the Cassirer Lectures. In fact, he went so far as to say that he thought he "really got Kant right this time." You need to understand what I took him to mean by this.

Sellars read Kant and thought about Kant's views all his life. In fact, he actually wore out two copies of *The Critique of Pure Reason*. (The older one, bought in the 30's when Sellars was at Oriel College, literally fell apart and was sent out by his wife, Susanna, for rebinding; the newer one, purchased in 1962, was well on the way to the same fate.) Both copies contain massive underlining, copious margin notes, and hundreds of references to other passages before and after a marked passage. Sellars published, all in all, several hundred pages on Kant and filled many pads (some the yellow, legal-sized he used for many years) with notes on Kant's work. In addition, it is clear that Sellars considered himself to be a modern defender of doctrines found in Kant. The remark that he "got it right" did not, in light of the above considerations, suggest to me that he had come to some entirely new construal of Kant. What he meant was that he had added refinements and further threads to a fabric on which he had long been working.

That, then, is the short story of how this volume came to be. It does not, however, explain some of its idiosyncrasies. For that, I must embark on a somewhat longer story.

In June (or, perhaps, early July) of 1990, I helped Susanna assemble the books and papers in Wilfrid's office at Pittsburgh. It was then that I discovered that I would not have anything more than the notes of the Cassirer Lectures (and a few other handwritten pads of the same period). Perhaps there is something more among his papers, but I could not find it then.

Obviously, I needed a plan. For me, part of that plan was decided before Wilfrid's death. The Cassirer Lectures, even had Sellars added quite a bit in re-writing his notes, would have been too short to constitute a reasonable volume. It occurred to me very early on that I should put the Cassirer Lectures together with Sellars' other post-*Science and Metaphysics* writings on Kant (and some other related papers from the same period). I was sure Wilfrid would agree since the other papers, written in the same period, would throw light on his developing views of Kant and thus on the Cassirer Lectures. I do think that I am right about this.

Another part of the plan was reached sometime shortly after that 1990 summer. The exact date is now unknown to me for the simple reason that all this is over a decade ago. Since the Cassirer Lectures notes were, in places, so incomplete, I concluded that the other papers would simply have to be used as a source to fill in the notes. I have literally pulled passages out the other papers (and also from *Science and Metaphysics*) and inserted them (in smaller type and with references) in paragraphs in the Cassirer Lectures. (This is especially the case at the beginning of the Cassirer Lectures where Sellars is "setting the stage" and therefore is reviewing what, from his point of view, are straightforward points.) Having confirmed that it was possible to find helpful passages, I resolved to go forward.

Even then I was not home free. There are places in the Cassirer Lectures where I simply had to add words, phrases and sometimes whole sentences. I have indicated these by (what I hope) is the simple and obvious device of using a san-serif type font whose general appearance is quite noticeably different from the type font of the text. (The Editorial Foreward explains, in more detail, all the devices that came to be utilized in the volume.)

Last (and perhaps least—I'll leave that to the reader), I decided to write an introduction which would attempt to state Sellars' position on Kant reasonably succinctly. (No doubt the reader of this Preface will have already discovered that I did not achieve that goal.) I also viewed it as of interest to consider some consequences of Sellars' account, consequences that he may, or may not, have himself considered.

By sometime in 1993, I had sufficiently regained my mastery of Wilfrid's hand to read all that I needed to read and to produce a working copy of the Cassirer Lectures notes. A few quandaries still remained, but I was confident that I could take care of them. By New Years 1999, the introduction was progressing, but had grown—what shall I say?—beyond my wildest dreams. Yes, at least that—still, I thought I saw the end. It was not to be.

Till then, my pace had been, to be complimentary, methodical. In my defense, from the end of 1991 to the end of 1999, I was the managing editor of a quarterly, *Noûs*; and from 1987, I was the publisher (till 1995) as well as the managing editor (till 2002) of an annual, *Philosophical Perspectives*.

But, as the joke goes, the light at the end of the tunnel turned out to be a train. Pedro Amaral, Sellars' last teaching assistant at Pittsburgh, informed me that he had transcribed (and recorded) Sellars' 1975 graduate lectures on Kant and other historical figures. No reader of that volume, *Kant and Pre-Kantian Themes*, can fail to see that no small amount of work went into it. Amaral had been so assiduous that, not only did we have the words, but we also had all the diagrams Sellars drew.

Despite the prospect of more work, I was not about to pass up such an opportunity. Yet, it did cross my mind that, never having heard Sellars' lectures on Kant, I might be surprised. What if I found my by now several hundred pages of introduction was in substantial disagreement with the lectures? I thought that unlikely to be so—I proved to be correct. Even worse, I reflected, was the other extreme: what if Wilfrid had, in effect, produced my introduction? Well, here, I was just lucky. There is some overlap between the introduction and the lectures, but since my introduction is directed to the papers that are in this volume, my introduction and his lectures diverge both in the choice of topics and in their organization and presentation. Of course, I do (though no doubt some will disagree) hold that it is all, at bottom, Sellars' view and so, in one way, agreement is part of the message.

I also got a gift: at one point, Amaral asks Sellars about "double affection". In the Cassirer Lectures notes, Sellars has an entry on that topic. But just an entry: it says "double affection". I was still mulling over what earlier writing to insert at that entry; his earlier remarks are to the point, but not all that long and the longest one is from "Some Remarks on Kant's Theory of Experience" (*KTE*, 67) which was published in 1967. Sellars' answer to Amaral's question came to the rescue. And as an extra bonus, a small part of his answer is a nearly verbatim quote from *KTE* (though Amaral says that Sellars did not have that essay with him to read from it). So, that passage from *Kant and Pre-Kantian Themes* appears in my introduction and a reader of the Cassirer Lectures notes can consult it at paragraph 741.

Thus, in 2002, Wilfrid is publishing two more works.

My thanks are due to many people. Of course, this project could not have gone forward at all without the help and support of Sellars' widow, Susanna Downie Felder. Charles Aston, the head of Special Collections of the Hillman Library at the University of Pittsburgh, and his associate, Jerry Heverly, showed great patience and restraint in allowing me the time I needed to work through Sellars' papers.

To Pedro Amaral, I owe great thanks for his work, judgment, and foresight and his comments on my introduction. I think all who have found Sellars' work important to them owe him thanks. Thanks go to Riitta Vepsalainen for the two computer drawn figures in my introduction. [Those of Sellars' figures included in this volume and not from *KPT*, I drew by hand. I find something appropriate in this, but there is no doubt that Riitta's artwork and Pedro's diagrams in *KPT* are very elegant and clear.]

To two colleagues, Daniel Sedey and Frank McGuinness, on whom I imposed for comments, goes credit for improving this volume. To others, Ronald McIntrye, James E. Tomberlin, and Takashi Yagisawa, go thanks for discussions that have helped shape my views (needless to say, not necessarily in ways they would approve). Finally, though I should like to find someone to take the blame for the shortcomings, I am afraid they must be laid to me.

EDITORIAL FOREWARD

Since most of organizational and editorial features of this volume were undertaken because of decisions made in editing the *Cassirer Lectures Notes* (*CLN*), I begin there.

As I mentioned in the Preface, I simply had to add passages from other of Sellars' works to supplement what are, in some cases, mere headings. These are typeset in a slightly smaller type with suitable references to show their origin.

Sellars had two pads in which he wrote his notes. In a side note, he referred to one of the pads as "I". It is this one I call "A" and, of course, the other I call "B". Sellars gave (not quite) each paragraph a number followed, sometimes, by a lower case letter. I have maintained all of this that I could, given a few problems. There are missing numbers, some re-numbering, and some duplication of content in paragraphs from the two manuscripts. Here is an example. The page of B finishing with (second) paragraph B20 is followed by another B page which has a note reading "in I 10" (meaning that it is page 10 of the first pad). Consequently, there is a page "10a" in part I (what I call "A") but no "10" and the original paragraph numbers in B fit with the last of "page 9f" in A which has paragraph 26f.

Basically, I decided that it would be best to indicate most of these editorial matters right where they occur in the notes. The major items needing prior notice are duplication and re-numbering.

Duplication: the paragraphs in the B manuscript numbered

B20 (the second one) through B32

appeared earlier intermixed with the paragraphs from the A manuscript numbered

A25 through A26f.

Since the duplication is not perfect, I sometimes have a part of an A paragraph and a part of B paragraph that are exact duplicates and parts that are not. At another place, because Sellars failed to number some paragraphs in A, I have interspersed them in B paragraphs.

Re-numbering: Sellars himself re-numbers

A26g through A26j   as   B33 through B36.

So, now, the next paragraph after A26f is A27. Then, in B, A26g appears re-numbered as B33 (=A26g).

Clearly I needed some simple device for making my editorial remarks identifiable. This need is made greater by having sentence fragments to complete and existing words in the manuscripts that I am not completely certain I have read correctly. All this I solved by using the sans serif font you are presently reading for my editorial remarks and additions. It stands out quite satisfactorily, but it is not as obtrusive as other devices I considered. Also in this type face are references in CLN to paragraphs in my introduction.

Once I decided to use the sans serif type in *CLN*, I found it convenient to continue with it in the other essays in the volume. So, even in these already published essays, you will see the occasional editorial point in sans serif type.

Besides correcting typographical errors in the other essays, I also numbered all the paragraphs in the essays which did not already have paragraph numbering. I thought of this as an easy way to solve any problems about references to the essays in the volume.

References to Sellars' other works is through the abbreviations appearing in the bibliography called "The Philosophical Works of Wilfrid Sellars" which is at the very end of the volume. Reference to anything but paragraphs (e.g., pages, sections) are so indicated. But if the work had paragraph numbers, they appear last in the reference without the word 'paragraph' preceding them. In addition, at the first occurrence of an abbreviation I append in parenthesis the number of that work in the bibliography. So, at first occurrence, a reference to paragraph 5 of chapter 3 of *Naturalism and Ontology* reads:

NAO (104), ch. 3, 5.

Another example:

EPM (31) in *SPR* (53), section 10

is a reference to section 10 of "Empiricism and the Philosophy of Mind" (31 in the bibliography) as reprinted in *Science, Perception and Reality* (53 in the bibliography).

References to works of authors other than Sellars are handled differently. For authors other than Kant, full references are given. At the end of the introduction is a bibliography of those works including works of Kant referred to in the introduction. To each of these works of Kant, I refer by a convenient abbreviation (along, of course, with the usual marginal numbering.)

Lastly, there is the question of references, in the introduction, to the introduction itself. Originally, I had imagined that sufficient sectioning and subsectioning would solve the problem. However, as the introduction became longer, I realized it was not enough (it got so that I couldn't find references by section).

In addition, it became clear that my scheme of organization unavoidably required me to cite earlier passages. As I explain in Part **I**, certain points get made in contexts which I try to make largely free of doctrines that are definitely Sellars' own and not Kant's. Then, after that first run through, they get another one with, shall I say, a full dose of Sellars. I didn't want to repeat the original discussion over again each time (though, in fact, there is some of that). Moreover, many of the earlier discussions contain many references, particularly to Kant, and I didn't want to have to repeat those too.

So, I numbered the paragraphs in the introduction. Then, to avoid using the word 'paragraph' or some abbreviation several hundreds of times, I decided to place these references *by themselves in parentheses* right within sentences. So, you find the following:

> **631.** I noted (201-4) that Sellars required a distinction between two senses of 'sensibility' and two senses of 'intuiting'. At the end of my treatment of sensory states (541-7), I cast these distinctions in the terminology of part **IV**. I restricted my use of the word 'sensibility' to that passive faculty, the affecting of which produces image-models (547) (with the help of the understanding, but sometimes without it (473, 544)).

All the numbers in this example are numbers of paragraphs within the introduction. In some small number cases, for the sake of sentence structure, I employ the word 'paragraph'. Finally, since I now had paragraph numbers, I refer to displayed items by their number and their paragraph (once I am in text after the paragraph in which the numbered item occurs). So,

> (446.TA4)   is   (TA4) in paragraph 446.

I probably should admit that, given the large number of references, my confidence that there are no typographical errors is not great. I have, however, done the best I could to make them accurate.

CONTENTS OF THE INTRODUCTION

Paragraph		Page
1	**I. Prologue: On reading Kant and Sellars**	19
1	A. The problem in general terms	19
11	B. An example	22
15	C. A small point	23
17	D. A special case	24
22	**II. A Look at the surface**	25
22	A. Transcendental Idealism	25
26	B. Some distinctions: ings versus eds	26
26	(I) REPRESENTINGS	26
38	(II) REPRESENTEDS	31
40	(III) REPRESENTEDS: "IDEAS" AND "CONTENT"	32
56	C. Back to Transcendental Idealism: Appearances as Representables	37
70	D. Things in Themselves	41
70	(I) THE EXEGETICAL PROBLEM	41
75	(II) TWO MORE THESES	43
80	(III) MORE TEXTUAL EVIDENCE AND RELATED CONSIDERATIONS	45
94	**III. "A Little Lower Layer"**	49
94	A. Concepts and Intuitions	49
94	(I) CONCEPTS	49
99	(II) INTUITIONS VERSUS CONCEPTS	50
104	(III) SOME COMPLICATIONS	51
107	(a) The term 'intuition' suffers from the '-ing-ed' ambiguity of all of Kant's terminology for representation.	52
108	(b) There are "inner" intuitings, a product of "inner sense", as well as "outer" intuitings, a product of "outer sense".	53
109	(c) There are both "pure" and "empirical" intuitings.	53
112	(d) There are concepts corresponding to (associated with?) all (most?) intuitions.	54
114	(e) Sensibility has both concepts and intuitions.	54
115	(f) Intellectual intuitions are possible.	54
116	(g) "All Sensible Intuitions are subject to the Categories" (B143).	55
121	B. Sellars' Account of Intuitions	57
121	(I) SELLARS ON INTUITIONS: STEP ONE	57
121	(a) Representings of this-suches	57
127	(b) Experiential derivation and intuitings	59
141	(c) Innateness, experiential derivation and rudimentary content	63
155	(d) Summary	68

16 Contents of the Introduction

157	(II) What Sellars' Account of Intuiting Is Not	69
166	(III) Does Sellars' Account Help with the Complications?	73
167	(a) The term 'intuition' suffers from the '-ing-ed' ambiguity of all of Kant's terminology for representation.	73
171	(b) There are "inner" intuitings, a product of "inner sense", as well as "outer" intuitings, a product of "outer sense".	74
182	(c) There are both "pure" and "empirical" intuitings.	77
190	(d) There are concepts corresponding to (associated with?) all (most?) intuitions.	80
201	(e) Sensibility has both concepts and intuitions.	83
205	(f) Intellectual intuitions are possible.	84
206	(g) "All Sensible Intuitions are subject to the Categories" (B143).	84
207	C. A Transcendental Logic: The Categories	84
207	(I) "To put it bluntly"	84
210	(II) They are "nothing but *forms of thought*" B305-6	86
215	(a) The table of judgments	87
217	(b) Not exactly THE categories	88
222	(III) A Metaphysical Deduction of Categories	91
222	(a) The forms of judging are the forms of thinking	91
227	(b) Step one: pure-pure categories	93
231	(c) A meta-logical point	95
238	(d) Category realism	98
244	(e) Step two: substance and causality	100
258	(f) Step three: kconcepts and intuitings	106
267	(g) Unity, apperception, and the forms of judging	109
275	(IV) A Transcendental Deduction of Categories	110
275	(a) 'Transcendental'? 'Deduction'? 'Possible experience'?	110
294	(b) The use in experience of the pure concepts of the understanding (B159)	116
294	(α) Two ways of having categorial structure	116
301	(β) Nature	119
308	(γ) An apperceptible synthetic unity	121
321	(c) Why the transcendental aesthetic is essential to the Sellarsian account	125
325	**IV. "Into the Heart"**	127
325	A. What does Kant Believe about Sensory States?	127
325	(I) Confusion amid the choices	127
325	(a) Are sensations spatial?	127
333	(b) Does matter have sensible qualities?	128
339	(II) A view no one ever held	131
346	B. What should Kant Believe about Sensory States?	134
346	(I) How to approach this question	134

348	(II) THE MANIFEST IMAGE AND THE SCIENTIFIC IMAGE	134
355	(III) SENSIBLE QUALITIES	136
355	(a) What are they not?	136
363	(b) What are they?	138
365	(α) Incompatibilities of determinates	139
370	(β) Generic incompatibility within families	140
372	(γ) Intensive magnitude (degree)	141
377	(δ) "filling" of space and togetherness	142
381	(ε) Causal relevance	144
401	(IV) SENSE IMAGE-MODELS: THE AESTHETIC	149
401	(a) Sellars' strategy	149
416	(b) Their analogical account as properties	154
416	(α) "Verb" theories of sensory states	154
422	(β) Concept construction analogically	156
441	(γ) The causal theme	161
454	(δ) Spatial connectedness	166
464	(ε) Image-models and synesthesia	169
471	(ζ) Back to the causal theme: a house	172
490	(η) Image-models and time	179
514	(V) IS THE AESTHETIC A "THEORY"?	187
527	(VI) IS THE "MYTH OF THE GIVEN" BACK?	191
527	(a) Qualia, phenomenal individuals, and their ilk	191
536	(b) What is the "myth of the given"?	193
541	(VII) GIVENNESS AND REPRESENTING: ARE IMAGE-MODELS GIVERS?	195
541	(a) The "blindness" of the image-models	195
551	(b) The "ontological impotence" of image-models	198
572	(VIII) GIVENNESS AND (ORDINARY) APPEARING: ARE IMAGE-MODELS GIVEN?	204
572	(a) Perceiving, ostensible perceiving, and appearing within the aesthetic	204
583	(b) Perceiving and appearing without the aesthetic	209
583	(α) A "vulgar" account of appearing	209
588	(β) "Noticing" sensory states: what Sellars is not denying	211
595	(γ) Cartesianism again	213
609	(IX) IMAGE-MODELS IN THE SCIENTIFIC IMAGE	218
625	**V. "Nothing of Him that doth Fade, but doth Suffer a Sea-change into Something Rich and Strange"**	223
625	*A. More Kantian Advantages from a Sellarsian Aesthetic*	223
625	(I) REMEMBRANCE OF THINGS ALMOST FORGOTTEN: AN EXEGETICAL POINT	223
631	(II) A REVIEW OF THE RELEVANT TERMINOLOGY	225

635	(III) ON THE RELATION OF THE SENSIBILITY AND THE UNDERSTANDING	228
657	B. *Thinkers and Perceivers in Themselves and as Part of Nature*	234
657	(I) THE SELF IN ITSELF VERSUS THE PHENOMENAL SELF	234
657	*(a) The self in itself*	234
667	*(b) Once more: "existence in thought"*	236
674	*(c) The doctrine of content as part of transcendental psychology*	238
679	*(d) A suggestion for Kant concerning the temporal*	239
687	(II) APPERCEPTION AGAIN	242
687	*(a) Perceiving the categorial*	242
687	(α) *What is perceptible for Kant?*	242
695	(β) *Back to "perceiving as"*	245
702	*(b) Apperceiving and the categorial*	248
702	(α) *apperception: purity, necessity, and spontaneity*	248
712	(β) *representing the self as a thinker*	250
722	(γ) *representing the self as a perceiver*	253
737	C. *Transcendental Idealism again*	257
737	(I) DOUBLE AFFECTION AND TRANSCENDENTAL APPEARING	257
737	*(a) "simple correlatives" (KPT, ch. 10, 8)*	257
742	*(b) Why not?*	263
754	(II) THE REFUTATIONS OF IDEALISM	266
754	*(a) Some obvious points*	266
765	*(b) Something a little different*	269
778	(III) THE UNDERSTANDING AS THE FACULTY OF RULES	274
778	*(a) An entering wedge: rules of criticism*	274
784	*(b) Rules of criticism as essential to thinking*	277
793	*(c) Rules of criticism and inferring*	280
811	*(d) Material rules of inferring*	285
818	*(e) The possibility of experience and the possibility of objects of experience (A158/B197)*	287
830	*(f) Practical reason, rules, and inductive inquiry*	291
841	*(g) Apperception and rules: the Platonic Strata*	296

Introduction

I. Prologue: On reading Kant and Sellars
A. The problem in general terms

1. Numerous problems beset a philosopher who wishes to write about Kant and even more beset one who wants to write about Sellars on Kant. If the quantity and scope of disagreements among Kant scholars are evidence, we must certainly incline to the view that Kant's writings are not only difficult, but capable of strikingly different interpretations by competent philosophers who have expended no small amount of effort. It would not be much of an exaggeration to say that Kant scholars disagree about almost everything.[1] They disagree about

(i) the meaning of Kant's philosophical terminology;
(ii) the central theses Kant wishes to defend;
(iii) the errors, confusions and "ambivalences"[2] in Kant's work;
(iv) Kant's arguments (both with regard to premisses and conclusions); and
(v) Kant's final word on philosophical positions (e.g., realism, idealism, rationalist metaphysics, skepticism).

My first problem, then, was what to do about the large body of Kant scholarship and the disagreements found therein. This problem solved itself by default.
2. I wrote this introduction to deal with Sellars on Kant, and only thereby with Kant. Nothing—certainly not an "introduction"—could be long enough to encompass an account of Sellars' writings on Kant, of other philosophers' writings on Kant, and of Kant's own writings. So, most of this introduction belongs to Sellars. Note 'most': I cannot avoid citing Kant. The textual sources of Sellars' understanding of Kant must be buttressed by reference to *CPR* ('*CPR*' is short for '*Critique of Pure Reason*') and other of Kant's works. It also seemed less than helpful to include no discussion of others' views on Kant and on Sellars. Here, however, I limit myself

---

[1] For a readable and penetrating account of some of these disagreements, see Karl Ameriks, "Recent Work on Kant's Theoretical Philosophy," *American Philosophical Quarterly*, 19, 1, January, 1982 which concentrates on the distinction between appearances and things in themselves and the transcendental deduction of the categories. Americks also includes an elaborate bibliography.
[2] I take this term from p. 39 of the subsection entitled "Kant's fundamental ambivalence" in Paul Guyer, *Kant and the Claims of Knowledge* (Cambridge University Press, 1987).

to very recent publications.³

3. Sellars provided a different sort of problem. It would, I think, be fair to say that Sellars usually tried, in his writings on historical figures, to do three things:

> (1) propound and defend his interpretation of a philosopher's writings, an interpretation which, among other things, explicates claims which appear to us unintelligible or obscure;
>
> (2) set out his interpretation so that is both accessible to modern readers and gives some insight into what is right and what is wrong in the philosopher's views;
>
> (3) explain his own position through agreement with or divergence from the views of the historical figure as these views have been formulated in his interpretation.

These three goals make Sellars' writings on historical figures more "philosophy" than "history" of philosophy.

4. That Sellars was aware of the consequences of these goals is shown in the Preface (written in 1978) to *Naturalism and Ontology* (*NAO*, 103).⁴ In talking about whether the contents of *NAO* will strike readers as distinctively new, he says:

> ... A reader who has struggled through some of my recent papers is bound to have a sense of *deja vu*. The same is true of the reader who has with difficulty penetrated the Kantian wrappings of a preceding attempt at synthesis.² [footnote 2 reads: *Science and Metaphysics*, London, 1968.] The present book may also be of assistance to the student of Kant who finds it difficult to penetrate the Sellarsian wrappings of Kantian themes in *SM*, but who nevertheless senses that the latter might throw some light on the *Critique*.

Though I cannot avoid dealing with both the Sellarsian and Kantian "wrappings", I try to state Sellars' views on Kant with little reference (at least at the time of stating them) to other of Sellars' views. When I undertake such discussion, I try to distinguish clearly what is Sellars and what is Sellars on Kant. For several reasons, this policy creates somewhat artificial organization and some repetition, especially since many points are put first in a preliminary fashion, and then, again later on, in a more developed and Sellarsian form.

5. One source of artificiality arises from Sellars' being a defender of Kant. Sup-

---

³ Examples of this policy include comments on John McDowell's "Having the World in View: Sellars, Kant, and Intentionality" (The Woodbridge Lectures 1997, *The Journal of Philosophy*, XCV, 9, September, 1998) and the use of positions and claims suggested by the writings of Dennett, Lycan, and Tye as contrasts for Sellars' views.

⁴ At the first mention of a work by Sellars, I append the number of that work in the bibliography of Sellars' works that appears at the end of this book.

pose you had said to Sellars: "You have a great many distinctive views of your own. Your problem is one many philosophers have had with historical writings: you want to read your views into the historical text." Sellars' response to this challenge would be complicated.

6. To begin with, he would point out that his own views grew while reading Kant. So, to a certain degree, he came to hold some of his views because, so he believes, he found them in Kant or Kant suggested something to him that, once reformulated, became his own. From his vantage point, he is, in part, just giving credit to Kant when, he thinks, credit is due.

7. Second, he was quite prepared to deal with Kantian text line by line and to supply passages supporting his interpretation. Sellars, however, was not inclined to imagine that incompatible interpretations can be sorted out just by looking at the text. Almost everyone who reads Kant is prepared, at some time or other, to find certain passages to be more important than others, or to be more obscure and confused than others, or to be outright errors of Kant's (that is, errors that Kant would have, or should have, agreed were errors). So, Sellars would have argued, *the building of interpretations of historical texts cannot be done apart from doing philosophy*. Relegation of a passage to the less important, to the obscure and confused, or to the erroneous is a judgment depending on substantive philosophical claims, not merely on purely textual claims. One's own philosophical views might make it impossible to find any even halfway satisfactory reading of a passage.

8. In addition, Sellars would press you to explain what Kant meant by the many philosophical terms which form Kant's technical vocabulary. Especially this task, Sellars would tell you, requires you to rely on your own philosophical predilections. Only your own philosophical work and judgment supply terminology, which you understand, to give the needed explanations.

9. Another source of artificiality concerns the point, just made, about Kant's technical jargon. Dealing with this problem is the main means by which Sellars achieves a great deal of goals (3.1), (3.2) and (3.3).[5] Bluntly put, Sellars was eager to explicate Kant's technical jargon, so far as it is possible, in contemporary terms. Such explication is a giant step in one's interpretation of Kant. In this introduction, then, none of these explications is "Sellars-free".

10. In sum, then, my attempt, in this introduction, to separate "Sellars on Kant" from "Sellars on Sellars" is an attempt to separate items which have some business being together.

---

[5] This is the first example of my device of referring to displayed material by paragraph number: '(3.1)' is to be read '(1) in paragraph 3'.

B. An example

11. Since I believe that explicating Kantian jargon is a central part of Sellars' strategy for achieving goals (3.1), (3.2) and (3.3), I want to provide an "argument" (speaking loosely) for the importance of doing that. Imagine listening to a conversation between two Kant scholars, A and B, in which they disagree about "intuitions" and the "categories". Everything these scholars say in this imaginary dialog has been said by someone somewhere.

> A: Kant tells us that sensibility is that faculty by which objects are "given" to us through intuition and that objects are "thought" by the understanding which uses concepts (A19/B33). Since intuitions belong to the sensibility and concepts to the understanding and since categories are (pure) concepts, intuitions as such cannot contain or in any way have a structure involving the categories, or, for that matter, any concepts.
>
> B: The passage you cite is at A19/B33. *CPR* goes to A856/B884. You can't defend your thesis by a passage that occurs before other crucial topics, like judging, are taken up. You can discover just how much difference this makes by looking at a well-known later passage in which Kant says that cognition is either intuition or concept. These two differ in that an intuition relates immediately (or directly) to an object and is "singular" whereas concepts are neither (A320/B377).
>
> Intuitions are thus classified by Kant as a kind of cognition and classified with concepts under that heading. But to speak more directly to your passage's distinction between sensibility and understanding, you will find that this distinction, though important to Kant, is not all that finally and unalterably drawn at the passage you cite. Consider the "Note to the Amphiboly of Concepts of Reflection" where we discover that concepts are transcendentally located either in the sensibility or in the understanding (A268/B324). So, there are concepts in the faculty of sensibility. The distinction your passage points to is a distinction of two different faculties of thinking, both of which have concepts but utilize them differently.
>
> A: Well, I am inclined to regard the passage in the Amphiboly as just carelessness. After all, it is not just A19/B33 that supports my claim. Let me give you two later passages, both of which show that I am right. At A89/B122, Kant says that the categories do not represent conditions for intuition. Objects may be given without the help of the understanding. At A253/B309, Kant tells us that if we remove the categories from an empirical cognition, only intuition remains and, through an intuition, no reference to any object is secured.
>
> B: The passage at A89/B122 says one thing that is correct: the categories are not the conditions of sensibility. Those conditions are space and time. The rest of the passage tells us only that, as far as "givenness" by itself is concerned, the categories are not involved. The rest of the passage describes something that the transcendental deduction will show to be incorrect. Remember, A89/B122 comes after the passage at A79/B104 which states that the same functions which give unity to judgments also give unity to intuitions. This unity is always a pure concept of the understanding, a category.
>
> Your second passage occurs in the section called "The Ground of the Distinction of

Introduction 23

all Objects in General into Phenomena and Noumena". By this time, Kant has come to enlarge his concept of representation insofar as it is essential to experience so that he is inclined to think of representation of objects as connected with the possibility of experience. One condition of the possibility of experience is the unity the pure concepts of the understanding provide. The categories are the concepts of "necessary synthetic unity". That intuition, by itself, is not considered a representation (as in the passage from A253/B309) is just Kant being a little careless by incorporating into representation what is required for judgments to express knowledge. So he is inclined to say, "Take thought away and with it the categories and you no longer have representation".

Let us leave our Kant scholars to their debate.

12. I note, first, that such debate is valuable. As the combatants range themselves in battle, we are supplied with passages from Kant and comments thereon that help us gain a sense of which interpretations are reasonable. We also find, in those passages and comments, threads leading us from item (intuitions, concepts, sensibility, understanding) to item (judgments, knowledge, synthesis). These threads are a kind of framework which we either respect or reinterpret in dealing with Kant and the remarks of others on Kant.

13. Yet, I take it, Sellars believed that such exchanges can continue, in principle, forever. The maneuvers of reinterpretation, of dismissal and relegation, of context and question, all of these can furnish, with ingenuity, nearly eternal life to an interpretation. (By the way, Sellars does not hesitate, like all—and it does appear to me that 'all' is the correct word—other commentators on Kant, to say that Kant is at times less than clear, at times confused, and at times downright wrong. Furthermore, Sellars' pronouncements on Kant were added to over time and were never stated with the rider "this and no more is what Kant is saying here".)

14. What brings it all home, however, is including Kant in the ongoing activities of philosophers. If you are pressed to tell other philosophers, in more or less contemporary terminology, what Kant is saying, then the ever more sophisticated weave of your interpretation is anchored somewhere—in your own philosophical views. Joining Kant to us in the contemporary philosophical scene is, for Sellars, essential to treating Kant as a philosopher, rather than merely as someone who wrote philosophy a long time ago.

C. A small point

15. My final organizational problem arises from a comment Sellars made: he said that, in working on the Cassirer lectures, he had "read the *Critique* backwards." Strange thoughts pop into mind when someone says something like that, but I had no opportunity to ask him a few obvious questions. So, I do not know the details of his "backward" reading of *CPR*.

16. Despite that, I think it is easy to understand the general purpose and point of what he did: he wished to reflect on Kant's doctrines in *CPR* as if they had been organized from the doctrines of method and the standpoint of reason and its ideas forward to empirical knowledge and the categories and then finally to sensibility. I think that this procedure makes a difference. It is not possible in this introduction to do all that much to reflect this difference. I have, though, organized my exposition to work, in some degree, from later passages back to the doctrine of sensibility in the Transcendental Aesthetic. My approach has the drawback that I must occasionally turn back in later parts of my introduction and reclaim some of the territory already gained, thus producing more repetition.

D. A special case

17. Much effort has been expended in attempting to construct Kantian arguments to defeat skepticism about the "external world". While Sellars makes comments about this, they do not fill much space in his writings. But since these matters loom large in Kantian commentary, I think it important to make a few points.

18. First, no doubt arguments are important in the elaboration of a philosophical position. But logic cannot tell us what to believe, only that it ought to be that we believe some further claim if we already believe thus and so. If we were in possession of premises commanding general philosophical assent, then we could hope to present our philosophy persuasively in *more geometrico*. The history of philosophy, however, has borne out the improbability of finding such indisputable premises. In the case of Kant, part of the intractable, and apparently ineradicable, disagreement among Kant scholars concerns whether Kant has any such premises at his disposal. Sellars thought it better to set out a philosophical position with an eye to providing as much philosophical insight and understanding as one could. Arguments make their appearance in such an exposition, but they are only one element in the framework of the exposition.

19. Second, skeptical arguments are in no better position than any other arguments—they need premises. Among Kant and his predecessors, skeptical arguments rested on premises derived in part from Descartes and, in most cases, concerned our access to human mental activities. No matter how strong Hume's empiricist credentials, he shares with Descartes a conviction about the utter reliability and *adequacy* of our concepts of and reports about the mental:

> Add to this, that every impression, external and internal, passions, affections, sensations, pains and pleasures, are originally on the same footing; and that whatever other differences we may observe among them, they appear, all of them, in their true colours, as impressions or perceptions. ...since all actions and sensations of the mind are known to us by consciousness, they must necessarily appear in every particular what they are,

and be what they appear.[6]

Sellars, I am convinced, believes that Kant's critical philosophy undercuts many skeptical premises by presenting an alternative view of our access to our minds, one which rejects such Cartesian claims. Not that this alone shows that Kant is correct. It does, however, relieve the pressure to provide Kantian arguments—against skepticism and (some sorts of) idealism—which are built on premises agreed to by Kant's predecessors.

20.   In fact, I will suggest that, by Sellars' lights, Kant's account of consciousness is sufficiently different from that of his predecessors that Kant cannot formulate premises that he holds to be true about consciousness and that his predecessors would agree to, if they understood these premises as he does. Kant and Descartes might, of course, share some words, e.g., 'I have empirical knowledge of my own existence' (B275), but shared words are not sufficient. So, Sellars, I believe, accounts himself as one of those who do not find it to be Kant's *principal* concern to provide *direct* arguments against skepticism.

21.   These two points (with later adornments) go some way in explaining why Sellars does not feature skepticism prominently even when he discusses the transcendental deduction.

II. A Look at the surface
A. Transcendental Idealism

22.   I start where Sellars, in most cases (*KTI* (98), in this volume, is an exception), does not: by formulating, in a preliminary fashion, the doctrine Kant calls "Transcendental Idealism". Kant's statement of this doctrine and his related remarks introduce some fundamental Sellarsian theses about Kant.

23.   In section 6 of the Antinomy of Pure Reason (A490-1/B518-9), Kant explains what Transcendental Idealism is. He says that he proved, in the Transcendental Aesthetic, that everything intuited in space or time and thus all objects of experience are appearances. Appearances, he continues, are "mere representations" (or, "presentations"[7]) which have no "independent existence" outside our thoughts. Similar remarks occur earlier, even in the Transcendental Aesthetic (e.g., A42/B59), but certainly in the first edition Paralogisms at A369 and in a note to A375 (both quoted by Sellars in section II of *KTI*). Such formulations occur later as well. The

---

[6] Page 190, David Hume, *A Treatise of Human Nature*, edited by L.A. Selby-Bigge (Oxford University Press, 1888).
[7] Though there is a point to the now common preference for the translation 'presentation' over the traditional 'representation', most readers will find that what I say about representation is far enough removed from traditional complications and confusions that my continuing use of 'representation' is not a problem.

"cosmological" antinomy, Kant says (A506-7/B534-5), provides another proof of the transcendental ideality of appearances, over and above the proof given in the Transcendental Aesthetic: appearances are "nothing outside our representations", i.e., they are transcendentally ideal.

24. Kant is quite firm that the transcendental ideality of appearances is proven by the considerations concerning space and time presented in the Transcendental Aesthetic (see also A378). In the Transcendental Aesthetic, however, Kant insists that the transcendental ideality of space and time can be consistently maintained with their "empirical reality" (or, "actuality") (A28/B44; A35-9/B52-6). Such an insistence is found in later passages accompanying the ones mentioned above (e.g., first edition Paralogisms, A370-9). The passage at A491-2/B520 features both claims at once: appearances, the objects of outer intuition and of inner intuition, are real and yet they are representations which cannot exist "outside our mind".

25. I think it beyond controversy that, unless we give some account of what Kant means by 'representation' (or, 'presentation'), we will not understand what Transcendental Idealism is. I now develop a piece of Sellars' account by a preliminary treatment of this question. Again, I emphasize that, though arguments are present in my account, my aim is to explicate Sellars' view by driving a line of thought through it, not to argue directly for this or that part.

B. Some distinctions: ings versus eds
(I) REPRESENTINGS

26. When Kant tells us that "appearances" are representations and that the Transcendental Realist treats representations as things in themselves, does he mean that the Transcendental Realist (mis?)takes mental items of some sort to be objects that are not mental and exist independently of thinking and thinking beings? It is possible to decide that the answer is "yes".

27. It is not unknown for commentators on Kant to decide that the mental items are "sensations". Indeed, Kant says that appearances are sensible representations and that nature is an collection of appearances.[8] These commentators conclude that appearances are sensations, more accurately, collections of sensations, and that nature is the system of such collections. On this view, a consequence of Kant's characterization of Transcendental Realism is that the Transcendental Realist literally holds that sensations exist independently of thinking beings.

28. Sellars denies that these passages require such an interpretation. Some of his reasons for this denial will be clearer shortly, but, to begin with, there is a distinction crucial to making this denial possible. It seems clear to Sellars that we must distinguish between

---

[8] See A104 and A114, and also A109, A127, B163-5.

represent*ings* and represent*eds*

and then elaborate this distinction by incorporating certain traditional concerns.⁹

29.   Let me tell a small story (the central item of which is taken from *SRPC*, 106, in this volume¹⁰):

> On a camping trip, you (Dick) take a short walk, at dusk, into the woods. Suddenly you hear a noise to your left and upon turning, you see (according to your later story in camp) a large, black bear. You think to yourself
>
> that large black bear is coming at me
>
> and, in your fright, yell out the very same thing. Having run back to camp, you are convinced by your friends to show them the place at which this "near bear attack" occurred. Careful search finds no traces of a bear. Further, Jane, who was, unknown to you, on your path only yards away, says, "when I heard you yell, I didn't see a black bear. There was, on your left, a large bush moving in the wind." Sis, your "bear-phobic" dog, finds no fresh traces of bear at the scene. Your friends agree that the large bush does exist and that the black bear did not exist and that's that.

In this story, Dick has produced two representings, one which is a thinking and the other which is a speaking. Both these representings are of the sort that Sellars, following Kant, calls a "judging". Each of these judgings has what I shall call a "subject" and a "predicate".

30.   The representing which is a speaking and the representing which is a thinking are, so most people would agree, quite different. For example, speaking involves the production of noises which can be heard; not so the thinking. Despite the considerable differences, most philosophers classify thinkings and speakings (and, as well, writings, typings, and so on) by a common vocabulary of such seman-

---

⁹ I will use my discussion of this distinction as an opportunity to "fix" a feature of the Cassirer Lecture notes (*CLN*, 116), a feature that I could not fix in the notes themselves. As I say in the Preface, Sellars' notes, particularly in the beginning of the lecture, are sketchy. In many cases, I was able to supplement a mere heading, or a drawn diagram, by inserting into the notes a paragraph or two from one of Sellars' other papers. In an early part of the notes where Sellars is discussing the philosophical background of Kant's views (in particular, the doctrine of "ideas"), he wishes to contrast two different "themes" in accounts of representation. At **A9**, where he commences his discussion of thinking as "mentalese" tokenings (the second "theme"), I found myself without a conveniently short excerpt that would be intelligible if torn from another paper. It is not that Sellars doesn't discuss the second theme elsewhere. In fact, it is just the opposite: for example, a substantial amount of chapter III of *SM* (62) is given over to one or another approaches to this topic. Nonetheless, I could not find any short passage which was intelligible out of context. Part of what I will be expounding in the following remarks is one formulation of the second theme.

¹⁰ This example, attended by remarks related to the ones I am making, also appears in chapter IV of Jay F. Rosenberg, *The Thinking Self* (Temple University Press, 1986).

tical and logical terms as

> is true; is false; is a conjunction; is a conditional; is universally quantified; is a monadic predicate; is a definite description; is a name,

and make claims about the relations of these representings using such phrases as

> is consistent with; is implied by; is more(less) certain than; is explained by.

True, philosophers have definite views about which representings are "fundamental" and which "derivative". For Kant and his predecessors, there is little doubt that thinkings are fundamental. Even if we give them this thesis, there seems little reason to believe that they did (or should) treat logical and semantical classifications and relations as different for speakings and thinkings.

31. The most determinate (or, more fashionably, "fine-grained") classifications of representings are the ones which allow us to say that two representings are the "same". Thus both Dick's thinking and speaking are 'that large black bear is coming at me' representings. The predicates of both representings are also the "same": they are 'is coming at me' predicates.

32. Since nothing in Sellars' remarks in the Cassirer Lectures notes (*CLN*) requires superior technical sophistication, Sellars makes use of single quotes (from **A9** on) as I just did. Single quotes, however, have such a history in philosophical literature that I fear their use conjures up commitments that are not mine. In addition, I find that, in certain constructions, the single quotes present a rather strange, and perhaps misleading, appearance. So, I will use a device devised by Sellars: dot quotes.

33. My *present* (as contrasted with Part **V**) use of dot quotes does not require all the claims that Sellars usually incorporates into his account of this sort of quotation. At the moment, I rely on what are *consequences* of Sellars' usual account of dot quotation: namely,

> (i) dot quotation, in forming predicates (not names), provides a means of classification, both gross and "fine-grained", for conceptual activities, whatever the natural properties of the activities;
> (ii) such predicates are capable of familiar grammatical transformations; and,
> (iii) these predicates are capable of handling the complexity of conceptual activities.

All these points, but particularly (ii) and (iii), are illustrated in what follows.

34. In conformity with the tradition, representings (tokenings) are activities of an object (commonly spoken of as the "subject" of the activities) and so "modifications" (properties) of that object (not necessarily, of course, an object which is a "substance"). A warning: that Kant agrees that representings are modifications of an object is borne out by many passages in *CPR*. In fact, one could take a hard line about passages in the First Analogy where Kant says that, in "all" appearances, the permanent is substance and the transitory is a determination of that object's existence (A182/B224) and that "all" change belongs only to the way in which substance exists (A183-4/B227).[11] Since Kant says 'all' in these passages, the hard line commits Kant to the claim that all alteration and change is a case of *substance* (or, individual portions of it) having properties and then losing them and gaining others. I mention this because whether it is so is not the question at issue but merely whether Kant holds that representings are modifications, or "determinations", of an *object*. This latter view is one that can be defended as Kant's.

35. Since dot-quote predicates are *verbs*, we can say (in the past tense) that

Dick •that large black bear is coming at me•ed twice

and Dick might, after the incident, say of himself

I was •that large black bear is coming at me•ing out loud and running simultaneously.

In general, dot-quote predicates have all the usual verb forms; thus, with 'V' as a dot-quote predicate, we can have:

S Vs, S is Ving, S was Ving, S Ved, S will V, and so on.

36. Changes involving representings (thinkings, speakings, typings, whatever) are no different from other changes. Thus, as

Dick walks and then Dick runs

records a change (loss and gain of properties), so does

Dick •that large black bear is coming at me•s and then Dick •I am back in camp•s.

Runnings are not walkings; similarly,

---

[11] Sellars comments on this passage in paragraph 39 of *I* (81, in this volume) to make a different, but related, point.

•that large black bear is coming at me•ings are not •that large black bear is coming at Dick•ings.

After all, •is coming at me•ings are not •is coming at Dick•ings; •me•ings are not •Dick•ings. Both

•that large black bear is coming at me•ings, and
•that large black bear is coming at Dick•ings

are combinings of •that large black bear•ings and a predicate. Such combining of a demonstrative phrase and a predicate is a familiar example of complexity in a representing.

37. Another familiar matter is the equivalence between tokenings with verbs and tokenings with so-called "nominalizations" of the verbs. Thus

S with solemn march goes slow and stately by them
S raised a sigh both piteous and profound

are equivalent to (respectively)

S solemnly marched slowly and stately by them
S sighed piteously and profoundly.[12]

In the case of dot-quote predicates, the equivalent form in which the predicate appears "nominalized" requires some verb like 'had' or 'wore' in 'S had a good row' or 'S wore a wan smile'. I sometimes employ the term 'token' for this task. So,

Dick •that large black bear is coming at me•s and then Dick •I am back in camp•s

is equivalent to

Dick tokens a •that large black bear is coming at me• and then Dick tokens a •I

---

[12] No defender of this equivalence is forced into supposing that any particular language, say English, contains presently all the words necessary for formulating both sides of the equivalence. Thus 'he wore a countenance more in sorrow than in anger' is an example where the present resources of English do not allow us to produce an idiomatic "unnominalized" equivalent.

am back in camp•.¹³

(II) REPRESENTEDS

38. The classificational account (26-37), which treats thinking as one form of tokening (mentalese tokening), does not allow us to say everything Kant and his predecessors wanted to say about represent*eds*. Indeed, what can be said about representeds on this account is rather slight:

(*eds1*) something is a represented if and only if there exists a representer, S, who represents it.

It might be helpful to consider a more long-winded, equivalent formulation:

(*eds2*) something is a represented if and only if there exists a representing by S such that this representing is a representing of it.

Thus, for example,

Santa Claus is a represented if and only there exists a representing by S such that this representing is a representing of Santa Claus.

So, consider

(1) S says "Santa Claus is coming down the chimney now", i.e.,
S •Santa Claus is coming down the chimney now•s (in English).

Since a •Santa Claus• is part of S's representing,

(2) S represents Santa Claus,

and so

---

¹³ Notice that, without delving into the machinery of dot quotation, it is not possible to provide the unnominalized equivalent of

Dick tokens a complex representing which is a •that large black bear• combined with a predicate.

The interested reader can consult, among other of Sellars' work on this topic, *AE* (reprinted in *PPME*, 101) and *NAO*. See also Johanna Seibt, *Properties as Processes: A Synoptic Study of Wilfrid Sellars' Nominalism* (Ridgeview Publishing Company, 1990), ch. 3 and Jeffrey F. Sicha, *A Metaphysics of Elementary Mathematics* (University of Massachusetts Press, 1974), chs. 2 and 3.

(3) Santa Claus is a represented (by S, of course).

39. Though not wishing to be the bearer of bad tidings, I hold that

(4) Santa Claus does not exist.

Both (4) and its negation

(5) Santa Claus exists

are consistent with (38.1), (38.2) and (38.3)[14] and, furthermore, consistent with the negations of (38.1), (38.2) and (38.3). Despite the apparently simple surface structure of (38.3), (5) does not follow from (38.3). In addition,

(6) there exists a represented item

does not follow from (38.3). However, part of the tradition concerning representeds, as defended by many of Descartes' successors and Descartes himself, is that *something like* (6) is a consequence of (38.3).

(III) REPRESENTEDS: "IDEAS" AND "CONTENT"

40. This brings us to the theme with which Sellars begins *CLN*: "ideas". Before pursuing the line of thought that will lead us back to something like (39.6), I emphasize that *much* of what post-Descartes defenders of "ideas" wish to say has a straightforward counterpart in the idiom which classifies representings. Paragraphs 29-37 make it clear that Sellars' classificational idiom can draw some version of distinctions traditionally used (and in some cases ignored). I will belabor this point a bit more.

41. Though the term 'idea', in one sense, has been used for such thinkings as are "about" or "of" things,[15] the term 'idea' is also used for an item that is "in" a thinking and that many thinkings can "share".[16] The term 'content' (even more than the term 'idea') suggests that the content of a representing is "in", or "is contained in", the representing of which it is the content. This by itself might be no more than a harmless metaphor.

---

[14] A reminder: '(38.1)' is '(1) in paragraph 38'.
[15] See Sellars' discussion of Descartes, section I of *BD* (95, in this volume).
[16] Kant does not like the indiscriminate use of the term 'idea'. Moreover, the upcoming discussion requires a more sophisticated approach to representing than that found in most of Kant's predecessors. These considerations motivate my switch from the term 'idea' to the term 'content', a term which also has the advantage of being presently employed in discussions of cognition.

Introduction 33

42. The harmless understanding of "content containing" can be illustrated by someone who builds an elaborate system for classifying, say, bodily movements. Among bodily movements are those that depend on extremities, e.g., the legs. Leg-involving bodily movements might be more determinately classified as walkings, joggings, trottings, sprintings, and so on. Then, to say of an individual leg-involving bodily movement that it "contains" the content ^jogging^ is just a long-winded way of saying that someone is jogging. Thus, in the case of representings, the biconditional

(7) the content ^that large black bear is coming at me^ is contained in a representing of a representer S if and only if S •that large black bear is coming at me•s

is, from Sellars' point of view, harmless in that it merely unpacks the "content containing" metaphor in classificational terms. Of course, the defender of the traditional doctrine of content (ideas) finds the same biconditional harmless, but for the reason that such a philosopher sees the dot-quotational classification as stemming from the representing's having the content it has.

43. In addition, Sellars and a proponent of the doctrine of content can agree on the "sameness" and "structure" of thinkings. The defender of content can claim that two thinkings, one of which is a

•that large black bear is coming at me•ing

and one of which is a

•that large black bear is coming at Dick•ing,

are, while not exactly the same, the same in the respect that both contain (share) the content ^coming at^ and the content ^large black bear^. The latter content includes (in specific arrangement) the content ^black bear^, the content ^large^, the content ^black^ and the content ^bear^. These four contents (ideas) are also contained in the two representings mentioned above.

44. Similarly on Sellars' account: since •black bear•ings are combinings of •black•ings and •bear•ings, when Dick •that large black bear is coming at me•s and when someone else •that large black bear is coming at Dick•s, both persons are •black bear•ing as well as •black•ing and •bear•ing. The specific kinds of combining need, of course, to be explicated. But whatever the correct account of different sorts of combinings, once it is incorporated into Sellars' classificational idiom, that idiom then matches the "content" ("idea") idiom in its delineation of conceptual complex-

34   *Introduction*

ity and sameness. (These remarks are not meant to attribute to all of Kant's predecessors an adequate grip on the various kinds of conceptual complexity.) In sum, there is a reasonably firm correspondence between claims that a representing contains contents combined in certain ways and a classification of the representing as being of a sort which involves complexity through combining.[17]

45.   There is, however, a venerable distinction found in the traditional doctrine of content. In the *Proslogium*, Anselm contrasts "existence in the understanding" and "existence in reality".[18] Descartes adopts a version of Anselm's contrast. In Meditation III and in the material appended to the Reply to Objections II, Descartes distinguishes between "objective reality" and "formal reality". While we might find much to argue about in Descartes' treatment of this distinction, it is drawn in such a way that Berkeley's tacit use of it in replying to the fifth envisaged objection (paragraph 49 of *A Treatise Concerning the Principles of Human Knowledge*) is intelligible. There Berkeley argues that though "extension and figure exist only in the mind", it does not follow that "the mind is extended and figured". These two qualities, he says, are in the mind, not as attributes of the mind, but "only by way of *idea*".

46.   Let me formulate an example. S represents as follows:

(8) this piece of wax is hard, cold and easily handled.

The content contributed by ^is hard^, i.e., hardness, is part of the content of (8). Therefore, hardness "exits in S's mind" (i.e., exists objectively) without it following either that S, the representer, is hard or that (8), the representing, is hard. If (8) were true (something that Descartes, when he •this piece of wax is hard, cold and easily handled•ed in French, claimed he was not in a position to know), then hardness would "exist in reality" (in that circumstance).

47.   This commentary on (46.8) does justice to one feature of the tradition: that the very same item (e.g., a property such as hardness) is capable of two kinds of reality or existence (objective and formal). A complication: remember that for most of Kant's predecessors (particularly Descartes), any representing (thinking) is a modification (property) of a thinking being. The claim

---

[17] Compare Sellars' remarks in chs. 3 and 4 of *KPT*.

[18] That this distinction is part and parcel of Kant's position, as one of its background assumptions, can, I think, be defended by passages from *CPR* (even those concerning the nature of "ideas" in Kant's technical sense). That Kant never gave up this distinction is supported by his paraphrase of the Anselmian idiom in passages in the *Opus Postumum (OP)* (e.g., 22:120, 22:55).

A small point: I hesitate to cite *OP* very much since I expect that it will be the subject of much disagreement and since Sellars may never have read it (though he did read German well). Nevertheless, there are passages in *OP* supporting Sellars' reading of Kant and I see no conclusive reason for not citing them.

Introduction 35

(9) a representer S is in a representational state whose content is the complex content ^this piece of wax is hard, cold and easily handled^

is a way of attributing a property to S. (This is part of what lies behind the biconditional (42.7).) Since the content ^is hard^ is part of the content ^this piece of wax is hard, cold and easily handled^, if (9) is true, it is also true of S that

(10) S is in a representational state whose content is (in part) the content ^is hard^.

Suppose there is no piece of wax. The representational state and the representer, as a thinking being, are the wrong sorts of things to have the property hardness. So, *even though (10) is true* and thus hardness exists in S's thought, there is nothing appropriate to have the property hardness.

48. As a consequence, it might seem that everyone should have settled for saying that the "existence in thought" of hardness is its existence, not (so to speak) as itself, but *as* the content ^is hard^ and that there is some satisfactory connection between hardness and ^is hard^—a connection that needed to be worked out. But this is not what happened. One reason it did not happen concerns a point that has been somewhat obscured in my discussion.

49. Though Berkeley's employment of the distinction between the two sorts of existence involved properties and relations (as do some of Descartes' discussions of objective and formal reality), all would have agreed that the same distinction applied to all contents: individual contents (such as ^that black bear^ and ^this piece of wax^) as well as "general" contents pertaining to properties and relations. No individual, be it black bear or piece of wax, can exist in your thought in any way differently from the way in which hardness or triangularity does, i.e., objectively rather than formally. Besides, what is represented as hard is a piece of wax, an individual.

50. So, if asked "What kind of item would exist in reality (formally) in the case of the contents ^this piece of wax^ and ^is hard^?", Kant's modern predecessors would have, nearly to a person, answered "In the first case, an individual, and in the second case, a property". When they then answered the companion question, "What kind of item would exist in thought (objectively) in case of the contents ^this piece of wax^ and ^is hard^?", they should have proceeded carefully and said, "In the first case, an individual as content, and in the second case, a property as content". But since the whole point of such a distinction as Anselm's is to get the very same item to be capable of two sorts of existence and since some of the distinctions made above were not well appreciated (especially by those who used the word 'idea' in loose ways), it seemed much more intuitively appealing to say simply, "In the first case, an individual, and in the second case, a property". In this way is born the conviction that 'exists in thought' and 'exists in reality' are predicates that can take (with no qualifications) *the very same subject.*[19]

51. I am not claiming that if you had asked any of these philosophers whether an item (individual, property, relation) is identical to that item as content or to an idea of that item, they would have replied "yes". Put thus baldly, the question would have been answered negatively. What this discussion and similar discussions in Sellars' writings do is bring out background philosophical commitments that sometimes lead philosophers to forget answers they would give to direct questions.

52. Another consideration encouraged these philosophers to take the "contained in" metaphor too seriously: an item which exists in thought (and which also might, or might not, exist in reality) seems to be an item, *with some sort of existence*, for the thought to be about. As we know from contemporary philosophy, many philosophers find it comforting to dig up actually existing objects where non-existence threatens.

53. In the theory of representing, familiar theses result from the doctrine of content ("ideas") and Anselm's distinction:

(I1) in general, items (individuals, properties and relations) are capable of two kinds of existence, "in thought" and "in reality";
(I2) any representing is guaranteed an object with at least existence in thought;
(I3) that an item "exists in thought" requires the existence in reality of a representing of it;
(I4) because thinkings (indeed, all representings) are activities of a representer, an item's "existence in thought" requires the existence in reality of a representer (the item is in this respect, as I shall say, "mind-dependent"); and
(I5) in any given circumstance, an item might have one kind of existence without the other or it might have both.

54. Once individual contents and general contents are accorded the same treatment, there seem to be little grounds for withholding it from judgment contents. Since the content ^that large black bear is coming at Dick^ is merely individual contents (^that large black bear^, ^Dick^) and general contents (^is coming at^) combined in a certain way, the status of the judgment content can hardly be any different from theirs. Though the existence in reality (the formal existence) of

---

[19] The metaphor "existence in thought/existence in reality" has no useful point in the Sellarsian classificational account and Sellars makes no serious use of it except in historical explication. Of course, nothing prevents introducing such a claim as "Santa Claus exists in (S's) thought" as, say, another way of putting (38.3). But no point is served in doing so: tracing (38.3) back to its roots in (38.1) would reveal that the 'exist' in the so introduced 'exists in thought' has only a tenuous connection with existence.

judgment contents might require some serious reflection, let me assume that one and the same item, which I shall call a state of affairs, can "exist in thought" and "exist in reality". When it exists in reality, it is a fact.

55. One final theme rounds out this discussion of representeds: representeds, as (53.I4) claims, are mind-dependent; their being is that of being in a representing. Compared to other items which are not mind-dependent, contents seem to be "second class" items as Sellars puts it.[20] Yet Sellars believes that Kant and his predecessors realized that it is entirely unsatisfactory to make representeds dependent on specific representings, yours, say, versus mine. Individuals, properties, relations, states of affairs, etc., are available to all ("intersubjective") and available to each of us over time: the same item can be represented over and over. Thus Sellars speaks of them as "represent*ables*". Though this availability does not remove their "second class" status, it pushes philosophers of the period to find some sort of "objectivity" for representables. Sellars thinks that Kant recognizes that if there is to be empirical knowledge, there must be some such objectivity for representables (though Kant cannot ensure that objectivity by, as Malebranche and others did, placing them in the mind of the supreme being) (*KPT*, ch. 4, section D). In addition, the domain of representables nicely accommodates items that are available to be actually represented but simply never have been (*KPT*, ch. 5).

C. Back to Transcendental Idealism: Appearances as Representables

56. We are now in a position to understand part of what Sellars takes Kant to be saying when he tells us that appearances are "representations" and "cannot exist outside our mind" (A491-2/B520). It is not a simple task to set out Sellars' full view on this matter, but we get a first approximation in this section.

57. Sellars thinks that the term 'Vorstellung' which is translated as 'representation' (or, in the newer translations, as 'presentation') is ambiguous. In fact, Sellars thinks that, in general, Kant's terminology pertaining to representation abounds in ambiguity. In section **A6** of the *CLN*, he makes a "four-fold distinction". First, there is representation as the activity, the representing, which is a property of an object, a representer. Second, there is representation as the content that each representing has: thus ^this piece of wax^ as part of the content of (46.8). It is, as I have said, the item represent*ed*. Third, since two or more representings can "share" content in common, the content ^this piece of wax^ is a represent*able*. Finally, there are items which exist when such a representing as (46.8) is true: e.g., a piece of wax. With regard to a representer, S, who truly represents (46.8), there is a piece of wax in the vicinity of S. The piece of wax in the vicinity of S is a represented object, but since a true representing represents it, it exists "in reality".

---

[20] For a blunt statement of these points, see chapter 4 of *KPT* (especially section C).

58. As I was at pains to set out in paragraphs 38 and 39, from

(11) O is a represented item

nothing much follows, on the classificational account by itself, about the status of O. In particular, there follows nothing about the (non)existence of O, nothing about what kind of item O is, and certainly nothing about whether O's (non)existence is "mind-dependent" or "mind-independent". Sellars thinks that the classificational account, or something *at least like* that account, makes itself felt in Kant's views, but that it is the characteristic theses of the doctrine of content (53.I1-I5) that drive most of Kant's account of appearances. The doctrine of content and the background distinctions Kant inherited make possible a philosophical frame of mind in which items (states of affairs, individuals, properties and relations) can have two ways of existing. Given (11), one way of existing is thereby guaranteed to the represented item and that way of existing, viz., "in thought", is a "mind-dependent" existence. So, given the traditional account of content, from (11) it does follow that O has (one kind of) existence.

59. That Kant believes he has good reasons for concluding that certain items, i.e., appearances, have no mind-independent existence is supported by many passages (see the references in 23-4). Whether Kant is correct that he has shown that appearances "have no independent existence outside our thoughts" is another matter. But, having so concluded, Kant then thinks himself entitled to the claim that appearances are "mere representations".

60. As a first approximation, Sellars takes this remark about appearances to say that appearances are represent*eds*, or, more generally, represent*ables*, not represent*ings* or other "mental" states. Long ago in *SM*, Sellars said

> ...the core of the Kantian notion of an appearance is that of an idea or content. Thus, when Kant tells us that spatial objects are appearances his claim is a remote cousin of Berkeley's claim that 'extension and figure...are in the mind *only as they are perceived by it*, that is, not by way of *mode* or *attribute*, but only by way of idea...'. *SM*, ch. II, 20[21]

Sellars has not given this view up, but he has elaborated it. So, reserving the right of later qualifications and additions, I shall, on Sellars' behalf, attribute to Kant the

---

[21] Sellars, in 1966, may well have been nearly alone in espousing this sort of view, but he has, perhaps, been joined by others. See Phillip Cummins, "Kant on Outer and Inner Intuition," *Noûs* 2, 1968, pp. 271-92; Richard Aquila, *Representational Mind: A Study in Kant's Theory of Knowledge* (Bloomington: Indiana University Press, 1983); James Van Cleve, "The Argument from Geometry, Transcendental Idealism, and Kant's Two Worlds," *Minds, Ideas, and Objects: Essays on the Theory of Representation in Modern Philosophy* (Volume 2, 1992, North American Kant Society Studies in Philosophy) edited by Phillip D. Cummins and Guenter Zoeller (Atascadero: Ridgeview Publishing Company, 1992), pp. 291-302.

theses that

> (K1) appearances are "mere" representeds (and, more generally, representables), not representings (or other "mental" states or collections thereof).
> (K2) appearances have "existence in thought", i.e., mind-dependent existence, but not "existence outside our thoughts", i.e., existence independent of representing.

A comment about the word 'mere': that

> Dick "merely" represented (thought about, spoke about) a black bear

implies that there was no black bear. So, if there were nothing more to say about appearances than that they are mere representeds or mere representables, we would seem to be forced to blame Kant for not concluding that appearances simply do not exist. Here, however, we must not forget that the line of thought that led to (K1) wound its way through the doctrine of content (ideas). Part of that doctrine is that items have two ways of existing and appearances as contents still have one of those.

61. As a first item in my list of additions, I consider what distinguishes Kant's view from others that might also merit the title "idealist". Besides contrasting transcendental idealism with transcendental realism, Kant distinguishes his idealism from the (empirical, or sceptical, or) *problematic* idealism, most closely associated with Descartes, and the *dogmatic* idealism of Berkeley.[22] I leave problematic idealism for later consideration.

62. Kant writes that Berkeley holds that a spatial thing is "in itself" impossible and so an imaginary entity (B274).[23] Kant himself argues not only that appearances cannot exist independently of the mind, but also that the same is true of space and time (see particularly A491-2/B520 and sections 2-6 of the Transcendental Aesthetic). So, if we treat dogmatic idealism as the thesis that space, time and all spatiotemporal items cannot "exist outside our mind", then Kant is a dogmatic idealist. Exactly what, then, in Berkeley's position is Kant complaining about?

63. On the usual phenomenalistic readings of Berkeley, Berkeley is driven (whether he likes it or not) to the view that space and time are features of mental items (i.e., spirits or ideas). Paragraphs 1 through 15 of Part 1 of *A Treatise Concerning the Principles of Human Knowledge* would leave little doubt in most readers' minds that this is so, though exactly how it may be that mental items have spatial properties is not clear (given, among other things, Berkeley's denial of this

---

[22] The relevant passages are: empirical (A491/B519); sceptical (A377); problematic (B274); dogmatic (A377 and B274).
[23] Sellars has a straightforward suggestion about this passage and Kant's surrounding discussion (see *KTI*, 20-36). My discussion is largely comments on this passage.

claim later in same work). In short, on phenomenalistic readings of Berkeley, space and time could not "exist outside our mind" because they are properties of mental items. According to Berkeley, at least some of the items that philosophers like Locke thought to "exist outside our mind" are ones with no mental properties, but are, nonetheless, in space and time. Therefore, the doctrine of these nonmental items "existing outside our mind" is, Berkeley says, incoherent and thus the supposedly nonmental items are, as Sellars puts it,

> a figment of the *philosophical* imagination. They would be radically imaginary, not just imaginary in the empirical sense. KTI, 33

64. So, it is not all that hard to come up with a thesis that can be attributed to Kant, but not to Berkeley:

> (K3) at least some appearances and their properties and relations, including spatial and temporal ones, are irreducibly material.[24]

Thesis (K3) requires considerable commentary and I begin some of it now.

65. (64.K3) is formulated as a claim that Berkeley is committed to denying. I think that I can, in the scope of this introduction, give sufficient content to the phrase 'irreducibly material' to substantiate this point. More pressing problems are: Why does it begin 'at least some'? What does (64.K3) say that (60.K1) doesn't? Is it in conflict with Kant's doctrine that space and time are "forms of intuition"?

66. The 'at least some' is required because Kant believes that there are appearances which are *not* through-and-through material items. These appearances I shall call "empirical selves". Very roughly speaking, an empirical self is an appearance that we each cognize through what Kant calls our "inner sense".

67. Support for the claim that empirical selves are appearances is easily found even in early passages in *CPR*. At B68, Kant says that anything we are aware of through the activity of a sense is appearance and thus that the object of inner sense must be appearance (see also B153-6, B428-9.) That our empirical selves are (at least) not through-and-through material items finds support in such passages as that at A386-7. There we discover that outer sense provides cognition of spatial relations while inner sense deals with thoughts which involve no spatial determinations whatsoever. (Compare also B66-7, A357, A379-80, and *MFNS*, 467-72.) Since Kant connects extension and materiality very strongly (a point I shall return to later), that inner sense supplies no spatial determinations argues that the empirical self, the self as appearance, is not simply (or wholly) material. (On the topic of

---

[24] Sometimes it seems to be claimed that the only way to avoid a "phenomenalistic" (i.e., Berkeleian) reduction of appearances is to accept the so-called "two-aspect" view of appearances and things in themselves. The account I am describing denies this claim.

matter, I suggest that, for the present, the reader consider A848/B876, and *MFNS*, 503 and 543-4.) Though these points are not conclusive, (60.K3) is formulated to allow for *some kind* of empirical "dualism" (see, e.g., A370 and A379).

68. Suppose that some such distinction between material objects and our empirical selves is a Kantian one. (60.K1) can be correct in that appearances in general, including our empirical self, are not represent*ings* of any sort and are not "constructions" out of represent*ings* or other "mental" states. Trivially, in being the *subject* of representings and other "mental" states, an empirical self might correctly be said to be a "mental" *something or other*; but, according to (60.K1), empirical selves are represented*s*, on a par with material items in not being reducible to some kind of (collection of) mental states. It is possible to maintain this point while not holding that the reason for this irreducibility is that empirical selves are thoroughly material. Thus I started (64.K3) 'at least some' and (64.K3) does not merely repeat (60.K1).[25]

69. A possible conflict with Kant's doctrine that space and time are "forms of intuition" I shall consider in a later section once I have examined Sellars' position on "intuitions". In order to finish up this first pass through Sellars' account of the doctrine of "Transcendental Idealism", I need to say a few words about "things in themselves".

D. Things in Themselves
(I) THE EXEGETICAL PROBLEM

70. Many criticisms of Kant have been launched from his remarks about things in themselves,[26] and some interpretations of Kant are built around a qualified partial rejection of any strong contrast of things in themselves with appearances. Sellars is convinced that things in themselves, as objects which are not empirical objects, are an essential part of Kant's view.[27] Despite this, Sellars counts, in one way, as a proponent of a "one-world" view though, since he rejects a main tenet of one-worldism, he also counts, in another way, as a "two-worlder". I shall place Sellars within this controversy after setting out a few main considerations.

71. That Kant draws *some* distinction between appearances (or phenomena) and things in themselves (or noumena) is clear. He tells us, in the preface to the second edition (Bxxff), that the distinction is absolutely necessary for the practical employ-

---

[25] I do not attempt to formulate a collection of theses that are completely non-overlapping in what they say; I am not convinced that such a project is a helpful one in an introduction.

[26] Once again, a helpful discussion of recent disagreements is the essay by Karl Ameriks, "Recent Work on Kant's Theoretical Philosophy," *American Philosophical Quarterly*, 19, 1, January, 1982. For a list of earlier commentators and their positions with respect to one issue concerning things in themselves, see Hoke Robinson, "Kant on Embodiment," in Phillip D. Cummins and Guenter Zoeller (eds.), *Minds, Ideas, and Objects: Essays on the Theory of Representation in Modern Philosophy* (Volume 2, 1992, North American Kant Society Studies in Philosophy) (Ridgeview Publishing Company, 1992).

[27] See *KPT*, chs. 9 and 10, in particular, his remark in paragraph 15 of ch. 9.

ment of reason and thus to morality and, in addition, devotes a chapter "The Ground of the Distinction of all Objects in general into Phenomena and Noumena" and an appendix "The Amphiboly of Concepts of Reflection" to this distinction and, particularly in the Amphiboly, says many things about the differences between appearances and things in themselves.[28]

72. In the second edition preface, though, Kant fuels future controversy in a footnote to Bviii; in discussing a priori concepts and principles, he argues the need to arrange that these concepts and principles can be used for viewing objects from two standpoints, that of experience and that of reason. His remark can be read as implying that it is the very same objects that are viewed from the two standpoints. Moreover, he speaks of things in themselves as "appearing" to us and this remark occurs in a context (Bxxvi-Bxxvii) in which it is plausible to think of "appearances" as "appearances of" things in themselves. In that same passage, as if to nail the point down, he says that it is part of the doctrine of *CPR* that an object be taken in two senses, as appearance and as thing in itself. If such language occurred only in the preface, the thought (not unknown among commentators) that Kant is easing his readers into an unfamiliar doctrine would gain more power to persuade, but similar turns of phrase are found throughout *CPR* (e.g., A258/B313-4, B306).

73. Equally impressive, though, are passages, like the Amphiboly, in which Kant stresses the differences between appearances and things in themselves. Space and time figure greatly into Kant's example of two drops of water (A263-4/B319-20 and A272/B328). As appearances in space, two drops of water can be nonidentical because of their spatial positions while being otherwise exactly the same; this, Kant tells us, cannot happen for things in themselves.[29] This view would seem a natural one for a philosopher like Kant who tells us that space is not a property of things in themselves (see, e.g., A26/B42).

74. The standard one-world view seems to require that empirically correct representings of appearances are truths about the only objects there are, truths about these objects "considered" with regard to the conditions of human sensibility (i.e., space and time).[30] It is possible, on this view, to "consider" these same objects without regard to those conditions of human sensibility and, at least in principle, to produce truths about these objects "considered" as they are in themselves. Thus the drops of water "considered" as empirical objects are not identical, but "considered"

---

[28] Van Cleve makes substantial use of the Amphiboly in constructing a criticism of the claims of the standard one-world view. See James Van Cleve, "The Argument from Geometry, Transcendental Idealism, and Kant's Two Worlds", *Minds, Ideas, and Objects: Essays on the Theory of Representation in Modern Philosophy* (Volume 2, 1992, North American Kant Society Studies in Philosophy), edited by Phillip D. Cummins and Guenter Zoeller (Ridgeview Publishing Company, 1992), pp. 291-302.

[29] See James Van Cleve's essay (mentioned in the previous footnote) for further argument concerning this point in the Amphiboly.

[30] See Henry E. Allison, *Kant's Transcendental Idealism: An Interpretation and Defense* (Yale University Press, 1983), ch. 1, section 1.

Introduction   43

as things in themselves are identical. This doctrine, as Van Cleve points out in some detail, is difficult to maintain. The heart of the difficulty is that, on this view, the very same objects are *correctly* represented as both having, and lacking, certain properties. It is difficult, Van Cleve argues, to understand how 'considered' is to be understood so that the obvious inconsistencies are avoided.

(II) TWO MORE THESES

75.   Sellars does not endorse the "same objects considered differently" claim and the attentive reader will have surmised that he would wish to deny any such doctrine. What Sellars wishes to attribute to Kant is the claim that

(K4.1) the objects of representings of appearances are not identical to the objects of representings of things in themselves.[31]

Let me explain why (K4.1) is put so complicatedly. Why not just say

(NK4) appearances are not identical to things in themselves?

First, (NK4)—the 'N' is meant to indicate a thesis which Sellars does *not* wish to ascribe to Kant—sounds too much like "sheep are not identical to goats", or "centaurs are not identical to satyrs". Both of these claims are about objects which do, or might, exist in our world and whose differences are to be elucidated by reference to empirical characteristics. Sellars cannot very well formulate the non-identity that I try to formulate by (K4.1) in these simple terms.

76.   Let me utilize a device introduced earlier. If someone asked "What are centaurs represented as?", one answer might be:

(12) From the waist down they are equine; but from the waist up, human.

Similarly, one answer to a slightly more specific question "What is the object represented by Dick represented as?", might be

(13) Well, as a bear and so with teeth and claws and so on; in addition, as

---

[31] Kant says things like this and things even stronger: "...this space and this time, and with them all appearances...cannot exist outside our mind" (492/B520) from which it would seem to follow that appearances *cannot* be identical to things in themselves. So, in the Amphiboly (A280/B336), it is no surprise to find Kant saying that, given what he has claimed, appearances "cannot" be things in themselves. (See also A740/B768 and A793/B821.) Notice, however, that the defender of the standard one-world view has no difficulty accommodating such remarks since they can be understood as expressing the *necessity* for having two ways of "considering" the same objects (see, e.g., Bxx).

44 *Introduction*

coming at Dick and therefore as moving, i.e., changing its spatial position over time.

When we consider such questions about a thing in itself, Kant's view is that we cannot provide any such answers as (12) or (13). I put this by saying that human beings do not "determinately" represent things in themselves (see *OP*, 22:33).

77. As in A26/B42, Kant sometimes puts one part of his point by saying that things in themselves are not in space. But this way of putting the point can make it seem that we do know determinate truths about things in themselves. What we can say is that

> (K4.2) spatial and temporal concepts and empirical concepts occur in determinate representations of appearances; we do not have determinate representings of things in themselves; and if there are any beings that do have such representings, our spatial and temporal concepts and empirical concepts do not appear in their representings of things in themselves.

78. Note that (77.K4.2) is not in conflict with the claim that we *do* represent things in themselves and that we *do* know something about things in themselves. Kant is sometimes portrayed as holding that we know *nothing* about things in themselves. This portrayal is aided and abetted by remarks from Bxxvi in the preface to the second edition to the effect that, though we cannot know things in themselves, we must be able to think things in themselves. Newer translations remove 'know' in favor of 'cognize' or 'have cognition of' (or, 'have rational cognition of'). But, since cognizings are states of us that, if not knowings, are at least essential for our knowing anything (or, perhaps, are part of any state that is a knowing[32]), the new translations still give the impression that as far as things in themselves are concerned, we are, so to speak, entirely out of luck.

79. Of course, it was always obvious that a commentator could say that by 'know' Kant had in mind a specific sort of knowledge (e.g., "empirical knowledge"). A similar point can be made about the word 'cognize': Kant uses this word mostly for states of the understanding connected with perception and thus with empirical knowledge. Sellars is, to some degree, in this camp:

> ... This unknowability [of things in themselves], however, must be compatible with the *philosophical* (transcendental) knowledge that there is an in-itself, and that it is structured in a way which can be *abstractly* represented—in some sense of 'abstractly'— and which accounts for the existence and character of experience. *SM*, II, 19 (see also

---

[32] See Patricia Kitcher, *Kant's Transcendental Psychology* (Oxford University Press, 1990), pp. 16-7, 135-8, and 146-7 and p. xxxiv of her introduction to Pluhar's translation of *CPR* (Werner S. Pluhar, translator, *Immanuel Kant, Critique of Pure Reason* (Hackett Publishing Company, 1996)).

section B, ch. 10 of *KPT*)

So, Sellars does want to attribute to Kant:

(K5) we represent things in themselves and we have philosophical knowledge of things in themselves.

I admit that (K5), without further commentary, can lead to confusion. This commentary must await my upcoming discussion of the categories.

(III) MORE TEXTUAL EVIDENCE AND RELATED CONSIDERATIONS

80. I conclude this section by setting out some of Sellars' reasons, partly textual, for attributing (75.K4.1), (77.K4.2) and (79.K5) to Kant.

81. There is a passage in section 26 of the second edition of the Transcendental Deduction of the Pure Categories of the Understanding that Sellars finds indicative of an entire facet of Kant's thought that commentators can ignore only at the peril of distorting Kant's position. Kant is explaining how it is that the categories can "prescribe" laws to appearances and thus to nature (B163). In passing, he remarks that things in themselves, necessarily and independently of any understanding, conform to "laws of their own" (B164). Such talk is hardly appropriate to anyone who would agree to the claim, put in ordinary terms, that "we don't know anything about" things in themselves.

82. This remark at B164 is prima facie in conflict with Kant's insistence that space and time pertain only to appearances. After all, it is hard to imagine things in themselves conforming to laws without something like time being involved. Now Sellars thinks that this is so. The catch, Sellars argues, is what we are to understand by space and time. In section 23, not long before B164, Kant observes that things in themselves can be represented as not having the characteristics of appearances and, in particular, about such objects it can be said that they are not spatial and that their "duration is not a time" (B149).

83. The phrase 'duration is not a time' is no fluke. Kant is fond of noting that our cognitive abilities are limited. These limitations insure that *we* cannot make any use of certain concepts, e.g., a non-spatial presence or a non-temporal duration (A770-1/B798-9), but he allows that these concepts are "not contradictory." Thus, though space and time, those "forms" connected with our sensibility, are limited to appearances, things in themselves can have a relational structure, a "form" of their own, so to speak, that were we different sorts of beings than we are, we would be able to give examples of.

84. Let me add a passage from the chapter, "The Ground of the Distinction of all Objects in general into Phenomena and Noumena". In this chapter, Kant is at pains to tell us what sort of access to things in themselves, noumena, we do *not* have and, as part of this account, to distinguish between a "positive" and a "negative" sense of 'noumenon'. In the process of contrasting these two senses of 'noumenon' and, in particular, in making a point about the negative sense, Kant flatly says that to sensible entities there correspond intelligible entities and that there may also be intelligible entities to which we have no relation through the senses (B308-9). Kant makes a similar remark in discussing "transcendental theology": there is "without doubt" something distinct from the world, something which is thinkable by the understanding and which is the transcendental "ground" (or "basis") of the order of appearances according to law (A696/B724).[33]

85. The passages just mentioned are reasonably striking and, when combined with Kant's remarks about the requirements of freedom and morality, provide clear support for a position of the sort Sellars defends. Sellars, however, thinks that there is another equally, or, perhaps, even more important, consideration: "transcendental psychology". One of Sellars' fundamental views about Kant's "transcendental psychology" is clearly expressed in section IX of *KTE* (66, in this volume). (Please keep in mind that *KTE* was written, in 1967, immediately after *SM*.) In this section, Sellars wants to put the notion of "transcendental psychology" in a better light. Though Sellars has altered some details of his account of transcendental psychology (particularly that part he calls Kant's "theory of empirical representation"), he sticks with the central point that, understood properly, "transcendental psychology" is not a dispensable part of the Kantian system. I quote from section IX:

> 39. It is often said today that Kant's *Critique* consists of important insights into the logical geography of our conceptual structure which are obscured almost to the point of invisibility by a tedious and fictitious "transcendental psychology". Kant is said to postulate a mechanism consisting of empirically inaccessible mental processes which "constructs" the world of experience out of sense impressions. If my argument is correct, this criticism is misdirected. The true situation can be seen by assessing the validity of a corresponding criticism directed against a linguistic version of Kant's position.
>
> 40. To construe the concepts of meaning, truth, and knowledge as meta-linguistic concepts pertaining to linguistic behavior (and dispositions to behave) involves construing the latter as governed by *ought-to-bes* which are actualized as uniformities by the training that transmits language from generation to generation. Thus, if logical and (more broadly) epistemic categories express general features of the *ought-to-bes* (and corresponding uniformities) which are necessary to the functioning of language as a cognitive instrument, epistemology, in this context, becomes the theory of this functioning—in short *transcendental linguistics*.
>
> 41. Transcendental linguistics differs from empirical linguistics in two ways: (1) it is

---

[33] See also A537-8/B565-6 where Kant insists that appearances must have transcendental grounds, and as well A278/B334, A288/B344, A494/B522, A740/B768, and A672/B700.

concerned with language as conforming to epistemic norms which are themselves formulated in the language; (2) it is general in the sense in which what Carnap describes as "general syntax" is general; i.e., it is not limited to the epistemic functioning of historical languages in the actual world. It attempts to delineate the general features that would be common to the epistemic functioning of any language in any possible world. As I once put it, epistemology, in the "new way of words," is the theory of what it is to be a language that is about a world in which it is used. Far from being an accidental excrescence, Kant's transcendental psychology is the heart of his system. He, too, seeks the general features any conceptual system must have in order to generate knowledge of a world to which it belongs. *KTE*, 39-41

86. I limit my commentary, for the moment, to answering the question, "Why does the existence of Kantian transcendental psychology lend support to attributing (79.K5) to Kant?". This question is made more pressing because the *KTE* passage compares transcendental psychology to a "linguistic version" of Kant's project, "transcendental linguistics". Are we to believe that Sellars thinks that transcendental linguistics, a subject which, in some form, as Sellars indicates, he subscribes to, must be committed to things in themselves? The short (though, I will argue, somewhat too easy) answer is "no". The analogy between "transcendental psychology" and "transcendental linguistics" has its limits.

87. But just as surely, Sellars believes that Kant thinks of transcendental psychology as connected with things in themselves. Too many to be ignored are passages in *CPR* which tell us that Kantian faculties and powers belong to us as intelligible objects, not as appearances (though, presumably, even these faculties and powers also "appear"). At A546-7/B574-5, Kant explicitly says that, though human beings are appearances, we can cognize ourselves by "pure apperception" and through this access to ourselves (whatever exactly that access may be) we know that we have powers that are not that of sensibility. These powers are understanding and reason and, since we possess these powers, we are, not just appearances, but intelligible objects. Also, many passages contrast the "spontaneous" activity of the understanding and the reason with the causality involved in the receptivity of sensibility. See, particularly, B153-9, especially the footnote to B158, where Kant says that it is because of this spontaneity that we are called intelligences.[34]

88. Further, despite the non-spontaneity of sensibility, there are passages in which Kant indicates that sensibility is a faculty of us as intelligible objects. Shortly after the passage at A491-2/B520 where Kant explains what transcendental idealism is, Kant remarks that inner sense provides, not the transcendental subject, but only

---

[34] Passages in which Kant speaks directly of intelligences and of the status and powers of thinking beings are spread throughout *CPR*. A sample that bears on my present topic is: B155, B158, footnote B158, B159, second footnote B415, B428-9, A492/B520, especially A546/B574, A566/B594, A641/B669, A742/B770, A815/B843 and compare also *OP*, 22:413-415, 22:78, and 22:81-2.

an appearance made possible through the activity of the sensibility of the transcendental subject, the self in itself. In "The Ground of the Distinction of all Objects in general into Phenomena and Noumena", Kant also says the doctrine of sensibility is part of doctrine of noumena and thus of things which we must think of, not as appearances, but as things in themselves (B307; see also A278/B334). The whole of his discussion makes it clear that the doctrine of sensibility and the doctrine of things in themselves (in at least the negative sense) belong together.

89. According to Sellars, Kant's transcendental psychology isolates what we contribute to "experience" and, once you realize just how much that is, you are bound to draw a strong distinction between appearances and things in themselves. *That distinction* is not one that can be treated as merely a matter of considering the "very same" objects in two different ways.

90. If we combine these passages with earlier quoted ones on Transcendental Idealism (and yet others in, for example, the Transcendental Deduction where Kant discusses synthesis), Sellars believes that a case (though, of course, not a conclusive one) can be made for attributing (75.K4.1) and (79.K5) to Kant. Sellars is firmly against the view that things-in-themselves are "static" or unchanging and that we know nothing at all about things in themselves. In fact, he believes that Kant's transcendental psychology requires that we know (but not empirically) a great deal about the soul-in-itself.[35]

91. The *one world* that exists ("in reality") is the world of things in themselves; in this sense, appearances do not exist. Thus it cannot be that appearances and things in themselves are the same objects "considered" in two different ways. So, as I said that the beginning of this section, in one way Sellars is a "one-worlder" though in another way he is not.

92. Complications, however, loom not far off: for example, besides the "existence in thought" which appearances have as representeds, Sellars holds that Kant attributes something else to appearances (namely, actuality) which, as we will discover, might be confused with existence.

93. All said and done though, this part of my introduction has attempted to lay out the surface of Sellars' account of Kant from the scenic vantage of transcendental idealism. I have utilized, in passing, quite a variety of Kantian terminology, a veritable white whale of complexity, that I have not shed light on. To this rather large task I now turn.

---

[35] Consider, in this light, the footnote to B155 which says, in part, that motion, not of an object in space, but as "the describing of a space" is an act of successive synthesis by the productive imagination and is a concept of transcendental philosophy.

III. "A Little Lower Layer"
A. Concepts and Intuitions
(I) CONCEPTS

94. Almost all commentaries on Kant discuss concepts and intuitions and seem to admit that one, or the other, of these figure, in one way or another, into nearly every Kantian doctrine. Perhaps because most commentators struggle with Kant's (as usual) competing remarks,[36] few come down to a reasonably contemporary formulation of Kant's account of the related notions of concepts, intuitions, and judgings. Sellars, as I said earlier, is committed to just this.

95. Sellars finds, not unexpectedly, that we need to employ the distinctions, made previously (26-55), to concepts. Concepts appear as parts of representations. Thus in a representing which is a •this piece of wax is hard, cold and easily handled•, the concept is a •is hard, cold and easily handled•. Concept*ings*, if I may so put it, are predicates in representations. Kant seems strongly committed to this view of concepts as predicates in representations. In fact, in a famous passage at A69/B94, he says just that: concepts are "predicates of possible judgments".[37]

96. Even so, though perhaps less clearly, Kant thinks of concepts as represent*eds* which he calls "characters", "characteristics", or "features" (see, e.g., B40).[38] Though Kant does not have a completely developed ontological terminology, it is not misleading to think of the represented characteristics, e.g., of being cold, hard and easily handled, as being involved in states of affairs, e.g., that this piece of wax is hard, cold and easily handled.

97. The terms for the represented characteristics in a •is hard, cold and easily handled• representing are 'hardness', 'coldness' and 'being easily handled'. These characteristics, as the contents ^is hard^, ^is cold^ and ^is easily handled^ (as well as the content ^and^) are treated as part of the content of the representing, as part of what "exists in the representing".

98. In sum, we must be prepared to find concepts as parts of representations (as predicates), concepts as involved in states of affairs (as characteristics or features, i.e., in general, properties and relations), and concepts as contents (which, of course,

---

[36] For an interesting display of someone struggling with all the various remarks Kant makes about intuitions and concepts, see chapter 4 of Henry E, Allison, *Kant's Transcendental Idealism: An Interpretation and Defense* (Yale University Press, 1983).
[37] In other places, Kant makes remarks that clearly involve such a view of concepts. See, e.g., the passages from the Reflexionen that Allison quotes (in pursuing a related point) on pages 146-7 of *Kant's Transcendental Idealism: An Interpretation and Defense* (Yale University Press, 1983).
[38] See also A19/B33, A25/B40, A320/B377, and A655/B683; the Jäsche Logic contains similar passages on pages 63-4 and 96-101. The Jäsche logic is one of Kant's series of lectures on logic, edited at his request by Jäsche. The translation I cite is *Immanuel Kant Logic*, translated by Robert Hartman and Wolfgang Schwarz (The Bobbs-Merrill Company, 1974). The letter I use for this work is '*L*'.

the tradition took as the very same properties and relations "existing in thought").[39] In what follows, this tripartite division occurs also in the case of intuitions. Intuitions, however, are an especially tough morsel and I will not be able to chew through it all at one bite.

(II) INTUITIONS VERSUS CONCEPTS

99. The exegetical cornerstone of Sellars' account of intuition is that intuitions are cognitive states on a par with concepts (A320/B377). If I were to use the terminology of *SM*, I would saying that both intuitions and concepts are "conceptual" representations. (The importance of this point will become clearer when I discuss sensory states which, in *SM*, Sellars calls "nonconceptual" representations.) We should keep in mind that out of what we might call "conceptual" items, the only ones that Kant officially uses the term 'concept' for are those that appear as, or correspond to, predicates in representations. Other items which we *now* might call "conceptual", such as those that "refer to" individual things, do not in the "official" Kantian sense count as conceptual items. This Kantian terminological preference does not show that intuitions and concepts are not both "conceptual" states in a contemporary sense.

100. The main logical contrast between concepts and intuitions is that, as Kant tells us in *CPR* and in the Jäsche Logic[40], concepts are general, but intuitions singular, representations. Second, an intuition relates "directly" (or "immediately") to an object; not so for concepts which relate to objects indirectly (A320/B377).[41]

101. Kant's seriousness about the singularity of intuitions shows not just in what he attributes to intuitions, but what he denies to concepts. At A655/B683, Kant claims that no species is the lowest. The reason he gives is that, since a species is a concept and a concept contains what is common to different things (see also A320/B377), it is not "completely" determined and so cannot relate directly to an individual. Shortly after A655/B683, in discussing what Kant calls the "logical horizon" of a concept, he says that, for concepts, this horizon can be narrowed to smaller horizons, i.e., subspecies, but not to individuals (A658/B686). For Kant, concepts are inherently general (not "completely" determined, as he would say) and thus cannot *as such* be cognitions of a single individual. This theme finds expres-

---

[39] In *KPT*, ch. 12, 1-4, Sellars suggests that Kant also occasionally uses 'begriff', the German word translated as 'concept', in a sense derived from its connection with 'begreifen' which means 'to grasp', and thus, metaphorically, 'to pull together', 'to get together'.
[40] See *L*, page 96 (section 1 of the General Doctrine of Elements).
[41] In a footnote in the Transcendental Deduction of Pure Concepts of the Understanding (B136), Kant says that space and time, are intuitions and, therefore, singular representations. (Notice that Sellars would *not* read this sentence as saying that space and time are intui*tings*.) Here the feature of singularity seems to have outweighed any question of immediateness. I will take it that intuitions in the full sense possess both properties. (See also Sellars' remarks in section *A*, ch. 8 of *KPT*.)

Introduction 51

sion in a passage of the Jäsche Logic[42] where Kant says that since single things require an "all-sided", i.e., "complete" determination, concepts cannot be cognitions of individuals. (See also A571/B599ff.)

102. Finally, the other property of intuitions, namely, that of being "immediately" or "directly" related to an object (A19/B33, B41 and A68/B93), serves to cut down the candidates for intuitions (in the full sense). Out of the various items that might count as singular representations, many would not appear to qualify under the criterion of "immediate relation": e.g., names and definite descriptions.

103. Before setting out Sellars' account of intuitings as singular, immediate representings of objects, I need to provide an overview of some complications in Kant's total view of intuitions.

(III) SOME COMPLICATIONS

104. A passage at A19/B33 has influenced many commentators. Intuitions occur, Kant explains, by our "sensibility" (a passive power, or capacity, for representing) being "affected" and, in this way, an object can be "given" to us. It is only the sensibility, not the understanding, which has the capacity to be caused to intuit and thus only the sensibility that "gives" us objects; the understanding, by contrast, thinks objects by using concepts. The association of intuitions with sensibility and concepts with understanding is seen in other passages as well. In often-quoted passages from the Introduction to Transcendental Logic, Kant seems to insist on a strict division of sensibility and understanding and, accordingly, a strict division of aesthetic, the science of the rules of sensibility, from logic, the science of the rules of the understanding (A52/B76).

105. Since Kant tells us at A19/B33 that the sensibility is the capacity for coming to have representations as a result of being "affected by objects" and since he goes on (A19-20/B34) to say that in the resulting effect there is "sensation," a certain conclusion can easily reached. Though no philosopher may ever have relied on *exactly* the following line of thought, it illustrates points which have been relied on and which I shall, in some measure, oppose.

> The sensibility is a passive power which produces representations by being affected; the understanding produces representations "from itself", "spontaneously". A51/B75
>
> What does the sensibility produce when affected? Sensations. A19-20/B34
>
> What is produced in the spontaneous activity of the understanding? Concepts. A50/B74 (And, as well, judgments.)
>
> What is the activity of sensibility called? Intuiting. What is the activity of the

---

[42] See *L*, page 105 (section 15 of the General Doctrine of Elements).

understanding called? Thinking. "The understanding can intuit nothing; the senses can think nothing". A51/B75

Intuitions belong solely to sensibility; concepts, solely to the understanding. A51/B75

Sensibility deals with the sensory; understanding, the intellectual.

Intuitings are sensory and nonconceptual; concepts are intellectual and nonsensory.

One might also be inclined to add, given the upshot of this line of thought, that

the immediacy of intuitings is a result of a "direct, nonconceptual mode of representing".[43]

106. In what follows, I do not wish to be construed (nor would Sellars) as arguing that the line of thought just surveyed is not reasonable. I do, however, claim that other lines of thought that are equally reasonable. As part of making a case for the reasonableness of Sellars' account of intuition, I present a laundry list of complications that, in one way or the other, bear on the contrasts, incorporated in the above line thought, between the pairs:

sensibility	understanding
sensation	thought
intuitions	concepts
sensory	intellectual
affection	spontaneity

(a) The term 'intuition' suffers from the '-ing-ed' ambiguity of all of Kant's terminology for representation.

107. When Kant remarks (as in the note to B136 mentioned in 100, footnote 41) that space and time are intuitions, Sellars does not read such a pronouncement as saying that space and time are intui*tings*. Intuitings are, after all, parts of representings which are modifications of thinking beings. Sellars' view is that Kant does not hold that thinking beings *as thinking beings* are, in any way, *literally* spatial. Thus, many of Kant's remarks about intuition, space and time, Sellars construes as being about intui*teds*.

---

[43] This phrase is quoted from page 67 of Henry E. Allison, *Kant's Transcendental Idealism: An Interpretation and Defense* (Yale University Press, 1983).

Introduction 53

(b) There are "inner" intuitings, a product of "inner sense", as well as "outer" intuitings, a product of "outer sense".

108. Inner sense, Kant tells us in the Transcendental Aesthetic, is that by which the mind "intuits itself or its inner state" (A22/B37 and also A33-4/B50-1). Kant has qualifications to add to this remark, particularly with regard to apperceiving, another way in which we can represent our minds and inner states such as thinkings (particularly relevant are B153-8 and B428-32). Whether, within the Kantian system, a neat line can be drawn between intuiting inwardly and apperceiving is a question I take up later. For the moment, I leave it at this: a view of intuitions should make it at least possible to make intelligible remarks about inner intuitings.

(c) There are both "pure" and "empirical" intuitings.

109. Kant says that the Aesthetic shows that our intuiting is sensible and that sensible intuiting is either pure or empirical (B146-7), but the distinction between pure and empirical intuition is not, in the end, all that easy to draw. Kant, in many places, simply indicates that purity is obtained by removing, or ignoring, what is empirical (see B3, B5-6, A14-5/B28-9). Luckily, he provides a more, at least prima facie, informative way of marking this distinction: an intuiting is empirical if its relation to an object involves sensation and it is pure if there is nothing in it that belongs to sensation (A20/B34; see also A22/B36 and B207-8.)

110. If we take these remarks seriously, we can provisionally say that the "empirical" is tied to what involves sensation. Note that the same distinction is applied by Kant to concepts: when they "contain" sensation, they are empirical and when they do not, they are pure (A50/B74). The problem is the province of "sensation" is all that clearly demarcated (see, e.g., the list at A20-1/B35). I have much more to say about this in Part **IV**.

111. But once Kant starts his exposition of general logic and transcendental logic (A50/B74) and notwithstanding the passages just mentioned, the "purity" that occupies much of his attention in no way involves space and time. The most general concepts and principles of the "pure understanding" are pure and not empirical in even in the widest sense (see A55-7/B79-81 and A64-5/B89-90).[44] Here, perhaps, what is important is the distinction between the "transcendental" and the "empirical", the "empirical" now being that which involves space and time or sensation.[45] Sorting out the kinds of "purity" that apply in the case of intuitings unfortunately depends on the answers to other questions about intuitings, especially those raised

---

[44] Even here there are perplexities: compare B3-5, A158-161/B197-200, and B232-3 on whether the concept of change is "pure".
[45] Note that the distinction between the "transcendental" and the "empirical" belongs to the understanding, indeed to "critique" (A57/B81).

by the last item, (g), in the present list.

(d) There are concepts corresponding to (associated with?) all (most?) intuitions.

112. As is well known, Kant places great importance on the role of intuition in mathematics.[46] This should not blind us to the fact that he thinks that there are concepts corresponding to (associated with) intuitions. In fact, in the famous discussion of '7 + 5 = 12', Kant speaks of the "concepts" of 5, of 7, and of 12 and mentions intuitions as "corresponding" to these concepts. Even more strikingly, though the Transcendental Aesthetic insists that space and time are not concepts, but pure intuitions (§2 of Section I and §4 of Section II), the word 'concept' appears regularly with regard to space and time, even in the titles of sections ("Metaphysical Exposition of this Concept", "The Transcendental Exposition of the Concept of Space", "Metaphysical Exposition of the Concept of Time", "The Transcendental Exposition of the Concept of Time").

113. Perhaps it is only that the "origin" of our concepts of space and time are in intuition (B40-1, A32/B47-8). This closeness of association between intuitions and concepts is reflected in a passage in the Introduction where, in explaining the limits of mathematics and its reliance on intuition, Kant notes that it is easy to overlook his point since the intuition in question is an a priori one and is therefore usually not distinguished from a "pure concept" (A4/B8). Moreover, and most importantly, in Chapter I, Section 1 of the Discipline of Pure Reason (see especially A713/B714 and A722-4/B750-2), Kant claims that mathematics "constructs" its concepts from a priori, nonempirical intuitions. Sellars' response to such remarks as these is to construct a view which allows intuitings a close connection with concepts.

(e) Sensibility has both concepts and intuitions.

114. Kant introduces a distinction which requires concepts in sensibility. The very first sentence of the Note to the Amphiboly of Concepts of Reflection says that the "transcendental location" of a concept is the position assigned to it in either sensibility or understanding (A268/B324) and the note goes on to explain how important it is to make this distinction.

(f) Intellectual intuitions are possible.

115. In the face of the foregoing complications, it is still possible to maintain a reasonably "hard" distinction between sensibility and understanding by

---

[46] With regard to mathematics, see B14-17 and chapter 1, The Discipline of Pure Reason, Transcendental Doctrine of Method.

leaning on Kant's insistence (illustrated above) that intuitions belong to sensibility,
admitting that sensibility is a more encompassing faculty than previously envisaged, and
holding that, in intuitions, sensibility has something all its own, not had by the understanding.

Even this move, however, faces major hurdles. One of them is: passages reveal Kant's belief that "intellectual intuition" is not a contradictory notion. Some mention of it appears even in the Transcendental Aesthetic: having noted that other thinking beings might have sensibilities different from ours (A27/B34), Kant concludes §8 of the Transcendental Aesthetic with a discussion of the possibility of a completely nonsensible, i.e., nonempirical in the widest sense, intuition. As his later remarks confirm,[47] such intellectual intuition, though not possessed by us but perhaps by a divine understanding, is not contradictory.[48] Further, as these same remarks make clear, such intellectual intuition belongs to an understanding, not to a sensibility. An account of intuiting should not, if possible, rule out *ab initio* intellectual intuitings.

(g) "All Sensible Intuitions are subject to the Categories" (B143).

116. This item of the laundry list is difficult to state in anything even approximating an uncontroversial manner. It returns us to my fictional debate (11). That debate, though mentioning some of the other items in my list, centered on the relation of intuitions to the pure concepts of the understanding, the "categories". Without more preparation, I do not think it possible to state the problem involved in (g) clearly. Nonetheless, I wish to survey some territory to introduce upcoming topics.

117. Almost any defense of sensibility as one of the "two stems of human knowledge" (A15/B29), capable of acting independently of the understanding, will argue that sensibility does not involve those very special concepts of the understanding, the categories. My fictional scholar A cited passages that seemed to say as much (e.g., A89/B122 where Kant says that appearances can be "given" to us independently of the understanding). Particularly in Kant's early remarks (B1-3, A19-2/B33-6, A50-2/B74-6), the overwhelming impression the reader receives is that by the "manifold of intuition" the sensibility provides the "raw material" (A1, B1) upon which the understanding is to work.

---

[47] B138-9, B145, B148-9, B158-9, B306-10, and A286-7/B342-3.
[48] The importance of this notion of intellectual intuition to Kant can be seen in sections 76 and 77 of *CJ* (*Critique of Judgment*).

56   *Introduction*

118.   Sellars agrees that this is part of what Kant wants. That, according to Sellars, Kant is not clear about how to work out such a doctrine of sensibility is revealed by many passages, some given by fictional scholar B. A case can be made that an attentive reader would receive from these passages just the opposite impression about intuition and therefore sensibility.

119.   One passage Sellars always cited comes from the section Kant later (B159) calls the "Metaphysical Deduction of the Categories". In discussing synthesis, Kant says that the same functions which unify representations in a judging also unify the representations in an intuiting; the unities at issue, Kant continues, are the pure concepts of the understanding (A79/B104). Sellars reads this as claiming that intuitings require synthesis and this synthesis is the same as that to be found in judgings. The consequences of this reading are far-reaching. Kant has, just before, explained the "The Logical Function of the Understanding in Judgments". The key to this logical function is the "Table of Judgments" with its concepts (A70/B95). Of course, it is the *understanding* that is the "faculty of judgment" (A69/B74). Moreover, just before A79/B104, Kant says that synthesis is a result of the operation of the imagination (A78/B103), but imagination, more precisely, the "productive" imagination, is the *understanding* acting on the sensibility (B152). Finally, Kant has another important discussion of synthesis at the beginning of the B edition Transcendental Deduction of the Categories (B129-31) in the section "The Possibility of Combination in General": combination of a manifold cannot be supplied by the senses; it is an act of the *understanding*. No matter what is being combined it is the understanding which is doing it.[49] It is this act which Kant calls "synthesis". Taking this passage with the one from A79/B104, we are left with the impression that the understanding contributes so much to intuitions through synthesis (combination)—so much that depends on the logical function of the understanding in judgments—that intuitions can hardly be items that the sensibility, acting *independently* of the understanding, produces.[50] Perhaps surprisingly, Sellars agrees that this second impression is also largely correct.

120.   His suggestion about intuition (and the obviously related items) is a complex one and it is meant, at the worst, not to rule out anything in my list of complications

---

[49] I am inclined to believe that this passage contains part of the characterization of judging that Kant talks about in the long note to 474 of *MFNS* (Immanuel Kant, *Metaphysical Foundations of Natural Science*, translated by James Ellington in *Immanuel Kant, Philosophy of Material Nature* (Hackett Publishing Company, 1985)). *MFNS* was written between the A and B editions of *CPR*. The note to 474 includes Kant's promise to change the exposition, not the content, of the transcendental deduction of the categories; the key to this revised exposition is, he claims, a definition of judgment.

[50] I am reasonably sure that these considerations, which point to the possibility of distinguishing two senses of 'sensibility', is part of what Sellars would say in response to McDowell's charge that Kant "never so much as mentions" sensibility and forms of sensibility in one of Sellars' senses (p. 456, "Having the World in View: Sellars, Kant and Intentionality", The Woodbridge Lectures 1997, *The Journal of Philosophy*, XCV, 9, September, 1998).

Introduction 57

and, at the best, to provide philosophical insight into the problems surrounding these items. It will take me some while to deal with his suggestion; I have to assemble the pieces one by one.

B. *Sellars' Account of Intuitions*
(I) SELLARS ON INTUITIONS: STEP ONE
(a) *Representings of this-suches*

121. Sellars' opening move accommodates two features of an intuition (99-102): its status as a singular representing and its "immediate" relation to an object. Since Sellars does not, I think, emphasize certain aspects of his suggestion sufficiently in *SM* and since the sort of suggestion that Sellars makes has a later history,[51] I need to differentiate Sellars' proposal from related ones and, in that process, deflect various criticisms.

122. I begin by quoting (severely hacked-up) several of Sellars' original remarks:

> ...'immediate relation' can be construed on the model of the demonstrative 'this'. On this model, which I take to be, on the whole, the correct interpretation, intuitions would be representations of *thises* and would be conceptual in that peculiar way in which to represent something as a *this* is conceptual. *SM*, ch. I, 7

> We seem, therefore, to be led to a distinction between intuitions which do and intuitions which do not involve something over and above sheer receptivity. It is the former, Kant tells us in the metaphysical deduction (A78/B104), which the understanding subsumes under general concepts. *SM*, ch. I, 10

> ...of intuitions those, at least, which are synthesized by the productive imagination would seem to have the form illustrated by
>
> this-cube
>
> ...which is a representation of a *this-such* nexus, specifically of *this as a cube*, though it is not a judgment and does not involve 'cube' in a predicative position.... . *SM*, ch. I, 11

What Sellars is *not* attributing to Kant is the thesis

---

[51] The interested reader can find part of this further history (and references to papers) in the following places: page 31 of Patricia Kitcher, *Kant's Transcendental Psychology* (Oxford University Press, 1990); pages 67-8 of Henry E. Allison, *Kant's Transcendental Idealism: An Interpretation and Defense* (Yale University Press, 1983); page 105 of Paul Guyer, *Kant and the Claims of Knowledge* (Cambridge University Press, 1987); and chapter 2 of Richard Aquila, *Representational Mind: A Study in Kant's Theory of Knowledge* (Indiana University Press, 1983).

(NK6) All intuitions are demonstrative phrases.

First, Sellars thinks that the 'all' is wrong. For example, sometimes when Kant talks about intuitions, particularly (but not uniformly) when he uses the phrase 'manifolds of intuition' (*KTE*, section II and *KTI*, 10), Sellars believes that Kant has in mind sensory states. These states, as I shall point out later, Sellars does not construe as conceptual states in the contemporary wide sense of 'conceptual'; Sellars characterizes these sensory states as ones that do "not involve something over and above sheer receptivity". Second, 'intuitions' is misleading: Sellars wishes to say something about some intuit*ings*. Third, 'are demonstrative phrases' is not what Sellars says in the above quotations.[52] What Sellars says is that the intuitings that the productive imagination synthesizes are representings of "this-suches" and our "model" for such representings is demonstrative phrases. Why does he put his point in this complicated way?

123.   There is little evidence, Sellars would agree, that Kant ever thought much about the logic of demonstratives or indexicals (except 'I') and he offers no account of their logical characteristics. So, Sellars would be the last to attribute to Kant a view of intuitings as demonstrative phrases (even as Mentalese demonstrative phrases) in the contemporary sense. What there is evidence for (e.g., in some of the passages mentioned in 99-101) is that Kant worried, in rather traditional ways, about individuality and generality and about individuals versus genera and species. Sellars' appeal is to that Aristotelian tradition[53] and his characterization of some intuitings as "representings of *this-suches*" is in the jargon of that tradition, not in contemporary terms, not in "formal" terms, and certainly not in "syntactical" terms.

124.   On the other hand, Sellars does claim that our contemporary understanding of demonstratives can provide insight into the notion of representings of *this-suches*. His use of 'model' indicates that such insight is not acquired without some work. All models come with a commentary, part of which tells what part of the model is inaccurate or misleading.

125.   The most inaccurate part of the model concerns something common to all (almost all?) present-day accounts of demonstrative phrases. Demonstrative words are treated as operators (syntactically analogous to the 'the' of definite descriptions) that produce complex expressions from predicates. By this account, a representing of a *this-such* is a demonstrative representing (e.g., a •that•) combined with a representing which is a concept (e.g., a •large black bear•). Kant would not find this suggestion acceptable without qualification.

---

[52] Though, when he is short of space as in *KTE*, he tends to put his view in this simple fashion. In *CLN*, the remarks he makes about intuitings are generally directed toward other relevant points.

[53] *SM*, ch. I, 11-16. That Sellars maintained his emphasis on the Aristotelian tradition is evident from *KPT*, ch. 6 where Sellars refers to an early essay of his, "Aristotelian Philosophies of Mind" (*APM* (5), reprinted in *KPT*). *APM* shows how seriously Sellars took this Aristotelian tradition.

126. I argued (99) that Kant's view of concepts (and thus of what is conceptual) is more restricted and narrower than that of contemporary philosophers. For the sake of compact expression, I indicate Kant's narrower sense by writing

    'kconcept' and 'kconceptual'.

Kant takes kconcepts to be general and to occur as predicates of judgings. So, intuitings, being representations of individuals, do not count as kconcepts.

(b) Experiential derivation and intuitings

127. A different question is: can intuitings be assembled ("synthesized") from other representations which include a kconcept? To answer positively implies that intuitings are complex conceptual representations in that they are assembled from other representations among which is a kconcept. Put in terms of content, intuitings have content part of which is a kconcept. (Note that such a thesis is in conflict with the position sketched in 105.)

128. As we have seen (109-111), Kant makes it clear that there are both pure intuitions and pure kconcepts (which are also, in some way, a priori) and empirical intuitions and empirical kconcepts. Though the empirical character of empirical kconcepts sometimes (A50/B74) has to do with a connection to sensation, Kant also says that empirical kconcepts are derived from experience (for some of his general remarks on empirical kconcepts, see B3-6).

129. Kant believes[54] that empirical kconcepts are the result of the understanding acting in certain ways on other representations. In section 6 of *L*, these acts of the understanding are said to be comparing, reflecting and abstracting. By these acts, we generate kconcepts.

130. Kant gives an example of the sort of thing he has in mind. He imagines situations in which he sees various trees, "a fir, a willow, and a linden." One compares these trees for their differences, reflects on what they have in common (trunk, branches, and leaves) and then abstracts from specific sizes, shapes, and so on. Thereby, he says, "I gain the concept of a tree." In another example, that of the kconcept of body, we abstract from "size, color, hardness or liquidity; in short, from all special determinations of special bodies."

131. No doubt, such remarks and examples are capable of many different construals.[55] For the moment, though, I return to the question I asked before: is there an

---

[54] *L*, sections 5 and 6, along with sections 99-105 and a similar passage in *CPR*, A727-9/B755-7.
[55] For a construal that attempts to place these remarks within the framework of modern cognitive science, see particularly chapter 8 of Patricia Kitcher, *Kant's Transcendental Psychology* (Oxford University Press, 1990) and also sections 3 and 4 of Kitcher's introduction to Werner S. Pluhar, translator, *Immanuel Kant, Critique of Pure Reason* (Hackett Publishing Company, 1996).

impediment to holding that intuitings—on Sellars' view, representings of *this-suches*, e.g., a •that large black bear• or a •this cube•—are complex representings combining a demonstrative with a kconcept? The answer is that, with some qualifications, one can hold such a view within a Kantian framework. The key to this answer is that

> the thesis that empirical kconcepts are "gained" by the understanding acting on contents

is consistent with the view that

> the contents, when acted upon, *need not* be kconcepts.

132. Do the activities of comparison, reflection, and abstraction accomplish alteration in the content(s) being acted upon? Doubtless Kant understands these activities as accomplishing *some* alteration. A less easily answered question is: how does one describe this alteration correctly?

133. Kant connects being a kconcept closely with being a predicate in a judging (A69/B94). I am strongly inclined to believe that he thinks of that connection as so tight that something which is not occurring in a predicate position[56] in a judging cannot be a kconcept. As a result, to the question "Can contents as they occur in intuitings occur as kconcepts?", I am convinced that Kant would answer "no". Notice, though, that this point can hardly settle the matter since Kant would not deny that the contents of intuitings have intelligible connections with kconcepts—such as the derivation from experience that is in question.[57]

134. Suppose we agree that no content that occurs in an intuiting is a kconcept. It can still be true that something which might correctly be called the content ^linden^ can occur both in an intuiting and in a judging although only in the judging is it occurring as a predicate and therefore as a kconcept.[58]

135. Combine these considerations with the fact that the doctrine of experiential derivation, as it comes down in the Aristotelian tradition, leans heavily toward the

---

[56] Notice that this turn of phrase allows for certain complications: e.g., that the occurrence of a term in the "subject" position of a *universal* judging is also in a predicate position and is thus occurring as a kconcept.

[57] Some might think the very idea that empirical kconcepts can be derived from experience insures that intuitings cannot involve kconcepts. After all, it might be said, if intuitings involved kconcepts, then the supposed "derivation" presupposes at least some kconcepts and cannot account for our possession of those. I address this point in the upcoming discussion.

[58] Notice the same point can be made in Sellars' model. The fine-grained classification provided by dot quotes can be so enhanced that •bear•s as they occur in demonstrative constructions—•bear•$_d$s—would not be the same items as •bear•s occurring as predicates in judgings—•bear•$_p$s—despite their otherwise enormous similarity which guarantees that they are all •bear•s.

view that this derivation is largely a matter, to use Locke's terms, of "discerning" and "distinguishing".[59] The "raw materials", as it were, appear in perception "mixed together" and what needs to be done is the "separating out" of the contents (ideas) from each other. Once you have compared, reflected and abstracted (separated out), you have a content that is now available for use alone, by itself, in other activities of your understanding, especially judging.

136. So, one change that comparison, reflection, and abstraction can make is that the content is now available for "separate" employment, crucially, as a predicate in judgings. Whether the three activities which comprise experiential derivation effect any other changes is not clear. It is clear, however, that other activities of the understanding need not leave the derived content as it is. Kant holds that the systematic purposes of human reason, particularly with regard to species and genera, not just can, but will, lead to changes in kconcepts.[60] Though this topic is a large one, involving Kant's doctrine of "The Regulative Employment of the Ideas of Pure Reason" (A642/B670ff), a specific example is found in his discussion of "the concept of *gold*" (A728/B756). Kant claims that characteristics are retained in a kconcept only so long as we find them adequate for distinguishing things; new observations can remove characteristics and can add others. The kconcept need never be finally fixed.

137. Let's reconsider Kant's example. I will assume that what is true of the kconcept ^tree^ is also true of the kconcept ^linden^. As an empirical kconcept, it too must be derived from experience. Since experiential derivation may alter contents, to be cautious we must say that *very nearly* the same content (e.g., ^linden^) can appear in intuitings as a candidate for experiential derivation (e.g., in a •this linden near me•) and also as a predicate in judgings as experientially derived (e.g., in a •this leaf is a linden leaf•, in a •all lindens are deciduous•).

138. But, once the understanding has derived the kconcept ^linden^, one can reconsider intuitings involving the content ^linden^ and treat them as, *in a secondary sense*, containing the kconcept ^linden^. After all, we can imagine Kant saying, the original contents of intuitings cannot escape critical reflection any more than anything else in our cognitive activities.

139. Using the example of the content ^linden^, I recast the above points incorporating the Sellarsian suggestion that intuitings are representings of *this-suches*:

(i) Consider T which is a •this linden near me• intuiting.
(ii) T contains the content ^linden^ which is not occurring in T as a predicate and thus not as a kconcept.
(iii) T and with it the content ^linden^ can occur in the mind of representer who

---

[59] Sellars comments on these topics in Appendix, Locke in *KPT*.
[60] See Kant's treatment of definition, A727-32/B755-60, and The General Doctrine of Method in *L*.

does not have the kconcept ^linden^.

(iv) But the kconcept ^linden^ is derived from such intuitings as T.

(v) This deriving of the kconcept ^linden^ is at least in part a "separating out" (comparing, reflecting, abstracting) of that content.

(vi) Though the "separating out" leaves the content ^linden^ very nearly as it originally appeared in intuitings such as T, subsequent modifying of that content is possible.

(vii) Notwithstanding this modifying, the kconcept ^linden^, because of its history, is tied to the content ^linden^ as it appeared, and as it will appear, in intuitings like T.

(viii) This historical connection is currently enshrined in the present logical structure of representings of a sophisticated, critical kconcept user by the fact that the truth of a judging like

> this linden near the side door of my house is old

requires the truth of the judging

> this linden [content as content of intuiting] near the side door of my house is a linden [content as kconcept]

and, in the circumstances, the truth of other judgings as, e.g.,

> the old tree near the side of my house is a linden [content as kconcept].

Thus, though the content ^linden^ in an intuiting is not strictly speaking a kconcept, it can be secondarily treated as the kconcept ^linden^.

140. The last point above must not be forgotten: for the sophisticated representer the content in an intuiting is now the same content which is a kconcept, but the content in an intuiting, *occurring as the content of an intuiting*, is not a predicate of a judging and is thus, in a really strict sense, not a kconcept. It is not that the content of the intuiting has no connection with predication; it is just that the content's occurrence as the content of an intuiting is not an occurrence as a predicate. With this much, Sellars certainly agrees. I have been at pains in previous paragraphs to separate this point from Sellars' claim that, in "mature experience" (*SM*, I, 16), the sophisticated representer finds the two contents to be the same.⁶¹

(c) Innateness, experiential derivation and rudimentary content

141. The previous subsection makes room in the Sellarsian account of intuitings as representings of *this-suches* for one sort of experiential derivation. It also allows for development in light of upcoming topics such as the connection of the categories to intuitings.

142. This account qualifies Kant as part of a long Aristotelian tradition of abstractionism (see Sellars' discussion in *SM*, ch. I, 11-16 and ch. 6 of *KPT*). One of the central tenets of this Aristotelian tradition is that the basic states brought about in our perceptual activity represent objects and represent them as being of kinds and as having properties. "Comparing, reflecting, and abstracting", perhaps aided by yet other operations of the understanding, provide us with "separate" contents such as ^linden^ and ^tree^ which we can incorporate into judgings as predicates.

143. As this view is generally cast, it has many shortcomings and limitations.⁶² My present interest is with two of these limitations. First, note that the sort of experiential derivation illustrated in Kant's example presupposes two things:

(i) The "special determinations", e.g., trunk, branches, and leaves (or, perhaps, being a trunk, being a branch, being a leaf), are there for your understanding to compare them, reflect on them and abstract from them.

(ii) The understanding is capable of recognizing these "special determinations" when they are there.

What (ii) tells us is essential to Kant's formulation. If your understanding does not recognize "special determinations" (being 1 inch on a side, being 6 feet on a side, being cold, being wet), how will it be able to compare an ice cube and a cube of marble for their differences? If it does not recognize the determination being square, how will it get started on reflecting on what they have in common? And then, finally, how will it know what to chuck out and what to keep?

---

⁶¹ These points, indeed even *some form* of experiential derivation, are consistent with Sellars' conviction, as McDowell puts it, that "the capacity to experience things as thus-and-so should be seen as coeval with the capacity to judge that they are thus-and-so" (note 3, page 454, "Having the World in View: Sellars, Kant and Intentionality", The Woodbridge Lectures 1997, *The Journal of Philosophy*, XCV, 9, September, 1998). Compare Sellars' remarks in sections 19, 36, 37 and 38 of *EPM* in *SPR*. Further, though, Sellars is a long-time foe of certain abstractionist views (see *PH* (64), toward the end of section V), it is not true he finds nothing in them (see *BLM* (108), sections I and VI, and *MEV* (112), 57; and compare *SM*, ch. I, 72).

⁶² For Sellars, one of the shortcomings is that it *lends* itself to one form of the "myth of the given" (see section A, ch. 6, *KPT*). To this, I return to in my later discussion of sensory states. Second, the terminology generally employed in the tradition gives, to me, the unwanted impression that experiential derivation must be a voluntary, or at least, conscious, process. To this I also return later.

144. It is, however, what is required by (143.i) which is crucial and which explains my practice, in the previous subsection, of linking experiential derivation and contents. The only way that a linden, its trunk, its branches, and its leaves (or the corresponding properties, being a linden, etc.) can "be there" for the understanding to act on them is by being contents. Lindens cannot be located in the understanding; the understanding can not have the property of being a linden. Of course, both a linden and its various properties can "exist in thought" as contents of representings. The experiential derivation is not, therefore, derivation from actual cases, e.g., from actual trees, actual trunks, branches and leaves, not from actual cubes of ice or of marble, and not even from actual shapes, expanses or the like; it is derivation from contents.[63] This is an important reason for taking intuitings to have contents of the same sort as the contents which occur in judgings. (Compare my remarks in 99-101 about taking seriously that intuitings are conceptual representings of individuals.)

145. The first limitation, then, is that:

> (EXD1) the best Kant's doctrine of experiential derivation can do is explain the possession of content which is an empirical kconcept on the basis of the possession of other content (that in intuitings).

Of course, it might be that some gain is made by accounting for "more generic" content (e.g., ^tree^) on the basis of "less generic" content (e.g., ^linden^). Even if we were to grant this, the doctrine does not even try to derive the content of judgings and other representings from something which is *not* content (i.e., not something of the same sort); the content of an intuiting does not occur as a predicate, but it's still just content.[64]

146. The second limitation is made apparent when we ask how much else, in light of (143.i) and (143.ii), has to be assumed to make the doctrine work. Since what is mentioned in (143.i) and (143.ii) is required for experiential derivation (is, as Kant would say, "necessary for" experiential derivation), the doctrine presupposes an array of abilities that must be there prior to any experiential derivation: humans, merely as humans, seem to need

> (14a)   abilities to represent objects as substances belonging to relatively determinate kinds (fir, willow, linden),

---

[63] Sellars is anxious to press home the distinction between abstraction from content and abstraction from actual cases; see *KPT*, Appendix, Locke, section *A*, and *APM*, section III (reprinted in *KPT*).

[64] In any case, the "more-less" generic hierarchy runs down to a bottom which has nothing "less generic" below it. That is one reason that, in the previous subsection, I found no reason not to treat the kconcept ^linden^ as derived from the content ^linden^ as opposed to some less generic contents. Such cases are bound to be part of the abstractionist view.

(14b) abilities to represent them as having "special determinations" (sizes, shapes, colors, etc.), and
(14c) abilities to "reflect" on these kinds and determinations as contents of representings, to "compare" them, and to "abstract" one from another.

To be sure, better examples than the kconcept of a tree might show that experiential derivation starts a lot lower down. Even so, in the end, there is a residue of abilities to represent substances as members of rock-bottom kinds with rock-bottom "special determinations" and intellectual abilities to reflect on these contents. Since these processes of experiential derivation depend on the active exercise of these abilities, experiential derivation can account for none of the contents required for the exercise of these abilities and certainly none of the abilities themselves despite the clear empirical connections of those in (14a) and (14b). These abilities are innate in, at least, the sense of "not being experientially derived".

147. The mere mention of innateness in connection with Kant rings warning bells. On a quick reading, Kant gives a portrayal of someone quite definitely opposed to innateness in any form. In *CPR* (B167-8), Kant rejects the divine implantation of the categories as dispositions to thought in favor of the claim that they are "self-thought". (In many passages, he also insists that the understanding derives the categories from itself, in contrast to deriving them from experience.) In *On a Discovery*[65] (*O*, 221-3), Kant goes so far as to say that *CPR* is committed to no divinely implanted or innate "representations".

148. Unfortunately, when these questions arise, the opponents Kant has in mind are ones for whom divine causation is really important and he spends time objecting to appeals to the "supersensible" in explanations of the properties of living beings.[66] Second, in a *On a Discovery*, he goes on, in the same passage, to make it clear that the "representations" he is centrally worried about are the "forms" of intuitings, i.e., space and time, and the categories. His main point is that the experiential derivation of determinate kconcepts of things presupposes these "representations". Finally, he claims that, with regard to space and time and the categories, their "ground" is innate (though he does not say anything about the general features of such a ground). His discussion leaves us, therefore, with rather substantial uncertainty as to the more delicate elements of his objections to innateness.

149. Out of the many possible positions compatible with Kant's remarks, I limit my comments to a position appropriate to this introduction: namely, that sketched

---

[65] Immanuel Kant, *On a Discover According to which Any New Critique of Pure Reason Has Been Made Superfluous by an Earlier One*, in Henry E. Allison, *The Kant-Eberhard Controvery: An English translation together with supplementary materials and a historical-analytic introduction* (The Johns Hopkins University Press, 1973).
[66] This point stands out in a pertinent section of *CJ*: section 81.

by Sellars in *CLN*. At **A43**ff in *CLN*,[67] Sellars suggests that Kant believes that we have innate abilities to represent in accordance with "recipes for constructing sequences of object behaviors". These recipes are formulable as principles of kinds of objects and their "determinations" and have *something like* the following form:

if object is a K, then if it φ's, it ψ's.

Two importantly different sorts of examples of such recipes are:[68]

if B is a billiard ball, then if B were tapped, it would roll in a straight line

and

if S is a sphere on a plane, then if S were tapped, it would roll in a straight line.

Sellars remarks that these recipes involve concepts of geometric shapes and concepts of (basic) kinds of physical objects and that

> **B11. We must** distinguish innate tendencies to represent in terms of basic kinds **characterized** by certain basic causal properties. **What is innate** is the *ability* to think in terms of specific kinds and causal properties pertaining to physical objects. If we didn't have these innate tendencies, we couldn't go on from there to formulate more sophisticated classifications in terms of more and more sophisticated causal properties. *CLN*, **B11**

150. Before getting to the major point, I note, first, that Sellars' suggestion is that Kant thinks certain abilities are innate, not any actual representations. Further, in order for such abilities to generate actual representings, there might need to be some kind of activation by sensory activity. Second, Sellars does not say that the ability to formulate the recipes themselves is innate. Let me, in Sellarsian fashion, call these recipes a "proto-theory of objects in space and time". The considerations supporting the belief in the innateness of the abilities specified by such a proto-theory also incline one to believe that the proto-theory must include a proto-theory of representers. In particular, the proto-theory might allow that representers have innate abilities to reflect on and compare their own representings, thus leading in the long run to their formulating the recipes.

---

[67] Lamentably, here uncertainties about the two separate manuscript pads are acute. The impression that I am *very* sure how Sellars would have fleshed out the upcoming points is not one I wish to give, particularly since Sellars has other manuscript pads of the same period which show that he was mulling over complicated and competing formulations.
[68] These examples come from one of the subsidiary manuscript pads of the same period as the *CLN* pads.

Introduction 67

151. Third, that these abilities are innate does not imply that their presence can be explained only by appeal to some non-natural, or supersensible, activity. Consider the lowly chicken egg: a natural object brought about by causal activities of chickens. Taking the word 'ability' in a rather wide sense, I can truly say that the abilities of a chicken egg are produced by the same causal activities that produce the egg. For example, chicken eggs are such that, once broken open, they supply a translucent viscous "white" which, if whipped, becomes opaque white stuff strong enough to support its own weight in little peaks. Such abilities are not immune to causality. For example, heating an egg for a moderate time in boiling water completely destroys the ability just described.

152. Fourth, the difference between the two principles (149) is a reminder that Kant has such strong convictions about Newtonian science that he might view only the second of the two as reflecting an ability that can be innate. The concept of a billiard ball might simply be too complicated (just as, say, the concept of a wheel is more complicated than that of a cylinder with a hole in the middle). This point leads me to a suggestion directly connected with the main point of this discussion.

153. Even the second, "Newtonian" principle might be too sophisticated. For a full-fledged representer, the representings, in temporal sequence,

> this sphere on a plane is tapped
> it will roll in a straight line

contain representings as parts which are concepts (e.g., sphere, plane, tapping, rolling, straight, line). Though far from neat and tidy in stating his requirements for concept possession, Kant believes that some empirical kconcepts are developed by experiential derivation, that kconcepts are the sort of representing that can appear as predicates in judgings (including all the constructions dictated by the forms of judging), and that (most?)(all?) kconcepts are capable of some (perhaps, partial) "analysis", or explication, by full-fledged representers. It is not implausible (and is certainly consistent with his views) to suggest that Kant's requirements for possessing kconcepts (being a kconcept user) are high enough that the usual distinction between apprentices and masters (e.g., between someone who is learning to play the piano and someone who is a pianist) can be drawn. Thus it might be that the representational repertoire of a fledgling representer lacks sufficient sophistication to qualify *any* representing of such a representer as a kconcept. The formulation that *we*, as full-fledged representers, give of *both* principles in paragraph 149 may be too sophisticated to capture the rudimentary content that appears in the representings that actualize the innate abilities of novice representers.

154. Nevertheless, the rudimentary content of the representings of apprentice representers is the same sort of content that appears in our representings, not a different sort. The distinction is that the apprentice representer fails to meet other standards, the meeting of which would qualify the representer as a kconcept user.[69] To indicate rudimentary content, I shall add the prefix 'ur-'. Thus, in my present example, there is the rudimentary content ^ur-sphere^. In an apprentice representer, no occurrence of the content ^ur-sphere^ is the occurrence of a kconcept. Yet like our content ^sphere^, the occurrence of the content ^ur-sphere^ is not the occurrence of something spherical or ur-spherical. Representings, whether their contents are rudimentary or sophisticated, are "of" items with "existence in thought". Since rudimentary content is of the same sort as our more sophisticated content, one impediment to the doctrine of experiential derivation that Kant favors has been removed. Furthermore, since all the content that occurs for an apprentice representer is rudimentary, the content of a representer's rudimentary representings of *this-suches* can provide content to "reflect" on, to "compare", and to "abstract" (to separate out).[70] So, while my suggestion concerning rudimentary content does not eliminate the innate abilities in the list of paragraph 146, it provides them with contents to transform into kconcepts, even though none of those contents qualifies as kconcepts in the beginning.

(d) Summary

155. With these points on the demonstrative model, empirical kconcepts, experiential derivation and rudimentary content in the background, I return to my main task and formulate an approximation of the thesis Sellars wishes to attribute to Kant.

> (K6) Of those representings that Kant calls "intuitions", some of them (primarily, though not exclusively, those he calls "intuitions of a manifold") are (singular and immediate) representings of *this-suches* and are complex in that they are the combining (synthesizing) of contents, one of which, were it occurring elsewhere would be a kconcept, but, as occurring in the intuiting, is not a kconcept.

---

[69] For Sellars' account of such matters in a context free from the impediments of classical doctrines of "abstraction", see section IV of *MEV* (112) and sections I and VI of *BLM* (108). Note that Sellars' discussion of meaning in section II of *MEV* is consistent with representers having innate abilities to classify rudimentarily their own representings. These points about apprentices and masters are part of the backdrop to Sellars' view that the ability to "experience things as thus-and-so" is "coeval" with the ability "to judge that they are thus-and-so". See footnote 61.

[70] Notice that the distinction between apprentice and master applies in the case of intuitings as well. Novice representers have ur-intuitings for the very same reason that they have ur-kconcepts: their representational repertoire is not sufficiently complex. In particular, they may not have sufficient grasp of the connections between intuitings and kconcepts such as that illustrated in (139.viii). I see this point as another addition to my remark in footnote 61.

As a codicil to (K6), I formulate a claim of Sellars' which Sellars does not, of course, attribute to Kant (which I indicate by adding an 'S' to the 'K'):

(SK6) The central properties of the intuitings mentioned in (K6), their complexity, singularity, and immediacy of relation to an object, are illuminated by using, as a model, contemporary accounts of demonstrative phrases.

In sum, Sellars thinks that the model of demonstrative phrases help us understand, in more detail than Kant supplied, how certain representings can be complex and, in addition, singular and in immediate relation to an object. We have some understanding thereby of how some representings can be representings of individuals *as individuals* (not as members of some kind).

156. Furthermore, I have sketched a view of empirical kconcepts in which they are gained by a process (the exact details of which are, admittedly, largely unspecified) from content sufficiently rudimentary that none of it qualifies as kconcepts. The main exegetical point of this excursus into the topic of the development of kconcepts is that nothing in Sellars' demonstrative model of intuitings is inconsistent with maintaining *some* doctrine of "experiential derivation" of empirical kconcepts. Moreover, as I shall argue in what follows, all of this, combined with my forthcoming discussion of Sellars on the categories, provides in the end at least one way of maintaining Kant's view that the categories are not innate and, as well, not derived from experience. Unfortunately, this is just a first step. Before I can make major headway on succeeding steps, I must clean up details.

(II) WHAT SELLARS' ACCOUNT OF INTUITING IS NOT

157. First, as the reader has ascertained from (155.K6), Sellars does not attribute to Kant a thesis that is, in the modern sense, formal (and certainly not one that is syntactical). Second, (155.K6) also makes provision for the claim that Kant is not always talking about representings of *this-suches* when he talks about intuitions. Sellars intends to handle other of Kant's remarks about intuitions by making distinctions where they were not, or were not clearly, made by Kant. Third, part of (155.K6) is a claim about the sort of thing these intuitions are: they are conceptual (intentional) states though not, we can agree with Kant, kconceptual. Even in full-fledged representers, occurrences of •bear•ings and •cube•ings, as well as •that•ings and •this•ings, in •that large black bear•ings and •this cube•ings are conceptual states of the representer, but none of them count as kconcepts.

158. Sellars' account stands in sharp contrast to accounts of intuiting, common to otherwise quite disparate interpretations of Kant, which aim to connect intuitings

with sensory states (104-6). The following discussion is intended to elaborate further this contrast.

159. In the most general terms, one traditional view of Kant's position is that the mind grapples with its own sensory states and, through its own contributions (loosely put, space, time, and the categories), organizes these sensory states and thus makes possible our knowledge of appearances.[71] These traditional views I call (somewhat inaccurately) "phenomenalistic" accounts of Kant. A different, contemporary interpretation (the "cognitive science" view), whose main champion is Patricia Kitcher, attempts to relate Kant's transcendental psychology to modern cognitive science. Despite the cognitive science view's scientific orientation, it seems to incorporate the thesis that the mind, according to its own principles, "processes" sensory states (or, perhaps better, "sensory data") to produce the kinds of higher cognitive states necessary for empirical knowledge.[72]

160. Both the phenomenalistic and the cognitive science accounts suggest several theses that Sellars does not adopt. A word of warning: I do not claim that any of the philosophers I have cited hold these theses. I simply mean that these theses are, at very least, suggested by these sorts of accounts. My primary aim is to set out the theses so I can indicate what Sellars does not hold.

161. I grant that much of the "organizing" or "processing" the mind contributes is something that we do not "notice". In fact, let me go further: the "unthinking and unphilosophical part of mankind," as Hume puts it, not only don't notice this activity, they have no well articulated beliefs about it. After all, the appreciation that all this epistemic (or cognitive) activity exists is an achievement, hard won by philosophical or scientific work. Nonetheless, on both accounts, all these unnoticed and unconceived processes are really taking place. I offer the following story about

---

[71] Philosophy does produce strange bedfellows. I think I can find the sort of view I have in mind in a wide variety of earlier Kant commentators, but I offer references to a few up-to-date writings in which I detect (perhaps incorrectly) this kind of view. See: page 66 of Otfried Höffe, *Immanual Kant*, translated by Marshall Farrier (State University of New York Press, 1994); pages 596-7 of David Bell, "Kant" in Nicholas Bunnin and E. P. Tsui-James (editors), *The Blackwell Companion to Philosophy* (Blackwell Publishers, 1996). With even less assurance, I also suggest pages 306-16 of Paul Guyer, *Kant and the Claims of Knowledge* (Cambridge University Press, 1987). I also worry about section 6 of chapter IV, "Kant and Phenomenalism" of Bruce Aune, *Knowledge of the External World* (Routledge, 1991).

[72] See pages 36-7, 84-6, 102-12, and particularly 113-4 and 117-8, of Patricia Kitcher, *Kant's Transcendental Psychology* (Oxford University Press, 1990) and pages xxxvi-xxxix of Kitcher's introduction to Werner S. Pluhar, translator, *Immanuel Kant, Critique of Pure Reason* (Hackett Publishing Company, 1996). Some such point also seems to be part of McDowell's view of Kant: in remarking on Kant's claim that "sensation" is the "matter" of intuition (or perception), he says that Kant "never suggests that this matter has its *own* form as the matter it is, independently of its being formed into intuitions, perceptions, and empirical knowledge...". McDowell compares the "forming" of sensation to the "forming" of "bronze" into "statues or spearheads" (pp. 456-6 and note 8, "Having the World in View: Sellars, Kant and Intentionality", The Woodbridge Lectures 1997, *The Journal of Philosophy*, XCV, 9, September, 1998).

part of what might be involved in a simple case where I see a house with green shingles and produce a •this house has green shingles• representing.

(1) The subject comes to be in sensory state S.
(2) The subject represents to itself: sensory state, S, has properties P1,...Pn and has occurred in relations R1,...,Rm to sensory states S1,...,Sk.
(3) The subject also represents to itself: the sensory states S1,...,Sk have thus-and-such properties and relations.
(4) Through the action of some principles concerning possible sensory states and their possible organization, the subject comes to represent to itself: sensory state, S, belongs to (is connected with) an organized item to which the concept house applies.
(5) Due to further properties of S and the action of additional principles, the subject finally comes to represent to itself: This house has green shingles.

Keep in mind that this tale is not one that we consciously tell ourselves on occasions on which we perceive objects; but it is at least one kind of tale that attempts to make sense of how all the purported unnoticed processing of sensory data fits into our coming, in a particular situation, to have a representing about a particular house.
162. One thesis this tale suggests is that singular representings of objects like houses are (though "immediate" in one respect) always derivative in that they require singular representings of sensory states. Let me put this another way around:

(Ph1) without the subject having singular representings of sensory states, the subject would never have singular representings of such spatiotemporal objects as houses or bears.

Sellars would agree that (Ph1) can seem plausible in light of various passages in *CPR*, but he finds no compelling reason to include it in his account. It is not that Sellars is against interpreting Kant as believing in unnoticed processing; the question is what the processing is. Moreover, Sellars subscribes, both in his own views and in his view of Kant, to some similar claims about sensory states. As a simple illustration, Sellars thinks that without the *existence* of sensory states, there would be no perceivings of houses with green shingles and no singular representings produced by the perceiver's causal involvement with these houses. What Sellars objects to in the present view is saddling Kant with the claim that the occurrence, say, of a •that large black bear is coming at me• requires the occurrence (at that time or earlier) of a *singular representing* of a sensory state. Representings of *this-suches* and other singular representings of appearances are not dependent on, or derivative from, singular representings of sensory states. (Later I will refer to this point as part of what Sellars has in mind when he says (*SM*, ch. I, 24) that sensory states are not "apperceived" and I will also take up the question of whether representings of bears and houses depend on *any* representings of sensory states.)

163. A second thesis, not suggested solely by my tale, makes a plausible showing when it is combined with some of Kant's remarks about sensibility. Kant says that the understanding works up the "raw material" the senses provide (A1 and B1) (see footnote 72). In addition, one of Kant's favorite contrasts is between "matter" and "form" (see, e.g., A19-22/B33-6). Much of what Kant claims as the contribution of the subject falls under the heading of "form" while the "matter" seems associated with the senses and thus, in some sense, originates from without. So, a natural accompaniment to my tale is the following train of thought:

> the senses supply the raw material of cognition; the subject processes this sensory "matter" only by adding "form"; but transforming something by merely adding form leaves the raw material still there; so, the sensory input supplies the empirical content (as opposed to the form) of any representing; so, for example, the content ^house^, the content ^green^, the content ^bear^, the content ^black^, and so on must be, at bottom, sensory.

Let me put the upshot of this line of thought as the thesis:

> (Ph2) all empirical content is (in some way) sensory content.

Thesis (Ph2) allows for nonempirical content as well, but the nonempirical kconcepts supplying such "pure" content would, presumably, have some strong connection with form (i.e., space, time, and the categories). (Ph2) is a fairly natural thesis for traditional portrayals of Kant as a unifier of empiricist and rationalist principles. A similar thesis about sensory "input" may also be part of some contemporary programs in cognitive science.

164. Once again, Sellars would agree that (163.Ph2) is a thesis that one can with some plausibility attribute to Kant, but (163.Ph2) is not part of Sellars' interpretation of Kant. Though I will show that the content ^house^, on Sellars' account, is connected with something one might call "sensory" content, it does not turn out, in my estimation, to be so in a tough enough sense to satisfy those who would wish to defend (163.Ph2).

165. Sellars' fundamental reasons for not adopting (163.Ph2) I cannot lay out at the moment. The reader will have noticed that I have said little about the sensory and it enters this subsection only because it seemed important to emphasize what is *not* built into Sellars' account of intuitings as representings of *this-suches*. The inherited impetus of my treatment propels me back to additional discussion of such representings and away, for the time being, from the sensory.

(III) DOES SELLARS' ACCOUNT HELP WITH THE COMPLICATIONS?

166. The complications set out earlier (104-120), I repeat below and move through them one by one to fill in more of Sellars' account of intuiting. In some cases, final discussion awaits later treatments of the categories and of the sensory.

(a) The term 'intuition' suffers from the '-ing-ed' ambiguity of all of Kant's terminology of representation.

167. Since I have remarked at length on this matter, I limit my present comments to a simple-seeming point, but one that leads down a road that many Kant scholars have not wished to travel. Kant regularly speaks in terms of "applying" kconcepts to items, or of kconcepts "being referred to" items, or of "determining" items.[73] Especially when Kant talks of applying kconcepts to intuitions, it is possible to generate considerable disagreement. On any view in which intuitions are sensory states, it is possible to think of the item to which the kconcept is being applied as the sensory state. While Kant may wish to say such things, in many cases it is more straightforward.

168. Thus the representing (a judging)—this house has green shingles—is an "applying" of a kconcept to an intuit*ing* in the sense that the judging is a combining (a synthesizing) of an intuiting (a representing of a *this-such*) and a kconcept(ing).

169. In related sense of 'applying', the kconcept of having green shingles is applied to, or is referred to, the object of the intuiting, i.e., the intuit*ed*. So, since the kconcept occurs as the predicate of the judging, the kconcept, as we could say in more contemporary terms, is "predicated of" the object, a house. "Determining" the object, in one sense, comes to the same thing. Moreover, if the judging is true, the object is "determined" in the sense that it does have green shingles.

170. Since judgings and parts of judgings have contents, we also have an example in the judging—this house has green shingles—of the actualizing of the contents ^this house^ and ^has green shingles^ in the content of the judging, i.e., the content ^this house has green shingles^. The judging actualizes the entire judgment content and its component contents and is also thereby an example of an "applying". (I take these remarks to be connected with what Sellars says at *CLN*, **A6a** and **A8**.)

---

[73] For a few examples, see A19-20/B33-4, A68-9/B93-4, and also various places in the Transcendental Deduction of the Categories, particularly sections 24 and 26 of the B version.

(b) There are "inner" intuitings, a product of "inner sense", as well as "outer" intuitings, a product of "outer sense".

171. Entry *(b)* proves to be something that Sellars can make sense of in several different ways. First, there is no reason why intuitings shouldn't be of events like accidents and stumbles:

> that accident on the other side of the 405 will close the northbound lanes of the freeway.
> this stumble by Jones is sending him off the lecture stage in our direction.

Kant holds that events as *thises* have a different status than substances as *thises* (see A182/B224ff.) Still and all, events seem to qualify (derivatively, perhaps) as *this-suches*. Representings are "determinations" of a representer and succeed one another temporally (A31-2/B46-7 and B67-9) and, therefore, occur. Second, there is no problem in there being representings of representings. Together these two points suggest that there is, in principle, no impediment on Sellars' account to there being "inner" intuitings, i.e., intuitings of representings (and, perhaps, intuitings of sensory states). The separation of intuitings as singular representings of *this-suches* from sensory states stops us from having to treat "inner sense" as involving some sort of "inner sensation".

172. Admittedly, the exact formulation of inner intuitings is not easy to come by. Kant enmeshes inner sense in a complicated web of restrictions and conditions. For example, inner intuitings do not involve anything about space. No determination of space (e.g., shape, place, motion) are to be found "within us", only "thoughts."[74] Many of these passages also emphasize the contrast with outer sense: in outer sense are only spatial determinations and forces leading to changes in spatial determinations such as change of place (see also *MFNS*, 523-4, 542-3). Inner intuitings represents the mind "as it appears to itself"[75] and appearances of inner sense are only temporal while appearances of outer sense are, when all is said and done, spatial and temporal (e.g., motion). Finally, Kant wishes to distinguish inner sense from another kind of access to our histories as representers, an access he calls "apperceiving" (see especially B152-9).

173. Nevertheless, one suggestion about inner intuitings is obviously tempting: they are singular representations of other representings. Inner intuitings, then, are the subject parts of judgings about the representings in our mental histories. Consider an example. Dick tokens an •I am back in camp• and then an •I am safe now•. If judgings about these representings are the results of the operation of inner sense,

---

[74] A386-87; also A23/B37, A34/B50, A49/B66, B67, A357-8, A380, and *MFNS*, 470-1.
[75] B69; see also A34/B50, A107, B152-7, A357-9, B429-30, and A546-7/B574-5.

they are as much caused as those judgings, like Dick's •that large black bear is coming at me•, which are results of the operation of outer sense. Judgings of inner sense are cases in which we inwardly affect ourselves (see B153-6). So, they should not be thought of as examples of "introspection" if introspection is understood, as it often is, as being a completely active, intentional process like deliberate searching.

174. If we combine the present suggestion with the Humean claim that all we ever discover in reflecting on our intellectual histories is "some particular perception or other",[76] then a judging involving an inner intuiting might be

> this •I am back in camp• occurred to me just a moment ago

and another might be

> that •I am back in camp• occurred to me immediately before this •I am safe now•.

On this account of inner intuitings, they can be distinguished from apperceivings: apperceivings always involve 'I think' as a indicator of *spontaneity*. Such a way of distinguishing inner intuitings from apperceivings apparently squares with part of the import of passages in *CPR*. Empirical consciousness of our ever-changing inner states is "inner sense, or empirical apperception" (A106). "Pure" (or, "transcendental" or, "original") apperception involves the possibility that the representing, 'I think', accompany my representations; but the representing 'I think' is an "act of spontaneity" and does not belong to sensibility and thus not to inner sense (B132; see also B139, B155-9.) Though this Humean account, if I may so call it, of inner intuitings seems to capture part of what the relevant passages say, these passages also suggest another way of distinguishing inner intuitings and apperceivings.

175. First, a reminder: all representings are determinations, i.e., properties, of a representer, not relations between an object and a representer.[77] True, the doctrine of content pushes toward some relational account of thinking.[78] But, even if one were to lean heavily on the relational aspects of the doctrine of content and decide that the properties of a mind are all, in some way, relational properties, the history of representings of a thinker would still be a history of alterations, the successive gaining and loosing of properties, of the subject.

176. The attempt to found the difference between inner sense and apperceiving

---

[76] The Humean theme seems to be a factor in Rosenberg's characterization of inner sense; see chapter II of Jay F. Rosenberg, *The Thinking Self* (Temple University Press, 1986).

[77] The reader can find an illustration of the importance of this point in the Second Analogy; see particularly A197/B242.

[78] Sellars discusses this in *KTI*, 16, in *CLN*, **A5**ff and in *KPT*, ch. 3, section *D* and ch. 4.

on the logical form of the representings provided by each of them faces major hurdles in later parts of *CPR*. Either because Kant's attention is now focussed on other issues or because some doctrines of the Aesthetic are superseded by later remarks, passages in the Deduction and in the Paralogisms treat 'I think' as a very general and, indeed, empirical vehicle of self-reporting. In particular, it is interesting to note that, in the footnote to B422, Kant says that the 'I think' expresses an "indeterminate empirical intuition".

177. Yet, is there not some distinction to be drawn between inner sense as empirical apperception and "pure" apperception? What are the central differences if they are not to be found in the logical form of the representings supplied by each? Passages at A107f and B132f suggest several differences and a major similarity.

178. The similarity, already mentioned (174), is that there is a wide sense of 'apperception' in which both inner sense and apperception (narrowly construed) count as kinds of apperception. Thus Kant characterizes inner sense as "empirical apperception" while apperception (in the narrower sense) is called "transcendental" and "pure" apperception. So, inner sense being empirical apperception can lay as much claim to the 'I think' as pure apperception. The differences concern spontaneity, purity (in one sense), and necessity. I pass, till later, on how these three are involved in apperception, but I need to make points about inner sense and the empirical.

179. One point is that representings of inner sense (at least) locate our representings in time and therefore are empirical in a wide sense (111). Another is that the representings of inner sense include empirical content, but not generally empirical content applying to the subject. That is, if my thinking has the content ^this piece of wax is hard, cold and easily handled^, nothing in that content is predicable of me, the thinker. As a thinker, I cannot be said to be said to be a piece of wax; as a thinker, the predicate 'is hard, cold and easily handled' is not of the correct sort to apply to me. In the terminology of the previous subsection, representings of inner sense do not "determine" the self by any properties other than properties which have the structure "thinks [content]".

180. Furthermore, since everything that is represented through a sense is appearance (B68), representings of inner sense never supply any content which can tell us what the noumenal self is (see B152ff, A357 and B429ff). But even in the case of the empirical self, judgings of inner sense do not supply any knowledge of anything determinate about what empirical sort of thing a thinker is (see B157ff and A357ff). In general, inner sense might supply us with truths about what an empirical representer represents and, perhaps, even be the source of empirical generalizations about such representings, but it is not the source of an answer to the question "What empirical sort of thing is a representer?"

181. All this being so, it does not seem to me necessary to construe the deliverances of inner sense as being about Humean (in some sense) "subjectless" events.[79] Thus, I shall, in my later remarks, follow Sellars (*I*, 43ff) in construing inner sense as providing such representations as

I •I am back in camp•ed just a moment ago.
(i.e., I just a moment ago thought that I am back in camp.)
I am •I am safe now•ing now.
(i.e., I am now thinking that I am now safe.)

This move does not force me to deny that inner sense *might* also give us the demonstrative representations previously illustrated (or, perhaps, representations which combine both demonstrative and indexical items). It does, however, require that Sellars' demonstrative model of intuitings be augmented to include indexical intuitings as well. As there are generally thought to be connections between indexicals and demonstratives, this addition seems reasonable.

(c) There are both "pure" and "empirical" intuitings.

182. There are at least three ways in which pure intuition can be accounted for on Sellars' characterization of intuitings as representations of *this-suches*. In the Transcendental Aesthetic, Kant describes "pure intuition" as the "pure forms" of sensibility. If one takes the empirical intuiting of a body and removes various properties (such as "substance, force, divisibility" and "impenetrability, hardness, colour"), extension and figure still remain as forms and thus belong to pure intuition (A20-1/B34-5; also A33/B49-50).

183. As a pure form, space, for example, can (indeed presumably must) be present in the intuiteds of outer sense, i.e., spatiotemporal appearances. Thus when I •this house to my left has green shingles•, the intuited, a house, i.e., a certain sort of "body", has "extension and figure." Moreover, the house is represented in the intuiting as in a certain spatial relation to me. And, finally, the intuited, as the subject of predication, has the spatial properties required by the having of shingles (as can be discovered by, to use a term of Kant's, analyzing the kconcepts house and shingles). Similar points about space and time apply to the intuiteds like accidents and stumbles (171). So, the "form" which is the pure intuition is present in empirical intuitings of *this-suches* as the form, i.e., the properties and relations, of the

---

[79] Notice that my formulations in paragraph 174 do not accomplish "subjectlessness" in that the phrase I found natural to use is 'occurred to me'. Notice, too, that it might not, on this model, be possible to maintain Kant's requirement of strict independence from spatial matters since the "me" to whom the representing occurred would seem to be the same "me" that is located in space, a space which also includes the camp and might have included a bear. Another, related issue is whether there can be •this•s which pertain solely to time and involve nothing about space.

intuit*eds*.

184. The second way in which space and time can be the form of intuition is that space and time can be built into the structure of the intui*ting*. Consider the intuiting

(15) this linden near the side door of my house

which appears as part of the judging

(16) this linden near the side door of my house is old.

The demonstrative •this• in (15) expresses the "here-now" presence of a linden which, as the remainder of (15) indicates, is in a spatial relation to the side door of my house. The expression of "here-now" presence is part of what Kant means when he says that intuitings are in "immediate" relation to an object. I cannot, of course, take this as an opportunity to argue about the exact account of principles pertaining to demonstratives and indexicals. But I think what I am about to say is simple enough that it will fit somewhere into nearly any such account, including Sellars'.

185. What has to be part of the principles, or a consequence of the principles, governing demonstratives is that the "here" and the "now" are determined by the place and the time at which the representer S tokens (184.16). So, for objects which are both spatial and temporal, the principles of demonstratives must build in such a connection with space and time that a correct representing by a representer S conforms to the rule that

(D1) it ought to be that

if a representer S produces a token T which is a •this [content] is [kconcept]•,

then a [content] is present in the place and at the time at which S produced T.

So, suppose I produce

(184.16) this linden near the side door of my house is old.

Then, an instance of the condition in (D1), namely,

I produced a token T which is a •this linden near the side door of my house is old•, is true and, given (D1), it is correct for me to token

> a linden near the side door of my house is present in the place and at the time at which I produced T.

Note that (D1) makes a connection (of the sort discussed in 139) between the content ^linden^ as it is actualized in an intuiting and as it is actualized as a kconcept. (D1) is thus a principle of the connection between contents occurring in intuitings and contents occurring as kconcepts.

186. Of course, the total account which includes (185.D1) would make further remarks about how the place and time are delineated. When I token (184.16), I can be standing inside my house, worrying about the consequences if the trees around it do not weather the upcoming winter winds. From certain vantage points it is possible to see the entire fourteen mile ridge of the Cuillins on the Isle of Skye. In such a case the "place" would be adjusted by the circumstances and would certainly be a largish one. Moreover, though the linden is a spatiotemporal object that can be perceived, I need not be perceiving it at the time. It might be pitch black outside and, even if I were standing at the side door of my house looking in the correct direction, I still would not be seeing the linden. (And, truth be told, there are few enough days when the Cuillins are out of clouds.)

187. We think of logical form as being explicated by principles. (185.D1) is a principle, or is a consequence of principles, governing the workings of demonstratives. The "logical form" of intuitings incorporates, through (185.D1), both space and time (at least in the case of spatiotemporal appearances but, perhaps, time only in the case of inner appearances.) Even though representings are not spatial, Sellars' account of intuitings allows those representings which are, or which contain, intuitings to have "spatial form" and "temporal form" as part of their logical form. Sellars thinks that Kant should agree that transcendental logic (instead of "general logic") includes such principles (and Sellars also holds, I think, that some such principles are part of what is at issue in the second and third Analogies).[80]

188. Finally, in yet a third sense, Sellars' account allows for items which are clear candidates for the status of pure intuitings. Consider a case in which (perhaps as Socrates did in the *Meno*) you draw, with a stick in the sand, a square. You then inquire: What square would have twice the area of this square? The intuited in this question is, without doubt, a square drawn in the sand. Yet since the intuiting omits all content save the geometrical content ^square^, we have an example of an intuiting of a square *as* merely a square and as nothing else. An intuiting of a drawn

---

[80] Needless to say, logical form is, for Kant, an example of "purity". Though (185.D1) incorporates reference to space and time, I believe that we can come to appreciate that this reference does not impugn the purity of such principles.

or an imagined geometrical figure can be pure in that it contains only mathematical content out of all the content it could contain. Omitting possible content is nothing particularly strange or unusual since we do it all the time in representing *this-suches* (see A714/B742).[81]

189. The topic of space and time as forms is not, of course, completed by this discussion. I remind the reader that Sellars thinks that Kant talks about sensory states as intuitings. These, too, as we shall discover, can, in a way, have space and time as their forms.

(d) There are concepts corresponding to (associated with?) all (most?) intuitions.

190. In effect, I have already commented on *(d)*: I claimed that it is at least possible that empirical kconcepts be derived from the content of intuitings (141-54). When, however, we remember that this claim depends on Kant's agreeing that we have abilities to "reflect" on, "compare" and "abstract" contents (145-6), we can find a line of thought that sheds light on other than empirical kconcepts. I observed, in my earlier discussion of *(d)* (112), that while Kant insists that space and time are "pure intuitions", it is evident that he also thinks of there being kconcepts of space and time. Moreover, it is part of the burden of my comments on *(c)* that spatial and temporal contents appear in empirical intuitings as the "forms", i.e., the properties and relations, of the intuiteds (182-3). But if this is all so and the activity of the understanding allows it to "derive" empirical kconcepts from empirical contents, why shouldn't it do the same for spatial and temporal contents? In fact, the passage at A20-1/B34-5 suggest that very possibility: we start with an empirical intuiting and "separate out" one property after another until we are left with extension and figure which belong to "pure" intuition. Is this not the same process that gives rise to empirical kconcepts?

191. I do think that this is so and that it gives us a partial understanding of what Kant thinks about the source of mathematical kconcepts and other non-empirical kconcepts. But before I continue with this line of thought, I must make clear what is not being claimed. I pointed out (149-50) that Sellars interprets Kant as believing that we have innate abilities to represent in terms of "recipes" connected with principles pertaining to physical objects. At the time, I did not emphasize two points. First, some of these recipes pertain to geometric items (*CLN* **A31-[A35] & B6**). Thus to intuit a square (188) is to be in a conceptual state that depends on a recipe for which, as we sophisticated kconcept users believe, there are correct principles pertaining to squares. Second, these recipes, *in their most rudimentary form,* allow

---

[81] Time is on a par with space with regard to being a form, but there is some question whether Kant would allow for pure intuitings of time in the sense just described. At A33/B50, he suggests that time provides nothing akin to the shapes of space and that we make up for this lack by conceiving time in spatial terms.

us to come to have representings of *this-suches* even though we may well be at a cognitive stage at which we cannot formulate these recipes and their attendant principles. As sophisticated kconcept users, we come to be able to formulate these principles and direct our cognitive activities in light of them.

192. In general terms, the point of paragraph 191 is that one sort of "combining" (synthesis) is a requirement of intuitings as representings of *this-suches*. The results of this combining, the content of the intuiting, is there for the understanding to "reflect" on. I need to expand this point. Item *(g)* in the original list of complications brings up the question of the relation of intuitings to the categories. In my earlier discussion (116-120), I took the position that two strains of thought compete in Kant's treatment of intuition. The strain being investigated at the moment insists that categories are required in the activity of intuiting.

193. Now, let me remind the reader of passages which Sellars takes very seriously (119). One says that combination, i.e., synthesis, of any manifold of representing is accomplished only by the understanding (B129-31). The second claims that intuitings require syntheses in order to be unified and these syntheses, supplied by the understanding, are the very syntheses which unify representations in judgings. The "synthetic unities" shared by intuitings and judgings are formulated in the "pure concepts of the understanding" (A79/B104). The overwhelming impression such passages convey, I claimed, is that intuitings are unified by combining utilizing the categories. Sellars' account of intuitings as representings of *this-suches*, as we shall see, allows for such a use of the categories. These points make the questions of paragraph 190 more pressing since, now, it seems that the understanding might stand a chance of "deriving" even the categories.

194. The answer requires coming to grips with Kant's view on the traditional contrast, "derived from experience" versus "innate".[82] Earlier (147ff.), I pointed out that Kant is adamant that there is a third possibility. A passage in the B Transcendental Deduction of the Categories expresses Kant's concern about someone's rejecting his view about the origin of the categories, namely, that they are "*self-thought* a priori first principles", and opting instead for the doctrine of innateness (B167). In the lines that follow, Kant rejects this possibility as firmly as he rejected, in the preceding lines, the doctrine that the categories are "derived from experience" (see also *PFM*, 260).

195. In that same passage (B167), Kant describes the position he favors in different terms: the categories "make experience possible". Just this conclusion, Kant informs us in section 14, "Transition to the Transcendental Deduction of the Categories", is a guide to the structure of the Transcendental Deduction: it should

---

[82] Sellars was a little cavalier and imprecise in his early remarks on this matter and even says that the categories are, for Kant, innate (*KTE*, section 7). But very shortly thereafter he came to see that he had to be more careful about exactly what Kant takes to be innate. In particular, Sellars subsequently says that the categories are not innate (*I*, 20).

show that the categories, as a priori concepts, are necessary conditions of experience and that the categories relate necessarily and a priori to objects of experience because only by the categories can any object of experience be *intuited* or *thought* (A93-4/B126).

196. One virtue of Sellars' view is that, in the end, all of this enjoys a noncontrived place in his account. For the present, I consider part of his strategy. On Sellars' view, intuitings as representings of *this-suches* involve space and time (184-187) as part of their transcendental-logical form. The same thing, Sellars also argues, is true of the categories. So, the central part of his strategy is to explain a sense of 'experience' in which experience requires intuitings of *this-suches*. In this sense of 'experience', therefore, space and time, and the categories, each in their own way, are "conditions of the possibility of experience." That is, with respect to "experience" in this sense, space, time and the categories are *a priori* in that, without them, there would be no experience.

197. So, on this strategy, the answer to questions, like those of paragraph 190, is straightforward: that the understanding should be able to "separate out" space, time and the categories from experience in this sense is irrelevant. To speak in terms that Kant sometimes uses, what is "put there" to make experience is a fortiori there to be recognized and separated out by activity of the understanding. (Kant also thinks that, about no concepts other than space, time, and the categories, can it be said that they are necessary for experience *in general*.)

198. Notice, first, that none of the above points deny what was said earlier (146ff): that Kant believes *something* to be *a priori* in the sense of being innate. But the sense of '*a priori*', the sense of 'being prior', that is crucial for space and time and the categories is not that which has to do with innateness, but rather with being necessary for "experience". How this might be so for the categories I attempt to explain later. For space and time, however, I have, even at this stage of the exposition, taken a step in the correct direction. Given that part of the Sellarsian strategy is to explain one sense of 'experience' in which experience requires intuitings, anything which is necessary for intuiting is necessary for experience. In discussing complication *(c)*, I offered (185.D1) as a principle required for intuitings of *this-suches*. (185.D1) is, then, at least a preliminary example of the sort of thing that is necessary for experience. In more Kantian terms, it is the transcendental- logical form (185.D1) supplies which is necessary for experience.

199. Second, that the understanding might "sort out" all sorts of different content from intuitings and other representings is, as far as I can tell, an advantage of Sellars' view. It can help us understand what Kant is saying at B167 where he tells us that, out of the triad "self-thought", "innate", "derived from experience", the categories are "self-thought": i.e., derived from reflection on intuitings as representings of *this-suches*. Moreover, Kant clearly thinks that the three members of the

triad are independent in that you can opt for one and deny the other two. For Kant, then, if "derivation from experience" is to stand as an independent member of the triad, it has to be, not just "finding something" in intuitings and, thus, in experience, but a matter of obtaining something from "experience" (in some sense) that, to put it crudely, isn't "put there" by the understanding.

200. To nail down these points, another part of Sellars' strategy must be to characterize a sense of 'experience' in which it can be seen to be plausible that space and time and the categories *cannot* be "derived from experience". Sellars wishes to do just this. As a result of the two senses of 'experience', the phrase 'derived from experience' also comes to have two senses. Though, here again, comment on the categories must wait, a small point about (185.D1) makes a beginning on this topic in the case of space and time. It is initially plausible that one can so characterize "experience" (in terms of sensory states) that the logical form contributed by a principle like (185.D1) is not the sort of thing that can be derived from it.

(e) Sensibility has both concepts and intuitions.

201. Clearly Sellars claims that Kant employs the term 'sensibility' ambiguously. Intuitings as representings of *this-suches* belong to sensibility as a faculty whose operation is not independent of the understanding (particularly of the understanding acting as the productive imagination). For now, let me borrow the term 'productive' and speak of this sensibility as the "productive sensibility". The other sensibility, as yet undiscussed in this introduction, I shall call the "passive sensibility".

202. Attributing kconcepts to the productive sensibility is in line with the passage at A268/B324, mentioned at the introduction of complication *(e)* (114). Kant's central concern is with those who would confound the objects of "pure" understanding with appearances (A269/B325ff). He drives home a very general contrast between things in themselves as objects of the pure understanding versus appearances as objects which we can intuit (e.g., A279/B335). Since appearances in general are at issue, it therefore is appropriate that any empirical kconcept might (for a sophisticated concept user) appear as the content of an intuiting. Just this (as we shall see in more detail) Sellars' account of intuitings as representings of *this-suches* obviously allows.

203. The other part of Sellars' strategy, the characterization of the passive sensibility, provides a way to draw a Kantian distinction between faculties that are not conceptual at all and ones like the understanding and the productive sensibility which are.

204. Two small points. First, the productive sensibility in producing intuitings with the aid of the productive imagination is not judging. Intuitings, on Sellars' account, can be the subjects of judgings; but without a predicate, there is no

84   Introduction

judging. Thus Kant's claim that sensibility does not judge (A293/B350) is preserved even for what I am calling the productive sensibility. Second, the productive sensibility need not be construed as acting independently of the "passive sensibility". Since, in general, Kant characterizes faculties by what job they get done, there is no obvious problem in one faculty depending on another for doing its job.

(f) Intellectual intuitions are possible.

205.   One impediment to through-and-through sensory accounts of intuitings is not an impediment for Sellars: a divine understanding has no sensory activity.[83] Lacking a passive sensibility, a divine understanding could nevertheless produce intuitings of *this-suches* without the aid of sensory states and be entirely active, or spontaneous, in its intuitings. While the details would be pure speculation (since Kant tells us too little about divine understandings), Sellars' account has found a possible place for such items.

(g) "All Sensible Intuitions are subject to the Categories" (B143).

206.   The distinction between intuitings as representings of *this-suches* and intuitings as sensory states and the correlated distinction between the productive sensibility and the passive sensibility are necessary, on Sellars' account, to making sense of *(g)* and, at the same time, to give due respect to the passages Kant scholar A cites in my fictitious dialog (11). The details of all this depend on Sellars' account of the categories, their involvement with representings of *this-suches*, and their noninvolvement with sensory states—all that will finally complete consideration of the list of complications, particularly item *(g)*.

C. A Transcendental Logic: The Categories
(1) "TO PUT IT BLUNTLY"

207.   Mostly, I use a meat cleaver where Sellars uses a scalpel. On the subject of the categories, Sellars forgoes medical instruments for munitions. Nothing I would say could outdo, in tone and directness, Sellars' own pronouncements:

> Metaphysical Deduction (the form of judgment). ...
>   The crucial point to appreciate here is, to put it bluntly, that the categories *are* the forms of judgment. *CLN*, **A26b**

True enough, Sellars qualifies this remark. But at the last and from the first, Sellars

---

[83] B71-2; see also A27/B34, B138-9, B145, B148-9, B158-9, B306-10, and A286-7/B342-3.

defended the thesis that, for Kant, the so-called "ontological" categories are (in some sense) "really" epistemic categories:

> Kantian "categories" are concepts of logical form, where 'logical' is to be taken in a broad sense, roughly equivalent to 'epistemic'. To say of a judging that it has a certain logical form is to classify it and its constituents with respect to their epistemic powers. *KTE*, 23

That the categories are, at bottom, the forms of judging is one element in Sellars' account of the "epistemological turn" in Kant's philosophy:

> Indeed, as we shall see, the core of Kant's "epistemological turn" is the claim that the distinction between epistemic and ontological categories is an illusion. All so-called ontological categories are in fact epistemic. They are "unified" by the concept of empirical knowledge because they are simply constituent moments of this one complex concept, the articulation of which is the major task of the constructive part of the *Critique*. *KTE*, 9 (See *CLN*, **A26b-A28a**.)

208. Further, Sellars' thesis about the categories as "epistemic" concepts is strongly connected with his account of part of what Kant is really doing in *CPR*:

> Thus he [Kant] thinks of the categories as together constituting the concept of an *object* of empirical knowledge. The extent to which this is so does not stand out in the Metaphysical Deduction. It isn't until the Analytic of Principles, as has often been pointed out, that one can grasp the full import of Kant's theory of the categories. The conception of the categories as the most general classifications of the logical powers that a conceptual system must have in order to generate empirical knowledge is the heart of the Kantian revolution. *KTE*, 29 (See also *TTC*, section I.)

This passage is a partner of the concluding remarks of the earlier long quotation (85) in which Sellars compares transcendental psychology to transcendental linguistics. The concluding sentences of that quotation describe the goal of transcendental linguistics:

> It attempts to delineate the general features that would be common to the epistemic functioning of any language in any possible world. As I once put it, epistemology, in the "new way of words" is the theory of what it is to be a language that is about a world in which it is used.[11] Far from being an accidental excrescence, Kant's transcendental psychology is the heart of his system. He, too, seeks the general features any conceptual system must have in order to generate knowledge of a world to which it belongs. *KTE*, 41

209. I deal with this web of claims by pulling it apart into simpler strands which

I will, in the end, reassemble. In addition, I intend to take perverse advantage of a point Sellars himself makes. He says, in describing Kant's theory of categories,

> ...it is to be noted that implicit in the above account of categories is a theory of abstract entities. *TTC*, 27

Sellars' strategy is to adumbrate this theory of abstract entities together with the theory of categories. To achieve a simpler and more accessible exposition, I intend to separate the account of the categories from that of abstract entities. Moreover, I will depart from Sellars' own formulation in order to highlight certain points in this theory. I have, though, found no way of avoiding rather complicated, and certainly contemporary, considerations and distinctions; and it is partly because of this that I introduced a soupçon of Sellarsian machinery, specifically dot quotation, earlier in this introduction.

(II) THEY ARE "NOTHING BUT *FORMS OF THOUGHT*" B305-6

210. That Kant subscribes, in some less than contemporary idiom, to the connection Sellars finds between the categories and the forms of judging is a thesis that has substantial textual support.

211. Kant tells us, in introducing the table of judgments, that the functions of the understanding are the "functions of unity in judgments" (A69/B94) and that these functions can be gathered under the four headings of the table of judgments (A70/B95). In addition, Kant makes it clear, in discussing general logic and transcendental logic (A50/B74ff), that both general logic and transcendental logic are disciplines that deal with, as Kant often puts it, the "forms of thought." Then in the Metaphysical Deduction of the Categories, at A79/B104, Kant says, not only that the functions which provide unity to judgings also provide unity to intuitings, but also that these "functions of unity", or concepts of synthesis (A80/B106), are the pure concepts of the understanding, the categories.[84]

212. Kant's emphasis on this connection between the categories and the functions of judgment is maintained in later passages. Just before the Transcendental Deduction, at B128, in elucidating the categories, Kant says that the categories are the means by which intuitings of objects are "*determined* in terms of one of the *logical functions* in judging." Particularly throughout the B version of the Transcendental Deduction, Kant makes statements that can, without any strong construing, be read as maintaining that the categories are the forms of judgment. For example, at B143, Kant claims to have made it clear (or perhaps demonstrated) that any intuiting is

---

[84] Thus Sellars has more than one reason for this being one of his favorite passages (see *KTE*, 29; *I*, 20; *CLN*, **A26b**).

(and he uses the phrase from B128) "*determined* in regard to one of the logical functions of judging." He then adds that the categories are just these functions of judging understood as applied to intuitings.

213. Since Kant claims that the categories are a priori concepts, he worries that someone might conclude that the categories give us the resources for gaining knowledge about things in themselves[85] and so he, quite early on, argues that the only objects the categories allow us to gain knowledge of are appearances, i.e., objects of intuitings. Quite frequently when he states this epistemic limitation of the categories, he explains why intuitings are necessary by pointing out that the categories are "mere forms of thought" (B150) and therefore are incapable by themselves of supplying knowledge of individual objects. Putting the same point the other way around, he sometimes says that were we to deprive the categories of their connection with intuitings, they would revert to being "mere logical forms" (A136/B175), or to having only "purely logical" significance (A147/B186) or to being mere "forms of thought" (B288; B305-6; A567/B595), or "pure form" of thought (B305). The Sellarsian reading of these passages is that being a category is just being a form of judging as it is applied in the case of intuitings.[86] A near summary of what I am propounding occurs at A321/B377-8 where Kant contrasts the categories and the transcendental ideas. He says that the Transcendental Analytic has given us an example of how "logical form" can be the "origin" of the categories; these forms of judging, "converted" so that they apply to intuitings, yield the categories and are concepts of the synthesis of intuitions. I intend to explain this characterization.

214. There are two hurdles standing in the way of elaborating the view of the categories as the forms of judging.

(a) The table of judgments

215. First, there is the table of judgments itself. Controversy has arisen partly from its inadequate account of the structure of judgments. Another problem is Kant's desire to arrange the entries of the table into four groups of three items each. (This raises questions that are difficult to answer: e.g., does each judgment have one feature from each group?) Sellars' position appears to be (see *TTC*, section I) that we should agree that the logical theory of Kant's time is inadequate and give Kant the benefit of later work in logic. In confirmation of this, note that Sellars nowhere, in all the pages he wrote on Kant, bothers to discuss in detail the specifics of the table of judgments. Thus, Sellars indicates that he sees no point in attempting to defend the exact items and structure of the table. I concur with this view.

---

[85] For what may be the earliest example, see A88/B120-1.
[86] Indeed, this very formulation is found in the long footnote to 474 of *MFNS* (*Metaphysical Foundations of Natural Science* translated by James Ellington in *Immanuel Kant, Philosophy of Material Nature*, Hackett Publishing Company, 1985).

88   Introduction

216. I shall, therefore, approach the doctrine of logical form in a generally contemporary fashion without, however, laboring through the details of any one approach. It is my hope that the points that I make will not be thought to hinge on complicated logical distinctions. Furthermore, from a contemporary perspective, Kant lumps together items which all, in some way, belong to logic, but not all in the same way. Thus, in these days, it is reasonably common to treat negations, disjunctions and conditionals together, within a logic of sentences (propositions, whatever). But Kant does not set matters up in this way. The disjunctive judgings he has in mind are ones that express mutual exclusion and might really be better formulated by saying "such and such judgings are mutually exclusive". Similarly, in the case of the hypothetical, it seems to me that given Kant's association of this logical form with causality, it is better to formulate judgings of this logical form as implications. (Of course, doing so would not prevent an equivalent formulation in terms of some sort of conditional.) I intend to handle all these matters without laboring over the details.

(b) Not exactly THE categories

217. Second, beginning in passages in the Preface to the Second Edition (Bxxviff), Kant emphasizes that our knowledge of individual objects and the principles which govern them is limited to appearances, i.e., objects of intuitings, and that, properly speaking, we have no such knowledge of things in themselves. He claims that all this is proved in the analytical part of *CPR* (Bxxvi). Equally though, he argues that we are able, indeed must, think about things in themselves. So, on the one hand, he secures for himself a position which stands against the traditional presumptions of metaphysics to supply us with determinate knowledge of a supersensible realm of objects while, on the other, he does not leave himself without some means, essential to both his transcendental psychology (75-90) and his account of morality, of dealing with things in themselves and such attendant concepts as freedom.

218. If we speak in a reasonably general way, few would disagree that this limitation of the categories to appearances is proclaimed loudly and regularly by Kant though with different emphasis and formulation from passage to passage.[87] Equally, though, Kant emphasizes, in sometimes the very same passages, that the categories allow us to think about things in themselves. The categories are not limited, in thought, by anything that is connected with intuiting or restricted by

---

[87] I list just a few of the more prominent places in which Kant makes this point: A130 (end of the Transcendental Deduction of the Pure Concepts of the Understanding in A); B146-7, B166 (both in the Transcendental Deduction of the Pure Concepts of the Understanding in B); A147/B186-7; A235/B288; throughout the chapter on the distinction between phenomena and noumena (A235/B294-A260/B315; see, e.g., B308); A567/B595; A696/B724; A719/B747ff.

anything having to do with sensibility.[88] Moreover, many passages require Kant himself to employ categorial terms in writing about things in themselves (80-8). Some noteworthy examples are later in *CPR*,[89] but the section on the Amphiboly of Concepts of Reflection (A260/B316-A289/B346), dealing with differences between appearances and things in themselves, is unavoidably filled with categorial terms, e.g., the term 'object'.

219. Part of the solution to this apparent tension is that it is not true that one can speak of *the* categories without qualification. At very least, the categories of the table of categories, what we might call the "pure" categories, are to be contrasted with what are usually called the "schematized" categories.[90] The chapter of the Schematism (A137/B176-A147/B187) explains how to connect time and the pure categories to produce restricted categories, the schematized categories.

220. Sellars thinks the situation is slightly more complicated than that. As noted earlier (115, 205), Kant believes that the concept of non-sensible, i.e., intellectual, intuitings is an intelligible concept though not one we can explicate in any determinate way. In addition, Kant thinks it possible for there to be other beings with sensible intuitings different from our own (A27/B43; A42/B59; B72). Presumably such beings would have schematized categories but not necessarily ours (see *PFM*, 351).

221. Taking into account all the above, Sellars suggests, in *CLN*, a scheme which distinguishes levels of categories. This suggestion is buried within a complicated passage. Since, in the next subsection, I frame my account by using this passage as a foil, I quote it at length though the presently pertinent points are near the end:

> **A26b. & B25.** *A word about the categories*: Metaphysical Deduction (the form of judgment). The Metaphysical Deduction is regarded as seriously flawed. Kant, it is said, simply fails to "derive" his categories from the forms of judgment.
>
> The crucial point to appreciate here is, to put it bluntly, that the categories *are* the forms of judgment.
>
> **A26c. & B26.** More delicately put, the categorial concepts,
>
> > substance, attribute, negation, plurality, etc.,
>
> are concepts of the *forms* of judgments (not always form in the sense of syntactical role).

---

[88] See, e.g., A96-7; A109; B147-8; B158; A147/B186; B224; A242; A245; B304-15; A286/B342-A288/B344; A771/B799.
[89] B431; A494/B522; A537-8/B565-6; A566/B594; A696/B724.
[90] The distinction between the "pure" and the "schematized" categories is crucial for Kant. Over and over again in the Transcendental Dialectic, he appeals to this distinction. In the Paralogisms, at A349-50, he contrasts the "pure" category of substance with the "empirically usable concept of a *substance*". (See also A356-7, A399-402, B421-2, B429, and B431-2.) Similarly, in the Antinomy, the distinction carries great weight and is sometimes appealed to directly (A499/B527-8), but sometimes, as in his explanation of how freedom is possible (A544/B572), it is tacitly required by the position he is defending.

The categories are concepts of the conceptual powers of a judgeable or of a representable-as-a-constituent-of-a-judgeable by virtue of a subject matter independent feature of the judgeable.

A26c. & B27. Thus if we use the phrase

> Category C applies to x

to mean

> Category C is true of x,

then what C is true of is always a judgeable or a representable as a constituent of a judgeable.

A26c. This is obviously true of negation:

> 'the sun is not hot' is the negation of 'the sun is hot'.

A26c. & B28. In scholastic terminology, the subject of categorizing judgments are terms taken in second intention.

> the sun is a substance
> 'the sun' is a subject

A26c. & B29. Notice that the categories are not limited to what we would call syntactical features of judgeables:

> it is necessary that every number is either (evenly) divisible or not (evenly) divisible by 4
> 'every number is either (evenly) divisible or not (evenly) divisible by 4' is unconditionally assertable (which involves reference to a judging mind)

> lightning is the cause of thunder
> 'there is lightning at t' causally implies 'there is thunder at $t + \Delta t$'

A26d. & B30. I said "subject matter independent". Obviously we must distinguish between the categories as features common to judgments about any subject matter, e.g., common to empirical, metaphysical, mathematical, theological, ethical judgments, e.g.,

> being a triangle is the ground of having an area equal one-half base times height
> being a case of promise keeping is a ground of being a duty,

from those which are specified as being about individuals in a spatio-temporal world. The latter are the schematized categories.

A26e. & B30. In between the pure-pure categories and the schematized categories are categorial concepts which concern the characteristic features of judgeables specified to a subject matter which consists of individuals (objects of possible experience), but where they are not specified to be *spatio-temporal*, i.e., might be experienced by *non-human* finite minds:

> pure-pure categories—completely subject matter independent;

> pure categories—apply to judgeables and representables which are possible objects of experience, but not necessarily spatio-temporal.

This is really a generalization of the concept of a schematized category: schematized categories—categories which apply to judgeables about the spatio-temporal world.

Thus the category of ground-consequence applies in the judgeable

> things in themselves are the ground of the manifold of sense

and that of subject-attribute in

> judgings are attributes of minds.

A26e. & B31. Obviously the judgments which belong to transcendental philosophy (the metaphysics of knowledge) have logical form and categorial concepts are true of and apply to the **terms** of such judgments.

> But none of this requires, or so Kant argues, that this world of things in themselves and thinking subjects in themselves have categorial form.

> Putting it bluntly, only judgeables and constituents of judgeables have categorial form. (Once again, how this thesis is to be understood is perhaps the central problem concerning Transcendental Idealism.)

> Once again, only judgeables—whatever their subject matter—have logical form.

(As a small aside, I should point out that the thesis that *only* judgings and their constituents (or, *only* judgeables and their constituents) have logical form and thus categorial form is not new to *CLN*. It also appears much earlier in *KTE* (*KTE*, 21 and 22). What does seem to be new is the position that Sellars assigns this thesis in his account of Kant's thought.)

(III) A METAPHYSICAL DEDUCTION OF CATEGORIES
(a) The forms of judging are the forms of thinking

222. The title of this section is a bit fanciful, but it complies with Kant's description of metaphysical deduction at B159 (compare B38): a metaphysical deduction shows the a priori origin of concepts. In the case of the categories, this is accomplished by showing their connection with the forms of thought, i.e., the forms of judging.

223. Though Kant calls these forms the forms of "judging", he associates these forms with the understanding and thus with thinking. Indeed, Kant says that all thinking of objects requires the categories (B165-6) and that the 'I think' is the "vehicle" of all concepts, not just transcendental ones (A341/B399). He further characterizes the thinking I as the object of inner sense (as contrasted with body which is the object of outer sense) (A342/B400)[91] and says that "this I or he or it" is known to us "only" through the thinkings which are its properties (A346/B404). When we put these comments together with Kant's remarks

> that the understanding is the faculty of thought (A51-2/B75-6; A69/B94; A126),
> that the understanding is a power of judgment (A69/B94),
> that the ability to judge is equivalent to our ability to think (A81/B106),
> that all different explications of the understanding (as a spontaneity, as a power to think, as a power of concepts, as a power of judgments, as a power of rules) come to the same thing (A126),
> that thinking is involved in all activity of the understanding (B131), and
> that our consciousness of ourselves is as thinking subjects (B155; footnote to B158; A341-2/B399-400; A357-8; B429),

it seems reasonable to attribute to Kant the thesis that

> (K7) the forms of judging are the forms of all thinking.[92]

(Actually, Kant remarks that all acts of the understanding can be reduced to judgings (A69/B94) and although (K7) might be part of what this remark means, it is not clear that is so).

224. A warning: (K7) might seem, to some, to be completely innocuous, but it has, in concert with other principles, consequences that others might not think to be innocuous. McDowell is, perhaps, an example in point. For him, judging is "making up our minds what to think" and is therefore an "exercise of freedom."[93] Neither Sellars nor I wishes to deny that there is such a notion as "making up our minds what to think"; and we do not wish to deny the possibility that sometimes Kant uses the term 'judge' for that very notion (see, for possible examples, A130-4/B169-173). Sellars, however, treats Kant as using a wider concept of judging, for which

---

[91] This point is briefly and forcefully repeated in *MFNS*, 467.
[92] At *PFM*, 304, Kant makes the stronger remark that thinking and judging are the same.
[93] John McDowell, "Having the World in View: Sellars, Kant and Intentionality", The Woodbridge Lectures 1997, *The Journal of Philosophy*, XCV, 9, September, 1998, 434 and 439.

Introduction 93

judgings are not all cases of "making up our minds what to think". Judgings, in this wider sense, are representings and some of them occur in examples of "making up one's mind".[94] Exactly what differences of importance mark off the user of the wider sense of 'judging' (the only one I will henceforward use) from the user of the narrow sense is not easy to set out since each will try to accommodate distinctions drawn with the competing terminology. For the present, I note that since perceptual experiences are not cases of "making up our minds what to think," McDowell must say that the "claims" that are a part of visual experiences are not cases of judging.[95] Sellars says that they are and, thus, as we shall see, treats perceptual experiences (in one sense of 'experience') as requiring the forms of judging.

225. Since I have treated thinking as one kind of representing, I would be satisfied to state (K7) as the thesis that

the forms of judging are the forms of representing.

Without some distinctions that I have not yet drawn, I am convinced that it is better to stick with (K7) for the moment.

226. Given (K7), forms of judging show up in all thinking, even that, say, about mathematics or morality. These forms of thinking are subject-matter independent. The first step is to connect them with the "pure-pure" categories.

(b) Step one: pure-pure categories

227. Consider an earlier example,

(46.8) this piece of wax is cold, hard, and easily handled.

Now consider various specific classificatory judgings:

(17) (46.8) is a judging,
(18) (46.8) is subject-predicate judging,
(19) the subject of (46.8) is a •this piece of wax•,
(20) the predicate of (46.8) is a •is cold, hard, and easily handled•.

In general,

---

[94] Of course, not all complete representings are judgings; e.g., some complete representings are questions. Questions can derivatively have the forms of judging without being judgings. Parts of judgings, e.g., predicates, also partake derivatively of the forms of judging.
[95] John McDowell, "Having the World in View: Sellars, Kant and Intentionality", The Woodbridge Lectures 1997, *The Journal of Philosophy*, XCV, 9, September, 1998, 434.

94   Introduction

   (21) •this piece of wax•s are singular terms,
   (22) •is cold, hard, and easily handled•s are predicates, and
   (23) •this piece of wax is cold, hard, and easily handled•s are judgings.

Sellars connects the categories with such classificatory judgings as (21)-(23). I depart from the details of Sellars' strategy (in, e.g., *TTC*, in this volume) to show that his account can be made to fit more closely the "content" account of representing (40-55) and to make distinctions that Sellars wants, but does not spell out.

228.   The rule for producing judgings about the *contents* of representings (in particular, thinkings) relies on classifications of representings; the truth of a categorial judging, thus produced, depends only on the truth of the classification of the representing. The classification of the representing determines the category of the content. So, given (227.21)-(227.23), the contents ("ideas") are classified as follows:

   (21^) ^this piece of wax^ is an individual,
   (22^) ^is cold, hard, and easily handled^ is a property, and
   (23^) ^this piece of wax is cold, hard, and easily handled^ is a state of affairs.

I claimed (50) that, when asked, Kant and his predecessors would have said that contents are simply individuals, properties, relations, states of affairs and so on. Further, they would have employed the customary singular constructions for these individuals, properties, relations, and states of affairs to formulate judgings about them. Thus from (21^), (22^) and (23^), they would move to:

   (21C) this piece of wax is an individual,
   (22C) being cold, hard, and easily handled is a property, and
   (23C) that this piece of wax is cold, hard, and easily handled is a state of affairs.

229.   By constructing the path from (46.8) and its classifications, (227.21)-(227.23), to (228.21C)-(228.23C) as I have, we can see that other "items" can be categorially classified from the appropriate "form of thinking". Thus, for example, consider

   (24) there are intelligent beings living on Mars,
   (46.8) this piece of wax is cold, hard, and easily handled, and
   (25) $5 + 7 = 12$,

and assume that

(26) •there are intelligent beings living on Mars•s are possibly true judgings,
(27) •this piece of wax is cold, hard, and easily handled•s are actually true judgings, and
(28) •5 + 7 = 12•s are necessarily true judgings.

Then following the route set out above, we arrive, first, at

(29^) ^there are intelligent beings living on Mars^ is a possibility (a possible state of affairs),
(30^) ^this piece of wax is cold, hard, and easily handled^ is an actuality (an actual state of affairs), and
(31^) ^5 + 7 = 12^ is a necessity (a necessary state of affairs).

and, in the end, at the categorial classifications

(29C) that there are intelligent beings living on Mars is a possibility (a possible state of affairs),
(30C) that this piece of wax is cold, hard, and easily handled is an actuality (an actual state of affairs), and
(31C) that 5 + 7 = 12 is a necessity (a necessary state of affairs).

230. The term 'individual' in (228.21^) and (228.21C) is meant to carry a contrast between individuals, on the one hand, and properties, relations, and states of affairs, on the other. But, since the tradition, right up to the present, employs singular constructions, such as those in (228.22C) and (228.23C), to occupy the subject positions in claims about properties, states of affairs and the like, there is pressure to recognize a wider sense of 'individual'. In effect, the reader will find that, in *TTC*, Sellars does just this. For present purposes, this elaboration heads in an interesting, but exegetically wrong, direction. I am concerned in what follows with individuals in the narrow sense and with the attempt, appropriate to Kant, to separate out an even narrower sense of 'individual'.

(c) A meta-logical point

231. Kant sets his account of the forms of judging and the categories in what he calls "transcendental logic". My introduction of "pure-pure" categories from the forms of judging gives categorial terms a status which it would not be unwarranted to call "logical" in a wide sense. This wide sense of 'logical' has, in part, the sense of 'pertaining to the structure of thinking (or, representing)'. Sellars prefers, we have seen, the term 'epistemic'. I prefer not to spend space arguing about which term is better, but I do think it necessary to emphasize a central similarity between categorial terms and logical ones (in a narrow sense of 'logical').

232. In order to avoid contemporary battles about logic, I shall assume that connectives are adequately characterized by principles only if these principles, along with other logical principles and, perhaps, other premisses, have as consequences statements about the truth-values of the compounds these connectives form. (Obviously, one possible way to satisfy this requirement is to use truth-value statements to characterize the connectives directly.) An example: the principles for characterizing a conjunctive connective must have the consequence that, in the case of a conjunctive connective that combines two judgings to form a complex judging (a conjunctive judging), the complex judging is true if and only if both judgings are true.

233. Given the premisses that

•and•s are conjunctive connectives,
•2 + 2 = 4•s are judgings, and
•5 + 7 = 12•s are judgings,

one can produce a conjunctive judging, thus:

(32) 2 + 2 = 4 and 5 + 7 = 12.[96]

From these premisses and the assumed adequate principles pertaining to conjunction, it follows, first, that

(33) •2 + 2 = 4 and 5 + 7 = 12•s are true if and only if •2 + 2 = 4•s are true and •5 + 7 = 12•s are true.

Then with the additional premiss that

(34) (32) is a combining of a •2 + 2 = 4• and a •5 + 7 = 12• with an •and•, and is thus a •2 + 2 = 4 and 5 + 7 = 12•,

if follows, second, that

(35) (32) is true if and only if the •2 + 2 = 4• in (32) is true and the •5 + 7 = 12• in (32) is true.

---

[96] The reader is to treat (32) as a tokening. It is true that all that appears on the page of the book are ink marks which are a result of a long process that includes a typing.

The generality (33) does not follow from (32) and even (35) does not follow from (32), but *against the background of assumed premises* the material equivalence of (32) and (35) can be shown.

234. Further, (233.32) cannot be rewritten using, let me call them, the "meta-conceptual" principles characterizing conjunction or any of the consequences of these principles, e.g., (233.33). No matter how strongly you characterize the job of these meta-conceptual principles (e.g., they explain what conjunction is; they explain the meaning of 'and'), they do not provide anything which "says the same thing" or "means the same thing" as (233.32). The material equivalence between (233.32) and (233.35) does not show that (233.32) and (233.35) "say the same thing".

235. One benefit of the meta-conceptual characterization of conjunction is that it enables us (with the help of some additional principles) to determine what is a logical consequence of a conjunctive judging and what is not. For example, we can show that the reasoning

(36) $2 + 2 = 4$
therefore, $2 + 2 = 4$ and $5 + 7 = 12$

is incorrect while the reasoning

(37) $2 + 2 = 4$ and $5 + 7 = 12$
therefore, $2 + 2 = 4$

is correct. All this is entirely compatible with my remarks in the previous paragraph. As an addition to those remarks, notice that the judgings of logical consequence (and lack thereof), for example,

•$2 + 2 = 4$ and $5 + 7 = 12$•s are not a logical consequence of •$2 + 2 = 4$•s, and
•$2 + 2 = 4$•s are a logical consequence of •$2 + 2 = 4$ and $5 + 7 = 12$•s,

are not to be confused with the corresponding reasonings. Also, •therefore•s are not •is a logical consequence of•s, though the correctness of tokenings of •therefore•s are to be ascertained by appealing to rules of logical consequence.

236. In essence, what I claim about the categorial terms 'individual', 'property', and 'state of affairs' is that my characterization of them is parallel to that of logical terms like connectives. *Within the context* of a transcendental psychology which, like its contemporary counterpart transcendental linguistics, contains principles of the classification of representings into singular terms, predicates, judgings and so on, (227.21), (227.22), and (227.23) provide what is necessary for determining the truth and logical relations of

(228.21C) this piece of wax is an individual,
(228.22C) being cold, hard, and easily handled is a property, and
(228.23C) that this piece of wax is cold, hard, and easily handled is a state of affairs.

But the judgings (228.21C), (228.22C), and (228.23C) cannot be rewritten, or replaced, by (227.21), (227.22), and (227.23), respectively.

237. One failure of logical consequence is particularly important to note: it does not follow from (228.21C) that

(38) an individual (namely, a piece of wax) exists.

Categorial judgings are true (or false) independently of questions of existence. This is as the tradition had it. Certainly Descartes needed an individual (as opposed to a property or state of affairs) to reflect upon even if no pieces of wax existed.

(d) Category realism

238. To many contemporary philosophers, there is a problem with what I have offered as the beginning of an account of the categories: my account presupposes that classifications of representings are, in some sense, "prior to" (or the "source of") classifications of the items representings are "of" or "about". Let's put this point the other way around. These philosophers would object that an item of language, or of thought, gets whatever status it has within a theory of representation *because* it stands for (is about, is associated with) a certain category of item. For example, predicates are predicates because they stand for properties or relations. So, for them, the sequence of steps from (227.21), (227.22) and (227.23) to (228.21C), (228.22C) and (228.23C) proceeds in the wrong direction. Let me call this view "category realism".

239. At this juncture, my contribution to the war between category realists and their opponents is to point out that Sellars is (rather obviously) correct in claiming that

(K8) Kant is not a category realist.

Kant's problem, as he sees it, is to give an account of the origin of the categories that makes them pure, a priori concepts of the understanding. Kant rejects (194-5, 199) what he thinks of as the other options—derivation from experience and innateness. With this exegetical point in mind, one purpose of the metaphysical deduction

I am carrying out is clear: without it, Kant has no answer about what the source of the categories really is. He has rejected, for the categories, the two then common accounts of their origin and now he needs some answer to his opponents' objection that there isn't any other source.

240. However, I believe another line of thought illuminates Kant's position better. Kant regularly says that the categories are the necessary conditions of possible experience (195). It is, of course, part of Sellars' strategy to argue that there is sense of 'experience' in which this is true. This sense of 'experience' (195-8) is one that involves intuitings in the sense of representings of *this-suches* and therefore thinking. For Kant, no object can be thought without the categories.[97] So, the categories must have their source in the understanding, and nowhere else, because the categories are part of what the understanding contributes so that it can think about objects. Kant believes that obtaining the categories from objects *of any sort* (concrete or abstract) requires the thinking (representing) of these objects and thus already assumes that the representer is utilizing the categories.[98] All said and done, that leaves Kant with no way to be a category realist.

241. This line of thought also sets the metaphysical deduction in a new light. My Sellarsian metaphysical deduction derives the categories from the forms of judging which I have claimed are the forms of all thinking (223.K7). So, if successful, the metaphysical deduction shows the categories to be part of the theory of thinking (representing) and to be akin to logical concepts. To put it bluntly, the categories are concepts necessary for understanding the concept of thinking (representing). I summarize this in a thesis attributable to Kant:

(K9) A metaphysical deduction of the pure concepts of the understanding (categories) shows them to be derived from concepts (forms of judging) belonging to the theory of thinking (a part of transcendental psychology) and thereby necessary for all thinking, including judging.

242. Further, my derivation of the categories holds out the possibility of demonstrating that the categories are a priori concepts (222) and also pure (without anything empirical in the wide sense) concepts by showing that such a status can be defended for the concepts of the theory of representing and, in particular, for the

---

[97] Passages in *CPR* which I read as saying this in so many words are: A92/B124-A94/B126; A109-111 (especially the second paragraph in A111); B164-5 (particularly the first sentences of section 27). There are other passages in which Kant mentions this claim in passing while discussing other issues: e.g., A199/B244-5; B309; A677/B705.

[98] There is, of course, a possible view which speaks directly to point: namely, the view that "abstract ideas", such as the categories, literally directly *cause* the soul to have the ability to produce representings using these ideas. Interestingly enough, Sellars believes that Plato at least flirted with this view (*KPT*, Appendix, Descartes, section *A*). Kant's remarks on Plato (A314/B370-A319/B375; A568-9/B596-7; A853-4/B881-2) make it clear he does not see this as a live option.

concepts of logic.[99] I admit that work needs to be done, but, for the moment, I am content that I have taken a step in the direction that Kant would surely desire.

243. Before I move onto the second step of my metaphysical deduction, I cannot resist a small aside about Sellars' own views. Sellars is not so concerned about the a priori and the pure as Kant was. Moreover, contemporary treatments of the categories are not playing on the same field as those of Kant's time. Almost all (all?) present-day category realists subscribe to some view about the acquisition of concepts through language. It is not obvious that there is any problem in a category realist's believing that the categories conceived realistically are learned as are any other concepts (though this is not to say that there might not be a problem). For Sellars, then, part of the importance of a "metaphysical deduction" of the sort he pursues is that it provides a bulwark against category realism by showing how the categories can be concepts in an "epistemic" theory that explains what is required for empirical knowledge. To drive this home, I repeat a part of paragraph 208:

> **208.** ... Thus he [Kant] thinks of the categories as together constituting the concept of an *object* of empirical knowledge. ... The conception of the categories as the most general classifications of the logical powers that a conceptual system must have in order to generate empirical knowledge is the heart of the Kantian revolution. *KTE*, 29 (See also *TTC*, section I.)

This passage is a partner of the concluding remarks of the earlier long quotation (paragraph 85) in which Sellars compares transcendental psychology to transcendental linguistics. The concluding sentences of that quotation describe the goal of transcendental linguistics:

> It attempts to delineate the general features that would be common to the epistemic functioning of any language in any possible world. As I once put it, epistemology, in the "new way of words" is the theory of what it is to be a language that is about a world in which it is used.[11] Far from being an accidental excrescence, Kant's transcendental psychology is the heart of his system. He, too, seeks the general features any conceptual system must have in order to generate knowledge of a world to which it belongs. *KTE*, 41

(e) Step two: substance and causality

244. As I promised (215-6), I do not intend to expend much energy on the details of the table of judgments and thus on the details of the table of categories, but two

---

[99] For Kant's thoughts on the "purity" of logic, see A50/B74-A57/B82 (and compare the opening paragraphs of the Preface of *G* (Immanual Kant, *Grounding of the Mataphysics of Morals*, translated by James W. Ellington (Hackett Publishing Company, 1981)). My account also holds out the hope that even more can be said about the description of the categories as "self-thought" (B167) and as arising from the "pure operations of thought" (*MFNS*, 472).

entries, substance and causality, play such a prominent role in later sections that I need to say a little about them. My sketch develops points in the long quotation from Sellars (221), in particular, with regard to the distinction between the pure-pure categories and our schematized categories. As I treat both kinds of categories together, my exposition is, by Kant's lights, out of order as the schematism of the categories appears only after the transcendental deduction of the categories. I hope that whatever my procedure lacks in fidelity to Kant, it gains in expositional clarity.

245. Kant says much about substance (a goodly amount in the First Analogy) that has been the source of disagreement, making thorough discussion out of the question. Instead, I take my start from a theme found in many disparate passages. In an Aristotelian turn of phrase, Kant remarks that the pure concept (pure-pure concept in Sellars' terminology) of substance is the concept of something that can be a subject of predication, but never a predicate.[100] Compare this with our schematized concept of substance, the concept Kant describes in the Schematism and then discusses in the First Analogy. Our schematized category of substance is the concept of that which is the subject of change and which is permanent (or enduring) through change. Change is a way of existing of an object succeeded by a different way of existing of that object (A187/B230).

246. The Aristotelian conception of substance seems to me to be, for present purposes, too encompassing. Literally, almost everything might count as individuals in the sense of being subjects and not predicates (something Kant comes very close to saying at A349). My present exposition is better served by dealing with a more circumscribed pure-pure concept of substance, one more tailored to our schematized concept.[101] Such a concept is constructed, on Sellars' view, by articulating and elaborating the theory of representing.

247. Using my earlier example,

(46.8) this piece of wax is cold, hard, and easily handled,

I set out a tripartite condition. First, consider two judgings which are combinings of two tokenings of a demonstrative singular term with tokenings of two different predicates: for example,

a •this piece of wax• with a •is cold•

---

[100] B129; B149; A147/B186; B288-9; A243/B301; A246; A349; A401; B412; B431; see also *MFNS*, 503.

[101] Actually, in terms of the tripartite division Sellars insists on in *CLN* (see **A26e & B30** in the long quote in paragraph 221), I explicate, in my general remarks, a "pure-pure" concept, but the illustration I give approximates more closely to an example of a "pure" concept of substance. For expositional purposes, I have simply ignored these complications.

and

>   a •this piece of wax• with a •is warm•.

Second, suppose that the two predicates are incompatible as a matter of principles of some sort; for example,

>   a judging that is any singular term combined with a •is cold and warm•

is guaranteed by principle to be false. (Kant, I think, believes there to be principles that apply to kconcepts as kconcepts. Of course, we are describing a situation generally; and, presumably, he would not consider the general specifications to depend on our having such principles in any given case.) Notice that the specifications do *not* require that the two judgings mentioned above are logically inconsistent. Third, on the demonstrative-phrase model of representings of *this-suches*, we are assured, by the rules of such representings (139, 185), that it ought to be that the representer is in a determinate relation to something of the correct sort in the case of each judging. In the example of Descartes' piece of wax, the determinate relation might be that of being in his hand. So, supposing that the tokenings have been produced correctly and thus that the representer is in a determinate relation to something of the appropriate sort in the case of each judging, I can construct an identity:

>   the something to which the representer is in determinate relation as tokener of the one judging is identical to the something that the representer is in determinate relation to as tokener of the other judging.

In terms of our example,

>   the piece of wax in the hand of Descartes as tokener of a •this piece of wax is cold• is identical to the piece of wax in the hand of Descartes as tokener of a •this piece of wax is warm•.

If this three-part condition obtains and, as well, *the two judgings made by the representer are both true*, then the meta-conceptual condition for a PP-substance is met. (The 'PP' indicates that we are dealing with the pure-pure category.) In terms of our example, it would be true that

>   (39) this piece of wax is a PP-substance.

(Properties do not satisfy these conditions and are not PP-substances though they are individuals in a wide sense.)

248. Of course, since it appears that the two judgings are inconsistent, it is hard to appreciate that the three-part condition can obtain and the two judgings also be true. But Kant believes that we have examples in our own case of all of this being so. What makes the examples possible is time. All I have done above to produce the pure-pure concept of substance is to leave out what pertains to time: Sch-substances ('Sch' indicates schematization) endure through time and are the subjects of change. In terms of my example, I have supposed all the following are true:

Descartes thinks that this piece of wax is cold,
Descartes thinks that this piece of wax is warm,
being warm and being cold are incompatible,
the piece of wax in the hand of Descartes as thinker that this piece of wax is cold is identical to the piece of wax in the hand of Descartes as thinker that this piece of wax is warm, and
both thoughts are true.

How? Well, he thinks one thought at one time and the other thought at another time: correspondingly, the piece of wax is cold and *thereafter* is warm. Our schematized category of substance requires that the formal conditions for being a substance are realized in time (A142/B181ff). To sum this up, Sch-substances can change, where the concept of change is the loss and temporally subsequent gain of modifications (see B48 and A187/B230).

249. Nonhuman schematizations are, as Sellars suggests, left open as possible by this account. Nonhuman finite minds with different sensibilities could take the concept of PP-substance and realize it in whatever order they use in place of time. I do not rule out that, if we knew of such an order, we might decide that it too was "temporal" in some sense of 'temporal' that allowed for different kinds of time, of which ours would be just one.

250. There is even, on this view, the possibility of a species of the pure-pure category of substance that no finite mind has. Kant, as I noted (218), often employs categorial terms in connection with things in themselves. These terms express, on this view, the pure-pure categories. The pure-pure categories make it possible for us to think things in themselves, i.e., to represent things in themselves (79). I argued (80-84) that *CPR* contains textual evidence to support the claim that things in themselves have their own order and even conform to their own laws. The present account of the pure-pure categories of substance requires that if things in themselves are to be PP-substances, then they must have relations among themselves (see the third condition) though we don't have a clue what those relations are. There is, however, a true counterfactual (with a "metaphysically" false antecedent): if we knew these relations, we would be able to form a restricted category that applied to things in themselves. (Technically, this restricted category is not a schematized category since Kant associates schematizing with sensibility.[102]) Neither we nor any other finite mind, so Kant tells us, can do this. I take this point to provide some insight into Kant's claim that we can think about things in themselves. It also reinforces my earlier point (75-9) that things in themselves are not some "airy-fairy" metaphysical items about which we can, in all possible senses of 'know', know nothing at all. (Cf. Sellars' remarks in *SM*, ch. II, section X.)

251. Another feature of my account of the categories is that space comes into the schematized category.[103] Perhaps my account can be recast to omit space and leave only time. It certainly is true that Kant insists that time is what is required in schematization (A138-9/B177-8; A144-5/B183-4), perhaps because inner sense supplies nothing spatial and deals only with the temporal (172). From my vantage, there is, in one way, no problem: the forms of judging apply to representings which, as actualizings by representers, are in time; that the really important concept in schematization is time seems natural. But I am not much moved by these reflections to think that space must not be mentioned at all in connection with the schematized categories.[104] The Transcendental Deductions (particularly the B version, sections 20 through 25) make it abundantly clear that the categories apply in the case of *all* intuiteds, inner and outer, and both deductions contain, near their ends, a discussion of how we "prescribe" (or "legislate"), through the understanding, laws to nature, i.e., laws to *all* objects of experience (A125ff; section 26 in the B deduction).

252. The category of causality presents a different expositional problem. It is easy enough to say what causality is on Sellars' account: it is causal implication. In the long quotation in paragraph 221, Sellars gives us an example of our schematized category at work:

lightning is the cause of thunder
'there is lightning at t' causally implies 'there is thunder at $t + \Delta t$'.

Such implications can be expressed by conditionals:

---

[102] A divine understanding has no schematized categories since divine beings do not have sensibilities. But such a being could, for example, create things in themselves and thus create the order underlying the restricted category without having any schematized category.

[103] Also, a determinate relation which might fit general restrictions sufficient for us to be willing to call it "spatial" in a generalized sense comes into the pure-pure category. This might not be an issue for Kant since no specific spatial relation of ours gets mentioned.

[104] I invite the reader to consider *OP*, 21:454 and 21:455. There Kant contrasts the pure concept of magnitude with our schematized concept of magnitude. He mentions only restriction to "sensible intuition", not to time alone. I also note, in passing, that his attempt to formulate this pure category by leaving out the restriction to sensible intuition is of a piece with my attempts in this subsection.

if there is lightning at t, then there is thunder at t + Δt.

By contrast, the unschematized category omits the reference to time.[105]

253. That much simply said, questions arise that cannot be answered in this introduction. Is the pure-pure category of causality to be understood as merely implication in general, with no involvement of anything even remotely similar to succession? An affirmative answer would incline us toward the claim that the pure-pure category is that of "ground-consequence" and applies in cases that are not causal at all. The quotation from Sellars contains something like this claim. His examples are:

> being a triangle is the ground of having an area equal one-half base times height;
> being a case of promise keeping is a ground of being a duty.

On the other hand, one might decide that, even at the level of the pure-pure category, something should be done to generate, much as in my treatment of substance above, a cut-down concept of implication that covered fewer sorts of cases. Of course, Kant provides no guidance about how one would proceed to accomplish this rather contemporary task.

254. But other contemporary questions are equally pressing. One of these Kant seems to be, to some degree, aware of. In a footnote in the Second Analogy (A297/B252), Kant says that his preceding discussion concerned changes of "state", and not just any old thing that might be called a "change". The example he gives is uniform motion of a body. Uniform motion, Kant says, involves changes in relations, but no change of "state"; only acceleration or deceleration of the body produces a change of state in the body. The problem is easily described in terms I have employed. Given Newtonian principles and the appropriate circumstances,

that body B is at place p at time t implies that B is at place q at t+Δ.

Nevertheless, it sounds a little odd to say that B's being at p at t "causes" B to be at q at t+Δ (though it would, perhaps, also be odd to suggest that the above implication had nothing do with causality). Pushing the body, and thus accelerating or decelerating it, is a cause and an appropriate implication is available. However, the above implication about places and times at least suggests that some such true implications may not correspond to causal claims.

255. There are a wide variety of responses to this problem. One might, in the spirit of Kant's remark, try to distinguish changes of "state" as a sub-group of changes in general. One might then use this distinction to help characterize both a narrow and a wide sense of 'cause'. Traveling down these philosophical avenues is

---

[105] Once again, I ignore the complexities that arise from Sellars' tripartite division; see footnote 101.

256. First, the central suggestion of Sellars' view is that the pure-pure categories are derived from the forms of thinking. Nothing I have sketched in paragraphs 253 and 254 shows that this derivation ("metaphysical deduction") cannot be done. Second, the complications do not show that Sellars is attributing to Kant a view Kant did not hold. After all, what Sellars is saying is that Kant had the idea, not that he worked the whole thing out. Many serious philosophical claims take more to set them on solid footing than their originators ever imagined.

257. A third, and somewhat different, point is that the view of the categories as, at bottom, the forms of thought might seem to give the categories too much separation from sensibility and perception and thus from empirical knowledge. I have stated this worry rather vaguely because I want it to be a reasonably general worry and because I don't know how to make it clearer. Perhaps the worry can be illustrated by an example. Suppose someone said: "Sometimes on the highway, one sees an accident. And, sometimes, as part of that, one sees an automobile hit another and dent its side. Is it not that one is perceiving substances (automobiles) in causal interaction (denting)?" (If you don't like the use of artifacts in the example, substitute an ancient battle in which people "dent" each other with blunt instruments.) The answer that Sellars would give to this question is "yes". Exactly how this fits into Sellars' view is what I hope to explain in upcoming sections and to do so in such a way that Sellars' response to this worry about categories and perception gives no succor to the category realist. Indeed, the response is aimed, in part, at removing one prop of category realism: namely, the thought that if the categories are involved in perception, they really can't be quasi-logical notions.

(f) Step three: kconcepts and intuitings

258. My metaphysical deduction has additional consequences for both kconcepts and intuitings. Kant is certainly aware that kconcepts have logical form though he tends to reserve comments on "logical form" to judgings.[106] In conformity with my policy of giving Kant the benefit of contemporary work in logic, I should like to make what I hope my readers will find to be tiresomely obvious points.

259. Consider the kconcept of a vehicular accident.[107] Vehicular accidents are a certain sort of occurrence and are individuals in the wide sense (though they are not substances and thus not individuals in the narrow sense). An explication of the kconcept of vehicular accident, while not at all easy, would seem to involve something like the following: at least one vehicle is moving and the vehicle hits

---

[106] See A712/B741ff and *Immanuel Kant Logic*, I. General Doctrine of Elements, First Section: Of Concepts and Second Section: Of Judgments.

[107] I say "vehicular accident" and not simply "accident" since it may be that the term 'accident' is associated with a family of related concepts and that there is no single concept of an "accident".

some other object (vehicle, pedestrian, tree, whatever) hard enough to damage one or the other. The contemporary reader, of course, notices 'at least one', 'and', 'some', and 'or'. Having logical form in concepts through the appearance of logical terms is now beyond the commonplace.

260. Something else shows up in this (partial) explication. If the concept of a vehicular accident includes that of a moving vehicle, then built into the concept of such an accident are the categories of individual and property. Further, the bringing about of damage requires that at least one individual start out the occurrence in, so to speak, better condition than it is at the end of the occurrence and that its change in condition at the end causally results from the motion of the vehicle.[108] In short, the change of state, as Kant would put it, of one of the individuals is causally implied by facts about a moving vehicle. So, in this way, the concept of a vehicular accident involves causal implication.

261. These observations are not a result of the example I chose. It is a twentieth-century example and it uses artifacts, but two prominent (of the few) examples in *CPR* are that of a house (A190/B235ff) and of a ship (A192/B237): complicated concepts and concepts of artifacts as well. Take the concept of a house. (Ignore some borderline cases and some contemporary architectural innovations.) Part of this concept is the concept of a roof and the concept of walls (or pillars, or arches) supporting the roof, or at least the concept of something that supports the roof. However you put it, the concept of supporting is a causal concept or, at least, a concept that involves causality in its explication. Take Descartes' piece of wax. Part of the concept of wax is that if something is a piece of wax, then being in your hand, at rest with respect to its immediate surroundings and at your body temperature, implies its being solid (i.e., not "runny"). The piece of wax, therefore, rests in Descartes' hand and does not "run off" (a change of state involving causality).

262. These points bear on intuitings as well. I argued (particularly 139-40) that Kant does not treat the contents of intuitings as kconcepts. (Even for the sophisticated kconcept user, the contents in intuitings are not occurring as predicates.) On the other hand, the connection between those contents and kconcepts is not that remote.[109] There seems to be no reason to saddle Kant with defending the claim that there is something wrong with

---

[108] Notice how inadequate my explication of vehicular accidents is: for all I have said so far, an earthquake that throws your automobile on top of another has just created a vehicular accident. Well, nothing hinges on my explicating the concept of vehicular accident adequately (though your insurance company cares).
[109] According to Kant, at least some kconcepts are derived from the contents of intuitings. Would this be true for the kconcept of a vehicular accident? a ship? a house? These kconcepts seem rather complex. Here, perhaps, we have examples where Kant would agree with the tradition and think that full-fledged kconcept employers get to construct by logic more complex kconcepts out of an already present stock of less complex ones (145) and, once constructed, these complex kconcepts are candidates for being contents of representings of *this-suches*.

> this ship ...
> this house ...
> this accident ... .

His own examples suggest the opposite. Sellars' account, as I claimed (202), allows practically any empirical kconcept to appear as the content in an intuiting of a full-fledged kconcept user.

263. I mentioned (210-214) that, in the Metaphysical Deduction of the categories, Kant tells us that the combinings, i.e., the syntheses (see A77/B103), in judgings are the same as those to found in intuitings (A79/B104-5). Now we see how this can very simply be so. The combinings of contents in kconcepts are logical combinings taken from the forms of judging.[110] There is no reason to think that these forms should change when that content comes to appear in an intuiting. In short,

> the combinings of contents, whether the combined contents occur as a kconcept or in an intuiting, are the same.

Of course, the combining of contents in an intuiting or in a kconcept can be done without the kind of conscious activity that sometimes goes into making a complex from simpler elements. The understanding, acting as the productive imagination, can do so in a way of which we not conscious, at least at the time it happens (see A78/B103 and compare A120, B151-2, and B164.) None of this shows that the combining is different in the two cases: Kant seems to insist on the opposite.

264. Moreover, in the case of rudimentary content (153-4), we should probably suppose that Kant would agree that such combinings in ur-intuitings and in ur-kconcepts cannot, as a matter of the impoverished cognitive status of neophyte representers, be done as sophisticated reflection.

265. I have illustrated a way in which the forms of judging (and of judgeables) appear in kconcepts and intuitings.[111] So, given the derivation, argued for above (227-30), of the categories from the forms of judging, I have exhibited the represent*eds* of these various representings as having categorial form. In particular,

> all intuitings involve the forms of judging and all intuiteds have categorial structure and a categorial classification, a "unity" (substance, property of sub-

---

[110] Once again, we can "fine-grain" our classifications so that, e.g., conjunction as it appears in concepts is *derived* from conjunction as it appears in judgings. Thus the two can, strictly speaking, be different even though enormously similar. Indeed, a more generic classification can be characterized such that both a "judging" conjunction and a "predicate" conjunction are simply conjunctions.

[111] It might be that this, too, is part of what Kant had in mind when he said, in the section before the Table of Judgments, that "all acts of the understanding can be reduced to judgments."

stance, etc.).

266. I have thereby imputed to Sellars the view that the Metaphysical Deduction does a fair amount of work for Kant. In particular, it accomplishes what is mentioned in the Transcendental Deduction at B143, "All Sensible Intuitions are subject to the Categories" and at B144, "Comment". There Kant says that a beginning is made on the deduction by showing that the logical functions of judging, which are the categories, determine intuitings. That is, by means of a category the understanding contributes a "unity" to an intuited: the intuited is a substance, or a property, or a quantity, or a modality, and so on. It is a natural outcome of Sellars' view of the Metaphysical Deduction that the Transcendental Deduction should be, in part, an unpacking of what went before (cf. *KPT*, ch. 11). What else, then, does the Transcendental Deduction do? Unfortunately, there are many candidates for answers to this question. Kant himself supplies some at B144 by referring to what he will do in section 26.[112] Reading section 26, one discovers that an important part of that section attempts to show that all synthesis is subject to the categories, even that in perception, and that the understanding through the categories makes "nature" possible by prescribing laws to it. I intend to make headway on just these matters in discussing the Transcendental Deduction.

(g) Unity, apperception, and the forms of judging

267. But, first, something more on "unities". The topic of this small subsection is a little off my main line of march, but it is a first salvo on a topic that returns on several later occasions.

268. Kant talks about "unity" in many different contexts in *CPR*. Of his remarks about unity, those that are presently relevant occur in the Metaphysical Deduction itself (A65-83/B90-116) and, perhaps, also in section 15, the beginning of the Transcendental Deduction in the B edition. Sellars has a suggestion about unities and the forms of judging that connect them with apperception.

269. Earlier (171-181), I noted that one of Kant's claims is that apperception is in some sense "pure". Of course, Kant thinks of the logical forms, the forms of thought, as pure and a priori. Logic, for Kant, is not derived from experience and its concepts do not have empirical admixture of any sort (242). An element of the Metaphysical Deduction is that we can have correct representations of other representations; these correct representations classify the other representations in logical terms. Let me review the pertinent points.

270. Jones judges, i.e., produces a synthesis, in a unique way (*CLN*, **A14ff**):

---

[112] Another one suggested by Kant is that making a case *that* something happens is not showing *how* it happens (see, e.g., *CPR*, B20-1, *MFNS*, 474 note, *PFM*, 276).

110   *Introduction*

the sun is hot.

This judging, like all judgings, is a unity in a straightforward sense: it is not a list. It is a combining of items into one item: a judging. More, of course, needs to be said about this kind of combination, but the present point is that it is possible for us to classify this representing as a judging. That is, this representing can be apperceived as a judging (*CLN*, **A13c**). Furthermore, the "mode" of unity, the kind of unity, can be further specified. The judging might be singular or universal, affirmative or negative, hypothetical or disjunctive, and so on.

271. The machinery of my metaphysical deduction applies the forms of judging to kconcepts and intuitings (258-66). So, the points I have just made about judgings transfer to kconcepts and to intuitings (as, of course, representings of *this-suches*). In particular, our ability to classify the content of intuitings by the forms of judging shows that they, too, are unities of apperception.

272. I mention all this now because of three considerations. First, a simple point: it gets us started on seeing how some apperceivings can be "pure" representations of our thinking selves. In part, they are "pure" because of the logical concepts that show up as the predicates of the apperceivings.

273. Second, a consequence of taking the metaphysical deduction seriously, which Sellars does, is that the logical classifyings of representings lead to categorial classifyings of contents. The contents (states of affairs, individuals, properties, relations, and so on) are, therefore, unities as well. (I will argue that they also have a different sort of unity, also due to the categories and definitely synthetic.)

274. Third, Sellars denies that the kind of synthesis involved in judgings is the only kind that is crucial to Kant's doctrines. I am not alluding to the point that there are more complicated examples of categorial combining. Let me characterize the kind of unity of representings, supplied by logical forms, as "intellectual". I will try to show in the next section that there is more intellectual unity to discover. But, in the end, Sellars is firmly on the side which holds that there is other unity and other synthesis than the intellectual.

(IV) A Transcendental Deduction of Categories
(a) 'Transcendental'? 'Deduction'? 'Possible experience'?

275. Again, the title of this section might also seem fanciful. Yet, I do something here that ought to be recognized as fitting some of Kant's stated requirements for a transcendental deduction.

276. To say that there is little agreement on the transcendental deduction (What premisses does it have? What is it supposed to prove? Is it really a deduction in our sense at all?) is an understatement.[113] And again, Kant is responsible for some of the problem. A case can be made that Kant does not use the word 'transcendental' in just one sense and that he does not use the word 'deduction' in a sense that would come to our minds at all.[114]

277. With regard to deductions, Kant observes that there are empirical deductions as well as transcendental deductions. At A85/B117ff, he explains that an empirical deduction traces the origin of a concept from experience and thus is unavailable to pure, a priori concepts such as the categories. This emphasis on the origins of concepts is maintained in late passages (for a very late one, see A762-2/B790-1), but it is frequently there earlier and, perhaps, explains why Kant thinks that the Transcendental Aesthetic contains a transcendental deduction of the concepts of space and time (A87/B119-20). In the Aesthetic, the transcendental "expositions" (the word 'deduction' is not in the headings of these sections) of the concepts of space and time speak of the origins of these concepts in pure intuition. (Since, in the previous sections, I trace the "origins" of the categories to forms of thinking, it is apparent that there are some reasons for believing that my metaphysical "exposition" is, at least, a *start* on a transcendental deduction.[115])

278. With regard to what is transcendental, Kant begins early by claiming that transcendental cognition concerns, not objects directly, but concepts of objects and (presumably) the principles with which these concepts are associated (A11-2/B25). It is therefore not much of a jump to think of the transcendental "exposition" of a concept as one that makes it clear how we can have "synthetic a priori" cognitions on the basis of that concept (B40).

279. Yet before long, one of Kant's strong convictions makes itself felt. Kant is convinced that ever so many interesting propositions of mathematics, of natural science, and of philosophy cannot be defended by simply "analyzing" the subject concepts of the propositions and, by this analysis, finding therein the other concepts in the propositions. In the B Introduction, he argues (A6/B10ff) that it just can't be done in general. In effect, I have loosely stated one of the points of Kant's discussion of analytic versus synthetic judgments.

280. When Kant comes later in *CPR* to reflect on the categories and the associated principles of the Transcendental Analytic, he puts the point again in the same,

---

[113] For a insightful sketch of some of the disagreements, see part II of Karl Ameriks, "Recent Work on Kant's Theoretical Philosophy," *American Philosophical Quarterly*, 19, 1, January, 1982.

[114] A useful example of someone grappling with these problems is Patricia Kitcher; see, e.g., pp. 184ff of *Kant's Transcendental Psychology* (Oxford University Press, 1990) and section 4.b. of her introduction to *Immanuel Kant, Critique of Pure Reason*, translated by Werner S. Pluhar (Hackett Publishing Company, 1996).

[115] That the difference between "metaphysical" and "transcendental" "expositions" is elusive, despite Kant's remarks (compare A23/B38 with B40), is evidenced by the fact that he admits that, in the metaphysical exposition of time, he has included items that should have been in the transcendental exposition of time (B48).

relatively simple way. At the end of the Analogies (A216-7/B263-4), he insists that the analogies can not be obtained by simply analyzing (or "dissecting") the pure concepts of the understanding. At the end of the long section "Systematic Presentation of All the Synthetic Principles of Pure Understanding", there is a small subsection "General Comment on the System of Principles" (B288ff). In that subsection, he makes the same point about all the principles: not one of them can be derived by merely analyzing pure concepts of the understanding. In the Transcendental Doctrine of Method (particularly, A720/B748ff, A736/B764ff, A766/B794, and A782/B810), Kant returns to this same point with the same message: interesting mathematical principles and the philosophical principles of *CPR* itself can not be obtained by simply reflecting on the concepts in the principles. Let me summarize this point in a thesis that would seem to be shared by both Hume and Kant:

> (K10) Analyzing categorial concepts (quantity, quality, substance, cause, etc.) does not put one in a position to defend principles of traditional metaphysics or, for that matter, important principles of philosophy, mathematics and natural science.

281. Since, however, Kant believes that we have knowledge of such principles, how do we acquire it? Kant's general way of answering is to say that such knowledge depends on having an additional something, "a third thing".[116] What is the "third" something?

282. In the case of mathematics, and all that depends on mathematics (such as natural science), pure intuitions of space and time allow us to construct concepts and (at least sometimes) to do proofs (see section I of Chapter I of the Transcendental Doctrine of Method and A782-3/B810-1; also *MFNS*, 469). It is important to recall the point (99, 126) that while contemporary philosophy is inclined to see the workings of representations of *this-suches* as conceptual, Kant thinks of intuitings as *not* kconcepts and as something additional to, and more fundamental than (127ff.), the mathematical kconcepts at issue.

283. In the case of the synthetic principles of the pure understanding, the third something is "possible experience". Possible experience (sometimes "the possibility of experience") and objects of possible experience are discussed widely in *CPR*. I limit my citations to passages in which it is clear that possible experience is the third something that Kant wants: A155-6/B194-5, A217/B264, B289, A737/B765, A766/B794, A783/B811ff.

284. How does possible experience help? Well, Kant maintains that he can show that the synthetic principles of the understanding are necessary for possible experi-

---

[116] An introductory version of the this point occurs at A8 and A9/B13, but more obvious statements of it are at A155/B194, A217/B264, B315, and A766/B794 where "third" is specifically mentioned.

ence or, to put it the other way around, without these principles, no experience is possible. Moreover, he tells us that this point is a touchstone for the Transcendental Deduction (A93-4/B126). At the end of the Transcendental Deduction in the A edition (A127-9) and in the B edition (B168-9), at the end of the Analogies (A216/B263), and at the end of the General Comment on the System of Principles (B294), Kant reiterates that exact point: the categories and the system of principles of the understanding (along with space and time) make experience possible. They are the principles of possible experience.[117]

285. I use a response to an objection as a foothold for making what Sellars takes to be important points about transcendental investigations. Imagine someone, reflecting on possible experience and the categories with their associated principles, who reasons that there is a dilemma facing defenders of Kant:

> On the one hand, Kant might be trying to prove that only by utilizing the categories and the principles associated with them can we have empirical cognitions (including some that express empirical knowledge). Hume has, however, made a good case for the point that from a rather "thin" concept of experience we can not validly obtain such principles as, e.g., the causal principle. It certainly is hard to think of what such a Kantian proof might look like, particularly since Kant seems to insist on there being *some* concept of experience which does not involve the understanding at all. On the other hand, Kant might be trying to argue for the philosophical reasonableness of employing a much "thicker" concept of possible experience which, in some reasonably direct way, includes the categories and the principles of the understanding. Then, though, it would appear that what Kant is really doing is arguing for a concept whose "analysis" includes the categories and the principles of the understanding. But that should be ruled out by Kant's insistence that *not one* of the principles of the understanding can be derived by analyzing concepts.

Sellars' response to such a objection comes in several parts.

286. Concerning the second horn of the dilemma, it has long been Sellars' contention that Kant is not doing anything like arguing that there is empirical knowledge, but rather explicating what is involved in the concept of empirical knowledge (*KTE*, 11 and 45). So, on the one hand, Sellars says "yes" to the claim that the synthetic principles of the pure understanding appear as items within the completely articulated explication of the concepts of empirical knowledge, of empirical cognition, of judging, and so on. On the other hand, this claim is not in conflict with Kant's claim that the principles of the understanding cannot be obtained by analyzing the

---

[117] In light of these points, the reader might wish to reconsider the strategy described in paragraphs 194-196.

categories *alone*. It is the categories *alone* that Kant mentions in the passages I cited above. Moreover, in a passage that Sellars cites in *CLN*, Kant commits himself explicitly to the claim that philosophy consists of judgments made on the basis of concepts. These points, along with the reference to *CPR* just mentioned, are contained in the follow paragraphs of *CLN*:

> **B40.** Once again, Kant isn't proving that there is knowledge. His strategy is to counter the arguments for the negation by showing that their basic *philosophical categories* are mistaken.
> **B41.** Finally, a question: are the propositions of Transcendental Metaphysics analytic or synthetic? (They are *a priori*.) Kant says that knowledge of principles through concepts only (as opposed to based on *experience*) is always analytic. Kant tells us that philosophical knowledge (Transcendental Metaphysics) is knowledge through concepts only.
>
> *Philosophical* knowledge is the *knowledge gained by reason from concepts*. (A713/B741)
>
> Therefore, it must be *analytic*.
> **B42.** We can't know the causal principle through the concepts of event and cause.
> **B43.** We need the concept of *"possible experience"*. (See A736-7/B764-5 and A788/B816) *CLN*, **B40-B43**

287. The first addendum to these points is that the concept of possible experience is *not* a part of the table of categories. The same is true of many other concepts of transcendental psychology: they are NOT among the "official" pure concepts of the understanding, the analysis of which, Kant tells us, is insufficient for obtaining the principles of the understanding.

288. Second, I intend, as I have said (196), to show that the view I am defending has a place for the claim that the concept of possible experience involves that of intuiting (as representing of *this-suches*). I hope that this claim has already, from my discussions, gained some plausibility. In addition, part of Sellars' interpretation is that the concept of possible experience includes other items and these items are not kconcepts and not conceptual even in the wide sense of 'conceptual'. In sum, it will turn out that an appeal to the concept of possible experience is an appeal to a concept which involves other concepts that *cannot* appear in the table of categories.

289. I return to the hypothetical objector. Sellars has, in effect, said both "yes" and "no" to the second horn of the objector's dilemma. "Yes", Kant believes (280.K10). "No", Kant can still maintain that philosophical principles are the result of "explicating" concepts, but the important concept in the case of the synthetic principles of the understanding is the concept of possible experience.

290. What about the first horn of the dilemma? Are there any Kantian arguments about empirical knowledge originating from the concept of possible experience? Here, too, Sellars answers both "yes" and "no". From a "thin" (or, we might be tempted to call it "empiricist") concept of possible experience? "No". (This point I will belabor unmercifully in upcoming sections.) From a concept of possible experience that involves the categories? "Yes". We can get an idea of the sort of thing Sellars has in mind by considering a passage from *TTC* (77, in this volume):

> 50. If empirical knowability is always knowability *by* a person *here* and *now*, whereas the *scope* of the knowable includes facts about the *there* and *then*; or if (to abstract from the specific conditions of human knowledge and move to the 'pure pragmatics' or 'transcendental logic' of empirical knowledge as such) knowability essentially involves a perspectival relationship between act of knowing and object known, must not the knowability of objects consist, in large part, of *inferential* knowability? ... On the other hand we have learned from Hume that facts about the *there* and *then* are never *logically* implied by facts about the *here* and *now*, but, at best, by the latter together with the general facts captured by true lawlike statements.
> 51. Now if we assume in the spirit of Hume that it is a contingent fact that such general facts obtain, it would seem to follow that it is a contingent fact that *there-then* objects are knowable. But if to be an object is to be a knowable, our conclusion would have to be that it is a contingent fact that there are *there-then* objects. But surely any *here-now* object is on its way to being a *there-then* object in the past and on its way *from* having been a *there-then* object in the future.
> 52. If so, then there would seem to be a logical inconsistency in granting the existence of *here-now* objects while denying that of *there-then* objects. A transcendental argument does not prove that there *is* empirical knowledge—what premises could such an argument have?—nor that there are *objects* of empirical knowledge. It simply explicates the concepts of *empirical knowledge* and *object of empirical knowledge*. Thus, to admit knowing that it *now* seems to me that there is a red and triangular object over there is to admit knowing that this *was about to* seem to me to be the case. If the skeptic (after making a similar move with respect to Space) attempts to replace the now of the seeming by the semblance of a now, by putting Time itself into the content of that which seems, does it not reappear (at least implicitly) outside this context—thus: *It (now) seems to me* that there is such a thing as Time (an order of before and after) in the *now* of which (and as Space in the *there* of which) there is a red and triangular object. (And does it merely seem to *me* that there is such a thing as I?)
> 53. What Kant takes himself to have proved is that the concept of empirical knowledge involves the concept of inferability in accordance with laws of nature. To grant that there is knowledge of the *here* and *now* is, he argues, to grant that there are general truths of the sort captured by lawlike statements. *TTC*, 50-53

It is not my intention to spend time assessing the above argument. What I want to point out is that Sellars' view—that part of Kant's business is explicating the concept of empirical knowledge (and related concepts)—is consistent with the claim that there can be all sorts of arguments as part of the total scheme of explication.

291. So, I propose a position on the question of what the Transcendental Deduction (in part) does: in the spirit of the above quotation from Sellars, I will take seriously that there is no overarching proof (in a strict sense) with which Kant is occupied in the Transcendental Deduction. Rather, he is attempting so to explicate the concept of possible experience (with whatever attendant arguments are useful) that we become convinced that possible experience, and thus empirical knowledge, require certain principles connected with the categories.

292. Just how much there is to do to accomplish this task is not clear.[118] Kant says, in the A edition, that what is required of the transcendental deduction of the categories is that it make intelligible the connection of the understanding and the sensibility (A128). Perhaps, a more specific form of this requirement shows up in section 26 of the B edition (B159ff): here Kant announces that section 20 has shown that objects of intuitings are subject to the categories. A similar remark occurs in the long footnote to 474 of *MFNS*: there Kant clearly says that one has done enough in the transcendental deduction once it has been shown that the categories, which are nothing but the forms of judgings, can be applied to intuitings; the categories and the forms of judging differ only in that, in intuitings, the forms of judging are used to determine an object. Finally, Kant describes the deduction as an exhibition of the pure concepts of the understanding as determining sensibility (B168-9).

293. I intend to take my cue from these comments and, as first step, continue my discussion (258-74) of the connection of the forms of thinking with representings of *this-suches*. The complete working out of my strategy requires, of course, that I finally get to sensibility, a topic Kant has already treated before beginning the Transcendental Deduction of the Categories.

(b) The use in experience of the pure concepts of the understanding (B159)
(α) Two ways of having categorial structure

294. I said (266) that I believe that my metaphysical deduction does part of the work that needs to be done in this section. I also hope that many of the points of the previous section and the present one are rather obvious, if one begins, as Sellars does, with a treatment of intuitings as representings of *this-suches*, elucidated by the model of demonstratives. The substantial amount of philosophical work in the Transcendental Deductions of the A and B editions gives evidence that Kant thought otherwise. The lack of obviousness for Kant is capable of being explained within

---

[118] It could be that Kant himself is not, as a result of all the different things he wants to get done, entirely clear about which parts he would like to call, strictly speaking, "the" transcendental deduction of the pure concepts of the understanding. It has been a matter of some controversy that, in section 26 of the deduction in the B edition, he refers to the earlier sections 20 and 21 as the transcendental deduction of the categories but then immediately announces that there is more to do.

Sellars' view. In addition to lacking the aid of modern logic, Kant labored under confusions, some concerning sensibility. I will argue, when I discuss sensory states, that there are considerations which might, correctly, incline Kant to think of intuitings as consorting with items dramatically different from kconcepts. Sellars' claim is that, in some substantial measure, Kant's lack of clarity about sensibility made the philosophical path harder for him than it need be.

295. Let us return to my example of the ubiquitous accident on the 405. You are driving north on the 405 when a multivehicle accident occurs. You think to yourself: This accident will make me late for dinner. Just a fraction of a second later, you think to yourself: I am about to get killed in this accident. Exercising skills honed by years of evasive maneuvering on Los Angeles freeways, you extricate yourself from immediate danger and stop on the righthand margin of the 405 while the over-medicated, the senile, the slow of reflex, the tired and distracted, the organ donors commonly known as motorcyclists, and their ilk become enmeshed in what enjoys, on the TV news, the title of "multicar pile-up". It all began, you later tell the police official, when a black panel truck, one lane to your left and several vehicle spaces ahead of you, veered left and hit the right-rear fender of a small red two-door sedan. The sedan, which was in the farthest left lane of the 405, skidded into the center divider. The red and the black might then have locked in an embrace that would have lent a limited privacy to their encounter. It was not to be. The van driver braked strenuously and the red automobile, in rebound from the divider, crossed cleanly in front of the van to crash into the left-front of one of those fashionable, suburban assault vehicles. At this point, you were too busy extricating yourself to notice the details of what then happened. Having thus provided your fragmentary account of the accident and now having an opportunity to look at the clock in your dashboard, you note that while you were wrong about this accident's killing you, you were right about its making you late for dinner.

296. Consider the black van's hitting the right-rear fender of the red vehicle, denting the fender, bending the axle, and doubtless doing other damage as well. Some of the relations, e.g., hitting, need spatial concepts for their explication. Even the ones that most clearly involve causality, denting and bending, also require the concept of space. Take denting. Something dented, like an automobile fender, is modified in that its surface is altered from one with only relatively large scale deviations from its major surface (wrapping around, flaring at the edge) to one with also small scale deviations, perhaps many. Using the common expression, I call these deviations 'dents'. Giving even a half-way decent explication of wrapping and flaring (curving in general) and dents is not easy, but they are spatial concepts and their explication, if achieved, would contain further spatial concepts.

297. What else is involved when one vehicle dents another? My answer, I hope, as I said before, strikes most as obvious: as a verb, 'dent' combines spatial rear-

118   *Introduction*

rangement with causation. Denting is an empirical causal relation: empirical in that it requires spatial alteration over time; causal in that it incorporates causal (a sort of physical) implication. So, part of the structure of

> black vehicle dents red vehicle

is made more apparent in

> that the black vehicle hit the red vehicle causally implies that part of the red vehicle's surface has dents.

298. There is much more though. It may well be that some items which can be said to "happen" or "occur" do not involve change. But the occurrences in which Kant is primarily interested are occurrences which do involve change. So, for example, both vehicles go from not being in contact with repulsion to being so. The red automobile undergoes other changes: its right-rear fender which (I have assumed) was (relatively) undented is now dented; its axle which was straight is now bent; its trajectory (direction of motion) was parallel to the center divider and is now in a direction which will lead to its hitting the divider. The black van also undergoes related changes. In cases of hitting, the hitter, as well as the hittee, change though changes in the hitter may be less pronounced. The accident, at very least, involves all these changes (and many more). (It has, as well, other properties since it is takes some time to happen and it is spread out in space.)

299. So, given the Sellarsian account of categories, categorial structure abounds in the representeds of the judgings that formulate the history of the accident.[119] Substance, property and relation, causality, quality, quantity, and even modality (possibilities that did not become actualities) figure prominently in the small piece of history I gave. (For present purposes, I assume that Kant would count automobiles, as well as, certainly, their drivers, as substances.)

300. Further, categorial structure shows up in your fragment of the history of the accident because of the logical form of the kconcept of an accident. I have supposed you had many thoughts containing intuitings of the accident. Among other things, you thought:

> This accident will make me late for dinner.
> I am about to get killed in this accident.
> This accident has made me late for dinner.

---

[119] Since the schematized categories are built from the pure-pure categories, any item which is an instance of a schematized category is also an instance of the pure-pure category. For example, if an automobile counts as a Sch-substance, it also counts as a PP-substance. Thus, though it is the schematized categories that are at issue in the present example, I speak simply of categories.

Introduction 119

Insofar as your intuitings have the content ^accident^, the intuited has categorial structure (258-66). The same is true of any other intuiteds: a house, a ship, a piece of wax, a vehicle, a highway, a center divider, and so on. To appreciate *another* way in which the accident has categorial structure, I need to weave in a topic that appears at the end of both versions of Kant's Transcendental Deduction.

(β) Nature

301. The history of our accident is not obtained from the kconcepts which occur in the judgings that tell that history. No explications of the kconcepts of an accident, of a red sedan, or a black van, or a freeway, or a hitting, or any of the others gives the history of the accident you intuited. It happened at 4 P.M. on a Wednesday. No explication of chronometric and of calenderic kconcepts offers up these kconcepts as providing us the judging that a certain black van hits a red sedan at that time on that day. Neither logic nor logic aided by the explication of concepts gets us to the history, in our world, of individuals (substances and events).

302. Back to the accident. You walk over to look at the black van and you think

that left front tire of the black van is flat

and you wonder when it became flat. For Kant, temporal principles guarantee that the tire went flat before, while or after the van hit the red sedan.[120] Neither just before the accident nor during, or immediately after, the accident did you think

that left front tire of the black van is flat.

Though you did not so think during that period of time, it would have at some time been correct for you to have so thought. The accident, and the changes in substances that make up the accident, are part of nature. As a part of nature, the accident has a correct history. This correct history, what Sellars calls the "true world story" (*CLN*, **A22a** and **A27**), contains judgings about the accident and judgings about representings which were not actual judgings by any representer at the time in question. As a part of nature, the accident's correct history far outruns the actual (as opposed to the possible) representations that occurred during, and immediately before or after, the accident.

303. First, nature in one sense is, for Kant, the aggregate of appearances (Bxix, A114, B163, footnote to B446, A845-6/B873-4), whether the appearances be substances or series of changes to substances, like our accident on the 405

---

[120] A30-3/B46-7; and compare A177/B219 and A188-9/B232.

(A491/B519). An important principle for Kant is that

> to represent individuals in space or time (or both) is to represent them as in nature.

After all, one of Kant's fundamental claims is that both space and time are conditions of the possibility of appearances, or, as he also puts it, as conditions of the possibility of experience (A24/B39, A28/B44, A31/B47, A49/B66-70). Since nature is the aggregate of appearances, i.e., objects of possible experience (see particularly A114 and *PFM*, section 16), nature is unavoidably spatial or temporal (or both) and all that is spatiotemporal is part of nature or possibly part of nature.
304. Second, nature involves laws (A114, A125-7, A216/B263, and A228/B280-1). In the preface to *MFNS* (468-9), Kant bluntly says that the concept of nature contains the concept of laws (which in its turn brings with it the concept of necessity). Section 14 of *PFM* opens with the same remark and succeeding sections elaborate on this point.
305. Thirdly, Kant also takes nature to be a dynamical *system* of appearances (A216/B263 and A418-9/B446-7). In this sense, nature as a whole is the object of experience. It is, I think, with this thought of nature in mind that Kant claims there is one single experience.[121] All experiences (in the plural) have their place in this single, coherent system of experience.[122]
306. As we know, Kant insists that space, time and appearances, and thus nature in one sense, are "representations" and thus dependent on us. Is nature, then, a system of representings (e.g., judgings)? I claimed (26-8, 56-60) that the answer is "no". However, the notion of a "true world story" allows us to characterize a sense of 'nature' in which an affirmative is correct. I need to make a few preparatory points.
307. First, not every judging represents something (a represented) that is in nature. Thus you might have (though you didn't), just before the van veered toward the red sedan, judged

> that left front tire of the black van is (going) flat.

---

[121] See A110, A230-2/B282-4, A582/B610. *OP*, being a selection of pages in which Kant repeatedly attempts to formulate his thoughts to his satisfaction, contains as a consequence substantial repetition. Though I have taken no strict count, the remark that there is only one experience (sometimes in conjunction with the remark that there is only one space and one time) must be in the running for the title "most repeated".

[122] Again, I remind the reader that here I am only mildly concerned with what might be derivative and what might be more fundamental in Kant's views; my main concern is to state what Sellars takes these views to be. Sellars' suggestions about how to understand Kant on nature are to be found in *CLN* at **A17ff** and at **B13ff** and in *KTE*, sections I, V, VII and VIII.

But if this judging is false, then the flattening of the tire does not belong to nature or, at least not to that time in the system of nature. That is why the word 'true' appears in the phrase is 'true world story'. Second, there just aren't enough actual representings. You did not, we have supposed, judge

> that left front tire of the van is flat

until well after the flattening of the tire happened. So, we turn our attention from actual judgings to judgeables. In the end, then,

> Nature, in one sense, is the system of true judgeables (i.e., the true world story as judgeable) and, in another sense, its categorial correlate, the system of correctly representable states of affairs.

Similarly, there is also a system of intuitables, those that appear in the true judgeables, and also their categorial correlate, the system of existing substances and events.[123] Since it is one of the consequences of the metaphysical deduction that Kant is not a category realist (238-43), it must be the case that the true world story is the more fundamental of the two. This is one understanding of Kant's remark that we make nature "possible" (A125-8, B159-165; see also B281).

(γ) An apperceptible synthetic unity

308. Out of all the judgings which could have occurred in the circumstances of the accident and which contain •this accident•s, you have contributed some nearly insignificant fraction (302). Why your contribution is so small is an important topic, but, whatever the reason, your contribution and that of everyone else's involved are fragmentary. Nature is not fragmentary and the accident as a series of changes to substances is not fragmentary.[124] When you and the police official discuss, as we say, "what happened", the accident has gone from being "here-now", as Sellars puts it (290), to "there-then". You and the police official now have an inferential access to segments of the accident. In the narrow sense of 'logic' (general logic, as Kant calls it), such inferences are secured neither by logic alone nor by logic aided by the analysis of concepts. As Sellars contends, we need true lawlike principles, i.e., laws of nature, to enable us to reason about substances and their changes through time and thereby to continue to fill out the true history of the accident.

309. In my example, the process of filling in the piece of the true world story that

---

[123] See *CLN*, **A21-22a**, **[A36]**, **A38-40**, **B10**, and **B19-20**. In making these points so bluntly, I am ignoring some necessary qualifications (cf. *CLN*, **[A36]** and **B10**).

[124] I take this to be part of what Kant has in mind when he talks of the "thoroughgoing" determination of individuals (*L*, part I, section 15; A571/B599ff, especially A582/B610).

pertains to the accident is the process of attempting to specify, from a later point in time, what would have been correct representings at an earlier point in time. Thus, at some stage in the accident, it would be correct for you to have represented:

(40) that left front tire of the black van is flat
(41) the right rear axle of this red sedan is bent

and so on. That is, from the point of view of what is true, the representational history of a representer of nature ought to contain representing that it did, in fact, not contain. As Sellars puts it,

> Roughly, the form of empirical knowledge is: an I thinking (however schematically) the thought of a temporal system of states of affairs to which any actual state of affairs belongs. (*I*, 9; see also *KTE*, 11.)[125]

310. In short, your representational history, as a representer of nature, is something that ought to have a coherent structure organized, in part, by reasoning depending on laws of nature (exactly which laws cannot, of course, be settled a priori). My metaphysical deduction of the categories insures that the system of true judgeables (the true world story) has a categorial correlate, a reflection, if you like, in terms of states of affairs and individuals (substances and events)—nature as a system of representeds, both states of affairs and individuals. The same is true for the lawlike component that introduces coherence in the system of true judgeables: causal implications have categorial correlates in terms of causality (cf. 221 and 252).

311. The representational structure, whose reflection is categorial structure, is capable of enormous refinement. The refinement I concentrate on is that pertaining to intuitings and thus to individuals. The judgings of the true history of the accident contain represesentings of *this-suches* which are correctly tokened in those circumstances: e.g., •this accident•s, •this black van•s, •that red sedan•s, •this veering left of the black van•s, •this rebounding of the red sedan off the center divider•s, •this bending of the right-rear axle of the red sedan•s, and so on. These judgings belonging to the true history of the accident require that these intuitings have "formal" (logical in the sense of 'transcendental logic') connections that cannot be ascertained from merely the content of the intuitings. A simple example:

> (in the circumstances) that this black van hit the right rear of that red sedan physically implies that the red sedan slid into the center divider.

---

[125] Sellars, by the way, holds that this point is part of an explanation of what is involved in the "transcendental unity of apperception" (*I*, 7); I will come back to this later.

This judgment has the categorial counterpart

> (in the circumstance) this black van's hitting the right rear of that red sedan caused the red sedan's sliding into the center divider,

or, perhaps more colloquially,

> (in the circumstances) this black van knocked that red van into the center divider.

So, •this black van•s and •that red sedan•s have (due to circumstances described in other parts of the story) a connection derived from the physical implication of judgings. In categorial terms, the intuiteds, the black van and the red sedan, have a causal relation, being knocked into.

312. Obviously, though, not all the intuiteds have this categorial connection. In particular, •this accident•s and •this rebounding of the red sedan off the center divider•s do not (in the circumstances) have a logical connection due to physical implication. What is true is that

> this rebounding of the red sedan off the center divider occurred during this accident.

In addition, the rebounding occurred because of something that also caused the accident. In categorial terms, the rebounding is part of the accident.

313. For Sellars, the philosophical insight that summarizes these points is that

> the assembling of the true history of the accident is an apperceptible synthetic assembling of (a manifold of) intuitings into a unity according to principles.

In representing yourself, in Sellars' formula, as

> an I thinking (however schematically) the thought of a temporal system of states of affairs to which any actual state of affairs belongs (*I*, 9; also *KTE*, 11),

you also represent yourself as representing the subjects of states of affairs. In the case we are discussing, the subjects are intuiteds: e.g., this accident.

314. First, since

> this accident is an individual

(though not a substance), it is an example of a unity.

315. Second, you can judge of yourself (apperceive) by thinking that

> I think that this accident is ... .

316. Third, the accident, though it is a unity, is a complex item (one sort of manifold). It can be assembled (combined) according to principles from the contents of other intuitings you can correctly token as the subject of judgings that belong to the true world story of the accident. So, (I ignore spatial and temporal structure) the intuited—this accident—is

> a complex (a manifold) that *can* be combined from the intuiteds
>
>> this black van, that red sedan, this veering left of the black van, this denting of the right rear of the red sedan, this knocking of the red sedan into the center divider, this rebounding of the red sedan off the center divider, ...

and so on. Let me make this point again. As above, I leave out, for simplicity, the temporal structure (and part of the spatial structure). What I have just claimed is that

> this accident

is

> this (veering left of the black van, denting the left rear of the red sedan, knocking the red sedan into the center divider, rebounding of the red sedan off the center divider, ...)

and much more that can be worked out by filling in the correct history of the accident, for example, by answering the question, "Does the bending of the right rear axle of the red sedan belong in the manifold?" For simplicity, I ignored the temporal features of the situation, but these need to be added. (When did the flattening of the left front tire of the van occur?)

317. Fourth, all of this can be apperceived by you. That is, in principle, you can judge:

> I combine (according to principles) such-and-such intuitings into an intuiting of so-and-so.

Introduction 125

318. Fifth, since this complexity is a result of combination by constructing part of the true world story, i.e., part of the history of nature as the system of appearances and their properties and relations, this combining counts as synthetic (if anything is to count as synthetic).

319. The accident, an intuited, is a synthetic combination of other intuiteds—substances, their properties and relations, happenings of all sorts including changes—all organized spatiotemporally and having categorial form. Put in the Kantian terms of A722/B750, the categories provide principles of the synthesis of possible empirical intuiteds. The *total* categorial form of the accident as intuited is a result of the categorial form of the combined intuiteds individually and the fact that the intuiting

this accident

is an intuiting (potentially) combined by an I constructing the true world story. The categorial form is a reflection of the "transcendental logical" form of the intuitings that can be tokened as part of the judgings which correctly belong to the histories of representers.

320. To sum up: some of the formal structure of the true world story is not the formal structure of whole judgings; it also includes formal structure as it appears in intuitings. Intuitings have formal structure (and thus intuiteds have categorial structure) not just in virtue of having certain content (e.g., the content ^accident^, the content ^vehicle^, and so on), but also as parts of the true world story. Thus, individuals, like accidents, houses,[126] and ships, have categorial features and categorial relations to other individuals (as well as spatiotemporal relations) as part of nature. This, I should like to suggest, is part of what Sellars takes Kant to be pointing out in the Transcendental Deduction.

(c) Why the transcendental aesthetic is essential to the Sellarsian account

321. I hardly need to remind the reader (though, as you can tell, I am about to) that Sellars sees conceptual structure, forms of thought, as basic and categorial structure as derivative. So, on Sellars' account, the crucial matter is saying something about true (vs. false) judgeables. Further, what he says about truth, given his account of the metaphysical deduction, cannot make truth depend, in any interesting way, on correspondence with the facts construed as independent entities having categorial structure (i.e., structure involving other independent entities like individuals, properties and relations). Of course, there *is a* trivial correspondence

---

[126] Rather than an accident, I maintain that I could have, with the same results, used Kant's example of the house and the history that went with your visiting the house.

of true judgeables with facts through the metaphysical deduction: the obtaining (or actuality) of a fact is dependent on the truth of a judgeable. (For a blunt statement of these points, see *CLN*, **A17** and **19**.)

322. Sellars elaborates this by introducing into the account of truth what Kant refers to under the rubrics "objective validity", or "universal validity", or, as the *Prolegomena* has it (section 18ff), "necessary universal validity" (*CLN*, **A16a-16g, A20a**). Such discussion inevitably embroils us in a variety of Kantian claims about necessary universal validity, in particular, the claim that he has completely and exhaustively set out in his transcendental psychology what the principles of cognition really are, i.e., how the sensibility and the understanding really work (for early remarks in this vein, see *CPR*, Axii-xx).

323. Setting those considerations apart, the crucial buttress of the entire account is an attack on the idea that an independent realm of items with categorial (or propositional) structure is any help with regard to empirical knowledge. I put this rather vaguely so that it is reminiscent of Kant's oft-repeated claim that making appearances (with their encumbrances of space, time and the categories) into things-in-themselves—this being the failing of the Transcendental Realist—leads to nothing helpful. What Kant's view needs to be defended against is the empiricist claim that, in some way, the "senses" supply all that is needed (or, perhaps, all there is to get). To give it its crudest formulation, the point that must be part of a Kantian account of sensibility is that nature and the objects in it do not "pass" what they are to us: rather, our understanding "puts" it there (A125-8, section 26 of the B deduction; see also Sellars' remarks in *KPT*, ch. 11).

324. That the indispensability of an "aesthetic" to Sellars' account of the transcendental deduction makes its appearance here is, in part, a natural outgrowth of the discussion of intuiting and the categories, but also, in part, a consequence of my "backward" sequence of topics. I laid out my remarks on the example of the accident with hardly a mention of perception. Yet the example would seem almost to cry out for such an addition to the narrative. In any case, no matter how complex an account of possible experience is, no one would be satisfied if it didn't mention perception. Kant would be dismayed, too, since both versions of the Transcendental Deduction and many of the succeeding sections put perception in a prominent position. Therefore, I have succeeded in only part of what I promised in this subsection: I have not yet managed to explicate fully the role of possible experience in a transcendental deduction. So, with the cracks in my organizational structure showing a bit, I have, nonetheless, worked my way (back, as it were) to the Transcendental Aesthetic.

IV. "Into the Heart"
A. What does Kant Believe about Sensory States?
(I) CONFUSION AMID THE CHOICES
(a) Are sensations spatial?

325. In spite of its relatively small size (or, perhaps, because of it), the Transcendental Aesthetic can be that journey into the heart of darkness we all hope to avoid. My organization of this introduction has the benefit of bringing me to questions of the Transcendental Aesthetic with some philosophical ground cleared. Moreover, this procedure shows the doctrines expounded earlier to be largely independent of anything said in this section. Though I will incorporate a doctrine of sensory consciousness into an encompassing position which includes theses defended earlier, still and all, what has come before is independent of what is to come in that very few earlier claims have even part of their defenses depending on anything concerning sensory consciousness.

326. As a first step, I sketch the main impediments to a satisfyingly unconvoluted answer to the question

> What, if anything, has spatial form besides (some) appearances?

Previously (182-9), I claimed that spatiotemporal concepts are built into the rules for intuitings understood as representings of *this-suches*; thus space and time are included in the logical form of such representings. But I understand the above question to be about literal spatiality and about whether anything besides certain appearances are literally in space.

327. A not unknown answer to the above question is: (some) sensations (such as sensations of colors). Berkeley, Sellars argues,[127] is pushed very hard toward this position though, officially, he rejects it (45, 60, 63).

328. It might seem that Kant could accept such a view. Consider the following line of thought:

> Kant repeatedly, especially in the Transcendental Aesthetic, characterizes space and time as "forms of sensibility". Further, Kant tends to describe sensation as that which, resulting from affection of sensibility, is the "matter" and space and time are its "forms" (see particularly A42/B60, but also A50-1/B74-5). Though the "form-matter" contrast is always slippery, it would seem that saying "the matter M has the form F" is a way of saying (or, at least implying) "M is F". So, if the matter is sensation and the form is triangularity, it would seem that sensations can be triangular.

---
[127] In this volume, *BD* (95), 98ff and 115.

Well, if this view is what Kant wanted, he certainly made it difficult for us to be sure that he did. I list the major obstacles.

329. (1) The centerpiece of the Anticipations of Perception (B207ff) is that sensations have only "intensive magnitude", i.e., degree, but no "extensive magnitude" (see, especially B208). The Axioms of Intuition (A162/B202ff) make it clear that the concept of extensive magnitude is that which involves the familiar principles of Euclidean geometry.

330. (2) I have to put this a bit loosely: sensations are some kind of state of consciousness. Kant characterizes them as "subjective representations" (B207-8) and as "modifications" of the subject (A320/B376; see also *CJ*, 189 and 294). Also, it is reasonable to expect Kant to say that "empirical apperception", i.e., inner sense (not transcendental apperception because of Kant's restrictions), supplies us with some sort of access, however indirect, to sensations. But Kant is firm that inner sense never supplies anything involving space, only time. He says this in the Transcendental Aesthetic (A22-3/B37, A33-4/B50, A37/B54 and B66-7) and repeats similar sentiments at A373, A379, A492/B520, and A682-3/B710-1. So, on the assumption that inner sense provides access to sensations, the results of this access never involve space. The empirical self is not revealed, through inner sense, as being in any way spatial.

331. (3) Kant divides the study of nature into two separate parts, one dealing with the objects of outer sense (this study is physics) and one with the objects of inner sense (this study is psychology) (A846/B874 and *MFNS*, 467-471). At *MFNS*, 471, Kant explains that psychology can never become a science because mathematics is not applicable to the objects of inner sense for the reason that the objects of inner sense are in time alone, which has but one dimension.

332. Kant has other, shall we say, "leanings" that get in the way of his providing us with definitive remarks on the topic of sensation. For example, when Kant comes to questions concerning the soul in the Paralogisms, his entire emphasis is on "the thing which thinks" and his remarks on sensation are scanty (e.g., A374-6) and do not serve to connect sensation with the main points of his exposition. In the Anticipations of Perception, where he announces that sensations are "subjective" representations with only intensive magnitude, he says (B207) that sensations provide *only* the consciousness that we have been "affected": sensations do not represent any object at all (see also A28/B44).

(b) Does matter have sensible qualities?

333. The flip side of questions about the spatiality of sensations is whether spatial appearances have color, texture, flavor, or, in general, as I will say, "sensible quali-

Introduction 129

ties". In the twentieth century at least, it has been argued that ordinary objects have sensible qualities. Among (some) defenders of common sense, this has meant that ordinary objects have properties (sensible qualities, as I call them) that are not identical to any spatial properties or to any causal properties characterizable in spatiotemporal terms (i.e., "secondary qualities"). It is conceivable that Kant might, in some fashion, agree that appearances have sensible qualities.

334. If so, the doctrine that appearances are spatial and have sensible qualities could be elaborated in something like the following way:

> Consider an opaque object, say, a book. Looking at this book, you think: that book has, on the side facing me, a grey, smooth, rectangular cover. You don't see all of the cover since, among other things, it wraps around to the back of the book which you don't presently see. You don't see the inside of the cover (or the inside of the book). What you see of the cover is grey and smooth. Further, since the grayness and the smoothness is in every part of the rectangle, there seems to be no impediment to saying that you see a rectangular expanse of greyness and smoothness. Without the greyness and the smoothness, there would be no perceptible expanse: they "fill" the expanse. Equally though, the boundaries of the greyness and smoothness form a rectangle. Thus, sensible qualities, as qualities of appearances, are literally spatial.

If this doctrine of sensible qualities as properties of appearances is what Kant wanted, he has, once again, made it difficult for us to believe so.

335. To begin with, there are passages in which Kant seems to deny outright that sensible qualities are properties of appearances (A28-9; B44-5).[128] In addition, passages about outer sense, mates of the ones about inner sense, claim that outer sense reveals only space (A22-3/B37 and B66-7). In fact, B66-7 emphasizes that the ideality of space is confirmed by the fact that outer sense provides nothing but "mere relations" (involving, e.g., places). If appearances have sensible qualities as properties, it would seem odd to suggest that the appearances of outer sense involve nothing but relations.[129] Kant makes similar remarks about appearances and relations at A265/B321, A277/B333, and A283-5/B339-41.

336. Other considerations arise from Kant's doctrine of substance, particularly as discussed in the First Analogy (A182-9/B224-32). In appearances, the "permanent" endures through variation and that permanent is substance. What is substance

---

[128] There are those who think these passages contain a view Kant is not attributing to himself. See, for example, Richard E. Aquila, "Intentional Objects and Kantian Appearances," *Essays on Kant's Critique of Pure Reason*, eds. J. N. Mohanty and R. W. Sheehan (Univ. of Oklahoma Press, 1982), p. 17, note 20.

[129] Sellars makes this exact point in ch. 7 of *KPT* (also compare, ch. 8).

among appearances? Substance in the world of appearance is matter.[130] Among other points made in *MFNS* is that what we know about matter is a result of forces (repulsion and attraction) acting to produce motions. Matter changes only through motion (*MFNS*, 543) and only through motion can our senses be affected (*MFNS*, 467). To use a recurrent formula of Kant's, matter is impenetrable extension (and, by the way, completely without an "internal principle" to determine itself, i.e., is "lifeless" or "inanimate").[131] These remarks about matter, all made without the least mention of sensible qualities, stand firmly in the way of a "yes" to the question which heads this subsection.[132]

337. The truth, though, is that Kant has great philosophical wiggling room available to him and that his remarks on sensation, sensible qualities, and matter generate more questions than answers. I intend to cut through this problem by setting out what Sellars thinks Kant *should* have said about sensation. Before I embark on that, I have one line of thought, with contemporary connections,[133] to explore. This line of thought serves as an indicator of just how much philosophical wiggling room Kant's remarks leave us and also provides a foil for later comments on Sellars' view.

338. The main goals of this view are to meet two requirements that *might*, as we have seen, be part of Kant's position:

sensible qualities exist *only* as sensations and have no extensive magnitude; material objects have extensive magnitude, but *no* sensible qualities.

---

[130] See B278, B291, A265/B321, A277/B333, A845-8/B873-6, and *MFNS*, 467, 470, 503 and 523. Sellars thinks it plausible that this is Kant's view and follows out a line of thought that bears on my present discussion and also on the problem of freedom (*I*, 38ff).
[131] See A265/B321, A848/B876, *MFNS*, 543-4, and compare *CJ*, 374, 383, 394, 411, and 424; for examples in *OP*, see 21:222, 21:227, 22:546, 22:548, 22:301, 22:373, 22:466, 22:481.
[132] As Sellars points out (*SM*, II, 40), it does not quite settle the issue. However, Sellars seems reasonably convinced that Kant's Newtonian commitments rule out colors and other sensible qualities as properties of appearances (see *KPT*, ch. 7, 11-2).
[133] The interested reader can find a recent debate over this contemporary line of thought in William G. Lycan, "In Defense of the Representational Theory of Qualia (Replies to Neander, Rey, and Tye)" in *Philosophical Perspectives, 12, Language, Mind, and Ontology, 1998*, edited by James E. Tomberlin (Blackwell Publishers, 1998), pp. 479-87 and in the essays by Neander, Rey, and Tye to which Lycan is replying in defense of his position in *Consciousness and Experience* (MIT Press, 1996). For an earlier statement of Lycan's view, the reader can consult p. 88ff of William G. Lycan, *Consciousness* (MIT Press, 1987).

The line of thought I describe utilizes a maneuver (for purposes Lycan would, maybe, reject) that is part of Lycan's view. I also believe that the view I will ascribe to Sellars is the one that Lycan finds "startling" and to which he claims only an "unreconstructed" sense data theorist could subscribe. Though I will have nothing to say about Lycan's being startled, I do think that I can show that his claim about Sellars' view and sense data theories is wrong.

(II) A VIEW NO ONE EVER HELD

339. For one who takes things in themselves seriously, there must be states (i.e., properties) of the soul in itself that result from interaction ("affection") by other things in themselves. In future exposition of Kant's views, I shall call these "noumenal states of sensibility" and reserve 'sensation' for the "phenomenal sensory states" of the empirical self. One source of the following line of thought is that sensations, for Kant, are states of the empirical self, the self as appearance.

340. Since I believe no actual philosopher has ever held the view I am about to describe, I attribute it to a possible philosopher, René William Kant (RWK, for short). On most interpretations of Kant, RWK would be in the "Kant family" (on the model of the "Bach family").[134] He is definitely not Sellars' Kant since he handles sensations as Sellars thinks Kant should not. RWK's given-name intellectual progenitors (Descartes and Lycan) are summoned to remind us that actual philosophers have made some of the moves by which RWK tries to maintain the two claims suggested in paragraph 338 and to square those claims with some seemingly obvious facts.

RWK, like Kant, holds that the soul can affect itself (B68) through its inner sense thereby producing representings of the empirical self, some of which represent the empirical self as having sensations. Consider an example:

(42) I am having a sensation of grey.

This representing attributes a property to the empirical self. This property, a state, comes in varying degrees. In addition to (42), however, some of the representings of inner sense have the form

(43) I am having a sensation of a grey rectangle.

RWK admits that (43) might, in some cases, seem to attribute correctly to the empirical self a state which has not only intensive magnitude, but also extensive magnitude. This, RWK claims, is not so.

To locate the error, RWK says, remember that the prejudices of childhood lead us to say things like

(44) that book has, on the side facing me, a grey rectangular cover

---

[134] The philosophical family of a philosopher has members with definite views on topics on which the philosopher may be confused or simply may not have asked questions that needed to be asked. The relationships between members of the family is, therefore, not simply some sort of similarity since some members maintain that they hold views that the others "ought to" have held, but didn't.

132 *Introduction*

and not simply

(45) that book has, on the side facing me, a rectangular cover.

While there is little doubt that the deity has arranged things for the best, our benefit in these matters does not require accuracy, but merely aid in survival. Philosophical reflection assures us that though the book may have a rectangular shape and whatever other geometrical features it needs to affect our sense organs, it does not have greyness or any other sensible quality. The same philosophical reflection assures us that empirical selves do not have extensive magnitude.

What has happened, RWK explains, is that the regular association of representings like (42) and (45) has led to confusion through an illicit borrowing of content from one representing to the other. By this borrowing, the representing (42) is added to and becomes (43) and, similarly, the representing (45) becomes (44). Thus are borne concepts of sensations, empirical selves, qualities and material objects that are confused.

Strictly, according to RWK, there is no *grey*, rectangular cover: it is an "intentional inexistent".[135] Similarly, there is no grey, *rectangular* sensation; it, too, is an intentional inexistent. Neither sensibly qualified material objects nor extensively quantified sensations exist, except, of course, in thought. We simply mis-represent appearances, both outer and inner. Philosophy shows us how we can overcome such mis-representation.

There are subtle aspects of RWK's view that he regards as pluses.

341. His thesis concerns the world of appearance, phenomenal objects, not noumenal ones. Both inner sense and outer sense involve systematic error, and this error arises, for the unphilosophical part of humankind (the "vulgar"), at the level of appearance. For example, the vulgar attribute shape to sensations and thus, since sensations are modifications of the empirical self, they attribute shape to the empirical self. On the other side of the coin, they attribute color, and other sensible qualities, to matter. Both these errors concern the world of appearance. When asked why such systematic errors should plague human beings, RWK says that answering such a question is for those who study our natural history as appearances in the spatiotemporal world. Someday, perhaps, someone may be able to tell us why it took us so long to reach, with the help of investigators like Newton, an appreciation

---

[135] Lycan uses this, by now traditional, phrase on p. 481 of William G. Lycan, "In Defense of the Representational Theory of Qualia (Replies to Neander, Rey, and Tye)" in *Philosophical Perspectives, 12, Language, Mind, and Ontology, 1998*, ed. by James E. Tomberlin (Blackwell Publishers, 1998), pp. 479-87 and on pp. 71 and 153 of *Consciousness and Experience* (The MIT Press, 1996).

of what matter is like and how thinking selves are different from material objects. What is obvious, RWK thinks, is that it did take many thousands of years for us to reach our present philosophically and scientifically enlightened state. Moreover, RWK believes that the illicit trading of content that he has pointed out will figure somewhere into the explanation of these systematic errors.

342. RWK claims that "neither sensibly qualified material objects nor extensively quantified sensations exist". He thinks it wrong to weaken this to: the vulgar merely think false thoughts about empirical selves and material objects. That way of putting it makes is sound as though the vulgar have an adequate conception of appearances. But the heart of the matter is that they don't have an adequate conception.

343. The vulgar really believe that empirical selves are the sorts of things that *can* have extensive properties like shape and that material objects are the sorts of things that *can* have color, taste, smell and so on. Principles of philosophy show these beliefs about the nature of empirical selves and material objects to be incorrect. While RWK is willing to treat such things as errors, he is concerned not to underestimate such fundamental errors. These errors are a result of inadequate and confused concepts of appearances. Put more carefully, what RWK wants to say is that both empirical selves *as conceived by the vulgar* and material objects *as conceived by the vulgar* do not exist, indeed, cannot exist in the spatiotemporal world of appearance. The correct principles of appearances rule them out as possible.

344. The severity of the confusion of the vulgar enables RWK to fend off an objection that Berkeley might well have put to RWK: do not perceived colors have shape and do not even the most transitory cases of perceived shape come with color, or some other sensible quality, as "filler", as the "matter" of which the shape is the "form"? RWK diagnoses Berkeley's objection as a failure to come to grips with the illicit borrowing of content and the confusion within the ordinary conception of appearances. RWK agrees that the vulgar think of extensive magnitude and qualitative "filler" as indissolubly joined. So what? Philosophy and science have shown us the confusion inherent in that whole view of appearances. It is important to remember that this confusion extends all the way to the concepts of the properties in question. Those properties, *as conceived by the vulgar*, are instantiated only by "intentionally inexistent" objects.

345. For future use, I note that RWK thinks of the ordinary, non-philosophically sophisticated conception of appearances as including *some* salvageable concept of sensation. Moreover, the vulgar are not so completely confused that they fail to identify sensations as sensations. When they have sensations of grey, they respond to them as sensations and employ their confused and inadequate concept of sensation. (Thus RWK subscribes to a claim very close to one built into what I called "phenomenalistic" accounts (157-165).) Admittedly, their concepts of sensations and empirical selves are confused enough that they must be abandoned. Still and all, the philosophically correct concept of sensation does not impugn the vulgar's access to sensations. All of us, sophisticated and vulgar alike, recognize sensations as states of the empirical self, but lack of philosophy has leaves the vulgar with concepts of sensation, of empirical self, of sensible quality and of material object tainted by the illicit borrowing of content among different representations.

B. What should Kant Believe about Sensory States?
(I) HOW TO APPROACH THIS QUESTION

346. Sellars' view, strictly speaking, precludes a simple answer to the question of this section. Kant has, according to Sellars, twined strands together in his accounts of perception, matter and empirical selves so thoroughly that nothing we would agree to be "minor" emendations would sort things out. Still, Sellars believes that he can make sense out of *most* of what Kant wants to say (*IKTE*, I, 1-2). The crux of the whole matter is an account of sensory states.

347. An even moderately careful exposition of Sellars' account of sensory states should shield his view from certain mis-conceptions and defend it against reasonably obvious criticisms. I do not know how such an exposition can be accomplished without explaining Sellars' distinction between the manifest image and the scientific image. Doing without this distinction has its benefits: those skeptical of the whole idea of conceptual frameworks might then find Sellars' account of sensory states couched in friendlier terms. Tempted though I am, I found that the result of trying to do this is that I am cast adrift from resources to fight off the sharks. Besides, Sellars himself aids and abets certain criticisms that can be countered only by some exposition of the differences between the two images.

(II) THE MANIFEST IMAGE AND THE SCIENTIFIC IMAGE

348. In his treatments of the two images, Sellars has said many things, sometimes in contexts in which he does not even use the terms 'manifest image' or 'scientific image' (for cases in point, see *SM*, ch. I, 21-59 and ch. VI, 44-61). That, in doing so, he has helped create confusion is beyond dispute.

349. Even the terminology itself, particularly the term 'scientific', engenders problems. For example, in *PSIM* (43) (in *SPR*, p. 6ff), Sellars no sooner begins to contrast the two images when he has to stop to point out that reserving the term 'scientific' for the scientific image makes it appear the manifest image is "unscientific". This is not so.

350. Attempting to explicate the contrast by employing the term 'theoretical' runs afoul of the fact that philosophers, including Sellars, use the word 'theory' now in narrower, now in more encompassing, senses. In a dialectical context sporting both

Behaviorists and defenders of early 20th-century instrumentalism as viable opponents, the term 'theoretical' can have a very weak gloss. In a passage where Behaviorism is on his mind, Sellars offers "theoretical—not definable in observational terms" (*EPM* (31), 58, in *SPR*): given the narrow group of observables favored by early 20th-century empiricists, that makes nearly everything theoretical.

351. Characterizing the difference by reference to the rational processes or forms of reasoning available in the images is misleading and in need of substantial qualification. One such difference Sellars picks on is that the manifest image does not use reasoning "which involves the postulation of imperceptible entities, and principles pertaining to them, to explain the behaviour of perceptible things" (*PSIM* in *SPR*, p. 7). This lies uneasily with Sellars' insistence that, in the manifest image, sensory states (sense impressions) and conceptual states (thinking) can be understood as items introduced in *very much* the "postulational" spirit. One can, of course, lean heavily on the phrase 'imperceptible entities', construe it as 'imperceptible objects', and then point out that such items as states are not "objects" in the tough sense (see *EPM*, 61(1)). While I think that this move is faithful to what Sellars had in mind, another consideration makes this point not as useful as it might be.

352. Sellars defends a position on the "postulation" of objects for scientific theories that utilizes the notion of a "model".[136] For Sellars, one purpose of models in the context of scientific theories is, surprisingly to some, concept construction by analogy.[137] That is, a model is a tool to help in the construction, by analogy, of the concepts needed by a new scientific theory. At some point, by Sellars' lights, the scientific image starts to be constructed and, at that point, the only concepts and objects one has are those of the manifest image. So, the manifest image must contain the *resources* for analogical construction of new concepts and thus for the postulation of new items (*EPM*, 51).

353. With these brief remarks as a prologue,[138] I proceed rather dogmatically to explain what I need of the distinction between the two images. The manifest image does *not* lack any resource for concept construction or any logical or semantical resources. It has no general problem about unobservables since it is part and parcel of the manifest image that manifest objects, including persons, have unobservable properties (to take one example, causal properties). What the manifest image, at any stage, lacks are the unobservable *objects*, the "dull little atoms in the void" (to use a phrase of Lycan's) and their successors and their attendant entities (e.g., electromagnetic fields), so prominent in the scientific image. This metaphysical point about fundamental kinds of objects differentiates the two images, not matters about

---

[136] See section III, *SRI* (58) in *PPME* (102).
[137] For other purposes of models, see section IV, *TE* (51) in *PPME*.
[138] I do not deny that there are other important points to be made, but they are simply too far off my present track. I recommend the discussion in Johanna Seibt's *Properties as Processes: A Synoptic Study of Wilfrid Sellars' Nominalism* (Ridgeview Publishing Company, 1990).

resources for reasoning or concept construction (compare *PSIM*, p. 9 in *SPR*).

354. The two images as conceptual frameworks differ most basically in their objects. The fundamental spatiotemporal objects of the manifest image are continuants that have such sensible qualities as colors, shapes, flavors, smells, textures and so on. As the fundamental objects of the manifest image, they are not assemblages of more fundamental objects though they may have parts in an ordinary sense. For my present purposes, I can ignore Sellars' thesis that, of spatiotemporal objects in the manifest image, the "primary" ones are persons (*PSIM*, pp. 9-14 in *SPR*).

(III) SENSIBLE QUALITIES
(a) What are they not?

355. A philosophically adequate differentiation of qualities from other sorts of properties is difficult. As a start, sensible qualities are different from what are sometimes called "dispositional" or,"causal" properties. On Sellars' view, the characterization of causal (and, in particular, dispositional) properties connects them so closely to conditionals (exactly how closely is controversial) that these properties merit being called "iffy" properties. In whatever sense causal properties are "iffy", sensible qualities are not "iffy", but count, in the terminology of the time, as "occurrent".

356. In addition, sensible qualities do not, in general, have definitions involving the connectives and quantifiers. Thus, given the usual logical distinction between defined and undefined items, the sensible qualities are, in general, undefined and nonrelational properties of objects. This is not to say that they are "metaphysically simple" in the sense of involving no complexity.

357. In this day and age, though not when Sellars first wrote about these matters in the nineteenfifties and early nineteensixties, it is important to point out that sensible qualities are not "functional" properties in what has come to be the standard sense of 'functional'.[139] In the standard sense, functional properties are defined either (a) by specifying "inputs" and "outputs" or (b) by including with this specification the "purpose" to be served (in the sense of the "job" to be done). These definitions find their implementation in what I shall call "the relational characterization":

(46) ___ is a property something has if and only if .....

where the second blank is filled in as in (a) or as in (b).

358. By denying that manifest image sensible qualities are functional or causal properties, Sellars is denying that, say, redness has any sort of definition like

---

[139] Sellars himself, though a very early user of the term, is not a functionalist in the now standard sense.

(47)   redness is a property a thing has if and only if, in standard conditions, that thing causes such-and-such response in human beings.

As a definition, (47) commits one to the claim that an object's being red consists in its being the case that *if* a human being were in thus-and-so conditions, *then* that object would cause the human being to be in such-and-such state. Redness thus becomes an "active" causal property, a "power" in traditional terms.

359.   *Some version* of (358.47) is true on Sellars' account, but it is not a definition of redness in the manifest image. One reason, but not the only one, that a definition of the form of (358.47) is unavailable for sensible qualities is that, *in the manifest image*, causal properties and functional properties depend on sensible qualities. Sometimes this dependence is direct: the antecedent or the consequent of conditionals associated with the causal or functional property includes sensible qualities.

360.   Sometimes it is less direct. Consider a causal property that involves in its specification another causal property. Wine has the property (intoxicativity?) that if it is ingested in sufficient quantities, then the drinker becomes "inebriated" ("drunk"). So, this causal property of wine involves another causal property, inebriation, a complicated causal property involving, inter alia, impairment of abilities, such as speech.[140] Characterizing speech impairment, however, requires a specification of the standard sounds produced by the speaker and the deviations from those sounds produced by the speaker when inebriated. Such deviations, like slurring, involve sound qualities, not just matters of duration. In the manifest image, at some point in any complicated chain of causal properties, one will unavoidably be brought back to sensible qualities. The actualizing of a causal property cannot be by other causal properties without end.

361.   Since the relations of functional properties and sensible qualities need greater exposition than I can afford to give it in this introduction, I cut through the morass to two central points. A relational characterization of, say, "being a doorstop" ("being a doorstop is a property a thing has if its job is to prevent doors from swinging closed") puts few constraints on doorstops. As a doorstop, you can use your well-trained dog while Captain Ahab can use a harpoon. But stopping doors—indeed doing any job—is not possible without the appropriate causal properties which are realized in circumstances pertaining to the job. Thus we are brought back to sensible qualities. Notice also that, in the manifest image, whatever is a "job-doer" is some kind of manifest object and thus has sensible qualities. It would not seem possible for objects to have merely functional properties.[141]

---

[140] "Breathalizers" and blood tests utilize modern chemistry and are thus items in the scientific image.
[141] Sensible qualities may, in a looser sense, be said to "have a function": i.e., they may contribute, in some way or other, to the object doing its job. That does not make the sensible qualities functional properties in the strict sense.

138   *Introduction*

362. More on the connections and differences of sensible qualities and other properties appears in upcoming subsections, but the moral is easily summed up: the manifest image, the unavoidable nonfunctional, noncausal properties of objects are sensible qualities. To encapsulate this logical status of sensible qualities, Sellars refers to them, in a terminology common at the time, as "occurrent" properties.[142]

(b) What are they?

363. Sellars was so concerned to argue about sensory states and their connection with sensory qualities that he devoted little space to sensible qualities themselves. The following is a late example of this tendency (an example also useful to me for other purposes):

> 44. Visual sensations, which are states of the perceiver, are not (for example) *literally* cubes of pink facing the perceiver edgewise. On the other hand it is not *simply false* that they are cubes of pink facing the perceiver edgewise. It is tempting to appeal to the tradition of analogy and say that the pinkness and cubicity of a sensation which belongs to the "of a cube of pink" kind are *analogous* to the pinkness and cubicity of its standard cause.
>
> 45. But analogies are useful only if they can be cashed or spelled out. One way of doing this is by saying—as I have said on a number of occasions—
>
> According to this version of the adverbial theory of sensing, then, sensing a-pink-cube-ly is sensing in a way which is normally brought about by the physical presence to the senses of a pink and cubical object, but which can also be brought about in abnormal circumstances by objects that are neither pink nor cubical, and, finally, according to this form of the adverbial theory, the manners of sensing are analogous to the common and proper sensibles in that they have a common conceptual structure. Thus, the color manners of sensing form a family of incompatibles, where the incompatibilities involved are to be understood in terms of the incompatibilities involved in the family of ordinary physical color attributes. And, correspondingly, the shape manners of sensing would exhibit, as do physical shapes, the abstract structure of a pure geometrical system.[3] [Sellars' footnote: "The Structure of

---

[142] In light of what I will explain about Sellars' account of colors and physical objects, one point is, it seems to me, without doubt: closing the refrigerator door is not causally sufficient to change the color of a pink ice cube or to destroy its pinkness, and the presence of a perceiver cannot create the pinkness of a pink ice cube. The ice cube is pink inside the refrigerator in the dark as it was outside the refrigerator in the light. I mention this because Daniel C. Dennett has claimed otherwise (p. 103 of "Wondering Where the Yellow Went", *Monist*, 64, 102-8 and p. 371 of *Consciousness Explained* (Little, Brown and Co., 1991)). The source of the misunderstanding, I believe, is that Dennett has taken the term 'occurrent' to be connected with 'occurrence'. Therefore, he thinks that the pink color "occurs" when someone opens the door and sees the pink ice cube. But 'occurrent', in the sense Sellars uses it in connection with sensible qualities, has always been a term for the logical classification of properties, as indicated above.

Knowledge: Perception," the first of a series of three Matchette Lectures. (*SK* (79), Lecture I, 64.)]

> 46. I have come to see, however, that we must be able so to formulate the analogy between manners of sensing and perceptual attributes of physical objects, that it is made evident that the analogy preserves in a strict sense the conceptual *content* of predicates pertaining to the perceptible attributes of physical objects, while transposing this content into the radically different categorial framework to which manners of sensings belong. Just what more (if anything) this would involve than spelling out in greater detail the analogies referred to above, and (perhaps) adding additional dimensions of analogy, I am not able to say. I believe, however, the problem is an important one, and that an adequate answer is necessary to explain the sense in which color concepts preserve their content throughout their migration from the manifest image to the scientific image. (*SRPC*, 44-6, in this volume)

Sellars' early remarks (e.g., *EPM*, sections IV and XVI and *SM*, ch. I, 37-51) are in basically the same vein, but without the new qualification about "preserving" "conceptual *content*". While one can understand Sellars' concern about arguing for the general idea of his position, his approach leaves us without part of what we need. After all, every analogy has two sides and what he did not fill out, in any detail, is the sensible quality side.

364. I do not suggest that I can do that here, but I think that I can sketch the range of required topics. I begin with items that Sellars nearly always mentions.

(a) Incompatibilities of determinates

365. There are "the incompatibilities involved in the family of ordinary physical color attributes": for example, the incompatibility of a region of a surface's (or, a volume's) being thoroughly (some determinate shade of) red and that same region of the surface's (or, the volume's) being (some determinate shade of) green, or any other color. The "thorough" redness of a region consists in every sub-region of that region being red. Similar incompatibilities can be found for tones and for flavors (with 'region' and 'sub-region' being replaced by 'duration' and 'sub-duration').

366. Such incompatibility does not occur with all properties. In fact, the structures of causal properties and functional properties seem considerably different from and, in some ways, dependent on that of sensible qualities.

367. Causal properties are not easily grouped into families at all. Moreover, even the slightest contemplation of examples suggests that compatibility is the rule, not the exception. The causal property of being brittle is possessed both by objects that do, and objects that do not, possess the property of floating if placed in water. Being toxic to humans (i.e., if there were human contact, e.g., ingestion, then the human being would be poisoned) is a property possessed by so many gases, liquids and solids that is hard to find any other causal properties that are incompatible with it.

368. Finally, what incompatibilities there are among causal properties can, many times it seems, be traced to the sensible qualities involved in the consequent of the associated conditional of the causal property. Take mushrooms as an example. Having a brown "spore print" (i.e., if placed on a sheet for several days, the mushroom drops a ring of *brown* spores) is incompatible with having a white spore print (i.e., if a placed on a sheet for several days, the mushroom drops a ring of *white* spores). (Interestingly, in mushrooms, having a brown spore print is incompatible with being toxic to humans, but having a white spore print is compatible with being nontoxic, as well as (usually) toxic, to humans.)

369. For functional properties, the situation is even more complicated. Suppose we were to agree, with Lycan, that the "job description" gives the function. So many things have more than one job, and where they don't usually, it could be so arranged. (Think of those pocket knives where one blade is a knife on one edge and fish-scaler on the other, the bottle opener is a screw driver, and so on.) True enough, when Ahab's harpoon is stopping the door, it is definitely not doing the job of a harpoon, and vice versa. But while some jobs cannot be done simultaneously, others can. To take a contemporary example, our livers simultaneously detoxify (e.g., alcohol), aid digestion (through the production of bile acid), and re-process lipoproteins circulating in the blood. Finally, as Lycan points out, jobs designed by nature come in a complicated hierarchy (the cells of a liver have various jobs that variously contribute to the jobs of the liver). All this presents a picture of a structure far different from the families of colors or tones.

(β) Generic incompatibility within families

370. In the case of colors, there may be other incompatibilities of a more generic sort (on which Sellars, as far as I know, does not explicitly comment). Thus, though there are reddish blues and bluish reds, it is usually held that there are no reddish greens or greenish reds. Whether this is so or not is debatable.[143] With tones, though, it seems to me reasonably clear that timbres come in kinds that are generically (or, familially) incompatible. The timbres of wood-wind reed instruments (e.g., clarinet, oboe, bassoon, contra-bassoon) and those of bowed string

---

[143] Danto, in his foreword to Hardin's book (p. xff., *Color for Philosophers: Unweaving the Rainbow*, Hackett Publishing Company, 1988), points out that there are experiments in which subjects report that their visual field has a single unitary color which is both red and green. I view this as a complicated matter. The experimenters did not accomplish their feat by making a perceptible object that is, say, both red and green on the side facing their subjects. What they did was illuminate, in a special way, the retinas of the subjects' eyes. Sellars' account leaves open the possibility that what the experiment shows is that colors as properties of manifest objects do not have *exactly* the same structure as some human sensory properties which also have a claim to being called colors.

instruments (e.g., violin, viola, violoncello, contrabass) are examples. (We commonly identify timbres by reference to instruments that most characteristically produce them; it is, nonetheless, possible for something else to produce those timbres.)

371. Flavors present examples of the incompatibility of determinates within a family and *may* provide examples of generic incompatibility. (Note that, without the aid of modern science, the common cold would convince anyone that many flavors owe more to the nose than to the mouth. That is, some flavors are principally aromas (or odors or fragrances) and not tastes.) For illustration, I take what I hope are reasonably familiar examples from wine and food. Among the flavors of grape wines are usually listed (with some characteristic possessors) the aromas

> fruitiness (lemon, apple, grapefruit, apricot, pear), floralness (mint, rose), herbaceousness (grass, bell pepper, green beans, asparagus), caramelness (honey, butterscotch, raisin, molasses), woodiness (oak, cedar, vanilla, almonds)

and the tastes

> sourness, sweetness, bitterness, astringency, yeastiness.

Some of the above flavors and tastes are determinately incompatible. For possible examples of generic incompatibility, we must turn to flavors that are conspicuously missing in writings about grape wine: flavors whose names come from the spices and herbs that have them—coriander, juniper, sage, dill, fennel, cardamon, clove. Also missing are the flavors of cheeses (some of whose names also derive from names of cheeses): cheddar, swiss, rancidity (blue cheese). Some of the distinctive flavors of spices, herbs, and cheeses seem to be generically incompatible with some of those of the wines. (Admittedly, there are complications concerning the mixing of foods with different flavors leading to "blendings" of flavors).

(γ) Intensive magnitude (degree)

372. I borrow the phrase 'intensive magnitude' from Kant though he might not like my use of it. Distinguishing intensive magnitude as it applies to sensible qualities from comparable scales for other properties is no small job since almost any property shows degree in one way or other.

373. For functional properties, where I have been assuming "job done" is central, the degree is "better-worse" by some standard of doing the job. A better catapult might: throw heavier payloads; throw present payloads farther; hit the target more often; break down less often; be easier to set up; be easier to move; be easier to repair. Though much grading of "job performance" is by standards which involve quantities (space, time, money), it need not be so. A bigger pot still might make more malt whisky faster, but if it changes the distinctive flavor of your whisky, then it will not be as good as the one you use now. Generally grading of job performance seems to flow from the "job description" plus whatever "external" purposes we might have for the objects being graded. (Making a living, as Plato reminds us, is not a purpose that is "internal" to the craft of medicine.)

374. Causal properties also have scales based on quantities. A more toxic substance takes less time to act or requires less amount to be effective. In other cases, quantity of force makes the difference: the more malleable the metal, the more fragile the china, the more volatile the liquid, the less force (or energy) that needs to be applied to actualize the causal property.

375. Sometimes the involvement of sensible qualities with time or space is much like that of other properties: the flavor of a certain wine may last longer in the back of the mouth ("a longer finish" as it is said). However, other examples of straightforward "more" and "less", with attendant relations, do not require space, time, or any of the other quantities mentioned in the above cases.

376. The color of one surface might be bluer than that of another of exactly the same size and shape; indeed, a single surface might have a gradient from less blue to more blue. Of two tones of the same pitch, loudness, and duration, one might be smoother, or harsher, or more piercing, or more sonorous than the other. Flavors of food and drink provide examples of more, or less, strength. So, in at least some cases, the degrees of sensible qualities need not be connected with anything else but having more (less) of the quality; neither space nor time are involved and nothing about "job performance" is at issue. In the manifest image, sensible qualities vary (are "more" or "less") independently of manifest image spatiotemporal features.

(δ) "filling" of space and togetherness

377. On Sellars' account of the manifest image, the question 'What are physical objects?' has a general, though qualified, answer. Sellars usually concentrates on vision since traditional treatments of perception featured that sense and therefore his answer is in terms of color: colors are the very "stuff" out of which physical objects are made; in the manifest image, physical objects are color stuff in space and time with causal properties (*FMPP* (110), I, sections II and III).

378. This answer must be augmented by including other sensible qualities besides color and qualified to allow for numerous complications beyond the scope of this introduction. I find one point reasonably clear:

> the sweetness, the fig-flavor, the warmth, and the reddish-brownness of the flesh

are all there *together* in the fig and can be together in all the sub-regions of the flesh.

The same is true of the redness, the coolness, and the many flavors of your glass of wine.[144] It is characteristic of sensible qualities that this sort of togetherness—in the same object—of sensible qualities from different families is common and is capable of tremendous variation. Red liquids can be warm or cold, sweet or bitter, salty or not, and so on. What necessary connections there are between items in different families are established, I shall argue, by causal processes.

379. One rather special form of *togetherness* is that involving the "filling" of shapes by color. Consider such sentences as

(48) object O has a red rectangular facing surface (or, has a facing surface which is a red rectangle).

(48) is not the same as

(49) object O has a red and rectangular facing surface.

(Of course, I admit that there might be contexts in which (48) comes to no more than (49)). Also note that (49) does not amount to

(50) object O has a red facing surface and object O has a rectangular facing surface.

Since it is not required that facing surfaces be parallel to a line connecting the outermost surface of the perceiver's eyes, (50) is consistent with O having two different facing surfaces (with an edge between them like the front cover and spine of a book), one of which is rectangular and the other of which is red. By comparison, (49) I understand to imply that the very same surface is red and rectangular. What (48) implies, but (49) does not (though it is consistent with it), is that the redness "fills" the rectangle and that there are no sub-regions of the rectangle which are not red. In some cases, though not all (e.g., the spine and cover of some books), the redness forms the boundaries of the rectangle.

380. The upshot of all this is that while (379.48) implies (379.49) and (379.50), both (379.49) and (379.50) are weaker than (379.48) and are not candidates for supplying anything which could qualify as an "analysis" of (379.48). Let me put it

---

[144] Yes, there are sub-regions too small to be tasted just as there are things to small to be seen. The manifest image incorporates many principles on size, distance, lighting, impairments of senses (age, disease, birth defect), and so on, that reflect limitations of the senses of humans.

144 *Introduction*

this way: the rules for •red rectangular•s and for •a red rectangle•s as they appear in judgings like (379.48) must allow that (379.48) implies both (379.49) and (379.50), but such rules cannot specify that the combining of •red rectangular•s and of •a red rectangle•s is simply a matter of conjunction. (Inattention to this point, I shall argue, leads some philosophers to attribute false importance to a criticism of certain doctrines of sensory states.)

(ε) Causal relevance

381. Since the rise of the scientific image, it has been commonplace to castigate colors and other sensible qualities for their causal ineptitude. In the manifest image, by contrast, sensible qualities are as "natural" and as causally efficacious as, say, shapes, and thus as deserving as any other properties of being called "physical".

382. Present-day concern with "natural" kinds may make part of what I am about to say about sensible qualities seem wrong. I invite you to consider that, in the manifest image, it is difficult to draw a clean line between artifacts and natural objects. Is the contemporary dairy cow a natural object? Well, the contemporary dairy cow is a result of thousands of years of human domestication which has transformed successive generations of cows into an animal vastly different from its earliest ancestor, so different, in fact, that, unlike its distant ancestors, it is unable to survive without man. As the domesticator did not make the raw material he started with, so the cook does not make the egg he soft-boils. Yet both domesticator and cook depend on natural, causal, processes to produce something different from what they began with and both produce something which is, therefore, in some way natural and in some way artificial.

383. Even in cases in which there is something everyone would call an artifact, causal processes are at work. The statue Michelangelo is creating emerges from the block of marble through the causal efficacy of a chisel. The shape, size and weight of the statue are, in part, the result of this causal process and no one, I presume, would deny these properties to the statue simply because the statue is an artifact.

384. It is the *thrusting* of the sword into your body that does the damage, not the shape of sword: so one might plausibly argue. Events of various sorts are the producers of effects. Even so, the shape and crosssection of the blade, along with its sharpness and rigidity, contribute in their own ways to the exact gash in your torso. Shapes, sizes and other properties are not, therefore, causally irrelevant: the account of why the sword thrust produced the damage it did mentions these properties to account for spatial and other properties of the gash.

385. In the manifest image, the whipping of so-called "egg whites" produces a container of frothy, white stuff that can support its own weight in little peaks if the cook pulls at it with the whip. Both the white color and the causal property are produced by the whipping. Tomatoes and mission figs start out green and ripen, respectively, to red, roughly spherical objects with a characteristic flavor and to black, pear-shaped objects with a characteristic flavor and sweetness. Both the flavors and the colors are the products of a lengthy causal process as is their presence together in the same object (378).

386. Examples of sensible qualities contributing to causal processes from the beginning rather than the end are easily found. You de-glaze your frying pan with a medium Madeira instead of red wine and, after adding other items, you produce a sauce. No doubt, like the thrusting of the sword, the *pouring* of the Madeira into the hot pan is the salient event. But as properties of the sword are not causally irrelevant, so too with properties of the Madeira: the account of why the sauce has the flavor it does mentions, among other things, the flavor of the Madeira (in contrast to the flavor a red wine might have imparted). Owners of fruit trees are regularly reminded that the ripening of certain fruits brings about colors that, as we colloquially say, "attract" birds. Such attraction is a causal process, whatever its details, to which color makes an irreplaceable (in the manifest image) contribution.

387. This last example, dealing as it does with causal processes involving living creatures, highlights that I have said precious little about sensible qualities and human beings. This omission was intentional. In the preceding paragraphs, my aim was to make a case for the position that there is much to say about sensible qualities without discussing human beings. In the manifest image, sensible qualities are as "objective" (whatever exactly that might mean) and as natural as any other properties. It is, however, true that sensible qualities are causally efficacious with regard to human beings.

388. Using sight as an example, I begin with a really inadequate formulation:

a red object causes a human being to think that the object is red.

The purpose of beginning with such an inadequate formulation is to emphasize that, as in the case of the birds and the fruit, it is the color of the object that is causally important. Shapes, too, can be, in the same way, causally important. Thus a red, rectangular object can cause a human being to think that the object is rectangular. To repeat my earlier point, that neither colors nor shapes are "doings" does not show them to be causally irrelevant.

389. The steps to a less inadequate formulation engage us in a familiar dialectic. According to my account of the category of causality, what are needed are sufficient refinements so that judgings about the sensible qualities of objects imply judgings about conceptual representings of thinkers. In my opinion, it is not all that easy to do this and, additionally, it requires much discussion. The view I will sketch places sensible qualities in an intelligible, but complicated, causal processes.

390. First, I trade in 'human being' for 'person'. The standards for being a human being are flexible and can be, for certain purposes, lowered to simply having human beings as parents. As I understand 'person', only full-fledged concept users count as persons. So, babies can be excluded as merely apprentice concept users.

391. Second, other relevant and well-known conditions, pertaining to perception, are: you can't see anything in the pitch dark; you can't hear much with your fingers in your ears or in a high wind; you've got to put it in your mouth to taste it; being unconscious drastically impairs sensory activity; and so on. Such matters lead to restrictions involving "normal" (or "standard") conditions:

> (51) in normal conditions and for a person, P, who is a normal perceiver, that O is red and rectangular implies that P thinks that O is red and rectangular.

392. Third, though (391.51) is start in the right direction, "normality" of conditions and persons would usually be characterized so generally that many things are left to be taken into account. In the case of sight, a person has to be, as we say, "looking at" the object, not just looking in the general direction ("if it were a snake, it would bite you"). Additionally, in the case of sight, it is facing surfaces of opaque objects that matter; an opaque object that has a red rectangular back side does not suffice. In the case of hearing, if you're not "paying attention", you may not hear sounds in your immediate vicinity. This, no teacher needs to be reminded of: "Pay attention. I'll say it again: the test is not next week; it's the week after next". Notice it hardly seems appropriate to treat not being in the required spatial orientation as "non-normality" of conditions and not paying attention as a case of "non-normality" for perceivers (not, at least, if my students are anything to judge by).

393. I shall assume that a case can be made for not gutting the concept of normality by making it into the concept of "whatever it takes" to secure the implication. Further, I shall assume that what is required for normal (or standard) conditions and perceivers can be generally and briefly, but flexibly, listed (thus, leaving open for, say, serious wine tasters the option of adding to the list). The other matters, such as orientation in space, directing one's attention and concentrating, etc., I shall collect under the phrase 'in suitable circumstances'.

394. In addition to "suitable circumstances", the person, P, must be in a "frame of mind" for which thoughts about the sensible qualities are relevant. The cognitive conditions at issue here are quite familiar. Suppose P, like so many of us, is looking for her keys. Coming upon them, P is caused to think "there are my keys over there". So much of our perceptual interaction is in contexts of goal-directed or problem-solving conduct where nothing about sensible qualities is pertinent to our frame of mind. Moreover, I find no reason to saddle myself with the principle that a sensible quality of an object always causes subjects to think about it and, only by some process of reasoning, subjects come to conclusions about other properties of objects.

(Sellars rejects such a principle, along with a related one, in *SM*, ch. I, section III.) Notice that rejecting this principle does *not* require me to accept that other properties of objects (being of a certain kind, having a certain function, having a certain disposition) are causally relevant with persons. What is true is that, in the manifest image, sensible qualities are sometimes causally responsible for persons' having thoughts which are not about these sensible qualities (or, not only about these sensible qualities), but are about other properties (or other properties as well). This point turns out to be very important in what follows.

395. So, with (at least) all those restrictions, (391.51) becomes

(P1) given that the circumstances are suitable, in normal conditions and for a person, P, who is a normal perceiver and in the appropriate frame of mind, that O is S implies that P thinks that O is S (where 'S' is a sensible quality predicate).

Under all the restrictions in (P1), a person's thinking that O is S, where 'S' is a sensible quality predicate, is an occurrence which is a reliable indicator of O's being S; that is, under all the restrictions, that P thinks that O is S makes it likely that O is S.[145]

396. Though I restrict (P1) and reliable indication to sensible qualities, I do not deny that *similar* principles can be stated for other sorts of properties. These principles, however, require further restrictions. Consider reliable indication. Gain, in normal conditions, a normal perceiver's complete attention; put before this person some what's-it with which the person is completely unfamiliar. Will the person's candidly expressed thoughts about the sensible qualities of the what's-it be a reliable indicator of the sensible qualities of the what's-it? Yes. Now ask the person: what kind of thing is the what's-it? what is its job? what would it do if so-and-so occurred? Given the ignorance I have assumed, the person may have not a clue about the answers to these questions.[146]

397. So, nothing with just the restrictions on (395.P1) works for other properties; thus, as formulated, (395.P1), and the reliable indication connected with it, help to

---

[145] This very point is one that figures prominently into Sellars' account (section VIII of *EPM*) of what is required for observational knowledge.

[146] For those who wish to see this little experiment enacted, there is a television program in which people bring in antiques to be evaluated by experts. The possessors of the antiques are, in some cases, the exact ignorant subjects of my described experiment. The experts, of course, satisfy further conditions that qualify them as experts.

mark off sensible qualities from other properties of objects. (I emphasize that (395.P1) deals with thinkings about, say, red objects, not with something called "experiences of red", as in, for example, principles David Lewis sets out.[147] Part of my account is to say what "experiences of red" are.)

398. A final point about reliable indication concerns failure in cases involving sensible qualities. Jones is caused to think that O is S, but it is not. Abnormality of conditions or of Jones may well be the source of this failure; or, Jones is rushed and gives insufficient attention. The manifest image contains causal principles, other than (395.P1), that relate Jones' thinking that O is S, in abnormal conditions, to objects that are not S or to other states of Jones (say, brought about by the ingestion of psycho-active substances). However, one of the inadequacies of the manifest image is that the system of relevant causal principles is incomplete: there are cases of failure not covered by any principle. Though one can conclude that something is wrong, it does not follow that, in the manifest image, one can formulate the conditions that are required to state principles for such cases. (In some cases, however, certain refinements in the system of principles are possible).

399. Do not confuse the sort of failure that is due to incompleteness of principles with failure of (395.P1). (395.P1) fails in cases in which O is S and Jones does *not* think O is S and yet the utmost scrutiny can detect nothing wrong with the conditions, with the subject or with anything else. There is nothing surprising in this: causal principles in the manifest image fail in cases for which no manifest image answers to the question 'what went wrong?' are available. For centuries, farmers and gardeners have planted their crops, protected them from pests, seen them get water and sunshine and everything else that the plants had last year. Yet, more die this year than last. Cooks, cheesemakers and winemakers have similar failures. Abandoning such causal principles wholesale is not a viable alternative: in the manifest image, they are the only ones you have. All said and done, the manifest image is inadequate to the task of formulating exceptionless causal principles.[148]

400. In these subsections, I have tried to hammer home the claim that philosophical investigation of the manifest image stands a chance of formulating an account of what characteristics mark off sensible qualities from other properties, i.e., an account of which properties are sensible qualities.

---

[147] Pages 326-7 of David Lewis, "Naming the Colours," *Australasian Journal of Philosophy*, 75 (1997), 325-342. Also I should emphasize that, in contrast to Lewis, my account does not even contemplate giving anything like "definitions" in terms of causal principles and definite descriptions. Such "definitions" are examples of the relational characterization I rejected. In passing, I note that the requirement Lewis sets down at the beginning of his article, viz., that an account of color be "both materialistic and commonsensical", is satisfied, I would argue, by my account so far. The question of materialism is one to which I will return.

[148] Of course, the various stages of the scientific image before the last are also inadequate in both the ways just discussed. Since one of the goals of the scientific enterprise is to remove such inadequacies, the last is free of such inadequacies by definition.

(IV) SENSE IMAGE-MODELS: THE AESTHETIC
(a) Sellars' strategy

401. Sellars' strategy in his later treatments of sense image-models and the sensory states that compose them is on display in essays from the nineteen-seventies and nineteen-eighties.[149] In the opening stages of this strategy, he distinguishes between "seeing that so-and-so" and "seeing an object", between what we see an object "as" and what we see "of" an object, and between "seeing" and "ostensibly seeing".

402. The distinction between "seeing that so-and-so" and "seeing an object" rests on familiar examples (which may be connected with other examples I discuss in connection with "seeing as"). One can see that there is a fire on the hills in the distance but be too far away to see the fire; one can see that a fish is near one's boat though the angle of the sunlight on the water makes is impossible to see the fish. An example Sellars uses is that of seeing that there is a plane flying overhead though the plane is too high to see (*SRPC*, 17; *FMPP*, I, 72). On Sellars' view, it is open whether all cases of "seeing that" are cases of seeing some object or other. On the other side of the coin, one can see an object without seeing that the object is so-and-so for any particular property. Sellars' account of seeing an object leaves it open that mature perceivers always "perceive that" when they perceive an object while not building "perceiving that" into perceiving an object.

403. Sellars believes that examples can convince us that what we see *of* objects is limited (*BD*, 70-5). We do not see *of* objects

> their kind;
> their causal properties;
> their functional properties;
> some of their relational properties; and
> even some of their sensible properties.

By contrast, we can see objects *as*

> dogs, bushes, bears, and wine;
> toxic, brittle, and soluble in water;
> doorstops, hammers, harpoons, and wine vats;
> too heavy to lift, aunts, and orbiting the earth; and
> scratchy, fragrant, sweet, bitter, and hot.

---

[149] Sections I-IV of *SSIS* (76), lecture I of *SK* (103), lecture I of *FMPP* (110), and sections I and II of *SSOP* (108); in this volume, sections I and II of *IKTE* (103) and sections I-IV in *SRPC* (106).

Seeing *of* is also limited in another way. We do not see *of* an opaque object its inside, its back side, or indeed any side that is not (perhaps, at an angle) facing us or that is obscured by something else whereas we do see books *as* having back sides, insides, and so on.

404. To find familiar and comfortable examples to shed light on the question "Do we see *of* objects their logical and categorial features?" is not so easy. That we see objects *as* not moving in a straight line, *as* denting something, *as* a sibling (sister or brother), *as* individuals and so on is appealing. Neither I nor Sellars is committed to the view that phenomenology takes us all the way. What will be clear is that Sellars' account of sensory states is so constructed that, when we latterly reflect on the distinction between seeing *of* and seeing *as*, the account gives a "no" to the question which begins this paragraph (*IKTE*, 37ff).

405. Sellars draws the last of his distinctions, that between "seeing" and "ostensibly seeing", in pretty much the same way in all his work since *EPM*. The "basic phenomenological fact" (*FMPP*, I, 69) to which Sellars appeals is that, like Dick in my story (29), we are sometimes perceptually "taken in".

406. Take Sellars' favorite object, this pink ice cube (*SRPC*, 28.) There are times when

(52) P sees that this ice cube is pink, and
(53) P sees this ice cube to be pink.

Both (52) and (53) are, for Sellars, judgments whose truth requires "achievement". In the case of (52), the "achievement" is at very least[150] that

it is true that there is an appropriately situated cube of ice and it is pink;

in the case of (53), it is additionally required that

the volume of pink is causally efficacious in S's seeing (or, as Sellars puts it, that the pink ice cube be "causally responsible" for S's seeing).

Cases Sellars describes as our being "taken in" are just those in which we would swear that we are seeing something, but the achievement fails (e.g., the ice cube is not pink or there is no ice cube at all). Let me speak in these cases of the failure of the "appropriate achievement".

407. Ostensible seeings, Sellars says (*SRPC*, 39; *FMPP*, I, 70), would be seeings

---

[150] I leave it open that we might be able to convince ourselves that what I say about (53) should have a version appropriate to (52).

if the appropriate achievement obtained; seeings and ostensible seeings are "intrinsically alike". The word 'intrinsic' cuts out other features of the situation which would be different from what they were if the appropriate achievement obtained. For example, in Dick's case, having a bear where there is really a bush brings about certain other changes in the *total* situation (e.g., bears salivate; bushes don't), but not in Dick's cognitive state (though, of course, his relational properties change since he is near a bear now, rather than a bush). Let me put this in another way. Sellars draws the distinction between seeing and ostensible seeing so that seeings are a subclass of ostensible seeings. Consider setting down all that is required for something to be a case of S's seeing (including the appropriate achievement); now take away the appropriate achievement (and whatever goes with it) and everything left is required for being an ostensible seeing.

408. A small complication lurks in the wings. We can say of Dick that

(54) Dick saw this black bush *as* a bear

and Dick can full well say this of himself afterwards, though he would deny it at the time. It is also true that

(55) Dick saw this black bush,

but it is false that

(56) Dick saw this black bush *as* a bush.

According to Dick's friends, (55) is true, but Dick cannot be accredited with any representings which begin with

this black bush is ...

though he did think

this black bear is ... .

This case suggests that we need to accommodate examples in which persons see an object though they would firmly deny it. It may be that whenever persons see an object, they see it *as* something (a bear) though, of course, not necessarily *as* what it is (bushes are not bears).

409. Not only are there mistakes of the sort Dick made, there are more radical mistakes in which someone claims to see a pink ice cube when there is no pink ice cube around and there is no object around to see *as* a pink ice cube. Part of Sellars' strategy is to argue that "phenomenologically speaking" such cases leave the unphilosophical user of the manifest image with very little to say (*SK*, I, 51-57; *FMPP*, I, 87-91). What Sellars thinks "phenomenology" can get us is well illustrated in a passage from *SRPC* (in this volume):

> 35. Sufficient to the occasion is an analysis of the sense in which we see of the pink ice cube its very pinkness. Here, I believe, sheer phenomenology or conceptual analysis takes us *part of* the way, but finally lets us down. How far does it take us? Only to the point of assuring us that *something, somehow* a cube of pink in physical space is present in the perception other than as merely *believed in*.
> 36. In traditional terminology, the *somehow* presence of a cube of pink does not consist in its intensional in-existence as the content of a conceptual act. Nor is its character as a cube of pink in physical space facing me edgewise a matter of its actually being a cube of pink in physical space. It is *somehow* a cube of pink in physical space facing me edgewise without *actually being* a cube of pink in physical space facing me edgewise, yet without merely being the content of a *belief in* a cube of pink in physical space facing me edgewise.
> 37. Seeing *of* the cube its very pinkness and its cubicity (from a point of view) would be analyzed in terms of this *somehow, other than merely believed in* presence of a cube of pink in physical space facing one edgewise in the visual experience.
> 38. I say "visual experience" because it is time to take into account, at least provisionally, the fact that we can seem to see a cube of pink ice from a point of view in physical space when there is, in point of fact, no cube of pink ice in the neighborhood.
> 39. We can use the phrase "*ostensible* seeing of a cube of pink ice facing one edgewise *as* a cube of pink ice facing one edgewise" to refer to a visual experience which would be a case of seeing a cube of pink ice facing one edgewise as a cube of pink ice facing one edgewise, if there was such a cube of pink ice and it was (in a sense requiring analysis) causally responsible for the ostensible seeing.
> 40. Thus the *somehow*, other than as believed in, presence of a cube of pink ice facing one edgewise would be common to what can provisionally be called veridical and non-veridical ostensible seeings of a cube of pink ice facing one edgewise. *SRPC*, 35-40

410. In short, that philosophical investigation of our experience which Sellars calls "phenomenological" brings us to the realization that there are actual cubes of pink in cases where there is no pink ice cube and even in cases in which there is no object to be seen *as* pink. Such reflection on our experience supplies us with no answer to the question of the status of these actual expanses and volumes of color. For this, Sellars holds, another sort of philosophical reflection is required, one which leads to an account of perception in which, *in some sense*, expanses and volumes of color can have a place as states of perceivers.

411. To me, it is clear that Sellars believes that the phenomenological distinctions addressed in his opening strategy *motivate* the further, different philosophical investigation of perception. For some philosophers, this may well be so. Sellars, therefore, can forge a dialectical connection that gives his subsequent treatment of sensory states a handhold in the rocky architecture of these philosophers' positions. Doubtless such a dialectical approach is a reasonable one. Sellars, though, knew that there are philosophers who are unmoved. The *"new*, new Materialists" whose views "surprised" him so much (*NAO* (104), p. 2) probably reject his conviction that volumes of pink are actual items whose existence is obvious and about which the crucial concern is their status (*FMPP*, III, 46 and also I, 87).[151] Given what these materialists reject, the remainder of Sellars' strategy does not work for them as he intended it to work.

412. Many of Sellars' subsequent arguments defend two claims: that, in the switch to the scientific image, the original sensible qualities of manifest objects are abandoned so that nothing in the scientific image has the sensible qualities of the objects of the manifest image and that, *in some way*, colors (and other sensible qualities) are preserved as constituents of neurophysiological states of sentient beings. For Sellars, the upshot of the views of the new materialists is that cases of sensible qualities, in the sense that I have been discussing, disappear *completely* in the scientific image as actual items. They might be "intentional inexistents", but nothing in the scientific image would actually have these properties and, among the properties actually had by objects, there would be none which might be accounted to be the sensible qualities with a new status.

413. I view the current dialectical situation as too complex to deal with in this introduction. So, I intend to unhitch my expository horse from the dialectical wagon. I will set out Sellars' account of sense image-models with an eye to its central claims, with a reasonable concern for how it differs from other accounts, and with the occasional remark intended to forestall misunderstanding and fend off obvious criticism.

414. As the first of these remarks, I state from the outset that I do not view the enterprise as one of "proving" the existence of sensory states.[152] Inasmuch as it will be plain that sense image-models are merely complex properties of persons, it is, to me, strange to think there might be a *philosophical* "proof" that certain objects had them. I provide an "argument", in a weaker sense, in that I expound the view and defend it from criticisms. (Further, Lycan's request that the antimaterialist, who holds that Lycan has failed to establish materialism, "show why" he (Lycan) has failed is not a satisfiable request: materialists would simply reject the premises of

---

[151] One such philosopher would seem to be Daniel C. Dennett. See his comments on Sellars' *FMPP* in "Wondering Where the Yellow Went", *Monist*, 64, 102-8.

[152] Some philosophers seem to construe the task of defenders of sensory states as being that of giving such a proof. See, e.g., p. 373 of Daniel C. Dennett, *Consciousness Explained* (Little, Brown and Co., 1991) and Lycan's long attack on p. 121 of *Consciousness* (MIT Press, 1987) where he also insists that defenders of "qualia" merely "posture" and are unmoved by argument.

any such "proof" an antimaterialist would attempt to construct.)

415. Once my task of exposition is accomplished, I turn to making a case for the claim that Sellars' account of sensory states, if set into the Kantian framework, supports many theses that Kant commits himself to.

(b) Their analogical account as properties
(a) "Verb" theories of sensory states

416. The quotation from *SRPC* (363) provides guidelines:

> (G1) the structure of sensory states is not literally spatial, but sensory states involve properties and relations analogous to literally spatial ones;
> (G2) sensory states correspond to sensory qualities (like color) and are similar to these sensory qualities in having some of the central features that differentiate sensible qualities from other properties;
> (G3) the total philosophical account, including the analogy, attributes to sensory states causal connections both "externally" and "internally".

I characterize (G1)-(G3) as guidelines since there is much in them to explicate.

417. One other point stands out in the quotation from *SRPC*: Sellars likes to set his entire account of sensory states within the framework of adverbialism. I am sure that there are dialectical situations in which adverbialism is important. The predicate 'sense' is as convenient as the predicate 'represent'.

418. So, too, if we had the predicate 'vis' (in analogy to 'move' as in 'P moves slowly'), we could introduce

> P vises smilingly
> P vises frowningly

as equivalents, respectively, of

> P smiles
> P frowns

and, on the model of 'move' and 'movement', as equivalents, respectively, of

> P has (does?, wears?) a smiling visage
> P has (does?, wears?) a frowning visage.

When I introduced dot-quoted expressions as predicates (32-37), I assumed that beginning with predicates does not cut one off from these familiar transformations just as starting with the predicate 'smiles' does not cut one off from the adjective 'smiling', the adverb 'smilingly', and the noun 'smile'.

419. Moreover, though not all properties of individuals are ones about which we can say that they "happen", or "take place", this is true of smiles. So, "P smiles" is true if and only if "a smile (or, a smiling) by P takes place". Sensory states are, on my account, also items that take place.[153] So, though my account concentrates on predicates, which I shall indicate thus,

S-( ),

and which appear in judgings thus,

P S-( )s,

I do not thereby think of myself as barred from

an S-( )ing by P takes place.

420. My general inclination, largely acquired through a desire to avoid common philosophical associations, is to abjure the term 'sense'. With this term, however, it is harmless, I hold, to make use of the forms

P senses S-( )ingly,
P has a S-( ) sensing (or, sensation), and
S-( )ings are sensings (or, sensations).

The additional complication of, as the phrase goes, "quantifying over" smiles or sensations or whatever, I would also argue is harmless.[154]

421. All this notwithstanding, I frame the account of sensory states without adverbialism.[155] Like one of Sellars' mythical philosophers (*SSOP*, 37-40), I pro-

---

[153] I repeat a point made earlier: though the terminology of properties classifies sensible qualities as "occurrent", it does not follow that sensible qualities "occur" or "take place". The properties which are sensory states are both occurrent in this logical sense *as well as* being items that take place.

[154] Note that, on the standard account of quantification, one explains what is in one's "domain of quantification" and then, well, one "quantifies". Using quantification does not alter (change, modify, do anything to) the entities being quantified over. What you had before is what you still have and my account obviously includes sensory states as properties.

[155] "Without adverbialism", meaning that the expressions for sensory states are not introduced as adverbs that modify the verb 'sense'. Of course, I have committed myself in paragraph 420 to there being equivalent forms that do involve adverbs. Moreover, whenever one treats complex properties, one might think of this as dealing with property "modifications" and therefore with adverbs in a related sense.

pound, not an "adverbial", but a "verb" account of sensory states.

(β) Concept construction analogically

422. Concentrating again on vision, I begin with (416.G1). There is a serious question of how much geometry one needs in dealing with perception, but I think that nothing much hinges on approaching this less than systematically.

423. I use the word 'scene' for the objects, with their properties and relations, which, along with the perceiver, are relevant to a perceptual situation. Roughly speaking, an object is in a scene if and only if the perceiver, P, would normally be credited with seeing the object. By some changes in position, P can change the scene; other changes of position simply reveal more of the scene. Were I to loosen my restriction to vision, I would include objects in the scene P did not see since it is possible to smell the skunk and hear the bear without seeing them. The term 'scene' is not meant to carry any great weight; its usefulness is in providing simpler exposition.

424. What the perceiver can see *of* the objects in a scene depends on the relative positions of the objects and the perceiver in the scene. Since perceivers can change their positions, I construct the analogy to accommodate all of what could be seen *of* any scene. In general, the analogy holds that to whatever physical properties and relations we can see *of* scenes, there correspond S-(spatial) properties and S-(spatial) relations ('S' to remind one of 'sensory').

425. The shape of a surface of an object in a scene might be a rectangle, a triangle, a circle, and so on. So, the analogy offers us corresponding properties and predicates to go with them: 'S-(is a rectangle)', 'S-(is a triangle)', 'S-(is a circle)' and so on. Properties of the shapes preserved by the analogy are, for example, those having to do with edges. A rectangle has four edges and a triangle only three; so it is with S-(rectangles), S-(triangles) and S-(edges). Some circle can be drawn inside a square so that the edge of the circle coincides with the edges of the square at four points; so, too, with S-(circles) and S-(squares). In general, the analogy preserves *many* (but not all) of the implications that are part of a system of geometry.[156]

426. For many shapes, we have no presently available predicates. Adapting a theme from Kant, I shall assume that we are all better at drawing and painting than we really are. Our drawings of shapes allow us to introduce, by definite description, predicates for the immense variety of shapes that the surfaces of objects have.

427. The objects in a scene, like all physical objects, are connected together in space and can be in many different spatial relations. Some of these relations are

---

[156] I have avoided mentioning angles since it would open up complicated questions. Is it Euclidean geometry that is in question? Even if it is, many of surfaces that confront us are not plane and thus some triangles on these surfaces do not have angles which sum to 180 degrees.

perspectival and some not.

428. An object O may have a largely flat surface with a blue rectangle adjoining a red square. Sellars' pink ice cube may be surrounded by pale green liquid so that the transparent cube of pink is enclosed within a wine-glass shape of green. The bite you take out of a mission fig displays a reddish-pink concavity of fig flesh framed by the remaining black skin on either side of the concavity. Since the perceiver is in the scene, perspectival spatial relations abound. The white billiard ball is to the left of the black, but the green ball is to the right of black and somewhat behind it. The analogical account offers us S-predicates for all these spatial relations.

429. I turn now to colors and other sensible qualities. I believe that the thrust of (416.G2) is that the analogy should maintain for sensory states the same "incompatibilities of determinates" and "generic incompatibilities" had by sensible qualities and also those arrangements of degree that are possessed by sensible qualities. So, whatever relations of degree there are with sensible qualities, these have analogs in the case of sensory states. Thus one sensory state, an S-(color), might be S-(bluer than) another sensory state, also an S-(color); an S-(tone) might be more (less) S-(strident than) another S-(tone).

430. Most importantly, what is true of sensible qualities regarding "togetherness" and "filling" is also true of sensory states. In paragraphs 379-80, I argued that

> (379.48) object O has a red rectangular facing surface (or, has a facing surface which is a red rectangle).

is not even equivalent to, much less analyzable into, either of

> (379.49) object O has a red and rectangular facing surface, or
> (379.50) object O has a red facing surface and object O has a rectangular facing surface.

I claimed that (379.48) tells us that red "fills" the rectangle. Such "togetherness", I argued, is not to be understood *merely* in terms of conjunction. Consider again the example of the fig. The sweetness, the fig-flavor, the warmth, and the reddish-brownness of the flesh are sometimes all there *together* in the fig and together *fill* the fig-shaped volume. So, in at least some cases, the attributing of sensible qualities to surfaces of objects or to the objects themselves requires combining parts of judgings with more than mere conjunction.

431. However exactly such combining is to be finally explicated, Sellars' analogy takes it over to the combining of predicates for sensory states. For example, that

> P S-(a red rectangle)s

158   *Introduction*

or that, in the adverbialized form,

   P sense S-(a red rectangle)ly

or that, in the nominalized form,

   P has a S-(a red rectangle) sensation

no doubt entails something involving conjunction, but it is not to be explicated in terms of conjunction.

432.   Compare the above to having predicates for total facial expressions. I use 'F' as an indicator for such predicates. We might say of someone, P, that

   (57) P F-(.........)s

where the dots are filled in by suitably combined terms like •smiles•s, •frowns•s, •winks•s, and so on. Once again, conjunction is not irrelevant to (57); some cases in which the token of (57) combines a •smiles• and a •winks• should be so understood that the token entails

   (58) P smiles and P winks.

433.   Also notice that, though a person can have only one total facial expression at a time, we are not thereby compelled to attribute that entire property to the person. To judge merely that P smiles is to attribute to P only "part" (in some sense of this widely used term) of what we can attribute to P. But I see this as no more problematic than judging

   object O has a red facing surface

when it would also have been true to judge

   (379.48) object O has a red rectangular facing surface (or, has a facing surface which is a red rectangle).

434.   The importance of these points is that, as I mentioned (380), inattention to them has led to criticisms.[157] If I were to analyze

   P S-(a red rectangle)s

as

   P S-(red)s and P S-(rectangle)s

and

   P S-(a blue triangle)s

as

   P S-(blue)s and P S-(triangle)s,

then I couldn't distinguish between

   P S-(a red rectangle)s and S-(a blue triangle)s, and
   P S-(a blue rectangle)s and S-(a red triangle)s

for the obvious reason that conjunction commutes. But it is just this analysis that I avoid for reasons that originally concern sensible qualities, not sensory states.

435. As its "negative" part, the analogy abandons for sensory states all the causal properties of sensible qualities. The causal interactions in the spatiotemporal world in which the perceiver also has a place are a large part of what insure that the sensible qualities are "physical" properties of manifest objects. It is not that the total philosophical account does not propose causal interaction for sensory states; it does. But the causal interactions that enmesh volumes and durations of sensible qualities with other properties of literally spatial objects changing over time are not the correct ones for sensory states.

436. I constructed the analogy to preserve *intact* part of the characterization of sensible qualities; this part is, on the analogy, literally *common* to both sensible qualities and sensory states. What is *different* in the two characterizations is that sensible qualities are properties of all manifest objects and participate in the literally

---

[157] See the discussion in Box 3.1 (p. 74ff.) of Michael Tye, *Ten Problems of Consciousness: a Representational Theory of the Phenomenal Mind* (MIT Press, 1995). Tye is there discussing some points made by Frank Jackson latterly in his book (to which Tye refers) and originally in an exchange of papers among Jackson, Tye, and Sellars in *Metaphilosophy*, April, 1975. Sellars' contribution to that exchange is *ATS* (96). Though I do not have the space to make all the relevant points, I direct my discussion at two of the more important criticisms.

spatial framework in which these objects have a place while the sensory states are properties of sentient beings only and, though they have an analogical spatiotemporal structure, their participation in the history of the literally spatiotemporal world is through the history of sentient beings. I propose this formulation as one way of explaining what Sellars had in mind in saying (363):

> 46. I have come to see, however, that we must be able so to formulate the analogy between manners of sensing and perceptual attributes of physical objects, that it is made evident that the analogy preserves in a strict sense the conceptual *content* of predicates pertaining to the perceptible attributes of physical objects, while transposing this content into the radically different categorial framework to which manners of sensings belong. *SRPC*, 46

I propose to call this common content the "quality dimension" of sensible qualities and sensory states.

437. I summarize what I have been saying to set out the segments of the analogy clearly. According to the analogy,

> sensible qualities and sensory states are properties which share the following properties:
>
> (TA1) having *some sort* of spatiotemporal structure;
> (TA2) having the *very same* incompatibilities and degrees;
> (TA3) having the *very same* structure of "togetherness" and "filling".

438. For reasons primarily connected with exposition, I stipulate that the "analogy" is the material of this subsection plus some related points to be discussed shortly. The analogy plus material that arises in discussing (416.G3) comprise the "total philosophical account" mentioned in that guideline. Continuing in my vein of purloining terminology from Kant, I call that total account the "aesthetic". Its completion takes more than this subsection.

439. I admit that I had second (third, fourth, and on) thoughts about whether to rearrange this subsection and the next. Doing that, I would have treated (416.G3) before the others. I could find expositional gains in that, but the losses would be large since it is difficult to formulate some of the material of the next subsection without terminology from this subsection. A convoluted mixture of the two subsections I rejected on the grounds that it muddies the structure of Sellars' aesthetic as a doctrine that separates intertwined issues pertaining to sensibility.

440. I repeat something I said a moment ago: the entire discussion of the aesthetic occupies more than this, and the next, subsection.

Introduction 161

(γ) The causal theme

441. What guides the causal part of the aesthetic is both the phenomenology of "seeing *of*" and an old theme that "strictly speaking" not really all that much has a causal impact on the senses. (Remember that, for the most part, I am restricting my remarks to vision.) Since we do not see *of* objects (403)

> their kind;
> their causal properties;
> their functional properties;
> some of their relational properties; and
> even some of their sensible properties,

these properties form the basis of a list of perceptually causally irrelevant properties (see paragraphs 394 and 396 for replies to some obvious objections). To this list, the account adds logical and categorial features as not affecting the senses. What remain (in the case of vision) are sensible qualities such as colors, some shapes and some perspectival and non-perspectival spatial relations.

442. It is familiar that many considerations of widely varying worth prompted members of the philosophical tradition to add the logical and categorial features to the list of perceptually causally irrelevant properties. For myself, one of the important points is that a principle like (395.P1) does not work for logical and categorial items (see 396-7). I cannot stress too much that such a position about perception would seem wrong unless one remembers the points of paragraphs 394 and 404:

> first, sensible qualities can be causally responsible for perceivers having thoughts that are not about the sensible qualities themselves;
> second, seeing *as* is not under the restrictions of seeing *of*.

(In section **V**, this point about perceiving *as* takes on greater weight.)

443. Now the question is: in any scene at a given time, what state is produced in the perceiver by the scene? What is caused is one (complex) sensory state of the perceiver; or, abiding by my restriction to the visual, I should say "one (complex) visual state". Optimally, sensible qualities and relations of the objects in the scene produce in the perceiver a state involving the corresponding S-qualities and S-relations supplied by the analogy. Since "seeing *of*" is limited to the facing surfaces of objects (those that are opaque) and by the position of the perceiver, the aesthetic supplies an idealized procedure.

444. For example, suppose that what the perceiver, P, can see *of* two objects which adjoin each other in a scene is a red rectangular facing surface of the one on the left and a blue square facing surface of the one on the right. So, "stripping out" all but (or, as Kant would say, "abstracting from" all but) the sensible qualities and relations as they are from the perspective of P, we have a description which leaves the objects out and includes only the following:

(59) a red rectangle adjoins left to right a blue square.

What is caused, in this example, is that

(60) P S-(a red rectangle adjoins left to right a blue square)s.

445. In general, of course, what perceivers can see *of* scenes varies from scene to scene and perceiver to perceiver. The causal doctrine of the aesthetic handles the required range of cases by idealizing and generalizing the steps of the procedure illustrated in the example. Take P's spatial position with respect to the scene into account; provide a total description of the objects of the scene restricting yourself to the sensible qualities of the facing surfaces (or volumes) of the objects and to the perspectivally available spatial relations involving these objects. (As we know, care must be taken with Sellars' transparent cube of pink ice and with concave surfaces of "bitten into" mission figs.) From this total description, produce the "stripped-down" description containing only the sensible qualities and their relations. (Remember that •red rectangle•s do not get turned into •red and rectangular•s.) The stripped-down description, assembled from the perspective[158] of the perceiver, provides what is used in the S-predicate for the visual sensory state of the perceiver. Let me indicate this last step as follows:

assembled stripped-down description

generates, under the analogy, the predicate

S-(assembled stripped-down description)s.

446. The optimal conditions mentioned in paragraph 443 are those discussed earlier in connection with sensible qualities: normal conditions, normal persons, and suitable circumstances (particularly 381-99). Among others, the aesthetic offers the following principle:

---

[158] Since some philosophers have used 'perspective' or 'point of view' for something they consider to be, in some sense, "subjective", I should point out that I have in mind only spatial position.

(TA4) given that the circumstances are suitable, in normal conditions and for a person, P, who is a normal perceiver,[159]

that the scene has D (which is an assembled stripped-down description)

implies

that P S-(assembled stripped-down description D)s.

I re-state (TA4) in the nominalized talk of "sensory states" (or, "sensations"). Optimally, a scene with the assembled stripped-down description D causes P to have a total visual sensory state (or, sensation) which is an S-(assembled stripped-down description D) state (or, sensation). The causal part of the aesthetic envisages that sensory states are part of the causal order in that they are brought about by objects whose causally relevant properties and relations are sensible qualities and relations.

447. As in paragraphs 381-99, there are points to be made about reliable indication. Optimally, that

P S-(assembled stripped-down description D)s,

makes is likely that the correct assembled stripped-down description of the scene is D. (Remember: the assembled stripped-down description depends on the spatial position of P in the scene.)

448. There are several topics which, in a fuller treatment, would be due considerable space. One is that the optimal does not always obtain. I like to believe that philosophers of perception, particularly those who defended commonsense accounts of perceiving, have beat this dog, if not dead, at least insensible. I hope, therefore, that it will suffice for me to say that the aesthetic account I am expounding plans to take over, and adapt as necessary, commonsense principles about less than optimal conditions and circumstances. Another is the topic of the failure of manifest image causal principles. What I have said about this matter in paragraphs 398 and 399 will have to suffice in this introduction.[160] I turn my attention to questions of more recent concern and then to other questions that finally return us to Kantian issues.

449. In the analogy, I pointed out (431-4) that, in general, conjunction is not irrelevant to predicates for sensory states. I likened that case to ones with predicates

---

[159] Notice that the qualification 'in an appropriate frame of mind' (394-5) does not appear here. The point is that the initially caused sensory state is not dependent on activity of the "understanding" and my account has to be capable of being extended to sentient individuals that have no "frame of mind".
[160] On both these topics, as well as on the topic of sensory states in general, I still find what was said in chapters V, VI and VII of Aune's *Knowledge, Mind, and Nature*, though written over thirty years ago, to be, with some qualifications, defensible.

for total facial expressions in which

> (432.57) P F-(.........)s

entails

> (432.58) P smiles and P winks.

In (432.58), we attribute to P, I am supposing, a correct, though not total, description of P's facial expression. Nothing prevents us from using the term 'facial expression' in such a way that (432.58) and

> (61) P smiles, and
> (62) P winks

all attribute facial expressions to P (though not total facial expressions). Under such a regimen, the nominalizations of (61) and (62) result in our treating both smiles and winks as facial expressions and, no doubt, would lead us to say that the total facial expression, which is a F-(.........), is composed of other facial expressions, in particular, a smile and a wink. If we do this, we cannot then balk at what might seem to be a little unpalatable: namely, that persons regularly have more than one facial expression at a time (though, of course, not more than one total facial expression). What we would have done is to have established a way of treating the complexity of total facial expressions.

450. Something similar happens in the case of scenes. There is, at least in principle, a total description, but as well there are partial descriptions. This carries over to assembled stripped-down descriptions. Consider a total assembled stripped-down description D of some scene. (There are, it should be noted, many equivalent such descriptions.) There are cases in which D entails

> (63) a red rectangle adjoins left to right a blue square and a green circle is above a brown triangle

and thus, of course, D entails both

> (444.59) a red rectangle adjoins left to right a blue square, and
> (64) a green circle is above a brown triangle.

451. This entailment carries over to sensory states. After all, no one can be compelled to describe perceivers completely any more than they can be compelled to describe scenes completely. So, in some cases,

(65) P S-(assembled stripped-down description D)s

entails

(66) P S-(a red rectangle adjoins left to right a blue square and a green circle is above a brown triangle)s

and thus, of course, entails both

(444.60) P S-(a red rectangle adjoins left to right a blue square)s, and
(67) P S-(a green circle is above a brown triangle)s.

Once nominalization is invoked, we have it that

(68) P has an S-(assembled stripped-down description D) visual sensation,
(69) P has an S-(a red rectangle adjoins left to right a blue square and a green circle is above a brown triangle) visual sensation,
(70) P has an S-(a red rectangle adjoins left to right a blue square) visual sensation, and
(71) P has an S-(a green circle is above a brown triangle) visual sensation.

Here again we stare complexity in the face. Nothing, I think, prevents us from invoking the fact that the total assembled stripped-down description is composed of partial descriptions to generate an analogous "composition" of the visual sensation, thus allowing us to say, in at least traditional-sounding terms, that some visual sensations are "composed" of other visual sensations.

452. If we decide that we have captured something important about this complexity, then, once again, we should not become queasy over one of its seemingly unpalatable consequences: namely, that a perceiver can, in the nominalized mode, have more than one visual sensation at a time, or, in the adverbial mode, have more than one sensing at a time.[161]

453. In this subsection, I have set out one part of the causal theme: more is to

---

[161] I refer again to the discussion in Box 3.1 (p. 74ff.) of Michael Tye, *Ten Problems of Consciousness: a Representational Theory of the Phenomenal Mind* (MIT Press, 1995). The original objection to allowing more than one sensing at a time was made by Frank Jackson in the exchange of papers among Jackson, Tye, and Sellars in *Metaphilosophy*, April, 1975. Sellars' contribution to that exchange is *ATS* (96). Tye repeats this objection in Box 3.1.

I should take this opportunity to note that I believe that I have reproduced what is essentially Sellars' strategy in *ATS*, but without the adverbialist trappings.

166 *Introduction*

come. One topic, however, emerges quite naturally from the present points and I take it up next, leaving another part of the causal theme to the subsection after.

(δ) Spatial connectedness

454. The manifest objects in a scene, being literally spatial objects, are spatially connected: that is, each object bears at least one spatial relation to every other, including the perceiver. With a little work, we could formulate this connectedness in terms of a path, starting at the perceiver, that led to each of the objects in the scene. That there are many such paths reflects the many different spatial relations the objects have to each other.

455. This connectedness is handed down, as it were, to the assembled stripped-down description. In the example of the previous subsection,

(450.64) a green circle is above a brown triangle.

The colored shapes of the objects have inherited spatial relations from their objects. Such a judgment as (450.64) formulates a partial stripped-down description of the scene and is part of the "dis-assembly" which we can practice with descriptions of scenes, whether stripped-down or not.

456. This dis-assembly can, with care, be continued. There is nothing by itself dangerous in treating the structure of (450.64) as

(72) individual spatial relation individual

provided that the sense of 'individual' is the wide one in which, maybe, everything is an individual. So, both the original description of the scene and the assembled stripped down description of the scene entail judgments whose structure can be indicated by (72) and by saying, in more or less traditional terminology, that these judgments are about individuals and their relations. By doing this, we do not commit ourselves to any special traditional theses: for example, a thesis that puts different sorts of individuals all on equal footing or a thesis about the nature of relations. If I say of Jones that

his wink is above left of his smile

and then think of this as a matter of individuals in spatial relation, I have not thereby committed myself to anything I did not independently believe about winks, smiles and spatial relations.

457. The same steps just negotiated are available in the case of sensory states.

After all, in some cases,

(451.65) P S-(assembled stripped-down description D)s

entails

(451.67) P S-(a green circle is above a brown triangle)s,

which becomes, once nominalized,

(451.71) P has an S-(a green circle is above a brown triangle) visual sensation.

Now comes the tricky part.

458. Do not sensory states also inherit spatial connectedness from the original description of the scene through the mediation of the assembled stripped-down description? Yes. In fact, I insist on this point. The entire structure of a (total) visual sensory state is analogically spatial, i.e., S-(spatial). With some qualifications, I wouldn't mind putting this by saying the visual sensory states have a structure which is S-(colored) S-(shapes) in S-(spatial) relations. For later purposes, I summarize this point about the S-(spatial) structure of visual sensory states (and some other points coming soon) in the slogan

(TA5) the structure of sensory states is empirical.

459. Next question: does not (451.67) entail both

(73) P S-(a green circle)s, and
(74) P S-(a brown triangle)s?

Or, put in terms of the nominalizations, does not

(451.71) P has an S-(a green circle is above a brown triangle) visual sensation

entail both

(75) P has an S-(a green circle) visual sensation, and
(76) P has an S-(a brown triangle) visual sensation?

A qualified "yes" to this question. The qualification concerns a point about the analogy that I did not include in my earlier discussion (only so much can be said without preparation). Every analogical construction has "negative" pieces that exclude, rather than include, certain features. From the judgment about an object, O, that

O has a facing surface which is a green circle,

it follows that O exists and no doubt we can be happy enough with the idea that from

(450.64) a green circle is above a brown triangle,

it follows that a green circle exists and a brown triangle exists. Under the analogy, however, this logical feature of (450.64) is dropped because the analogy constructs *predicates*, not subject terms. From

(451.67) P S-(a green circle is above a brown triangle)s,

it follows only that P exists and the same is true of (73) and (74).
460. The analogy maintains only that (451.67) entails both (459.73) and (459.74) and, similarly, (451.67) entails

(77) P S-(is above)s.

Given that I have been free in using nominalizations, I find it, to that extent, unproblematic that

(78) P has an S-(is above) sensation.

461. The final question: since the structure of (450.64) was diagrammed as

(456.72)   individual   spatial relation   individual,

would not the same diagram do for the predicate of (451.67) and the adjective of its nominalized counterpart

(451.71) P has an S-(a green circle is above a brown triangle) visual sensation?

My answer to the previous question shows, I think, why the answer to this question must be a qualified "no". I say "qualified" only because I can think of construals of (451.71) which are harmless even in this context. But most construals of (451.71)

that I can think of incline one to treat sensory states in a way that befits the manifest image objects that occur in scenes. No such objects are available in the analogical construction: only properties. These properties are properties of objects, viz., perceivers, that are in the scene.

462. In recent paragraphs I may seem to be making a rather large issue out of virtually nothing. I did so, first, because the view of sensory states I am putting together supports theses which give the appearance of qualifying it, in Lycan's phrase, as one to which only an "unreconstructed" sense data theorist could subscribe.[162] To this point I will return.

463. Second, ridding oneself of the topic of complexity is not that easy. Once we have ground our way down to

(459.74) P S-(a brown triangle)s,

it seems reasonable to inquire even further. Suppose we give due weight to my earlier points about the "togetherness" of •brown•s and •triangle•s in •a brown triangle•s. It still seems possible to worry about the kind of complexity that such "togetherness" brings with it. Even more interesting is that it would seem that (459.74) must, somehow or other, involve (imply?)

(79) P S-(triangle)s.

But aren't triangles (rectangles, squares, etc.) complex as well? While I can not take on all these problems, to this last one I will return. Now, though, back to another piece of the aesthetic.

(ε) Image-models and synesthesia

464. Disheartening as it may be, the truth is that I have not yet reached the points which explain most clearly why Sellars' decided to use the term 'image-model'. To tackle these points, I need to say something about synesthesia.

465. When, some years back, I came across the term 'synesthesia' in Sellars' writings (*FMPP*, I, 112 and *SRPC*, 34), I knew what he was talking about and was not particularly surprised to find him appealing to this phenomenon. Well, I should have been surprised.[163] Synesthesia, though noted more than two hundred years ago

---

[162] See page 481 of William G. Lycan, "In Defense of the Representational Theory of Qualia (Replies to Neander, Rey, and Tye)" in *Philosophical Perspectives, 12, Language, Mind, and Ontology, 1998*, edited by James E. Tomberlin (Blackwell Publishers, 1998).

[163] As an undergraduate in a psychology class, I came across a reference to synesthesia and chose to do a paper on it. As an illustration, perhaps, of the vagaries of statistics, the very first person I interrogated was a true synesthete who had the most common form, sound-color synesthesia.

and discussed in nineteenth-century psychological literature, fell into obscurity with the rise of Behaviorism in the twentieth century. As a topic in neuroscience, it was resurrected almost single-handedly by the neurologist, Richard E. Cytowic, in the nineteen-eighties.[164]

466. True synesthetes are rare, maybe, ten in a million, and have a neurological condition that is not to be confused with more familiar conditions such as: pathological states (classical migraine, epilepsy, drug- or deprivation-induced states and so on), "holes" (lesions) in the brain, hyperactive imagination abetted by literary association (as advanced in the Symbolist Movement) or by musical association (as in Scriabin's music), or one or another garden-variety psychoses. Synesthesia, as the etymology of the word for it suggests, is a union of senses: stimulation in one sense (such as hearing) produces responses in another (such a sight). The sensory response of a synesthete is involuntary, durable (lifelong), invariable (always caused by the same stimulus subject, of course, to restrictions on conditions), "generic" (described in terms of the sensible qualities, not other properties such as kinds), vividly remembered, and occurs much as it would if the appropriate sense had been suitably stimulated.

467. Several passages show why Sellars wants to appeal to something different from synesthesia, but *like* it in several respects:

> 32. Even more interesting is the fact that in seeing the cube *as* a cube of ice we are seeing it *as* cool. But do we see *of* the cube its coolness? Here we are torn in a familiar manner. On the one hand we want to say that the pinkness and coolness are "phenomenologically speaking" on a par, and are tempted to say that the idea that we don't see its coolness is a matter not of phenomenology, but of scientific theory. On the other hand, when asked point blank whether we see its coolness, we find an affirmative answer intuitively implausible and are tempted to fall back on the idea that its coolness is *believed in,* i.e., that it is *taken as* cool.
> 33. Obviously we want to say that the ice cube's very coolness is not *merely* believed in, even though its very coolness is not seen. It clearly won't do to say that we feel or imagine a coolness on seeing the cube, what is in question is *its* coolness. (*SRPC*, 32-3, in this volume.)
>
> 13. But what of the volume of white apple flesh which the apple is seen *as* containing? Many philosophers would be tempted to say that it is present *in the experience* merely by virtue of being believed in. It has, of course, actual existence as a constituent of the apple, but, they would insist, it is not present in its actuality. Phenomenologists have long insisted that this would be a mistake. As they see it, an actual volume of white is

---

[164] For a rather personal report of Cytowic's work on synesthesia (with references to more austerely scientific reports), see Richard E. Cytowic, *The Man Who Tasted Shapes* (MIT Press, 1998). Part One of his book is pertinent to my discussion, not the attempt at a neurophysiological explanation of synesthesia in Part Two.

present in the experience in a way which parallels the red. We experience the red *as containing the white*.

14. But if what is experienced is red-containing-white *as* red-containing-white, and if both the red and the white are actualities actually present, how are we to account for the fact that there is a legitimate sense in which we don't *see the inside of the apple*? To be sure, we see the apple *as* white inside, but we don't *see* the whiteness of the inside of the apple. .....

16. How can a volume of white apple flesh be present *as actuality* in the visual experience if it is not seen? The answer should be obvious. It is present by virtue of being *imagined*. (Notice that to get where we have arrived, much more phenomenology must have been done than is explicitly being done on this occasion. We are drawing on a store of accumulated wisdom.) ...

19. Notice that to say that it is present in the experience by virtue of being imagined is not to say that it is *presented as* imagined. The fruits of careful phenomenological description are not to be read from experience by one who runs. Red may present itself *as* red and white present itself *as* white; but sensations do not present themselves *as* sensations, nor images *as* images. Otherwise philosophy would be far easier than it is.
...

21. Let us combine our results into one example. We see the cool red apple. We see it *as* red on the facing side, *as* red on the opposite side, and *as* containing a volume of cool white apple flesh. We do not see *of* the apple its opposite side, or its inside, or its internal whiteness, or its coolness, or its juiciness. But while these features are not seen, they are not *merely* believed in. These features are present in the object of perception as actualities. They are present by virtue of being imagined.

23. To draw the proper consequences of this we must distinguish between imagining and imaging, just as we distinguish between perceiving and sensing. Indeed the distinction to be drawn is essentially the same in both cases. Roughly imagining is an intimate blend of imaging and conceptualization, whereas perceiving is an intimate blend of sensing *and* imaging *and* conceptualization. Thus, imagining a cool juicy red apple (*as* a cool juicy red apple) is a matter of (a) *imaging* a unified structure containing as aspects images of a volume of white, surrounded by red, and of mutually pervading volumes of juiciness and coolth, (b) *conceptualizing* this unified image-structure as a cool juicy red apple. Notice that the proper and common sensible features enter in *both* by virtue of being *actual features* of the image and by virtue of being items thought of or conceptualized. The applehood enters in only by virtue of being *thought of* (intentional in-existence). (*IKTE*, 13-23, in this volume.)

Let me put the presently pertinent points of these passages in the context of my discussion.

468. Imaging is a process that augments a perceiver's sensory state. *Sometimes the augmentation crosses sensory boundaries as in cases of being S-(is juicy) and being S-(is cool). Other times, unlike synesthesia, a visual sensory state is augmented in a purely visual manner as in the cases of being S-(is red containing white) and being S-(is white surrounded by red).* In the case of the perceiver's own body, the imaging includes both S-properties that pertain to vision as well as ones pertaining to other bodily states.

469. Unlike synesthesia, imaging might vary widely throughout a person's life. It is entirely consistent with Sellars' account of imaging that babies pop into this world satisfying a version of a traditional empiricist principle: their visual states (for example) are completely unaugmented by imaging. A baby's visual image-model might be merely the visual state produced by objects of a scene. Only "experience", in some sense of this term, might make it possible for the augmentation of visual states to go on. Equally though, the account is consistent with more rationalist principles which would endow babies with innate concepts and principles which, in some way, guide the construction of image-models.[165]

470. What stands out in Kant's case, Sellars argues, is that the part of the image-model produced by imaging is, to use a term of Kant's, a case of the understanding "affecting" the sensibility.[166] This affecting is part of the job of what Kant calls the "productive imagination" and Kant is firm on the point that the productive imagination is an active (spontaneous) faculty of a priori synthesis that uses "schemata" to produce images.[167] I return to this point after another topic.

(ζ) Back to the causal theme: a house

471. The aesthetic has a place, I suggested (435), for "internal" causal involvement of sensory states, or rather, as I shall say now, image-models. In imitation of present-day functionalists, I put this in terms of a faculty (which I shall call after Kant) the "productive imagination", a faculty of the perceiver whose "job" is to respond to sensory states (119). This response is rather complicated and varies depending on the principles available to the perceiver.

472. Suppose the perceiver, P, is a full-fledged manifest-image concept user. In optimal conditions, P is looking at a house from such a position that P sees two rectangular sides, joined at a corner, a triangular end portion of the roof, and one side of the roof. The roof is brown and the rectangular sides and the triangular roof end are white. Assuming charity for my inadequacies as an artist, I draw the following:

---

[165] Of course, even the rationalist account is consistent with individuals augmenting their sensory states in ways that are idiosyncratic or personal. "Association" thus has a place in almost any account of sensory activity.
[166] See A118-124, particularly the footnote to A120, B151-2, B162 with its footnote, and B164.
[167] A120-123, B151-2, note to B162, A142/B181, and A224/B271.

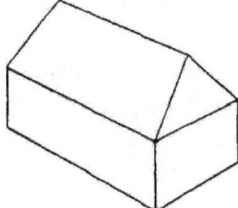

(Compare Sellars' own drawings in *IKTE*.)

473. Ignore the remainder of the scene and concentrate on the house. A rough-and-ready stripped-down description of the house (assembled by a path that begins at the white triangle, goes down, then left, and then up) is:

white triangle bottom-to-top-adjoining white rectangle left-edge-adjoining larger white rectangle top-to-bottom-adjoining brown rectangle left-to-right- adjoining white triangle.

The house, with the various sensible qualities of its facing surfaces, is causally responsible for P being in a

S-(white triangle bottom-to-top-adjoining white rectangle left-edge-adjoining larger white rectangle top-to-bottom-adjoining brown rectangle left-to-right-adjoining white triangle)

visual sensory state. That P (who, I assume, is in an appropriate frame of mind) is in such a state causes

(TA6) the productive imagination to

(i) augment the visual sensory state in accordance with principles (the schema) associated with the (complex) concept of a house-in-relation-to-a-perceiver, and (ii) generate an intuiting, i.e., a representing of a *this-such*, whose content is determined by the concept of a house and the S-(colored), S-(spatial) structure of P's visual image-model.

A reminder: I have supposed that I am discussing a full-fledged manifest-image concept user in optimal conditions. For neonatal humans, the sensory state might cause none of the above; for novices, some augmentation, compatible with rudimentary content, might be caused. (Also a warning: do not think of the activities of the

174   Introduction

productive imagination as actions that the productive imagination can deliberate over. What is being characterized are complicated cognitive processes only indirectly under our control.)

474. Other facets of P's frame of mind can influence the augmenting of P's visual sensory state (that for which the house is causally responsible). P might have come to view the house as a possible purchase and thus have read a description of it. Though such idiosyncrasies make themselves important in determining details of the image-model, my present concern is about what is required ("necessary", Kant would say) given the concept of a house and the spatial position of P. It is not easy to "analyze" the concept of a house adequately, but the principle that

> (80) a house has a foundation and bearing walls which in turn support a roof

has claim to be part of any explication of the concept. Ignoring the cavils we might have about (80), I shall assume that it is within P's repertoire. With (80) and information about the position of P with respect to the house, roughly,

> that the edge of the house, closest to P, is the edge which is made by the walls facing P and which is at the left bottom of the triangular roof end,

there is another principle (graspable but complicated) which goes roughly as follows:

> (81) the roof is supported at the back of the house furthest from P by walls that adjoin the walls facing P.

I shall suppose (for reasons having to do with other states of P) that P's productive imagination utilizes a rectangular shape for the horizontal cross-section of the house. Thus, once again with apologies for my drawing, P's image-model is augmented S-(spatially) as indicated by the dashed lines:

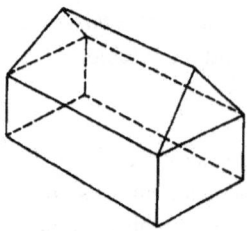

475. Further, in addition to the S-(spatial) augmentation, there is S-(color) augmentation. So, *except in one case*, P's productive imagination augments P's state so that *now*

P S-(white triangle)s

in any case in which the S-(spatial) augmentation gave

P S-(triangle)s

and *now*

P S-(white rectangle)s

in any case in which the S-(spatial) augmentation gave

P S-(rectangle)s.

The exception is the case which involves the roof rectangle that P does not presently see. In this case, the S-(color) augmentation has it that

P S-(brown rectangle adjoining far-right top of white triangle)s.

(To put it in terms of the house, the rectangular walls are white, but both rectangular roof portions are brown.[168])

476. In Sellars' reading of Kant, (474.81) is part of the *schema* of the concept of a house (*IKTE*, 33):

> the schema of a house is the entire family of principles like (474.81) which are derived from the concept of a house, or the concept of a kind of house (cape, bungalow, etc.), *plus* information about the position of the perceiver with respect to the house.

477. Though neither the concept of a house nor the concept of a perceiver is a

---

[168] Note that P has an "idiosyncrasy" which may be reasonably common: P believes that the portion of the roof not presently seen is the same color (brown) as the side presently seen and that the far triangular roof end is the same color (white) as the near triangular roof end. I have allowed such an idiosyncratic "association" just to show that the account allows sensory states to be "affected" by more than what is dictated by concepts. Of course, P may think that the concept of a house does require such uniformity of coloring: in that case, P is in for a surprise in my part of the country where half re-roofed and partly re-painted houses are not all that uncommon.

concept of something perspectival, the principles of a schema (e.g., (474.81)) are perspectival. The productive imagination has in its repertoire the schema of the concept of a house, i.e., principles about the perspectival structure of a spatiotemporal object, and these principles guide the productive imagination in augmenting the original sensory state. Described in the philosophical terms of the aesthetic, the productive imagination strips-down (474.81) to the sensible qualities and relations (including the perspectival ones) and it uses these in "affecting" the sensory state of P (i.e., in bring about changes in the sensory state that lead to the full image-model). The original sensory state is perspectival through the derivation from the assembled stripped-down description of the scene; and the image-model is augmented by the guidance of principles, like (474.81), of the schema which maintain the point-of-viewishness.

478. According to (473.TA6(ii)), the productive imagination generates a representing of a *this-such*, i.e., an intuiting, which depends for its content on both the concept whose schema is employed in producing the image-model and the empirical structure of the image-model. Again, so many other states of P are relevant that P's productive imagination might produce the uncomplicated intuiting,

> this white house.

Let me, though, treat the idealized case in which an attentive perceiver's productive imagination makes full use of the structure of the image-model.

479. Kant's treatment of perception relies on the metaphor of drawing[169]. I follow Sellars in describing the gross spatial structure of the image-model in terms of drawing and painting. Draw a rectangle in perspective; draw four straight, parallel, equal lines up from each vertex of the rectangle; connect the tops of these lines with straight lines to form a four-sided polyhedron with a horizontal cross-section that is rectangular; put, in perspective, at the top of the polyhedron two triangles whose bases are the short sides of the polyhedron; connect the top vertices of the two triangles by a straight line. The rectangular sides of the polyhedron and the two triangles should be painted white and two rectangular sides between the two triangles brown. (What you get is roughly my drawing in paragraph 474, but with the dashed lines replaced.)

480. In the philosophical terms of the aesthetic, the combining (the "synthesizing") which forms the intuiting moves back from S-(colored) S-(shapes) to sensible qualities and relations and utilizes concepts which are part of the concept of a house as a spatiotemporal object (e.g., walls, roof, foundation). The idealized intuiting is:

---

[169] See particularly, A105, B162 and A141/B180); Sellars utilizes drawing to advantage in his discussions of Kant (*IKTE*, 31ff, *KTI*, 42ff and *CLN*, **A32dff**).

(82) this house, with a rectangular foundation, whose sides and roof ends are white and whose roof is brown.

(82) is the result of a process that, beginning with the causal involvement of the house with the perceiver's eyes, causes a sensory state, augments it to produce an image-model, and generates the intuiting. (For future reference, I observe that there is, clearly, room for errors of one sort or another in this complex process.)

481. Note: the object of the intuiting is the house. The S-(colored), S-(spatial) structure of the image-model is reflected in the literally colored and spatial structure of the represented *this-such*. As Sellars puts it in his example of an apple (467),

> the proper and common sensible features enter in *both* by virtue of being *actual features* of the image and by virtue of being items thought of or conceptualized. The applehood enters in only by virtue of being *thought of* (intentional in-existence). (*IKTE*, 23, in this volume)

482. Unlike the position of RWK (339-45), no fundamental "confusion" due to the prejudices of childhood or anything similar is involved in the activity of the productive imagination. It is not some "association" of thinkings that leads to the intuiting (480.82). Sellars constructed the analogy (a point I emphasize in my version) so that S-properties and S-relations, on the one hand, and sensible qualities and relations, on the other, literally share properties in common; they have a common core, the "quality dimension" (436), that is neutral between the two. The productive imagination is thus caused to move from S-properties and S-relations in the image-models to the corresponding sensible properties and relations of manifest objects.

483. What I have just said is not in conflict with the productive imagination's actively contributing to the image-model.

484. The productive imagination, one is tempted to say, "selects" a concept once P has been caused to be in a sensory state. The trouble is that the word 'select' suggests deliberation, choice, and, worst of all, reflection on the sensory state. *Nothing of this sort is at issue.* The sensory state "affects"—causes—the productive imagination to commence its activity. In general, causal principles incorporate conditions; the result of affection depends on those conditions. In this case, the result of that affection is dependent on complicated states of P: on what P believes, on what P expects, on P's present state of cognitive preparation—in general, on P's frame of mind.[170] This process is indirectly under our control since we can do things to change our general cognitive state. (For an extreme example, it you didn't have the concept of a house, you can take steps to acquire that concept.)

---

[170] It is, perhaps, worth pointing out the obvious: that frames of mind are described by attributing representings to perceivers. Thus, on my account, being in a certain frame of mind is *not* a matter of, say, having certain "behavioral dispositions" or being in certain "neurophysiological states".

485. This process of selection (construed as indicated) is part of what Kant has in mind when he speaks "recognition in a concept".[171] Cognition, Kant says (A106), requires a concept, no matter how "imperfect or obscure", that provides a "rule", namely, the concept's own structure. The productive imagination implements this rule in augmenting the original sensory state. The finished image-model then guides the productive imagination in synthesizing an (admittedly idealized) intuiting like (480.82). Of course, once the concept of a house is selected, the sensible qualities and relations involved in (480.82) are the ones which correspond to the sensory qualities and relations of the image-model (which, as I have noted, may have elements that are not dictated by the concept).

486. While I am on this topic, I take the opportunity to add to earlier denials. On this understanding of "recognition in a concept", what is being "recognized" is *not* the image-model. Image-models are not even the right sort of item to be houses. The intuiting (480.82) is about a house and its production requires not one single *conscious thinking about* the image-model or the original sensory state. On the other hand, I agree that the philosophically sophisticated (the "non-vulgar") are not prohibited from philosophically reflecting on the process and saying things like "Given the doctrines of the aesthetic and noticing that my judging contained (480.82), my image-model must have been so-and-so". But *none* of this judging and reasoning by the non-vulgar is part of the activity of the productive imagination.

487. A point, for future use, also hinges on my claim that (480.82) is about a house. A house is a literally spatiotemporal object which, unless something happens to it, will be around for further perceptual investigation. Suppose such future perceptual investigation occurs (say, by walking around the house). Under that supposition, the schema of the concept of a house, the family of principles for augmenting sensory states, guarantees a succession of image-models and leads, in the end, to more possible intuitings about the house. I observe that this possible future scenario is neither "haphazard" nor "arbitrary" (A104); it is obtained from premises, some of which are the principles of the aesthetic and some of which are about the perceiver and involve the concept of a house and the concept of perceiver in spatial relation to a house.[172] Given the premises, the conclusions follow and are therefore, in one simple sense, "necessary" (A104).

488. Further, as I shall argue later, the principles of the aesthetic turn out to be part of what is necessary to explain what perceiving and "experience" are. To use an oft-repeated phrase of Kant's, these are some of the principles of the "possibility of experience", the necessary conditions of experience. Therefore, when we attribute to ourselves perceivings, these attributions imply, according to the aesthetic, the

---

[171] See A103ff, especially A103-106, and A120.
[172] The only, in a sense, "arbitrary" element is that which is provided by the perceiver's personal history. However, even such "associations" are associations with a kind of *object*, an "object of experience", and thus depend on the non-arbitrary elements being discussed.

Introduction 179

correctness of these principles (whether we know it or not). So, again, they are, in that sense, "necessary" (A93-94/B126, A213/B259-260, B294); they are part of a philosophical account of what perceiving and experience are.

489. A consequence of the point of the previous paragraph, when combined with a feature of the aesthetic's account of the construction of image-models and the generation of intuitings by the productive imagination, sets it off from the accounts of perception given by Kant's predecessors (and most of his successors): concepts of literally spatiotemporal objects, houses as appearances and perceivers as appearances, along with the concepts of their spatial relations are built right into the concept of perception. (This is in addition to the fact that the concepts of sensory states are derived by analogical concept construction form the concepts of sensible qualities.) I sum this up (subject to elaboration in the next subsection) by saying:

concepts of the literally spatial and temporal are necessary to perceiving.

The elaboration of this requires one more topic has to be added to my sketch of the aesthetic: time.

(η) Image-models and time

490. No reader of *CPR* doubts the need for a discussion of time and sensibility. On a more mundane level, had I chosen an example different from the house (say, gone back to the automobile accident), the need to address the topic of time would have been immediately obvious. Personally, I find the issues here quite interesting and would happily go on for many pages. I intend to restrain myself and sketch the needed elaboration of the aesthetic and its motivation without much adornment.

491. The primary intent of Sellars' comments on time and sensory states is to include, within the aesthetic, principles which accommodate a perceiver's seeing temporally extended items. It is clear that perceivers are often credited with seeing processes of some duration, e.g., motions. Sellars also thinks that such principles enable constructive remarks on the "specious present" (*SM*, Appendix, 9).[173] Remember, at present, my topic is sensory states, not perceiving. Sensory states are merely elements in the process of perceiving; consequently, principles of time in the

---

[173] Sellars likes to refer to this "temporal" aspect of sensory states as the "τ-dimension" (*SM*, Appendix, 14; *FMPP*, II, 131ff); and he sometimes refers to S-(spatial) properties and S-(spatial) relations as "σ-characteristics" (*SM*, Appendix, 18 and *KPT*, chs. 13-15). In *KPT*, Sellars deals extensively with issues pertaining to time. I do not attempt to follow his discussion since, in these chapters, his formulations pertain first and foremost to Kant and Kant's predecessors whereas, in the present subsections, I am expounding Sellars' views and will turn back to Kant only in the next section.

aesthetic formulate what is generally necessary for perceiving changing things.[174]

492. I extend the analogy to include analogical temporal relations which I shall call S-(precedence) and S-(simultaneity). The aesthetic allows for (at least) two cases. Out of sensory states that are "retained" and thus in some sense "persist", some of the literally simultaneous acquire an ordering and form a sequence of S-(precedence); on the other hand, other sensory states, which did not originally occur simultaneously, also "persist" but are ordered as S-(simultaneous). To avoid delicate and complicated exact details, I intend to conduct the requisite work primarily through examples.

493. Let me take two simple examples which illustrate part of what is involved in Kant's examples of the house and the ship (A190-3/B235-8). Consider a red billiard ball sitting in the middle of the green felt surface of a billiard table. I skip other features of the scene having to do with the cushions of the table, the legs of the table, the room containing the table, and so on. Suppose that the billiard ball and the perceiver, P, are stationary with respect to the table and so stationary with respect to each other. The assembled stripped-down description of the part of the scene I am considering is

> red hemisphere in middle of green rectangle

and, in the circumstances, what is caused is that

> (83) P S-(red hemisphere in middle of green rectangle)s.

494. Utilizing the concepts of billiard ball and of billiard table, P's productive imagination augments P's visual sensory state directed by the principles of the schema of the (complex) concept

> red billiard ball stationary in middle of green rectangular surface of billiard table in front of stationary perceiver (me).

What Kant says about the house, namely, that no one grants that the "manifold" *of the house* is successive (A190/B235), is true of billiard balls (and, of course, billiard tables). As the backside of the house co-exists with front, so the back hemisphere of the billiard ball co-exists with the facing one. So, P's productive imagination augments the sensory state so that a partial description of P is that

---

[174] In an essay on adverbial theories of sensing, Butchvarov adduces many objections to treating perception as adverbialized sensing and takes up an example of motion. Such criticisms might apply to Chisholm, who appears to be Butchvarov's main target, but, as I am about to show, they do not apply to Sellars (see section III of "Adverbial Theories of Consciousness," *Midwest Studies in Philosophy, volume 5, Studies in Epistemology* (University of Minnesota Press, 1980), pp. 261-280).

P S-(red sphere in middle of green rectangle)s.

(Remember I am ignoring a lot about the total scene.) Given the total image-model, the productive imagination, ideally again, generates the intuiting

> this red billiard ball in the middle of the green rectangular top surface of this billiard table.

495. The Sellarsian aesthetic can agree with Kant that sensory states are successive (A182/B225) and even, maybe, in constant "flux" (B291). So, I can allow that the process that culminates in the image-model, as we commonly say, takes a little time. In fact, in my previous house example, it seems reasonable to suppose that even looking at the facing sides of the house takes a little time. After all, the house has rectangular and triangular facing surfaces and is large enough that time passes in perceiving them.

496. The usual move to handle such psychological processes which take time is to talk about some kind of "retention".[175] While, on Kant's view, there is nothing contradictory about the empirical self "persisting", in the sense of remaining in a state over some period of time, Kant's predilection is to treat sensory states as being very short in duration (see, e.g., A167-5/B209-10).[176] So, it might be that a sensory state "persists" only by being "reproduced" over and over very quickly. Since I don't think that this issue cuts any ice in the present context, I intend to use the word 'retention' so that it is neutral with regard to these two ways of persisting.

497. So, in a case in which the perceiver continues to look at the billiard ball, or the house, without anything else happening, a process occurs which culminates in an image-model. This whole process has literally non-simultaneous as well as literally simultaneous elements. The aesthetic, however, incorporates a temporal dimension, the "τ-dimension" as Sellars calls it, in which the states which make up the image-model are S-(simultaneous). One source of the S-(simultaneity) is the concepts—billiard ball, billiard table, house—whose schemas are employed by the productive imagination to augment the original sensory states. These are concepts

---

[175] Perhaps, this sort of "retention" is something Kant wanted to be part of his discussion of "reproduction" (A100ff). I do not think it appropriate to use the term 'memory' in these cases because of its association with consciousness and its activity in producing judgings ("I remember: I left my keys in my office.") Nothing about what is required for judging is part of my present discussion though I would readily agree that questions similar to the present ones arise in the case of judging (see section II of the Appendix in *SM*).

[176] He actually says "in the blink of an eye". Even if we think of this as meaning "in an instant", we cannot wring too much out of this remark. When someone says that something "happened in an instant", they usually mean that it happened very quickly, not that it happened, in some technical sense, "instantaneously".

into which co-existence is built.

498. I wish to speak briefly on this topic, but I do not want to mislead. The roots of S-(simultaneity) lie well back in doctrines of the aesthetic. Assembled stripped-down descriptions are taken from descriptions of scenes that are formulated in the present tense. No other tenses are allowed. This restriction stems from a long-pressed phenomenological point: we do not see *of* objects their past, their future, or any of what I might call their "temporal connections". (Seeing *as* is, as usual, different: you can see someone *as* having aged since you last met.) Indeed, I would argue that, strictly, we do not see *of* objects their "presentness". But they *are* present and the assembled stripped-down description continues in the present tense so that it carries with it the "presentness" of the original description. The assembled stripped-down description is, then, incorporated into the S-predicate for the image-model. This is one element in making it possible for the principles of the aesthetic to provide that the perceiver S-(simultaneously) has the sensory states that go into the image-model despite the fact that it does take time to produce the image-model and thus, strictly, these sensory states may have occurred at literally different times and been "retained" for varying periods.

499. Notice, by the way, that there are other judgings that are true of scenes, but these, too, the aesthetic bans from the descriptions used to generate the assembled stripped-down descriptions. In the present billiard ball example, it might be true that

> P stands by the side of the table nearest the door while the red billiard ball is in the center of the table.

The term 'while', though entirely appropriate, is, like its cousins 'after' and 'before', not allowed in descriptions that are to be stripped-down. Once again, this restriction is due partly to the phenomenology of seeing *of*. (It is also helpful in partially explaining Kant's oft-repeated claim that time cannot be perceived.[177])

500. All this is not to say that the aesthetic has no use for such temporal expressions. Given the "verb" approach I have employed, S-(precedence) and S-(simultaneity) appear as 'S-(before)' (or, 'S-(after)') and 'S-(while)'. These terms are modelled on 'before' ('after') and 'while' as they occur, not between singular terms, but between *complete* judgings (as 'while' does above or, to use Sellars' example, in "Nero fiddled while Rome burned").[178] I shall call 'while' and its ilk as

---

[177] See B207; B219; B225; A183/B226; B233; A200/B245; B257; A215/B262; A292/B349. There are similar remarks about space; see, especially, A292/B349, the note to B457 and *OP*, 22:475.

[178] I admit that there is a boatload of metaphysics to do here. Some would argue that "Nero fiddled while Rome burned" *must be analyzed* as "the fiddling of Nero was simultaneous with the burning of Rome". I do not agree. Note, however, that even if this analysis were correct, I find no argument to show that modelling one item on another item requires taking over *all* the properties of the item one begins with.

Introduction 183

they appear as generators of judgings from judgings "temporal connectives".
501. So, in the above billiard ball example, take the (partial) description of P's image-model (494)

P S-(red sphere in middle of green rectangle)s.

and abbreviate it to

(84) P S-(RSmidGR)s.

As in the example of the house, (84) implies all the partial descriptions of P such as

(85) P S-(red sphere)s, and
(86) P S-(green rectangle)s.

What I said earlier then amounts to this: in the example given,

(87) P S-(red sphere)s S-(while) P S-(green rectangle)s

even though the two (partial) states described by (85) and (86) might not have occurred originally literally simultaneously and might have different histories in the process that culminates in the image-model. Their "retention" *in the process which culminates in the full image-model* (495, 497) qualifies them as S-(simultaneous). The productive imagination of a perceiver responds to S-(simultaneity), in this example, by generating the intuiting

this red billiard ball in the middle of the green rectangular top surface of this billiard table.

which, by the principles pertaining to demonstratives, implies the co-existence of this red billiard ball and the green rectangular top surface of this billiard table.
502. A warning is in order: (501.87) is a judging formulated within the confines of the philosophical doctrines of the aesthetic. None of what I have said above requires that perceivers, in general, know philosophy. Even more, the aesthetic does not require that persons be capable of "noticing", or "introspecting", S-(simultaneity), only that they be capable of responding to it. It is this, as Sellars would put it, "theoretical" relation that the perceiver responds to, not the literal simultaneity of "retained" sensory states.
503. In general, the process in the case of the billiard ball and the case of my

example of the house[179] is this:

> (TA6.iii) the productive imagination of a perceiver in the appropriate frame of mind
>
> (a) augments original sensory states (whose correct description is derived from a present-tense assembled stripped-down description) by utilizing concepts (billiard ball, house) and being guided by the principles of a schema whose general form is
>
>> such-and-such stationary object(s) (billiard ball, house) confronting stationary perceiver (me),
>
> (b) produces an image-model,
>
>> a complex of S-(properties) which the perceiver has S-(simultaneously),
>
> (c) and responds to the image-model and the S-(simultaneity) of its complex by generating the intuiting (whose content is determined by the concept of a stationary object (billiard ball, house) and the S-(colored), S-(spatial) structure of P's visual image-model)
>
>> this such-and-such object(s) (billiard ball, house)
>
> where coexistence of properties and object(s) is implied.

(The "manifold" of the house is not "successive"; its "manifold" co-exists. The billiard ball and the billiard table co-exist.)

504. Now, let's contrast this with a billiard ball example like that of the ship sailing (moving) downstream. The cue ball hits the red billiard ball which then rolls (moves) to the cushion of the table on P's left. Notice that the example *assumes* that the red billiard ball is moving to the table cushion to P's left just as Kant *assumes* in his example that the ship is moving downstream to one side of the perceiver and not the other. What is at issue here is the perception of motion, a kind of change.

505. Most of what went on in the example of the stationary ball also goes on in this example. What is different is that the productive imagination augments P's *successive* visual sensory states directed by the principles of the schema of the (complex) concept

---

[179] "My example of the house": i.e., one that has a perceiver stationary with respect to the house; in Kant's example, the perceiver is not stationary with respect to the house (A192-3/B237-8).

red billiard ball rolling to my left from middle of green rectangular surface of billiard table confronting stationary perceiver (me)

and thus produces a *succession* of image-models (compare A192/B237) as the ball rolls left across the table.

506. The usual suggestion about perceiving motion is that the earlier sensory states of P are "retained" as the motion goes on.[180] Sellars does think that this is so,[181] but alone this usual suggestion is inadequate for reasons which concern the fact that it involves only literal temporality.

507. First, no one of the image-models of all those generated is adequate, by itself, to allow for the perception of motion. Each one is an image-model that would generate an intuiting of a red billiard ball at a certain position on a green billiard table. Keep in mind that (visual) image-models have only S-(colors) with S-(spatial) structure and the properties in each image-model all occur S-(simultaneously). (Compare *KPT*, ch. 13, section *A*.)

508. Second, as retention has ordinarily been characterized, the result of the retention of the whole sequence would be a literally simultaneous collection of image-models. The literal simultaneity of such a group of image-models is also inadequate to allow for the perceiving motion either of the billiard ball, or to use Sellars' example, of a hand going up (that is, a hand at the end of an arm going up). In the case of the hand going up, you might consider a "fusion" of the image-models into one. But, then, the "fused" image-model would be like the single image-model you get by looking successively at the many, differently positioned arms of a Hindu god (*SM*, Appendix, 12-14; *KPT*, ch. 13, section *A*). Perceiving a change, like motion, requires, so to speak, that which is past.

509. Finally, the collection of image-models in this example is no different from the one which would be generated if the ball had rolled from the left cushion to the middle of the table. Compare: the succession of image-models in the case of the ship floating downstream (e.g., to my left) versus the ones that would be obtained were the ship moving (under power) sternward upstream (e.g., to my right).

510. What Sellars suggests is that mere retention must be modified to allow that literally simultaneous (retained) image-models incorporate S-(precedence): in short, a sensory temporal ordering analogous to literal temporal precedence. In my example, the first image-model is the image-model discussed in the stationary ball example and it is S-(before) all the others. So, in the example, what is true about the first image-model ("RSmidGR") and the last one (call it "RSleftGR") is that

---

[180] I repeat my disclaimer: I do not think it appropriate to use the term 'memory' in these cases because of its association with consciousness and its activity in producing judgings. No judgings are part of the succession of image-models and their preservation.
[181] *SM*, Appendix, 6-13; *FMPP*, II, 130ff; *KPT*, chs. 13 and 14.

(88) P S-(RSmidGR)s S-(before) P S-(RSleftGR)s.

The productive imagination responds to the total sequence of literally simultaneous image-models ordered by S-(precedence) (again in the ideal case) with the following representing of a *this-such*:

(89) this red billiard ball rolling (moving) from the middle to the left side of the green rectangular top surface of this billiard table.

Such representings of a *this-such* are ingredients in perceivings of temporally extended processes such as motion.[182]

511. Let us compare the general description of the case of the stationary billiard ball (house) with that of the moving billiard ball (ship).

(TA6.iv) the productive imagination of a perceiver in the appropriate frame of mind

(a) augments original sensory states (whose correct description is derived from a present-tense assembled stripped-down description) by utilizing concepts (billiard ball, ship) and being guided by the principles of a schema whose general form is

such-and-such moving object(s) (billiard ball, ship) confronting stationary perceiver (me),

(b) produces a sequence of image-models, each of which individually is

a complex of S-(properties) which the perceiver has S-(simultaneously),

(c) and responds to the sequence of image-models and the S-(precedence) in the sequence by generating the intuiting (whose content is determined by the concept of a moving object (billiard ball, ship) and the S-(colored), S-(spatial) structure of P's visual image-models)

this moving (changing) of such-and-such object(s) (billiard ball, ship)

---

[182] I find reason to include in the account the continuation of sequences of image-models into the S-(future). The image-models that are S-(after) the one whose original sensory state is being caused now are a result of the productive imagination being familiar with certain causal sequences. Such S-(futurity) forms an element, not only in the perception of motion, but also in an account of several familiar phenomena, including what is usually called "anticipation" in sports.

where the represented is an item, a change, which requires a succession of properties (and, as well, the co-existence of others).

The S-(simultaneity) cannot be dropped out of (b) since changes are the gaining and losing of properties by substances; so, to represent a change, you also must represent something which is the subject of a change (a billiard ball, a ship). Further, a crucial difference is that the first case (503) utilizes, in addition to the concepts of billiard balls and ships, the concept of being stationary while the present case has the productive imagination utilize those concepts with the concept of moving.

512. In generating (510.89), the productive imagination is guided by both S-(spatial) and S-(temporal) structure of image-models. It is *not* literal spatial and temporal structure that does the guiding. The generated representing of a *this-such* is about literal spatial and temporal structure, but it is the S-(spatial) and S-(temporal) structure that guides. I repeat: nothing in the aesthetic requires that the perceiver be "aware of", or "notice", any of the process that I have discussed.[183]

513. Kant says, at (A193/B238), that "subjective" succession must be derived from "objective" succession of appearances. The account above gives one interpretation of that remark: concepts pertaining to appearances and their permanence and their alteration guide the productive imagination in establishing the S-(temporal) orderings to which the productive imagination then responds in producing representings of co-existence and of change. For future use, I sum this up in a principle I use in explicating perceiving; it is a more elaborate version of the point made in paragraph 489:

> (TA7) the process of perceiving objects and events builds in the concepts of the literally spatial and temporal, i.e., of spatiotemporal appearances (through the analogical construction of S-predicates and through their utilization by the productive imagination both in augmenting sensory states and in producing representings of *this-suches*).

(See (473.TA6(i) and (ii)), (503.TA6(iii)) and (511.TA6(iv)). Compare Sellars' discussion of the Second Analogy in *KPT*, ch. 16, section *J* where he says that the key to working out the Second Analogy is "*the physical in space and time*".)

(V) IS THE AESTHETIC A "THEORY"?

514. I suggested (350) that Sellars swam with the dialectical stream of his time

---

[183] For a discussion, with a different beginning, of the topics of this and preceding subsections, I recommend chapter VI and the appendix to chapter VI in Jay Rosenberg's *The Thinking Self* (Temple University Press, 1986).

and employed the term 'theory' in now narrower, in now wider senses. Consequently, Sellars sometimes describes his aesthetic as a "theory" and even embellishes that appellation with rhetoric suggesting he means something toughly scientific (see, e.g., *SM*, I, 22 and 29ff). That said, he also, even his early formulations of this doctrine, flat-out denies that he is constructing a theory in the tough sense (see *EPM*, 51(2) and 59). Clarification of this matter starts the parade of Kantian principles supported by Sellars' aesthetic.

515. The principles of the aesthetic are formulable—indeed are formulated above—within the manifest image. I appealed to no chemistry, no physics, no neurophysiology: nothing our philosophical ancestors could not have appreciated. I constructed a complicated piece of philosophy, a piece of "transcendental psychology". Such products of philosophy are often called "theories". In addition, some of the intellectual activities that comprise philosophy (e.g., concept construction by analogy) are present in all organized and systematic thought, including modern science and its theories. Whatever term we decide to use, clearly philosophical reflection on the manifest image can lead to such philosophical "sophistication" as the aesthetic I have been constructing. In fact, I reached into arcane points to show that no small amount of sophistication is possible.[184]

516. For the very same reasons, it is a mistake to think that the aesthetic is appreciated by the non-philosophical (the "vulgar"). Like Sellars, I offer the aesthetic as a correct philosophical account of part of the manifest image. If, as we think, it is correct, then sensory states as states of persons (and, with qualifications, of other sentient beings) are part of the furniture of the manifest world and contribute causally to it. True, the "vulgar" are causally connected to their own sensory states, but this causal involvement does not require that they have the philosophical sophistication to appreciate the concepts of the aesthetic. (Compare the familiar point about constructing grammatical sentences and understanding grammatical theories.) So, Sellars' use of the word 'theory' has another point: the aesthetic is not something one learns, as the expression has it, at "one's mother's knee". (Turn it around: if humans had from time immemorial spouted quantum physics in their cradles, no one would have talked about "quantum *theory*".)

517. In passing, I note that I have provided support for my contention (414) that a "proof" of Sellars' aesthetic doctrines cannot be produced. Other philosophical "theories" of perception are obviously possible. This point I shall further elaborate

---

[184] I am not sure that I understand what the charge of "scientism" amounts to (p. 469, footnote 23, of John McDowell, "Having the World in View: Sellars, Kant, and Intentionality", The Woodbridge Lectures 1997, *The Journal of Philosophy*, XCV, 9, September, 1998). That Sellars believes that the scientific image will, in time, provide a more adequate account of the material world is true. That somehow appealing to this more adequate picture solves the philosophical problems here at issue, that Sellars does not believe. In any case, Sellars insists (e.g., *FMPP*, I, note 6 and II, 1), and I have tried to illustrate, that his doctrine of sensory states emerges from reflecting on the manifest image and is a philosophical option even if renaissance science had never come to be.

in the next subsection.

518. Last, but certainly not least, Sellars' predilection for the word 'theory' is a sign of wishing to mark how different his (and, he takes it, Kant's) view on sensory states is from a popular kind of view which he would call "Cartesian". In addition to that Cartesian principle so well rendered by Hume (19), other Cartesian principles Sellars rejects are:

> (C1) our concepts of psychological states and of their kinds and modifications are not derived in any manner from other concepts (in particular, not from concepts of extended objects);
> (C2) to respond to a psychological state is to have an "awareness" of that state and of those properties of it which pertain to whatever kind of state it is; and
> (C3) this awareness is adequate in that there are no other concepts that would enable us to formulate additional truths about these states, truths over and above what we can formulate with our present concepts (perhaps, "made clearer" by suitable reflection).

(I used the phrase 'psychological state' to avoid complicated questions about the exact views of cartesians on thinking versus sensory states.) For sensory states (and, with qualifications, for thinkings), Sellars rejects C1 through C3.

519. To (518.C1): The analogy phase of the aesthetic derives (not, of course, by definition) the determinate concepts pertaining to sensory states and image-models from concepts pertaining to physical objects. This is even true of such qualities as S-(colors). These qualities are "colors" shorn of the causal features that make them properties of physical objects. The analogy "abstracts" from sensible qualities a central core to carry-over into the account of sensory states (436, 482).

520. Without the philosophical sophistication provided by the aesthetic, the manifest image has no determinate category of quality other than that which pertains to physical objects. That is, for the philosophically unreflective, the only determinate categorial classification of qualities is as sensible qualities, namely, physical object "stuff" that is causally active, most interestingly with persons (and, with qualifications, other sentient beings) (381-400). Moreover, the "abstraction" practiced on sensible qualities by the aesthetic introduces no new category for sensory states. They are still properties, indeed still properties of those perfectly good manifest image objects, persons. The aesthetic has no pretensions to supplying a determinate category, like "thinking stuff", to stand on equal footing with the determinate category, "physical (extended) stuff".

521. To (518.C2): The aesthetic describes many "responses" to sensory states. Most of the responses of the productive imagination are not "awarenesses" at all. (It is hardly a good reason for treating them as awarenesses that a blow to the side of head with a two-by-four generally interferes with them). But, if I were to count as "awarenesses" those responses that are intuitings, i.e., representings of *this-suches*, then, as awareness, they would, generally, be awarenesses of spatiotemporal objects such as houses and bears, not sensory states.

522. On the other hand, I will shortly admit that it is possible for the philosophically unreflective perceiver to respond to a sensory state with a representing that, *with other premises*, implies something about the perceiver's sensory state. Such cases provide, I will claim, no solace for the Cartesian. Having the property of implying something about one's sensory states is too little to qualify a representing as an "awareness". Further, since such a representing implies something about a sensory state only in company with other premises, it does not provide that sort of "unmediated" and "unsullied" awareness of one's own sensory states that is desired by the Cartesian.

523. Actually, the aesthetic is more non-Cartesian than that. To the extent that it allows the characterizatioin of a sense of 'awareness' in which the vulgar are "aware" of sensory states, their "awareness" is inadequate (though not "confused"). It is not, as RWK worried (339-345), that the vulgar mix shape and color in completely confused ways; on that score, (visual) sensory states are S-(shapes) "filled" with S-(color) just as the surfaces of physical objects have sensible quality shapes "filled" with sensible quality color. It is rather that the vulgar, being by definition without philosophy, have no articulated conception of S-properties and S-relations and, thus, no such conception of what they are really responding to. In part, it is this lack of understanding that prompts Sellars to say in *SM* (I, 24) that sensory states are "never apperceived", i.e., never noticed *as such* by the non-philosophical. (See paragraphs 588ff for additional unpacking of this point.)

524. To (518.C3): I have tried to formulate with (518.C3) the Cartesian conviction that, in a very important sense, there can be no *conceptual* "surprises" in our investigation of psychological states. Philosophical reflection, aided by science, may help us, the Cartesian admits, in making "clearer" our concepts of psychological states and in weeding out "confusions", but the stock of such concepts, though in need of some work, will not (maybe, cannot) be augmented by "new" concepts. Clearly the aesthetic I have attributed to Sellars gives a scope to philosophical reflection greater than that of "tidying up" and imputes to our stock of commonsense psychological concepts a deficiency that cannot be rectified by making them more "clear and distinct".

525. In (518.C1), (518.C2), and (518.C3), I have tried to capture something of the simplicity, immediacy and adequacy that Cartesians usually associate with our awareness of our own psychological states. It is no news that Sellars is not a Cartesian. Nonetheless, it is not plain to me that readers of Sellars have appreciated just how thoroughly non-Cartesian he is and how fundamentally what Sellars would describe as his Kantian alternative rejects Cartesianism. The central burden of this subsection has been to start the exploration of the magnitude of this rejection and, along the way, to explain why Sellars chooses to speak in very non-Cartesian terms in characterizing his account of sensory states as a "theory" (or, as he sometimes says, a "proto-theory").

526. Kant commentators have been in disagreement on the extent to which Kant rejects Cartesianism. Sellars is, I think, quite determined to maintain that Kant's views provide at least the beginnings for thoroughgoing non-Cartesianism.[185] More on how to understand this is forthcoming. Other problems still stand in the way.

(VI) IS THE "MYTH OF THE GIVEN" BACK?
(a) Qualia, phenomenal individuals, and their ilk

527. To entertain a doctrine of perception including sensory states as an central element is to open oneself to the charge of returning to the "bad old days" of "sense data" theories and their ilk. It may seem especially troublesome in Sellars' case since one of his widely read essays, *EPM* (in *SPR*), attacks what Sellars calls the "myth of the given". Is not Sellars' dalliance with sensory states to step on the primrose path to the "given" and thus to show that he does not reck his own rede?[186] I may have a surprise for some of my readers: in what follows, I shall claim that Sellars believes that the aesthetic is a great (and perhaps essential) step to avoiding the myth of the given and thus to defending many claims of Kant's.

528. As preparation, I think it only prudent to show, at very least, that Sellars' view is not to be classed with those of the defenders of "qualia" with whom materialists, like Lycan and Dennett, have so often done battle.

529. In the contemporary literature on qualia, you will discover a wide vocabulary for characterizing qualia and differentiating qualia from other items. The list that follows is taken from an essay of Dennett's,[187] but it is quite indicative of the general literature. Qualia are

> the way things seem to us, directly or immediately apprehensible, ineffable, intrinsic, private, and phenomenal.

My response here is simple: Sellars did not, and I certainly did not in my preceding

---

[185] That Sellars has concerns over lingering Cartesianism in Kant is shown in *KTE*, 36(6) and in *KPT*, ch. 14, section *A*.

[186] Very recently, two authors, Patricia Kitcher (in section I of "Kant's Epistemological Problem and Its Coherent Solution, *Philosophical Perspectives, 13, Epistemology, 1999* (Blackwell Publishers, 1999)) and John McDowell (p. 467 of "Having the World in View: Sellars, Kant, and Intentionality", *The Journal of Philosophy*, XCV, 9, September, 1998) appear to have just such concerns.

[187] "Quining Qualia", *The Nature of Consciousness: Philosophical Debates*, edited by Ned Block, Owen Flanagan, and Güven Güzeldere (MIT Press, 1998), 619-642.

exposition, make any such claims about image-models. I have been at pains to point out that Sellars rejects (and he thinks that Kant rejects) principles, (518.C1) - (518.C3), that have been undergirding for doctrines of "direct awareness" or "direct apprehension". In the subsection after next, I shall point out that the account Sellars builds of "appears" ("seems", "looks") provides no handhold for the attribution of any of the above epithets to image-models. So, as a multiple-choice answer, I pick for image-models "none of the above".

530. Despite my unequivocal denial, I confess that I do not know what some of the terms in the above list mean. Worse, I am not sure I know the answer to the question: what do some people mean by the term 'qualia'? Lycan, I fear, is in constant danger of being impounded by animal regulation since the very mention of this question sends him into a frothing paroxysm.[188] I am bound to agree that he has a point: it is immensely clear that not everyone writing on "qualia" means the same thing by the term. It is largely for these reasons that I have not used the term and constructing of Sellars' account without it shows that its absence loses us nothing.

531. What, by the way, does Lycan mean by the term? Cleaving to ancient lore (if not, perhaps, wisdom) and following the lead of a more ancient Lewis (i.e., C.I.), Lycan tells us that a quale is an "introspectible monadic qualitative property" of a "phenomenal" individual, such as a sense datum might be.[189] I suppose, though I am not sure, that the simplest thing to say here is that neither Sellars nor I want any such items in the manifest image: no sense data, no "phenomenal" individuals, no properties of such individuals, and, finally, no "introspectible" properties of such individuals. Well, I think that firm denials have their place, but I also agree that there is more to say.

532. I am particularly struck by Lycan's insistence that "apparent" reference to "phenomenal individuals" is genuine and that, therefore, we must deal with these "phenomenal individuals" and their qualia. Lycan's choice is to make them "intentional inexistents".[190] I cannot deal with all these points in an introduction like this one. Let me make the following observations and one promise.

533. The first observation is that, if your view doesn't commit you to them, you don't have the problem. I have flatly denied that the aesthetic as I have set it out

---

[188] If you don't believe me, read note 3 of chapter 4 of *Consciousness and Experience* where he suggests a "prison sentence" as fitting the crime of "wanton neologism" of such a technical term as 'quale'. Another matter than energizes him almost as much is the phrase 'what it's like'. See page 77 where he describes this phrase, within the compass of sentence, as "worse than useless" and "pernicious and harmful". Lycan is our nonpareil practitioner of "take no prisoners" philosophy. Not surprisingly, I feel the urge to point out that neither I nor Sellars has ever used that phrase.

[189] See pp. 69-70, note 3 in chapter 4, and note 2 in chapter 6 of William G. Lycan, *Consciousness and Experience* (The MIT Press, 1996).

[190] My worries are centered around passages in section I of chapter 4 of *Consciousness and Experience* and pp. 480-1 of "In Defense of the Representational Theory of Qualia (Replies to Neander, Rey, and Tye)" in *Philosophical Perspectives, 12, Language, Mind, and Ontology, 1998*, edited by James E. Tomberlin (Blackwell Publishers, 1998).

encompasses any individuals that should be described as "phenomenal".[191]

534. Second, I agree that smiles, waltzes, the fountain of youth, orcs, elves, Hobbits, Grendel and Beowulf (and all the inhabitants of any Middle Earth), numbers, properties, relations, and anything that can be what is being talked about, or thought about, are individuals in the broadest sense. But if they are that sort of individual that is a property, then, well, that's what they are. Image-models and sensory states are properties of perceivers in the manifest image.

535. Finally, I promise to discuss, at least briefly, what happens when we consider what Sellars calls the "scientific image".

(b) What is the "myth of the given"?

536. Now I have more pressing questions to answer: what is the "myth of the given"? what is the "given"? It is quite natural to take the view that belief in the given (by Sellars' account something which does not exist) is a tenet of certain theories of perception, for example, sense data theories. Sellars' approach at the start of *EPM* seems to confirm that view since almost immediately his attention turns to sense data theories. Careful reading of the opening paragraphs of *EPM* shows that this is a mistake:

> Many things have been said to be 'given': sense contents, material objects, universals, propositions, real connections, first principles, even givenness itself. ... Often what is attacked under its name are only specific varieties of 'given'. Intuited first principles and synthetic necessary connections were the first to come under attack. And many who today attack 'the whole idea of givenness'—and they are an increasing number—are really only attacking sense data. For they transfer to other items, say physical objects or relations of appearing, the characteristic features of the 'given'. (*EPM*, 1)

So, the first moral is that practically anything, not just psychological states, can be held to be "given".

537. So, by the "given", Sellars has in mind something sufficiently abstractly characterized that it can show up in different "forms" (*EPM*, 32). In very late oeuvres, Sellars' emphasis is on a form of the myth, the statement of which makes explicit mention of categories. Thus he takes to saying that a very basic "form" of the myth is that if a person is "directly aware" of something which does, in fact, belong to a certain category, then that person is aware of that item *as* being of that category (*FMPP*, I, 43-45; *BLM*, 118-123). This formulation of the myth is, of course, most pertinent when Sellars is pursuing adversaries, such as Cartesians, who

---

[191] Though I admit that I have little grasp on what 'phenomenal' is supposed to mean, I assume that Kant's sense of 'phenomenal' is not at issue here since, after all, in Kant's sense, the entire world of appearances is phenomenal.

incorporate "direct awareness" of some sort into their views. Rejecting this form of the myth allows Sellars to argue that just because a persons responds to an inner state with a representing, it does not follow that the person's representing is about that inner state and even if, in some way, it is about that inner state, then it need not characterize the state *as* it really is (see, for example, 19 of *IKTE* quoted above in paragraph 467 and my remarks in paragraph 523).

538. To characterize the given adequately is no easy matter: so many manifestations of the given in differing philosophies insure that. I shall present an approximation by answering the question "What do you receive philosophically if you purchase what Sellars' claims to be a myth?" The philosophical benefits are of two sorts (though, admittedly, a mythologizer of the given might be more concerned with one, rather than the other, of these benefits). The first is epistemic: the given supplies us (not necessarily infallibly) with true premises on which we can construct the edifice of knowledge, particularly empirical knowledge. So, Sellars commonly describes epistemological views that incorporate the given as trying to provide a "foundation" for knowledge. Though mostly metaphysical, the second benefit might, in certain views, arise from the first, or might, in yet other views, be the source of the first: our access to the given secures for us access to at least some of what exists and to some of the features of those existents (i.e., their relations, their kinds and other properties).

539. I briefly describe a position on human perception which readily lends itself to the adoption of the given, in this case, with respect to what is traditionally called the "external world". The sort of view I have in mind incorporates the "banal"[192] claim that the function of the senses is to "inform" us (or, perhaps, our brains) about the external world. For present purposes, I want to take the word 'inform' in a commonsensical way: information is formulated by sentences (or, to use the terminology of this introduction, by judgings) as in "I was just informed: the Supreme Court refused to hear our case". This view ascribes to the senses, and the senses alone, the passive task of providing judgings on the occasion of their "stimulation". The causal activity of the world on the senses produces judgings about individuals and their properties and relations.

540. Consider the following (let me call it) "Aristotelian" line of thought:

> The senses (at least sometimes) provide correct information about the external world: that is, at least some of the judgings produced by the causal activity of the external world are true. Their truth depends *only* on this causal activity and the senses themselves, not on the understanding (or, in modern terms, on any

---

[192] The term is from pages 337-8 of Kathleen Akins, "Of Sensory Systems and the "Aboutness" of Mental States", *Journal of Philosophy*, XCIII, 7, July, 1996, pp. 337-372. Though Akins main target is naturalistic views of the senses, the "banal" view of sensory function has been a part of many philosophies.

"higher" cognitive processing). That being so, these judgings have, as a group, a fundamental status in the edifice of empirical knowledge. Moreover, the true ones must be telling us about items that "really" exist and that "really" have the properties and relations ascribed to them.

It would take very little to see this line of thought as putting us in a position to obtain the two "benefits" described in paragraph 538. How does the aesthetic block any such line of thought?

(VII) GIVENNESS AND REPRESENTING: ARE IMAGE-MODELS GIVERS?
(a) The "blindness" of the image-models

541. A reminder: I said (201-4) that Sellars' view of Kant requires distinguishing two senses of word 'sensibility'. In terms sufficient to my earlier discussion, I called them the "productive sensibility" and the "passive sensibility". This dichotomy is now too simple. Let me review the elements of the Sellarsian aesthetic:

(Ea) the bringing about of sensory states of a perceiver;
(Eb) the augmenting of sensory states to produce an image-model or a sequence of image-models;
(Ec) the producing of a representing of a *this-such*;
(Ed) the producing of a judging which has the representing, mentioned in (Ec), as its subject term.

Let me call the representing in (Ec) a "perceptual taking" and the judging in (Ed) a "perceptual judging". (Remember: all the elements (Ea)-(Ed), being processes, are of some duration, however small, and I allow that the temporal relations of these processes might be quite complicated).

542. Sellars takes Kant to use the term 'intuition' for, on the one hand, sensory states and image-models, (541.Ea) and (541.Eb), and, on the other hand, for perceptual takings, (541.Ec).[193] Similarly, the term 'sensibility' can be used cover (541.Ea) and (541.Eb) alone, (541.Ea), (541.Eb) and (541.Ec) together—or, indeed,

---

[193] I myself would not rule out, despite Kant's repeated insistence that the senses do not judge, that some passages in *CPR* are at least consistent with a reading that treats intuitions as perceptual judgings, i.e., the judgings mentioned (541.Ed). Without laboring over the details, I point out that Kant regularly speaks of the understanding as concerning itself with very general concepts (like the categories) and with general principles. If the dividing line between the understanding and the sensibility were to follow the contrast "specific-general", then it would not be surprising to find that Kant occasionally thought of intuitings as perceptual judgings. As I indicated earlier (114, 201-4), the Note to the Amphiboly of Concepts of Reflection illustrates Kant's inclination to free the sensibility, and presumably its attendant terminology, from his official restrictions (in particular, concepts are assigned to sensibility (A268/B324)).

all four. After all, the "banal" view, which goes all the way back to Aristotle, is so well established that it should be no surprise that some philosophers talk of the operation of the senses as something that issues in perceptual judgings. Sellars has no objection to someone talking about the senses, or sensibility, in such a way that it includes all of (541.Ea) through (541.Ed). BUT! if you do that, you have NOT distinguished sensibility as something distinct from the understanding: all of (541.Eb), (541.Ec) and (541.Ed) involve the activity of the understanding (in different ways, of course, in each case).

543. Sellars' point is that we ought to make a clear distinction, one that Kant was making but not clearly enough.

544. First, recall one point about the process in (541.Eb). The understanding, as the productive imagination, is bring about the augmentation given the sensory state of the perceiver and the perceiver's frame of mind. So, image-models are not, in that way, independent of the understanding. (Since it is possible that newborn humans do not augment (473), I here limit myself to persons (390).) Notwithstanding that, the result of the "affection" by the understanding on the perceiver's sensory state is the image-model, i.e., an augmented sensory state. The image-model contains no properties and has no structure different in kind from that which sensory states have. Let me put this by saying that, though an image-model can be distinguished from the original sensory state, it is basically just "more of the same sort of thing". So, henceforth (unless some context demands otherwise),

> I will lump (541.Ea) and (541.Eb) together and use the phrase 'image-model' to cover both original sensory states and augmented sensory states (image-models in the narrow sense).

545. I now add to the aesthetic principles about image-models:

> (TA8)
> (B1) image-models have empirical structure, primarily, S-(spatial) and S-(temporal) structure.
> (B2) image-models have no categorial structure (and thus no logical structure): no subjects, no predicates, no truth-functional structure, no quantificational structure, no modal structure—in short, no categories apply to them.

My strict sense of the word 'represent' (30-7, 222-37, and 267-74) requires that representings have categorial (thus logical) structure. So,

> (B3) image-models are not representing (so, they are not thinkings).

Introduction 197

Moreover, since they are not representings,

> (B4) image-models are not representings of *this-suches* and they are not judgings.

I want to summarize these theses, and their consequences, under the slogan

> (B) image-models are blind.

(I have, of course, borrowed this term from a very famous passage in *CPR*, A51/B75.)

546. In addition, I suggest that the phrase 'image-model' provides an adequate gloss of 'sensation' in some passages in which Kant uses that term. Previously (325-332), I discussed some of what Kant says about sensations:

> (1) sensation is that which, resulting from affection of sensibility, is the "matter" and space (and, perhaps, time) are its "forms" (see particularly A42/B60);
> (2) sensations have only "intensive magnitude", i.e., degree (B208), but no "extensive magnitude" (162/B202ff);
> (3) sensations are states, or modifications, of a perceiver (A320/B376; see also *CJ*, 189 and 294);
> (4) sensations are "subjective representations" (B207-8) which provide *only* the consciousness that we have be "affected": sensations do not represent any object at all (A28/B44).

The Sellarsian aesthetic makes sense of all these claims for image-models. Note that, on Sellars' account, (1) and (2) are consistent. Image-models have S-(spatial) and S-(temporal) form; so, they have *a* spatiotemporal structure. All states of a perceiver are in physical space and time with the perceiver (and thus, in that way, are physical themselves), but the important structure of image-models (480, 502-3, 511-2) is not that *physical* spatiality and temporality which Kant counts as "extensive magnitude".

547. Having the clear distinction Sellars wants between image-models and representings in the strict sense, I now restrict

> 'sensibility' to that passive faculty, the affecting of which produces (alone, unaugmented; with the help of the understanding, augmented) image-models.

Remember both Sellars and I agree that no one can be stopped from using 'sensibility' to cover all, or any two or three, of (541.Ea) through (541.Ed), but it one of the points of the aesthetic is that we can use 'sensibility' to cover just that faculty which produces the results described in (541.Ea) and (541.Eb).

548. Back to my question: how does Sellars' aesthetic block the line of thought sketched in paragraph 540? That is, how does the above account of image-models and sensibility block the Aristotelian line of thought that so easily can lead to the givenness of external items and their features? The crux of those Aristotelian reflections is that items in the world cause, independently of our intellects, judgings, some of which are true. Nothing so direct happens according to the aesthetic: image-models are blind. The sensibility does not judge at all: no premisses, true or false, arise immediately and independently, from the action of the world on our sensibility. No information (in the "informed that" sense) arises merely from sensibility: not even so much as the representing of an individual. There is nothing on which to begin the "foundations" of empirical knowledge; there are no individuals, properties and relations on which to build a metaphysic of what there is. A curtain of genuine conceptual blindness falls.

549. I have thus shown how Sellars' account of image-models shields his view from a plausible traditional line of thought leading to the given. Though I wish that I could say "that's that", there are other forms of the myth of the given, ones that do not aim at the givenness of items in the "external world", but rather at the givenness of such items as sensations themselves. Certainly, as Sellars himself points out in the quotation from *EPM* (536), most of the worries about givenness have been about just such things. I cannot take on this point without further preparation.

550. The route to dealing with the possible givenness of sensations leads through further discussion of representing and then of perception. The first topic is a possible objection that tries to maintain that image-models are "representings" in some sense of the word, thus denying that they are as blind as I have made them out to be.

(b) The "ontological impotence" of image-models

551. Well, aren't image-models representings of some sort? Kant, as I have noted (332, 546), says that sensations are "subjective representations" (B207-8) and classifies them as "representation" (A320/B376). Sellars, in *SM* (e.g., I, 55 and I, 73), speaks of sensory states as "non-conceptual representations". Sellars' predilection for contrasting "conceptual" and "non-conceptual" representation does not manifest mere convenience in exposition, runs far back in his work, and is founded on his views about hierarchies of representational systems.[194]

552. In contrast, in this introduction I have reserved the term 'representing' for

---

[194] One early discussion of representational systems is found in *SRLG* (in *SPR*). A short, but pointed treatment is in *BLM*, 105ff and more elaborate expositions which relate the topic to other elements of Sellars' thought are in chapter 5 of *NAO* and in *MEV*.

items in a system that, in Sellars' hierarchy of representation, is of the most sophisticated, or highest, grade. I intend not to depart from that decision. In my estimation, the points I am pursuing are more dramatically made by having a stark all-or-nothing contrast, rather than by setting the whole discussion in the more elaborate context of grades of representational systems. Moreover, it will be clear that, even in this more elaborate context, the distinction "conceptual vs. non-conceptual" is as all-or-nothing as my distinction of "representing vs. non-representing".

553. In this subsection, I roughly characterize something that some talk about as "representation" and that, in another setting and with some qualifications, I would be happy enough to call "representation", but here I don't. First, I summarize, *as drawn in this introduction*, the central contrast between representings on the one hand and image-models on the other.

554. Representings are judgings or components of judgings (e.g., predicates) or other items whose structure is connected, in some way, to judgings and the components of judgings (questions, commands, etc.). Since judgings have logical form, they come in various logical kinds (singular, general, negative, conjunctive, disjunctive, conditional, etc.). Besides logical structure of the sort just indicated, judgings (and their components) also can differ in regard to modality, tense, indexicality, and truth value and are capable of fine-grained classification reflecting what is commonly talked about as their "meaning".

555. Image-models have in and of themselves none of the above. In particular, they are not judgings and thus, for example, do not incorporate predication. I had to include the qualification 'in and of themselves' because I agree that one point of the following discussion is that we are able to characterize for image-models (and, in fact, for other items) analogs of some features of representings. These characterizations, it will turn out, are parasitic on representing.

556. "Indicating" (395ff) or, in older terminology, "being a sign of" provides a start: to cite a well-worn example, a property of a thermometer, the height of its column of liquid, indicates another property, the temperature of the surrounding air; e.g., if the column has risen to the mark '70 degrees F', then it is very likely the temperature of the surrounding air is 70 degrees F. Several obvious considerations push amendments to mere indicating.

557. First, the causal processes involved work for a range of properties in some (not all) conditions. Second, the property of the object does not indicate the one it is supposed to indicate if the property of the object has been produced in the wrong way. Take the convenient example (if you're old enough) of phonograph records. The recording process produces spatial variations in the walls of a long helical groove in a disk. The only relevant properties of the disk are spatial variations in the walls of the groove, not, say, small differences in the height of the walls of the grove. Under "optimal" conditions, a given spatial variation indicates, for example, a given note in a recorded symphony. If the conditions are not optimal because, say, the microphones distort the sound of the orchestra, then the presence of a certain spatial variation at some place in the groove does not make it likely that a certain note occurred at a certain time. Finally, a spatial variation caused by an earthquake, not by an orchestral sound, is not an indicator of any note.

558. The idea that emerges is that of, as Tye puts it, "causal covariation" for two sets of properties under optimal conditions.[195] His definition is something like this:

> S (in P) "represents" that Q if and only if, if optimal conditions were to obtain, then
>> S would occur in P if and only if that Q were the case, and
>> S would occur in P because that Q is the case.

So, assume that optimal conditions obtain. Then, this spatial variation (S) in the groove (P) "represents" that a note occurred in the symphony (that Q) just in case that spatial variation (S) in record grooves (P) would occur if and only if a certain note were to occur (that Q were the case) and this spatial variation (S) occurred because the relevant note occurred (that Q is the case). The general idea is clear: causal covariation of properties. Two different groups of properties are such that, in optimal conditions, there would be causal connections between properties in the two groups. Furthermore, in actual cases of "representing", the causal connection actually obtains.

560. Something very much like this can be worked out for image-models. First, a traditional theme: because of the analogy that introduces S-(properties) and S-(relations), image-models are, in general, similar to the sensible qualities of objects in a scene.[196] Ignoring the complications of concavities, transparent objects and so on, I could *almost* put this by saying that (visual) image-models are isomorphic to the surface structure of objects in scenes if it weren't for the suggestion of mere

---

[195] See chapter 4 (and the other authors referred to there) of Michael Tye, *Ten Problems of Consciousness: a Representational Theory of the Phenomenal Mind* (MIT Press, 1995), particularly section 4.2. The following definition is one that reflects the formulation Tye gives in note 6 of chapter 4.

   In passing, I must say that I do not see how Tye's definition supports his line on afterimages in section 4.3. In the optimal conditions described by Tye (p. 105), one can produce, say, a green afterimage when there is no appropriate green something around (or, indeed, no green things at all). Yet Tye tells us that a green afterimage "represents" that something is green (p. 107). But his definition requires that, if optimal conditions obtain (and we are supposing they do), the green afterimage occurs if and only if something is green and the green afterimage occurs because of that green something. Maybe I am being excessively dim here, but I do not find the requisite green item in most optimal green afterimage cases. (By the way, if there were a green something causing the image, it wouldn't be an afterimage—would it?)

[196] To formulate this in a completely general way would require that I take account of the similarity between sequences of image-models ordered by S-(precedence) and changes in objects such as their motion. The lack of such generality does not, I think, interfere with the points of this subsection.

structural similarity. Remember that S-(colors), for example, are similar to physical colors (436, 482); they are, so to speak, those colors without the physical locations and causal properties that would include them among the physical. So, I prefer the term 'replicas' since such a term suggests similarity, to use a Kantian turn of phrase, of both "form and matter". Thus, the view I am defending takes Berkeley to be wrong when he said that nothing can be like an "idea" but another "idea".

560. Though causality is not directly part of the characterization of similarity for replicas and objects, causality has a place in characterizing a kind of "accuracy" for image-models. Consider again the phonograph record. You are at the house of a friend, a recording engineer, who in the "good old days" actually lugged around equipment to produce phonograph records. While waiting for your friend who is busy in the kitchen, you choose an ancient-looking disk, a recording of a Beethoven symphony the jacket says, and place it in the player. You are appalled by the awfulness of the music. When your friend appears, you observe that the recording conditions must have been terrible. "No, no," says your friend, "the conditions were great. My child was in the third grade at the time and the music teacher thought the children would benefit from trying something a bit more demanding. They were terrible, but the recording is near perfect."

561. Optimal conditions (443-8) and causality can be used to specify those occasions on which an image-model is an *accurate* replica. Accuracy for replicas is akin to truth for representings. Optimal conditions and the causal responsibility of an object, or objects, for producing an image-model makes it highly probable that the image-model is an accurate replica of the causally responsible object, or objects. Consider the case of a single object. If the conditions are optimal and a (visual) image-model occurs because of the object O, then it is highly likely that the image-model is an accurate replica of the surfaces of the object.[197]

562. The limitations on this sort of accuracy are severe. Consider (545.TA8):

(545.B1) image-models have empirical structure, primarily, S-(spatial) and S-(temporal) structure.

(545.B2) image-models have no categorial structure (and thus no logical structure): no subjects, no predicates, no truth-functional structure, no quantificational structure, no modal structure.

Image-models are unlike intuitings (representings of *this-suches*) and other repre-

---

[197] Keep in mind that I am ignoring complications like transparent objects. Second, notice that, for the original sensory state, the correct phrase would be 'facing surfaces' and that the augmentation to an image-model proper no doubt decreases the probability in question. Finally, I note that, in this introduction, I resist all temptations to gnaw on the common turns of phrase involving probability (or, being likely). That my point is one that might be better expressed by conditional probabilities, rather than, as it might seem, by a conditional with probability in its consequent is a topic for another time.

sentings of individuals and of kinds of individuals. Nothing indicating individuality or kind membership is present in image-models. Even surgeons who have full S-(3-dimensional) image-models of (i.e., as they say, "visualized") a heart they are operating on have nothing in their image-models but "superficial" similarities and, at that, similarities to any objects which have the internal spatial structure and sensible qualities of a heart. The fact that they "visualize" internal S-(spatial) surfaces filled with S-(colors) makes it no less superficial. Of course, most of us would have image-models of hearts which had no internal augmentation at all and thus which were replicas of the surfaces of hearts and so "superficial" not just in the present sense but in the original meaning of the term.[198]

563. Notwithstanding, it is possible to invoke the causal theme to provide for image-models something, once again, *analogous* to being "of", or "about", individuals. In doing so, we can explain that inclination of many philosophers to talk in terms of sensations "of", or sense impressions "of" chairs, houses, bears, what have you (cf. *SM*, I, 52ff). The 'of' indicates a classification of the image-model by what caused it.[199]

564. Well, again, I should say: by what would have caused it if optimal conditions were to obtain. Dick's augmentation, in less than optimal conditions, results in an image-model to which he responds with the intuiting "that large black bear". Nonetheless, the cause is a bush. Choosing the actual cause places his image-model in the "of a bush" variety. Even less attractive classifications are made if Dick's entire episode in the woods is caused, not even by a bush, but by the ingestion of local mushrooms. The subjunctive version allows us to classify Dick's image-model as "of a bear" on the grounds that the image-model would, in optimal conditions, be caused by a bear. (I have some qualms about this subjunctive, but nothing important enough to mention here.)

565. The subjunctive causal construal of 'of' does not, by itself, allow picking out of specific individuals since many different bears would, if optimal conditions were to obtain, lead to the same image-model. In addition, just as in the case of replication, the existence of "imitators", "fakes", "counterfeits", and so on, shows that the subjunctive approach does not limit the classification of sensory states and image-models to single kinds. Species of amanita mushrooms make their poisonous way in this world by being accurate imitators of other species of mushrooms. ("There are old mushroom hunters and bold mushroom hunters, but there are no old, bold

---

[198] The superficiality is not diminished by the inclusion of other sensory qualities or structure. Neither Sellars' (467) image-model of an apple which includes S-(cool) and S-(juicy) S-(volumes) nor the S-(temporality) of image-models of the moving billiard ball save us from the superficiality of an empirical (S_s-spatiotemporal) structure of empirical (sensory qualities) properties.

[199] In cases of imagining, the following account has to be supplanted by one that allows the "of" to be borrowed directly from the thought *of* the item that you wish to imagine (467). In this case, too, there is causality but one that is "internal" rather than "external".

mushroom hunters.") None of this is much of a surprise since, as replicas, image-models are, as I said above, "superficial".

566. With the subjunctive causal construal of 'of', I can state another analogy between representings and sensory replicas. From the mere occurrence of a representing of an object, it does not follow that the object exists (38-9). Similarly, from the mere occurrence of a sensory replica, it does not follow that what the replica is "of" exists. If, however, we add to the subjunctive construal something like the second condition in Tye's definition (559), then we achieve a sense of 'of' in which image-models can be "of" existing individuals. An image-model is "of" this bear just in case,

in optimal conditions, this bear would cause that image-model, and
this bear is actually causally responsible for that image-model.

Now, of course, the existence of the bear in question is built into this characterization of 'of'.

567. Finally, Sellars can also agree that since sensory replicas are causally efficacious, they provide "information" to the organism in which they occur in that the causal process of which they are a part may well, in some cases, result in true representings (as well as other alterations in the organism). Let me call this the "input" sense of information to distinguish it from the sense which occurs in the phrase 'inform that'. Sensory replicas provide "input" by occurring in an organism which can respond to them with representings; it is these representings which can be premisses, not the sensory replicas. Image-models are blind.

568. The analogies and similarities between sensory replicas and representings are part of what inclines Sellars to place them as species, so to speak, under the genus "representations". (That this is not the whole story is made plain by the works cited in the footnote to 551.) So, Sellars can join in a common form of words and say that image-models are "representations", but "non-conceptual" ones.

569. The "ofness" of sensory replicas, their "accuracy" and their ability to provide "input"—indeed, their very status as replicas—are all explicated in terms that presuppose (in one way or another) a conceptual framework (e.g., the manifest image) in which it is possible to represent (in my strict sense) individuals, kinds, and the causal activities of nature. We cannot make an assessment, for an image-model, of "ofness", "accuracy", and "input" without utilizing such representings for the simple reason that "ofness", "accuracy", and "input" for image-models are characterized (not all in the same way) so that representing (in my strict sense) is required. The conceptual framework determines what image-modes are "of" and is therefore also necessary to the determination of their degree of "accuracy" and the determination of what "input" they provide. In imitation of contemporary termin-

ology, I call the "ofness", "accuracy", and "input" the "semantic" properties of sensory replicas: so, semantically, image models are parasitic on representings.
570. To the slogan, (545.TA8)(B) image-models are blind, I now add that

>(S) as replicas, image-models are "superficial", and
>(P) as regards "ofness", "accuracy", and "input", image-models are semantically parasitic on representings.

Collectively, these three, (545.TA8)(B), (S) and (P), are what I summarize as ontological impotence:

>(I) image-models are ontologically impotent (blind, superficial, and parasitic on representing).

571. The news of this subsection brings no joy to a Cartesian or Humean Mudville. In the Sellarsian aesthetic, fashioning for image-models analogs of the characteristics of representings serves to impede treating image-models as items which "give" anything. They have nothing to "give": they are ontologically impotent. Perhaps, though, as I suggested at the end of the previous subsection (550), rather than sensory states being the "givers", they are themselves the "given". To that battle I am still marching, but first something to smooth the way forward.

(VIII) GIVENNESS AND (ORDINARY) APPEARING: ARE IMAGE-MODELS GIVEN?
(a) Perceiving, ostensible perceiving, and appearing within the aesthetic

572. I quoted Sellars at length (467) on the topic of image-models, and in those remarks is a clear statement of what Sellars takes to be *one sense* of the term 'perceive'. I cannot emphasize too much that *these remarks are part of that piece of philosophical sophistication I have called the aesthetic*. Sellars is showing in that passage that his philosophical view, an integral part of which is the aesthetic (a philosophical "theory" committed to image-models), can deliver an account of perceiving and appearing:

>23. To draw the proper consequences of this we must distinguish between imagining and imaging, just as we distinguish between perceiving and sensing. Indeed the distinction to be drawn is essentially the same in both cases. Roughly imagining is an intimate blend of imaging and conceptualization, whereas perceiving is an intimate blend of sensing *and* imaging *and* conceptualization. Thus, imagining a cool juicy red apple (*as* a cool juicy red apple) is a matter of (a) *imaging* a unified structure containing as aspects images of a volume of white, surrounded by red, and of mutually pervading volumes of juiciness and coolth, (b) *conceptualizing* this unified image-structure as a cool juicy red

apple. Notice that the proper and common sensible features enter in *both* by virtue of being *actual features* of the image and by virtue of being items thought of or conceptualized. The applehood enters in only by virtue of being *thought of* (intentional in-existence). (*IKTE*, 23, in this volume.)

573. I re-state this account in terms of the elements of the Sellarsian aesthetic:

(541.Ea) the bringing about of a sensory state of the perceiver;
(541.Eb) the augmenting of sensory states to produce an image-model or a sequence of image-models;
(541.Ec) the producing of a representing of a *this-such*;
(541.Ed) the producing of a judging which has the representing, mentioned in (Ec), as its subject term.

In the above quotation, Sellars is concerned with perceiving (specifically, seeing) an object (a cool juicy red apple). (As I have largely concentrated on vision, so will I continue.) A "visual taking" of a cool juicy red apple requires (541.Ea), (541.Eb) and (541.Ec) where the representing of a *this-such* in (541.Ec) is a •this cool juicy red apple•. In one sense of the term 'perceive', visual (and, in general, perceptual) takings are perceivings of objects. A "visual judging" (or, a "seeing that"), e.g., that this cool juicy red apple is near me on the table, requires (541.Ed) as well as the other three. A perceptual judging (in this strict sense) has the singular representing of (541.Ec) as its subject. In one sense of 'perceive that', visual (and, in general, perceptual) judgings are "perceivings that".[200]

574. (541.Ea) through (541.Ed) include nothing about what I previously called "achievement" (406-7). What is being explicated is, thus, "ostensible seeing (perceiving)" and "ostensible seeing (perceiving) that" (401-9). Thus Dick can be said (ostensibly) to see a bear and (ostensibly) to see that the bear is coming toward him. The "achievement" sense of 'perceive' (and 'see') is ostensible perceiving plus what I called the "appropriate achievement". So, the aesthetic characterizes ostensible perceiving which in turn can be used in the characterizations of other senses of 'perceive' including the achievement sense.

575. Part of the philosophical importance of ostensible perceiving is that some ostensible perceivings are *perceptual* errors, but others are cases in which no perceptual error occurs and other conditions, e.g., appropriate achievement, are satisfied. Dick is making a perceptual error. He's not lying or making something up for a joke. He's not dreaming, not even daydreaming or fantasizing. He's not hallu-

---

[200] My continued qualification ("in one sense") is due to the various complications that are all too evident in Sellars' essays from *EPM* to *SRPC* and *FMPP*. I manage to handle some of these complications in upcoming paragraphs. But I ignore one of the most important: perceptual takings must be extended to include representings with indexicals.

cinating (though admittedly people do now employ this word in a jocular sense which would cover such cases as Dick's). Hallucinations, properly so-called, are brought about classifiable causes such as hysteria, febricity (fever), delirium tremens, some psychoses and some ingested substances. On this view, we do not have to claim that perceptual lack of success is due to something generally outside the perceptual process. (That some of these other occurrences such as hallucinating utilize parts of the perceptual apparatus does not weaken this point.)

576. The dialectical situations in which Sellars found himself explains one feature of the quote from *IKTE* (573): Sellars clearly uses the word 'perceive' and explicates it in the weak sense of "ostensibly perceive". That we confront such weak uses of 'perceive' ('see') is, I think, without doubt. To take but one example, in the 1960's people were fond of describing what they "saw" while under the influence of then fashionable exotic chemicals. Of course, they were under no illusions about those largely green yet iridescent monsters they said they were "seeing". It was to misunderstand to say to them, "Green monster! In the room? Where?"

577. In other dialectical situations (see, especially, *FMPP*) where Sellars confronts opponents who subscribe to doctrines of "appearing", Sellars treats the explication I have just gone through as an explication of 'appears' ('seems') in the perceptual sense.[201] In Dick's situation, as I described it, he is "taken in". So, had he thought to himself that I see that this large black bear is coming at me, the appropriate construal of this thought understands 'see' in its achievement sense. As the situation is described, he is wrong. Of course, like the "green monster see-ers," he might, if he had earlier eaten "magic" mushrooms, think to himself

it (visually) appears (seems) to me that there is a large black bear coming at me.

Sellars' construal of this thought is

I ostensibly see that there is a large black bear coming at me.

In the situation described, that thought is right. Moreover, in the situation described, it is a case of "mere" ostensible seeing since there is no bear there doing anything.[202]

578. Of course, Sellars knew that some philosophers have built views in which perceiving is understood in even a weaker sense: that is, as sensing. Expressed in the terms of the aesthetic, 'perceive' is being explicated by such philosophers as requiring only (541.Ea) alone or, as well, (541.Eb). That construal of 'perceive' is

---

[201] That is, "in the perceptual sense" as opposed to a sense in which 'appears' and 'seems' mean something like "on the available evidence I am inclined to believe that...".

[202] Complicated cases abound: for example, someone might think "this so-and-so appears to me to be such-and-such", rather than "it appears to me that this so-and-so is such-and-such". These matters will not affect my central point.

one that includes in perceiving *no representings* (in my strict sense).[203] Put in traditional terms, perceiving construed as sensing (i.e., having an image-model) includes no thinking. Perceiving as ostensible perceiving or ostensible perceiving with achievement does include thinking (either representings of *this-suches* or full judgings). It is part of the burden of the general argument of *EPM* that treating perceiving as merely sensing (i.e., having an image-model) is an inadequate account of perceiving.[204]

579. To tame the beast of terminology, I restrict mine to:

(P1) having image-models (sensory states and image-models proper) (541.Ea and 541.Eb),

(P2) ostensibly perceiving:
   (P2.a) perceptually taking (541.Ea, 541.Eb, and 541.Ec)[205]
   (P2.b) perceptually judging (541.Ea, 541.Eb, 541.Ec, and 541.Ed),

and

(P3) perceiving: ostensible perceiving with achievement (adjusted to take care of (P2.a) and (P2.b)).

Occasionally, I will remind the reader that, from Sellars' vantage, (P1) supplies a correct account of what others have sometimes called "sensing" and (P2), a correct account of various senses of 'appear' ('seem') though sometimes the word 'perceive' has occurred in place of 'sense' or 'appear'.

580. That the Aristotelian meditations sketched in paragraphs 539-40 have no foothold in the aesthetic is, in part, due to the role attributed to the understanding in the formation of image-models and in the production of perceptual takings and perceptual judging. A crucial element in the Aristotelian line of thought is commitment to a "clean" (in cognitive science terms, "free of higher processing") level of "information that". It is the "cleanness" of the operation of the senses, according to the Aristotelian, that shows that it has a grip on something that is "really there". By contrast, the only level, according to the aesthetic, that is "clean" is (541.Ea), the

---

[203] This is another way of formulating one of major points of section I of *EPM*.
[204] This point is crucial to appreciating that criticisms such as those in Butchvarov's essay ("Adverbial Theories of Consciousness," *Midwest Studies in Philosophy, volume 5, Studies in Epistemology* (University of Minnesota Press, 1980), pp. 261-280) are not relevant to Sellars' position.
[205] Again: among other qualifications that would be needed in a fuller treatment is one that allows perceptual takings to be formulated by more than representings of *this-suches*. Indexicals need to be included as well as terms like 'over there' as in 'there's a bear over there'. All I have tried to do here is to explicate a limited class of perceptual takings which have claim on being reasonably basic and which fit into my exegesis of Sellars on Kant.

original sensory state. But, at that level, there is no "information that" and thus no truths. All the remaining stages are "contaminated" by the ("higher") processes of the understanding. (To an elaboration of this point I shall return when I comment briefly on the scientific image.)

581. The upshot of this subsection is that, not surprisingly, when the aesthetic tells us about perceiving and (ordinary) appearing, it does so by invoking image-models. After all, that's part of its philosophical point. But the aesthetic itself is constructed in an entirely non-Cartesian fashion, a point I made earlier (518-26). Of particular importance is that the truths about image-models that the aesthetic makes available have no special epistemological or ontological status. Moreover, the aesthetic derives (though does not define) its concepts from those pertaining to physical objects; further it sets down principles which causally connect image-models as properties of physical objects with other physical objects. So, the metaphor of epistemological "foundation" so common among views which accept the "myth of the given" is inappropriate to image-models as characterized by the aesthetic.

582. What perceivers perceive or what appears to them provide premises which, when *combined with other premises and the principles of the aesthetic*, get us conclusions about states of the perceivers.[206] In utilizing the resources of the aesthetic, we make use of principles that treat a perceiver as part of system of spatiotemporal objects that evolves causally. (This includes the limiting case in which the system is just the object which is the perceiver.) The aesthetic sets down certain constraints involving causality (physical implication). For example, given the total situation (Dick's history, Dick's place in space and time, and the rest of the circumstances) and given that, in the total situation, we eliminate as possibilities an actual bear and "magic" mushrooms,

that Dick has an image-model "of" a bear and a perceptual taking of a bear
and
that a certain bush is in a certain spatiotemporal relation to Dick

mutually imply each other.[207] Image-models and our access to them, therefore, lack that "independence" of physical objects and processes so characteristically attributed to the "given".

---

[206] Principles of the aesthetic are now involved and so the reasoning now at issue is considerably more complicated than what was envisaged in the treatment of manifest image principles (388-400) without the aesthetic.

[207] For the purposes of this illustration, I assume that the world is simpler than we know it to be. I have treated Dick's case as if the only possibilities are: bear; no bear but some other object; no object apart from Dick's body. (My present remarks are a commentary on paragraphs 52 and 53 of *KTI* (in this volume)).

(b) Perceiving and appearing without the aesthetic
(α) A "vulgar" account of appearing

583. Well, you might ask, what about "appearing" as it is in the manifest image *without* the philosophical addition of the aesthetic? Might not judgings about "appearing" provide a foothold for the givenness of sensory states? The essential point (without the complications[208]) is that the philosophically unaugmented manifest image has, according to Sellars, very little to offer on the topic of appearing and what it does offer is no solace to the doctrine of givenness.

584. Take Sellars' pink ice cube. Suppose that I look, in the dim light, over at a nearby table and think

> (90) it appears to me that there is a pink ice cube in that glass.

Ignoring complication about epistemic attitudes such as endorsement or lack of endorsement (*EPM*, III, 16), I offer the following as something that is true of me given (90) and that is formulated without the help of the aesthetic:

> (91) I am in a complex visual state which is such that
> (a) it includes the thought that there is a pink ice cube in that glass,
> (b) the thought is brought about by some visual process (i.e., a process normally eye-involving), and
> (c) if the appropriate achievement obtained (in particular, if it were true that there is a pink ice cube in that glass), then the total state would be a case of seeing (in particular, seeing that there is a pink ice cube in that glass). (See *EPM*, III, 17 and 22.)

(91) is a philosophically unsophisticated counterpart of what showed up in the previous subsection as ostensible seeing.

585. Crudely speaking (i.e., absent questions of epistemic attitudes), cases of seeing and cases of appearing are alike except for the appropriate achievement. So, (91) upholds what Sellars describes as

> ...the simple but fundamental point that the sense of 'red' in which things *look* red is, on the face of it, that same as that in which things *are* red (*EPM*, III, 12)

and, I might add, the same as that in which things are seen to be red. In concert with this point, note that the thought that occurs as part of the total visual experience is

---

[208] For those interested in the complications, see especially lecture I of *FMPP* though as my further references show many of these complications already show up in *EPM*.

about a pink ice cube (whether there is one there or not). So, the pinkness in question is a sensible quality which, if it is exemplified, is so by a physical object. On this account, the concepts involved in appearings are those involved in seeings and are just those that pertain to spatiotemporal objects. Thus it can be the case that it appears to me that there is a pink ice cube in that glass and actually there is.

586. Second, (91) reflects that fact that, without the philosophical sophistication of the aesthetic, I am not in a position to do two things. I are not able to "answer a question about" (explain) what further similarities the pair of states

(92) I see that there is a pink ice cube in that glass, and
(584.90) it appears to me that there is a pink ice cube in that glass

might have. After all, this is part of what that piece of transcendental psychology I have called the aesthetic does. For the same reason, I am also not in a position to supply any very illuminating remarks about what is happening if it is pointed out to me that there is no ice cube, pink or otherwise, in the glass (and, maybe, no glass either). I can talk about abnormal perceivers and invoke familiar generalizations about what having "one too many" does to a perceiver. I can swear that it "was just as if I were seeing a pink ice cube in the glass." Of course, since the case described is a case of perceptual error, when asked whether I "made up out of whole cloth" there being something pink and cubical, I will deny that and say that I was not making up a story. My judging, the one mentioned in (584.91a), is brought about by something that is a part of the total visual experience. As Sellars puts it, "somehow" there is actually something which is a cube of pink though that is the end of what "phenomenological" reflection can do for us (*SRPC*, 35-42 and *FMPP*, I, 89-92).

587. The moral is that there is no reason to believe that "appears" (or, "looks") talk provides us with any other qualities but sensible qualities or with any other subjects for sensible qualities than physical objects. For colors and other sensible qualities, there is nothing more fundamental than, or more basic than, or prior to, the physical (519-20). The aesthetic is entirely in line with this moral: it commences under the assumption that sensible qualities are the very stuff of physical objects and, then, "separates out" the features that make the "physicality" of these qualities and leaves others of their features to be transferred to other properties which are psychological states of perceivers. In addition, original sensory states are augmented using schemas derived from concepts of physical objects (including that of a perceiver). All that reflects the fundamental conceptual position of the physical in the manifest image.

Introduction 211

(β) "Noticing" sensory states: what Sellars is not denying

588. I have been explaining the conceptual limitations of philosophically unsophisticated manifest-image users in dealing with their own sensory states. It might be concluded from my above remarks that manifest-image users have, to put it loosely, no "resources at all" for judging about the image-models the aesthetic attributes to them. I will show why this conclusion, thus baldly phrased, is wrong and also show that what is correct is, once again, no aid to a defender of "givenness".

589. As an addendum to these points, I unpack a remark of Sellars that might seem, at face value, to be rather perplexing. In chapter I, section II of *SM* (*SM*, I, 22ff), Sellars comments on the very topics at issue here and on what I have been arguing for: that image-models (sense impressions, as he calls them there) are not "found" by introspecting, but come to be appreciated as the result of epistemological (or, as he calls it, "transcendental") sophistication, i.e., the aesthetic. In setting up these topics, he suggests that one gloss of the phrase 'object of consciousness' is "noticed" which (as his next sentence shows) he treats as one sense of the term 'apperceived'. Reminding his readers that there is nothing contradictory about the idea that there are states of consciousness that are unapperceived (unnoticed) by subjects of these states, Sellars then warns his readers that he intends to push "to the hilt" the view that image-models (sense impressions) are "never apperceived" (523). What I will show is that this remark is consistent with the vulgar having the resources to construct judgings which the philosophically sophisticated user of the aesthetic, the "aesthete", would agree to be about image-models.

590. Consider once again my situation with the pink ice cube in the glass. Suppose, like Dick, I am taken in and think that

> (586.92) I see that there is a pink ice cube in that glass.

I am then informed that there is no ice cube, pink or otherwise, in the glass. As I mentioned above, the case is one in which I can correctly swear that it "was just as if I were seeing a pink ice cube in the glass." So, agreeing that the relevant achievement failed, I can say about my total visual state that

> besides the thought that there is a pink ice cube in that glass, it includes something that would normally be brought about by a pink ice cube in that glass.

591. What I have just formulated is an unsophisticated version of the (subjunctive) causal sense of 'of' (556-69). So, more or less, using 'of' as an abbreviation for 'that would normally be brought about by', I can characterize my state as one that includes an item "of" a pink ice cube. I can insist that this item "of" a pink ice cube would also have been present if I had been actually seeing a pink ice cube in that glass. Further, I can also insist that this item "of" a pink ice cube is relevant to my thinking that there is a pink ice cube in that glass (as opposed to, say, a golden ice sphere). Since this item "of" is relevant to my thinking about pink ice cubes, I can be willing to follow Sellars and say that "somehow" there is actually something which is a cube of pink.

592. In effect, what has been indirectly devised is a definite description. These items "of" a pink ice cube are

the sort of item that is common to both the total state of

my seeing that there is a pink ice cube in that glass

and the total state of

its appearing to me that there is a pink ice cube in that glass,

while not being the thinking that there is a pink ice cube in that glass and, moreover, somehow being (at least partly) responsible for my thinking about pink cubes.

The Sellarsian "aesthete" can construe my remarks as being at least partially correct descriptions of image-models. Definite descriptions being what they are, others of competing philosophical persuasions can construe them as about, say, neurophysiological states. Such a definite description is a cousin of the "relational characterizations" which I rejected for sensible qualities (357-9). Those characterizations, like the above definite description, do not provide an account of what is being referred to.

593. Nothing in this subsection gives an account of image-models. Only the aesthetic does that. Most importantly, no term, like 'pink' or 'cube', that occurs above occurs in a sense other than its usual manifest-image one. To recast my point in paragraph 587, there is no reason to believe that this "of" talk provides us with any other qualities but sensible qualities or with any other subjects for sensible qualities than physical objects. In fact, the unsophisticated "of" is as "parasitic" as is the sophisticated version (569-70). Again, there is nothing here to help the defender of the given.

594. So, by Sellars' own account, the "vulgar" have the intellectual resources to make judgings which would (in at least some circumstances) qualify them as "noticing" the sort of thing that philosophers have discussed under the topic of "sensations" (522). Sellars' own aesthetic doctrines agree to this. What, then, is he claiming when he says that they are "never apperceived" (noticed)? I use RWK, as a foil (339-45), to answer this question. What Sellars wishes to deny is a cluster of Cartesian attitudes and principles which I attributed to RWK.

(γ) Cartesianism again

595. RWK maintains that the philosophically reflective notice sensations and can recognize them for what they really are, "in their true colours" (19). The philosophical feat that allows them to achieve this is, though, of a rather limited kind. The philosophically astute have merely clarified by philosophy something they share with the "vulgar". Even the "vulgar", despite their serious "confusion" (345), recognize sensations as sensations. By comparison, for Sellars, such recognition is a result of philosophical sophistication that literally attempts to give an account of what image-models are and an account of how we come to appreciate such sensory qualities given that we began with sensible qualities of physical objects. So, while one cannot just find image-models by "screwing up one's mental eye" (*FMPP*, I, 82) in a cool hour, one can come to know of their existence (and, at least in principle, come to respond to these states with the terminology supplied by the aesthetic). So, one thing Sellars is denying is that human beings come into this world with "clear and distinct ideas" of sensations (and other states of themselves), ideas then obscured and confused by childhood prejudices and lack of philosophy.

596. The topic of "confusion" versus "clearness and distinctness" runs through early modern philosophy, but Sellars, unlike RWK, finds no "confusion of content" and, in one respect, no "inadequacy". Judgments about appearing, such as (584.90), involve no confusion. The embedded judging

> there is a pink ice cube in that glass

attributes the sensible qualities of color and shape to a piece of ice. In the manifest image, there is nothing, in general, wrong with that: pieces of ice can be pink cubes. Similarly, the aesthetic allows us, in certain circumstances, to attribute to a person an image-model which is a complex of S-(color) and S-(shape). There is no confusion there either (523). Both the philosophically inspired judgings involving image-models and ordinary judgings about sensible qualities are, within the manifest image, perfectly adequate. (Of course, that does not imply that the image as a whole is adequate.)

597. For Sellars, in the manifest image, color and shape in the physical object are "seamless" and S-(color) and S-(shape) are "seamless" as well. Since RWK accepts the Cartesian principle that we start *ab initio* with clear and distinct concepts (indeed, two systems of such concepts, one pertaining to thinking and unextended substance and one pertaining to extended and unthinking substance) needing merely reflection in a calm hour to remove any "obscurities", he has insured that the "seamless" union of color and shape in perceptual experience is a problem for him. Obviously, nothing could be further from the views Sellars defends.

598. Moreover, I think that the Sellarsian account of what sort of noticings the vulgar have of sensory states lets us penetrate deeper into RWK's position. Here is a piece of philosophical "fictionalized" history; it is akin to an historical novel in that it is a mixture of actual history and of plausible story telling. The aim is a tale which might illuminate a source of a philosophical view. My tale opens with what seems to me to be actual history. RWK, and his actual early modern contemporaries, had no doubt that our access to the contents of our representings (in my strict sense) is direct and accurate. Am I thinking of a piece of wax? That is, does my representing have the content ^piece of wax^? "Reflection" (perhaps in a quiet hour without the distractions of ordinary life) delivers the answer to any such question. This view makes RWK reasonably complacent about the idea of direct and accurate access to our inner selves. It also makes RWK very confident about knowing the answers to similar questions.

599. The story continues in a plausible, but speculative vein. All of us, RWK, and his early modern contemporaries, began life as "vulgar". It is not so implausible, then, to think of RWK's concept of "sensation" as beginning its life as the concept of an "item "of" so-and-so" (591). Thus, when RWK speaks of a "sensation" of a grey rectangle (340), we can understand him to have in mind an ancestor of the vulgar item "of" a grey rectangle, that item which is common to cases of seeing a grey rectangle and having it merely appear that there is a grey rectangle (591-2). He has transformed these items a bit because his reflections on human nature have convinced him that these items belong in the same general class as pains, pleasures and "feelings".[209]

600. The plot thickens. When RWK ask himself, "does every one of the representings

(340.42) I am having a sensation of grey
(340.43) I am having a sensation of a grey rectangle
(340.44) that book has, on the side facing me, a grey rectangular cover

contain the content ^grey^?", he follows the manifest-image phenomenology inherited by 'sensation of' and says "sure; what else?". To put it another way, since the lineage of the 'of' in 'sensation of' is the manifest-image causal one in 'item

---

[209] This is not to say that the items in this class are all the same; the class can be further subdivided. In particular, the involvement of sensations in the perceptual process marks them off from the others in the class. Kant appears to have just some such division in mind; see *CJ*, 189, 203, 206, 325, and 224'. An earlier version of these points may be hinted at in *CPR*, A28/B44 and A29.

"of"', its source in 'normally caused by' carries the day. Despite RWK's convictions about the confusions inherent in the vulgars' attribution of color to physical objects, the causal characterization of 'of' places at RWK's disposal only one property, the sensible quality greyness.

601. Notice that part of Sellars' position is that without the work of the aesthetic, a philosopher like RWK is simply depending on his ordinary grasp of manifest-image sensible qualities. So, on Sellars' view, when RWK thinks about the content ^grey^ (the property greyness), he is considering the only one he has, namely, that sensible quality of physical objects that figures in the "vulgar" treatment of sensation (591). In one way, then, the inclination of RWK to answer the question of paragraph 600 "yes" is understandable.

602. Once again, Sellars has something to deny. If (340.42) and (340.43) are construed within the Sellarsian aesthetic and not by means of the manifest-image causal 'of', then it is false that (340.42) and (340.43) contain the content ^grey^. What the representings (340.42) and (340.43) do contain is the content ^S-(grey)^. The representer is, in a nominalized version, giving a (partial) description of himself:

(93) I S-(grey).

By contrast, the representing (340.44) has the content ^grey^. In this introduction, I have acquiesced with the identification by RWK and his contemporaries of the content ^grey^ as the property "greyness" (49-50). Continuing to speak in this way, what the aesthetic directs me to say is that (340.44) is about the sensible quality greyness and not about a different property, the sensory quality S-(grey)ness. The content ^grey^ is not identical to the content ^S-(grey)^ (though, of course, these properties are very similar).

603. What RWK and his actual colleagues did is to take the traditional philosophical idea of a class of human states which included pains, pleasures and "feelings" and combine that with their "un-aesthetic" manifest-image account of appearing and perceiving (584-7), all the while using the causal sense of 'of' to make a philosophical package. Consider the following "first act" of RWK's intellectual history:

> I am presently in a complex state which I was caused to be in and which includes the (confused) thought that the facing side of a book over there is a grey rectangle. In this case, I know (for other reasons) that there is no book over there and nothing that is even rectangular. However, were there truly what the "vulgar" would call a book with a grey rectangular facing cover, I would be seeing that grey rectangular cover. What I want to say about this complex state is that, besides the confused and false thought, it also includes a part that would,

in optimal conditions, be caused by a grey rectangle, such as a cover of a book. So, I want to call it a

sensation "of" a grey rectangle,

and treat it, first, as a part of my present total state, a part that contributes to my thinking of a grey rectangle even though there isn't one there, and, second, as a part of my total state if I were really seeing a grey rectangle.

The causal sense of 'of' has a characterization that employs the content ^grey rectangle^ as it unsophisticatedly understood and therefore involves no properties other than those of physical objects.

604. Upon second thought, RWK realizes that his other commitments do not allow him peace and quiet. First, the "new" physics assures him that those sensible qualities such as colors which loom so large in the discourse of the "vulgar" are not in the physical world and not even in the bodies of thinking beings and, therefore, not there with the shapes to which they seem to be "seamlessly" joined. Second, the thinking being which is the empirical self is not, RWK holds, extended. Besides, even without that problem, could a thinking being really be colored—maybe, smelly? No. It is at this intellectual juncture that we first caught up with RWK (339).

605. Since RWK is a part of the Kant family, he is not tempted by a maneuver that appeals to Descartes. This maneuver treats all mental states as representings (in my strict sense). In traditional terms, RWK does not assimilate the 'of' in

sensation "of"

and to the 'of' in

thought (representing) of.

If one does so, sensations become a subset of thinkings, "confused" thinkings: confused because they are of items which really can not exist and which form part of an inadequate view of the world, both in regard to thinking beings and to extended beings. The dialectic described in paragraphs 339-45 attempts to solve the problems described above and yet keep a distinction between sensations and thoughts.

606. In Kantian terms, the doctrine that sensations have content (in the same sense thoughts do) is the "intellectualizing" of sense (*CPR*, Amphiboly of the Concepts of Reflection). Of course, those who "intellectualize" sensations will tend to find confirmed many of their prior opinions about our having as direct and accurate access to our sensations as to our thoughts. Such direct and accurate access is one of the hallmarks of being "given" (19):

> Add to this, that every impression, external and internal, passions, affections, sensations, pains and pleasures, are originally on the same footing; and that whatever other differences we may observe among them, they appear, all of them, in their true colours, as impressions or perceptions. ...since all actions and sensations of the mind are known to us by consciousness, they must necessarily appear in every particular what they are, and be what they appear.[210]

607. Despite RWK's resistance to the intellectualizing of sense, RWK is not entirely impervious to this siren's call. RWK is unwilling (in contrast to his contemporary namesake Lycan) to accept the idea that *all there is to say about* colors, tastes, and other sensible qualities is that they are properties only of "intentional inexistents" and have thus completely disappeared from the world. He thinks that there really are sensations in the world of appearance. Therefore, he happily talks about them without really having an account of the qualities that they are supposed to involve. (What is greyness as a property of the empirical self?) Furthermore, by neglecting the vulgar roots of the causal 'of', he never has qualms about direct and accurate access to these qualities. Finally, he is convinced that difficulties about "seamlessness" can be countered by the line of thought described earlier (339-45) even though that line of thought does nothing to set out the correct view, one which would replace the confused and inadequate one embraced by the vulgar.

608. I trust it is abundantly clear that the Sellarsian aesthetic is directly in conflict with the intellectual journey in my fictionalized history and provides no such foothold for a doctrine of the givenness of image-models. Far from being "given" on Sellars' account, image-models are indirectly indicated by unphilosophical users of the manifest image through their reference to the sensible qualities of physical objects. In the phrase from *SM*, the vulgar "never notice" image-models meaning by that phrase that these unphilosophical persons do not even have the concepts by which they can formulate judgings about image-models "in their true colours". Moreover, the maneuvers of early modern philosophers are no advance on this state of affairs. The transcendental psychologist has in the aesthetic (at least a start on) the appropriate concepts, but the aesthetic provides a formulation of these concepts which, as I have argued, makes them neither "givers" nor "given". One more nail in the coffin of givenness appears in the next subsection.

---

[210] Page 190, David Hume, *A Treatise of Human Nature*, edited by L.A. Selby-Bigge (Oxford University Press, 1888).

(IX) IMAGE-MODELS IN THE SCIENTIFIC IMAGE

609. For Sellars, one goal of the scientific image is to provide concepts which are "successors" to concepts of the manifest image. The manifest image concept of ice (for short, the concept of MI-ice) has a "successor" concept in the scientific image (SI-ice). These two concepts are certainly not identical, but the concept of SI-ice, Sellars holds, is in a explicable sense, a "successor" of the concept of MI-ice.[211]

610. Manifest image cubes of ice are "counterparts" of scientific image cubes of ice. In the scientific image, cubes of ice are literally assemblages of more fundamental entities (such as, microphysical particles). Since this metaphysical difference concerning basic objects is the crucial difference of the two images (348-54), the bluntest thing to say is that, strictly speaking, there are no manifest objects at all in the scientific image. Manifest objects do not consist of, are not systems of, say, microphysical particles or, of any other items from the scientific image. The point of characterizing a "counterpart" relationship is to explicate what is meant by the scientific image user who claims that such-and-such systems of scientific items are what the manifest image user, though without the least inkling, has been talking about all along.

611. Making my points about image-models does not hinge on addressing any specific stage of the scientific image. For definiteness and convenience, I take that stage of the Newtonian version of the scientific image favored by Kant; central to this stage, as Kant understood it, is that matter is impenetrable extension (336). In this stage of the scientific image, portions of matter endowed with appropriate causal powers are the "counterparts" of manifest objects.

612. I agree with Sellars that the evidence leans heavily toward the conclusion that Kant, and the great majority of philosopher-scientists of the modern period, thought that portions of matter lack all sensible qualities (333-8). Even for Sellars, in fact, that portions of matter do not have sensible qualities is a hallmark of the scientific image. It is not that Sellars believes other accounts of matter to be impos-

---

[211] See *SSIS* (76), pp. 407, 412, and 429. Sellars admits that "spelling out" the notion of "successor" concepts in two different conceptual frameworks is a large task on which he has done only a little; he correctly refers the reader to ch. V of *SM* (*SSIS*, p. 407). In "Sellarsian Realism" (*Philosophical Studies*, 54(1988), 229-256), I address some of these issues. In this introduction, I simply hack my way through the Gordian knot of complexities.

I heartily recommend *SSIS* to anyone interested in these issues. Sellars had discussed them elsewhere (see his references on p. 394 of *SSIS*), but here he is replying to an essay of Cornman's (reference on p. 395 of *SSIS*). That Cornman has missed (and misconstrued) fundamental points from Sellars' earlier papers is disconcerting to Sellars, who concludes that he must bear part of the responsibility in that some of his earlier expositions were "unclear and indistinct" (*SSIS*, p. 391). To correct this, Sellars moves slowly through all the details and painstakingly contrasts his views with others. For my own part, I should like to emphasize that one central error of Cornman's was to fail to take seriously Sellars' repeated assertions about the importance of the manifest image and the nature of manifest objects (*SSIS*, pp. 394-5 and footnote 7).

sible; they just didn't seem plausible to him (*SSIS*, p. 437). And, he might have added, those early modern scientists who made such arrangements had good reasons for doing so. (As for other possible views, the "new" new materialists managed to convince Sellars that no philosophical positions in this arena had been laid to rest and would not return from the grave to haunt you (*FMPP*, I, 150).)

613. Sketching a philosophical path to get to Sellars' final position on image-models involves taking on too many issues about why Sellars believes that competing positions are to be rejected. Instead, I list the elements of his position without much regard to how he comes to them.

(A) Sensible qualities:
(i) Since no portion of matter has sensible qualities, no assemblage of such portions does either.[212] So, no scientific image counterpart of any manifest image object has sensible qualities and thus no sensible qualities are exemplified by any scientific image object. Though, as philosophical archeologists of the manifest image, we have no trouble thinking about sensible qualities, sensible qualities are, so to speak, completely absent in the framework of the scientific image.
(ii) There is no "successor" concept, e.g., SI-pinkness of the sensible quality MI-pinkness, such that SI-pinkness preserves MI-pinkness in such a way that

(a) a scientific image counterpart of a manifest object is SI-pink if and only if the manifest object is MI-pink, and
(b) SI-pinkness has sufficient features to insure that it is a quality.

To sum up crudely, there is no way to define qualities from the properties of impenetrable extension; the defined properties will lack the required features.[213]

---

[212] Compare an atomist version: since no atom has sensible qualities, no assemblage of atoms does. My bald statement of this point is intended to hide the fact that metaphysical arguments about qualities of wholes and qualities of their "parts" occupies a great space in Sellars' reply to Cornman. (It is, of course, not properties in general at issue there.) Suffice it to say that, in some senses of 'emergence', Sellars wanted to argue against emergence. See lecture III of *FMPP* where my present remark appears as item 4 in paragraph 17.
    Nota Bene: Sellars constructs most of his argument in *SSIS* and his preceding essays on these issues, under the assumption that the scientific image—up to this point—contains "particles" (atoms, sub-atomic particles, etc.) as basic objects. Well, it has. But that is not so important to his argument, as his conviction that (A)(i) is essential to avoiding emergence of a sort that he finds metaphysically objectionable, regardless of what the scientific image basic objects are.
[213] It is usually at this point that Sellars stresses aspects of the "particulate" nature of objects of current and past stages of the scientific image (*SSIS*, p. 440 and *FMPP*, III, section VII). I do not deny that the notion of particles provides extra complications. My point is that Sellars would arrive at the same end point—particles, or no.

(B) Image-models:
(i) The aesthetic transfers to image-models the "sensible quality" dimension (482) of the properties I call by that very phrase. Image-models are not sensible qualities, but they are sensory qualities.
(ii) Since no portion of matter has sensory qualities, no assemblage of such portions does either. So, *as merely assemblages of portions of matter*, scientific image counterparts of persons do not have image-models.[214]
(iii) There is no "successor" concept, e.g., SI-S-(pink)ness of the sensory quality MI-S-(pink)ness, such that SI-S-(pink)ness preserves MI-S-(pink)ness as required by suitably adjusted versions of (A)(ii)(a) and (A)(ii)(b). (Actually, (B)(ii) and (B)(iii) are, at bottom, the problems from (A)(i) and (A)(ii) all over again.)

Should we, then, conclude that the "quality dimension" (482, 587) which the aesthetic gleans from sensible qualities and transfers to image-models is to be eliminated completely from the world? That no user of the scientific image would ever employ such concepts? We know from the history of philosophy that not everyone has joined the "new" new materialists and answered "yes, so much the worse for sensible and sensory qualities and what they share in common." Sellars counts himself among those who answer "no". His reasons are of basically of three sorts.
614. First, he believes there are, for example, volumes of pink (*FMPP*, I, 87 and III, 44-7). The question he thinks needs answering is what their ultimate status is.
615. Second, he holds image-models—more accurately, their successors—necessary to a scientific view of the world that would account for everything that needs to be accounted for in the case of animate objects (*IAMB* (56), section VI in *PPME*; *SSIS*, pp. 400 and 424). In particular, Sellars has in mind that at least some of what I have described in discussing image-models and perception will find its way into a scientifically sophisticated account of human perceptual activity. The account of the aesthetic is thus a part of the defense of the indispensability—in altered form—of sensible qualities.
616. Third, no one has such insight into the future of science as to be able to legislate now what the "physical" (or, "material") should encompass. Thus, Sellars sees no impediment to providing a "successor" to image-models in the scientific image. This successor allows both the preservation of the "quality dimension" of sensible qualities (inherited through image-models) and a construction of a philo-

---

[214] On p. 409 of *SSIS*, using a slightly different terminology from my present one, Sellars says: "...if we accept the principle of reducibility, for a system of scientific objects to sense-redly must *consist* in its constituents being in certain states and standing in certain relations to each other. Now sensing-redly as conceived in the Manifest Image does not consist in a relationship of objects in states other than sensings. A sensing can *include other sensings*, as when we sense a-red-circle-in-a-green-square, but it cannot *consist of non-sensings*."

Introduction 221

sophical position which is a non-trivial sort of "materialism" (*SSIS*, pp. 438-9 and 445-6; *FMPP*, III, 126).

617. The essentials of Sellars' position on the future role of the successors of image-models are:

(C) Neurophysiological states and sensa:
(i) The scientific image counterparts of persons and other animate objects of the manifest image are assemblages of portions of matter, some sub-portions of which are the central nervous system (CNS).
(ii) The successor concepts to those of image-models are concepts of

> CNS complex states that include other particulars (sensa) which are not portions of matter, which exist only in connection with neurophysiological processes, which have inherited the "quality dimension" of sensible qualities and image-models, and with which portions of matter of the CNS are in causal interaction.[215]

A neurophysiology that incorporates sensa has not thereby acquired entities or properties that are not "physical" though sensa are not "toughly" physical ("physical$_2$," as Sellars calls it (*SSIS*, p. 393)) in that they and their properties can not be reduced to portions of matter and their properties. From the beginning, neither sensible qualities nor image-models were described as in any way non-physical. All of them—sensible qualities, image-models, sensa—are involved in space and time and in causal interactions. None of them are described as having the intentionality of representings and thus none of them jump a traditional hurdle for being mental.

618. The sticking point for many philosophers, Sellars believes, is causal interaction.[216] He is convinced that traditional philosophical mistakes about the sensory combined with a commitment to a mechanical model of causation and a belief in the "autonomy of the mechanical" led philosophers to the conclusion that nothing involving the sensory (as Sellars has explained it) can be causally efficacious. The account of causality sketched in this introduction (244-57) is free of any such commitments. So, on Sellars' Kantian construal of causality, there is no impediment to the sort of causal interaction required of sensa.

619. All the above notwithstanding, Sellars is worried that the "last refuge of metaphysical dualism" (such as epiphenomenalism which elevates to metaphysics

---

[215] The neurophysiological part is essential as Sellars says (*SSIS*). No doubt Sellars would be pleased, given his account of the relation of perceiving and imagining (467, 572) by recent work showing that the usual visual neural areas are stimulated in cases in which subject merely imagines (*Nature*, November 16, 2000, pp. 357-9).

[216] My remarks for the next few paragraphs are a commentary on sections VI through VIII of lecture III of *FMPP*.

the causal impotence of the sensory and the autonomy of the mechanical) is the contrast between objects and object-bound processes. Sellars believes (for a variety of reasons) that the final account in the world should be in terms of "pure process". In "pure process" accounts of the world, objects become "constructions" out of processes.[217] The "thing-iness" of objects (especially, "particles") in the present stage of the scientific image disappears from this final view. As all fundamental items would be processes, the last philosophical impediment to viewing sensory processes, which Sellars now calls "σ-ings", as fundamental to the scientific account of sentient beings would be removed. These pure processes, "σ-ings", are the final inheritors of the quality-dimension which started with sensible qualities.

620. I have pursued questions about the place of the sensory in the scientific image for some paragraphs now. These questions lead away from the main interests of this introduction. Why, then, have I pursued them?

621. First, since the distinction between the manifest image and the scientific image looms so large in Sellars' views and since the distinction bears on the Sellarsian aesthetic, I just couldn't see myself saying nothing. Second, I have agreed with Sellars that the preponderance of evidence, put in Sellars' terms, is that Kant subscribes to (a stage of) the scientific image. So, on that score as well, I couldn't see myself sticking with the account of image-models in the manifest image.

622. Third, and most importantly, there is the question of "givenness". No interpretation of Kant's "transcendental metaphysics" can be complete without an account of sensibility. Were this account of sensibility to commit Kant to some form of "givenness", especially a Cartesian form, Sellars would face a problem. He thinks of the "critical philosophy" as requiring the abandonment of many of the Cartesian assumptions of Kant's predecessors. Once again, it's not that Sellars believes that Kant has all these matters straightened out, but he believes that Kant started in the right direction and that there is an interpretation that continues in that direction. So, I said (608), this subsection drives one more nail into the coffin of givenness. I hereby get my hammer.

623. Sellars believes that an account of the world as "pure process" is an element in the final stage of the scientific image (see, e.g., *PSIM* in *SPR*, p. 37). This account of the world as pure process is not some piece of metaphysics, but rather a stage in the scientific understanding of the world in which particles, like electrons and quarks, are constructed from pure processes and in which the fundamental laws are formulated solely in terms of pure processes. Nobody has such a view yet. Moreover, the present stage of the scientific image contains neurophysiology as a subject in its infancy. Here, too, Sellars does not think that anyone can foresee the details of future science.

624. So, Sellars is prepared to argue, in general ways, about the need for sensa

---

[217] Of course, this distinction depends on not employing the word 'object' in the widest sense.

in neurophysiology and for "σ-ings" in final science, but he never dreams of saying that he knows, in any detail, what the relevant concepts of the sensory will be. Scientific work generates new principles as well as putting them to test and alters concepts as well as merely employing them. Unlike the Cartesian (518), Sellars describes a view in which the very concepts of the sensory undergo elaboration and change. Such a position is surely one that no defenders of the "given" would find congenial. In Sellars' view, nothing merits being called "given" as the "given" was traditionally understood and nothing in Sellars' view of science, sensa and, σ-ings would purchase what the "given" was intended to purchase, viz., a "foundation" for empirical knowledge.

V. "Nothing of Him that doth Fade, but doth Suffer a Sea-change into Something Rich and Strange"
A. More Kantian Advantages from a Sellarsian Aesthetic
(I) REMEMBRANCE OF THINGS ALMOST FORGOTTEN: AN EXEGETICAL POINT

625. At the very beginning (1-21), I explained why Sellars' writing on the history of philosophy is a complicated intertwining of both philosophy and exegesis. Later (346) I warned that Sellars' approach precluded simple answers to questions about Kant's views on sensory states and perception. I have explained something about what Sellars takes to be right and wrong in Kant's account of "experience" and, in this part, proceed further with this task.

626. Sellars himself provides good guidance. I quote, from the *Preface* to *SM*, Sellars' description of the contents of chapter I of that book:

> Chapter I combines a sympathetic but critical account of Kant's attempt to disentangle the respective roles in experience of sensibility and understanding, intuitions and concepts, with *an independent discussion of the issues involved*. I argue that many of the *confusions* of his treatment of Space and Time can be traced to a failure to do justice to the complexities of the distinctions required, but that *when they are more adequately drawn they maintain their Kantian flavour, and that when his views are correspondingly reformulated they are substantially correct*. The heart of the chapter is a clarification and defense of the Kantian concept of a 'manifold of sense'. [Italics are mine, not Sellars'.]

Sellars is quite accurate in his description of chapter I. After introductory paragraphs (I, 1-20) devoted almost exclusively to exegetical remarks on Kant, Sellars embarks on his promised "independent discussion of the issues" which continues for fifty-two paragraphs (sections II through VI). Only in the final six paragraphs (I, 73-8, sections VII and VIII) Sellars returns to a direct treatment of Kant.

224   *Introduction*

627. In sections VII and VIII, Sellars bluntly and unqualifiedly describes the "confusions" in Kant's treatment—perhaps, with too little qualification.[218] I summarize his main point. What Kant lacks—and what the Sellarsian aesthetic supplies—is an account that maintains a clear distinction between the sensibility and the understanding and between space and time as "forms" in representations of *this-suches* and those "forms" of sensory states and image-models which also deserve to be called "spatial" and "temporal". This lack has some simple consequences.

628. First, it makes it difficult for Kant to keep in focus the fact that he uses the term 'intuition' ambiguously, on the one hand, for sensory states and, on the other, for representations of *this-suches*. Secondarily, it then becomes unclear how the distinction between intuit*ing* and intuit*ed* is to be drawn.

629. Moreover, it also tempts Kant to contemplate that intuitings of temporal *this-suches* are originally so limited in what they can represent, that they can be about only states of the self.[219] Anything intuitively represented in time would be a state of a self and all representations of spatial objects in time would arise from some activity of the understanding that depended on those intuitings of states of selves. Avoiding phenomenalistic doctrines, as I have called them (159-65, and 345), is made much harder by this line of thought (see *SM*, Appendix, 17-22). Further, that what Kant calls the "objective" order of time should derive from operations of the understanding in dealing with representations of states of the self as temporal also seems to be difficult to reconcile with theses of the Refutation of Idealism: viz., that states of the self are located in the "objective" time order (i.e., officially for Kant, the only time order) and that determinate locatings of temporal states of the self are dependent on (or, at least rely on) representations of spatiotemporal objects in time. So, keeping a clear distinction between the sensibility and the understanding and the respective manifestations of spatiotemporality is not only demanded by passages after the Aesthetic, but also loses Kant nothing but temptations toward an idealism like Berkeley's, a position which he stoutly rejects.

630. The purpose of this section is to show that the more "adequately drawn" distinctions of the Sellarsian aesthetic allow me to "reformulate" some basic Kantian theses so that their correctness *within the view as described* is without doubt. In the process, I lay the groundwork for this part's more controversial matters which complete items from part **III** that were left hanging when part **IV** was begun.

---

[218] The reader of *KPT* will find a slightly different emphasis in Sellars' remarks on Kant's "confusions" and it is these remarks that my following reformulation most resembles. See, in particular, chapters 14 and 15 of *KPT*.

[219] See, for example, Kant's claim that time is directly only a form of the mind and its determinations and not of outer appearances (A33-4/B49-51; see also A42/B59-60). Probably, it is such passages as these that Sellars has in mind in chapter 14 of *KPT* when he says that Kant should have gone back, once he had finished the Analogies, to rewrite the Aesthetic.

Introduction 225

(II) A REVIEW OF THE RELEVANT TERMINOLOGY

631. I noted (201-4) that Sellars required a distinction between two senses of 'sensibility' and two senses of 'intuiting'. At the end of my treatment of sensory states (541-7), I cast these distinctions in the terminology of part **IV**. I restricted my use of the word 'sensibility' to that passive faculty, the affecting of which produces image-models (547) (with the help of the understanding, but sometimes without it (473, 544)). I shall continue using 'sensibility' for this passive faculty. To the sensibility in this sense belong "intuitings" as sensory states and image-models.

632. I shall continue (116-20 and 471ff) to employ the phrase 'productive imagination' for the understanding in its function of affecting, and being affected by, the sensibility, especially in connection with the production of intuitings as representings of *this-suches*. Ostensible perceiving and perceiving (579) as the process of perceptual taking and perceptual judging is thus a result of the action of both the sensibility and the productive imagination.

633. As representings (in my strict sense), representings of *this-suches* are characterized in terms of the forms of judgings and, therefore, in Kantian terms, belong to the understanding alone. So, one sense of 'intuition' is explicated by saying that intuitings are representings of *this-suches*. But Kant, in discussing perceptual situations, often uses the term 'intuition' in the richer sense of "perceptual taking" (542). In this sense, intuitings are representings of *this-suches*, but not merely representings of *this-suches*. They are those brought about by a causal process initiated in the sensibility alone and then continued by the sensibility and the productive imagination acting in concert. In this sense the faculty of intuiting is not the understanding alone, but rather the combination of sensibility and productive imagination that results in what I have called "perception" (especially, perceptual taking).

634. The relative contributions of the sensibility and the productive imagination to perception are spelled out in the principles of the aesthetic. Since, in the following, I refer regularly to various processes that are part of perceiving, I review aesthetic theses that illustrate the central points.

446. ...
(446.TA4) given that the circumstances are suitable, in normal conditions and for a person, P, who is a normal perceiver,

  that the scene has D (which is an assembled stripped-down description)

implies

  that P S-(assembled stripped-down description D)s.

473. Ignore the remainder of the scene and concentrate on the house. A rough-and-ready stripped-down description of the house (assembled by a path that begins at the white triangle, goes down, then left, and then up) is:

> white triangle bottom-to-top-adjoining white rectangle left-edge-adjoining larger white rectangle top-to-bottom-adjoining brown rectangle left-to-right-adjoining white triangle.

The house, with the various sensible qualities of its facing surfaces, is causally responsible for P being in a

> S-(white triangle bottom-to-top-adjoining white rectangle left-edge-adjoining larger white rectangle top-to-bottom-adjoining brown rectangle left-to-right-adjoining white triangle)

visual sensory state. That P (who, I assume, is in an appropriate frame of mind) is in such a state causes

(TA6) the productive imagination to

> (i) augment the visual sensory state in accordance with principles (the schema) associated with the (complex) concept of a house-in-relation-to-a-perceiver, and
> (ii) generate an intuiting, i.e., a representing of a *this-such*, whose content is determined by the concept of a house and the S-(colored), S-(spatial) structure of P's visual image-model.

503. ...
(503.TA6.iii) the productive imagination of a perceiver in the appropriate frame of mind

> (a) augments original sensory states (whose correct description is derived from a present-tense assembled stripped-down description) by utilizing concepts (billiard ball, house) and being guided by the principles of a schema whose general form is
>
>> such-and-such stationary object(s) (billiard ball and table, house) confronting stationary perceiver (me),

Introduction

(b) produces an image-model,

a complex of S-(properties) which the perceiver has S-(simultaneously),

(c) and responds to the image-model and the S-(simultaneity) of its complex by generating the intuiting (whose content is determined by the concept of a stationary object (billiard ball, house) and the S-(colored), S-(spatial) structure of P's visual image-model)

this such-and-such object(s) (billiard ball and table, house)

where coexistence of properties and object(s) is implied.

511. ...
(511.TA6.iv) the productive imagination of a perceiver in the appropriate frame of mind

(a) augments original sensory states (whose correct description is derived from a present-tense assembled stripped-down description) by utilizing concepts (billiard ball, ship) and being guided by the principles of a schema whose general form is

such-and-such moving object(s) (billiard ball, ship) confronting stationary perceiver (me),

(b) produces a sequence of image-models, each of which individually is

a complex of S-(properties) which the perceiver has S-(simultaneously),

(c) and responds to the sequence of image-models and the S-(precedence) in the sequence by generating the intuiting (whose content is determined by the concept of a moving object (billiard ball, ship) and the S-(colored), S-(spatial) structure of P's visual image-models)

this moving (changing) of such-and-such object(s) (billiard ball, ship)

where the represented is an item, a change, which requires a succession of properties (and, as well, the co-existence of others).

228 *Introduction*

(III) ON THE RELATION OF THE SENSIBILITY AND THE UNDERSTANDING

635. The Sellarsian aesthetic maintains the sensibility as a faculty of "receptivity". In perceiving, the original sensory state is caused and requires no activity whatsoever by the productive imagination.[220] In this sense, then, the sensibility is independent of the understanding. Even the augmentation of the original sensory state accomplished with the help of the productive imagination results in a state of the perceiver which is not different in kind from that of the original sensory state; it is more of the same (544).

636. That sensations represent no objects at all is, I have argued (546), true for image-models. Image-models are not representings (in my strict sense) and therefore not judgings or parts of judgings. As states of a perceiver, they have structure, but that structure is not conceptual structure of any kind and thus not categorial structure (545.TA8). They can be said to be "of" objects, but such characterization is by their (normal) cause (551-70 and 591-4). So, they can, as Kant says, be "referred" to objects (A23/B38), but such "reference" is parasitic on the reference to individuals secured by representings, particularly representings of *this-suches*. Image-models are ontologically impotent (570(S)).

637. Abundantly important though the contribution of image-models to perceiving is, this contribution is through their causal interaction with the productive imagination in its wielding schemas of concepts which the productive imagination brings to that interaction. The S-(spatial) and S-(temporal) structure and the sensory qualities (S-(colors), etc.) thus structured that causally guide the productive imagination are actually there in perceiving: they guide by being "actual". If I were to talk in terms of "content" in the case of an image-model, such talk would be no more than another way of saying what (complex) property a perceiver has (446.TA4). For example, for perceiver P's image-model to have the "content" S-(blue)-ness is no more than that the (partial) description of P is that P S-(blue)s (449-56). Compare my example of the "contents" of leg-involving bodily movements in paragraph 42.

638. Contrast this with "contents" of thinkings. Thinkings as modifications of a subject can be as "actual" as sensory states. However, these modifications do not reveal any other properties of the subject than those which have the form "thinks [content]" (180-1) or which are consequent to the general principles of transcendental psychology (such as, that thinking has logical form). Though a thinking must have other properties, these are not supplied either by specifying the content or by the general principles of representing. What we know about a thinking as an actuality is, in traditional terms, what its content is (including its form). Thinking is a

---

[220] The word 'activity' is important. For a full-fledged concept user, the total state of such a person, including states of the understanding, can serve as conditions in the principles which spell out which sensory states are caused in which circumstances.

synthesizing (combining) of contents (263-5) and an actual thinking is an actualization of the contents in it, but not as properties of the thinker.

639. That concepts (and other contents of thinkings) have a special way of being actualized in thinking is part of the import of Kant's claim that all concepts must be included within the "I think" and that "I think" is included in our conceiving of concepts (A341-2/B399-400).[221] Concepts, empirical or not, are the materials which, along with the forms of judging, comprise thinkings and differentiate one thinking from another. Kant puts this by saying that concepts are the "matter" which is "determined" by forms of judging (A266/B322): i.e., concepts are capable of being "synthesized" ("combined"), according to the forms of judging, into determinate thinkings. (This point is highlighted by the classificatory structure of dot quotation.)

640. Care must be taken with cases in which a thinker actualizes contents about thinkers or about itself as a thinker: e.g., when what is being actualized is a content of the form "[thinks [content]]"; this is not a case of actualizing either embedded content as a property of the thinker. The simplest example is one in which a thinker thinks that he has a determinate thought. For example, consider my thinking that I am thinking that B is a bear. In the content notation, what is true is that

I am thinking a thought with the content ^I am thinking that B is a bear^,

i.e., equivalently,

I am thinking that I am thinking that B is a bear.

Just as thinking the content ^I am thinking that B is a bear^ is not to think

B is a bear,

so thinking the content ^I am thinking that I am thinking that B is a bear^ is not to think

I am thinking that B is a bear.[222]

The present tense throughout provides a temptation that other tenses do not. Compare

I am thinking that I thought that B is a bear, and

---

[221] See Sellars' comments on A341/B399 in section *D* of chapter 17 of *KPT*, in *KTE*, 22-5, and in *CLN*, A13c-15a.
[222] Of course, I can imagine conversational situations in which the through-and-through present tense construction could be understood as a cute way of admitting that you are thinking that B is a bear.

230   *Introduction*

I am thinking that I will think that B is a bear.

The point of this paragraph comes back to haunt us later (767), but for the moment these comments will have to suffice.[223]

641. What is true of concepts must also be true of other conceptual items such as intuitings as representations of *this-suches*. In fact, A341/B399 may be a passage in which Kant departs from his majority inclination and uses the term 'concept' so that it covers non-general conceptual items. In any case, Kant is well aware that there are singular judgings and includes singularity in his classification of representations (A320/B377). (The Sellarsian interpretation incorporated this point at the outset (31-7)). In sum and with careful concern for the cases mentioned in paragraph 640, the actualizing of contents in thinking is never the actualizing of properties of the thinking subject.[224] In characterizing the self as thinking, our only, available actual properties of the subject are of the form "thinks [content]".

642. Turning back to image-models, I note that, in addition to the Sellarsian aesthetic securing a "non-intellectualized" sensibility (606) and a "non-sensualized" understanding, it provides a buttress against both empiricist attack and the need for what Kant calls "transcendental realism". Image-models are ontologically impotent (570(I)): i.e., they are blind, superficial and semantically parasitic (323). Nothing is "passed" through image-models; they are not "givers" of anything. On the Sellarsian account, the structure of properties, relations and states of affairs cannot, as Kant puts it (*PFM*, 282), "migrate" through the processes of sensibility.

643. The non-conceptuality of image-models and their status as "non-givers" leaves, as Kant wishes, all "synthesizing"—all "combining"—to the understanding whether we are "conscious" of the synthesizing or not (B129-130). Even in the perceptual process, where the causal activity of original sensory states and image-models guides the producing of representations of *this-suches*, these representations are through-and-through conceptual items, belong within the 'I think', and their com-

---

[223] The points of the present paragraphs have straightforward formulations by means of the device of dot quotation. (Remember that image-models are not classifiable through dot quotation; that is, they are not capable of falling within the "I think".) The classification provided by dot quotation puts all conceptual items within the "I think" though the distinction between "form" and "content" is turned into the contrast between more versus less generic classification (*KTE*, 24). I resisted putting my present points in Sellars' terminology since that would have lost touch with the more traditional formulations of Kant and his predecessors. In addition, I have resisted the temptation to include in this introduction an investigation of the relationships of "I am •B is a bear•ing", and "I am •I am •B is a bear•ing•ing" and so on.

[224] A contemporary qualification might be necessary because of the possibility of the self-reference of a thinking to itself. Such cases must not, of course, be confused with a doctrine of direct or "non-representational awareness" of the soul. Though Sellars worries that all the philosophers of the modern period, including Kant (see *KPT*, Appendix, Descartes), are tempted by such direct awareness accounts, self-reference is, by contrast, a very twentieth-century topic that appears even within the confines of representational theories.

plexity is due to combining done by the understanding (263-5).

644. Further, the Sellarsian aesthetic is consistent with Kant's position on "experiential derivation" (127-156). I argued earlier that experiential derivation of empirical kconcepts such as that of a tree must be from states that have "content" in the sense relevant to representings (in my strict sense) (141-5). Image-models do not have such "content" and thus cannot be worked on by "comparing, reflecting and abstracting". In any case, image-models are, as replicas, "superficial" (see (570(S)) in (545.TA8)) and are (complex) properties merely "analogous" to the properties that would need to be abstracted. So, on this account, sensibility alone cannot provide for the experiential derivation of even empirical kconcepts (200).

645. On the other hand, that empirical kconcepts can be "experientially derived" from *intuitings* as *perceptual takings* is at least possible on my account of perceiving (196-200). The understanding, as the productive imagination, augments a sensory state by employing a content which is a kconcept or, in the case of novice perceivers, by employing an ur-content which at that stage is not a kconcept (141-54). The resulting perceptual taking, a representing of a *this-such*, contains that logically structured ("synthesized") content which makes it the kind of representing it is. That the understanding by "reflecting, comparing, and abstracting" should identify such content and "separate" some of it out for use as a kconcept is not, as I argued earlier, impossible. What the understanding "puts" there, it is not impossible that it should unearth (199, 307, 323).

646. Equally, Kant has great concern that spatiotemporal concepts and, especially, the categories (A86-7/B119; B127-8) be attributed a "birth certificate" (194ff) other than that ascribed to them by "sensualists" like Locke (A853-4/B881-2). I will show that the Sellarsian aesthetic secures part of what Kant wants. (Another part awaits further discussion of inner sense and apperceiving.)

647. Officially, what Kant has in mind by space and time are not the analogical concepts of S-(spatiality) and S-(temporality). Kant's official spatiotemporal order is the literal one which contains perceivers and objects being perceived, in short, "appearances". The cognitively efficacious structure of image-models is, however, the S-(spatial) and S-(temporal) structure (see the parts of (TA6) reviewed in 634). Even if—contrary to Sellars' view—we had some direct, philosophically unmediated access to image-models, notice how hard it would be to articulate a useful account of abstraction. How could you "abstract" the properties and relations that are the official spatiotemporal order unless you could distinguish the S-(spatiotemporal) from the literally spatiotemporal? Thus, rather than spatiotemporal concepts "arising" (by abstraction) from image-models, their "priority" would be required.[225]

648. The categories are easier: no categorial structure (and no logical structure)

---

[225] As I shall note, Sellars has a suggestion for Kant that would make the "abstraction" of the spatiotemporal order from image-models impossible. See the second note to paragraph 683.

232   *Introduction*

is present in image-models (545.TA8). Putting it crudely, if we could get to image-models, we would not find the categories. The Sellarsian aesthetic thus insures that whatever "birth certificates" spatiotemporal concepts and the categories have, they cannot be ones that show them arising from sensibility. (My earlier claim (239-40) that Kant cannot be a category realist has thus found further support.)

649. The key to the birth certificate of both spatiotemporal concepts and the categories lies, as Kant says (B167), in their "making experience possible" (147, 194-7). This is most definitely true on Sellars' construal of that mixture of sensibility and understanding which leads to "experience".

650. One might easily argue that Kant does not employ the term 'experience' unequivocally. Nevertheless, his considered inclination is to claim that there is just "one experience" and that experiences (plural) are elements in the single, coherent system of experience (A110, A230-2/B282-4, A582/B610). If we take experience, at first approximation, to be the system of empirical knowledge, then we can understand why Kant treats perceivings as providing possible elements of this system. So, if experience requires perceiving, then it can be shown that space, time and the categories are "prior" to experience: they make it possible. In *one sense* of Kant's phrase, they are principles of the possibility of experience[226] (283-293, especially 288). I review briefly the crucial points.

651. First, literal space and time are involved (149-154) in perceiving:

> (513.TA7) the process of perceiving objects and events builds in the concepts of the literally spatial and temporal, i.e., of spatiotemporal appearances (through their role in the analogical construction of S-predicates and through their utilization by the productive imagination both in augmenting sensory states and in producing representings of *this-suches*).

Whether it's rudimentary content (e.g., the content ^ur-sphere^) or a kconcept (e.g., ^house^) in a perceptual taking, the content pertains to literally spatiotemporal objects. As well, a perceptual taking is a representing of a *this-such* whose *logical form* is intelligible only through principles involving space and time (182-9). So, without spatial and temporal concepts, there would be no perceiving.

652. For spatiotemporality in general, the above point holds in a different way. Though literal space and time are part of the content of representings of *this-suches* and, on the demonstrative model, are built into the explication of the logical form of these representings, none of this makes anything spatial and temporal an actual, causally efficacious structure of *sensibility*. According to the aesthetic, however, S-(spatiality) and S-(temporality) are the "forms" of image-models. So, S-(spatiotem-

---

[226] See, e.g., B168-9, but also A128, both passages at the ends of their respective versions of the deduction of the categories.

Introduction 233

porality), though not the literal space and time of appearances, becomes in this way part of perceiving and thus "necessary" to experience as an actual feature, not just as a represented feature or as a feature of representations (in my strict sense).

653. Second, as a consequence of my metaphysical deduction and transcendental deduction rounded-out by the explication of perceiving as perceptual taking and thus as involving representings of *this-suches*, the categories, too, are "necessary for experience" in that without them, there would be no perceiving. That is, "all sensible intuitions are subject to the categories" (116-20 and 206) is borne out both for "sensible intuitions" as perceptual takings and for the represent*eds* of the perceptual takings (cf. *BD*, 73-8). The categories are built into the process of perceiving because the kconcepts employed in perception by the productive imagination have categorial form as do the contents that are assembled ("synthesized") in the representings of *this-suches*. The represent*eds* of perceptual takings are part of the system of nature (301-7), that is, a dynamical system of intuitables being synthesized as a coherent system of which the perceptual represent*eds* are a fragmentary part (308-20). I repeat what I said about one perceptual represent*ed*, an accident:

> **319.** The accident, an intuited, is a synthetic combination of other intuiteds—substances, their properties and relations, happenings of all sorts including changes—all organized spatiotemporally and having categorial form. Put in the Kantian terms of A722/B750, the categories provide principles of the synthesis of possible empirical intuiteds. The *total* categorial form of the accident as intuited is a result of the categorial form of the combined intuiteds individually and the fact that the intuiting
>
> this accident
>
> is an intuiting (potentially) combined by an I constructing the true world story. The categorial form is a reflection of the "transcendental logical" form of the intuitings that can be tokened as part of the judgings which correctly belong to the histories of representers.

654. Kant can, notwithstanding, plausibly deny that *CPR* contains a doctrine of innate principles and concepts *as opposed to* capacities and abilities to represent and, in particular, to represent *this-suches* (146). Of course, he must admit abilities of the understanding to reflect on its operations and so to come to appreciate the principles and the concepts involved in perceiving and to understand the logical structure of perceptual takings. Having eliminated the possibilities of derivation from sensory states and innateness, Kant can take what he considers to be the remaining option: the concepts of space, time, and the categories arise from this reflection and thus, in his phrase, are "self-thought" (199).

655. The material of parts **III** and **IV**, especially,

> the account of image-models and the distinction between them and intuitings as representing of *this-suches*,
> the account of S-(spatiotemporality) as the "form" of image-models,
> the account of the categories as, at bottom, the forms of judging, and
> the account of perceptual taking and perceptual judging built on these other accounts,

have made it possible to provide a coherent explication of most of the points that my mythical philosophers A and B (11) disagreed about. It is my contention that the passages scholars A and B cited contain distinctions and theses that when "*more adequately drawn...maintain their Kantian flavour, and...are substantially correct.*" In light of this claim which I adopt from *SM*, I intend, henceforth, to treat the materials of parts **III** and **IV** as if they were Kant's (with one or two exceptions to be noted). Only in this way can I keep reasonable control of my exposition as I wring from Sellars' interpretation further consequences.

656. Nothing in this section (625-656) stands or falls because of the distinction between, or questions about, the in itself versus appearance. All my points about the sensibility and the understanding, the source of concepts, and the "necessary conditions" of experience are independent of this distinction. In the next section, the in itself returns to center stage.

B. Thinkers and Perceivers in Themselves and as Part of Nature
(I) THE SELF IN ITSELF VERSUS THE PHENOMENAL SELF
(a) The self in itself

657. At the beginning of section *B* of chapter 10 in *KPT*, Sellars says something that might surprise those familiar with standard views on the doctrine of the in itself:

> 8. You see the interesting thing is that Kant claims that we can know an awful lot about the in itself. People often get hung up on that. We have philosophical knowledge about the in itself. First, we know that there is the in itself, and we know what its role is. The role of the in itself is to act on itself: to generate sense impressions and we take over from there. The metaphor that I have always used is that the in itself is like sand in the ocean, and, then, sand creeps and crawls into our shells and irritates us and we construct pearls. And the world of experience is the pearl that we construct on the occasion of being acted on by the in itself. According to Kant, we know that there is the in itself but *we can only know of it*—leaving aside the chief effect of it—we can only know of it what it must be like to account for there being such a thing as a public, intersubjective world

of experience. He thinks that he has principles in terms of which he answers this question. *KPT*, ch. 10, 8.

658. On Sellars' account, Kant believes that we have philosophical knowledge of the in itself, but not, of course, ordinary empirical knowledge (77-9). Some of this philosophical knowledge is of a very special sort. I quoted (85) a long passage from *KTE* comparing Kant's "transcendental psychology" to "transcendental linguistics". The point of transcendental psychology, Sellars says, is to set out what is required for a being to have "knowledge" of its world: in Kantian terms, it sets out what is "necessary" for experience. Some of this concerns the in itself. As the above quote from *KPT* says, a large part of what we can know about the in itself stems from a structured investigation (an "argument" in a loose sense) about what the in itself must be like in order to generate the world of experience.

659. What, then, according to Sellars do we know about the noumenal self, the self in itself? Paragraphs 70-93 are the *mis en scène* for answering this question. I draw from those paragraphs three central points: Sellars takes seriously that things in themselves conform to "laws of their own" (81); although our space and time are not to found among things in themselves, they do have a "form" which, given a more general viewpoint, might count as "spatiotemporal", e.g., a duration which "is not a time" (82-3); and the sensibility and the understanding (as well, of course, as reason) are faculties of the self in itself (87-8).

660. Further, as the quote in paragraph 657 shows, Sellars also thinks that the in itself acts on itself, in particular, on us. What is almost, but not quite, correct is: the self in itself is affected by intelligible objects and, as a result of some of this affection, has sensations; it also thinks and some of its thinkings are brought about through the causal influence of intelligible objects on the sensibility.

661. I admit that I can imagine an interpretation of Kant that leans very heavily on Kant's insistence that we have no determinate "cognition" of the in itself and so concludes that the self in itself does nothing even remotely like thinking. Adjudication of such a view would be too large an undertaking here. Let me simply register my opinion that it contributes to the doctrine that the in itself has no philosophical point and is, perhaps, unintelligible, and thus makes a hash out of large sections of *CPR* as well as Kant's account of freedom and morality.

662. A similar view about states of sensibility is also conceivable. It, too, might be prompted by the thesis of our lack of determinate knowledge of the in itself, or by the conviction that the in itself is static and unchanging. Sellars sees no reason to impute to Kant such a thesis. Moreover, it would omit, when combined with Sellars' attribution of thinking to the noumenal self, an element of "passivity" that Kant insists is a feature of beings such as us who are not completely active.

663. The sort of view I am defending is supported by passages in which Kant is reacting to the suggestion that everything, even the self, might be appearance. One such passage, B155-9, ends on a theme taken up again at B428-9 and at A546/B574 (which culminates a long discussion starting at A538/B566): we exist as intelligences among whose most important activities are those involving "combination" (B158-9, B428). I think I can make a comprehensible package of this theme and others already scouted in this introduction.

664. I begin with qualifications to my "almost correct" claim in paragraph 660. First, our remarks about noumenal "affection" of the sensibility, whether "inner" or "outer", must be understood in terms of the "pure-pure" category, not the "schematized" category, of cause (in the footnote to paragraph 219, I give references to passages in which Kant does exactly that). Similarly, any talk of the self in itself as "substance" or "subject of thought" must also be in terms of the "pure-pure" category of substance (B429).

665. Second, Kant's remarks at A538/B566ff make it necessary to admit "phenomenal" as well "noumenal" faculties of sensibility and understanding. These "powers", as powers of humans beings, have "empirical character" as well as "intelligible character". To put it in terms that I will make more of in this part, since human beings are "appearances", sensibility and understanding also "appear". (This raises the possibility that some transcendental truths might work for both the noumenal and the phenomenal faculty.)

666. What is, at bottom, wrong with my direct statement in paragraph 660, concerns the fact that, according to Kant, both "thinkings" and phenomenal sensory states (i.e., "sensations") are in time.[227] In fact, if the causal sense of "of" is needed to identify sensations, then it would seem that space is also involved. Straightening this out takes us to the heart of the transcendental psychology of the self. Before I attempt this operation, I intend to kill two birds with one stone by considering an argument whose conclusion is that Kant is committed to noumenal representations for a reason other than those so far suggested.

(b) Once more: "existence in thought"

667. Obviously, the concept of "dependent existence" ("existence in thought") gets us, by negation, the concept of "independent existence" ("existence not in thought"). If there were something incoherent about the latter concept, there would be something incoherent about the former.

668. Sellars argues that the Cartesian doctrine of "existence in thought" leads to a commitment to the existence of "unrepresented" representations. To put it as Sellars

---

[227] That Sellars knows that there something to straighten out is clear from notes 17 and 18 to paragraph 43 in *I*. In that note, he says in so many words (actually, he employs the word 'thought') that the noumenal self thinks, but his immediate remarks show that, in that context, he uses the term 'thinking' so that it does not imply being literally temporal. That is the crux of my qualification.

does in *CLN*,[228] that something can be "dependent for its being on being thought of" requires that at least some representings do not have their being in that dependent way. In Kantian terms, the claim that everything has "thought-dependent" being is to say that everything is "appearance". Not only does that seem to be impossible, we also know how negatively Kant responded to that suggestion (B155ff and particularly B428-9).

669. One might think that the notion of being representable can stave off this conclusion. Being a representable is, Sellars argues, an important concept to the philosophers of the early modern period since the demands of intersubjectivity pushed them to allow contents to be actualized in many different minds (*KPT*, ch. 4). Thus contents in individual minds, *as actualizings of representables*, have a status that breaks them loose from dependence on any finite mind.

670. Kant's elucidation of the concept of actuality for appearances also utilizes representables. There are representables which pertain to distant stars, items in the past (A495-6/B523-4) and "magnetic matter" (A225-6/B272-3). If, in certain circumstances, these contents are actualized or *would be* actualized in perceiving, then the appearances in question are actual (92). In all these cases, the actuality of an appearance depends on a lawlike connection between it and the actualizing of representables in perceiving (and hence between it and sensation) (A218/B266, A225-6/B272-4, A491-5/B520-3).

671. On the other hand, *merely* being a representable does not guarantee the actuality of any appearance. Even the *mere* actualizing of a representable does not guarantee the actuality of the appearance. In the circumstances in which Dick finds himself, he actually thinks that that black bear is coming at him and actually has a sensation correctly characterized as a sensation "of" a black bear (564, 590-2), but there is no actual bear.

672. The relation between the actualizing of the content ^that black bear is coming at me^ and the actuality of an appearance is mediated by laws of nature. In certain circumstances and given the laws of nature, the actuality of the black bear implies that Dick actualizes the content ^that black bear is coming at me^. Conversely, given the laws of nature and that the circumstances, including Dick's state and history, are described to eliminate other possible causes of Dick's actualizing the content ^that black bear is coming at me^, then the actualizing of ^that black bear is coming at me^ implies the actuality of the black bear coming at Dick.[229] What we have is a system of two appearances, Dick and a bear, set within a part of nature: given the laws of nature, some of the properties of the two elements of the

---

[228] *CLN*, **B37**. Sellars has always argued that, for Kant, there are representings that do not depend for their existence on being represented or on their being able to be represented (*SM*, ch. II, 14, 24, 27-9; *KPT*, ch. 10, 11-14).

[229] Remember that we are envisaging a principle that is different from the ones in paragraphs 388-400. See the notes to paragraph 582.

system are not independent (compare 582).

673. While all this reminds us that the notions of representable and actuality are interestingly connected, it does not stand in the way of Sellars' point. If you have items with "second-class being", it is impossible not to have items with "first-class being"; and when representing is the source of second-class being, then (at least some) representing is part of first-class being. There might be sense to be made out of the claim that any such representing can be represented by another representing, but then the second representing presents the very same difficulty all over again (*CLN*, **B37**). So, Kant concludes, "in mere thought I am the *being itself*" (B429).

(c) The doctrine of content as part of transcendental psychology

674. Twice (180-1 and 638-41), I have discussed the crucial point that the contents of thinkings supply nothing concerning the subject of the thinking. This seems to me just a reformulation of Kant's repeated assertion in the Paralogisms that the "I think", which is the "vehicle of all concepts" (A341/B399), yields no determinate classifications of a thinking being (A398-402, B406-13, particularly B407-9). No analysis of thinking and its contents gives us an answer to the question "What kind of thing is a thinking being?". This is true whether the subject is the self in itself or the phenomenal self.

675. I have argued that Kant, in one way, treats all concepts, indeed all the conceptual, as on a par: the "I think" is the "vehicle" of *all* the conceptual regardless of its status. Combining is an intellectual activity solely of the understanding (B130-3) (though, in the case of perception, with causal "guidance" from the sensibility) and the combining of concepts in a judging, or in any complex conceptual item, also falls within the "I think" (222-3, 258-65, 639-43). If we express this in terms of "form" and "matter", then we must not be misled into concluding that the concepts which are the "matter" have status *as conceptual* different from the "form". The Sellarsian view is sealed off from any speculation that sensory states might be the "matter" on which the understanding imposes conceptual "form", thus producing empirical concepts. Such speculation aims, with at least some of the conceptual, to derive it from, or reduce it to, that which is not conceptual. The conceptual is conceptual through and through and not obtainable from, or reducible to, something which is originally something else (see my discussion of ur-content in 141-54).[230]

676. Transcendental psychology is, in some large measure, the elucidation of principles of representing which fall within the purview of transcendental logic. In a broad sense of 'logic', then, the entirety of representing is, as Kant says (B428-9), a "logical function". Representing, according to the principles of this logical function, is independent of the sort of being doing the representing. The contents of

---

[230] Sellars argues for essentially the same point in *KTE*, 23-25.

representings are linked neither to appearances nor to things in themselves. Thus the attributing of representings to a being does not "exhibit" the being as "appearance" (B429) simply because it does not exhibit it as any *sort* of being at all (unless, of course, being a representer is to allowed to count a sort of being).

(K11) The doctrine of contents of representings is a (transcendental) logical doctrine of "function" and, in particular, of "combining" (synthesizing) which is independent of the noumenal-phenomenal distinction.

677. Sellars makes this point to his contemporary readers by describing Kant's account of thinking as "functional" (*I*, 43, note 18; *MP*, 48f). This can be misleading. Sellars is not seriously attributing to Kant an up-to-date functionalist view of the mental.[231] He merely has in mind a salient feature of all (almost all?) contemporary functionalisms: that functional characterizations of mental states put next to no restrictions on the sorts of individuals that can have these states. Thus he is trying to make accessible just the point I have belabored in more traditional terms.

678. Given (676.K11), it is understandable that Sellars thinks it literally correct to say that one form of the "transcendental unity of apperception" is

an *unrestricted* principle in the philosophy of mind, which transcends the distinction between the noumenal and phenomenal self, to the effect that

an I thinks of a manifold

is not to be confused with

an I has a manifold of thoughts.

Thus an I thinking that Socrates is wise is not to be confused with the "coexistence" in the I of a thought of Socrates and a thought of wisdom. Nor, for that matter, a thinking that p and q with a thinking that p and a thinking that q. (*I*, 7)

(d) A suggestion for Kant concerning the temporal

679. Of course, the soul in itself represents itself empirically in the only way, according to Kant, that it can: namely, in time and at least indirectly in space (because of the spatial perspective of the perceiver). So, as represent*eds* both the thinkings of the phenomenal self and the sensory states of the phenomenal self are in time (and indirectly in space). But if part of the concepts of thinking and sensa-

---

[231] Another reason that it might mislead is that Sellars, as I shall shortly show, is not a "functionalist" in the presently dominant meaning of this term.

tion is occurrence in literal time, then we cannot use them to characterize the noumenal self (660-6). Kant, impressed by this very point (and with certain of his opponents in the forefront of his mind), says as much about thinking (A379-80).[232] In one way, there is no real problem: we can simply adopt other terms, 'noumenal representings' and 'noumenal states of sensibility', with the stipulation that the states ascribed by that terminology are not literally spatiotemporal. It's another case where a pure-pure category is at issue: the category of property ("modification"). In contrast, properties which are thoughts or sensations belong to sub-categories of the schematized category of property. But more needs to be said.

680. I start with sensibility. My subsection title is put in terms of a "suggestion" because the relevant questions have uninformative answers. Should the Sellarsian aesthetic, as it is, be placed within an *unamended* Kantian scheme as a doctrine of the self in itself? Or, as a doctrine of the empirical self? The answer is, as Sellars himself insists, nowhere (see the quote from *SM* in paragraph 626). After all, Sellars' point is that Kant does not draw the requisite distinctions and fails to see the possibilities of analogy except in theological contexts (*SM*, I, 77).[233] The question must be addressed to its place in a "reformulated" Kantian doctrine, the doctrine to which I previously addressed myself (635-56).

681. I'll try again and, in the process, introduce a qualification. It's not impossible that a philosopher find attractive parts of another philosopher's view without even conceiving, much less accepting, the whole view. Sellars believes that Kant should consider the benefits of S-(spatiotemporality) even though he might not care for all the Sellarsian trappings, particularly those pertaining to the manifest image.

682. Sellars' suggestion is that Kant should treat S-(spatiotemporality) as a feature of noumenal states of sensibility. By doing so, Kant would be able to maintain that these noumenal states had *some sort* of relational structure which contributes to their guiding conceptualization. Perhaps Sellars thinks that Kant was on the verge of just such a doctrine (*KPT*, ch. 15). After all, Kant says that things in themselves conform to their own laws and might have an order that is not literally spatiotemporal ("a duration which is not a time") (80-4).

683. In addition, by conceiving of image-models in the Kantian framework as

---

[232] That he does not repeat this remark in quite this way in the second edition may reflect his realization it has the construal I rejected in paragraph 661.

[233] A similar question put about Sellars' own position has too complicated an answer to give in this introduction. I offer two cautionary points. First, the aesthetic begins its life as a doctrine within the manifest image. Second, one distinction that Sellars draws between "appearances" (what, as the metaphor has it, exists "in thought") and the "in itself" (what really is) is, in crucial respects, different from Kant's. Third, the aesthetic is a piece of philosophical sophistication (a "theory" as Sellars likes to say) that is a part of an account of perceiving as an epistemic notion within "transcendental linguistics". Later, I shall show that Sellars thinks that Kant missed a philosophical opportunity of some importance in articulating the doctrine of representing within "transcendental psychology", an opportunity that Sellars does not overlook in his version of the Kantian program.

elements in a doctrine of the in itself, literal space and time can be confined to represent*eds*, i.e., appearances. Two exegetical birds are killed with one stone. First, transcendental reflection, a kind of philosophical sophistication about what is necessary for "there being such a thing as a public, intersubjective world of experience," enables us to come to philosophical knowledge about the structure of states of the noumenal sensibility, even though with our sensibility and understanding we have no way of filling in (making empirically "determinate") this knowledge.[234] Second, objections to the in itself as an unknowable "static", "unchanging" philosophical extra wheel are countered while not making any moves which impede maintaining a central Kantian thesis that space and time, and "everything in it", is appearance.[235]

684. What about states of the understanding as a faculty of the self in itself? Any noumenal representing, not having existence which is dependent upon being represented, is not, on Kant's account, literally in time. Sellars believes that the doctrine of the S-(temporality) of image-models (what he calls the "τ-dimension") should be extended to conceptual episodes (see *SM*, Appendix, II). For Sellars, thinkings partake in a mode of "retention" and "analogical temporality" which is responded to in literally temporal terms. (I remind the reader that, as before, this account is formulated, in the beginning, in the manifest image.)

685. Again, imagine a Kant who is attracted to this part of Sellars' view (without all the Sellarsian trappings). This Kant believes that noumenal representations, though not literally temporal, can participate in a structure which, like S-(temporality), involves both "successiveness" and "simultaneity". Thus, for example, though we represent the *thinking*

that black bear is coming at me

as both located in time and as being temporally extended ("taking some time", as the phrase has it), the conceptual parts of the noumenal representing, which is being responded to, can be "S-(simultaneous)" (earlier parts having been "retained"). We *respond* to this "noumenal simultaneity" with such representings of ourselves as

I am •that black bear is coming at me•ing now.
(i.e., I am now thinking that that black bear is coming at me),

---

[234] Remember I am assuming that Kant would not be thrilled by Sellars' views on the manifest image. For Sellars, there is no doubt that image-models are characterized "determinately".

[235] A third bird also falls: on Sellars' suggestion, the literally spatiotemporal is not there at all in image-models. Thus it would be impossible to "abstract" it from *them* under any suppositions about our access to image-models. Of course, it might be possible to "abstract" it from *representings* of image-models, but this would simply be another case of the sort of abstracting from the representings (in my strict sense) that I allowed earlier (645 and 654).

rather than with the sequence of representings

> I •that•ed a while back,
> I •black•ed after that,
> I •bear•ed after that,

and so on. Notice the importance of (676.K11): an explanation of the "τ-dimension" for noumenal representings requires that noumenal representings have the same representational classifications that thinkings (i.e., representings of the empirical self) have (cf. 262-5).

686. In one way, then, it should be no surprise that, on Sellars' view, we know an "awful lot" about the in itself. For a "one-worlder" (91) like Sellars, finding within Kant doctrines that elaborate themes belonging to the in itself is directly in accord with other parts of his interpretation. On the other hand, there can be no doubt that my return to questions about the in itself throws open various possibilities that I have not yet considered. One of these involves apperception and inner sense.

(II) APPERCEPTION AGAIN
(a) Perceiving the categorial
(α) What is perceptible for Kant?

687. To prepare for a point concerning apperception, I investigate what might be portrayed as an objection to the account of the categories as, at bottom, the forms of judging. I set out this objection in no great detail and without any great refinement; I hope bluntness gives it an appeal from which qualifications might detract:

> Our experience quite obviously includes the categories, particularly substance, property, negation, and causality. It is not merely that our descriptions of empirical objects can be fashioned in categorial terms, but we also perceive objects in categorial terms as the example of the accident (295ff) bears out. By contrast, the forms of judging are logical forms utilized by the understanding in its reflection on judgings and other representings. Logical form is not something that is perceptible and we do not perceive the world in terms of logical form.

So goes the objection. Note that this objection concerns the question of whether anything similar to logical form could be perceptible, *not* whether perceptual takings and perceptual judgings *have* logical form (cf. *BD*, 76-8).

688. It treads on dangerous ground within a Kantian preserve. Clarifying Kant's views on what is perceptible, and what is not, is not all that easy. Kant's official view is that space and time are not perceptible.²³⁶ Time particularly is singled out in the Analogies, but in *MFNS* (481-2, 559-60), it's space. Kant carefully qualifies these remarks by adding "by themselves", "by itself", or, "absolute". In the passages from *MFNS*, "absolute", "pure", "nonempirical" are the qualifications that contrast with spaces that are "material".

689. The history of the word 'absolute', especially in the debates between Leibniz and the Newtonians, might mislead. I see no reason to treat the occurrence of this term as showing that Kant has some space and time in mind different from those two "pure" items of the Aesthetic. First, Kant claims there is only one time and one space.²³⁷ Second, the contrast he wishes to mark is that between the "pure" space (and time) and, as he says in *MFNS* (480-1), the "material" spaces. These material spaces are indicated in the only way possible which is by "material bodies".²³⁸

690. This last point is reinforced by noting that, for Kant, points and other parts of space and moments and durations of time are delimited items in the one space and the one time. A particular space can be the space of some body; a line, or a point, a "termination" of a body, where the body is "not" (A25/B39; A32/B47-8). So, in the example of the accident (295ff), a particular space is

the space of the black van,
the space of the red sedan,

and so on. These "material" spaces are as "movable" as the extended beings which make the spaces "material".

691. Exactly the same is true of time. At B156²³⁹ (a passage that prefigures part of the Refutation of Idealism), Kant says that we must determine moments and periods of time by changes that occur to extended bodies in space, i.e., material bodies. Without all the needed qualifications, the upshot is that moments of time and durations are such items as

the moment at which the black van struck the rear of the red sedan,
the period of time in which the red sedan crossed in front of the van,

---

²³⁶ He says this at B207. The point about time alone is repeated regularly (B219; B225; A183/B226; B233; A200/B245; B257; A215/B262). Both space and time are said in *OP* not to be objects of perception; see, e.g., 22:434, 22:435, and 22:436. However, that space (and presumably time) are, in one sense, "perceivable" conforms to Kant's characterization of one sort of space as "material" (*MFNS*, 559; compare *MFNS*, 481, 554-6).
²³⁷ See A25/B39, A110, A188/B232. In *OP*, this is a much repeated claim; see, e.g., 21:224, 21:227, 22:554 note, 22:495, and 22:514.
²³⁸ In *OP*, he puts this point very bluntly by saying that it is matter that makes space a "sensible" object ("an object of the senses"), i.e., a perceptible object. Without matter, space would be a mere "form", an "intelligible" object (only an "idea"), not a "sensible" object. See, for starters, 22:475, 22:507, 22:508, 22:514 (where he mentions *MFNS*), and 22:535.
²³⁹ See also B277-8 and A292/B349.

and so on. Sellars argues (*KPT*, ch. 16) that it is this doctrine about time that is incorporated into the larger framework of a structural "analogy" between time and primarily the causal structure of substances, events and processes. The "Analogies" are so-called, Sellars argues, because they connect the structure of changes to substances with the structure of time and thus insure that the one imperceptible time can be accessible to us through extended beings. (Cf. *KTE*, 37, #7.)

692. *CPR* has many other passages supporting such an account of the difference between "intelligible" space and time on the one hand and "sensible" space and time on the other. First, space and time are all classified by Kant as "forms". At the end of the Amphiboly (A290-2/B346-9), there is a table of "nothing" with accompanying commentary. The items mentioned in the table are not literally "nothing", but they are "no things". The two most important "no things" are "pure" space and "pure" time; these are indeed "something", but they are not objects, "things". As "forms", none of these "no things" are capable, *by themselves*, of being perceived. To be perceptible, these "forms" depend on what they are forms of.

693. Second, Kant's scientific commitments convince him that our senses are "affected" only by motion.[240] Now, forms are hardly the sort of item that seem capable of motion *by themselves*. What moves are extended bodies.

694. I think that Kant takes these points about space and time to apply to anything that is a "form" including the forms of judging. It is noteworthy that, in the passage at the end of the Amphiboly (A290-2/B346-9), Kant mentions negation in the same breath with space and time. The conclusion I draw is that Kant is willing to talk about "perceiving" in a tough sense such that "forms" are not perceptible. I do not conclude that Kant believes that there is no sense of 'perceive' in which space, time and, the forms of judging are perceived. Whatever is true of the "tough" sense of 'perceive', it must also be true (in presumably a related sense of 'perceive') that in perceiving "material spaces", extended bodies and the changes and processes they participate in ("a ship floating downstream"), we do perceive space, time and, I will argue, the forms of judging.[241] Therefore, I turn my attention to showing that on the account of perceiving constructed within the Sellarsian aesthetic, the perceiving of "forms", and, in fact, many other items, is not a problem.

---

[240] He says this in so many words at *MFNS*, 476. This claim may be, for Kant, a simple corollary of the more general claim that matter is changed only by motion (*MFNS*, 524 and especially 543-4).

[241] A more complete discussion would consider stronger theses. For example, one of Kant's remarks at (A292/B349) suggests the thesis that perceiving extended beings is in some way a necessary condition of our representing space. Note the similar remark about time at the end of B277 (and compare B156).

(β) *Back to "perceiving as"*

695. Neither Sellars nor I see any compelling reason to attribute to Kant the kind of account of perceiving that has been part of many of what I have called "phenomenalistic" views (though we admit that such an interpretation is possible and that Kant sometimes displays a recessive inclination toward them). I have been particularly anxious to reject (159-62) principles which require that the perceiving of spatiotemporal objects be a result of being "aware of" sensory states and from thence proceeding by some form of "reasoning process" to judgings about spatiotemporal objects.

696. In the same vein, I reject, on Kant's behalf, any principle which requires that, *in general*, perceivings are restricted to containing representings of some limited group of properties, such as the sensible qualities of spatiotemporal objects. I have already rejected such principles on Sellars' and my own behalf. Let me quote what I said about "seeing *as*" as compared with "seeing *of*":

> 403. Sellars believes that examples can convince us that what we see *of* objects is limited. We do not see *of* objects
>
> > their kind;
> > their causal (e.g., dispositional) properties;
> > their functional properties;
> > some of their relational properties; and
> > even some of their sensible properties.
>
> By contrast, we can see objects *as*
>
> > dogs, bushes, bears, and wine;
> > toxic, brittle, and soluble in water;
> > doorstops, hammers, harpoons, and wine vats;
> > too heavy to lift, aunts, and orbiting the earth; and
> > scratchy, fragrant, sweet, bitter, and hot.
>
> Seeing *of* is also limited in another way. We do not see *of* an opaque object its inside, its back side, or indeed any side that is not (perhaps, at an angle) facing us or that is obscured by something else whereas we do see books *as* having back sides, insides, and so on.
>
> 404. To find familiar and comfortable examples to shed light on the question "Do we see *of* objects their logical and categorial features?" is not so easy. That we see objects *as* not moving in a straight line, *as* denting something, *as* a sibling (sister or brother), *as* individuals and so on is appealing.

Let me take an example of seeing *as* that illustrates the point at issue.

697. Right in front of you in clear daylight, Jones repays Smith the fifty dollars he owes Smith. Given the exact circumstances and your frame of mind, any one of a vast variety of perceptual takings might have occurred to you. Let me select a few:

> this fifty dollar bill,
> this person holding a fifty dollar bill,
> this person, Jones, handing a fifty dollar bill to Smith,
> this fifty dollar bill being handed to Smith by Jones,
> this person, Jones, repaying his debt to Smith,

and so on. Well, you see something *as* a fifty dollar bill, something *as* a person holding a fifty dollar bill, Jones *as* a person handing a fifty dollar bill to Smith, something *as* fifty dollar bill being handed to Smith by Jones, or something *as* a person, Jones, repaying a debt to Smith. What items can be perceived *as* depends on what the productive imagination packs into the representing of the *this-such* which is the perceptual taking (487-513). Further, that a philosopher can see something *as* a substance, *as* a property, *as* a change, and so on is just as possible on the account of perceiving of part **IV**. "Shoes and ships and sealing wax, cabbages and kings", as the represent*eds* of perceptual takings, are all perceptible items as well as their spatiotemporal properties, categorial (logical) features, moral and legal features, and so on.

698. Note, too, that there is even a wider sense of "perceiving *as*". Let me call this the "enlarged *as*". In the example, you saw something *as* a fifty dollar bill. Fifty dollar bills are legal tender. So, you, and others, may report that you saw something (enlarged) *as* legal tender. You saw someone *as* repaying a debt. When asked, you say that you saw someone (enlarged) *as* doing what he or she ought to do. After all, repaying a debt is a case of doing what ought to be done. Other sorts of enlargement can occur. Handing a fifty dollar bill over requires motion, a change in place of the fifty dollar bill. Motion, as change, involves negation ("was there, but is not there now, and is here"). Thus, you can lay claim to having seen something (enlarged) *as* having been over there and not being there now. The difference between the enlarged and the unenlarged senses is that the unenlarged attributes to you a perceptual taking as an item in your history whereas the enlarged merely claims that

> a certain perceptual taking, given your conceptual status and repertoire and given that another perceptual taking *is* part of your history, *would correctly have been* part of your history.

I say 'correctly' because the phrase after the enlarged *as* is, roughly speaking, a consequence, given other truths, of the phrase after the unenlarged *as* (*as* a cow;

cows are animals; so, *as* an animal).

699. Resistance to this account of the "widely" perceptible can have a source I rejected in my discussion of the "given". It has, I think, seemed to some that natural objects really do "pass" something conceptual to perceivers in perception, something involving the nature and structure of those objects (323, 539-40). Views of this sort have regularly put limitations on what could be so passed: thus, sensible qualities might be said to passed, but not, say, moral or legal features. On the account of perception in the Sellarsian aesthetic, nothing is, in this sense, "passed" through the perceptual process.[242]

700. Let me repeat what I said about an Aristotelian line of thought:

> 548. ... The crux of those Aristotelian reflections is that items in the world cause, independently of our intellects, judgings, some of which are true. Nothing so direct happens according to the aesthetic: image-models are blind. The sensibility does not judge at all: no premisses, true or false, arise immediately and independently, from the action of the world on our sensibility. No information (in the "informed that" sense) arises merely from sensibility: not even so much as the representing of an individual. There is nothing on which to begin the "foundations" of empirical knowledge; there are no individuals, properties and relations on which to build a metaphysic of what there is. A curtain of genuine conceptual blindness falls.

In terms of my present crude formulation, nothing conceptual about the world is "passed" through the process of perception; the sensory part of perceiving is impervious to conceptual information, i.e., "information that" (567). (Of course, sensory activity and sensory changes are in the world and are causally connected to other items in the world.)

701. In Kantian terms, the creating by the productive imagination of representings of *this-suches* under the causal guidance of the sensibility is the creating of states of the self which have "content". These contents are identified by Kant and his predecessors (48ff) as represented items (in these examples, as intuiteds). Since Kant believes that he can show that such intuiteds *cannot* exist independently of thought, these intuiteds, with all their properties and features, exist "only in thought" and thus, derivatively, the intuiteds are created as well (323, 642).

---

[242] I am not denying that sensible qualities have a special place in the perceptual process. My remarks on "perceiving *of*" show otherwise. Second, the many connections of sensible qualities to the sensory qualities mark them off from other properties. Finally, in the manifest image, they are the very "stuff" of manifest objects (377).

(b) Apperceiving and the categorial
(α) apperception: purity, necessity, and spontaneity

702. Paragraphs 108 and 171-81 illustrate how difficult it is to pin Kant down on apperception and on the differences between apperception and inner sense. One could, I think, adequately defend one, or another, of many different partitions of our self-reflection into the province of inner sense ("empirical apperception") and the province of ("pure") apperception.[243] Not wishing to sort through all the possibilities and considerations, I intend to aim for a view which, though incomplete, is well enough elaborated that I can pursue the line I began in paragraphs 267-72.

703. Most widely conceived, apperception is the faculty of attributing to oneself states of the understanding or the sensibility. I shall attribute to "empirical apperception" a task that certainly is empirical by Kant's standards: namely, delivering representations of "sensations".[244] I take it that Kant is happy enough to identify sensations by their standard causes (e.g., a sensation "of" "green grass" (*CJ*, 224)).[245] For the moment, I drop the topic of states of sensibility and turn to attributing to oneself states of representing (in my strict sense).

704. A thinking is a representing in time; thinkings are thus examples of our schematized category of property (679). In apperceiving thinkings, we attribute to ourselves states that, for example, succeed one another in time. To use my earlier examples, we can imagine Dick apperceiving as follows:

> a moment ago: I think that I am back in camp. (i.e., I •I am back in camp•.)
> now: I think that I am now safe. (i.e., I •I am safe now•.)

705. Principle (676.K11) and the "transcendental doctrine of content" (638-41, 674-8) require that the temporal aspect of such attributions to the empirical self is carried by the temporal structure of the verb 'think', not by the "[content]" part of "thinks [content]".[246] Further, attributions of thinkings do not *by themselves require* that the empirical self have other *empirical* properties than temporal ones (674). So, we can agree with Kant (172) that such attributions reveal no determination of space (e.g., shape, place, motion), and thus nothing material, "within us". In one sense,

---

[243] The interested reader should look at Sellars (*I*, 42-67) and Rosenberg's *The Thinking Self*.
[244] Kant's remarks about inner sense in *CJ* suggest that he may have pondered this matter, but they are hardly conclusive (see *CJ*, 225, 228, 291, 226′).
[245] See paragraphs 591-2. On this issue, then, I am taking it that Kant shares an unreflected-upon commitment of RWK's (599-601).
[246] The Sellarsian version of these attributions involves tense because the dot-quoted terms are verbs (35). Note a principle that applies in both the Sellarsian version and the content formulation: the time involved in the verb 'thinks', or in the dot quotation, *need not*—notice "need not"—be the time involved *inside* the content or within the dot quotation.

then, apperceptive representings partake of "purity".²⁴⁷

706. One sort of "necessity" present in apperceivings is a kind of "non-arbitrariness" which results from the classifications made available by the principles of the transcendental logical doctrine of representing. To claim that a judging has a content which is an individual with a property is to classify that judging very generically. To claim that the content is a *this-such* which is a bear combined with a property is merely another classifying of the judging, a not so generic classifying. As Sellars emphasizes (*CLN*, **A20**ff), these classifications of the combinings found in representations are not "arbitrary" and not a consequence of the happenstances of history, but are non-arbitrary and intersubjective since they are a matter of the principles of ordinary logic and transcendental logic.

707. That "purity" and "necessity" are brought together can be seen in Kant's discussion of "empirical" laws (A126-8, B164-5, A159/B198). Kant tells us that these laws are "determinations" of the pure laws of the understanding.²⁴⁸ Empirical laws reside in a hierarchy of genera and species the apex of which is the category of causality (the "logical form", physical implication). So, to think an empirical law is to have a thought which is classifiable as having a content of the sort "example of the genus *principle of causality*". Similarly, to think of a bear is to have a thought which is classifiable as having a content of the sort "example of the genus of substance". All classifications of representations by content are classifications within the structure of the categories, i.e., the forms of judging.²⁴⁹ What apperceivings attribute to an "I" is always within a structure determined by the categories. (Other examples show up in my metaphysical and transcendental deductions .)

708. What, then, about "spontaneity"? In some passages (e.g., A445/B473ff., A533/B561 and A548/B576), Kant takes freedom to be a pristine example of spontaneity. But we should not conclude that examples of freedom in some strict sense are all that Kant has in mind by "spontaneity". In many passages, Kant emphasizes activity of the understanding which is "spontaneous" as contrasted with the causality involved in the receptivity of sensibility.²⁵⁰

709. We also know that at least some cases in which we judge about what we are thinking are cases in which causality is involved; that is, such judgings are cases in

---

²⁴⁷ These passages are partial payment on my promise to discuss Kant's remark that "pure apperception" involves "purity, necessity, and spontaneity" (198).

²⁴⁸ An interesting point, to which I shall return, is that this is true even though such laws must (usually? always?) be "learned" through "experience".

²⁴⁹ We may well need "experience" to be able to think such "determinations" of the categories. That does not show them to be "empirical". After all, we may need "experience" to be able to think the concepts of logic and mathematics (B1); that does not impugn their status as non-empirical.

²⁵⁰ See B153-9, especially the footnote to B158, where Kant also says that it is *"this"* spontaneity which is essential for treating ourselves as "intelligences". Compare with A546/B574 where, in speaking again of "inner determinations", Kant remarks that these cannot be thought of a result of the senses. (See also B68, A50-1/B74-5, and A97.) Finally, consult the interesting passage at B430-1 where he describes the possibility that there is "a spontaneity" that is different from that of the understanding.

which we inwardly affect ourselves (see particularly B153-6). This is one reason I maintained that apperceiving should not be thought of "introspection" since introspection is often understood as an active, intentional process like deliberate searching (173). So, I conclude that the spontaneity involved in apperceiving is not lack of causality, but lack of that causality that comes through the operation of the sensibility alone. The causality in some cases in which we judge about what we think is contributed by the activity of the understanding, not the sensibility as I have characterized the sensibility in this introduction (631-4).

710. These points suggest a distinction between a more, and a less, encompassing sense of 'apperceive'. Out of all the attributions of thinkings to the self, judgings which begin "I think" (or, "I represent"), no matter what their source, can be said, in the widest sense, to be apperceivings. But, in what follows, I shall limit the term 'apperceive' to such judgings as are brought about by "self-affection" where the occurrence which is the cause of the apperceiving is the representing that the apperceiving represents. Thus apperceivings have a similarity to perceivings in that they are representings which are "caused". (That, even though the apperceiving represents the representing as in time, this "causation" can be "noumenal causation" is a point which, for the moment, I reserve comment on.)

711. Since Sellars believes that Kant's account includes a commitment to the noumenal self as a representer (657-78), apperceivings in classifying thinkings by content *can* get something about the noumenal self right. On this view, transcendental psychology provides in such classifications an access to the in itself. Consonantly with Kant's view that the represent*ed* thinking is an "appearance", I sum this up in Kantian terms by saying that the represent*ed* thinking is "an appearance of" a noumenal representing.

(β) *representing the self as a thinker*

712. Suppose I represent myself as now

thinking that black bear is coming at me.

That is, my representing is that

(94) I am now thinking that that black bear is coming at me (i.e., I am •that black bear is coming at me•ing now).

According to transcendental psychology, so representing myself is representing myself as in a complex state, a "combining" (a "synthesizing") of a •that•, a •black•, a •bear•, and so on. I represent myself as complex just as when I think that black bear is coming at me,

I represent something as a bear and thus as complex.[251] In effect (676-8), I have claimed that this is true for both the noumenal self and the phenomenal self.

713. Since the state with the complex content ^that black bear is coming at me^ requires, by transcendental logic, "synthesizing" ("combining"), if (712.94) is true, then there are other things that must be true of me with regard to the content ^that black bear is coming at me^. As just one example, it must be true that

(95) in accordance with such-and-such rules, I combined such-and-such contents to produce the complex content ^that black bear is coming at me^.

Though I need to leave the topic of "rules" up in the air for the moment, one point is obvious: some of the rules I have in mind are (in a broad sense of 'logic') rules of logic such as those that specify what judgings are, what representings of *this-suches* are, and so on.

714. This also applies to that sub-class of representings of thinkings that are apperceivings. For (712.94) to be an apperceiving, the self causes itself to be in the state (712.94). This makes no difference to my claim about (713.95). The judging (712.94) *along with premisses from the transcendental logic* imply (713.95) or, more accurately, examples of (713.95) in which "such-and-such" has been filled in.

715. It does not follow from this that the synthesizings (and, indeed, the rules) mentioned in (713.95) are *apperceived* or, in fact, represented at all by the subject of (712.94). Not that it follows they are not apperceived (they are apperceptible (313-7)). Thus it is not ruled out that examples of synthesizing are apperceived—of course, not by representers who lack the appropriate concepts or, at least, not *adequately* by representers who lack the appropriate concepts.[252] But whichever is the case, what is formulated in (713.95) is, *within the confines of transcendental psychology*, a consequence of (712.94). So, if (712.94) is true, then (713.95) tells us something about what went on in the subject of (712.94).

---

[251] Note that here is a yet wider "enlarged *as*" (698). What has been dropped is the requirement that the representer's repertoire extends to the needed truths. In claiming that someone represents something as complex, I do not make any claims about the representer's ability to explicate that complexity by setting out the pertinent principles. For an earlier example, see 303.

[252] Out of all the needed qualifications, I confine myself to noting that my concern here is with apperceiving, not with the more general question of what a representer need believe in order to be a representer. Moreover, my discussion is meant not to trespass on the simple point that human beings can think, speak, write, whatever, without having any very sophisticated beliefs about those activities. This is part of what Sellars has in mind when, in a different context, he says (*CLN*, **B12**), "We must distinguish carefully between what is psychologically necessary in order for us to have *beliefs about* objects and events in nature and what is **necessary for** truth about nature and the classification of nature."

716. Compare a "strict" Cartesian (of which there may be no actual instances). A strict Cartesian, SC, takes the sentiment, expressed by Hume (19), seriously: "all actions and sensations of the mind are known to us by consciousness". Further, SC also takes it that "synthesizing" is an "act" of the mind. (Kant would agree: all "combining" in representations (in my strict sense) is supplied by the understanding.) Thus anything described by a true example of (713.95), should, according to SC, be apperceived by any attentive representer in a cool hour. The implausibility of this is not my concern. My concern is that though Kant holds that "combining" is an activity of the understanding, he does not hold that it is generally apperceived or, even, can be apperceived by some given their present conceptual status. (Compare Sellars' remarks on a related matter in ch. 14 of *KPT*.)

717. There seems to me no substantial reason not to employ the word 'represent' to cover all conceptual activity that contributes to the production of representations such as judgings. Thus all the activity of the understanding in "synthesizing" is representing (see the references on the understanding (119)). So, the following might very well be true:

> my understanding is representing in that it is combining such-and-such contents to produce the complex content ^that black bear is coming at me^ in accordance with such-and-such rules, the result of which is my representing that that black bear is coming at me and, even though I now apperceive my representing that that black bear is coming at me, I do not, and did not, apperceive anything involved in the process of combining.

In short, there can all sorts of conceptual activity which is not, to use Sellars' word, "noticed" (523).

718. All that said, apperceivings are, in one way, "direct": they occur through causal activity unmediated by the apperceiving (or, even, the representing) of other states of the subject. No processes of representing "simpler", or "more basic", items intervene to make an apperceiving occur (of course, there can be states of the apperceiver which interfere with the causal process). Further, apperceivings—being caused, but *not caused by representations* of any of the representational activity pertaining to apperceiving—cannot be the result of inference.

719. Moreover, I find no thesis like the following to be one Kant is compelled to adopt: because of all the processes required for the truth of an apperceiving, we really cannot trust any apperceiving to express even justified true belief, much less knowledge.[253] It is true that apperceivings lack that simplicity and independence of

---

[253] But I do not think that Kant ever had in mind "proving" that apperceivings express knowledge (or, justified true belief). This is one example of the general point that Sellars had in mind when he said that Kant is not trying to "prove that there is empirical knowledge" (*KTE*, 11, 38, 45).

other states hoped for by some of Kant's predecessors. Denying such simplicity and independence is another element in a view that abjures the "given" in all its forms.

720. I find lurking in the views of some of Kant's predecessors a conviction concerning our "access" to that part of the world which is ourselves. The image, appropriate to some views of perceiving, of something "passing" (699-700) through from the world, though crude, is, in the case of ourselves, not crude enough. The metaphor appropriate to our own selves seems to have been that, since we are, as it were, "there" to ourselves, we can simply reach and "grab" what is really there. Such a metaphor enshrines something that Sellars would class as part of some forms of the myth of the given.

721. Nothing of the sort is part of the Kantian account as I have described it. Another indication of just how different the Kantian view is can be obtained from reflecting on a point which would be anathema to at least some of Kant's predecessors. In general, apperceivings, even in cases where they are true, can be like perceivings in being incomplete, or inadequate, in their characterization of the world. I elaborate on this theme in the next subsection.

(γ) *representing the self as a perceiver*

722. That we sometimes *represent* ourselves as perceivers, that is, we have such thoughts as

(96) I see (perceive) that that black bear is coming at me,

is clear enough. From here, the progression of considerations matches that of the previous subsection.

723. According to part **IV**, being a perceiver adds to the conceptual complexity of thinking the complexity of processes involving image-models. I characterized seeing (579) (in the achievement sense and adjusted to the visual case) in (P3) of

(579.P1) having image-models (sensory states and image-models proper) (541.Ea and 541.Eb),

(579.P2) ostensibly perceiving:
(P2.a) perceptually taking (541.Ea, 541.Eb, and 541.Ec)
(P2.b) perceptually judging (541.Ea, 541.Eb, 541.Ec, and 541.Ed), and

(579.P3) perceiving: ostensible perceiving with achievement (adjusted to take care of the (P2.a) and (P2.b)).

724. The references to paragraph 541 are to the processes that lead to perceptual takings and judgings. These I reviewed in paragraph 634 where I reproduced, from part **IV**, examples of principles pertaining to image-models. I remind the reader that I am working through some of Kant's doctrines under the assumption that he is willing to give S-(spatiotemporality) a place in the operations of the noumenal self. Nevertheless, much of what I have to say in this subsection is independent of whether we consider the sensory processes from the vantage of the Sellarsian aesthetic or from that of the "vulgar" (583-94).

725. If, as in Dick's case, the judging (722.96) is false due to failure of achievement, one is still attributing to oneself an ostensible perceiving (with the qualification that principles concerning abnormality take over). Even if I am merely ostensibly seeing, I have "synthesized" according to rules, not only a judging, but also the subject of that judging, i.e., a representing of a *this-such*. In addition, the perceptual judging is brought about by a complicated process involving image-models, i.e., augmented sensory states.[254] So, I have progressed through rather complicated activities orchestrated by the sensibility and the understanding together. My understanding has utilized rules, e.g., the "schema" associated with a (complex) concept of a spatiotemporal-object-in-relation-to-a-perceiver. Therefore, even the weaker claim, *within the context of transcendental psychology*,

(97) I ostensibly see (perceive) that that black bear is coming at me,

implies that I have undergone quite complex processes (exactly which ones depend on the circumstances). Once again, none of the *conceptual* activity need even be represented, much less apperceived, by me.

726. Do we sometimes *apperceive* ourselves as perceivers? That is, are we sometimes caused by the process of perceiving to represent as in (723.96) or (725.97)? My view is that the Kantian answer is "yes." Despite the complexity of what such judgings imply, I find no reason to hold that we must, or always, infer such things as (723.96) and (725.97). This affirmative answer requires an extension of term 'apperceive' to cover judgings which accomplish two things: attributing a representing to the subject and implying activity of the subject's sensibility. Put another way, the apperceivings of perceiving, *with the aid of principles of the aesthetic*, imply that some empirical apperceivings would be true.

727. Apperceivings are a sub-class of representings of the self as thinking. So, image-models, or, in the vulgar, "sensations", cannot be apperceived in this sense.

---

[254] By the way, Sellars is willing to agree (*IKTE*, 51) that Kant uses the word 'synthesize' for activities which, on Sellars' account, are the augmenting of sensory states in perceiving and in imagining (see 730). The only reason I don't talk about "conceptual synthesis" versus "sensory synthesis" is that I am concerned to make the terminology for the conceptual different from that for the sensory. As I have hewed to my strict sense of 'represent', so I have restricted 'synthesize' and 'combine' in the same way.

Introduction   255

They are not within the 'I think'. They can, however, be "empirically apperceived" (703). Thus Dick can be caused to think (in the vulgar)

(98) I am having a sensation of a black bear.

728. However, as with the case of the conceptual activity in perceiving (725), it need not be that I empirically apperceive, or even represent, any of the sensory states involved in ostensible perceiving. Judging (725.97) implies that sensory activity of a certain sort has taken place and, without doubt, the total state to which I am *responding* with (725.97) includes that sensory activity. Nonetheless, I need not empirically apperceive any of the sensory activity.

729. On the other hand, as I said before about (pure) apperceiving (715), it is not part of my account that such conceptual activities and such sensory activities cannot be, respectively, apperceived and empirically apperceived. Here is one kind of case in which it can happen.

730. Sellars holds that imagining (467) employs the same resources as perceiving but under the control of the subject. Sellars considers an example in which someone is imaginatively "constructing" a triangle (*CLN*, **A32d-[A35.] & B6**). Sellars illustrates this sort of case "pictorially", because in addition to the "synthesizing" of representings of lines required by the (rule for) the concept of a triangle, there is the constructing of the image-model of a triangle. Imagining, like perceiving, is from a point of view: e.g., "face on". The productive imagination of the subject follows the schema of the concept of a triangle-face-on-to-perceiver and assembles an image-model of a triangle facing the subject. In these cases, it seems reasonable to hold that much of the conceptual process is apperceived and much of the sensory process is empirically apperceived.

731. Whatever the full story of such cases of imagining, they do not show that we must apperceive or empirically apperceive the processes implied by apperceiving ourselves as perceiving. I sum up a central point of this account as follows:

(K12) (a) Both perceivings and apperceivings are "direct" in that the representings which occur in perceivings and apperceiving are brought about by (complex) processes that have no part which is inference.

(b) No perceiving (or, ostensible perceiving) or apperceiving need be accompanied by any representings of the conceptual or sensory processes involved in perceiving or apperceiving.

(c) Despite (a) and (b), the judgings which formulate the apperceivings of ourselves as thinkers and perceivers (successful or ostensible) imply that processes such as synthesizing judgings and constructing image-models have taken place.

732. The second major point of this subsection is that, with the principles of transcendental psychology (including the Sellarsian aesthetic), the judging made in apperceiving oneself as perceiving implies that the phenomenal self has categorial structure and is part of nature (301-7). Our representings of the activities of the sensibility and of the understanding in being "affected" by and "affecting" the sensibility involve natural laws. Any phenomenal self as perceiver is a subject of changes (loss and gain of properties) and it persists through these changes in ways specified by natural laws.[255]

733. If the circumstances are suitable, Dick is a normal perceiver and in an appropriate frame of mind, the conditions are normal, and there is a black bear coming at Dick, then Dick changes in various ways, the final upshot of which is that Dick judges

>that black bear is coming at me

and if further conditions obtain, also judges

>I see that that black bear is coming at me.

The same two judgings can be brought about if there is no black bear, but then the circumstances are not suitable, or Dick, or the conditions, are not normal. In such cases, Dick only ostensibly perceives that a black bear is coming at him; that is, it merely appears to Dick that a black bear is coming at him.

734. In the case in which Dick makes a perceptual error (575), nothing apperceptible by Dick at that time need settle that it is a case of his making an error. Neither the (pure) apperceiving of his thinking nor the empirical apperceiving of his sensory states in the error case *need be* any different from that which would occur in the case in which there is a bear coming at him. Yet, because perceivers are natural beings in space and time, the natural laws that apply in perceptual situations guarantee one sort of pertinent "intersubjectivity".

735. Jane, another being of (approximately) the same understanding and sensibility in (approximately) the same place at the same time, saw no bear. Sis, a being

---

[255] It cannot be different "I"s that are the subjects of the various states. If that were so, then there would be no single self to be a perceiver. It is the same problem that occurs if one thinker •that•s, another thinker •black•s, another thinker •bear•s, and so on; there is no thinker who •that black bear is coming at me•s. Compare Sellars' remark on the transcendental unity of apperception (678). A point Sellars explicates in the case of the noumenal self also applies in the case of the phenomenal self: a self can be a series, a composite or some kind of plurality, but it cannot be a series, composite, or plurality of "I"s (*MP*, 51-55). It is true that the possibility Kant considers at A363 requires a series of "I"s, each of which bequeaths all its activity to its successor. It is, however, only the last one in the series that can be said to think a complete thought or to have perceived; about that one, what I have said is correct.

with a sensibility having similarities to ours, smelled no bear. For Kant, natural laws are universal. Even admitting that the philosophers of his period might be too optimistic on this topic, we can still appreciate that Jane's and Sis's causal response to the circumstance is relevant to whether Dick is in error. This relevance is not "social" in the sense of emanating, in some way, from social acts which confer obligations. Our representing of a thinking as an element in a perceiving implies that it occurs in processes governed by natural law, and thus has a claim to an "objectivity" arising from "necessary universal validity" (322). As Kant puts it (*PFM*, 299), in certain circumstances, what any one of us is taught by nature, every one of us must, in those circumstances, be taught.

736. The necessity arises from the non-arbitrariness of natural law. The perceptual process is through and through as universal and as general as any other natural process (however much that might be). That there are variations in individuals of any kind can be admitted. Dick's error is one that, according to Kant, is as subject to natural laws as his successes (582). We may not be in a position to state all the laws that apply, but they are, in principle, available. That the laws are very complicated is clear from the Sellarsian account in that the understanding (as the productive imagination) is involved in the perceptual process, not just the sensibility. The conditions required to formulate adequately the relevant laws might well, indeed, does, outrun our present grasp of cognitive processes. Thus, in most cases, we must balance Dick's perceptual judgings against those of Jane and Sis.

C. Transcendental Idealism again
(I) DOUBLE AFFECTION AND TRANSCENDENTAL APPEARING
(a) "simple correlatives" (KPT, ch. 10, 8)

737. My account of apperceiving thinkings and perceivings involves *something similar* to what is usually thought of as "double affection". Take perceiving as an example. The sensibility comes to be in noumenal states (on Sellars' suggestion, states that are S-(spatiotemporal)) and, as a result, "affects" the understanding. The understanding acting as the productive imagination initiates cognitive processes, including that of "affecting" the sensibility. The result of all this noumenal causal (pure-pure category) activity is a noumenal representing (though, of course, a representing *of* the phenomenal, not *of* the noumenal).

738. Our understandings work in a certain way. We represent whatever of the perceptual process we happen to represent on any given occasion in literal space and time, and thus as appearances. Our (vulgar) empirical apperceivings of "sensations" as modifications of our spatiotemporal selves characterize these "sensations" in terms of their standard, literally spatiotemporal causes. Our (pure) apperceivings place thinkings in time (and indirectly in space). The characterization of perceiving as a process in the spatiotemporal world of appearances implies that thinkings, as elements of the perceptual process, are caused, depending on the circumstances, by one or another of appearances (including, in certain cases, our own central nervous system as affected by our gastrointestinal tract and circulatory system).

739. As appearances, the sensory and conceptual occurrences involved in perceiving are given a causal account in terms of the schematized category of causality. By contrast, what is *"really* going on", as Sellars puts (*KPT*, ch. 17, 31), is the activity among noumenal objects and our only characterizations of these are supplied by transcendental philosophy and formulated by us in terms of the pure-pure categories. The two accounts are counterparts, but only the noumenal one, unknown to us in any determinate form, is an account of what is "really going on".

740. The notion of transcendental "appearing" flows from this account of double affection. The activity of the noumenal non-self on the noumenal self and of the noumenal self on itself causes the noumenal self to produce representings of a spatiotemporal objects, "appearances". There is a correspondence (transcendental appearing) between, for example, such spatiotemporal items as a house, myself as perceiver, and the causal activity of the house in changing me as perceiver and *something or other* in the in itself. Though we cannot say what the *something or other* is, we can be assured by transcendental philosophy that we are representing in accord with the principles of our understanding and sensibility in response to the non-temporal non-spatial "affection" of the in itself. In short, we are doing the best we can, with the conceptual and sensory equipment we have, to produce representings of the in itself. It is just that the best we can do is to represent appearances, items in space and time, whose only existence is that of "existence in thought" (cf. A551/B579, A556-7/B584-5.)[256]

741. These points are clearly contained in Sellars' comments in chapter 17 of *KPT*. I reproduce several paragraphs with attendant figures.[257]

> 29. When we experience states of the empirical self and we are particularly concerned here with the *perceptual* states of the empirical self, we think of them as caused. What I am doing is spelling out what I was saying last time. We think of our perceptions in the sense of *perceptual* states as being brought about by the material world of which our body is a part. Here (Figure 7) is my body. You

---

[256] There is, in Sellars' own view, a rough-and-ready analog of this point. Consider the following: those ignorant of "natural philosophy" exist in an enormously complex world of particles, fields, and so on, but with their present conceptual and sensory equipment they represent objects of the manifest image. That some version of this is correct is the burden of a great number of Sellars' papers and also of chapters of *SM* after I and II.

[257] I have omitted Amaral's notes. My figure numbers are not the same as those in *KPT* and this discrepancy has been adjusted in the captions. We owe these figures and Sellars' accompanying discussion to a question by Amaral. Sellars' answer merely elaborates, with the addition of figures, Sellars' established view of double affection and transcendental appearing.

see, here is my body and here is a book and I am looking at a book. Why do I have these perceptual states? Because I am confronted by a book, a tough book, and it is having an impact on me.

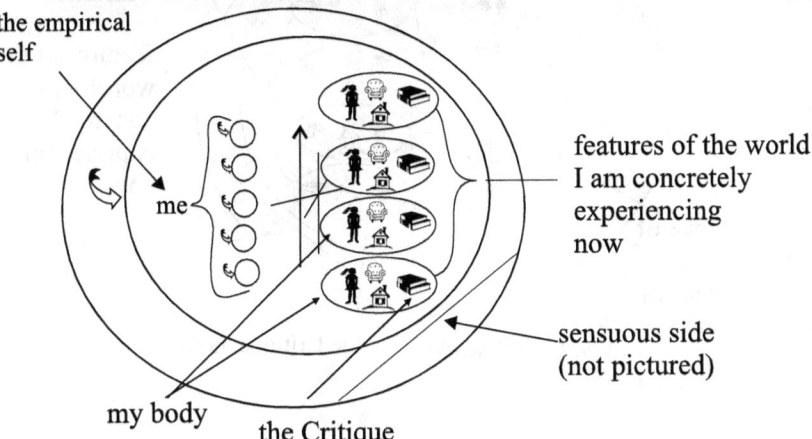

Figure 3=Figure 7

So here is the sense in which one's perceptual states are, in the phenomenal world, caused by material things acting on my eye generating the buzzings in the brain and generating perceptual states. That is what we are going to call the empirical level of affection (Figure 8).

260 *Introduction*

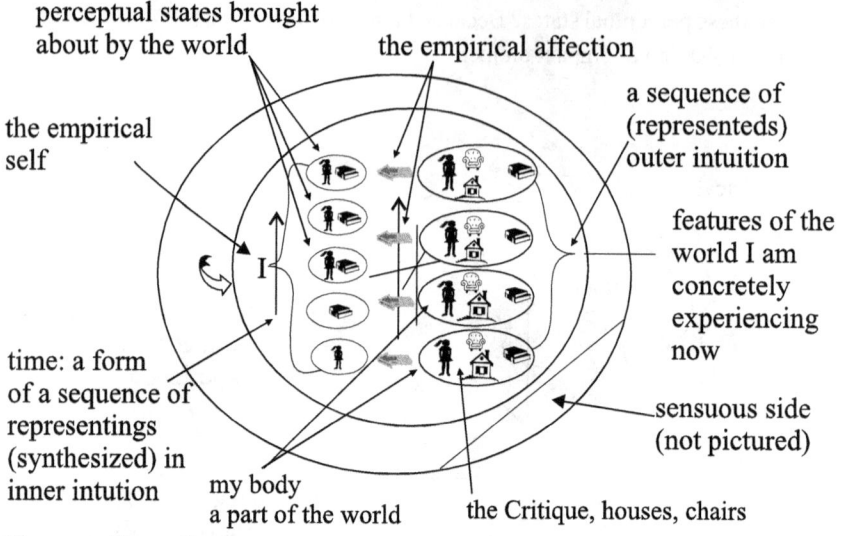

Figure 4=Figure 8

F. Double affection: the in itself

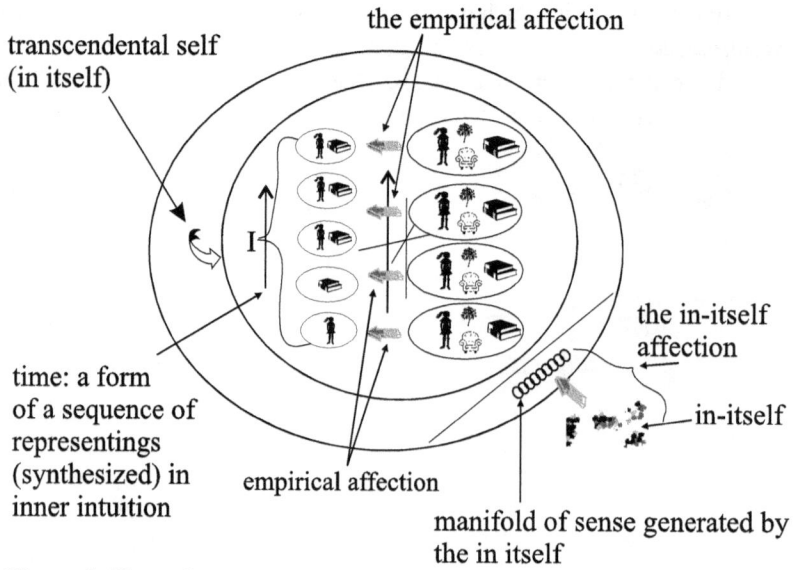

Figure 5=Figure 9

Introduction 261

30. Of course, all this structure has been inspired, as it were, by the presence of the manifold of sense that is generated by the in itself. And there (Figure 9) we have, in the pure-pure category sense, the in itself as the *cause* of the manifold of sense. And that we can call the other level in which there is an affection of the mind in experience.

31.   This is an "in itself" kind of affection. I mean, this is what is *really* going on: namely,

> a non-spatial, non-temporal in itself is non-spatially and non-temporally impinging on my faculty of sensibility which is itself non-spatial and non-temporal and is generating in it a manifold to which I am responding by constructing a spatial and temporal world.

This is what is meant by the doctrine of double affection. Here (Figure 10) is the, as it were, *in itself* action.

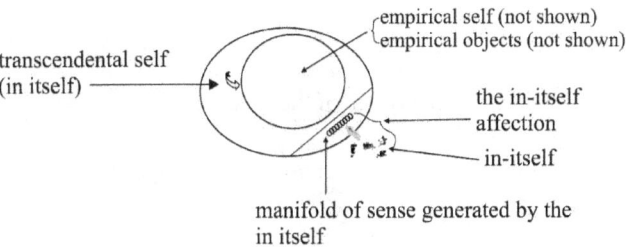

Figure 6=Figure 10

32. And here (Figure 11) is the empirical action.

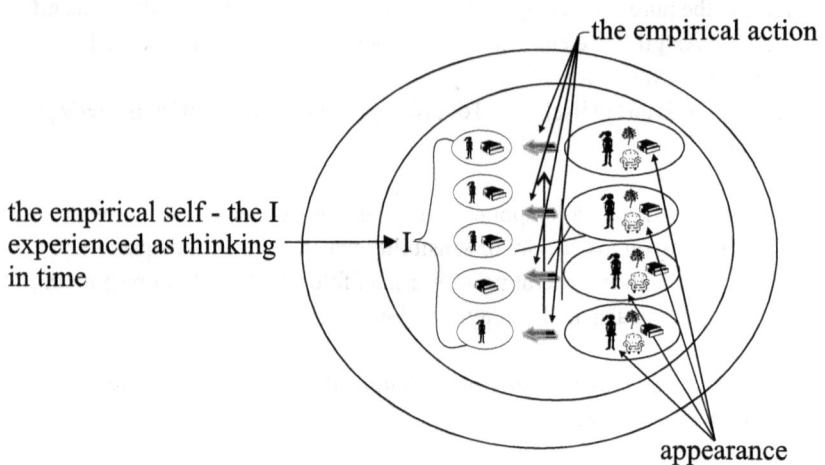

Figure 7=Figure 11

33. The one could be the *appearance* of the other. In other words,

> this sort of relationship between material things in space and time and my empirical self

is

> the way in which, to my mind with its faculties, this kind of action, the action of the in itself on my faculty of sensibility, appears.

So, as I would like to put it, the *empirical* action of material things, on our body and on our mind, is the appearance of a real in itself relationship of impingement by the in itself on my faculty of sensibility.

34. As I said in *Some Remarks on Kant's Theory of Experience*, Kant is in a position to grant that empirical knowledge involves a uniformity of conceptual response to extra conceptual items and even to grant that extra conceptual items conform to general laws, without granting that the character of the items to which we conceptually respond, or the laws to which God knows them to conform, are accessible to finite minds.

35. This idea is implicit in the transcendental principle of the affinity of the manifold of sense and finds its explicit formulation in B164 where Kant, in a little noted passage, wrote that

Things in themselves would necessarily [that is, as a necessary truth of transcendental logic, ws] apart from any understanding that knows them, conform to laws of their own.

We are led to think of the Newtonian framework of the world as we experience it as a projection of a system of laws to which things in themselves conform and which are known only to God. (*KPT*, ch. 17, 29-35)

(b) Why not?

742. As explained, "double affection" and transcendental appearing are quite natural consequences for someone like Sellars who, as I have said, holds a "one-world" view of a certain sort (91, 686). I believe that much more can be said to elaborate Sellars' account, but I also believe that this is not much to the point. If previous commentary on Kant is any guide, the point would seem to be that many philosophers have found it difficult to accept any such account no matter how well elaborated. I, therefore, turn briefly to observations which, I hope, bear on some of the difficulties philosophers have had.

743. One source of difficulty may be the rarity with which it is said that something much like "double affection" and something much like "transcendental appearing" is part of many philosophical positions since Descartes. Let me take Leibniz as an example.[258]

744. Leibniz has the belief, to which Kant objects, that he can tell us the nature of mind-independent existence. Leibniz holds that the in itself, i.e., that which exits independently of representing by mind, is monads, "simple subjects" capable of representing (A266/B322). Leibniz's view is a thus a form of idealism according to one of Kant's characterizations of "idealism" (*PFM*, 288-9): the in itself is nothing but thinking beings (of various grades).

745. We, as Kant says (*PFM*, 289), believe that we perceive all sorts of spatial objects which, on Leibniz's account, simply do not exist. Space and spatial objects show up only as represented objects in the thoughts of some monads. These spatial relations are "bene fundata" in that to represented spatial arrangements there "correspond" relations of representings among monads.[259] But there is even more.

746. Imagine that, at dinner, the conversation between you and Leibniz turned to winemaking. Being generally knowledgeable, Leibniz is able to converse on the finer points of the winemaker's art and even to speculate on some rather recondite matters about fermentation, a causal process only rudimentarily understood at the

---

[258] I use Leibniz since Sellars fills in many details of Leibniz's position that I presuppose, but do not take up here. See *ML* (57) in *PPHP* and *KPT*, Appendix, Leibniz.
[259] See *KPT*, Appendix, Leibniz for an illustration of one example of this "correspondence".

time. Suddenly turning the conversation in a more philosophical direction, you observe that since wine and all the appurtenances of the winemaker's trade are spatial items, none of what we normally believe about these items can be true and speculation about which additional principles might belong in the winemaker's art is just the articulation of falsehood. Here, I think Leibniz would maintain that it is more complicated than that.

747. Yes, he would say, no spatial items exist as we represent them: i.e., independently of thinking beings. Yet this kind of inadequacy, or falsehood, in our everyday thoughts is built into the sort of being we are. Those of our "perceptions" of which we are aware do not represent monads as they are and our philosophical reflection is unable to engage the world as it is except in very general terms. Yet, Leibniz would insist that his philosophy shows that in separating out, as we normally do, the true from the false in, say, winemaking, we are *indirectly* finding out about monads. To the changes caused in spatial items correspond alterations of a quite different sort in monads, alterations whose causal basis is in the choice of this best of all possible worlds by the creator.

748. *In broad outline*, this view is not very different from Kant's. A philosophical view that will involve something like double affection and something like transcendental appearing has, if I may so put it, a basic formula. On the one hand, maintain that the world is really not at all as we usually conceive it to be or perceive it to be and consequently that the objects we treat of in our "ordinary" life do not really exist. (It is has been historically popular to exclude certain items, such as thinking beings, from this general censure.) On the other hand, be unwilling, for one reason or another, to discover nothing in our ordinary intellectual history but confusion and falsehood. Therefore, attribute the gulf between our common understanding of the world and that philosophical glimpse of what is real to our present, or permanent, conceptual and perceptual apparatus. At best, then, our conceptual and perceptual endowment as the sort of beings we (presently or permanently) are filters our grasp of what really is (and its causal processes) through that endowment, leaving us, philosophically speaking, with a story of causal process and objects which are not part of what is "really going on". Philosophy (like the experts most ordinary computer users believe) assures you that to the causal history of objects you generate (like the changing shapes and colors on the computer screen) there corresponds a causal history that is quite different (like the electrical activity of the computer).

749. A second source of difficulty may arise from the very point just mentioned: namely, that the causal history of appearances is different from the (for Kant, to us inaccessible) causal history of the in itself. If an inchoate worry about this point is combined with a mechanical view of causality, it is easy to heighten the discomfort. Consider the gears within, as we say, some "mechanical" gadget. The tooth of one gear "pushes" upon the tooth of another; the second gear moves. It seems impossible to imagine another "pusher" in the process. How would the second pusher "get into the act" to cause the motion of the second gear? Isn't the first "pusher" already causing the motion of the second gear? Yes, two people can "push" an automobile, but then neither individually is the cause of the motion. This image of "mechanical causation" seems to lower a veil of incoherence over Kant's account.

750. Insight might be found in describing certain cases of causality as "mechanical" and in using the image of a "pusher". It is, however, an error, Sellars holds, to attempt to understand causality as "mechanism" simpliciter. According to the metaphysical deduction, the basis of the concept of causality is physical implication (85-90). So, Sellars starts out with an account which abjures the mechanical image.

751. Further, the inchoate worry may be enhanced by a "one-worldism" of the kind Sellars rejects (74ff, 91). To see how different Sellars' account is, consider, again, what Sellars says at the end of *KTE* and repeats in the quote from *KPT* (741):

> We are led to think of the Newtonian framework of the world as we experience it as a projection of a system of laws to which things in themselves conform and which are known only to God. (*KPT*, 35)

Let me put this differently. There are two systems of laws, one that we have in principle, and one that we don't have (and, in principle, so Kant thinks, cannot get). Not only are these two systems of laws compatible, the one we have (the "Newtonian" one as Sellars says) is a "projection" of the other. What does that mean? If we could (metaphysically impossible for us, Kant thinks) consider the system of laws of the in itself, *including us*, then we would discover that

> the laws of the in itself imply that beings such as us employ as laws of our represent*eds* the laws of appearances (for Kant, the Newtonian system).

This claim does not say that the laws of the in itself imply the laws of appearances. What it says is that the laws of things in themselves and, specifically, those laws concerning such beings as us imply that we have a certain complicated property. To alter my formulation slightly, that property is that of being such as to represent objects that conform to the laws of appearances. The laws of things in themselves imply that beings such as us, i.e., with our understanding and our sensibility, represent spatiotemporal objects, i.e., appearances, when, for example, our sensibility is "affected" and, moreover, these spatiotemporal objects conform to a certain laws, the ones I have called the laws of appearances.

752. Finally, the special case of our own thinking, if not carefully handled, provides a prop for the worries about double affection. Every reader of Kant on free-

266 *Introduction*

dom[260] can appreciate the temptation to conclude that one and same representing, a willing, is as a noumenal representing free but as a thinking of the empirical self not free. Kant belabors the theme of "natural necessity" and its application to all the occurrences of nature.[261] Insofar as all the thinking of the phenomenal self is part of nature, natural necessity and thus lack of freedom must apply throughout the activities of the phenomenal self. But Kant's description of freedom makes it clear that freedom requires noumenal causality and thus Kant seems committed to having both kinds of causality with regard to the same event (A537/B565, A544/B572, *PFM*, 343-4, and *G*, 455ff).

753. In general,[262] the points made above (750ff) hold for the phenomenal self. The phenomenal self is a represent*ed* and the "laws" (Newtonian or otherwise) that govern its changes are what I have called laws of appearances. Since a thinking by the phenomenal self and a representing of the self in itself can share exactly the same content, we are tempted to assimilate the two. This is a mistake on Sellars' account. Even in the case of ourselves, we build, under the impact of noumenal causality, a spatiotemporal world, a represent*ed* world which includes a represent*ed* self. So, we get a glimpse of what "is really going on" filtered through the "projection" provided by our sensibility and understanding. Nothing in the realm of appearance, i.e., in the realm of "being dependent of being thought", is an item in the realm of "being independent of being thought" (75-9, 667-73).[263]

(II) THE REFUTATIONS OF IDEALISM
(a) Some obvious points

754. This section's title is intentionally plural: refutations. Despite the amount of ink devoted to the relevant sections of *CPR*, I am not convinced that there is much common ground on what Kant should be trying to show and on what basis he should

---

[260] For example, A532/B560-A557/B585, *PFM*, 343-6, and *G*, Third Section.
[261] Sellars, by the way, is quite concerned about the theme of "passivity" that runs through these passages in Kant; see *I*, 45ff.
[262] Whether my following remarks help Kant with the problem of freedom is a topic I do not take up. The topic of freedom shows up only because of its connection with double affection. I offer one observation that is, to some degree, taken up in what follows: Kant fails to give much attention to the question of how practical principles, including moral principles, operate in the world of appearance. There are problems here that Sellars sees as overlooked by Kant and is anxious to pursue in his own account (see 776ff and the references collected in the footnote to 786).
[263] I repeat my earlier point that double affection and transcendental appearance have *analogs* within Sellars' account of the manifest image and the scientific image. The later chapters of *SM*, especially chapter V, are meant to fill in important aspects of the relevant issues, aspects that are not handled by Kant. Moreover, even my point in this paragraph has an analog in Sellars' view. It is not often noted that Sellars holds that a part of the goal of the scientific image is an account (which the manifest image proved incapable of supplying) which would explain how it is that human beings ever came to employ the principles of the manifest image. (See sections III and VII of *PSIM* in *SPR*.)

be trying to show it.[264] Consequently, I confine my remarks to arguing for the claim that, as Kant specifies his problems with idealism, the materials for his rejection of Berkeley's view and of Descartes' view are present in this introduction.

755. This exempts me from the burden of "refuting" "dogmatic" idealism and "problematic" idealism (61) by, say, demonstrating that they are inconsistent. Such a demonstration could be achieved by showing that principles to which the idealism ascribes lead to conclusions inconsistent with those same principles or with other consequences of those principles. Such a demonstration would be a "Kantian" demonstration in the strong sense if its premises are in common to Kant's view and the view which is the subject of the demonstration. My hesitation (17-21) about such common premises is on the grounds that they are very hard to come by, especially in the case at issue.[265] Since no philosopher is unfamiliar with modus tollens, anyone who reflects on what Berkeley or Descartes would say to many points made in this introduction should, it seems to me, agree. My purpose, by contrast, is to show that Kant's idealism can be reliably shown, within his own doctrines, to be neither one of the other two. I organize my remarks by considering what Kant says he is worried about in the views of Berkeley and of Descartes.

756. Kant's issue with "empirical" idealists is over appearances. He is inclined to believe that all empirical idealists start as "transcendental realists", i.e., as ones who treat what, for Kant, are appearances as mind-independent objects, and then become entangled in worries about how to "infer" the existence of such objects from their supposed effects on us (A367-73). So, Kant's issue is that of the existence of "objects in space and time".[266] In any case, he thinks that none of these idealists can reasonably ask for a proof that things in themselves exist (A375-6).[267]

757. About the "dogmatic idealism" of Berkeley, little needs to be added to my earlier discussion (62-4). Berkeley's idealism conforms to one of Kant's characterizations of idealism: viz., the only existents are thinking beings (*PFM*, 288). Extension, then, either exists as a modification of thinking beings or exists only in the, perhaps confused, thinkings of such beings. When pressed, Berkeley opts for the

---

[264] As grist for my mill, I point to the elaborate and interesting discussions of the "refutation" to be found in Part IV, chapter 14 of Henry E. Allison, *Kant's Transcendental Idealism: An Interpretation and Defense* (Yale University Press, 1983) and in Part IV, chapters 12-14 of Paul Guyer, *Kant and the Claims of Knowledge* (Cambridge University Press, 1987).

[265] Kant's remark about hoisting problematic idealism on its own petard (B276) seems to suggest that he thinks that he can do just this. On the other hand, such remarks are common rhetorical flourishes among philosophers and we do not know what Kant would have replied had he been asked to supply the goods in more detail.

[266] Most particularly, of the existence of objects in space as Kant realized that empirical idealists generally took inner experience to prove the existence of objects in time (A491/B519).

[267] At the end of *CLN*, **B37**ff, Sellars correctly points out that, on his interpretation, Kant's adherence to a doctrine of the in itself does make him some sort of realist. Kant's realism differs from that of his predecessors in that he vigorously maintains the view that our knowledge of the in itself is philosophical and not of that determinate kind his predecessors believed they had.

latter (45) though his position pushes him very hard toward the first option. Those interpretations of Berkeley that commit him to the doctrine that material objects are temporally extended "congeries" of such mental items as sense impressions would seem to envisage him accepting the first option.

758. That, on Sellars' interpretation, Kant's view is not an example of any such phenomenalism has been emphasized over and over in this introduction. Second, it has often been noted that Kant believes that there is nothing "confused" about the concept of extension and nothing contradictory or, generally amiss, in the science of extension as a non-mental property. Among appearances are spatially extended objects whose actuality is on a par with the actuality of empirical selves (582, 672). On the other side of the coin, Kant must view Berkeley as not appreciating the complications of a correct account of thinking being. If Berkeley's idealism contains an example of that doctrine of the self in itself that Kant calls "rational psychology" (A341/B399ff), then Kant argues, in the Paralogisms, that it must fail of its goal and, moreover, that his own view is clearly different. If, however, Berkeley is propounding a doctrine of the empirical self, then, at very least, Sellars' Kant can point out (as I shall in more detail in connection with problematic idealism below) that his own account of perceiving and apperceiving shows that his view is not like Berkeley's. The empirical self as perceiver and apperceiver is part of nature and so caught up in Kant's "official" spatiotemporal order and thus, as perceiver, the empirical self must have a spatial location.

759. When Kant comes to worry about Descartes' "problematic idealism", his concerns are, at least on the surface, quite different. Whether our representings of spatial entities are all results of a process of "inference" from our own states, and thus not "direct", is the centerpiece of the A edition refutation (A366-380) and is in the background in the B edition refutation (A225/B272ff). Such inferences from "effects" to "causes" insure that the epistemologically status of our convictions about the existence of spatial objects is "doubtful" (B276, A366-7).

760. First, I repeat (718, 731): it is no part of the account of this introduction that perceiving (or, apperceiving) is a matter of "inference" from states of the self (or, anything else). Throughout this introduction, I have lumped, for convenience, such views as require inference from states of the self under the heading "phenomenalistic" and maintained that no such thing need be part of Kant's account (159-65, 345, 695). I have characterized perceiving as "direct" for just that reason and held that the complexity of the processes is no impediment to this sort of directness.

761. Second, the supposed "indubitable" access (B275) to our own states that makes the picture suggested by (some) phenomenalisms more tempting is not there on the Kantian account. It is not that apperceiving is any less direct than perceiving. It is rather that both are of the same standing in that they involve causal processes of some complexity and the states attributed to the self in apperceiving are also complex (712-731). (Not to mention that, on Sellars' suggestions to Kant, part of the process involves the self in itself.)

762. These two points go a long way to showing that Kant's view cannot be a form of "problematic idealism". A third point is even more important in that it strikes against one of Descartes' central principles. As Sellars says (*I*, 53; *KTI*, 51-53) and in conformity with my explication of the concept of perceiving, the self as perceiver and perceptible objects form law-governed systems in which the perceptual takings of the perceiver and the properties of the perceptible objects are not independent (582, 672, 733-4). Out of all the possible states of the empirical self as perceiver, only some of them are "actual", i.e., can be held truly to be part of the history of the perceiver; among the actual ones are those perceptual takings which, in the circumstances, are implied by actual states of perceptible objects. If Kant were to adopt the Cartesian terminology of "clearness and distinctness", he would deny, contrary to Descartes' view, that we have a "clear and distinct" conception of a thinking being as a perceiver apart from extended being.

763. This denial is not inconsistent with the transcendental doctrine of content. All that is required by that doctrine is that the reflection on content *alone* does not allow you to draw the kinds of conclusions about the subjects of the content that some philosophers thought you could draw. Transcendental psychology helps to "clarify" and make "distinct" the concepts of thinking and perceiving but not, as Kant himself points out, in a way that leads to a Cartesian conception of "thinking substance" (518-26, 595-608, 674-6).

764. As Kant reminds us in the Refutation (as amended at Bxxxix, note), all representings are determinations (modifications) which require a subject. I have stressed that, in attributing a content, e.g., ^that black bear is coming at me^, to a subject, we are not attributing to the subject any of the spatial properties and relations within the content (172, 180-1, 638-41, 674-8). So, Kant can say that reflection on thinking and its content reveals nothing spatial because what he means is that such reflection reveals nothing spatial about the subject of the modification. Of course, he does not mean that reflecting on represent*ed* objects does not reveal spatial properties and relations and he does not mean that reflecting on the subject *as perceiver* reveals nothing about the spatial properties of the subject.

(b) Something a little different

765. I intentionally omitted detailed consideration of what has been a hotly debated feature of the second edition Refutation: Kant's claim that he can "prove" the "existence of objects in space" from the consciousness of time determination of the self. So much disagreement surrounds this claim that any competent discussion of it would be so lengthy that it would tend to obscure more straightforward points flowing from the interpretation being developed in this introduction. But, in pursuing other topics, Sellars navigates his way through waters to open up a thought-provoking vista on these matters (*I*, 41 ff). Worrying about the consequences of the Analogies, especially the First Analogy, for Kant's account of the empirical self and hearkening to Kant's expressed preference for a "dualistic" account of the empirical self,[268] Sellars, correctly I think, contemplates the possibility that, at some level, part of the point of the Refutation of Idealism is to find a way to get the temporal alterations of the empirical self into the "objective" time order. Two preparatory points hint at why this might be more difficult for Kant than one might initially imagine.

766. First (687-694), Kant holds that, strictly, time is not perceptible and, of course, not apperceptible either. Moreover, nothing spatial, and thus nothing material, is revealed in reflecting on thinking.[269] These points, which seem never to be far from his mind, may help explain why, at B156, well before the Refutation, Kant bluntly says that all fixing of determinate temporal positions or durations for "inner perceptions" depends on changes pertaining to "outer things", i.e., material items in space (691).

767. Second, one can be carried away by the transcendental doctrine of content (674ff): a mistake exacerbated by not keeping firmly in mind what is, and what is not, required by transcendental appearing. Kant and most of his predecessors—certainly Descartes, Berkeley, and Leibniz—view the doctrine of content as insuring that a thinking being cannot be "contaminated" by what it thinks about. In terms of this medical metaphor, a thinker can't "catch" space by representing it. Kant surely contemplates that this prophylactic protection applies to time as well. The self in itself can *represent* his official time and not *be* officially temporal. But it might also seem to Kant that representings by the self in itself, in no way, involve the self in a structure which would have some similarity to the structure of the officially temporal. Thus, even though Kant claims that time is the "form" of inner sense, it might come to seem quite difficult to obtain "official" temporal status for thinkings in general, including the unrepresented ones. (That this line of thought would be an

---

[268] A367, A370, A379 and compare *MFNS*, 467-471.
[269] I have now brought this point up in so many different contexts that references to earlier paragraphs are quite lengthy: 67, 172, 179-80, 638-41, 674-5, and 764. It should also be remembered that, for Kant, matter is impenetrable extension (336).

error is part of the burden of paragraphs 742-53.[270])

768. With this background, Sellars' line of thought is easy enough to appreciate.

(i) The First Analogy claims, without restriction, that all alteration pertains to material substance (matter). (*I*, 31, 38, 39)

(ii) Kant does not wish to deny that reflection on thinking reveals alteration in the thinking subject (*I*, 39).

(iii) To preserve alteration in our mental life, Kant could attempt to reduce thinking to the properties of matter (i.e., more or less, extension) or to treat thinkings as irreducible states (properties) of material substance. (*I*, 40).

(iv) Kant is not a reductive materialist. (*I*, 40) [The numeral '(v)' was accidentally omitted.]

(vi) Since Kant finds that nothing concerning extension is revealed in reflection on our thinking, he is unwilling to treat thinkings as irreducible properties of matter. (*I*, 40, 41)

(vii) With these two options out, thinkings have lost their connection with the "permanent", i.e., material substance, that persists through change and thus they have lost what is, by the First Analogy, the standard connection with the "official" temporal order. (*I*, 40, 41)

(viii) The remaining available choice for Kant is that thinkings are something like "epiphenomena" that gain a non-standard grip on the temporal order by being a by-product of material changes. So, temporal location of any thinking and thus of any alteration in our mental lives requires material substance. (*I*, 41, 51, and 53)

One could make, as Sellars says (*I*, 53), a "good case" for (viii)'s being Kant's position. (If so, then a spin-off is that Kant would, to say the least, have no problem

---

[270] Certain contemporary examples correctly, I think, put complete prophylaxis in doubt. While there is no dealing here with all the details, I note that the cases in which contemporary analysis claims some logical connection between, in traditional terms, what's inside the content and what's outside are not ones which would favor Descartes over Kant.

Moreover, on Sellars' account, Kant need not subscribe to the strong principle about time. After all, the self in itself is a representer and therefore, must be subject to the general, "pure" principles of transcendental psychology (for examples of what is at issue, see 676-8, 682-5, and 712-21). The representings of the self in itself must have the kind of "pure" structure demanded by a general doctrine of representing. So, in complicated cases involving tense ("I assure you that I will do what I promised I would do" (i.e., take out the garbage)), that some structure ("form" as Kant would say), conceived in "pure" terms, should be common to the representings of the self in itself and those of the empirical self is no problem. The transcendental doctrine of content identifies the "I" as the subject of content and thus independently of the distinction between the self not in the official temporal order (the self in itself) and the self in the official temporal order (the phenomenal self) (674-8). All that Kant needs is that the self in itself *not be in* his official temporal order. (I note that this move also helps with worries that Kant expresses at B155 just before the passage mentioned in paragraph 766.) As I shall show (778ff), Sellars has definite, worked-out ideas about what such "pure" principles are.

showing that his view is not "dogmatic" or "problematic" idealism.) But, Sellars immediately (*I*, 54) points out that there is another "thread in Kant's thought" which leads away from epiphenomenalism: spontaneity.

769. I want to be reasonably clear about how this opposition is to be understood. One core tenet of epiphenomenalism is that the mental—thinking in all its forms—is brought about by that which is not mental. Sellars argues (767) that Kant is driven toward this view by his other commitments, particularly by the general thrust of the Analogies that our access to imperceptible time is through material substance (*I*, 44; see also *KPT*, ch. 16). But apart from the Analogies, Kant construes the opposition of natural necessity and freedom so that some kind of epiphenomenalism seems almost inevitable. Kant says that natural necessity always involves "alien" (or, "foreign") causes (*G*, 446). The context makes it clear that what he has in mind are causes outside the understanding. Indeed, the prominence which he gives to sensibility (*G*, 449ff; A534/B562) confirms Sellars' evaluation (*I*, 51) that Kant tends to conceive all thinking of the phenomenal self on the model of perceiving where, in some sense, "alien" causes are always pertinent.

770. That it is an error (*I*, 45-52) to adopt this model is not my present concern. My present concern is that Kant surely understands spontaneity in such a way that it does not involve "alien" causes or, perhaps I need to say, *solely* alien causes. Kant agrees that there are different kinds of spontaneity, one that is, in some sense, "pure" and belongs to the reason, and one that belongs to the understanding (*G*, 452; see the references in the footnotes to paragraphs 87 and 708). Spontaneity of the understanding seems to be what is mostly at issue in *CPR* since, by Kant's own design, *CPR* is almost exclusively about "theoretical" reason and not "practical" reason, the faculty which, in some way, depends on "pure" spontaneity.

771. Further, spontaneity does not require lack of causality. I do not mean the obvious point that even "pure" spontaneity is a form of causality.[271] I mean that Kant is not committed to understanding 'spontaneous' as 'completely uncaused'. It is true that, in perception, the activity of the understanding can be caused by the activity of the sensibility in the sense of being *initiated* by it and being *guided* by it. But I cannot stress too much that the Sellarsian aesthetic leaves the content of the resulting conceptual states of the representer *entirely* up to what Kant would call the understanding. Image-models are ontologically impotent (570) and, in particular, blind (545). *All* synthesizing of content belongs to the understanding, not to the sensibility, and no content is derived from that which is not already conceptual (642-3, 675). So, the conceptual content of even perceivings is really the result of the understanding, as the productive imagination, "affecting" the sensibility. For example, this shows up in the fact that the frame of mind of the perceiver deter-

---

[271] Kant's insistence on freedom as a form of causality appears at the beginning of the Third Antinomy (A444/B472) and continues in subsequent discussions (A532/B60ff; see also *G*, 446, 457-8).

mines even which concept (bear vs. bush) is used to "augment" the original sensory state (look back at the review of aesthetic principles in 634). The dichotomy "determined by alien causes"–"not determined by any cause at all" is a spurious one. What really needs to be worried about is what I would call in Kantian terms the "causality of the understanding" and being "active" in the sense of being "determined" by other states of myself.[272] It is these points that are the crucial background to what follows.

772. To complicate matters, Sellars has a diagnosis that attributes part of Kant's problems on the total topic of "epiphenomenal; determined by alien causes; passive; spontaneous" to his struggling with what Sellars (677) likes to refer to as the "functional" character of content attributions. Confusion about contents being functional states can lead to misconstruing their character in such a way that states with contents become candidates for being "non-material" (and so epiphenomenal) states.

773. Notice how well *some sort* of functional characterization of mental states fits with Kant's requirements. Consider the negative requirements. First, on *some* functionalist views, functional states are not definable in terms of "matter" (more about this in a moment). Second, it is not part of the concept of any object conceived in non-functional terms that it have functional states. (Of course, a representer, on this view, is conceived in functional terms and, thus, has functional states.) Moreover, functionally characterized states are not restrictive about the nature of the objects to which they are attributed. They can be attributed to objects whose other properties are presently completely unconceived by us or, as in Kant's case, to the self in itself of which he holds we can never have a determinate conception. In sum, the introduction of *some* notion of functionality leaves the concept of a representer with nothing that constrains it to be a being with, in traditional terms, a specific "nature". (Even if it turned out that functional characterization requires that representers are objects in *some sort* of spatiotemporal framework, the noumenal self, on Sellars' account, would still qualify for content attribution.)

774. On the positive side, functional characterization does not preclude functional states from being attributed to material objects. So, the phenomenal self as representer need not be cut off from a connection with the appearance which is the human body.

775. Moreover, all this is consistent with Kant's point that there is nothing in the concept of representing or of a representer that gets us anything about determinate temporal locations for representings. What we find here is another example of what Sellars takes to be a fundamental thesis of Kant's view: what does the philosophical work is the concept of a representer as having "experience", i.e., empirical knowledge, and thus as being a perceiver. Certainly in perceiving we clearly find causal principles that connect the thinkings that occur in perceivings with changes in

---

[272] Roughly, "on one's own" (A533-4/BB561-2, A541/B569) in Kant's phrase.

material objects. So, it is in representing ourselves as perceivers that we find, given the Sellarsian explication of perceiving, a connection (by causal principle) between our own states and those of material substances.

776. Another facet of these topics raises yet other serious questions. I have found it quite natural (indeed, almost unavoidable), on and off,[273] to refer to "rules". There seemed little harm in this when discussing a philosopher like Kant who is happy to announce that the understanding is the faculty of rules.[274] In addition, I have been free with my use of the term 'principle', particularly in the phrase 'causal principle'. This, too, seemed relatively harmless. No doubt it is a contemporary cavil to complain that Kant does not treat us to an organized logical discussion of rules, principles, and related items. It is a little closer to the target to complain that he does not elaborate on the activity of the understanding in utilizing rules, principles and so on. In terms of the doctrine of content, causal principles tell us that, in certain circumstances, one content implies another content. I have argued that such principles are essential to certain sorts of "syntheses". And aren't (some) logical principles essential to syntheses? We are entitled to get some idea of how such rules, principles, and so on, are really involved in the operations of the understanding and it seems entirely unlikely that remarks about either "natural necessity" as the influence of "alien causes" or "transcendental freedom" will be much help. At bottom, what we really need is at least a start on an answer to the question of what Kant has in mind when he says the understanding is the faculty of rules and, in addition, how it is that such principles can be "efficacious".

777. Sellars has expended much time and energy on just this question. Moreover, his line on this matter is connected with the sort of functionalism that he thinks Kant really needs. Finally, it will be clear that his resulting view features rules in such a way that at least a beginning has been made on the project of leaving room for *some sort* of "spontaneity" in our mental activity.[275] So, my final introductory act is to sketch Sellars' account of rules with pertinent addenda. As a by-product, I fulfill one obligation of an introduction writer: I get to explain the presence, and importance, of *OAPK* and *OAFP* in this volume (and why *KTE* was originally part of larger essay which began with *OAPK*).

(III) THE UNDERSTANDING AS THE FACULTY OF RULES
(a) An entering wedge: rules of criticism

778. The Kantian term usually translated 'rule' appears in passages in *CPR* of quite different sorts. In the ones cited in footnote 274, what stands out is Kant's

---

[273] Here is a sample of paragraphs: 104, 185, 223, 326, 380, 485, 713, 717, and 725.
[274] A126; see also B159-60, B164-5, A159/B198, A216/B263.
[275] Whether all this helps with metaphysical freedom is something Sellars is willing to discuss, but which I leave aside. In this volume, consult *MP*, 34ff, *KBDW*, and *I*, 57ff; see also ch. VII of *SM*.

willingness to treat a wide range of "principles" under the heading of "rules of the understanding". Moreover, his exposition in these passages slides effortlessly from rules as laws of nature to rules as necessary for the operation of the understanding in cognizing objects and nature.[276] Other passages, particularly those dealing with logic (e.g., in the introduction to the "Transcendental Logic" (A50/B74)), continue the theme of rules for the operation of the understanding since there his emphasis is on rules of logic as providing a "canon" of correctness. This theme is also reinforced by Kant's early (A11/B24ff) and late (A795/B823) assessment of the "critique of pure reason" as a "canon" for the understanding and the reason.

779. Kant's *Logic* treats the rules of logic as merely one group of rules, singled out by being those which the understanding needs in all its activities (i.e., the rules of logic are completely subject-matter neutral). In addition, Kant unequivocally says that they are rules of correctness in that they tell us what "ought" to be with regard to our thinking.[277] Thus the understanding operates by rules of correctness, a "canon", which the understanding can formulate and thus reflect upon, along with other rules including ones which also, in some sense, govern nature.

780. Exactly when Sellars came to conceive one of his philosophical projects as making a coherent package out of the foregoing could be debated.[278] It is possible that only somewhat after the fact did he come to see the place of some of his mature views within a Kantian framework. Whatever may be the case, there can be no doubt that, by the time of *SM* and *KTE*, Sellars was more than willing to inject his own work on rules into his expositions of Kant.[279] My presentation is tailored to fit this introduction and is aimed is at the Kantian elements of the total ensemble.

781. It must have been a surprise to the audience of *KTE* when Sellars, in its very

---

[276] Other passages in which Kant slides from "law" to "rule" are in the Third Antinomy (A444/B472, A447/B475) and in its "solution" (A532/B560).

[277] See *L*, Introduction, Section I, The Concept of Logic.

[278] See, for example, his remarks about Kant on p. 446 and at the very end of *RNWW* (3) and on pp. 299-300 of *LRB* (6), both reprinted in *PPPW* (112).

[279] Of course, Sellars' work on the topic of rules is spread throughout the decades of his philosophical activity and though I make no pretense to discuss anything more than what is relevant to this introduction, here are a few references. To begin with, for the reader who is unfamiliar with Sellars, I recommend *SRLG* (24) reprinted in *SPR* and *AE* (48) reprinted in *PPME*. For those who wish to dig in further, there are *CIL* (4), *LRB* (6), and *IM* (22), all in *PPPW*, and, of course, *SM* (63) and, among later works *LTC* (74), *AAE* (78), *MFC* (89), *NAO* (104), *BLM* (109), and *MEV* (113). In addition, the reader can consult the appropriate chapters in Jay F. Rosenberg, *Linguistic Representation* (D. Reidel Publishing Co., 1974 and 1981), Johanna Seibt, *Properties as Processes: A Synoptic Study of Wilfrid Sellars' Nominalism* (Ridgeview Publishing Company, 1990) and Jeffrey F. Sicha, *A Metaphysics of Elementary Mathematics* (University of Massachusetts Press, 1974).

last paragraphs, refers prominently to "ought-to-bes" (*KTE*, section IX).[280] Sellars intended to pave the way for these references in an opening part. This first part (which I now call *OAPK*) of a paper entitled, "Ontology, the A Priori, and Kant," contained a discussion of "ought-to-bes", but he removed it leaving the second part which became *KTE*, a paper by itself of suitable length for presentation.[281]

782. After an opening section to clear the ground, Sellars explains an important characteristic of "ought-to-bes":

> 10. Importantly different from rules of the above form—which may be called, in a straightforward sense, rules of action—are rules that specify not what someone ought to do, but how something ought to be. Of these an important sub-class has the form
>
> Xs ought to be in state S, whenever such and such is the case.
>
> The purpose of such a rule is achieved to the extent that it comes to be the case that Xs are in state S when such and such is indeed the case. This time, however, the conformity of actual existence to the ought does not, in general, require that the Xs which are, in a sense, the *subjects* of the rule, i.e., that to which it applies, have the concept of what it is to be in state S or of what it is for such and such to be the case. This is obvious when the Xs in question are inanimate objects, as in the example,
>
> Clock chimes ought to strike on the quarter hour.
>
> 11. Now ought-to-bes (or 'rules of criticism' as I shall also call them), though categorical in form, point beyond themselves in two ways. In the first place they imply (in some sense of this protean term) a *reason*, a *because* clause. The exploration of this theme would soon take us back to the excluded topic of hypothetical imperatives. In the second place, though ought-to-bes are carefully to be distinguished from ought-to-dos they have an essential connection with them. The connection is, roughly, that ought-to-bes imply ought-to-dos. Thus the ought-to-be about clock chimes implies, roughly,
>
> (Other things being equal and where possible) one ought to bring it about that clock chimes strike on the quarter hour.
>
> 12. *This* rule belongs in our previous category and is a rule of action. As such it requires

---

[280] I did not notice a similar response in the audience for *SM* when, at the end of chapter IV, Sellars launched into a table of various kinds of "rules of criticism". Of course, the preceding chapters had prepared the audience for such references (see, especially, sections V and VI of III). The footnote to that table of rules of criticism in *SM* cites "Some Reflections on Language Games" (*SRLG*), reprinted in *SPR*) as containing an "earlier version" of what is in that table. Parts of my ensuing discussion reformulate points from *SRLG*. It is my view, and I think Sellars', that what he said in *SRLG* is largely correct though in need of a better setting by removal from some of what seemed to be pressing concerns in 1950's philosophy and by emendation of the false assumption that "a rule is always a rule for doing something in some circumstances" (see also *IM* (22), p. 329).

[281] Eastern Division APA symposium on Kant, 1967.

Introduction   277

that the item to which *it* applies (persons rather than chimes) have the appropriate concepts or recognitional capacities. (*OAPK*, 10-12)

783. Sellars then extends the contrast between rules of action and rules of criticism to examples which involve persons rather than inanimate objects. Where persons are the objects of ought-to-bes, the importance of rules of criticism for Sellars is to be found, on the one hand, in connection with a thesis that he normally sets out as a thesis about language and, on the other hand, in an analogy to games.

(b) Rules of criticism as essential to thinking

784. The thesis about language is mentioned in *OAPK* and is the centerpiece of the discussion in paragraphs 1 through 17 of *SRLG*. Sellars notes:

> 17. It is obvious, from the above considerations, that if *all* rules of language, were ought-to-dos we would be precluded from explaining what it is to have concepts in terms of rules of language. Now many rules of language *are* ought-to-dos thus,
>
> (Other things being equal) one ought to say such and such, if in C
>
> and as such they can be efficacious in linguistic activity only to the extent that people have the relevant concepts. It is therefore of the utmost importance to note that many of the rules of language which are of special interest to the epistemologist are ought-to-bes rather than ought-to-dos. For only by taking this fact into account is it possible to carry out a program according to which (a) linguistic activity is, in a primary sense, conceptual activity; (b) linguistic activity is through and through rule governed.
> 18. ...All I'm concerned to point out is that to approach language in terms of the paradigm of *action* is to make a commitment which, if the concept of action is taken seriously and the concept of rule is taken seriously, leads to (a) the Cartesian idea of linguistic episodes as *essentially* the sort of thing brought about by an agent whose conceptualizing is not linguistic; (b) the inability to understand the rule governed character of this conceptualizing, as contrasted with its overt expression. For if thought is analogous to linguistic activity to the extent implied by Plato's metaphor of 'discourse in the soul', the idea that overt speech is *action* and its rules *rules of action* will generate the idea that all inner speech is *action* and *its* rules *rules of action*, which leads to paradox and absurdity without end. (*OAPK*, 17-18)

Clearly Sellars' formulation was directed to then current concerns over language learning, linguistic structure, and its relationship to thought. In what follows, I largely avoid reference to language[282] and so restate Sellars' central point that it is

---

[282] Here I have in mind a sense of the word 'language' in which it is appropriate to contrast language with thought. In a more general sense (the one that I have leaned on in this introduction), speaking, writing, typing, signing, and so on, as well as thinking, are all examples of representing.

clearly sensible in the context of his interpretation of Kant and is set in terms more congenial to early modern philosophy.

785. To take "the concept of rule" "seriously", in this context, is, at very least, to hold that talk about rules is not reducible to talk about uniformities (e.g., like those achieved by association) and to maintain that activities of the understanding are thoroughly "rule governed".[283] That is, Sellars takes the thesis that the understanding is the faculty of rules as claiming more than merely that some activities of the understanding exhibit regularity; formulable rules must, in some significant and essential way, be involved in *all* thinking, *all* activities of the understanding.

786. One way to achieve such a view—a way Sellars rejects—is to treat all thinking as action and all the rules of the understanding as rules of action.[284] The application of a rule of action (either prior to the action or after it) requires subjects to think the rule, i.e., to think that a certain action is demanded of certain subjects by the rule, and to think that, in the circumstances they find themselves (if any are relevant), they and their action are of the sort covered by the rule. They can then contemplate what they ought to do or what they ought to have done. Thus what is commonly called "obeying a rule" requires thinking and, in particular, reasoning. So, the view that all rules of thinking are rules of action would seem to present one with two choices neither of which should be palatable to Kant.

787. Choice one: at least some thinking goes on without *any* involvement of rules and at very least the concept of thinking does not require through and through rule-governedness. As formulated, this choice seems to fit Hume reasonably well. In nearly any sense of 'rule', rules involve generality and Hume insists that our grasp of any generality is derived from thoughts which involve no generality in any way and so nothing that would merit being called a "rule". On Sellars' interpretation of Kant, this choice simply eviscerates the straightforward reading of the thesis that the understanding is faculty of rules. In any case, if some thinking can go on without rules being involved, why not all of it?

788. Choice two: thinkers are "up and running" right from the beginning and have all the concepts necessary for obeying rules (though, as many a rationalist would have insisted, it may take some causal activity from "without" to get the full package running). As we know, such an *inclusive* doctrine of innateness is rejected by

---

[283] For extended discussion of what Sellars has in mind by 'rule governed', see paragraphs 1-17 of *SRLG*.

[284] The view Sellars rejects has many variants, but a reasonably thorough canvassing of them out of the question. For a partial account of action, see 35-45 of *MP*. For more, see *SRLG*, 1-17; *SM*, ch. III, 31-41, ch. VI, 13-8, 62-4, and ch. VII, 5ff; *NAO*, ch. IV.

The topics of action, intending, willing, freedom, and morality are bound together for Sellars in such a way that many of this works treat one, or more, of these topics. In addition to the references just given, I here provide a list of Sellars' works which touch, more or less extensively, on these topics: in this volume, *OAPK*, *KBDW*, and *OAFP*; also *OM* (13), *OMR* (15), *IIO* (29), *IIOR* (39), *TA* (59), *FD* (60), *CDI* (70), *AAE* (78), *VR* (97), *ORAV* (107), *BLM* (109), and *CPCI* (111).

Kant (141-54, 654).

789. In addition, the second choice is, in one way, a sham and returns us to a consequence of the first choice. Obeying a rule of action requires thinking (e.g., of the rule itself, of the circumstances, and of oneself). Now suppose all thinking requires obeying rules. To avoid the regress that looms—the "paradox and absurdity" Sellars mentions (784)—adherents to this choice, (usually) adopt the doctrine that at least some thinking occurs without any rules being invoked. In any case of thinking, rules might be invoked, but they cannot be invoked in all cases. But once the thesis that all thinking and all activity of the understanding is rule governed is abandoned, it can easily become unclear why you need anything that would properly be called rules of thinking at all.

790. For Sellars, there are two errors to avoid. One is that the only relevant rules are rules of action, i.e., what Sellars also calls "ought-to-dos". Rules of criticism, "ought-to-bes", are erroneously ignored as an option despite their aptness to the problem. Rules of criticism require no obeying to be relevant. They provide a canon of correct thinking. Sellars generally sets these points within an account of language as a community activity in which there are learners and also those who are full-fledged wielders of the canon. So, he can mention well-known features about language learning:

> ...The answer should be obvious: the members of a linguistic community are *first* language *learners* and only potentially 'people', but *subsequently* language *teachers*, possessed of the rich conceptual framework this implies. They start out by being the *subject-matter* subjects of the ought-to-dos and graduate to the status of *agent* subjects of the ought-to-dos. Linguistic ought-to-bes are translated into *uniformities* by training. As Wittgenstein has stressed, it is the linguistic community as a self-perpetuating whole which is the minimum unit in terms of which conceptual activity can be understood.[285] (*OAPK*, 25)

That this canon is not available equally to all thinkers at all times does not argue against its being essential to thinking.

791. The second mistake is taking all thinkings to be actions. The example Sellars is fond of citing is perceiving. Perceiving is a causal process and the thinkings that occur in perceivings are caused.[286] Not uncommonly, Sellars takes a very simple formulation to illustrate his point. In *OAPK*, he says,

---

[285] Sellars has written extensively on how such a community might be accounted for. He takes the question of how such a community should ever have come about as needing an answer that does not require the prior existence of language teachers. For starters, try *SRLG*, 1-17 and *PSIM* (43), both in *SPR*; for related issues, try *NAO* (104), ch. 4, *BLM* (108), and *MEV* (112).

[286] As I said earlier (e.g., 389ff), there are many conditions that must obtain for the causal process to work. Some of these may well be actions or be consequences of actions. Thus, we can intentionally look in one place, rather than another. Of course, that in no way shows that perceiving is an action.

21. To fix our ideas, let us consider an example which, though simplified to its bare bones contains the essence of the matter:

(*Ceteris paribus*) one ought to respond to red objects in sunlight by uttering or being disposed to utter 'this is red'.

This ought-to-be rule must not be confused with the (fictitious) ought-to-do rule,

(*Ceteris paribus*) one ought to say 'this is red' in the presence of red objects in sunlight.

The latter presupposes that those to whom it applies have the concepts of 'red objects', 'sunlight', and, even more important, of what it is to *say* 'this is red'. In other words, they must already have the conceptual framework of what it is to do something in a circumstance. (*OAPK*, 21)

(My appeal to the more elaborate account of this introduction to add flesh to the "bare bones" of Sellars' example leaves his point unaffected.) Perceptual takings and perceptual judgings are non-actions though they are "acts" in the sense of actualities (as contrasted with potentialities). Since they are not actions, the appropriate rules are rules of criticism.

792. I draw two morals. First, the two errors are, according to Sellars, connected. Non-actions are not directly within the purview of "ought-to-dos". Second, the central point Sellars is making does not depend on a context concerning language, language learning, and its relation to thinking. Setting the point in that context brings in, right from the beginning, the idea of a community and makes a congenial background against which to explicate the intersubjectivity involved in "ought-to-bes".[287] Rules of criticism are general and their subjects are "all of us".

(c) Rules of criticism and inferring

793. Even before Sellars worked out his views on "ought-to-bes", he described inferring as a process, but not as an action.[288] The view of inferring we find in *OAPK* fuses the themes of rules of criticism and activities that are not actions:

26. Furthermore there are radically different kinds of linguistic ought-to-bes: not only word-object ought-to-bes (or, as I have called them elsewhere, language entry transi-

---

[287] Sellars clearly thinks that, though the tradition appreciated the importance of intersubjectivity (and related concepts), a reasonable approach to this topic was not generally present. See Sellars' comments in ch. 4 of *KPT*. Also the topic of "trainers" brings in a connection between "ought-to-bes" and "ought-to-dos" since the "trainers" need to perform "training" actions to which "ought-to-dos" are relevant.
[288] See, e.g., *SRLG*, 18ff.

tions) [a footnote at this point refers to *SRLG*], but also the ought-to-bes formulated by formation and transformation rules.

27. The oughts governing utterances as perceptual responses to the environment are not ought-to-dos.... Similarly the oughts governing inference are not ought-to-dos. Inferring is not a *doing* in the conduct sense—which, however, by no means implies that it is not a *process*. Again, as the pragmatists have stressed, inference as an element in enquiry occurs in the context of action, epistemic and otherwise. (*OAPK*, 26, 27)

794. A small disclaimer: Sellars is not denying that we use the term 'infer' in the sense of "draw (reach, come to) a conclusion", a phrase often enough used in cases where an action is occurring. A common example is one where we are "making up our mind" on the basis of evidence, principles and a weighing of reasonableness of various relevant alternatives. (Many examples of just this sort are found in legal cases.) All of this is fine with Sellars. (In particular, it explains his references to the pragmatists and their emphasis on the conduct of "enquiry"). What Sellars has in mind by inference is a more fundamental process in that it operates at the same causal level as perceiving. Inferring is, in categorial terms, a causal process. It can no more be an action (as opposed to an "act", an "actuality") than perceiving.

795. To illustrate the distinctions needed, I take an earlier example (231ff) that qualifies as a "logical" inference (i.e., for Sellars, an inference governed by an "ought-to-be" that can be defended as belonging to "logic").

796. At rock bottom and without necessary qualifications, a representer whose judging is conjunctive, e.g.,

(233.32) $2 + 2 = 4$ and $5 + 7 = 12$

is caused (*in certain conditions, of course*) to judge (inter alia)

$2 + 2 = 4$.

In general, what is required is that a representer's conjunctive thinkings cause thinkings of the conjuncts of the conjunctive thinkings.

797. A small idealization will make our life easier. The conditions which need to appear on such a causal principle are many and various. First, there are the cognitive conditions collected under the heading of "frame of mind" (394, 474, 485). For example, the representer cannot be, as we say, attending to other matters and pondering other questions or in one of the many other states that can "distract" the representer (fear, anger, and all the emotional states not present in "a cool hour"). Second, those "ills flesh is heir to" can intrude. So, in the manner of logic texts (in which such matters are given short shrift), I wish to "abstract", or "idealize", by assuming that the cognitive condition of the representer is whatever is needed.

Sellars himself does this by regularly including the phrase 'is disposed to' (791), a maneuver which hides the conditions in the antecedent of the "if,then" associated with the disposition. In addition, I suppress the temporal element.

798. By the metaphysical deduction (252ff), the preceding (causal) principle is really a causal implication. In traditional terms (and idealized), it is:

(99) that a representer, R, has a thought with the content ^2 + 2 = 4 and 5 + 7 = 12^ implies that R has a thought with the content ^2 + 2 = 4^.

Traditionally, the root idea is that one state of the representer R "necessitates" ("requires") another (though no extended treatment of this kind of necessity was then available).

799. In one way, we are not far from the non-empiricists of the early modern tradition. A representer is a being that conforms to what, without emendations such as "so-called", can be termed "laws of thought". In perceiving and in reasoning,[289] the states of a representer are constrained by a "necessity"—something not *directly* under the representer's control, something intersubjective, non-idiosyncratic, and not accidental. The principles of such changes are causal laws, i.e., implications, and it is conceptual states that are caused by *other conceptual states*.

800. For the non-empiricist part of the tradition, the implicational connections between contents (properties, relations, "natures" as Descartes would have it) are, as Sellars puts it,[290] "internal." By contrast, "association" forms connections between contents that are "external": one content is "associated" with another by showing up in reasonably regular succession in the history of a representer (*CLN*, **A16b**ff). One need not deny that there is an association in the cases covered by (798.99); it is rather that the association is, in some sense, *because of* the implication. Exactly how the implication should be involved in the genesis and maintenance of such an association is a question where, I think it is fair to say, Sellars thinks that Kant missed an opportunity. Kant should have asked himself about the relation of causal implications to the rules which are the canon of correct thinking.

801. Sellars has often been content to state the connection between implications like (798.99) and rules of criticism by simply saying that implications like (798.99) really are normative principles, indeed, ought-to-bes.[291] I shall follow him in this treatment of the intuitive notion of implication (but, as I show below, there is more to say on this topic). For my purposes, I shall assume that nothing is lost by treating the relevant ought-to-be as the following:

---

[289] As well, of course, in deliberate action in which willing is involved. I omit this element. See the references in the footnote to paragraph 786.

[290] See *KPT*, Appendix, Descartes, sections F, G, and particularly J.

[291] For a late example, see *AEE*, 30. I intend to ignore the question of whether each implication is a single ought-to-be or a conjunction of ought-to-bes.

(100) it ought to be that, for any one of us representers, given we •2 + 2 = 4 and 5 + 7 = 12•, then we •2 + 2 = 4•.[292]

If I were to put this as Sellars did in his example (791), (100) would read as follow:

(*Ceteris paribus*) one ought to respond to '2 + 2= 4 and 5 + 7 = 12' by uttering or being disposed to utter '2 + 2= 4'.

My (idealized) version is intended to avoid some of what, for my present purposes, are irrelevant questions and problems.

802. On Sellars' account, (801.100) is a logical principle in the sense of being a rule of the canon of correct representing, in particular, of correct reasoning.[293] These examples are an illustration of a general thesis that implications, logical or otherwise, are rules of inference, where inference is understood as a non-action.

803. In the case of the rules of logic, the general considerations about ought-to-bes versus ought-to-dos reappear (786-90). Suppose that logical inferences are actions and that the rules of logical inference are ought-to-dos. Being obeyed is how ought-to-dos enter into the history of a representer in order to generate action. The threatened regress looms as a consequence of rule-obeying requiring reasoning which requires obeying rules and thus, again, reasoning, and so on. At this point, in all probability, the threatened regress would force opting for the thesis that such inference can go on without obeying rules; it is but a small step to decide that all inference can go on without any rules. Sellars' avoids the choice by treating rules of inference as rules of criticism and inference as process which is not an action.

804. In one sense, then, a rule of logic is an implication and thus, on Sellars' account, an ought-to-be rule of inferring, but nothing, so far as I can tell, prevents us from also treating other judgments as "principles" of logic in a slightly different sense. Leaving further elaboration of the following points to later subsections, I forge a connection between Sellars' account of inference and a more contemporary account of principles of logic.

805. I have already "idealized" by ignoring the conditions on the principles I began with (797) and this idealization I carried over to the ought-to-bes (801). I also ignored the temporal element in the structure of the rule and thus, in Kant's sense, produced an "unschematized" rule (801.100). Now, I take one more step by "sepa-

---

[292] The word 'given' appears in the present formulation merely as a sign of conditionality and of my conviction that it is possible to envisage substantial disagreement over what the conditionality is.
[293] Actually, we might not want to dignify (798.99) and (801.100) by calling them principles and rules. They would presumably be more accurately described as examples of the more general items which are the principles or rules. I don't wish to go to the trouble of setting out all the machinery needed; so I will continue with specific examples.

rating out" (abstracting) the "core" of the rule as it applies to the judgings involved. So, ignoring everything in (801.100) which pertains to representers, to what ought to be and to the status of dot quotation as forming predicates of representers, we find that, *against this background of rules of criticism*, we can construct a very "abstract" system of relations among contents, or, in Sellars' terms, relations involving dot-quoted terms.

806. Against the background of rules of criticism, we can ask ourselves what to say about a relation (symbolized by '$\Rightarrow$') between judgings, e.g.,

(101) •2 + 2 = 4 and 5 + 7 = 12•s $\Rightarrow$ •2 + 2 = 4•s.

One story (with many variants) is that what is required for $\Rightarrow$-hood, in my example, is that, with respect to possible "something or others" (worlds, circumstances, valuations, whatever), there is not one of these in which

•2 + 2 = 4 and 5 + 7 = 12•s are true and •2 + 2 = 4•s false.

The elaboration of this story is familiar. The $\Rightarrow$-judgment (101) has a claim to being called a principle of logic though it is not a rule. For convenience and because it contains a kind of quotation, I will call this one a "meta-principle of logic" (see footnote to paragraph 802 for the appropriate qualification).

807. In addition, we can take one more step and produce yet another judging that also merits inclusion within logic. We have moved from (801.100) to (806.101) which can be called the "non-rulish meta-core" of (801.100). In the next step, one moves from the dot-quoted predicates like

•2 + 2 = 4 and 5 + 7 = 12• and •2 + 2 = 4•

to items which the predicates are true of. I assume that we can provide an intelligible story that links $\Rightarrow$-hood to some sort of conditionality (for which I shall again use the word 'given') in such a way that the truth of the meta-principle and the conditional are linked. Doing so, we get:

(102) ^{R}(given 2 + 2 = 4 and 5 + 7 = 12, 2 + 2 = 4).

The judging (102) incorporates a "non-rulish core" (without the 'meta' qualification). I assume that our accompanying story (perhaps with some qualifications) insures that (806.101) is true if and only if (807.102) is true.

808. The superscript 'R' indicates the special status of (807.102) as something "pulled out" of a rule of criticism. I shall call (807.102) a "logical principle" (see footnote to paragraph 802 for the relevant qualification). Note that (807.102) is not a rule despite the superscripted indicator of its status and despite, by its characterization, being connected to a rule of inferring.

809. The centerpiece of Sellars' story is (801.100). The philosophical movement in Sellars' account is from the categorial causal principle to the causal implication and thence to the ought-to-be, what I call a rule of logic. From the rule one gets a meta-principle of logic and then, finally, a conditional, suitably annotated to show its lineage. As in my discussion of category realism (238-43), I do not deny that "realists" of some stripe wish to see the story written in the opposite direction.

810. In sum, I have a fivefold classification of judgings relating to my example:

(i) the categorial causal principle pertaining to cognition (in 796);
(ii) the implication (under the metaphysical deduction) (798.99);
(iii) the ought-to-be—a rule of logic (801.100);
(iv) the meta-core of the ought-to-be—a meta-principle of logic (806.101).
(v) the ^{R}conditional—a principle of logic (807.102)

Of course, there are also the inferrings, thus:

2 + 2 = 4 and 5 + 7 = 12
2 + 2 = 4.

I have intentionally omitted an important comment about the connection between (iii) and (iv). It is easier to take up this point in what follows.

(d) Material rules of inferring

811. Sellars has principles in cases where cognitive states are causally connected, but not by a subject-matter neutral principle like the one lying behind my example in the previous subsection. In these cases, the inferences are what Sellars sometimes called "material inferences" and the corresponding rules are "material" (as contrasted with "formal") rules of inference. Over the years, Sellars discussed many reasons for accepting the doctrine of material rules of inference. (As we shall see, one of these reasons is in *OAFP*; for others, consult the references in second footnote to paragraph 780.)

812. One remark, which I hope sets the whole enterprise in a helpful light, concerns the extent to which Sellars sees material rules of inference as crucial to what he calls a "functional" account of thinking and of abstract objects.[294] In traditional terms, Sellars wants his doctrine of what I shall call "normative functionalism" to account for the contents of thoughts. Since the contents of thinkings obviously include much more than just logical contents, having your view encompass merely "formal" rules of inference would be insufficient.

813. I noted (783) that an analogy between language and games is important to Sellars' elaboration of his account of rules of criticism.[295] Games like chess, Sellars thinks, have rules that specify what ought to be and what ought not to be in the game. The rules of the game form a canon of what ought to be with respect to the players and the items of the game and thereby *constrain* the players' actions which result from their deliberations about the end of winning (or losing) the game.

814. The crucial point is that the pieces of chess—the bishop, the pawn, the king, the queen, and so on—are characterized by what is promulgated in the rules of chess. So, the chess analogy *illustrates* a concept—the concept of items for which the answer to the question "What is that?" is given by setting out the rules which are relevant to that item. In addition, it illustrates the way in which a "game" terminology figures into the formulation of these rules.

815. Of course, a certain kind of "parochialism" must be avoided. Chess, Sellars supposes, is played in Texas where it is called "Tess". There, the board is Texas counties and the counters which replace the common, shaped items of wood (or, something or other) are automobiles. In Tess, Volkswagens are pawns, Cadillacs are queens, and so on. Despite the different "embodiments", it is nonetheless true that Tess is just chess.[296] We "ordinary", non-Texan chess players may have, initially, too constricted a conception of chess. (Parochialism is also not unknown among Texans.) We may have thought that having a certain shape is required of pawns. Reflection on the existence of Tess leads us without great intellectual effort to a more refined conception: that the properties of pawns set down in the rules require no particular shapes, sizes or other, we might say, "material" properties. The rules can be understood, to borrow from Kant again, as "pure".

816. It is this refined conception of rules of criticism, utilizing dot quotation, which figure into Sellars' "normative functional" account of representation. By dot quotation, we can construct predicates that, like the predicates 'bishop', 'pawn', and so on, appear in sufficiently refined rules. Dot-quotation predicates, as I explained (30), are true of an unlimited variety of "materially" different counters.

---

[294] Within this volume, see *KTE*, section IX and *TTC*, 27ff. Remember that, as I remarked earlier (677), Sellars is not a "functionalist" in the presently accepted meanings of that term and the present account of rules shows why that is so.

[295] Once again, the origin of Sellars' account of games and rules can be seen in *SRLG* (in *SPR*); some of the crucial elaboration of this account can be found in *AE* (in *PPME*).

[296] "Embodiment" is not "multiple realizability". Those who speak about "multiple realization" tend to say that "properties realize other properties". No such matter is at issue here. It is merely that a Volkswagen—or indeed a toy model of a Volkswagen—can be a pawn. (Cf. *MP*, 49.)

817. The chess analogy also illustrates the importance of "material" inferences (or, "transitions"[297]) and their rules. The inferences, or transitions, enjoined by subject-matter neutral rules could never serve to distinguish other than items of logic. Similarly, you cannot distinguish pawns and bishops by logic alone. Compare the non-empiricist tradition on this very point: it is not through one's understanding of logic that one appreciates the domain of non-logical properties and relations. On the contrary, our grasp of the domain of empirical thinkables is built, according to that tradition, on a grasp of natural laws. It is a *version* of this view that Sellars wishes to capture by invoking material inferences and their principles. In its "idealized" formulation, Sellars' normative functionalism supports a version of the theses of the "transcendental doctrine of content" (674ff). So, part of the point of material inference rules is to aid a philosophical account of content: what content is like and how it is that it can be "functional" and intersubjective.

(e) The possibility of experience and the possibility of objects of experience (A158/B197)

818. I take a simple example from the realm of commonsense "chemistry", i.e., cooking, and then follow out, in generalized form, the steps in the example of the "formal" rule of inference (793-810).

819. In the example of conjunction, I "idealized" away the conditions pertaining to the frame of mind of the representer (797) in order to simplify my presentation and to emphasize the crude point (796) that conjunctive judgings cause judgings of the conjuncts. This idealization works because no conditions *other* than those pertaining to the representer's frame of mind are needed. Clearly nothing about, say, the temperature of the room, its altitude above sea level, or other things of that sort, is relevant. Yet, in cooking, a wide variety of such conditions are relevant.

820. What is the categorial causal principle and the implication in the case of frying eggs? Very crudely, a representer who judges

> that egg is in this hot skillet

is caused to judge

> that egg will shortly be a solid disk with a yellow center surrounded by an opaque white ring.[298]

---

[297] See *NAO*, ch. 4, sections II and III.
[298] Notice that "idealizing" away the temporal within the representer does not remove the temporal element *within* the judgings. Getting rid of *that* temporal element is "un-schematizing" change in general and doing that is not helpful in this context. In addition, I have ignored options in the cooking of eggs.

While we can imagine such an unadorned causal connection within a representer, a more realistic rendering would include many conditions, thus: that the egg has been laid in recent times; that the heat source has raised the temperature of the pan to a certain level, but not too high; and so on. In general, many of the needed conditions have been "built into" the arrangements of present-day terrestrial kitchens.

821. I shall call these conditions, in contrast to those pertaining to the frame of mind of the representer, "material conditions" (and abbreviate this to "MC"). Furthermore, to put my example more generally (and to adopt a standardized format the details of which I do not want to argue about here), I intend to use the word 'in' to indicate some sort of conditionality. In general, then, the relevant categorial causal principle of cognition (see 810.i) has the form

(103) in MC, a representer who thinks that this K is F is caused to think that this K will be G.

Recast as a causal implication (see 810.ii), (103) becomes

(104) in MC, that a representer, R, has a thought with the content ^this K is F^ implies that R has a thought with the content ^this K will be G^.

Compare (798.99). (Admittedly, the occurrences of the letters 'K', 'F', and 'G' are not correct, but it requires too much machinery to correct this deficiency.)

822. What ought-to-be (see 810.iii) is the above causal implication? In (821.104), I used 'in' to indicate some sort of conditionality. I had already done something similar in stating the ought-to-be (801.100) by using the word 'given'. The topic of whether these two forms of conditionality are the same, or not, is too far a reach for this introduction.[299] Without further logic-chopping, I formulate the ought-to-be as:

(105) in MC, it ought to be that, for any one of us representers, given we •this K is F•, then we •this K will be G•

823. To obtain the non-rulish meta-core, once again, everything pertaining to obligation and representers must be ignored:

(106) in MC, •this K is F• C⇒ •this K will be G•

(where the story told about 'C⇒' is a restricted form of the story told about '⇒'). One more step eliminates the dot quoting and produces the conditional which uses the non-rulish core:

---

[299] I am also determined to ignore problems about the exact logical form of the ought-to-bes.

(107) ^{R}(in MC, given this K is F, this K will be G).

Once again, I assume that the story told about 'C⇒' and about the appropriate conditionality mesh in such a way that (with, perhaps, some qualifications) (106) is true if and only if (107) is true.

824. The ought-to-be (822.105) is a "material" rule of inference and not, of course, a rule of logic. It is, on Sellars' account, a "rule of nature". Equally, (823.106) and (823.107) deserve to be called "principles of nature". To distinguish the two (and to follow my previous example), I shall call (823.106) a "natural meta-principle" and (823.107) a "natural principle". When I wish to speak of both indiscriminately, I shall simply say "law of nature".

825. In sum, then, the fivefold classification of judgings in the case of "material" principles resembles that in the case of "formal" principles:

(i) the categorial causal principle (with material conditions) (821.103);
(ii) the implication (with material conditions) (821.104);
(iii) the conditional ought-to-be—a rule of nature (822.105);
(iv) the conditional meta-core of the ought-to-be—a natural meta-principle (823.106).
(v) the ^{R}conditional—a natural principle (823.107)

826. My presentation of these judgings contains a mixture of the traditional (in terms of content) and the Sellarsian (in terms of dot quotation). I so proceed in order to highlight certain differences and to keep in touch with the passages quoted from Sellars. Put roughly and without contemporary sophistication, all five, in one way or another, concern a connection between representings of the forms

this K is F, and
this K will be G.

Given their common ground in these two representings and the reasonably simple connections among the five, it is, on Sellars' view, not surprising to find a philosopher sliding from one to another. It is something of this sort that Kant has done (777). While it is true, Sellars would say, that Kant should have been more careful, a sympathetic reading of pertinent passages, in light of the above distinctions, also shows that Kant is not much led astray. Even more, the connections among (821.103), (821.104), (822.105), (823.106), and (823.107) are such that taking them as a "package" is—though hardly the most careful way of doing things—not all that philosophically unreasonable. In sum, we can interpret Kant as, now, making remarks pertaining, strictly speaking, to one judging in the package and, then, to a different one in the package.

827. At a less surface level, Sellars can hold that his account provides cash for *some* of the promissory notes issued by Kant. Since (822.105) is directly a rule for representers, it would merit the title "principle of the possibility of experience". On the other hand, for Sellars, material rules of inference are essential for the existence of content, in particular, that content pertaining to natural objects.[300] Thus such a rule is also a "principle of the possibility of objects of experience". It is crucial to remember an element of Sellars' interpretation I discussed long ago at the very beginning of this introduction (40-55): the "objects of experience" in question are "mind-dependent" items, i.e. kinds of contents.

828. Near the ends of both versions of the transcendental deduction (A125ff, B164ff), Kant expresses his view about the status of appearances as nature in a fashion that suggests the understanding has a hand in "creating" them. At the end of my transcendental deduction (301-7) and elsewhere (323, 642, 701), I offered some explication of this claim. The Sellarsian account of rules offers the prospect of fitting in another piece. On Sellars' "normative functionalism", the ought-to-bes are what determine content. Consider a false supposition about the status of these rules: they are created by the understanding (or, better, in Kantian terms, the reason). Appearances would thus gain another direct dependence on the workings of finite intellects. No such simple supposition can be defended.[301] But something reasonably close to it can be: finite intelligences are "responsible" for the rules that guide their epistemic activities. To put the point somewhat dramatically, we have the epistemic opportunity to continue with a rule we have—and thus, in a sense, to admit that it is one we would have "made" if that were possible—or to abandon it for another one that we do "make" (still not, of course, from that impossible standpoint where we have no rules at all).

829. An account of this epistemic opportunity has an important philosophical by-product. A standard, and perhaps the dominant, empiricist criticism of any view that incorporates some *version* of the doctrine that laws of nature carry a status that, in some sense, deserves to be characterized as "necessary" is that such necessity cannot be "obtained from experience". This criticism would seem to apply with even greater force to the doctrine of rules that Sellars is recommending to Kant. Sellars' reply is thus intended to kill two birds while quite neatly falling within a framework with substantial claims to being Kantian. (It also allows me to forge the still missing account of a relationship between (825.iii) and (825.iv).)

---

[300] See *TTC*, 27ff where Sellars argues that the insight of the metaphysical deduction is completed by a doctrine of content (individuals, properties, and relations) that places them in a hierarchy of conceptual "powers" formulated by rules. See also the end of *KTE*.
[301] To find Sellars arguing this, early on and in a context which features language learning, see *SRLG*, 1-19. By way of contrast, compare *PSIM*, section II, *MP*, 60, and *BLM*, 106ff.

(f) Practical reason, rules, and inductive inquiry

830. In *CLN* (at **B18**), Sellars has a margin note to discuss a rationalist-oriented account of laws of nature by comparing Kant and Descartes on what would amount to "inductive" reasoning. Lamentably, that was all his note said. But we can, I believe, see in the essay "On Accepting First Principles" (*OAFP*) the kind of view Sellars would think appropriate.[302]

831. Very generally, Sellars account of reasoning leading to the acceptance, or rejection, of "generalizations" and, indeed, even theories, is part of an account of practical reasoning which sets center-stage, not desires, wants, wishes and so on, but intending.[303] Sellars regiments the expressions of intendings by using the word 'shall'. In *OAFP*, he is particularly concerned with intersubjective intendings which begin with the phrase 'we shall'. These intersubjective intendings are also general in other respects. They would not misleadingly be called "epistemic policies."

832. I quote the essential points from several paragraphs in *OAFP*[304] which occur after Sellars discusses, with the help of the example of scientific theories, the framework of practical reasoning he requires:

> 30. ..... I want, therefore, to show how this approach can be extended to the probability of empirical generalizations. It is my conviction that once we get a feeling for what probability amounts to in the case of theories, then the classical problem of induction with respect to empirical generalizations turns out to be much more manageable, and many things fall into place which would otherwise remain a tangled mess.
> 31. Let's suppose therefore that to say of a law-like statement, LL_1, that it is probable means something like this:
>
> There is a good and sufficient argument of a certain kind for accepting LL_1.
>
> This would itself be the conclusion of an argument of the type represented by (β) in our earlier discussion. And the argument which is asserted to exist will be a practical syllogism of the type represented by (γ).
> 32. The practical argument in question has the form:
>
> We shall bring about E.
> Bringing about E involves accepting law-like statements which are ψ.

---

[302] See, also, *NDL*(73) and *IV*(54), the latter of which he cites in *OAFP*. Sellars sets his position on "inductive" reasoning on a wider stage than I can produce here. My remarks are limited to countering the empiricist challenge and setting the stage for the questions of the following subsection.
[303] Here Sellars has a large selection of essays running from the early to the late; see the references in the footnote to paragraph 786.
[304] The fact that, though *OAFP* was published in 1988, it was written in the 1960's explains some of the tenor and formulations of the paper.

LL_1 is ψ.
Therefore, we shall accept LL_1.

This schema raises the questions,

What is E?

and

What is the character, ψ?

To take up the latter question first, it is clear that ψ has something to do with the relation of LL_1 to observation. This relation is a logical relation, R_L. Let us put it by saying that the law-like statement must 'accord' with the observational evidence. To determine what 'according', R_L, might be, we must first come to some conclusion about the form of a law-like statement. And, curiously enough, to do this we must come to some conclusion about the nature of the end-in-view, E.

33. Is it, perhaps, the state of possessing true beliefs about the limit frequency of a quaesitum property, Q, in an infinite reference class, R? In other words, the relative frequency of cases of Q among cases of R "in the long run"? Is it, limiting ourselves for simplicity to non-statistical law-like statements, the state of having true beliefs of the form:

$(x)(fx \to gx)$,

i.e., (roughly) for all values of 'x', if x is f then x is g? Whichever line we take we run into the difficulty that the end is one we could never know ourselves to have reached, and I submit that any end with reference to which the doing of a certain action is to be justified must be the sort of thing that can be known to be realized.

34. The general point is related to our earlier attempt to distinguish between a *good* practical argument and one which was *merely* valid, i.e., to specify something which would play a role analogous to "having true premises" in the case of good non-practical arguments. There we suggested that it was a matter of the actual existence of the intention to bring about E. But it now appears that the appraisal of a practical argument as good requires that we say not only that the agent had the intention and that he *believed* that the action would realize it, but that it is actually realized. Thus, "Jones' action was justified *because it brought about E*".

35. Instead of the phantom ends considered above I suggest that the end-in-view, E, in the case of the acceptance of law-like statements is the state of being in a position to draw inferences concerning new cases, in a way which explains the observed cases. In other words, our proximate end-in-view is to have a principle of inference which applies in the same way to 'new' and 'old' cases. And the state of having such a principle *is* the sort of thing that we can know that we are in. And to be in this state requires *accepting* principles of inference which conform to this criterion. This *accepting* is what in our

terminology is called the *terminal* outcome of a practical syllogism which has as its *logical* outcome or conclusion, "I shall accept LL_1".

36. Thus, reflection on the proximate end-in-view of inductive reasoning supports the view, which, as we shall see, has independent support, that law-like statements have the form of principles of inference. In the case of non-statistical law-like statements, we can suppose that they have the form (roughly):

From 'x is f', it may be inferred that 'x is g'.

...

37. Now new evidence may well lead us to abandon one inference ticket and accept another. But the point is that as long as we have the evidence we do have, and this evidence is that all observed cases of f are g, we know that we have an inference ticket which accords with evidence and applies to the cases we expect to encounter.

38. As I see it, then reflection on the probability of law-like statements reinforces a conception which arises independently in the exploration of problems pertaining to counterfactual conditionals, the intuitive distinction between accidental and non-accidental uniformities and the concept of 'natural necessity'. For this exploration has constantly generated the idea (rejected only because it treads on radical empiricist toes) that law-like statements are inference tickets. Unlike the inference tickets of formal logic, they are empirically based in the sense that they are accepted because it is reasonable to accept them, given the evidence and given our proximate end-in-view.

39. Law-like statements, therefore, are empirically based principles of inference which authorize such inferences as, to use a crude example, 'Lightning now, therefore thunder shortly'. It also authorizes such conditionals as 'If there had been lightning then, there would have been thunder shortly' and such statements as 'There was thunder then *because* there had been lightning shortly before' and 'That there was lightning shortly before made it necessary that there be thunder then'.

833. Sellars' view of inductive inquiry helps in making good on the Kantian claim that theoretical reason is set within practical reason. Inductive inquiry is, for Sellars, part of the province of practical reason and thus practical reasonings are to be found in inductive inquiry. But the one "reasoning" David Hume worried so much about, "induction" as he understood it, is not there. So, it cannot, I think, be too much emphasized that the fundamentals of Sellars' account of inductive inquiry depart from the empiricist model right from the beginning.

834. This fundamental difference undercuts the empiricist criticism (829). Whatever status a material rule can be defended as having, that status is not derived from its being a conclusion of an argument whose premises concern individual objects, their properties and relations. To many, non-empiricist accounts of natural law seem to depend on *validly* getting something—"necessity" (and "universality")—out of premises which lacked it. No such attempt is part of Sellars' account.

835. On the other hand, what an empiricist would have considered "experience"

294   *Introduction*

is relevant to material rules. Material rules must "accord" with, loosely speaking, "past experience" (*OAFP*, 32, 37). There is an acceptable sense in which material rules have their "source" in experience while not having *what they are*, and thus *their status*, derive from that experience.[305]

836. In addition, item (825.iv)[306] has a feature hard to incorporate within traditional empiricism. The tale that provides the characterization of 'C⇒' invokes "possible" somethings—worlds, circumstances, valuations, whatever (823). Let me use the term 'world' without any of the stronger commitments occurring in some views on possible worlds. The judging

(823.106) in MC, •this K is F• C⇒ •this K will be G•

is true just in case, putting it crudely, in certain possible worlds, when MC obtains,

given •this K is F•s are true, then •this K will be G•s are true.

837. Of course, neither (823.106) nor the possible worlds characterization that goes with it directly form any part of the practical reasoning for accepting a material rule of inference. Still, (823.106) and its attendant unpacking are not irrelevant to the practical reasoning. What they do is, first, to answer the question: which cases are relevant to our acceptance of a material rule of inference? In terms of my example, the answer they offer is that in any world in the collection of possible worlds, when MC obtains, and

given •this K is F•s are true,

then the question is whether •this K will be G•s are true. At bottom, then, as representers, we must concern ourselves with sequences of judgings in MC,

this K is F
this K is G

where the second judging concerns a "now" after the "now" of the first judging. Second, the characterization of what it means to say that "the law-like statement must 'accord' with the observational evidence" (*OAFP*, 32) is in hand: it is that in the appropriate sort of cases in which the circumstances MC are "actual", given it is true that

---

[305] I take these points to firm up the point that Kant makes about Hume at A766/B794.
[306] I conduct the following discussion in terms of item (iv) in the list pertaining to material rules of inference. I do take it that most of my remarks apply, with certain amendments, to item (iv) in the list pertaining to formal rules of inference.

this K is F,

then it is true that

this K will be G.

The failure of this conditional with regard to any "actual" case of the appropriate sort stands in the way of acceptance for a material rule of inference.[307]

838. No attempt is here being made to "define" rules of inference in terms which are not "rule-ish". All that is being laid out is the background of standards that material rules of inference must meet. So, even if it should turn out that there is no way to specify the appropriate worlds apart from the material rules of inference themselves, that will make no difference. Since no "definition" in a strict sense is being attempted, circularity is not at issue.

839. The standard (823.106) specifies what must be in order for the material rule of inference (822.105) to be correct.[308] To appreciate what is being claimed here, ignore the operations of the understanding as the productive imagination; consider only the understanding acting on its own.[309] By the standard of acceptance for material rules of inference, any representer, in *any* appropriate world, who accepts, and conforms to, only correct material rules of inference constructs a story of that world (301-7) containing successions of representings (inferrings) that *always* "accord" with successions that are "actual" in that world. Given the standard, then, in any appropriate world, that the material rule (822.105) is correct implies (823.106), and (823.106) implies that the material rule (822.105) is correct.

840. I have been adumbrating some of what Sellars takes to be packed into Kant's ideal of "critique" in so far as that pertains to what is required for representers to have sufficient "cognitive wherewithal" so that some of their representations can count as knowledge (or, at least, justified true belief). In at least a rudimentary form, they must appreciate what it is to be "responsible" for the rules that govern their intellectual activities. Motivating this part of Sellars' account is a concern for the claim that the "understanding is the faculty of rules" and that the understanding (or,

---

[307] Yes, there are other requirements that would need to be considered in a more detailed account. Also, it is not correct that failure is a simple matter of believing that we have, in MC, a K which is F but is not later G. It is obviously part of the burden of the account of appropriate cases that we must support the claim that we have a genuine case. Moreover, I follow a strict terminology in which what might ordinarily be called the "revising" (or, "refining") of a rule (by, e.g., adding additional conditions) is really the abandoning of one rule and the accepting of another.

[308] I have no qualms about using the word 'true' here instead of 'correct'. Since others do, I thought it easier to avoid the distraction by using the word 'correct'.

[309] It is exactly this that Kant suggests at A293-4/B350. There he says that, in an understanding which is unfettered by the senses and which "accords" with its own "laws", there is no error.

296   *Introduction*

the reason) has a claim to being the "creator" of appearances. It will come as no surprise that the theses of this subsection have rather substantial consequences for other parts of Sellars' Kantian edifice.

(g) Apperception and rules: the Platonic strata

841. When Sellars says that the basic form of empirical knowledge is "an I" thinking a state of affairs as an element of a system (nature) which includes states of that very "I"(*KTE*, 11; *I*, 9), he has in mind a subject (a representer) that fits his remark in *OAPK*:

> ...The answer should be obvious: the members of a linguistic community are *first* language *learners* and only potentially 'people', but *subsequently* language *teachers*, possessed of the rich conceptual framework this implies. They start out by being the *subject-matter* subjects of the ought-to-dos and graduate to the status of *agent* subjects of the ought-to-dos. Linguistic ought-to-bes are translated into *uniformities* by training. As Wittgenstein has stressed, it is the linguistic community as a self-perpetuating whole which is the minimum unit in terms of which conceptual activity can be understood.[310] (*OAPK*, 25)

Full-fledged representers conceive of themselves as governed by ought-to-bes and, through their epistemic policies, as accepters and rejecters of ought-to-bes, and thus as beings, at least in part, in control of their epistemic destiny.

842. These points must, however, be combined with points discussed earlier (816, 828): Sellars account of rules of criticism is a part of his "normative functional" account of the content of thinking. The dot-quoted verbs are characterized, like chess terminology, by the rules and are thus part of the vocabulary of practical reason: they are, if you like, "prescriptive" terms. In apperceiving, we are caused to think, thus:

> I think [content], e.g.,
> I have a thought with the content $^{\wedge}2 + 2 = 4^{\wedge}$, i.e.,
> I think that $2 + 2 = 4$.

For Sellars, however, this apperceptive thinking is just:

> I •$2 + 2 = 4$•.

---

[310] Sellars, of course, has written extensively on the matter of how such a community might be accounted for. Just for starters, try *SRLG*, 1-17 and *PSIM* (43), both in *SPR*; for related issues, try *NAO* (104) (ch. 4), *BLM* (108), and *MEV* (112).

So, in apperceiving our own thoughts, we are locating ourselves within practical reason, not within—what might be construed narrowly as—theoretical reason.

843. Even more importantly, in apperceiving, the framework of rules is brought within the causal order (771).[311] Let me put the point of paragraph 842 in traditional terms: in attributing contents to thinkings, even in apperceivings, we are attributing to ourselves states that essentially involve rules. The Sellarsian aesthetic provides an unproblematic place for such a thesis, a place made possible, Sellars would claim, by rejecting the Myth of the "given" in all its forms.

844. Games illustrate part of what Sellars has in mind. Among the many things we do not see *of* objects (696), we do not see *of* them that they are pawns. As I have repeatedly stressed (696-8), no such limits apply to seeing *as*. We do see little pieces of plastic, of wood, or of whatever, and Volkswagens (in Texas) *as* pawns. This is NOT a matter of inference (718, 731, 760).

845. In any particular embodiment of a game, there are true biconditionals that reflect the fact that it is that embodiment, rather than some other embodiment. So, in Texas among Tess players, it is true that

something is a pawn if and only if it is a Volkswagen.

No one is precluded from utilizing such a biconditional in their reasoning. But someone who thinks that Jones just moved a pawn as a conclusion of piece of reasoning that employs the biconditional as a premiss, or indeed as a conclusion of any piece of reasoning, is *not* perceiving. On the Sellarsian aesthetic, no reasonings are part of perceiving (572-87, 731); yet it can be that

Jones just moved this pawn

is a perceiving by Smith. Admittedly, it is not impossible to imagine a person, Brown, who has been trained to forego chess concepts in perceiving and, while in Texas, perceives items as Volkswagens and only then reasons to

Jones just moved this pawn.

That does not show that the rest of us are not like Smith who perceives that Jones has just moved a pawn and thus perceives directly in "game" concepts.

846. An analogous point obtains in case of apperceivings. In certain circumstances, I am caused to think

---

[311] Again I omit the topic of intentional action and the causality involved therein even though it is an obviously relevant topic. See the references in the footnote to paragraph 786.

I •2 + 2 = 4•.

This, too, is not a matter of inference (731), but it is a response utilizing a predicate characterized "normatively". We can, with some justification, believe that, for human beings, it will be possible some day to fill in the biconditional

S •2 + 2 = 4•s if and only if S ...(something neurophysiological)... .

Our confidence has not yet been rewarded.[312] There are two points that should not be confused.

847. If (or, when, if you're optimistic) our confidence is rewarded, the "goods" on the neurophysiology will surely be immensely complicated. Except in rare experimental situations, no one will think thoughts about "something neurophysiological" as premises for conclusions about thinking.[313] Setting up these situations depends on many things including the experimenters' having an appreciation of what they are thinking. Without the experimental situation "up and running", their beliefs about what they are thinking have as their source apperceiving. And this again is not a matter a reasoning, but a direct normative response.

848. But suppose we hold it possible to have an analog of Brown for the case of thinking. That possibility won't show that we are all like that. The central point, on Sellars' account, is that we apperceive ourselves as beings of practical reason subject to rules; moreover, such a doctrine is an outgrowth of, and consonant with, other parts of his view. I can think of philosophical views on which such a result would be a source of worry. I have one in mind to which I can reply here.

849. I contrast a mostly, but not exclusively, empiricist line of thought with the Sellarsian one I have been describing. This line of thought maintains, contrary to what it considers a naive approach, that the entire structure of our thought about the world—about anything—is "built upon" and, so to speak, "driven" by the "really" empirical. The "really" empirical is what philosophers, mostly in the empiricist tradition, have taken to be "there" in the world; these are the items that are, in some way, elements in "facts". Of course, variation in convictions about what is "really" there in the world is not unknown. Still and all, the thrust of this idea is that one can discover what sorts of items are "really there" in the "facts" of the world. At least some of these are what we obtain access to, more or less successfully, in perception. Usually it is held that these "really there" items are rather limited and certainly do not require anything from us. Our distinctive "contribution" to the natural world is

---

[312] For Kant, of course, all this pertains to appearances since he believes that it is literally not possible for us to fill in the right side of any such biconditional for the in itself.
[313] We are not even guaranteed that the "something neurophysiological" is exactly the same when I •2 + 2 = 4• as when you do. A common enough case of such differences may be provided by those who are deaf from birth and whose maturation as thinkers has depended on learning a "sign" language.

the possession of desires which direct ("drive"?) us to reason about how to satisfy them by obtaining items that either are, or depend on, what's "really there". "The reason is, and ought to be, the slave of the passions." This line of thought has been elevated to full stature in discussions of morals, politics, and economics, but it has its feet in epistemology and metaphysics.

850. Against this rather fuzzy, but familiar, philosophical stance, I set what I should like to call the "Platonic" alternative (in some ways, I admit, equally fuzzy). Here I employ the term 'platonic' in a sense quite unlike the ones it has in its most common philosophical occurrences. Plato's dialogues, especially *Republic*, present us with a long, elaborated example of a structure that Sellars takes very seriously. Contemporary doctrines tend to carve the structure of thought (or, language), and with it perception, along lines that reflect commitments that arose during the modern period. Even the most casual survey of *Republic* shows that Plato had in mind something that allows our "contribution" to have considerably more scope.

851. First, judgings (to use a Kantian term) about individual objects and their properties and relations form an assumed background against which "dialogue" went on. In Plato's examples of judgings about individual objects, one finds almost no invidious philosophical distinguishing: more or less natural properties, moral and political attributes—none are relegated to the inferior or "less than real" status.[314] What Sellars and I look upon as Procrustean relegation, based largely on combining a faulty doctrine of perception with a philosophical wish to have the "empirically real" *dictate* the content of our experience, is simply not there (see (163.Ph2), a similar thesis which I rejected).

852. Second, it is possible, so Socrates (if we are to believe the literary presentation) discovered, to elicit from not all that reflective people principles of various sorts. Some of these principles might, not without reason, be classed as "definitions": justice (morality) is repaying what you owe; justice (morality) is what is to the advantage of stronger. Other principles are of a quite different sort. They are, broadly speaking, causal principles. In *Republic*, some of them have the form illustrated by "generally, starting with young human specimens of this sort and training (educating) them in such-and-such a way produces mature individuals of a certain sort". Large parts of *Republic* are devoted to Socrates' obtaining educated and tolerably reflective assent to such principles.

853. Third, however, is yet a different strata of judging which invokes reflection of a more refined sort. Not yet midway through *Republic* (449a), we are told that the questions being raised by Socrates' companions will require them to "start over" from the beginning. For literary effect, Plato drags all this out, into three "waves" each worse than the one before, to emphasize the climax in which he declares

---

[314] Except, of course, to the extent that the entire world of "becoming" might be inferior.

(473d) that philosophers are to be kings of their constructed community.[315] From a more contemporary perspective,[316] what strikes us is that Plato is having Socrates take into account reasonably astute objections to the principles they have set out. In general, the question being asked is: "why do you think that this principle is correct?" Reflection on principles, with an eye to their improvement or replacement, is an obvious step from the utilization of principles one has.

854. Being an intelligence with the concepts needed to navigate this three-strata Platonic structure is necessary in order to be a representer whose representings formulate knowledge (or, justified true belief). These strata are *not* like the layers of a cake in which the upper layers are "built on" the bottom one:

> ... There is clearly *some* point to the picture of human knowledge as resting on a level of propositions—observation reports—which do not rest on other propositions in the same way as other propositions rest on them. On the other hand, I do wish to insist that the metaphor of 'foundation' is misleading in that it keeps us from seeing that if there is a logical dimension in which other empirical propositions rest on observation reports, there is another logical dimension in which the latter rest on the former. (*EPM*, 38)

As Sellars sees it, one Kantian point about empirical knowledge is that only the sufficiently epistemologically "critical" can have it. Part of achieving that level of "critical" sophistication is being a representer that responds to itself in normative (practical) terms and thus conceives of itself as subject to rules and as responsible for their acceptance and rejection. To illustrate the complexity Sellars has in mind, I develop an example arising directly from the concerns of this introduction.

855. In *OAPK*, Sellars is willing to work with the a very simple example:

> 21. To fix our ideas, let us consider an example which, though simplified to its bare bones, contains the essence of the matter:
>
> (*Ceteris paribus*) one ought to respond to red objects in sunlight by uttering or being disposed to utter 'this is red'. (*OAPK*, 21)

I should like an example that harks back to my earlier discussions (379ff, 395ff). In terms of my present treatment, the ought-to-be I want as an example is:

---

[315] I put this as a matter of "literary effect" because readers of *Republic* would not find Plato's point very exciting once they reflect that the needs of a city, and a soul, are "producing, protecting, and ruling". By definition (474aff), the philosophical part of complex entity (city or soul) is just that in the entity which cares about knowledge, about getting it right, and is committed to acting in light of knowledge. Who else would you want to rule?

[316] Perhaps, as Kant says (A314/B370), we understand Plato better than he understood himself. Perhaps, perhaps...but I am always suspicious that, with Plato, we find someone who quite regularly understood himself very well indeed.

Introduction 301

(108) in MC, it ought to be that, given O has a red rectangular facing surface, we •O has a red rectangular facing surface•.

Continuing my policy of idealizing away (797) the factors collected under "frame of mind", I assume the persons I am discussing are in the required frame of mind. All the other conditions (see the qualifications leading up to (395.P1)), I collect, as I have now been doing (821), under the heading "material conditions" (MC).

856. I set out a principle which bears directly on "the present testimony of our senses", which incorporates the ought-to-be (855.108), and which displays the importance of the top strata of the Platonic structure for any sufficiently reflective and "critical" perceiver. This principle reformulates my earlier remarks (762) on the connection between perceptual states and empirical objects in light of the claim that we need to be sufficiently "critical" of the rules to which we are subject.

857. I separate the parts of this principle and comment as I go. The first is:

(109) I am in MC.

In this case, MC are the various, suitable circumstances, normal conditions and normal state of the perceiver that I discussed in connection with (395.P1). In general, the conditions and the state of the perceiver need not be normal and the circumstances need not be suitable. Whatever the material conditions might be, (109) does, because of the spatiotemporal elements that cannot be avoided, place me in nature as subject to the "objective unity of apperception" (301ff; *CLN*, **A21-22a**).

858. The second is:

(110) I accept

(855.108) in MC, it ought to be that, given O has a red rectangular facing surface, we •O has a red rectangular facing surface•

and, through the "criticism" required by (855.108), my cognitive activity conforms to it.[317]

Formulating (110) with (855.108) is merely a matter of convenience; the "vulgar" can be thought of as using equivalent forms, even though these forms do not make

---

[317] Sellars' comments, in *OAPK*, on the relationship of ought-to-bes to ought-to-dos fill in part of the story here. Nothing in my present remarks commits me to anything about how we got to that cognitive sophistication required by (110) (learning a language, innate endowment, or, à la St. Augustine, illumination). Note, too, that the intersubjectivity of the "we" in (110) guarantees that the "criticisms" of others must be taken into account.

evident everything that Sellars takes to be involved. (110) captures my realization that part of my general cognitive state occurs because of an activity, "cognitive husbandry", which I, as a natural being, am required to perform.

859. To sum up: (857.109) says that I am in the conditions required by the ought-to-be (855.108); (858.110) says that (854.108) is a rule I accept, and with respect to my cognitive state and that rule, everything is as it ought to be. (In addition, I am assuming that I am in the appropriate frame of mind.) Suppose that

(111) an •O has a red rectangular facing surface• just occurred to me and it is a case of ostensible perceiving.

The differences in the accounts of perceiving suitable for the "aesthetically sophisticated" and for the "vulgar" (572-94) are not important here. What is important is that (111) says that I apperceive a thinking (which is an ostensible perceiving); my apperceiving requires that some "empirical" apperceivings are also true (703, 722-31).[318] I am responding to my thinking that O has a red rectangular facing surface by thinking that I just thought that and, *as a response to my total state*, I judge that I am ostensibly perceiving.[319] Judging (111) specifies the way in which my thinking came about and is inconsistent with my thinking having come about in other ways (daydreaming, deliberating, or whatever).

860. The transcendental principle is a conditional with a biconditional consequent (it is of the form "given A and B, C if and only if D"). The principle is:

(113) given

A (857.109) I am in MC, and
B (858.110) I accept

(855.108) in MC, it ought to be that, given O has a red rectangular facing surface, we •O has a red rectangular facing surface•

and, through the "criticism" required by (855.108), my cognitive activity conforms to it,

C (859.111) an •O has a red rectangular facing surface• just occurred to me and it is case of ostensible perceiving

---

[318] Of course, a Kantian story about the in itself can be included at this juncture (656-86), but it would not effect the major points I am about to make.
[319] Remember that the claim to even ostensible perceiving involves claims about causality (572-94).

if and only if

D (112) O has a red rectangular facing surface.

The principle thus connects a

•O has a red rectangular facing surface•

that comes about as an ostensible perceiving to a

•O has a red rectangular facing surface• (i.e., (112))

that comes about through thinking a principle of transcendental philosophy.

861.   In terms of the three-strata Platonic structure, the principle belongs to the third stratum as it involves a part which is about a rule. The subject who, even rudimentarily, understands the principle must conceive itself as an "I" subject to rules of criticism ("ought-to-bes") as well as a natural object. Also, the subject must treat "we" as including "me".

862.   Indeed, it must be the same "I" throughout the principle as thinks the principle. This "unity" is, on Sellars' account, another manifestation of the transcendental unity of apperception. (The simplest statement of the principle of the transcendental unity is the one given by Sellars (678)).

863.   Consider the epistemic impact of a situation in which an "I" that can think (860.113) is confronted with the failure of the biconditional within (860.113). Broadly speaking and once again assuming the appropriate frame of mind, I find that my choices are that:

> the true world story (302ff) and nature (its categorial correlate) (307), including my own states, are not what I think they are

or

> the rules of criticism which I accept and which guide my cognitive husbandry are incorrect.

864.   Principle (860.113) articulates part of the framework within which epistemic betterment can be achieved. The tools for this are the principles and concepts of the understanding, basically the principles of logic and of nature including those that pertain to the operations of the sensibility and the productive imagination and the concepts of space and time, and the categories. It is not that (860.113), or anything like it, enables us to prove that there is empirical knowledge (or, even justified true belief). Rather, it is an example of something which is necessary in order for a thinking which occurs in an ostensible perceiving to be a piece of empirical knowledge (or, justified true belief) (*TTC*, 54-5). So, though

> there is a logical dimension in which other empirical propositions rest on observation reports, there is another logical dimension in which the latter rest on the former. (*EPM*, section 38)

865. The normative elements of Sellars' account are, in many ways, the heart of his, if I may so put it, recommendations to Kant. The common construal of the opposition between Kant and Hume as arising from a disagreement over synthetic a priori judgments misses, by Sellars' lights, a deeper and more fundamental conflict, that over the status of practical reason:

> 1. Practical reasoning, in a broad sense, brings particular matters of fact, empirical generalizations, scientific laws and logical principles to bear on values. ... A full theory of practical reasoning would bring out, for example, its involvement in scientific reasoning, where the values involved are epistemic. ...
> 2. Theoretical reason is...a structure of many levels. ...yet, as I have indicated, these structures exist in an ambience of rules of criticism, which themselves belong to the domain of practical reason, *qua* concerned with epistemic values. ...
> 3. But my aim is this chapter is...to explore the fundamental principles of a metaphysics of practice, with particular reference to the values in terms of which we lead not just one compartment of our lives but our lives *sans phrase*. I have said enough, however, to indicate that in my opinion the metaphysics of morals is but a fragment of a broader critique of practical reason. A philosophical interpretation of 'ought to be' and 'ought to do' with respect to everyday living must ultimately cohere with an account of theoretical reason which makes intelligible the truth and intersubjectivity of epistemic evaluation.
> 4. And, indeed, a theory of practical reasoning in morals which denies the *in principle* intersubjectivity and truth of the ought-to-be's and ought-to-do's of everyday life must face the challenge of the ought-to-be's and ought-to-do's of theoretical reason. This challenge has largely been ignored. ... I think...the facing of this challenge is the culmination of the philosophical enterprise... . (*SM*, ch. VII, 1-4)

Bibliography

Works of Kant

CPR	Immanuel Kant, *Critique of Pure Reason*, translated by Werner S. Pluhar (Hackett Publishing Company, 1996).
G	*Grounding of the Mataphysics of Morals*, translated by James W. Ellington (Hackett Publishing Company, 1981).
L	*Immanuel Kant Logic*, translated by Robert Hartman and Wolfgang Schwarz (The Bobbs-Merrill Company, 1974).
MFNS	Immanuel Kant, *Metaphysical Foundations of Natural Science*, translated by James Ellington in *Immanuel Kant, Philosophy of Material Nature* (Hackett Publishing Company, 1985).
O	Immanuel Kant, *On a Discover According to which Any New Critique of Pure Reason Has Been Made Superfluous by an Earlier One*, in Henry E. Allison, *The Kant-Eberhard Controvery: An English translation together with supplementary materials and a historical-analytic introduction* (The Johns Hopkins University Press, 1973).
OP	Immanuel Kant, *Opus Postumum*, edited, with an introduction and notes, by Eckart Förster and translated by Eckart Förster and Michael Rosen (Cambridge University Press, 1993).
PFM	Immanuel Kant, *Prolegomena to Any Future Metaphysics*, translated by James Ellington in *Immanuel Kant, Philosophy of Material Nature* (Hackett Publishing Company, 1985).

Other Works

Kathleen Akins, "Of Sensory Systems and the "Aboutness" of Mental States", *Journal of Philosophy*, XCIII, 7, July, 1996, pp. 337-372.
Henry E. Allison, *Kant's Transcendental Idealism: An Interpretation and Defense* (Yale University Press, 1983).
Karl Ameriks, "Recent Work on Kant's Theoretical Philosophy, *American Philosophical Quarterly*, 19, 1, January, 1982.
Richard Aquila, *Representational Mind: A Study in Kant's Theory of Knowledge* (Indiana University Press, 1983).
Bruce Aune, *Knowledge, Mind, and Nature* (Random House, 1967; thereafter reprinted by Ridgeview Publishing Company).
Bruce Aune, *Knowledge of the External World* (Routledge, 1991).
David Bell, "Kant" in Nicholas Bunnin and E.P. Tsui-James (editors), *The Blackwell Companion to Philosophy* (Blackwell Publishers, 1996).
Panayot Butchvarov, "Adverbial Theories of Consciousness," *Midwest Studies in Philosophy*, volume 5, *Studies in Epistemology* (University of Minnesota Press, 1980), pp. 261-280.
Richard E. Cytowic, *The Man Who Tasted Shapes* (MIT Press, 1998).
Phillip D. Cummins and Guenter Zoeller (eds), *Minds, Ideas, and Objects: Essays on the Theory of Representation in Modern Philosophy* (Volume 2, 1992, North American Kant Society Studies in Philosophy) (Ridgeview Publishing Company, 1992).
Daniel C. Dennett, *Consciousness Explained* (Little, Brown and Co., 1991).
Daniel C. Dennett, "Wondering Where the Yellow Went", *Monist*, 64, 102-8.
Daniel C. Dennett, *Consciousness Explained* (Little, Brown and Co., 1991).
Daniel C. Dennett, "Quining Qualia", *The Nature of Consciousness: Philosophical Debates*, edited by

Ned Block, Owen Flanagan, and Güven Güzekdere (MIT Press, 1998), 619-642.

Paul Guyer, *Kant and the Claims of Knowledge* (Cambridge University Press, 1987).

C. L. Hardin, *Color for Philosophers: Unweaving the Rainbow* (Hackett Publishing Company, 1988).

Otfried Höffe, *Immanual Kant*, translated by Marshall Farrier (State University of New York Press, 1994).

David Hume, *A Treatise of Human Nature*, edited by L.A. Selby-Bigge (Oxford University Press, 1888).

Patricia Kitcher, *Kant's Transcendental Psychology* (Oxford University Press, 1990).

David Lewis, "Naming the Colours," *Australasian Journal of Philosophy*, 75 (1997), 325-342.

William G. Lycan, *Consciousness* (The MIT Press, 1987).

William G. Lycan, *Consciousness and Experience* (The MIT Press, 1996).

William G. Lycan, "In Defense of the Representational Theory of Qualia (Replies to Neander, Rey, and Tye)" in *Philosophical Perspectives, 12, Language, Mind, and Ontology, 1998*, edited by James E. Tomberlin (Blackwell Publishers, 1998), pp. 479-87.

John McDowell, "Having the World in View: Sellars, Kant, and Intentionality", The Woodbridge Lectures 1997, *The Journal of Philosophy*, XCV, 9, September, 1998.

Hoke Robinson, "Kant on Embodiment", in Phillip D. Cummins and Guenter Zoeller (eds), *Minds, Ideas, and Objects: Essays on the Theory of Representation in Modern Philosophy* (Volume 2, 1992, North American Kant Society Studies in Philosophy) (Ridgeview Publishing Company, 1992).

Jay F. Rosenberg, *Linguistic Representation* (D. Reidel Publishing Co., 1974 and 1981).

Jay F. Rosenberg, *The Thinking Self* (Temple University Press, 1986).

Johanna Seibt, *Properties as Processes: A Synoptic Study of Wilfrid Sellars' Nominalism* (Ridgeview Publishing Company, 1990).

Jeffrey F. Sicha, *A Metaphysics of Elementary Mathematics* (University of Massachusetts Press, 1974).

Michael Tye, *Ten Problems of Consciousness: a Representational Theory of the Phenomenal Mind* (MIT Press, 1995).

James Van Cleve, "The Argument from Geometry, Transcendental Idealism, and Kant's Two Worlds," in Phillip D. Cummins and Guenter Zoeller (eds), *Minds, Ideas, and Objects: Essays on the Theory of Representation in Modern Philosophy* (Volume 2, 1992, North American Kant Society Studies in Philosophy) (Ridgeview Publishing Company, 1992).

ONTOLOGY, THE A PRIORI AND KANT

Part One[1]

1. Kant's theory of knowledge belongs squarely in the platonic tradition. It is a doctrine of innate conceptual abilities and propensities. These abilities and propensities are brought into play by the impressions of sense, but are in no way derived from these impressions. They form a systematic unity the elements of which are radically diverse and play radically different roles in human knowing. It has long been found fruitful to compare this innate structure to a language and to use linguistic parallels in explicating the forms and functions of its various parts. My contribution to this symposium will be no exception.

2. On the other hand, many recent accounts of Kant's theory of knowledge, by concentrating their attention on the extent to which Kantian things can be said about language—which, after all, is a part of the public, spatial-temporal world—cut themselves off from an understanding of the sense in which Kant was an idealist who believed himself to have shown that nature is a system of human thoughts. It would indeed be paradoxical to say that nature is a system of sentences, which is what Kant's thesis becomes when the linguistic model is taken to be the substance of his views. Thus the second half of my essay will highlight some of the features of Kant's ontology which are obscured by the linguistic approach.

I

3. The understanding, Kant tells us, is the faculty of rules. He also says that concepts have the character of rules. It seems appropriate, therefore, to begin these remarks with some reflections on the concepts of rule and of following a rule. In accordance with the program sketched above, my initial aim will be to see what these concepts amount to in the context of linguistic behavior.

4. There are many interesting questions about the exact meaning or meanings of the term 'rule' in non-philosophical contexts. What, for example, is the difference between a "rule" and a "principle"? Are prin-

---

[1] [Part Two of this typescript became 67, *KTE*. The date on the mimeographed copy of Part One is 1970. Part Two, *KTE*, was, however, published in 1967. Perhaps Sellars revised Part One in 1970 and thus it came to bear that later date.]

ciples simply "first" rules in that they are not special applications of more general rules? Or is the primary difference that rules can be arbitrary? Or are principles rules for choosing rules, the principle of induction, for example, a (non-arbitrary?) rule for choosing law-like statements, themselves construed as extra-logical rules of inference? Though these questions are intrinsically interesting and relevant to the general topic of this paper, I shall not discuss them. For however the domain of norms and standards is to be stratified and botanized, the term 'rule' has acquired over the years a technical and generic sense in which it applies to general statements concerning that which ought or ought not to be done or to be the case, or to be permissible or not permissible—distinctions which can be put in many different ways.

5. For our purposes, then, a rule is roughly a general 'ought' statement. Such statements have been traditionally divided into hypothetical and categorical 'ought's, or, as it has often misleadingly been put, 'imperatives'. The distinction between hypothetical and categorical oughts is an important one, though I believe that they are far more intimately related than is ordinarily taken to be the case.

6. Hypothetical oughts have the form 'if one wants X, one ought to do Y'. They transpose the relation of implication between a state of affairs X and a doing of Y into an implication appropriate to practical reasoning. In spite of their crucial importance to a theory of normative discourse, I shall have nothing to say about them, save by implication.

7. As far as anything I have so far said is concerned, a categorical ought is simply one that is not, in the familiar Kantian sense, a hypothetical ought. I shall continue my division informally by calling attention to the most familiar variety of general categorical oughts, those, namely, of the form

> If one is in C, one ought to do A.

Notice that although this proposition is conditional in form, it is not, in the Kantian sense, a hypothetical ought; and it is as contrasted with the latter that, even though it is conditional, it is called categorical. By application and the use of modus ponens one can derive conclusions of the form

> x ought to do A

which not only are not hypothetical oughts, but are categorical (non-iffy) statements.

8. The important feature, for our purposes, of general categorical oughts of the above form is that for actual existence to conform to these oughts is a matter of the agents to which they apply doing A when they are in the specified circumstance C; and this, in turn, a matter of their setting about doing A when they believe that the circumstances are C.

9. It follows that the "subjects" to which these rules apply must have the concepts of *doing A* and *being in C*. They must have, to use a current turn of phrase, the appropriate 'recognitional capacities'. Furthermore, for the rule itself to play a role in bringing about the conformity of 'is' to 'ought', the agents in question must conceive of actions A as what ought to be done in circumstances C. This requires that they have the concept of what it is for an action to be called for by a certain kind of circumstance.

II

10. Importantly different from rules of the above form—which may be called, in a straightforward sense, rules of action—are rules that specify not what someone ought to do, but how something ought to be. Of these an important sub-class has the form

Xs ought to be in state S, whenever such and such is the case.

The purpose of such a rule is achieved to the extent that it comes to be the case that Xs are in state S when such and such is indeed the case. This time, however, the conformity of actual existence to the ought does not, in general, require that the Xs which are, in a sense, the *subjects* of the rule, i.e., that to which it applies, have the concept of what it is to be in state S or of what it is for such and such to be the case. This is obvious when the Xs in question are inanimate objects, as in the example,

Clock chimes ought to strike on the quarter hour.

11. Now ought-to-bes (or "rules of criticism" as I shall also call them), though categorical in form, point beyond themselves in two ways. In the first place they imply (in some sense of this protean term) a *reason*, a *because* clause. The exploration of this theme would soon take us back to the excluded topic of hypothetical imperatives. In the second place, though ought-to-bes are carefully to be distinguished from ought-to-dos they have

an essential connection with them. The connection is, roughly, that ought-to-bes imply ought-to-dos. Thus the ought-to-be about clock chimes implies, roughly,

> (Other things being equal and where possible) one ought to bring it about that clock chimes strike on the quarter hour.

12. *This* rule belongs in our previous category and is a rule of action. As such it requires that the item to which *it* applies (persons rather than chimes) have the appropriate concepts or recognitional capacities.

13. The distinction between ought-to-dos (rules of action) and ought-to-bes (rules of criticism) stands out clearly when the examples are suitably chosen. A possibility of confusion arises, however, when the ought-to-bes concern persons rather than inanimate objects. Consider, for example,

> One ought to feel sympathy for bereaved people.

This example is interesting for two reasons: (1) It is a rule conformity to which requires that the subjects to which it applies have the concept of what it is to be bereaved. In this respect it is like a rule of action. (2) In the absence of a clear theory of action one might think of *feeling sympathy* as an action. Thus a casual and uninformed look might lead to the subsumption of the example under the form

> One ought to do A, if C.

It is clear on reflection, however, that feeling sympathy is an action only in that broad sense in which anything expressed by a verb in the active voice is an action.

14. Nor should it be assumed that all ought-to-bes which apply to persons and concern their being in a certain state whenever a certain circumstance obtains are such that the conformity to them of actual fact requires that the persons in question have the concept of this circumstance. The point is of decisive importance for our problem. To set the stage, consider ought-to-bes pertaining to the training of animals

> These rats ought to be in state S, whenever C.

The conformity of the rats in question to this rule does not require that they have a concept of C, though it does require that they be able to respond differentially to cues emanating from C. Since the term 'recognitional capacity' is one of those accordion words which can be used now in one sense now in another, it is a menace to sound philosophy.

15. On the other hand, the subjects of the ought-to-dos corresponding to these ought-to-bes, i.e., the trainers, must have the concept both of the desirable state S and of the circumstances in which the animals are to be in it.

16. If we now return to the sympathy example, we notice another interesting feature. If we compare the ought-to-be with the corresponding ought-to-do,

> (Other things being equal and where possible) one ought to bring it about that people feel sympathy for the bereaved,

we see that the "subjects" of the ought-to-be (i.e., those who ought to feel sympathy) coincide with the 'subjects' of the corresponding ought-to-do (i.e., those who ought to bring it about that people feel sympathy for the bereaved). It is the same items (people) who are the *agent* subjects of the ought-to-do and the *subject-matter* subjects of the ought-to-be.

III

17. It is obvious, from the above considerations, that if *all* rules of language, were ought-to-dos we would be precluded from explaining what it is to have concepts in terms of rules of language. Now many rules of language *are* ought-to-dos thus,

> (Other things being equal) one ought to say such and such, if in C

and as such they can be efficacious in linguistic activity only to the extent that people have the relevant concepts. It is therefore of the utmost importance to note that many of the rules of language which are of special interest to the epistemologist are ought-to-bes rather than ought-to-dos. For only by taking this fact into account is it possible to carry out a program according to which (a) linguistic activity is, in a primary sense, conceptual activity; (b) linguistic activity is through and through rule governed.

18. Much attention has been devoted of late to linguistic *actions* where the term 'action' is taken in the strict sense of what an agent does, a piece of

conduct, a performance—the *practical* sense of action, as contrasted with that general metaphysical sense in which action is contrasted with passion. The topic of linguistic actions, whether performatory, locutionary, illocutionary, perlocutionary, or perhaps, elocutionary is an important one. Indeed, it is important not only for a theory of communication, but for epistemology, for there are, indeed, linguistic *actions* which are of essential interest to the epistemologist: thus, asking questions and seeking to answer them. All I'm concerned to point out is that to approach language in terms of the paradigm of *action* is to make a commitment which, if the concept of action is taken seriously and the concept of rule is taken seriously, leads to (a) the Cartesian idea of linguistic episodes as *essentially* the sort of thing brought about by an agent whose conceptualizing is not linguistic; (b) the inability to understand the rule governed character of this conceptualizing, as contrasted with its overt expression. For if thought is analogous to linguistic activity to the extent implied by Plato's metaphor of "discourse in the soul," the idea that overt speech is *action* and its rules *rules of action* will generate the idea that all inner speech is *action* and *its* rules *rules of action*, which leads to paradox and absurdity without end.

19. The epistemologist, therefore, while recognizing that language is an instrument of communication, will focus attention on language as the bearer of conceptual activity. This is not to say that the two aspects can be separated as with a knife. Indeed, by pointing out that ought-to-bes imply ought-to-dos, we have already recognized that language users exist at the level of agents. Roughly, to be a being capable of conceptual activity is to be a being which acts, which recognizes norms and standards and engages in practical reasoning. It is, as Kant pointed out, one and the same reason which is in some of its activities "theoretical," and in some of its activities "practical." Of course, if one gives to 'practical' the specific meaning *ethical*, then a fairly sharp separation of these activities can be maintained. But if one means by 'practical' *pertaining to norms*, then so-called theoretical reason is as larded with the practical as is practical reasoning itself.

IV

20. Even if it be granted that many of the linguistic oughts which are of special interest to an epistemologist are ought-to-bes, the fact that ought-to-bes and ought-to-dos are conceptually inseparable might be thought to preclude a linguistic approach to conceptual abilities. Clearly *primary* epis-

temic ought-to-dos (and by calling them 'primary' I mean simply that they are not the unfolding of ought-to-bes), whether as primary they are categorical or hypothetical, pertaining to the systematic use of linguistic abilities and propensities to arrive at correct linguistic representations of the way things are, presuppose the possession of concepts by the agents to which they apply. And since all ought-to-bes unfold into ought-to-dos, which, in their turn, presuppose concepts, the outlook for linguistic theory of concepts would seem to be dark indeed. Yet the fundamental clues for a resolution of the problem have already been given.

21. To fix our ideas, let us consider an example which, though simplified to its bare bones, contains the essence of the matter:

> (*Ceteris paribus*) one ought to respond to red objects in sunlight by uttering or being disposed to utter 'this is red'.

This ought-to-be rule must not be confused with the (fictitious) ought-to-do rule,

> (*Ceteris paribus*) one ought to say 'this is red' in the presence of red objects in sunlight.

The latter presupposes that those to whom it applies have the concepts of 'red objects', 'sunlight', and, even more important, of what it is to *say* 'this is red'. In other words, they must already have the conceptual framework of what it is to do something in a circumstance.

22. The distinction between *saying* and *uttering* or being disposed to utter, is diagnostic of the difference between the 'ought-to-be' and the 'ought-to-do'. It might be objected that to use language meaningfully is to *say* rather than merely utter. But to *merely* utter is to parrot, and we need a concept which mediates between merely uttering and saying.

23. Notice that the ought-to-do which corresponds to the above ought-to-be, namely

> One ought to bring it about (*ceteris paribus*) that people respond to red objects in sunlight by uttering or being disposed to utter 'this is red'

presupposes that *its* agent subjects have a conceptual framework which includes the concepts of a red object, of sunlight, of uttering 'this is red' of what it is to do or bring about something, and of what it is for an action to be called for by a circumstance.

24. On the other hand, this ought-to-do does *not* presuppose that the subjects in which the disposition to utter 'this is red' in the presence of red objects in sunlight is to be brought about have any of these concepts.

25. But what of the objection that the *subject-matter* subjects of the ought-to-do are the *agent* subjects, and hence that they too must have the concepts in question? The answer should be obvious: the members of a linguistic community are *first* language *learners* and only potentially "people," but *subsequently* language *teachers*, possessed of the rich conceptual framework this implies. They start out by being the *subject-matter* subjects of the ought-to-dos and graduate to the status of *agent* subjects of the ought-to-dos. Linguistic ought-to-bes are translated into *uniformities* by training. As Wittgenstein has stressed, it is the linguistic community as a self-perpetuating whole which is the minimum unit in terms of which conceptual activity can be understood.

26. Furthermore there are radically different kinds of linguistic ought-to-bes: not only word-object ought-to-bes (or, as I have called them elsewhere, language entry transitions)[2], but also the ought-to-bes formulated by formation and transformation rules.

27. The oughts governing utterances as perceptual responses to the environment are not ought-to-dos—though, as the pragmatists have emphasized, perception as an element in enquiry occurs in a context of actions, epistemic and otherwise. Similarly the oughts governing inference are not ought-to-dos. Inferring is not a *doing* in the conduct sense—which, however, by no means implies that it is not a *process*. Again, as the pragmatists have stressed, inference as an element in enquiry occurs in the context of action, epistemic and otherwise.

28. A language is a many leveled structure. There are not only the ought-to-bes which connect linguistic responses to extra-linguistic objects, but also the equally essential ought-to-bes which connect linguistic responses to *linguistic* objects. There could be no training of language users unless this were the case. Finally, there would be no language training unless there were the uniformities pertaining to the use of practical language, the language of action, intention, of 'shall' and 'ought', which, as embodying epistemic norms and standards, is but one small (but essential) part of the

---

[2] "Some Reflections on Language Games," *Philosophy of Science*, Vol. 21, No. 3, 1954 (reprinted as Chapter 11 in *Science, Perception and Reality*). It is important to note that a full discussion would refer to may-bes (or permitteds) as well as ought-to-bes—otherwise the concept of "free," as opposed to "tied" (stimulus bound) linguistic activity, which is essential to any account of the functioning of a conceptual system, would be left out of the picture.

conceptual structure of human agency.

29. One isn't a full-fledged member of the linguistic community until one not only *conforms* to linguistic ought-to-bes (and may-bes) by exhibiting the required uniformities, but grasps these ought-to-bes and may-bes themselves (i.e., knows the rules of the language.) One must therefore, have the concept of oneself as an agent, as not only the *subject-matter* subject of ought-to-bes, but the *agent*-subject of ought-to-dos. Thus, even though conceptual activity rests on a foundation of *conforming* to ought-to-bes, of *uniformities* in linguistic behavior, these uniformities exist in an ambience of action, epistemic or otherwise. To be a language user is to conceive of oneself as an agent subject to rules. My point has been that one can grant this without holding that all meaningful linguistic episodes are *actions* in the conduct sense, and all linguistic rules, rules for doing.

30. A living language is a system of elements which play many different types of roles, and no one of these types of role make sense apart from the others. Thus, while the mere concept of a kind of vocalizing being a response by a human organism in specified circumstances to a certain kind of object does make sense in isolation, this concept is not as such the concept of the vocalizing as a *linguistic response*. For to classify an item as linguistic involves relating it to just such a system as I have been sketching. 'Word' goes not only with 'object' but with 'person', 'ought-to-bes', 'ought-to-dos' and much, much more.

31. Implicit in the above conception of language as a rule governed system are a number of important implications for a linguistically oriented epistemology. Instead, however, of developing these implications directly, I shall explore certain features of Kant's epistemology which will turn out to be their counterparts. For once it is appreciated that Kant's account of the conceptual structures involved in experience can be given a linguistic turn and, purged of the commitment to innateness to which, given his historical setting he was inevitably led, his theory can be seen to add essential elements to an analytic account of the resources a language must have to be the bearer of empirical meaning, empirical truth, and, to bring things to their proper focus, empirical knowledge.

[Here followed Part II which was published as *KTE*, the next paper in this volume.]

SOME REMARKS ON KANT'S THEORY OF EXPERIENCE

Presented in an APA symposium on Kant, December 28, 1967.

I

1. Kant never tires of telling us that Nature and the Space and Time which are its forms exist as a system of "representations." Now a representation is either a represent*ing* or a something represent*ed*. Does Kant mean that nature is a system of representings? Or that it is a system of representeds? And, in any case, what would the claim amount to?

2. Representings are "mental acts." Does Kant think of nature as a system of mental acts? At one level the answer is clearly No. For, although nature does include representings—thus, at least, the sensory representings that are states of the empirical self—its primary constituents are material things and events, and Kant would agree with the Cartesians that the idea that a material event could be a represent*ing*, or, equivalently, that a mental act could have shape and size, is absurd.

3. In the second-edition Refutation of Idealism Kant clearly contrasts material objects and events with the sense impressions correlated with them in the history of the empirical self. The former are extended and located in space; the latter are neither extended nor in space,[1] though they do have temporal location. He argues that spatial structures are as directly or intuitively represented as are the non-spatial states of the empirical self, thus attacking the view, lurking in the Cartesian tradition, that the intuitive awareness involved in perceptual experience is an awareness of non-spatial sense impressions. This thesis is by no means new to the Second Edition, though the distinction between physical events and sense impressions is drawn in a clearer and less misleading way.

4. Shall we then say that nature is a system, not of represent*ings*, but of represent*eds*? What would this mean? One's first reaction is to point out that not everything in nature is represented, and that not everything which is represented as being in nature *is* in nature. To the first of these objections, the natural reply is to distinguish between "actually represented" and "representable" and define nature as a system of representables. To the

---

[1] Kant's treatment of sensation is notoriously inadequate and inept. From the premise that sense impressions as mental states are neither literally extended nor in physical space, he infers that they are in no sense spatial, i.e., that they in no way have a structure which conforms to a geometrical axiomatics. The idea that sensations are "purely intensive magnitudes" has always made it difficult to understand how sense impressions could have a meaningful connection with physical states of affairs.

second, the natural reply is that while not everything which is represented as being in nature is in nature, everything which is represented by a *true* representing as being in nature is in nature. These considerations merge; for not every system of empirical representables constitutes nature, but only that system of empirical representables, the representings of which would be true.

5. The conception thus arises of nature as the system of those representable spatial and/or temporal states of affairs which *did, do,* or *will obtain,* whether or not they *were, are,* or *will be* actually represented. An actual representing is true if the state of affairs it represents belongs to this privileged set of representable states of affairs.

6. The trouble with this picture, as Kant saw, is not that it is false but that it is so thin that it scarcely begins to illuminate the concept of nature as the object of empirical knowledge. Yet unilluminating though the idea may be that an empirical judging is true if the state of affairs it represents is one which did, does, or will obtain, i.e., was, is, or will be actual, it is the initial datum for analysis. Kant saw that this truism must be submitted to the closest scrutiny if the specter of skepticism is to be laid to rest. This scrutiny must aim at clarifying the concepts of an empirical judging, of truth, of a state of affairs, and of what it is for a state of affairs to obtain or be actual. This Kant proceeds to do with important, indeed, dramatic results.

7. The central theme of the Analytic is that unless one is clear about what it is to judge, one is doomed to remain in the labyrinth of traditional metaphysics. On the other hand, to be clear about what it is to judge is to have Ariadne's thread in one's hand.

8. Now from the Kantian point of view, the above concepts pair up in an interesting way: *judging* with *state of affairs,* and *truth* with *actuality.* Indeed to say that they pair up is to understate the closeness of their relationships. For, Kant argues, in effect, that the pairs turn out, on close examination, to be identities.

II

9. Before following through with this claim, we must take into account another concept which ties them together and gives them point, that of *empirical knowledge.* On any view there is the closest of connections between the concepts of knowledge and truth. The above remarks suggest that for Kant the connection between the concept of empirical knowledge and the "category" of actuality is at least as close. Indeed, as we shall see,

the core of Kant's "epistemological turn" is the claim that the distinction between epistemic and ontological categories is an illusion. All so-called ontological categories are in fact epistemic. They are "unified" by the concept of empirical knowledge because they are simply constituent moments of this one complex concept, the articulation of which is the major task of the constructive part of the *Critique*.

10. It is obvious to the beginning student that the truths of "transcendental logic" cannot themselves be "synthetic a priori." If they were, then any transcendental demonstration that objects of empirical knowledge conform to synthetic universal principles in the modality of necessity would be question-begging. It must in a *tough* sense be an *analytic* truth that objects of empirical knowledge conform to logically synthetic universal principles. It must, however, also be an *illuminating* analytic truth, far removed from the trivialities established by the unpacking of 'body' into 'extended substance' and 'brother' into 'male sibling'.[2]

11. It is also obvious, on reflection, that Kant is not seeking to *prove* that there is empirical knowledge, but only to show that the concept is a coherent one and that it is such as to rule out the possibility that there could be empirical knowledge not implicitly of the form 'such and such a state of affairs belongs to a coherent system of states of affairs of which my perceptual experiences are a part'. By showing this, he undercuts both the skeptic and the "problematic idealist" who, after taking as paradigms of empirical knowledge items that seem to involve no intrinsic commitment to such a larger context, raise the illegitimate question of how one can justifiably move from these items to the larger context to which we *believe* them to belong.

12. Before developing these themes, we must take into account the familiar fact that truth is a necessary but not sufficient condition for knowledge. A judgment, to be a case of knowledge, not only must be true; we must, in some sense, be justified in making it. The problem posed is as old as the hills and as new as tomorrow. It is not my purpose to claim that Kant found all the essentials of the solution. He did, however, show convincingly that certain traditional lines of thought are blind alleys, and in so doing discovered the general lines of a successful strategy.

13. The task of "transcendental logic" is to explicate the concept of a mind that gains knowledge of the world of which it is a part. The acquisition of knowledge by such a mind involves its being acted on or "affected" by the

---

[2] Kant's discussion of philosophical method in the concluding chapters of the *Critique* shows that he was fully aware of these facts, and realized as well that "transcendental logic" as knowledge about knowledge could consist of analytic knowledge about synthetic knowledge.

objects it knows.[3] There are, of course, any number of stages at which one can go wrong with respect to the structure of Kant's thought—and Kant himself is not always a reliable guide—but the sooner one makes a wrong choice of roads, the more difficult it is to get back on the right track. And the first major "choice-point" concerns the concept of "receptivity." What is it, exactly, that is brought about when our "receptivity" (inner or outer) is "affected?" It has always been easy to answer, "impressions of sense," and to continue by construing these as non-conceptual states, states that belong to the same family as tickles and aches, but differ in that unlike the latter they are constituents of the perceptual experience of physical things.

14. Even though there is an element of truth in this interpretation, its total effect is to distort Kant's thought in a way that obscures its most distinctive features. In the first place, it makes nonsense of the idea that space is the form of outer receptivity. For sense impressions, being mental states, are, for Kant, no more capable of being extended that they were for Descartes. In the second place, it makes nonsense of the idea of inner sense. For when Kant tells us that the contents of "inner sense" come from "outer sense," this would mean, on the above interpretation, that certain extended (but not temporal) sensations "cause" a further set of non-conceptual states (sensations) which are unextended though temporally related.

15. It is often taken for granted that Kant was clear about the distinction between conceptual and non-conceptual mental states or representings. "Empirical intuitions" are interpreted as non-conceptual and construed, on the above lines, as the epistemically more important members of the sensation family. Actually the pattern of Kant's thought stands out far more clearly if we interpret him as clear about the difference between *general* conceptual representings (sortal and attributive), on the one hand, and, on the other, *intuition* as a special class of *non-general* conceptual representings, but add to this interpretation the idea that he was *not* clear about the difference between intuitions in this sense and sensations. "Intuitive" representings would consist of those conceptual representings of individuals (roughly, individual concepts) which have the form illustrated by

    this-line

as contrasted with

---

[3] That it also involves action in relation to these objects—if only by changing one's relative position—is a point to which he pays less attention than it deserves. Compare C. I. Lewis's treatment of this topic in the first chapter of *An Analysis of Knowledge and Valuation*.

>   the line I drew yesterday

which is an individual concept having the form of a definite description.

16. Notice that the above line of interpretation enables us to make sense of Kant's claim that "intuitions of a manifold"[4] have categorial form; for there is an obvious sense in which

>   this-line

has the subject-predicate form, even though it is not a subject-predicate judgment. It is familiar fact that in the judgment

>   This book is red

the subject-predicate form enters twice, a fact which can be made explicit by the paraphrase

>   This is a book and it is red.

17. According to the above interpretation, the representings that are brought about by the "affection" of "receptivity" would, as intuitions, already be, in a broad sense, conceptual. To make *this* move, however, is to give a radical reinterpretation to the concept of "receptivity" and to the contrast between "receptivity" and "spontaneity." This can be brought out by comparing Kant's conception of the affection of receptivity by things in themselves with what I have elsewhere called "language entry transitions." A language entry transition is an evoking, for example, of the response 'this is red' by a red object in sunlight from a person who knows the language to which this sentence belongs. As an element in a rule-governed linguistic system the utterance is no *mere* conditioned response to the environment. Its occurrence is a function not only of the environment but of the conceptual set of the perceiver. To know the language of perception is to be in a position to let one's thoughts be guided by the world in a way that contrasts with free association, with day-dreaming, and, more interestingly, with the coherent imaginings of the storyteller.

18. It is Kant's contention that the conceptual structures we develop in perceptual experience, under the influence of independent reality, are of a

---

[4] "Intuitions of a manifold" are to be contrasted with "manifolds of intuition" (see, for example, B135). The lumping of manifolds of sense with the latter, though a confusion, would at least keep them distinct from the intuitive representings synthesized by the productive imagination.

piece with the conceptual structures we freely or spontaneously develop in imagination. A useful parallel is provided by the difference between counting *objects* and "counting" in that unconstrained way (repeating the numbers) which is a rehearsing in imagination of actual counting procedures. Another parallel is the difference between perceiving a triangle and imagining a particular triangle (which must not be confused with "having a triangular image," whatever *that* is). In receptivity we do the same sort of thing we do in the "spontaneity" of imagination, but we do it as receptive to guidance by the objects we come to represent.

19. Kant claims, in other words, that the very same rule-governed conceptual activity that occurs in the free play of imagination constitutes perceptual experience, when it is guided by independent reality. According to this interpretation, the "productive imagination" (which is Kant's term for the faculty that generates intuitive representings of the form 'this cube') provides the subject-terms of perceptual judgments; thus, for example

This cube is a piece of ice.

III

20. According to the above interpretation Kant thinks of the products of that peculiar blend of the passivity of sense and the spontaneity of the understanding which is "receptivity" in the sense defined above as consisting of representings of the form

this-φ

rather than full-fledged judgments. But, since it is clear that he thinks of these representings as involving the categorial forms that occur in full-fledged judgment, it will simplify matters if, for our present purposes, we abstract from this special feature of his theory and suppose that, as in our linguistic model, it is perceptual judgments themselves which are evoked by the action of objects in our perceptual capacities. We are thus enabled to focus our attention on Kant's theory of what judgings are.

21. I shall begin by summarizing this theory as four closely related theses:

1. Judgings are complex representings in a very special sense of 'complex', which distinguishes them from the mere co-occurrence of representings in the same mind at the same time, as when an association is

aroused. Kant believed, not without justification, that this distinction was not clearly drawn by his predecessors—particularly David Hume.

2. Judgings have a variety of forms which Kant clearly conceives by analogy with the logical forms of the statements that express them.

3. Not only do judgings have these forms; anything (with the exception of intuitive representings) that has these forms is a judging.

4. To judge, for example, that snow is white is not just to represent *snow* and represent *white*; it is to be committed to the idea that the representable *snow* and the representable *white* belong together regardless of what anyone happens to think. It is, in other words, to be committed to the idea that representings that snow is white are (epistemically) correct and representings that snow is not white, (epistemically) incorrect. This thesis finds its clearest expression in section 19 of the Second Edition *Deduction*, entitled "The Logical Form of All Judgments Consists in the Objective Unity of the Apperception of the Concepts which They Contain" (B141-142).

The first two theses need little if any elaboration. The third and fourth, however, are of crucial importance to Kant's argument and require a closer look. At first sight the statement that only judgings have the forms that judgings have, may have the appearance of tautology. But it is not a triviality, and, indeed, is the very heart of the *Critique*.
22. It will be illuminating, I believe, to compare this thesis with its counterpart in a linguistic version of the Kantian position, i.e., one that speaks in terms of (meaningful) expressions rather than (conceptual) representations:

Statings have certain logical forms and everything which has these forms is a stating.

The logical form of a stating is clearly not the empirical configuration of the sentence it illustrates, though having an appropriate empirical configuration is a necessary condition of the stating's having the logical form it does, in the language to which it belongs. For a stating to have a certain logical form is for it to have certain logical powers, and, if so, the idea that anything having this form must be a stating has the ring of truth rather than paradox.

23. Kantian "categories" are concepts of logical form, where 'logical' is to be taken in a broad sense, roughly equivalent to 'epistemic'. To say of a judging that it has a certain logical form is to classify it and its constituents with respect to their epistemic powers.

24. If judgings qua conceptual acts have "form," they also have "content." Of all the metaphors that philosophers have employed, this is one of the most dangerous, and few have used it without to some extent being taken in by it. The temptation is to think of the "content" of an act as an entity that is "contained" by it. But if the "form" of a judging is the structure by virtue of which it is possessed of certain *generic* logical or epistemic powers, surely the content must be the character by virtue of which the act has *specific* modes of these generic logical or epistemic powers.

25. Thus, a judging that Tom is tall would, in its generic character, be a judging of the subject-predicate form. It is a judging that a certain substance has a certain attribute. (These two ways of putting it are equivalent.) If we focus our attention on the predicate we can characterize the judging more specifically as a judging that a certain substance has the attribute *tall*. Thus, just as to say that a judging is a judging that a certain substance has a certain attribute is to say that the judging is of a certain generic kind (i.e., has certain generic logical powers); so to say that a judging is a judging that a certain substance is tall is to classify the judging as one of the *such and such is tall* kind, i.e., to classify it in a way that ascribes to it the more specific conceptual powers distinctive of the concept of being tall. Indeed, for the judging to "contain the concept of being tall" is nothing more nor less than for it to have these specific powers.[5]

26. Kant correctly concludes from the above that there is no such thing as comparing a judging with an actual state of affairs and finding the judging to be "correct" or "justified." For, according to the above analysis, an "actual state of affairs," since it has judgmental form, is simply a true species of judging, i.e., to use Peircean terminology, a judging-type that it would be (epistemically) correct to token.[6] Thus "comparing a judging with

---

[5] The above remarks on categories and concepts can be construed as a commentary on the passage in the *Paralogisms* where Kant writes: "We now come to a concept which was not included in the general list of transcendental concepts but which must yet be counted as belonging to that list, without, however, in the least altering it or declaring it defective. This is the concept or, if the term be preferred, the judgment, 'I think.' As is easily seen, this is the vehicle of all concepts, and therefore also of transcendental concepts, and so is always included in the conceiving of these latter, and is itself transcendental" (A341; B399).

[6] Put in linguistic terms, an "actual state of affairs" is a true species of stating, i.e., a stating-type that it would be epistemically correct to token.

a state of affairs" could only be comparing a judging with another judging of the same specific kind, and this would no more be a verification than would checking one copy of today's *Times* by reading another.

27. In evaluating the significance of this point, it should be borne in mind that linguistic episodes have not only logical powers but also, and necessarily, matter-of-factual characteristics, e.g., shape, size, color, internal structure, and that they exhibit empirical uniformities both among themselves and in relation to the environment in which they occur. They can be compared as objects in nature with other objects in nature with respect to their matter-of-factual characteristics. I mention this, because the fact that we tend to think of conceptual acts as having *only* logical form, as lacking matter-of-factual characteristics, i.e., as, to use Moore's expression, diaphanous, makes it difficult to appreciate that the ultimate point of all the logical powers pertaining to conceptual activity in its epistemic orientation is to generate conceptual structures which as objects in nature stand in certain matter-of-factual relations to other objects in nature.[7]

IV

28. Aristotle seems to have thought of his categories as the most generic sortal concepts that can occur in statements about the objects around us. Thus

    Tom is a substance

would belong to the same family of statements as

    Tom is an animal

and would stand to the latter as

    Tom is an animal

stands to

---

[7] The basic flaw in the Kantian system (as in that of Peirce) is in its inability to do justice to this fact. The insight that *logical* form belongs only to conceptual acts (i.e., belongs to "thoughts" rather than to "things") must be supplemented by the insight that "thoughts" as well as "things" must have *empirical* form if they are to mesh with each other in that way which is essential to empirical knowledge. I have developed this point in Chapter 6 of *Science, Perception and Reality* [reprinted by Ridgeview Publishing Company, 1991] and, more recently in Chapter 5 of *Science and Metaphysics* [reprinted by Ridgeview Publishing Company, 1992].

Tom is a man.

If one attempts to carry through this model with the other categories, one is led to postulate such puzzling entities as quality-individuals and (*horrible dictu*) relation-individuals to be the subjects of statements of the form

... is a quality
... is a relation.

29. Medieval logicians began the process of reinterpreting the categories that culminated in Kant's *Critique*, by recognizing that certain statements (thus 'Man is a species') which seem to be about queer entities in the world are actually statements that classify constituents of conceptual acts. The insights of terminist logicians were largely lost in the post-Cartesian period. Kant not only rediscovered these insights, but extended them in such a way as to connect categories not only with the logical forms in the narrowest sense (roughly, syntactical powers) studied by formal logicians, but, to an extent not always recognized, with the logical powers in a broader sense which are essential to a conceptual framework the employment of which generates knowledge of matter of fact. Thus he thinks of the categories as together constituting the concept of an *object* of empirical knowledge. The extent to which this is so does not stand out in the Metaphysical Deduction. It isn't until the Analytic of Principles, as has often been pointed out, that one can grasp the full import of Kant's theory of the categories. The conception of the categories as the most general classifications of the logical powers that a conceptual system must have in order to generate empirical knowledge is the heart of the Kantian revolution.

30. It is, we have seen, in the literal sense a category mistake to construe 'substance', for example, as an object-language sortal word that differs from ordinary empirical predicates by being a *summum genus*. However, once the Kantian turn is taken, and substance-attribute is seen to be a classification of judgings, it becomes possible to interpret at least some categories as meta-conceptual *summa genera*, and to look for the "differences" that generate their species. It is along these lines that the obscure doctrine of the Schematism is to be understood. Roughly, the *schemata* turn out to be specific differences, and the schematized categories a classification of the epistemic powers of judgings in so far as they pertain to events in time.

V

31. Once it is recognized that intuitive representings are, in a generic sense, conceptual, though not sortal or attributive, other parts of the Kantian system begin to fall into place. To intuit is to represent a *this*, i.e., if I may so put it, to have a representing of the "this" kind. But no representing is, so to speak, a sheer "this" representing. To suppose the contrary is to treat 'this' as a mere label devoid of any but the most meager logical powers. Space and time are "forms of intuition," not by virtue of being attributes of or relations between things or events in nature, but by virtue of the fact that the logical powers distinctive of "this" representings are specified in terms of concepts pertaining to relative location in space and time. *The "transcendental," or epistemic function, of spatio-temporal concepts as forms of representing must be distinguished from their empirical function in matter-of-factual judgments about historical fact.*

32. In linguistic terms this means roughly that spatiotemporal predicates are essential not only to object-language statements, but to the metalinguistic statements that ascribe logical (epistemic) powers to linguistic forms. It is a familiar, but important, fact that the logical powers of demonstratives and tenses essentially involve the manner of their occurrence in space and time, and, hence, the conceptual structure of space and time is built into their logical powers.

33. To be an intuitive representing is to represent something as located in space or time, as being *here* and *now* with *me* as contrasted with *there* and *then*. But, by the same token, it is to represent it as on the way to being *there* and *then* and no longer with *me now*. We must remember that, although time does not change in the sense that one temporal system is replaced by another (there is only one time), it does, moving image of eternity that it is, constantly change with respect to the A-characteristics of pastness, presentness, and futurity.

34. Now to be represented as having a location in space and time is to be represented as an *object*, as something with respect to which there is truth or falsity. It is sufficient to note that so to represent an item is to commit oneself to the idea that it *is* so located. In the Analogies Kant argues, among other things, that such truth and falsity involves the concept of Nature as the object *par excellence* of empirical knowledge (A129). [A129 is, of course, in section 3 of the A edition Transcendental Deduction. Either Sellars meant to refer to A127 in that same section or he

meant to refer to A216/B263 in the Analogies.]

VI

35. Since a "this" representing is an object-of-knowledge representing, intuitions have the form

>this-*object*.

But just as nothing is represented as a mere "this," for the conceptual framework of space, time and of *myself* as confronted by *this* is involved, so nothing is represented in perception as merely

>this (here now) *object*.

To make the obvious point, *object* is an epistemic concept, and we *experience* objects in terms of *empirical* concepts. Thus, in giving an example of an intuition, we should offer not

>this *object*

but, say,

>this cube

where the concept of a cube, unlike its pure geometrical counterpart, is the concept of an object in nature. Kant seems to have taken for granted that the intuitive representings must be absolutely determinate and that to represent an absolutely determinate cube, for example, is to "draw it in thought" (A102, B138, B162). This difficult doctrine requires that the logical powers of the concept *cube* involve not only the inferential powers characteristic of its role as the predicate of full-fledged judgment, but also the powers involved in "constructing" or "drawing" determinate "this-cube" representings in accordance with a rule, and knowing that this is what one is doing.[8]

---

[8] One is struck by Brouwer's parallel point that to have temporal concepts is to be able not only to make judgments involving temporal predicates but to "construct" determinate representings of the form "this-after-that". But I must leave the details of Kant's theory of intuitive conceptualization and how it fits in with his theory of concepts as rules to another occasion.

VII

36. To be able to have intuitive representings, then, is to have all the conceptual apparatus involved in representing oneself as acquiring empirical knowledge of a world one never made. We are a long way from the Humean notion that merely by virtue of having a sense impression one has is good a piece of knowledge as one can get, not to mention the Cartesian notion that the intuitive knowledge of one's present *cogitationes* is logically independent of any knowledge of the context in which they occur. Some familiar Kantian theses follow as corollaries from the above considerations:

> 1. Having particular intuitions involves having the conceptual framework of space and time. Hence the possession of the latter cannot be accounted for in terms of the former. Kant infers that the ability to represent items as in space and time is innate.

> 2. The fact that concepts have categorial form undercuts any abstractionism that derives them from non-conceptual representations. As for forming concepts and categories by abstraction from intuitive representings of manifolds, this makes sense because the latter already have a conceptual and categorial character. By confusing the synopsis of sense (A97) with the intuitive representing of a manifold Locke mistakenly concluded that concepts and categories could be abstracted from sheer sensibility. Kant infers that the framework of basic concepts and categories is innate.

> 3. Induction, the process of forming generalizations about objects and events, presupposes the conceptual framework involved in thinking of objects and events as located in space and time. Since any present event will be a past event, it must, if it is to have truth and knowability, be inferentially as well as intuitively accessible. Since such inferential access involves laws of nature, the domain of objects of empirical knowledge must conform to knowable laws. The knowledge of these laws cannot be inductive, for, as was pointed out above, induction presupposes knowable objects. The knowledge of these laws must be innate in the sense in which geometry was innate in Meno's slave.

4. To conceive of an event as occurring at a time is to commit oneself to the idea that the *concept* of that event and the *concept* of that time belong together regardless of what one happens to think. But there is nothing about the sheer concept of a particular time which requires that it be occupied by a certain event. The belonging must, Kant concludes, be a matter of the temporal location of the event relative to other events and, *as belonging*, be the inferability (in principle) of its occurrence at that location from the occurrence of the events to which it is thus related.

5. Association of ideas is association of concepts (not images), and hence presupposes and cannot account for the framework features of a conceptual structure.

6. Even our consciousness of what is going on in our own mind is a conceptual *response* which must be distinguished from that which evokes the response. Not even in this context does it make sense to speak of verifying judgments by comparing them with the actual state of affairs to which we are responding. Kant tends to limit this point to the introspection of sense impressions and other sensory states of the empirical self. Thus he tells us in A456 [the correct reference is A546] that we have knowledge "by pure apperception" of our conceptual acts. Indeed, he repeatedly implies that we have (or can have) an unproblematic awareness of all acts of spontaneity or synthesis[9] (e.g., A108, B130, B153). And in B430 he even seems to suggest that in pure apperception the mental activity known and the knowing of it are somehow one and the same, a thesis which is surely inconsistent with critical principles.[10]

7. The application of the fourth corollary above to the special case of

---

[9] It has often been noted that Kant's references to successive acts of synthesis is in *prima facie* conflict with his dictum that everything in time is appearance. This conflict, however, merely points up the extent to which Kant's system calls for a distinction between Newtonian time as a form of nature and the successiveness involved in the activity by which the mind represents nature. The reference to *motion* as a transcendental concept (as contrasted with the motion of objects in space) in B155 and the accompanying note is particularly important in this connection.

[10] Kant could insist that the knowledge gained by pure apperception is not knowledge of an *object* by arguing that the mind qua rational, i.e., qua capable of spontaneous conceptual activity, is not a part of nature. In the terminology of the third Antinomy, its causality is not caused. A rational being qua rational does not have a nature in the sense in which, for example, gold and *aqua regia* have natures. Such natures as rational beings has is a matter of *abilities* (and the "second nature" of habit) rather than causal properties.

sensory states of the empirical self gives the *coup de grace* to the problematic idealism of Descartes. For since the only inferability there is pertaining to the occurrence of sense impressions concerns their law-like relation to the stimulation of our sense organs by material things, the *belonging together* of the individual concept of a particular sense impression and the individual concept of a certain moment involves the distinction between material things and the sense impressions that represent them in the empirical self (B274ff).

VIII

37. Nature, we have said, is the system of *actual* basic empirical states of affairs. There are two themes in Kant's account of what it is to be an actual basic state of affairs:

(a) It is one the intuiting of which would be a correct *intuiting*. In terms of our linguistic model, this amounts to saying that a true basic statement is one which, *in here-now form*, as contrasted with the *there-then* counterparts which make the same statement, would be a correct "language entry transition" by a person appropriately located with respect to the object.

(b) An actual basic state of affairs is one that is correctly inferable from correct present intuitive representings. In terms of our linguistic model, this amounts to saying that a true basic empirical statement is one that is correctly derivable by means of true law-like statements from true basic here-now statements.

38. Once again, it must be borne in mind that Kant's aim has not been to prove that there is knowledge of the *there-then*, but to show, by articulating the concept of empirical knowledge, that knowing the *here-now* involves knowing it as an element in a system that includes *there-thens*.

IX

39. It is often said today that Kant's *Critique* consists of important insights into the logical geography of our conceptual structure which are obscured almost to the point of invisibility by a tedious and fictitious "transcendental psychology." Kant is said to postulate a mechanism consisting of empiri-

cally inaccessible mental processes which "constructs" the world of experience out of sense impressions. If my argument is correct, this criticism is misdirected. The true situation can be seen by assessing the validity of a corresponding criticism directed against a linguistic version of Kant's position.

40. To construe the concepts of meaning, truth, and knowledge as metalinguistic concepts pertaining to linguistic behavior (and dispositions to behave) involves construing the latter as governed by *ought-to-bes* which are actualized as uniformities by the training that transmits language from generation to generation. Thus, if logical and (more broadly) epistemic categories express general features of the *ought-to-bes* (and corresponding uniformities) which are necessary to the functioning of language as a cognitive instrument, epistemology, in this context, becomes the theory of this functioning—in short *transcendental linguistics*.

41. Transcendental linguistics differs from empirical linguistics in two ways: (1) it is concerned with language as conforming to epistemic norms which are themselves formulated in the language; (2) it is general in the sense in which what Carnap describes as "general syntax" is general; i.e., it is not limited to the epistemic functioning of historical languages in the actual world. It attempts to delineate the general features that would be common to the epistemic functioning of any language in any possible world. As I once put it, epistemology, in the "new way of words," is the theory of what it is to be a language that is about a world in which it is used.[11] Far from being an accidental excrescence, Kant's transcendental psychology is the heart of his system. He, too, seeks the general features any conceptual system must have in order to generate knowledge of a world to which it belongs.

42. An essential requirement of the transmission of a language from generation to generation is that its mature users be able to identify both extra-linguistic items and the utterances that are correct responses to them. This mobilizes the familiar fact, stressed in the last paragraph of section III above, that, in addition to their logical powers, linguistic expressions have an empirical character as items in the world. We can ascertain, for example, that a person does in point of fact respond as he ought to red objects in sunlight by uttering or being disposed to utter 'this is red'. Again, we can ascertain that, other things being equal, he is not disposed to enlarge, as he

---

[11] "Realism and the New Way of Words," *Philosophy and Phenomenological Research*, VIII, 4 (June 1948); reprinted, with alterations, in *Readings in Philosophical Analysis*, edited by Herbert Feigl and Wilfrid Sellars (New York: Appleton-Century-Crofts, 1949) [also reprinted in *Pure Pragmatics and Possible Worlds*, Ridgeview Publishing Company, 1980].

ought not, utterances of 'it is raining' into 'it is raining and it is not raining'.

43. Kant's agnosticism, however, if taken seriously—i.e., construed as the view that we have no determinate concepts of how things are in themselves—means that no conceptual response can be evaluated, in the above manner, as correct or incorrect. Rules of the form

> (*Ceteris paribus*) one ought to respond to φ items with conceptual acts of kind *C*

could never be rules in accordance with which people criticize conceptual responses; for, on his official view, the *esse* of any item to which any empirical predicate applies is already *to be a conceptual response, not something that is responded to*. To put it bluntly, only God could envisage the *ought-to-bes* in terms of which our conceptual responses are to be criticized.

44. But, although any contemporary Kantian must take seriously the critique of agnosticism implicit in the preceding remarks, its force would have been obscured by the innatist features of Kant's transcendental "inner-linguistics." For him there is no problem concerning the cultural transmission of basic conceptual abilities. There is, in his system, no place for this role of the *ought-to-bes* of language entry transitions. Thus Kant is in a position to grant that empirical knowledge involves a uniformity of conceptual response to extra-conceptual items and even that extra-conceptual items conform to general laws,[12] without granting that the character of the items to which we conceptually respond, or the laws to which God knows them to conform, are accessible to finite minds.

45. We could expect Kant to say that, *if* there is empirical knowledge, there must be such uniformities (once again, he is not attempting to prove that there is empirical knowledge, but to articulate its structure) and that, in the absence of particular reasons for thinking that something has gone wrong, we are entitled to suppose that our conceptual machinery is functioning properly.

---

[12] This idea is implicit in the transcendental principle of the affinity of the manifold of sense and finds its explicit formulation in B164, where Kant in a little noted passage wrote that "things in themselves would necessarily" [i.e., as a necessary truth of transcendental logic (WS)] "apart from any understanding that knows them, conform to laws of their own." We are led to think of the Newtonian framework of the world as we experience it as a projection of a system of laws to which things in themselves conform and which are known only to God.

METAPHYSICS AND THE CONCEPT OF A PERSON

I

1. In the first edition "Paralogisms of Pure Reason" Kant suggests that "the substance which in relation to outer sense possesses extension" might be "in itself the possessor of thoughts and that these thoughts can by means of its own inner sense be consciously represented." On this hypothesis, which is a purely speculative one, "the thesis that only souls (as particular kinds of substances) think would have to be given up, and we should have to fall back on the common expression that *men* think, that is, that the very same being which, as outer appearance is extended is, in itself, internally a subject and is not composite, but is simple and thinks." (A359-60)

2. Kant, of course, does not commit himself to this hypothesis. Indeed it is a part of his methodology to advance alternative hypotheses concerning things as they are in themselves, which hypotheses can be neither refuted nor established by speculative reason, as a means of keeping what he calls dogmatic metaphysics in check. Thus, another such speculative hypotheses would be a dualistic one to the effect that as things in themselves, persons consist of a real mind and a real body, the latter appearing in perception as a complex material thing. In the course of his critique of traditional metaphysical theories of mind and body, he suggests still other hypotheses that are of even greater interest, a theme to which I shall return.

3. To set the stage for an appreciation of Kant's insights, both critical and constructive, let us take as our point of departure his reference to the "common expression" that *men* think, that is, "that the very same being which is...extended is...a subject...and thinks." This "common expression" is, of course, characteristic of the Aristotelian tradition, extending from antiquity to the Oxford Aristotelianism being reborn before our very eyes. According to this tradition it is the same thing, a *man* or, as we now say (since the equality of the sexes has moved into the higher levels of ideological superstructure), a *person,* which both thinks and runs.

4. Even a Cartesian dualist, of course, can acknowledge that it is one and the same thing, a person, which runs and thinks, for sameness is ubiquitous. Thus it is one and the same thing, a family, which gets and spends. But perhaps the family gets by the husband getting and spends by the wife spending. The Aristotelian counterpart would be the bachelor who does both the getting and the spending. The dualist thinks of the person as a

family or team, a mind that thinks and a body that runs. The Aristotelian, on the other hand, construes reference to minds as reference to persons qua having those states and capacities which are distinctive of rational animals, and references to human bodies as references to persons qua having those states and capacities by virtue of which they belong to the larger family of corporeal substances. The Aristotelian can grant, then, that there are minds and bodies without being in any more interesting sense a dualist. References to minds and bodies are *façons de parler*. They have a derivative existence or "mode of being."

5. It is worth pausing to note that since one must, as Aristotle himself emphasizes, be careful to distinguish between priority in the order of knowing, or conception, and priority in the order of being, a dualist could grant that our primary concept of a person is Aristotelian and yet insist that when we explore the behavior of the things to which we apply this concept, we discover facts that force us to postulate a dualism of minds and bodies. A useful parallel is provided by the development of microphysical theory. It is clear that in the order of knowing concepts pertaining to perceptual objects are primary. Yet, from the standpoint of Scientific Realism, perceptual objects are derivative and secondary—however these terms are to be construed—in the order of being.

6. Considerations of many different types have been advanced to support dualism—ranging from the interpretation of dreams and religious experience to abstruse metaphysical arguments. In the modern period, the mechanistic revolution in physical science provided the chief motive power for mind-body dualism. If the body is a cloud of particles, must not the unitary thinking, feeling subject be a distinct existent perhaps, as some have thought, like a captain in his ship; perhaps, as others thought, like a dog tied to a chariot.

7. My aim here is to do some hard-core metaphysics. I shall therefore begin by taking the Aristotelian framework seriously and assume that persons are, in the toughest of senses, single logical subjects: that persons are in no sense systems of logical subjects. If it is objected that according to well-confirmed scientific theory persons are, at least in part, made up of 'molecules and as such are systems of individual things, I shall take temporary refuge in the familiar line that such scientific objects are "conceptual fictions"—useful symbolic devices.

8. As for such perceptible "parts" as arms, legs etc., your true Aristotelian construes them as merely potential parts, much as the two sides of a uniformly colored expanse are potential parts—a line could be drawn

dividing it in two. And just as statements can be made about the two sides of the expanse without presupposing that it is actually divided in two, so, on strict Aristotelian principles, statements can be made about the arms or legs of a person without presupposing that they are distinct and individual things in their own right. Of course, the arms or legs can be made really distinct from the person by cutting them off; but then, as Aristotle points out, they would no longer be arms or legs in the primary sense—any more than a corpse is a man.

9. A person, then, according to the Aristotelian analysis, is a single individual which does not have subordinate individuals as its parts. Its unity is not that of a system. A person is a complex individual, of course, but his complexity is a matter of the many predicates applying to that one individual who is the person.

10. Identity or sameness is one of the least informative of concepts. As Bishop Butler pointed out long ago, "everything is what it is and not another thing." Thus, even if a person were a system he would be self-identical, for anything—even a system—is self-identical. Consider identity through time. Philosophers often attempt to distinguish between a "loose" and a "strict" sense of identity. The language is misguided, although the contrast they have in mind is sound. As far as I can see, to insist that a person is literally identical through time—as the Aristotelians do—is simply to insist that a person is not a system of successive "person-stages." On the other hand, even if a person were a series of person-stages, he would still be self-identical through time, for he would be the same series with respect to each moment of his existence.

11. It has sometimes been argued that anything which endures through time must be a series. If this is presented not as revisionary metaphysics, but as an analysis of the conceptual framework we learned at our mother's knee, it is sheer confusion. One such argument, recently elaborated by Gustav Bergmann,[1] is interesting as an example of how mistaken a metaphysical argument can be even when buttressed by all the technical resources of the new logic. It has the form of a *reductio ad absurdum* and goes as follows:

> (1) Suppose (contrary to fact) a Substance S—a logical subject of which the identity through time is *not* that of a series—and suppose that S becomes successively red and green.

---

[1] "Some Reflections on Time," in *Meaning and Existence* (Madison, University of Wisconsin Press, 1960).

(2) Then redness and greenness would both be true of S.
(3) But redness and greenness are incompatible.
(4) To be coherent, then, we must say that redness is true of S at one moment or period of time t_1 and that greenness is true of S at another moment or period of time t_2.
(5) Thus, to describe S coherently we must mention moments or periods of time.
(6) But [argues Bergmann] moments or periods of time are conceptual constructions and must not be mentioned in a list of ontological ultimates.
(7) Hence basic statements about the world must not mention moments or periods of time.
(8) But, according to the substance theory, this is exactly what basic statements about substances must do.
(9) Hence the theory of substance commits one to a false ontology and must be rejected.

Roughly, a substance ontology is committed to a "container" or "absolute" theory of time.

12. The flaw in this argument is that, in its attempt to formulate a substance ontology within the tidy language of *Principia Mathematica*, it overlooks the role of tenses and temporal connectives in actual usage. Thus, to take account of the incompatibility of redness and greenness, a substance theorist is not forced to move directly to propositions of the form

S is red at t_1
S is green at t_2,

let alone to such supposititious PMese counterparts as

$Red(S, t_1)$
$Green(S, t_2)$.

The latter, indeed, are counter-intuitive, for they present colors as relations between substances and times, rather than as qualitative characteristics. If a substance theorist were forced to make this move, he would indeed be in trouble.

13. If, on the other hand, we introduce the relational predicates 'red at' and 'green at', and write

Red at (S, t_1)
Green at (S, t_2),

we see intuitively that these locutions presuppose the propriety of the non-relational forms

Red(S)
Green(S).

But is this not to admit that the substance theorist cannot solve the incompatibility problem without countenancing times as ontological ultimates and doing violence to the intrinsic grammar of color predicates?

14. The answer is "no," for he needs only point to the availability of such forms as

S is red
S will be green

which preserve the non-relational character of color predicates.

15. It might be objected to this that sentences containing the tensed verbs 'is', 'was', and 'will be' are covertly relational. Thus one might be tempted to construe

S is red

as

S be red *now*

where 'be' is a "tenseless" (or "pure") copula; and the latter, in turn, as

Red(S, *now*)

and as unfolding into

Red(S, t_1) and Simul(t_1, context of utterance).

Similarly, one might construe

S will be green

as

  S be green after *now*

and as unfolding into

  (Et) Green (*S*, *t*) and After(*t*, context of utterance).

But once one sees that the job done by sentences involving tokens of 'now' requires not that they *mention* a relation to the context of utterance, but rather that they *stand* in a relation to the situation they describe, it becomes clear that the same is true of the tensed verbs 'is', 'was', and 'will be'. The concept of a pure tenseless copula is a myth—at least as far as our ordinary conceptual framework is concerned.[2]

16. Again, the substance theorist can point to the related forms

  S was red before it was green
  S is red and will be green
  S will be green after it is red.

It is surely a mistake to assume that 'before', 'while', 'after', and other temporal connectives[3] are to be analyzed in terms of a reference to moments or periods of time, as we saw it to be a mistake to assume that 'is', 'was', and 'will be' are to be analyzed in terms of a tenseless copula and a reference to a relation.

17. Thus it is open to the Aristotelian to agree with Bergmann that moments and periods of time are conceptual constructions, but to claim that they are constructible within the framework of a substance ontology in terms of such concepts as before, after, while—rather than in terms of relations between events, where "event" is taken to be the basic ontological category.

18. Even more transparent is a closely related argument for the thesis that the identity of a person is the identity of a series. It involves a confusion between a person and his history. The history of a person is the sequence

---

[2] That there might be a use for such a copula in a contrived conceptual framework is argued in "Time and the World Order," in *Minnesota Studies in the Philosophy of Science*, III (Minneapolis, University of Minnesota Press, 1963), pp. 577-93. For a discussion of the copula 'is' as a pseudotenseless copula equivalent to the 'be' introduced by the equivalence 'S be P ≡ S was P or S is P or S will be P', see p. 533.

[3] I speak of them as connectives, for unlike relation words they are not contexts calling for abstract singular terms (e.g. that-clauses). A broad theory of temporal and other nonlogical connectives is urgently needed. See pp. 550-51 of the essay cited above.

of events in which he is relevantly involved. There clearly are such things as events; and the events in which a person participates *do* constitute a series. But if we look at one such event, say,

> the event of Caesar crossing the Rubicon,

it becomes apparent that what can be said by referring to the event in which Caesar participated can also be put without such reference. Thus, instead of saying,

> The event of Caesar crossing the Rubicon took place

we can simply say,

> Caesar crossed the Rubicon.

19. Indeed, it is clear that in ordinary discourse event-talk is in some sense derivative from substance-talk. If one did not understand the simple subject-predicate sentence

> Socrates ran,

one could not understand the more complex locution

> (The event of) Socrates running took place.

The latter presupposes the former in a very straightforward sense. Indeed, it contains it, with a slight grammatical modification.

20. To appreciate the sense in which the latter statement contains the former, as well as to understand how the two statements can be strongly equivalent without having the same sense, an analogy will help. Consider the pair of statements

> Snow is white
> It is true that snow is white.

These statements are strongly equivalent, but not identical in meaning. Furthermore, the second statement in some sense contains the former. (In a literal sense it contains the sign design of the former.)

21. I have argued in a number of places[4] that '-ity', '-hood', '-ness', and 'that' (as used to form propositional clauses) are to be regarded as quoting devices which (a) form sortal predicates which apply to expression tokens in any language or conceptual scheme which are doing in that language or conceptual scheme that which is done in our language by the design with which they are conjoined; (b) turn these sortal predicates into distributive singular terms. Thus "andness" is to be construed as 'the •and•' where '•and•' is the sortal predicate formed from the design *and*. On this analysis the singular term

>that snow is white

becomes

>the •snow is white•

and

>That snow is white is true

becomes

>The •snow is white• is true.

22. Since statements which have distributive singular terms as subjects

>The lion is tawny

can be "reduced" to statements which have the sortal predicate from which the singular term is constructed as their grammatical subjects,

>Lions are tawny,

the above analysis enables the reduction of

>That snow is white is true

to

---

[4] Most recently in *Science and Metaphysics* (London, 1968), Chapter 3 [reprinted in 1992 by Ridgeview Publishing Company].

•snow is white•s are true

which tells us that in a relevant mode of correctness

•snow is white•s are correctly assertible,

i.e., authorizes one, so to speak, to step down from one's metalinguistic stilts and *use* a •snow is white•, which is, in our language, to use a 'snow is white'. My generic term for such assertibility is "semantic assertibility" (abbreviated to "*S*-assertibility").[5]

23. To focus these considerations on our original topic of events, notice first that there are a number of locutions which, used in appropriate contexts, are equivalent to the predicate 'true'. Thus:

That snow is white is the case.

Of particular interest are examples in which it seems appropriate to take seriously the prima facie tensed character of the copula in 'is the case'. Consider, for example, the statements

That Socrates runs is the case (right now).
That Socrates runs was the case (yesterday at 2 PM).
That Socrates runs will be the case (tomorrow at 3 PM).

The suggestion I wish to make is that 'is taking place', 'took place', and 'will take place' are to be construed as specialized truth-predicates that are used in connection with statements in which the predicate is a verb standing for a kind of change, activity, or process. The most interesting case, as we shall see, is that of statements in which the predicate stands for a kind of action.

24. To return to our example of event talk, the statement

(The event of) Socrates running took place

has, in the first place, the form

That Socrates runs was true

---

[5] For an elaboration of this account of truth, see *Science and Metaphysics*, Chapter 4.

and, more penetratingly considered, the form

> The •Socrates runs• was true.

A further step in the analysis (though by no means the final one) takes us to

> The •Socrates runs• was S-assertible

and

> •Socrates runs•s were S-assertible.

To develop this analysis into a full-fledged theory of event-talk would take us into problems pertaining to quantifying into statements containing abstract singular terms. My present purpose has been to sketch a strategy for explaining the sense in which event-talk is dependent on substance-talk, and the sense in which statements about events taking place can be strongly equivalent to statements about substances changing, without being synonymous with the latter. It may be possible, as I have indicated above, to construct a conceptual framework and a use of 'event' in which events are more basic than their counterparts in the substance framework of ordinary discourse. But to construct such a framework would not be to analyze the concept of event which we actually employ.[6]

II

25. Having taken the metaphysical bit into our teeth, let us turn to issues more directly related to the topic of persons. Consider, for example, the endless perplexities which have arisen about the ownership-relation between persons and their "experiences". The fundamental point to be made is of a piece with the considerations advanced above: Philosophers should be wary of verbal nouns. Failure to do so has generated about as much bad metaphysics as has been sponsored by 'is' and 'not'. Words like 'sensation', 'feeling', 'thought', and 'impression' in such contexts as

---

[6] In the essay referred to in note 2, however, I failed to appreciate the kinship of event-expressions with abstract singular terms. With this exception, the argument of the essay and the distinctions it draws still seem to me to stand up reasonably well.

> Jones has a sensation (feeling, etc.)

have mesmerized philosophers into wondering what Jones' mind is, as contrasted with his sensations, feelings, etc. If Jones qua mind is a haver of "experiences", then, since to be a haver is to have a relational property, must not the mind be a *mere* haver—in other words a "bare particular"? Are we not confronted by a choice between accepting bare particulars[7] with ontological piety, and avoiding them at the price of committing ourselves to a "bundle theory" of the self?

26. Since the above dialectic is a special case of a more general dialectic pertaining to subject-predicate statements, we find philosophers pressing their brows in anguish over the dilemma of choosing between "things are havers (bare particulars)" and "things are bundles of what they are said to have". The fundamental mistake, of course, is that of construing subject-predicate statements as relational. It is that of construing, for example,

> Tom is tall

as expressing a relation between two objects, Tom and tallness. The issues involved are complex, and I cannot do justice to them here.[8] I shall simply point out that if we consider the contexts listed at the beginning of this section, it is surely implausible to take such statements as

> Tom has a feeling

to be anything but a derivative (but legitimate) way of saying what is said adequately and non-relationally by such statements as

> Tom feels ... .

---

[7] The term 'bare particular' has come to be ambiguous. Traditionally it was used in connection with the view that ordinary things (e.g. horses) are composites of a *this* factor and a *such* factor, where the *this* factor was conceived to be a pure substratum in the sense that it has no empirical character, but only the metaphysical character of standing in the *having* relation (or *nexus*) to a *such* factor. Neither the *this* nor the *such* factor would be the horse.

Recently, however, the term has come to be used in connection with the view that particularity is an irreducible category, i.e., that particulars are not "complexes of universals." To accept bare particulars in the first sense is to accept them in the second, but not vice versa.

[8] I have examined it in some detail in Chapter 7 of *Science, Perception and Reality*, (London, 1963) [reprinted in 1991 by Ridgeview Publishing Company]. See also *Philosophical Perspectives* (Springfield, IL., 1967), Chapter 6 [in *Philosophical Perspectives: Metaphysics and Epistemology* (Ridgeview Publishing Company, 1979)].

Thus, in general,

> Tom has a V-tion,

where 'V-tion' is a verbal noun for a kind of "experience," would be a derivative (but legitimate) way of saying what is said adequately and non-relationally by

> Tom Vs.

Clearly there is a strong equivalence between

> Tom feels

and
> Tom has a feeling

and, in general, between

> Tom Vs (e.g., Tom senses)

and
> Tom has a V-tion (e.g., Tom has a sensation),

but this is no more a sign of synonymy than is the strong equivalence between

> Snow is white

and
> It is true that snow is white.

Clearly, 'Snow is white' is, in a straightforward sense, more basic than 'It is true that snow is white'. The strategy employed above with respect to events suggests that the sense in which 'Tom Vs' is more basic than 'Tom has a V-tion' is essentially the same. According to such an analysis,

> Tom has a sensation

would be reconstructed as

> That he senses is true of Tom.

We have already construed *events* as a special kind of proposition, and *taking place* as a special form of truth. It is but a small step along this path to construe an object's *participating in* an event as a special case of an attribute being true of the object.

27. Now it might be objected that what I have been advancing is interesting and possibly even true—but irrelevant. It might be conceded that the relational locution

> Tom has a V-tion

can, in many cases, be "reduced" to the "more basic"

> Tom Vs,

but urged that the latter statement is itself—when made explicit—relational. In other words it might be urged that the basic thesis of the relational theory of "experiencing" concerns *not* the metaphysical relation of *having*, but the *empirical* relations of feeling, sensing, thinking, etc. For even if we turn our attention from

> Tom has a V-tion (sensation)

to

> Tom Vs (senses),

we see, on reflection, that the latter is equivalent to

> Tom senses *something*

which, prima facie, has the form

> (Ex) Senses(Tom,x).

28. Here is where the so-called "adverbial" theory of the objects of sensation becomes relevant. For, joining in the move from

> Tom has a sensation of a red triangle

to

> Tom senses a red triangle,

the adverbial theory denies that the latter has the form

(Ex) x is a red triangle and Tom senses x.

To take a more intuitive example, the adverbial theory denies that

Tom feels pain

has the form

Feels(Tom, pain)

but interprets it rather as

Tom feels-pain

and, thus, ascribes to it the form

Tom Vs.

The example is more intuitive because we are struck by the rough equivalence of 'Tom feels pain' to 'Tom hurts'.
29. To make this move is to construe 'pain', in the above context, as a special kind of adverb; one which modified 'feels' to form a verbal expression which stands to the latter as "determinate" to "determinable": roughly, as species to genus.
30. If the verb in

Tom feels pain

is 'feels-pain' thus construed, then in the context

Tom has a feeling of pain

the 'of pain' must be construed as the corresponding adjective which makes a specific verbal noun out of the verbal noun root 'feeling'.
31. The adverbial theory views such verbs as 'feels', 'experiences', 'senses'—and, as we shall see, 'thinks'—as generic verbs, and the expres-

sions formed from them by "adding a reference to the objects felt, experienced, etc." as specific verbs. It follows from this that in a perspicuous language, we would not use the generic verb in forming its species, but, instead, say

>   Tom pains

rather than

>   Tom feels pain,

just as we say

>   The book is rectangular

rather than

>   The book is rectangularly shaped.

In this perspicuous language we would not say,

>   Tom senses a red triangle

but
>   Tom a-red-triangles

where the verb 'a-red-triangle' stands for that kind of sensing which is brought about in standard conditions, and in standard perceivers, by the presence of a literally red and triangular object.

32. In the case of conceptual activity, on the assumption that thinking is to be construed as "inner speech,"[9] parallel considerations lead to parallel results. In the first place,

> S has the thought that snow is white

or
>   The thought that snow is white occurs to S

would be the higher-order equivalents of

---

[9] For a discussion of the concept of thinking as a quasi-theoretical concept modeled on the concept of meaningful verbal behavior, see Chapter 5 of *Science, Perception and Reality*; also Chapter 6 of *Science and Metaphysics*.

S thinks (i.e., is thinking) that snow is white.

And, in the second place, the latter statement would not have the form

Thinks(S, that snow is white)

but rather

S Vs.

For 'thinks that snow is white' would stand to 'thinks' as specific verb to generic verb. Here, again, we are to construe the expression following the verb as a special kind of adverb. And, as before, in a perspicuous language the verb root 'thinks' would drop out of the specific verbs. What would the perspicuous specific verb be? The answer lies in our previous account of abstract singular terms as classifying expressions. There we abstracted from the fact that the primary mode of being of language was non-parroting verbal activity by one who knows the language, and construed

as
    That snow is white

    The •snow is white•

where '•snow is white•' applies to any expression in any language which does the job done in ours by the design *snow is white*. But, as we must now realize, the primary mode of being of "expressions" is people speaking (writing, etc.). Thus what we are really classifying are linguistic activities. To take this into account, instead of saying

'Schnee ist weiss's (in German) are •snow is white•s,

we should say

'Schnee ist weiss'ings (in G) are •snow is white•ings

and once we have these verbal nouns we are led to form the corresponding verbs. Thus when all the proper moves have been made,

>   Jones said that snow is white

becomes

>   Jones •snow is white•ed.

Parallel considerations lead to parallel results in the case of thinking as inner speech. Thus,

>   The thought that snow is white occurred to Jones,

which is doubly relational in appearance, turns out to have as its foundation the non-relational state of affairs expressed by

>   Jones •snow is white•ed.[10]

33. The above considerations will play a crucial role in the argument to follow. As a preliminary means of grasping their significance, consider the following objection often raised against Descartes. It is argued that instead of claiming that

>   I think (*cogito*)

formulates a piece of primary knowledge, Descartes should have given this role to something like

>   This thought exists.

To get to the existence of the "I", then, we would have to make the inferential move

>   This thought exists
>   So, a thinker (i.e., the thinker of this thought) exists.

"I" would then be identified as the thinker who "has" the thought. To start down this path is obviously to raise the question: what would justify this

---

[10] The dot-quoted expressions in the context of inner speech are analogical counterparts of dot-quoted expressions in the context of speech proper. For an elaboration of this point see Chapter 6 of *Science and Metaphysics*.

inference?

34. From the perspective we have reached we can see that this objection overlooks the fact that reference to thoughts is derivative from references to thinkers thinking. Thus the fundamental form of the mental is not

>There are thoughts (or, more generally, representations)

but rather, as Kant saw,

>x thinks (represents),

of which a special case is

>I think (represent).

III

35. Before I turn my attention to Kant's treatment of the "I" and the relevance of this treatment to the views I have been developing, I must enlarge my canvass to take into account other features of the Aristotelian metaphysics of the person. The theme I have particularly in mind is that of causation.

36. Offhand, one would be inclined to say that Richard Taylor belongs in the mainstream of the perennial tradition, and, indeed, his recent study of *Action and Purpose* contains much to warm the hearts of those who seek to defend classical insights against the dogmas of reductionist empiricism and naturalism. Yet in spite of the many positive virtues of his analysis, the total effect must be counted a failure, largely because of the inadequate account of causation on which it rests. Actually, this comment is a bit unfair, since Taylor has many interesting and perceptive things to say about causation. The trouble is that he overlooks the ambiguity of the term, the fact that it stands for a whole family of concepts. Once he commits himself to a paradigm it becomes the paradigm of all causality and blurs key distinctions.

37. One familiar sense of "cause" is embodied in locutions of the form

>X caused Y to Z by doing A,

e.g.,

>Jones caused the match to light by striking it.

This concept of causation can be called "interventionist." In its primary form, as the illustration suggests, the cause *is* a person and a person causes something to happen by *doing* something. This concept, by a metaphorical extension, is applied to inanimate objects, thus

> The stone caused the glass to shatter by striking it.

The extended use, as a frozen metaphor, is invaluable, but philosophers have often sensed in it the original life. This accounts for the traditional conviction that, strictly speaking, only persons can be causes.

38. Now I take it as obvious that persons are or can be causes in this sense of "cause". Let us, therefore, explore it by means of examples, thus

> Jones caused the pawn to move by pushing it.

This is an excellent example of personal causation, of a piece with many Taylor gives. But at a critical stage in his argument, we find him arguing that, on occasion at least, persons cause their actions. Thus, as he sees it, when Jones moves his finger, we can appropriately say

> Jones caused his finger to move.

Now if we were to ask

> By doing what?

which our original paradigm requires, the answer must surely be "nothing." For if we were to say, for example,

> Jones caused his finger to move by pushing it,

Taylor would, correctly, object that in this event the motion of the finger would not be an action, but the result of an action—the pushing. This indicates that something is wrong. Our previous concept of a person as a cause is out of place in this context. The point must, however, be made carefully, for when we leave the context of "minimal actions," this concept of persons as causes *is* relevant. Thus the assertion that

> Jones killed Smith

can be met with the question

> By doing what?,

that is,

> What did Jones do which caused Smith to die?

to which the answer,

> Jones caused Smith to die *by firing the gun at him*,

is appropriate and falls under our canonical form. A minimal action is exactly one to which the question

> By doing what?

is inappropriate. And for this reason the concept of persons as causes with which we have been working is inapplicable.

39. Notice that to admit that in the context of non-minimal actions a person caused something to happen is not to admit that what the person caused is an action. Minimal actions are not the causes of nonminimal actions, they are rather the initial stages of nonminimal actions. (Of course, not every "initial stage" of an action is itself an action; consider nerve impulses or, more to the point, volitions.) Thus granting, for the moment, that crooking one's trigger finger is a minimal action, whereas the action of firing a gun is not, the relation of the former to the latter is not that of cause to effect, but that of an action to a larger action of which it is a part. To be sure, the crooking of the finger causes the firing of the gun in the sense of the gun's going off. But in *this* sense the firing of the gun is not an action, but a purely physical event. The relation of minimal actions to nonminimal actions should not be pictured *thusly*,

```
      MA                 A
      --------->--------->
```

but rather thusly,

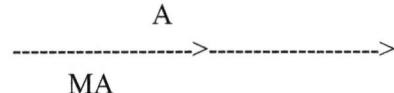

40. Now it might be said that by using the paradigm

X caused Y to Z by A-ing

to explore Taylor's idea that persons cause their actions, I am being seriously unfair. After all, it could be pointed out, Taylor explicitly contrasts "personal" causation with "natural" causation, whereas my comments amount to the idea that he fails to draw this distinction. There is some truth to this charge. I do claim that Taylor falls to draw this distinction; but as I see it this is because his concept of personal causation is vacuous. For, in effect, I have been arguing that the sense in which, according to Taylor, persons cause their actions amounts to no more than that they do them; indeed, in the last analysis, to no more than that persons act. Thus, as used by Taylor,

Jones caused action A

is a misleading way of saying

Jones did action A

which amounts to

Jones did an A-ing

and is, as I put it, the higher order equivalent of

Jones Ad.

Nobody would think of dancing a waltz as causing a waltz. Taylor may have been misled by the fact that we do speak, for example, of "making" a gesture, and "making" in some contexts is certainly "causing." But, surely,

Jones made a gesture

stands to

Jones gesticulated

as "Jones performed a waltz" stands to "Jones waltzed," and the appearance of causation is an illusion.

41. I conclude that persons do not cause their actions, though, except in the case of minimal actions, by doing one thing they can cause something else to happen, and can, therefore, be said to have done a correspondingly more complex action. Thus, by firing a gun and causing a death, one kills.

42. If persons do not cause their actions, does anything else cause them? On occasion, yes. I can be caused to do something by someone else, as when I am caused by someone in authority to make amends. By a metaphorical extension of this usage, inanimate objects can also cause one to do something. Two points must, however, be made in this connection. In the first place, it is obvious that not every action is in *this* sense caused. And in the second, one must be careful to distinguish between those cases in which an action is caused, and those in which one is not, properly speaking, an agent at all, but rather a patient, as when one is overpowered by superior force.

43. If, now, we turn to other senses of 'cause', and take Aristotle as our guide, we find it quite sensible to say that actions have causes indeed, in Aristotle's sense, *efficient* causes. For not all efficient causation is to be construed on the above model.

44. Taylor's account of the teleological explanation of purposive behavior consists of two theses:

(1) A negative thesis to the effect that purposive behavior is not caused by anything other than the agent, i.e., he is not caused to do it;
(2) A positive thesis to the effect that purposive behavior is to be explained in terms of such locutions as 'X did Y in order to bring about Z'.

Unfortunately, he leaves the latter thesis unexplicated except in tautologous ways, thus 'X did Y with the aim of bringing about Z'.

45. Taylor does consider the possibility that actions are caused by volitions. But his account of volitions and causation by volition is a

caricature. The following points need to be made:

> (1) Taylor assumes that volitions are actions in the practical sense, pieces of conduct (in this case mental conduct)—the sort of thing which, *if there were any*, could themselves be caused by volition. Thus he argues that according to the theory of volitions, in order to do one action (*A*) one must first do another (willing to do *A*). This, he points out, if taken seriously, would generate a vicious regress.

To this the answer is simple and straightforward. Volitions are not to be construed as pieces of conduct. They are "actions" only in that broadest sense in which anything expressed by a verb in the active voice (e.g., sleeping) is an action. They are actualities, indeed episodes, but not actions in any more interesting sense.[11]

> (2) Taylor assumes that because playing a phrase on the piano consists of striking successive notes, the willing that causes the playing of the phrase must consist of a volition for each note.

To this, the obvious answer is that learning to play a piece of music, and, in general, learning to play the piano, involves the building of behavioral elements into patterns which can be intended as wholes. It is only the beginner who has to think out each step as he goes along. The point is familiar to anyone who has learned to ride a bicycle or to swim.

> (3) Taylor agrees (with Melden) that since (with the necessary qualifications) there is no logical connection between cause and effect, and since there is a logical connection between the volition to raise one's arm and the raising of the arm, the volition cannot be the cause of the action.

To this the proper reply is that the so-called "logical" connection between the volition and the action is the "aboutness" relation between a thought and the state of affairs it represents, and not a putative relation of entailment between events. If Taylor's argument were correct, it would follow that a red book couldn't be the cause of the perceptual belief that one is confronted by a red book. Taylor, indeed, overlooks the point that

---

[11] For a more complete account of this and other matters pertaining to volition, see *Science and Metaphysics*, Chapter 7.

volitions are to be construed as thoughts and have intensionality. It is obvious that when we act purposively we must be thinking of the state of affairs to be realized. This thinking can't be merely matter-of-factual thinking about the future. What generates action is not descriptive thinking to which has been added a non-conceptual impetus or push. It is practical thinking.

> (4) Taylor ridicules volitions by arguing that all that can be said of the volition which causes ones finger to go up is that it is a "finger-raising volition."

This claim overlooks the complex logical and conceptual relations that can be traced between volitions and other modes of practical thinking.[12] For our present purposes, it is sufficient to note that Taylor's objection could also be raised against the concept of perceptual taking or belief. What is the perceptual taking (normally) caused by a red book in front of one? It is a red-book-in-front-of-one taking. Why not?

> (5) Taylor argues that if volitions are the causes of our actions, they must cause us to do them.

This argument is a simple consequence of his assimilation of all senses of 'cause' to his paradigm. His conclusion that if volitions are the cause of actions then we are not free, but are caused or compelled to do what we do, is sheer confusion.

46. Finally, it should be noted that just as motions are things moving, so volitions are persons willing. To suppose that in "personal" causation (or "agency") one is confronted by a mode of causation which can be schematized as

> Person causes event

and contrasted with "natural" causation, the latter being schematized as

> Event causes event

is to make a radical mistake. Even in the case of purely physical causation

---

[12] I have discussed these relations in some detail in "Thought and Action," in Keith Lehrer, ed., *Freedom and Determinism* (New York, Random House, 1966).

it is permissible to say, for example

> The bomb caused the disaster

which has the form

> Thing caused event.

Here, however, we recognize that although this form of statement is legitimate, the truth of such statements requires that of statements of the form

> Event caused event

thus,

> The explosion of the bomb caused the disaster.

It is, therefore, essential to see that exactly the same situation obtains in the case of personal causation. The truth of statements of the form

> Jones brought about E

requires that of statements of the form

> (In the circumstances) Jones' willing to bring about E' caused E

which also has the form

> Event caused event.

That the causing event is a volition, i.e., a conceptual event of the kind which is central to practical thinking, is what distinguishes 'actions' from 'mere events'. To construe the difference in terms of the contrast between 'person causes event' and 'event causes event' is sheer error.

IV

47. I shall now return to the Kantian idea that "I think" or "I represent" is

the basic and irreducible form of self-awareness with respect to distinctively human states of one's person. Traditional metaphysicians had argued that the subject of representations (the representer) is a simple, non-composite substance which is "strictly" or, as it is sometimes put, "literally" identical through time—i.e. does not have the identity of a series. Kant argues, *per contra*, that for all we know the subject or representer might be:

(a) an attribute of something more basic
(b) a system (composite)
(c) a series.

48. Of these possibilities, the first (although it has other overtones) amounts to the idea that from God's point of view a person's mind might be an Aristotelian unitary person qua having mental states and capacities, as contrasted with those states and capacities which are the real counterparts of bodily states and capacities. Kant defends this possibility by showing that a traditional argument to the contrary is a fallacy. His reconstruction of this fallacy or "paralogism" can be paraphrased as follows:

(1) The concept of the "I" (representer) is the concept of a subject of representations.
(2) The concept of the "I" is not the concept of derivative or dependent logical subject.
(3) Therefore, the concept of the "I" is the concept of a non-derivative subject.[13]

Kant concedes that the argument would not be a fallacy if we could add the premise that our concept of the "I" is the concept of a determinate kind of object, as the concept of a species of material thing is the concept of a determinate kind of object. For this premise would entail that the concept of the "I" is the concept of a specific type of logical subject; and from this, together with the premise that it is not the concept of a logical subject of specific type T, one could establish that it is the concept of a logical subject

---

[13] To get an initial insight into the surface structure of the argument, consider the following:

We conceive of x as colored.
We do not conceive of x as red.
Therefore we conceive of x as non-red.

of specific type T′, if these were the only relevant alternatives.

49. But the concept of the "I" is the concept of that which thinks (thus, as Kant uses the term 'I', it is equivalent to 'mind'), and concepts pertaining to mental acts are "functional" in a way which leaves open the question as to the "qualitative" or, as I prefer to say, contentual character of the items that function in such a way as to be the kind of mental act they are. To use a well-worn analogy, one may distinguish between the contentual and the functional aspects of the activities involved in a game of chess. The contentual aspects concern the material out of which the pieces and the board are made, and the specific kinds of changes which are to count as the various moves. We can conceive of widely different contentual embodiments of chess, i.e., we can conceive of the functionings in ways which abstract from specific embodiments, though they lay down abstract requirements which any specific embodiments must satisfy. Notice that these abstractly conceived functionings could be embodied in different types of logical subject. Thus there could be a game of chess in which the pieces were simple substances, or composite substances, or persons qua bodies, or, in the case of mental chess, conceptual entities. This can be put by saying that these abstractly conceived functionings are "transcategorial" with respect to the type of logical subjects in which they might be embodied (e.g., simple, complex, person qua moveable).

50. Now the peculiar feature of concepts pertaining to conceptual activity is that they are purely functional. To get purely functional concepts pertaining to chess, we start with concepts involving specific content and proceed by abstraction. Our concepts pertaining to conceptual activity, on the other hand, are purely functional *ab initio*. This lack of a specific contentual aspect is what lies behind the temptation to think of mental acts as "diaphanous." And Kant's point can be put by saying that conceptual acts are transcategorial with respect to the type of logical subject which might engage in them (e.g., simple, complex, person qua capable of conceptual activity).

51. Thus, to represent the mind as a substance (as contrasted with a person qua capable of conceptual acts) is not to know that the mind is such a substance. For to know that latter we would have to have an adequate contentual concept of mental activity (i.e., we would have to know the mind "as a determinate object"), and this we do not have. Thus, from the standpoint of knowledge, "representing the mind as a substance" amounts to no more than "not representing it as a contentually specific dependent subject." Indeed, by parity of reasoning, "representing the mind as a dependent

subject" would amount to no more than "not representing it as a contentually specific substance."

52. To sum up, if we conceive of the "I" (or mind) determinately as a determinate object of knowledge, without conceiving of it as a dependent logical subject, we must be conceiving of it as an independent or non-derivative object of knowledge. Thus Kant traces the fallacy to a failure to note that the term 'I' (or 'mind') does not express the concept of a determinate kind of object. It is because of this that, even granted that we do not conceive of the "I" as a derivative subject, it does not follow that we are conceiving of it as a non-derivative subject, or substance.

53. Kant finds a similar fallacy in the argument "rational psychologists" had used to prove the simplicity of the "I"—to prove that its identity is not that of a system or composite. His reconstruction of the argument can be paraphrased as follows:

(1) The concept of the "I" (representer) is the concept of one subject.
(2) The concept of the "I" is not the concept of a composite.
(3) Therefore, the concept of the "I" is the concept of a non-composite entity. Its unity is not that of a system.

54. As before, Kant concedes that if our concept of the "I", as *one* subject, were the contentually determinate concept of a determinate object, then the conclusion would be established. If we are not conceiving of it as a system or composite, we must be conceiving of it as a determinate non-composite or simple object of knowledge. But, again, our knowledge of the mind is the knowledge of that which acts in ways which we conceive of in purely functional terms. And since these functions could, in principle, be activities of either (a) a simple substance, (b) a composite substance, or (c) a substance (simple or composite) qua capable of conceptual activity, our knowledge does not determine to which of these types of logical subject the "I" belongs.

55. In connection with this second Paralogism, Kant makes two points that show the subtlety of his thought. It is, he argues, indeed true that the subject of thoughts cannot be a *many* in the sense of *many subjects of thought*. To make the point in terms of a familiar type of example, if one thinker thinks 'Tom', another thinks 'is', and yet another thinks 'tall', this does not entail that there is an "I" which thinks 'Tom is tall'. But, Kant points out, it does not follow that the "I" which thinks cannot be a plurality or system.

Metaphysics and the Concept of a Person (MP, 68) 361

The subject of thoughts, the "I", is a plurality

is not the same as

The subject of thoughts is a plurality of "I"s.

56. The third Paralogism concerns the claim that the identity of the "I" through its successive states is not the identity of a series. It has a similar form, and Kant's treatment of it is equally sound and illuminating. Here, too, it should be noted that the idea that the "I" is a series must not be confused with the idea that it is a series of "I"s.

V

57. I have often characterized my metaphysical views as strongly Kantian in structure. Thus I have argued that the common-sense world, the world of the "manifest image" is, in the Kantian sense, phenomenal; the way in which things as they really are appear to minds endowed with a certain conceptual framework. The fact that this framework is a subtle one, particularly in those respects which concern action and practice, by no means guarantees that its ontology is an adequate representation of the way things are.

58. In the manifest image, our concept of a person is not the concept of something of which the behavior can be assimilated to the triggering off of causal properties in the interaction of material things. Persons acquire second natures—in the literal sense, dispositions. But their *first* nature is not that of a system of causal properties—dispositions in the metaphorical sense—but rather that of a system of capacities pertaining to the various modes of thinking.

59. In the Paralogisms Kant has kept the way clear for the view that in reality the "I" is a system, and, in particular, for the view that it is a system of scientific objects, the true counterparts of Kant's things-in-themselves. Again he has kept the way clear for the view that thoughts and other representations are in reality complex states of a system and, in particular, of a neurophysiological system. Here again one must beware of assimilating scientific intelligibility to Taylor's paradigm of causation. Kant also kept the way clear for the view that in reality the identity of the "I" through its successive acts of representation is the identity of a series.

60. Kant's fundamental error was to construe the phenomenal world in

Cartesian terms. The Aristotelian-Strawsonian reconstruction is along sounder lines. But, as I see it, this (unavoidable) error was but one more symptom of his pre-evolutionary commitments. Correctly rejecting standard empiricism, he was forced into the platonic alternative of innate ideas. This led him to tie together in one bundle the diversity of concepts in terms of which we explain the course of nature. Different levels of spatial and temporal concepts were identified and construed in terms of the Space and Time of Newtonian mechanics. The framework of emerging microphysics was assumed to be already in the mind awaiting its Socrates, as did geometry in the soul of Meno's slave.

61. Today we are in a better position to distinguish between the conceptual framework of which nature was the cause, and the freely elaborate conceptual frameworks with which we now challenge nature. It is the greater explanatory power of the latter which stands behind the claim that things as they are in themselves are things as ideal science would find them to be. But the details of this neo-Peircean conception of truth and reality must be left to another occasion.[14]

---

[14] For an initial attempt see Chapters 3-5 of my *Science and Metaphysics*.

ON KNOWING THE BETTER AND DOING THE WORSE

The revised text of the 1969 Suarez Philosophy Lecture delivered at Fordham University.

I

1. The title of my paper describes an experience common to all of us, whether we be saints, sinners, or run of the mill members of the moral community. One might think that such a common experience would be quite unproblematic, raising no problems except *per accidens,* as when a person makes a foolish mistake about what is in front of his nose. What could be more obvious than that people often do what they know perfectly well they ought not to do? And if the *fact* be obvious, why does it not lie quietly in the philosopher's collection of specimens, while he turns his attention to puzzles which, so to speak, jump out at him like nightmares in the dark?

2. The answer is a familiar story. Just as the heart of tragedy lies in the fact that death and desolation can result from a clash between parties, each of which, in no superficial sense, has right on his side, so in philosophy the most disturbing problems arise when obvious truths begin to twist and turn and fight among themselves.

3. But what obvious truth or truths conflict with the all too human phenomenon echoed by my title? Surely, if the history of philosophy is a reliable guide,

> (A) To know that course *A* is better than course *B* is to have reason for following *A* rather than *B*;

and

> (B) If a person has reason for following course *A* rather than course *B* he will follow *A* rather than *B*.

For, together, these imply

> (C) To know that course *A* is better than course *B* is to follow *A* rather than *B*

which logically conflicts with the idea that there is such a thing as knowing the better and doing the worse.

4. But, it will be said, the second truth (B) is obvious only if it is qualified. It should read

> (B_1) If a person has reason for following course A rather than course B he will do A rather than B—unless he is overcome by impulse.

Since impulsive action is as common as blackberries, the paradox, it will be said, disappears; for the qualification, itself obvious, reconciles our new principles with the obviousness with which we began.

5. It does, however, only if *all* cases in which a person who, knowing the better, does the worse, are cases of action "on impulse." But is this true? Surely there are cases in which, to use Bishop Butler's phrase, a person "sits down in a cool hour" and after careful deliberation resolves to do that which he nevertheless knows to be worse. This is what gives our problem its bite; for, man being what he is, the fact that impulse can lead him to fly in the face of reason is a sobering rather than a puzzling consideration.

6. This is not to say that there are *no* puzzles about the idea that impulse can lead men to act "against their better judgement." Like other general truths about behavior it needs to be fitted into a coherent philosophy of mind, along with, for example, the fact that men on occasion do act in accordance with their better judgement. Aristotle's account of the incontinent man can be viewed as just such an attempt. But does it touch our problem?

7. For our problem is posed by the fact—at least I shall assume it to be a fact—that we are confronted by an "inconsistent triad," i.e., by three propositions which separately command assent, but which cannot live together in the reflective mind:

> (1) People know the better yet deliberately do the worse.
> (2) To know that course A is better than course B is to have reason for following A rather than B.
> (3) To have reason for following A rather than B is (impulse aside) to follow A rather than B.

II

8. But I probably have not yet persuaded you that these principles have that *prima facie* obviousness which makes it so difficult to lay them aside. Or, to put it differently, I may have concealed their claims by clumsy

formulation. Let me try again by making them more explicit. Consider

> (A_1) To know that course A is, *all things considered*, better than course B is to have a *conclusive* reason for following A rather than B

for, obviously, one thing may seem to be better than another with respect to certain considerations, but not seem to be so when a larger context is taken into account.

9. To make our first principle thus explicit calls for a corresponding revision in the second, which becomes

> (B_2) If a person has a *conclusive* reason for following course A rather than course B, he will (impulse aside) follow A rather than B.

Combined, these revised principles entail, as before, that, impulse aside, there is no such thing as knowing the better but doing the worse.

III

10. You will not have failed to notice that I have drawn heavily on the powers of that little word 'know'—one of the few four letter words which is not as "in" as it used to be. Is there such a thing as *knowing*—in a genuinely cognitive sense—that one thing or course of action is better than another? To convince the skeptic—and I don't mean the professional skeptic who would die rather than admit that he knows anything of substance, but rather one who has found grounds to question the possibility of such knowledge—would require that larger dialogue which, if Santayana is to be believed, goes on endlessly in Limbo—but, fortunately, not in the lecture hall. I shall, therefore, content myself with the reflection that the possibility of such knowledge—the knowledge that one thing is, all things considered, better than another—is really one of the *prima facie* obviousnesses with which philosophers begin.

11. But once we grant this possibility, it is bound to occur to us that it involves a distinction which might resolve our puzzle. For 'knowledge' contrasts with '(mere) belief'. Indeed, while we are at it, we might note that 'all things considered' can mean 'all things in point of fact considered for what they are thought to be' or (ideally) 'all *relevant* things considered for *what they really are*'.

12. Perhaps, then, what is "obvious" is that

(A₂) To *know* (rather than merely believe) that course A is, all relevant things considered for what they really are, better than course B is to have a *conclusive* reason for following A rather than B

which, together with

(B₂) If a person has a conclusive reason for following course A rather than course B he will (impulse aside) follow A rather than B

would entail that, impulse aside, there is no such thing as *knowing* the better but doing the worse. This time, then, the *prima facie* existence of exceptions could, perhaps, be accounted for by saying that the 'knowledge' of these agents wasn't *really* knowledge, but rather 'knowledge loosely speaking', a dignified form of mere opinion.

IV

13. I have already brought us face to face with the Socratic thesis that virtue is knowledge. I propose to examine it; not, however, as an exercise in exegesis, but because, being a card-carrying member of the Platonic tradition, I subscribe to the view that Plato wrong is usually closer to the truth than other philosophers right. But before embarking on this task, I shall sound a more contemporary note by reminding you of the distinction, baptized but not discovered by David Falk, between 'externalist' and 'internalist' theories of the relation between 'ought' and motivation.[1]

14. Roughly, the 'externalist' holds that it is *logically* possible for a person to 'know'—in a reasonable sense of this term—that he ought to do a certain action A, and yet have no motive for doing A. This means that the idea that he ought to do A fails, as such, to attract him toward the doing of A. The 'externalist' grants that in point of fact a person might be attracted towards doing A by the knowledge that A is what he ought to do. Such people, he would say, have a 'desire' to do what they know to be right. But the existence of this desire in people who have this knowledge would be a *contingent* fact. People could know that was right and lack any tendency to be moved to act by this knowledge.

15. 'Internalism', on the other hand, is the view that to know that a course

---

[1] "'Ought' and Motivation," *Proceedings of the Aristotelian Society*, **48** (1947-48); reprinted in *Readings in Ethical Theory*, edited by Wilfrid Sellars and John Hospers (New York, 1952).

of action A is one's duty is, *ipso facto*, to be moved toward the doing of A—is, *ipso facto*, to have a reason for doing A. For there is a perfectly legitimate and familiar sense in which to be moved toward doing an action by the idea that the action is of a certain character is to have its being of that character as a reason for doing it. The reason may be good or bad, but it is one's reason.

16. Notice that internalism was defined above as the view that to know that A is one's duty is, *ipso facto*, to have *a* reason for doing A. This leaves open the possibility that even if one knows that one ought to do A, one might have other reasons which point in other directions, say to the doing of B. Thus internalism, thus defined, is compatible with the view that one can know that one ought to do A (the better) and yet be moved to do B (the worse). Indeed, the internalist need not limit such occasions to impulsive action. A person can know that he ought to do A (the better), the internalist might hold, and yet *deliberately* do B (the worse). All we have committed him to is the view that if a person knows that he ought to do A, then he, *ipso facto*, as a matter of *logical* necessity, has *a* reason for doing A.

17. But once he goes this far, can the internalist avoid the more radical view that if a person knows that he ought to do A he has a *conclusive* reason for doing A, where this means that he has a reason for doing A which must 'overpower'—so to speak—all the reasons which incline him in other directions?

18. For, as William Frankena has reminded us,[2] we think that the fact that a person *ought* to do A is a *conclusive* reason for him to do A, and hence, that to know that one ought to do A is to *have* (i.e., be in mental possession of) a conclusive reason for doing A.

19. The connection between radical internalism and the topics with which I began is obvious. For if radical internalism is correct, then, if a person knows that course of action A is the *best* available alternative, the one he *ought* to pursue, then he has a *conclusive* reason for A, and hence a prevailing motive for this course of action, and will necessarily follow it.

20. Now the standard criticism of internalism, formulated most acutely by Frankena, is that it confuses two senses of 'having a reason for doing A':

(1) having (by virtue of certain facts) a *justification* for doing A
(2) having a *motive* for doing A.

---

[2] "Obligation and Motivation," in *Essays in Moral Philosophy*, edited by A. Melden (Seattle: University of Washington Press, 1958).

This confusion, the critic contends, leads internalists to move mistakenly from the idea that a person would (in certain respects) be *justified* in doing *A* to the idea that he *has a motive* for doing *A*, indeed, to think that being justified in doing *A* is *ipso facto* having a motive for doing *A*.

21. Now the distinction to which Frankena calls attention is a proper one, but far from supporting the idea that the phrase 'having a reason for doing *A*' is ambiguous, it points in the opposite direction. For surely

> *S* has (by virtue of certain facts) a justification for doing *A*

is equivalent, *not* to a sense of

> *S* has a reason for doing *A*

but rather to

> *S* has (by virtue of certain facts) a *good* reason for doing *A*.

Thus the difference between (1) and (2) is to be accounted for, *not* by different senses of 'having a reason', but by the difference between 'having a reason' and 'having a good reason', the sense of 'having a reason' being the same. And if so, then it follows from the critic's own remarks that *in this sense* to have a reason *is* to have a motive.

22. Now there is a perfectly obvious sense in which one can 'have a motive' without being moved. Thus, to say, for example, of Jones that he has a motive for killing his aunt is not to imply that Jones is being moved to kill his aunt, nor even that the idea of killing his aunt is tugging at his will. The statement commits itself only to the existence of a certain hypothetical fact—roughly—that:

> If Jones knew such and such facts (e.g., she has made a will in his favor but is about to change it), then he would have a motive—in the occurrent sense—for killing his aunt.

23. Thus, if to be justified in doing *A* is to have a good reason for doing *A*, then, building as before on the critic's remarks, to say that Jones has a good reason for doing *A* is to affirm the existence of a hypothetical fact, this time to the effect—roughly—that

If Jones knew such and such facts then he would have a good motive—in the occurrent sense—for doing A.

24. But if this is correct, then, taking account of the fact that to be *justified* in doing A is not merely to have *a* good reason but to have a *conclusive* reason, i.e., a good reason all things considered, for doing A, the 'conclusiveness' is seen to concern the *goodness* of the reason, and not its 'strength'. Thus

S is justified in doing A

would have the sense of

If S knew all relevant facts, S would have a *conclusively good* motive—in the occurrent sense—for doing A.

25. Thus we see that implicit in the critic's remarks is a valid point, *not* however against internalism, but against *extreme* internalism. For the latter is indeed confused; *not*, as the critic contends, by confusing two senses of 'having a reason', but rather two senses of 'having a *conclusive* reason':

(1) having a conclusively *good* reason
(2) having a necessarily *prevailing* reason.

26. For it is because of this confusion that the extreme internalist moves from

S knows that he ought to do A

to

S knows a conclusive reason for doing A

to

S has—in the occurrent sense—a prevailing motive for doing A

to

S does A.

VI

27. The upshot of the preceding remarks is that internalism, the view that knowing that one ought to do A entails being moved toward doing A, remains a viable position, even after Frankena's criticism has been taken

into account. We have seen the proper target of the criticism to be *extreme internalism*, but if the latter has lost one of its supports—a confusion between 'conclusively *good*' and 'conclusively powerful'—it is not without recourse. For it is open to the extreme internalist to argue that while these concepts are *different*, they are connected in such a way that if a reason is conclusively *good*, then, when known, it is, of necessity, *conclusively powerful*.

28. This brings me back to the Socratic thesis that Virtue is Knowledge. This thesis sums up a complex train of thought in which the following subordinate themes can be discerned:

> (1) Virtue is, in the first instance (Virtue$_1$), the propensity to do right actions.
> (2) Virtue is, in the second instance (Virtue$_2$), the state of the soul which ensures the presence of Virtue$_1$.

Clearly, when Virtue is said to be Knowledge, it is not meant that the propensity to do right actions *is* knowledge, but rather that the state of the soul which ensures the presence of this propensity is knowledge. The propensity to do right actions can exist in the absence of knowledge, for example, as the result of training by stick and carrot, given that the agent has true belief concerning what actions are in point of fact right. But, in the absence of the relevant *knowledge*, the propensity would have a precarious existence, and be at the mercy of the honeyed words of orators and poets.

29. If the true ground of Virtue is Knowledge—Knowledge of *what*? In the first instance, as one would expect, of the principles of right action. If, and to the extent that, one is mistaken about these, one's beliefs about what ought to be done would be false, and one's actions wrong. But the Knowledge which grounds Virtue includes not only knowledge of the principles of right action, but also knowledge of what makes for a satisfying life. Let me take these two modes of knowledge in order.

VII

30. So far as the principles of right action are concerned, Plato is, in a suitably broad sense, a utilitarian. By this I mean that he takes for granted that in each circumstance one ought to do that action which is for the good of the relevant community, which he tends to equate with the City (πολις).

As I have argued elsewhere,[3] conventions and positive law do not, as the Sophists tended to think, *constitute* principles of right action. They merely provide special circumstances which, like any circumstances (though more important than most, partly because they simplify many decisions), are relevant to determining what ought to be done as elements in the total circumstance in which one must do it. Principles of right action are, for Plato as for Socrates, a special case of the principles of a craft. Indeed, they are the principles of the craft of shaping and maintaining a City which lives well. The principles of any craft have the form:

To make and maintain E, one *ought*:
if in C_1, to do A_1
if in C_2, to do A_2
....

and if the 'product' of the craft has any complexity, the principles will be correspondingly numerous and varied, for they must take account of all foreseeable contingencies.

31. The situation is exactly parallel in the case of the art of the citizen; the form of a principle of right action is:

To promote the welfare of the City, one ought:
if in C_1, to do A_1
if in C_2, to do A_2
....

Thus the practical necessity of doing A_i if C_i is a necessity which is relative to promoting the welfare of the City. Abstracted from this context, the formulae

One ought:
if in C_1, to do A_1
if in C_2, to do A_2
....

---

[3] "Reason and the Art of Living in Plato," presented in a conference on "Greece: The Critical Spirit, 450-350 B.C.," held at Ohio State University, April 5 and 6, 1968. A discussion of closely related issues is to be found in my essay "The Soul as Craftsman," in *Philosophical Perspectives* (Springfield, IL.: Thomas, 1967) [in *Philosophical Perspectives: History of Philosophy* (Ridgeview Publishing Company)].

lose their intelligibility, and though they can be embedded in training and tradition, they can no longer be the objects of knowledge nor the purposes of informed action.

32. Thus one can *know* what one ought to do only by *knowing* that by doing it in the circumstance in which one finds oneself, one will be promoting the welfare of the City—or, to use a Socratic turn of phrase, that one will be effectively pursuing the citizen's craft.

33. The foregoing has been an explication of Plato's conception of justice in the sense of right action, i.e., justice as an attribute of actions. The latter must not be confused with justice as a virtue of the individual, nor with justice as a virtue of the City. As a virtue of the City, justice is that character which ensures that the City has the propensity to act justly. Plato, as is well known, conceives this character to consist in the agreement of all free men that the wise are to rule.

34. The City being the individual writ large, justice as an individual virtue would, accordingly, be the agreement of all 'parts' of the soul that reason is to rule.

35. But justice thus conceived as *one* virtue among *many* is not yet the true Virtue for which Plato is looking. For Virtue, as we saw, is that which guarantees right action, and hence which guarantees that the soul is, in the above sense, just, i.e., that all 'parts' of the soul agree that reason is to rule. Where is such a guarantee to be found?

36. Plato's answer, of course, is that Virtue in this ultimate sense is Knowledge—Knowledge, he tells us, of the Good. To many this has seemed to be the uninformative formula 'the Good is knowledge of the Good', and has been ridiculed as such. But Plato, of course, meant that Virtue is Knowledge of what constitutes a satisfying way of life. Thus the 'Good for man' is a 'satisfying human life', that which Aristotle called *eudaimonia* or, as this term is usually rendered, 'happiness'.[4]

37. But how does knowledge—even of the good for man—relate to action—let alone right action? Another premise is required, and again it is familiar: Each man 'wills' his own good. In other words, each man seeks to live a satisfying life. Each man sketches, more or less clearly, a life plan, an overarching end-in-view, for which particular appetites, inclinations, desires, and aversions are the raw materials which are to be shaped into a coherent and satisfying whole. When Plato says, then, that Virtue is Knowledge, he means that the frame of mind which guarantees right action

---

[4] For an interpretation of Plato's theory of the nature and role of the Idea of the Good, see the chapter on "The Soul as Craftsman," in my *Philosophical Perspectives* (note 3).

consists in knowing the nature of, and hence striving to realize, a truly satisfying life.

38. Thus the art of living takes its place at the peak of the Platonic edifice. For although, as we shall see, the art of living essentially involves the art of the citizen (the statesman's craft), the prime mover of all craftsmanship is the individual's search for happiness as defined by his plan of life.

39. But if this is the reality of Virtue when the veils of appearance have been stripped away, how does it guarantee right action?

40. Clearly, if Plato could show that a truly satisfying life is one which has as its primary end-in-view the welfare of the City, he would have proved his point. But, as we have seen, a major premise of his argument is that each person's ultimate end-in-view is his own happiness, a continuing sequence of satisfying states of mind. What kind of necessary connection would there be between such a goal and the welfare of the City?

41. One might point out that the wise man's satisfactions are non-competitive; that his living is a practice of dying; that the penalty of abstaining from the statesman's craft is to be ruled by knaves and fools. But none of these considerations does more than prepare the way for Plato's positive account of the incorporation of the welfare of the City into the truly satisfying life.

42. The ultimate irony of Plato's expulsion of the poets from the ideal City is that it is the contemplation of Beauty which constitutes the *sine qua non* of its existence. Among the raw materials of human life is the love of harmony and proportion. Indeed, the wise man's satisfactions primarily consist of those in which 'pure' or 'unmixed' pleasure colors the contemplation of intelligible order, not only in the world of Forms, but also in the world of Becoming. And it is clear that for Plato the complex harmony of a happy City is particularly pleasant to contemplate, and the contemplation of the disorders of timocratic, oligarchic, democratic, and tyrannized cities increasingly unpleasant as we go down the scale.

43. Must we not say, then, that the cash value of the Platonic thesis that Virtue is Knowledge is the claim that the wise man will do right actions because that to which right action is the means, namely the welfare of the City, is his end—not *directly* (for it is the direct end of the statesman's craft rather than of the art of living), but as *that the contemplation of which*—a most satisfying contemplation—is a necessary constituent of a well-crafted life.

VIII

44. The Platonic doctrine, is, it is clear, a form of 'extreme internalism', the view that

> to know, all things considered for what they really are, that course of action *A* is what ought to be done, is to have a conclusively *powerful* reason for following it.

45. But if, in the last analysis, Plato's attempt to prove, by an appeal to an intellectual aesthetics, that to know the good for man and to know what actions are right is to have a conclusively *powerful* reason (motive) for doing what is right must be counted a failure, has he, perhaps, prepared the way for a more satisfying solution?

46. The answer is, on the whole, "yes," for he has called attention to the fact that unless we can in some sense take the welfare of the City as our end, there will be no logical connection between that which we aim at, all things considered, and doing in each circumstance the action which is conducive to the general welfare. Furthermore, he has given the problem its clearest, its most (so to speak) *undiluted* formulation by relating the two questions:

> (1) What ought one to do, *all things considered as they really are*?
> (2) What would we be moved to do, *all things considered as they really are*?

47. But whereas the art of the citizen (which is concerned to discover the principles of right action) views the welfare of the City from an impersonal point of view, that of a *craftsman qua* craftsman, Plato assumes that an account of what a person would be moved to do, all things considered as they really are, essentially involves a *personal point of view*. For the ultimate end-in-view is the agent's own well-being or 'happiness'.

48. Nevertheless, there is a sense in which this personal point of view becomes, in the sage, 'impersonal', in that the state of affairs which he enjoys contemplating and the enjoyment of the contemplation of which is a constituent of his well-being, is defined in impersonal terms. When the sage enjoys contemplating a happy city he does so from the statesman's point of view, and the well-being of those who are to benefit by his actions is not dependent on their being persons who are for example, *familiar* to

him, or who *resemble him in their tastes or inclinations*. It is not a matter of their being the *particular* persons they are, any more than the carpenter's choice of which piece of wood to place where is a function of its being the particular piece of wood it is. The choice is regulated by the general principles of the craft.

49. Thus, the art of the citizen defines right action in the spirit of the utilitarian maxim 'each person to count for one'. The tastes and inclinations of the citizens who constitute the raw material of the city are relevant, not as the tastes and inclinations of particular people who stand in contingent relations to the craftsman, but as tastes and inclinations the coherent satisfaction of which is to constitute the well-being of the city.

50. All this is according to the letter—if not the spirit—of the golden rule and the categorical imperative. But when it comes to the carrying out of this program, the motive is not *that the welfare of the city be promoted*, but *that I enjoy contemplating the promoted welfare*. Thus, though in one sense the formula of the end-in-view is the promotion of the general welfare, when its full character is made explicit, the motive is personal in its point of view, the search for one's own happiness.

IX

51. But what is the alternative? It is to find in the members of the moral community a *mode of motivation* which is not impersonal in the Platonic sense—a subordinate impersonal moment in a personal satisfaction sought for as such—but is, rather, *directly* impersonal, or, better, *inter-personal*, as directly oriented toward the welfare of the community. This new mode of motivation would be that in which the individual views himself and the world from the standpoint of 'one of the community' or, as I have elsewhere put it, from the standpoint of 'one of us'.

52. This alternative would open the possibility that even after 'all things have been considered as they really are', there would be two coherent motives:

> (1) the welfare of our community viewed as related to the actions of each of us (inter-personal benevolence)
> (2) one's own happiness or well-being, viewed from a personal point of view *as* one's own happiness or well-being—in traditional terms, self-love.

These would constitute over-arching motives in their own dimensions or points of view, but would be *incomparable*, and not only *capable* of conflict but typically conflicting, though often to an undramatic degree.

53. Obviously, there is a sense in which these overarching motives could, and would, overlap. Thus the satisfaction of the inter-personal motive would be a personal satisfaction, and personal satisfaction would be a relevant element in the general welfare which is the object of the inter-personal aim. But these dialectical points are familiar to students of Bishop Butler's thought.

X

54. The position I have been sketching would be a form of 'internalism', but not of that 'extreme internalism' which equates 'conclusively *good* reason' with 'conclusively *powerful* reason'. To know that one ought to do *A*—i.e., to know that it is conducive to the welfare of the community that in these circumstances one does *A*—would be to have a conclusively *good* reason for doing *A*; but not, necessarily, alas, a conclusively *powerful* reason (i.e., motive).

55. What might it mean to say that the reason (motive) is conclusively good? The true answer to this question would obviously be the keystone of a successful moral philosophy, indeed the philosopher's stone itself. I have wrestled with this problem at length elsewhere.[5] I shall limit myself at present to an abstract, and hence inevitably disappointing, statement of my conclusions.

56. First, two remarks which indicate the general strategy:

> (1) If the ultimate answer is to satisfy the intellect it must follow from the meanings of the terms involved, for otherwise it would simply lead us on to new problems without end.
>
> (2) The goodness of a *reason* is always, in the last analysis as the term 'reason' implies, a *logical* goodness.

57. Applied to our problem, the strategy involves pointing out that to think of oneself as a member of a community is to think of oneself as one of a many who view each other from what I have called the inter-personal point of view and who, therefore, share the mode of motivation described above.

---

[5] *Form and Content in Ethical Theory*, the 1967 Lindley Lecture delivered at the University of Kansas, and available from the Philosophy Department; also *Science and Metaphysics* (New York: Humanities Press, 1968), Chapter 7 [reprinted by Ridgeview Publishing Company].

It is, therefore, a conceptual truth that to will that each of us does that which promotes our general welfare is to have that reason for acting the having of which constitutes being one of us.

58. But enough of promissory notes! I must devote the remaining moments to rounding off with pennies the payments I have been making on the promissory notes with which I began.

59. The bite of the traditional problem with which I have been concerned lies exactly in the fact that a conclusively *good* reason (i.e., a conclusively good motive) need not be a conclusively *powerful* reason (i.e., a conclusively powerful motive). One *can* know the better and do the worse; not just from *impulse*, but from self-love, all things considered for what they really are. It is for this reason that genuine moral conflict is imaginatively pictured as a conflict between two persons—one representing interpersonal commitment to one's community, the other, personal commitment to one's own happiness on the whole. At the moment of decision, one or the other of these candidates for an orientation of the self-in-action—each in its own way overarching—predominates. The choice is, in an important sense, between incommensurables. Which choice one makes is a revelation of what one, at that moment, *is*. It is often surprising, sometimes exhilarating, or disconcerting, even devastating—but always a revelation.

TOWARD A THEORY OF THE CATEGORIES

I

1. Kant is clearly not an "empiricist," yet the concept of experience is central to his philosophy. This dissociation of the terms 'empiricism' and 'experience' is an interesting feature of how they have come to be used, not only in the Kantian tradition, but also, for example, in the pragmatic tradition according to John Dewey. The latter, as is well known, equated 'empiricism' with the 'atomistic' sensationalism of Hume and Mill, but used the term 'experience' in the spirit of German idealism and made it the central concept of his naturalistic pragmatism.

2. Philosophical 'isms' are as difficult to define as their political counterparts, and 'empiricism' is no exception; yet paradigm cases are presented by Hume, Mill and, more recently, by logical positivism. The Wittgenstein of the *Tractatus* is a particularly interesting case, because although he is clearly, in some respects, in the Humean tradition, he nevertheless conceives of the task of philosophy as that of giving an a priori account of what it is to be an object of empirical knowledge. In this respect he belongs in the tradition of Kant, for whom, as far as theoretical reason is concerned, the task of philosophy is exactly that of explicating the concept of an object of experience. Kant emphasizes that this task does not belong to empirical psychology; like Wittgenstein he conceives of it as a nonempirical enterprise. In effect he is convinced that it is possible to delineate the essential features of anything that could count as an object of empirical knowledge in any possible world, that is, for any finite mind, however different the world it inhabits might be from ours in its generic traits. Notice that these differences between possible worlds would concern not just their histories, but the very qualities, relations, and nomological connections which characterize the objects which make it up. In other words, Kant aimed at delineating the conceptual structure of the most generic features of the concept of an object of experience. Needless to say, however, he was also concerned to understand how these most generic features take specific form to constitute the concept of an object of *human* experience.

3. If we can say, as I think we can, that the *pure* categories are essential moments in the definition of an object of experience in general, then *schemata* are to be construed as the *differentia* which specify these generic

moments into the specific categories of a variety of finite mind in its possible world; and the 'schematized categories' described by Kant become the categories involved in the explication of the concept of human experience, or, roughly, the experience of those finite centers of experience which share Space and, particularly, Time as forms of intuition. For, as Kant sees it, the distinctive feature of human experience is that it is experience of a world of spatio-temporal objects. In evaluating this conception, it must be remembered that Kant equates Space and Time with Newtonian Space and Time, and that he would grant that a world of experience might have a structure which, though not in this sense 'spatial' or 'temporal', has properties which are analogous to the latter in ways which make possible a schematizing of the pure categories and hence which satisfy the abstract requirements of a concept of a world of experience which has been purified of all contingent features.

4. The points I have been making so far can be summed up in the following statement. Both Kant and Wittgenstein think it possible to give an a priori account of what it is to be an object of empirical knowledge. Obviously the accounts they give differ in interesting ways—ways which reflect the different conceptual resources on which they could draw. For the intervening century saw two intellectual revolutions which have already wrought irreversible changes in the philosopher's environment. Of these revolutions the most important was the impact of evolutionary theory on what are now called "The Life Sciences."

5. Less important, but by no means insignificant—though its significance has been exaggerated—was the revolution in logical theory which triumphed with the *Principia Mathematica* of Whitehead and Russell; for both Kant and Wittgenstein took, as their point of departure in explicating the concept of an object of empirical knowledge, the forms and operations in terms of which the logical theory of their time interpreted the structure of statements and the validity of inferences.

II

6. I have pointed out that Kant believed it possible to explicate the concept of an object of empirical knowledge in a way which abstracts from the specifics of human experience. I shall now proceed to argue that the same is true of the Wittgenstein of the *Tractatus*. To begin with, it is a familiar and tantalizing fact that he gives an account of *objects*, not only without giving any examples, but without even indicating what sort of

examples it would be appropriate to give. Thus, whereas Kant does tie his abstract account to distinctive features of human experience, Wittgenstein makes no such concession and does indeed give an account of what it is to be an object *überhaupt*.

7.   Many contemporary philosophers think of themselves as belonging to the 'empiricist tradition', and yet are increasingly attracted to those features of Kant's thought which are not peripheral to but, indeed, central to his clash with 'empiricism'. It is, I would argue, no mere coincidence that this phenomenon has been accompanied by a revival of interest in the *Tractatus* and a growing awareness of the extent to which it diverges from classical empiricism and is profoundly Kantian in character.

8.   Are we to interpret this trend as an absorption of Kantian themes into empiricism or as a reinterpretation of Kantian themes along empiricist lines? These questions call for decisions rather than answers. Which gives us more insight: a contrast between empiricised Kant and historical Kant; or a contrast between Kantanised empiricism and historical empiricism? One thing is clear. The traditions are merging and neither will ever again be the same.

III

9.   I pointed out that for Kant, the explication of the concept of an object of empirical knowledge requires a theory of 'categories'. The same is no less true of Wittgenstein, and, indeed, I have been implying that their treatment of 'categories' is importantly similar. Yet on what principle do philosophers collect certain concepts together and label them 'categories'? For offering a theory of categories presupposes that one has such a principle of collection in mind. Historically, the principle has evolved with the theory. The initial clumsiness with which it was formulated reflected the inadequacies of early theory. Indeed, the sophistication of the principle of collection is just the sophistication of the theory. The initial move toward a collection of and a theory of categories is to be found in Plato's *Sophist*. The approach is a subtle one. Indeed as in the case of so many other aspects of Plato's thought, it achieved a degree of insight which was not soon to be equalled. Yet its explication would require an elaborate scholarly apparatus, and in a paper to fit the allotted space, two is company and three a crowd. On the other hand, a reference to the Aristotelian tradition is indispensable, though when Aristotle characterizes the categories as 'highest kinds' (*summa genera*) of entity he is building, as usual, on

Platonic ground. It is this conception of the categories which is one of the abiding themes, if not the abiding theme, of traditional *Kategorienlehre*.

10. To approach the conception of categories as *summa genera* in terms of what have been traditionally regarded as paradigmatic examples—thus, substance, quality, and relation—is to embark on a sea of perplexity. What would it be to construe substance as a *summum genus*? The natural temptation is to think of such a series of classificatory statements as

>   Fido is a dachshund
>   Fido is a dog
>   Fido is a brute
>   Fido is an animal
>   Fido is a corporeal substance
>   Fido is a substance.

11. Parity of reasoning would lead us, in the case of quality, to some such sequence as

> x is a red
> x is a color
> x is a perceptual quality
> x is a quality,

for if we tried

> x is red
> x is colored
>   .
>   .
>   .

it would be necessary at some stage to make a radical change in syntax in order to end up with

> x is a quality.

12. On the other hand, if we stick with

> x is a red,

what sort of item could x be? One answer trips readily off the tongue: x is an abstract entity, a universal. On the other hand, we can appeal to the familiar, but heterodox, idea of what have been called 'particularized qualities', or 'qualitative particulars'. Actually we have no choice, as we soon discover if we attempt to apply the second strategy to the case of relations. Only a series of even more desperate moves can keep us from falling immediately into the obvious absurdities exploited by Bradley.[1] We are, therefore, committed to the former alternative, that is that what belongs in the place of 'x' is an expression which refers to an abstract entity. Our search for *summa genera* leads us to the sequences

Red(ness)[2] is a color
Red(ness) is a perceptible quality
Red(ness) is a quality,

and

Juxtaposition is a spatial relation
Juxtaposition is a dyadic relation
Juxtaposition is a relation.

But if the entities which belong to the categories of quality and relation are *universals*, then to assert that there are qualities would seem to be to make an 'ontological commitment' to abstract entities.

13. Now I take it as obvious that there are, in some sense of 'are', qualities and relations. So I take it as obvious that there are, in some sense of 'are', universals, and, in general, abstract entities. Yet is it so clear that the statements

There are qualities
There are relations

make an 'ontological commitment'? Or is it possible for a philosopher consistently to assert

---

[1] I have discussed some of these expedients in "Meditations Leibnitziennes," *American Philosophical Quarterly*, II (1965), reprinted in my *Philosophical Perspectives* (Springfield, IL, 1967) [reprinted in *Philosophical Perspectives: History of Philosophy*, Ridgeview Publishing Company].

[2] Color words are notoriously ambiguous in the sense that they function sometimes as adjectives, sometimes as singular terms (as above), sometimes as common nouns (for example in 'crimson is a shade of red').

There are qualities

but add, in a different philosophical tone of voice, there *really* are no such things as qualities and relations? I shall pick up this theme shortly.

IV

14. The empiricist tradition had little light to throw on categorial concepts. Much of what they had to say can be regarded as a *reductio ad absurdum* of the principle: *nihil in intellectu quod non fuit prius in sensu*. Roughly this principle tells us that, in the case of simple and most specific concepts, expressions which belong in the context

concept of x

must also belong in the context

impression of x.

Obviously, the more limited the scope of the latter context, the more limited the scope of the former. At the hands of Hume the principle led to a rejection of the traditional interpretation of substance as a simple idea. Yet even in his reinterpretation of substance it remains a *summum genus*, and, in general, the Aristotelean conception of categories as *summa genera* and, hence, of categorial concepts as most generic concepts, lingered on, though particular categories were pruned or reconstrued. Thus Hume's intriguing account of generic ideas was intended to apply not only, for example, to the generic idea of triangularity, but also to such philosophically interesting ideas as those of substance, quality, relation, unity and even, it would seem, existence.

15. It is not my purpose in this essay to criticize radical concept empiricism. It is so vulnerable, indeed, that it is no easy task to relocate its insights in a correct account of the conceptual order. One would expect that, properly understood, it would turn out to be true a priori, like the theory of categories. Historically, of course, empiricists have never been clear as to the status of their fundamental principles. Are they, perhaps, appeals to Ockham's razor? Or are they sweeping generalizations?

16. Another feature of the empiricist tradition is its 'logical atomism',

according to which every basic piece of empirical knowledge is logically independent of every other. Notice that this independence concerns not only *what* is known, but the *knowing* of it. The second dimension of this 'atomism' is of particular importance for understanding Kant's rejection of empiricism, although its relation to his theory of categories has not always been clearly understood. That the Wittgenstein of the *Tractatus* agrees with Kant in rejecting this dimension of the 'logical atomism' of the empiricist tradition—not without raising unanswered questions about what is to count as a *logical* connection[3]—is equally relevant to *his* theory of categories. But this, also, is a topic for which preparation must be made.

V

17. The first major breakthrough in the theory of categories came, as one might expect, in the late Middle Ages, when logic, like knighthood, was in flower. A new strategy was developed for coping with certain puzzling concepts which were the common concern of logicians and metaphysicians. This strategy is illustrated by Ockham's explication of such statements as

(A) Man is a species.

Roughly, he construes it to have the sense of

(B) •Man• is a sortal mental term,

where, since mental terms are to be conceived as analogous to linguistic expressions in overt speech, the quotation marks are designed to make it clear that in statement (A) we are *mentioning* a concept rather than *using* it, as we would be if we were to judge that Tom is a man.

18. To this we must add, I believe, that whereas in (B) the expression '•Man•' presents itself as a name, it need not, and should not, be so construed. Its 'depth grammar' places it in quite a different box. A parallel will, perhaps, be helpful. Consider the statement

(C) 'And' is a logical expression.

It is clear that although the grammatical subject of this statement is a *singular term*, it need not be construed as a *name*. For, clearly, to talk about

---

[3] Is 'transcendental logic' just another *application* of 'ordinary logic'?

'and' is to talk about occurrences of 'and', (that is, 'and's). We might, therefore, be tempted to say that in this context "'and'" is functioning as a *general term*. Taken seriously, however, this suggestion would require us to reformulate (C) as

(C_1) 'And's are logical expressions.

But, then, we remember the 'institutional' use of 'the' and see that we can have our cake and eat it too. For we can interpret our original statement (C) to have the form

(C_2) (The) 'and' is a logical expression,

which is the equivalent of

(C_3) 'And's are logical expressions,

in the sense in which 'The lion is tawny' is equivalent to 'lions are tawny'.
19. If, now, we take seriously the concept of thinkings as 'inner speech' (Plato's 'dialogue within the soul'), then Ockham's analysis of

Man is a species,

when developed along the lines just indicated, would construe (B) as

(B_1) The •man• is a sortal mental term

and, hence, as equivalent to

(B_2) •Man•s are sortal terms.

20. Notice that although, according to this account, the original statement (A) is to be construed as referring to conceptual items, so that, *in a sense*, the expression 'man' in this context is equivalent to the expression 'the •man•', it would be a mistake to rewrite the original statement to read

(A_1) The •man• is a species,

for the context

----- is a species

already does the quoting, so that (A₁) is, according to the analysis, to be construed as

(A₂) The •the•man•• is a mental sortal term

that is,

(A₃) •The•man••s are mental sortal terms

which is, however, false, since •the•man••s are mental singular terms. Thus if we introduce the phrase 'distributive singular term' for expressions formed by prefixing the institutional 'the' to a sortal expression, for example 'the lion', then •the•man••s would be mental distributive singular terms.

21. Exactly the same point must be made about the statement

(D) Socrates is a substance, that is, a primary individual.

By parity of reasoning it would have, using the above strategy, the form

(D₁) •Socrates• is a basic mental singular term,

in other words,

(D₂) The •Socrates• is a basic mental singular term,

or, again,

(D₃) •Socrates•s are basic mental singular terms.[4]

22. Here, again, it would be a mistake to assume that if (D) is, in a sense, about conceptual items, that is, •Socrates•s, then it would be legitimate to

---

[4] Examples of singular terms which are *not* basic would be, for example, 'the average man', 'the tallest building in Manhattan', 'the lion', and 'Jack and Jill' as in 'Jack and Jill is a team'. (Of course in ordinary English we would say 'Jack and Jill are a team', but then it is quite clear that the 'are' is not functioning as it would in 'Jack and Jill are children', which simply abbreviates 'Jack is a child and Jill is a child'.)

rewrite it as

(D₄) The •Socrates• is a substance, that is, a primary individual.

For according to the analysis, this would be equivalent in sense to

•The•Socrates•• is a basic mental singular term,

that is,

•The•Socrates••s are basic mental singular terms.

But the latter are false, for although •the•Socrates••s *are* singular terms, they are not *basic* singular terms, but rather distributive singular terms, and, as such, to be classified with defined expressions. Thus, according to the above analysis, mental assertions or judgments with

•The•Socrates••s

as their subjects are dispensable in favor of statements with

••Socrates••s

as their subject, just as, in overt speech, statements with 'The pawn's as their subject, for example,

The pawn is a chess piece

are dispensable in favor of statements with 'pawns' as their subject, for example

Pawns are chess pieces.

23. What all this amounts to is that to apply Ockham's strategy to the theory of categories is to construe categories as classifications of conceptual items. This becomes, in Kant's hands, the idea that categories are the most generic functional classifications of the elements of judgments.
24. One might put this by saying that instead of being *summa genera* of entities which are objects 'in the world', a notion which, as we saw, would

force us to construe qualities, relations, and so forth as empirical objects, categories are *summa genera* of conceptual items. But while this is, I believe, the correct move to make, it raises the further question—what is the sense of 'in the world' which applies to 'empirical objects' but not to conceptual items? Indeed, *in the world* seems to be another category which, if we are to be consistent, must itself be construed as applying to conceptual items.

25. Assuming, however, that this apparent difficulty can be met, let us watch the theory grow. In the first place, once we take this general line, we see that we might be able to distinguish between 'formal' and 'material' categories. For just as it is plausible to say that

> Quality is a *summum genus* of entity,

so it seems proper to say that

> Color is a *summum genus* of perceptual quality.

This suggests that an adequate theory of categories would involve a distinction between 'determinables' and 'determinates'.

26. In the second place, the theory suggests that in addition to such standard examples as 'substance', 'quality', 'relation', and so forth, this list of categories should be expanded to include not only the 'modalities' but also 'state of affairs' as a 'formal' category, with 'event' and, perhaps, 'action' as 'material' categories subsumed under it.[5]

27. In the third place, it is to be noted that implicit in the above account of categories is a theory of abstract entities. For if

> Man is a species

is tantamount to

> The •man• is a sortal conceptual item,

then we are committed to the idea that statements about the abstract entity *man* are dispensable in favor of statements about conceptual items, that is, those acts and dispositions which involve 'predicates' to which the general

---

[5] It is worth noting at this point that 'species' as a classification of conceptual items would not be a category in the sense of *summum genus*, for it falls under the more generic notion of 'character'. For both 'man' and 'animal', not to mention 'white', are ways of characterizing individual things.

term

•man•

would apply.

28. Of course, there is always the temptation to say that to be a mental term of the sort to which the general term '•man•' applies is to be a mental term which stands for the abstract entity *man*, or the character *being human*. But the above approach can be generalized into the idea that *every* use of abstract singular terms is essentially classificatory, a matter of classifying conceptual items. Thus, to return to the linguistic level,

'*Gelb*' (in G) means yellow,

and its more regimented counterpart

'*Gelb*' (in G) stands for yellowness,

can be construed as classifying '*gelb*'s (in G) as •yellow•s, that is, as doing in German the job done in our language by the predicate 'yellow'.

29. If so, then

Yellow (yellowness) is a quality

would have the sense of

The •yellow• is a (one-place) predicate (in mentalese),

and 'reduce' to

•Yellow•s are predicates,

where to be a •yellow• is to be an item having a certain conceptual job, which would ultimately be explained in terms of the word-word and word-world uniformities by virtue of which 'yellow's in one language and '*gelb*'s in German function as they do in basic matter-of-factual statements.⁶

30. In the fourth place, while the theory permits us to say

> Yellow is an entity,

ascribing to this, roughly, the sense of

> The •yellow• is a meaningful mentalese term,

it must deny

> Yellow is an individual,

for the latter would have the sense of

> The •yellow• is a mentalese singular term,

which is false. In other words, 'Yellow is a primary entity' might be true, but not 'Yellow is a primary individual'. It would, therefore, be correct to say that *there are entities which are not individuals*, an ostensibly paradoxical statement which, nevertheless, many perceptive philosophers have been led by intuitive, if not always perspicuous, considerations to make.

31. Finally, notice that the theory would enable us to explain how a philosopher could be justified in acknowledging that

> There are qualities, for example, triangularity

while denying that there *really* are qualities. For such statements about qualities as have the form

> The •triangular• is ...

can be paraphrased without the use of a singular term. Might one not acknowledge that there are chess pieces, for example, the pawn, while

---

[6] Note that linguistic items proper—and not just 'inner speech' episodes—are now being treated as conceptual items. For a defense of the thesis that overt verbal behavior—which is the primary mode of being of the linguistic proper—is *as such* conceptual in character, see my "Language as Thought and as Communication," *Philosophy and Phenomenological Research*, XXIX (1969), pp. 506-527. For an exploration of the relation between the concept of thought as 'inner speech' and the concept of thinking-out-loud (candid overt speech) see my *Science and Metaphysics*, ch. III.

denying that there *really* are chess pieces, for example, the pawn? Thus a respectable and philosophically important sense could be given to the claim that although there *really are* particular conceptual episodes of thinking that something is triangular, there *really* is no such entity as the quality of being triangular.

VI

32. To appreciate the distinctive features of Kant's 'metaphysics of experience', it is helpful to approach it *via* the early Wittgenstein, although this might seem an attempt to illuminate the obscure through the more obscure. For, contrary to the usual conception, Wittgenstein's views are actually as clear and straightforward as he thought them to be.[7]

33. Wittgenstein conceives of basic empirical truths as consisting of expressions referring to simple objects and predicates which stand for simple matter-of-factual qualities and relations. Expressions for complex individuals and complex characters can in principle be eliminated in favor of these 'elementary' expressions. Wittgenstein does not deny, as is often thought, that expressions which do not occur in basic statements (or are not definable in terms of them) can be meaningful. He simply denies that they refer to or describe objects *in the world*. Their meaningfulness may consist in the fact that they enable us to formulate truths about *our thoughts about* objects in the world. One must also carefully distinguish between the way in which logical connectives are meaningful, although they do not refer to or characterize objects in the world, from that in which such meta-conceptual terms as 'object', 'quality', and 'fact' are meaningful.

34. This philosophical denial of existence to complex individuals and characters underlies Wittgenstein's claim that it is an essential feature of the objects of empirical knowledge that they be simple and have simple matter-of-factual characters. Another essential feature is that these objects be the referents of a referring expression in the living language (and of the corresponding mental terms) of those for whom they are objects. Yet just as simplicity and individuality are not attributes of objects, although objects are simple individuals, so *being the referent* of a referring expression is not a *relation* between an object and the expression.

35. This feature of Wittgenstein's thought has seemed to many to be a most intolerable paradox, for the following two statements are obviously

---

[7] That it was not easy to appreciate this at the time is but one more illustration of the fact that the more intelligible in the order of being does not always coincide with the more intelligible in the order of knowing.

true:

> (A) The objects of empirical knowledge include referring expressions as linguistic or mentalese tokens (tokenings).
>
> (B) Referring expressions would not refer to objects unless they stood in matter-of-factual relations to objects.

It is only too tempting to conclude from the truth of (A) and (B) that *reference* is a matter-of-factual relation, and hence that the character of referring to an object is a matter-of-factual relational property. Surely, if

> (C) Expression E denotes something

entails

> (C′) Expression E stands in matter-of-factual relations to something

and

> (D) Expression E denotes something

entails

> (D′) There is something, for example Socrates, to which E refers,

then

> E refers to Socrates

must have the form

> $R(E, \text{Socrates})$.

But this would be a mistake, as can be seen from certain parallels. Consider

> '*Oder*' (in G) stands for something,

that is,

There is something for which '*oder*' (in G) stands, that is, disjunction.

Clearly this entails that certain empirical facts hold of '*oder*' in German. Yet it would be implausible to suggest that *standing for* is an empirical relation between the German word '*oder*' and disjunction, or alternation or, to simplify the point, or-ness.

36. For, according to our strategy, to say what '*oder*' specifically means or stands for is to classify '*oder*'s (in German) as •or•s. And it is by virtue of being •or•s, and not by virtue of standing in a supposed empirical relation of *standing for*, that certain empirical facts must be true of '*oder*'s.

37. Consider another parallel:

(In our games of chess) tall cones play (serve as) bishops.

Clearly in order for tall cones to play the bishop, certain empirical truths must hold of tall cones (in the relevant contexts). But it is the criteria for *being a bishop* which carry these empirical requirements, not the supposed relation of *playing* or *serving as*. Indeed

Tall cones play (serve as) the bishop

can be paraphrased as

Tall cones *are* bishops,

and, obviously, '*are*' is not a word for an empirical relation.[8]

38. One who is half convinced might say that this is all very well and good with respect to the context

----- stands for .....

but does it throw light on 'denotes'? And, indeed, 'denotes', or 'refers to', unlike 'stands for' or its Fregean counterpart 'expresses', is no mere specialized version of the copula. But one can grant this without granting that reference or denotation is an empirical relation.

39. Consider the contrast between

---

[8] It is philosophically of the utmost importance that 'men are animals' when translated into PMese becomes 'man $\subset$ animal' which is short for '(x) (x is a man $\supset x$ is an animal)'. In this sense 'are' dissolves into connectives (not relations) and quantification.

'Centaur' (in E) denotes (or refers to) nothing,

and

'Centaur' (in E) stands for the property of being a centaur.

The former differs from the latter not by saying that 'centaur' fails to stand in a certain empirical relation to anything, but by telling us that the kind—left open—for which 'centaur' stands is empty, that is, is not exemplified by or true of anything. Again,

'Man' (in E) denotes featherless biped

differs from

'Man' (in E) stands for rational animal

not by doing the radically different job of telling us that certain items stand in an empirical relation, but by telling us that the kind—left open—for which 'man' stands is exemplified by or true of all and only those items which also exemplify the character of being a featherless biped.

40. The same general account can be given of the denotation of singular terms, though the details must be left for *another* occasion.[9] Thus

'*Parigi*' (in Italian) denotes the capital of France

would be construed as

'*Parigi*' (in Italian) stands for a concept which is materially equivalent to the •the capital of France•.

Accordingly, although

'*Parigi*' (in Italian) denotes something

would entail that the word '*Parigi*' (in Italian) stands in empirical relations, these relations would not *constitute* a relation of denoting but would serve

---

[9] See *Science and Metaphysics*, ch. III.

as criteria for the classification which is left unspecified by the statement. The cash for such denotation statements would be of the form

> '*Parigi*' (in Italian) stands for the •Paris• and the •Paris• is materially equivalent to the •the capital of France•,

which imparts the information that '*Parigi*'s (in Italian) are •Paris•s, and hence satisfy the criteria associated with this classification.

41. I conclude that Wittgenstein was right in claiming that *reference* is not a matter-of-factual relation, although the fact that a term refers entails that it stands in certain matter-of-factual relations. That it stands, at least contingently, in such and such matter-of-factual relations to objects in the world is known by knowing its *reference*. Those in which it *necessarily* stands can only be determined by tracing out the implications of its *sense*, that is, what it stands for.

42. Parallel points can be made with respect to predicates. Thus, for '*dreieckig*'s (in G) to stand for triangularity it must be true that they are caught up in certain word-word and word-thing uniformities. No more than in the other cases, however, do the latter constitute a supposed empirical relation of *standing for*.

VII

43. We can now turn our attention to the fact that for something to be an object of empirical knowledge, statements about it must be verifiable. There must, that is, be a method or strategy for deciding whether it is true or false. Here, again, the correct account has an initial appearance of paradox. Surely, to determine that a statement is true is to determine that it corresponds to a fact. Yet facts are not objects, and on Tractarian principles only objects can have matter-of-factual attributes and stand in matter-of-factual relations.

44. On the other hand, it is presumably a contingent or matter-of-factual fact that a given statement is true. How can we render consistent the ideas that

(a) facts are not objects;
(b) only objects can stand in matter-of-factual relations;
(c) the truth of a statement is a matter-of-factual relation between the statement and a fact?

Are not true statements those which correspond to facts?

45. The above treatment of *categories, standing for,* and *denotation* suggests the way out. According to it

'a is φ' (in L) corresponds to (the fact) that a is φ

no more *asserts* that 'a is φ' (in L) stands in a matter-of-factual relation to something in the world than

E denotes O

asserts that E and something in the world stand in a matter-of-factual relation of denotation. 'That a is φ' is to be construed as a distributive singular term ('the •a is φ•'), which, like 'the •triangular•', applies to conceptual items. Again, 'that a is φ is a fact' is to be construed, in first approximation, as having the sense of 'the •a is φ• is correctly[10] assertible'. Thus the original statement does two things:

(a) it classifies 'a is φ's (in L) as •a is φ•s;
(b) it tells us that the latter, which according to (a) include 'a is φ's (in L), are correctly assertible.

46. On the other hand, just as

E denotes O,

though it does not *assert* a matter-of-factual relation to obtain between E and O, nevertheless entails that E stands in a complex empirical relationship to O, so

'a is φ' (in L) corresponds to the fact that a is φ,

while it does not assert that a relation obtains between 'a is φ' and the fact, nevertheless entails that certain matter-of-factual relations hold between 'a is φ's as belonging to L, and the object a—not the fact that a is φ. It entails,

---

[10] The relevant correctnesses are those which "give meaning to expressions" and are to be distinguished from the correctnesses which concern the role of language in communication and personal interaction. For an elaboration of this point, see *Science and Metaphysics*, ch. IV; also "Language as Thought and as Communication," *Philosophy and Phenomenological Research*, XXIX (1969), pp. 506-527.

that is, that 'a is φ's as conceptual objects stand in certain complex empirical relationships to other objects. *Which* objects is determined by the *empirical relationships* which must be satisfied if 'φ' is to stand (in L) for a certain characteristic and 'a' is to denote (in L) a certain object.

47. Thus the matter-of-factual characteristics of 'a is φ's (in L) as conceptual objects which are entailed by their truth do not constitute a supposed relation of "correspondence to a fact." They are, rather, matter-of-factual relations to genuine objects. In the case of basic empirical truths, on which the above account has been focused, these relations are different in each case, although they can all be subsumed under the general formula:

> Tokens of 'x is f' (and 'xRy') as expressions (in L) (or in mentalese) have matter-of-factual characteristics by virtue of which they are linguistic projections—in accordance with certain semantical uniformities—of the objects to which these expressions refer.

48. We can sum this up as follows: In the case of basic empirical statements, unless the linguistic episodes which are their tokens stand in a projective relation to other objects in the world, they would not be true. On the other hand, to characterize these statements as true (that is as corresponding to facts) is not to specify the projective relation in question.

49. The above line of thought is reinforced by considerations pertaining to logical and mathematical truth. Thus it is a fact that $2 + 2 = 4$. And

'II + II = IV' (in L) corresponds to the fact that $2 + 2 = 4$

trips readily off the tongue. Yet it is implausible in the extreme to suppose that in this context 'corresponds' stands for a matter-of-factual relation between 'II + II = IV' (in L) and an extraconceptual entity. As before, 'corresponds to fact' dissolves into classification,

'II + II = IV's (in L) are •$2 + 2 = 4$•s,

and the ascription of correct assertibility to •$2 + 2 = 4$•s. This time, however, the relevant criteria of correctness are intralinguistic (or syntactical) and do not concern word-thing connections.

VIII

50. As the final step in this exploration of the concept of an object of empirical knowledge, I turn to considerations which were at the very center of Kant's thought,[11] but at best implicit in the *Tractatus*, lurking, if at all, in Wittgenstein's obscure dicta concerning the metaphysical 'I' and the status of the causal principle.

51. If empirical knowability is always knowability *by* a person *here* and *now*, whereas the *scope* of the knowable includes facts about the *there* and *then*, or if (to abstract from the specific conditions of human knowledge and move to the 'pure pragmatics' or 'transcendental logic' of empirical knowledge as such) knowability essentially involves a perspectival relationship between act of knowing and object known, must not the knowability of objects consist, in large part, of *inferential* knowability? (One can, of course, recognize the *essential* and *irreducible* role of inference without denying the existence of non-inferential knowledge of the *here-now*.) On the other hand, we have learned from Hume that facts about the *there* and *then* are never *logically* implied by facts about the *here* and *now*, but, at best, by the latter together with the general facts captured by true lawlike statements.

52. Now if we assume in the spirit of Hume that it is a contingent fact that such general facts obtain, it would seem to follow that it is a contingent fact that *there-then* objects are knowable. But if to be an object is to be a knowable, our conclusion would have to be that it is a contingent fact that there are *there-then* objects. But surely any *here-now* object is on its way to being a *there-then* object in the past and on its way *from* having been a *there-then* object in the future.

53. If so, then there would seem to be a logical inconsistency in granting the existence of *here-now* objects while denying that of *there-then* objects. A transcendental argument does not prove that there *is* empirical knowledge—what premises could such an argument have?—nor that there are *objects* of empirical knowledge. It simply explicates the concepts of *empirical knowledge* and *object of empirical knowledge*. Thus, to admit knowing that it *now* seems to me that there is a red and triangular object over there is to admit knowing that this *was about to* seem to me to be the case. If the skeptic (after making a similar move with respect to Space) attempts to replace the now of the seeming by the semblance of a now, by putting Time

---

[11] For an elaboration of the points I am about to make which brings out their specifically Kantian character, see "Some Reflections on Kant's Theory of Experience," *The Journal of Philosophy*, LXIV (1967), pp. 633-647 [*KTE*, in this volume].

itself into the content of that which seems, does it not reappear (at least implicitly) outside this context?—thus: *It (now) seems to me* that there is such a thing as Time (an order of before and after) in the *now* of which (and as Space in the *there* of which) there is a red and triangular object. (And does it merely seem to *me* that there is such a thing as I?)

54. What Kant takes himself to have proved is that the concept of empirical knowledge involves the concept of inferability in accordance with laws of nature. To grant that there is knowledge of the *here* and *now* is, he argues, to grant that there are general truths of the sort captured by lawlike statements. As far as specifically human knowledge is concerned, he was convinced that the idea that knowable objects are located in Space and Time carries with it certain general commitments as to the *form* of these laws. These commitments could, he thought, be known a priori or non-inductively. Thus, the transcendental knowledge that spatio-temporal objects of knowledge must conform to certain generalizations *which are themselves logically synthetic* is itself, according to Kant, analytic.

55. Notice that the full expression of what is known in synthetic a priori knowledge has the form:

> Spatio-temporal knowables must conform to (synthetic) general truths satisfying such and such conditions.

That is:

> *If* there is knowledge of spatio-temporal objects, then these objects conform to general truths satisfying such and such conditions.

This statement as a whole is an analytic or explicative statement belonging to transcendental philosophy. If we are willing to affirm the antecedent—that is, if we are willing to grant, as even Hume does, that we do have knowledge of the *here* and *now*, then we can affirm the consequent, that is:

> Spatio-temporal objects in my world conform to general truths satisfying such and such conditions.

It is, however, essential to note that the latter, *by itself*, is not a necessary truth, except in the derivative sense that it is necessary *relative to the antecedent*. To construe it as *intrinsically* necessary is to commit a modal fallacy of a piece with

Necessary (if all men are bipeds, then all Texans are bipeds);
All men are bipeds;
So, necessary (all Texans are bipeds).

56. It is this conception of transcendental philosophy which distinguishes the critical rationalism of Kant (and the Wittgenstein of the *Tractatus*) from both dogmatic rationalism and the naive empiricism which thinks that empiricism is an empirical 'ism'.

"... this I or he or it (the thing) which thinks ..."

Immanuel Kant, *Critique of Pure Reason* (A346; B404)

Presidential address delivered before the Sixty-seventh Annual Eastern Meeting of the American Philosophical Association in Philadelphia, December 28, 1970.

1. The quotation which I have taken as my text occurs in the opening paragraphs of the Paralogisms of Pure Reason in which Kant undertakes a critique of what he calls 'Rational Psychology'. These paragraphs are common to the two editions of the *Critique of Pure Reason*, and the formulations they contain may be presumed to have continued to satisfy him—at least as introductory remarks.

2. The paragraph in which the quoted passage occurs opens with a reference to "a transcendental psychology" which, "wrongly regarded as a science of pure reason", is characterized by "four paralogisms...concerning the nature of our thinking being". In other words, 'Rational Psychology' is a distorted version of an enterprise which, properly understood, does belong in the *Critique*, but only in the framework of the principles expounded in the Transcendental Analytic.

3. Notice that the subject matter of transcendental psychology is characterized, by implication, as "the nature of our thinking being". If we permit ourselves to use the referring expression 'I' as a common noun, meaning roughly whatever can be referred to by an appropriate tokening of 'I'—much as philosophers in the Aristotelian tradition speak of primary substances as *thises*—we can rephrase the question to read 'What sort of being is an I?'.

4. More accurately, 'What sort of being can we know an I to be without any appeal to experience?'. The question might also be rephrased, with still less ambiguity, as 'What can we know *a priori*, through sheer reflection on the relevant concepts, about the sort of being an I is?'.

5. Now if the relevant concepts are taken to include such concepts as that of a "necessary condition of the possibility of experience", not to go further afield, there is much that can be known *a priori* about an I. In this restricted sense there is indeed, according to Kant, a body of knowledge which can be called 'transcendental psychology'. Rational Psychology, on the other hand, takes the relevant concepts to be that of an I and that of a thought and purports to tell us what an I is "in itself". In other words, as Kant puts it, the rational psychologist takes as his "sole text" (A343; B401) "the proposition 'I think'" (A348; B405) and seeks, by explicating it, to answer certain

traditional metaphysical questions regarding "the nature of our thinking being".

6. Now it is no news that Kant denies that Rational Psychology can achieve its goal. On the other hand, his argument shares many of the obscurities of the transcendental deduction of the categories—to which it is closely related—and has been the subject of almost as many controversies and misunderstandings.[1] Thus, the concept of the "transcendental unity of apperception" plays a key role in both the Deduction and the Paralogisms, and, while it is, perhaps, the central concept of the *Critique*, only recently has British and American philosophy freed itself sufficiently, first from its positivistic heritage, then from its anti-systematic bias, to be in a position to translate it into congenial terms.

7. I shall not undertake any such translation on the present occasion, for it would take us into the technicalities of epistemic logic—a phrase which, incidentally, is on its way to becoming the contemporary counterpart of Kant's 'transcendental logic'.[2] I shall write in the traditional idiom, leaving for another occasion this more ambitious enterprise. Let me begin, therefore, by pointing out that the transcendental unity of apperception plays two closely related roles in the *Critique*. In the first place, it is an *unrestricted* principle in the philosophy of mind, which transcends the distinction between the noumenal and the phenomenal self, to the effect that

an I thinks of a manifold

is not to be confused with

an I has a manifold of thoughts.

Thus, an I thinking that Socrates is wise is not to be confused with the "coexistence" in the I of a thought of Socrates and a thought of wisdom. Nor, for that matter, a thinking that p and q with a thinking that p and a thinking that q.

8. This principle is, of course, compatible with the idea that a thinking

---

[1] It is therefore interesting to note that in the second edition the chapter on the paralogisms, like the transcendental deduction, was completely rewritten and transformed from a groping sequence of arguments, designed as much to persuade as to demonstrate, into a relatively brief argument, confident in tone, which marches along in single-minded style from beginning to end. This development is epitomized by the transformation of the fourth paralogism into the second edition refutation of Idealism.

[2] Hector-Neri Castañeda's highly original study of the logic of 'I' (and cognate expressions) in epistemic contexts is bound to develop, as he himself realizes, in a Kantian direction.

that Socrates is wise unifies, in a unique way, a thinking of Socrates with a thinking of wisdom. The ways in which many thinkings constitute one thinking are the "forms of thought,", e.g., the categories. The recognition of the radical difference between categorial forms and matter-of-factual relationships is the *pons asinorum* of the Critical Philosophy.

9. In epistemology, which, as concerned with good thinking in its various modes, is *a fortiori* concerned with thinking as such, this general principle becomes the epistemic principle that any true content of thought, e.g., that Socrates is wise, must, in principle, be an element in a certain kind of larger context, e.g.,

> an I thinks the true thought of a world in which Socrates is wise.

Roughly, the form of empirical knowledge is:

> an I thinking (however schematically) the thought of a temporal system of states of affairs to which any actual state of affairs belongs.[3]

10. Thus, in the Transcendental Analytic, the above unrestricted principle about thinking provides the clue to the form of the phenomenal world. This world is a represented world, and Space, Time, and the Categories are its "forms". These latter, however, are no mere collection of "forms of experience". They are but *moments* (to use Hegel's term) in its larger form:

> An I thinking a complex spatial-temporal-causal system of states of affairs—including, say, α and β. (The *synthetic* unity of apperception).

From this synthetic unity, as Kant points out, it follows analytically that

> The I which thinks α is identical with the I which thinks β. (The *analytic* unity of apperception).

11. A moment ago I said that for Kant the sole text of rational psychology is the proposition "I think". He brings this claim to sharper focus by writing,

---

[3] For an elaboration of the ontological framework which supports this analysis see my essay, "Some Remarks on Kant's Theory of Experience," *Journal of Philosophy*, 64 (1967), 633-48 [*KTE*, in this volume]; also Chapter 2 of *Science and Metaphysics* (London and New York, 1968) [reprinted by Ridgeview Publishing Company].

> ... We can assign no other basis for this teaching than the simple, and in itself completely empty, representation 'I'.

To which he adds that

> ... We cannot even say that this is a concept, but only that it is a bare consciousness which accompanies all concepts. Through this I or he or it (the thing) which thinks, nothing further is represented than a transcendental subject of thoughts = X. It is known only through the thoughts which are its predicates, and of it, apart from them, we cannot have any concept whatsoever. (A345-6; B404)

12. Now it has sometimes been thought that in this passage Kant is relying on a "substratum" theory of predication, a theory which sees every predicate in the light of the schema

$$x \text{ has attribute } A$$

and which therefore rebuffs every attempt to answer the question '*What* is it which has A?'—thus "It is a *stone* which has A"—by transforming the predicate—in this case, 'is a stone'—in its turn into

$$x \text{ has attributes } A_1 \ldots A_n,$$

a procedure which characteristically (and with flagrant inconsistency) culminates by permitting only the metaphysical predicate 'is a bare particular', asserting that

> it is bare particulars which have *empirical* attributes.

13. Kant most certainly does not make *this* mistake. He is not above speaking in scholastic vein of adjectival predicates and even verbs as true of objects by virtue of the "inherence" in them of "accidents". But he nowhere implies that the subject in which these accidents inhere is a bare particular. And he explicitly warns against construing predication in terms of a relation of inherence between accidents and substance,[4] insisting, rather, that a so-called accident, instead of being an entity, is "the *way* in which the existence of a substance is determined" (italics mine). While this does not amount to an adequate theory of predication it is certainly on the right track.

14. Thus, Kant's contention in the passage we are examining rests not on

---

[4] A187; B230. See also A182, the first edition formulation of the First Analogy.

a general theory of predication, but on the specific nature of the representation 'I'. He tells us, in effect, that the conceptual burden of the "proposition 'I think'" is carried by the verb 'to think'. He means that the only answer to the question

> What sort of being is an I which thinks?

which is yielded by *a priori* reflection is

> a thinker.

15. By contrast, consider the statement

> This moves.

If asked

> *What* sort of thing is a *this* which moves?,

we can answer not just

> a mover,

i.e., a thing capable of motion, but by using such sortals as 'a car' or, which, perhaps, comes to the same thing, 'a missile', we can draw a meaningful distinction between what a material object is and what it *does*, or is capable of doing. For Kant, the ultimate cash value of what a material object is, is to be given in terms of intensive and extensive physical magnitudes, roughly in terms of the traditional "primary qualities" of which the core consists of geometrical attributes constructible in external intuition.

16. Kant's point, then, is that our concept of an I is the concept of *that which thinks*, in the various modes of thinking, or, perhaps, to use a more general expression, *that which represents*, in the various modes of representing. Thus, we cannot answer

> *What* is it that represents?

save, tautologously, by

a representer.

17. Now before I go on to spell out what I think to be important about this, it should be noted that Kant did consider a less empty answer to the question 'What sort of being is it that thinks?', namely,

a person

where a person in construed not as a team, but as a single subject which has both mental and non-mental attributes. Kant does not reject this answer without qualification. For he specifically tells us that it *might* be true of the noumenal self. On the other hand, he does reject this answer as an account of the empirical self, on the ground that all the attributes of the objects of external perception must, as indicated above, be construed in terms of primary qualities. Although this answer conflicts with the flexibility of his concept of "matter", and his sensitivity to the possibilities of sophisticated physical theory, he never seriously questions it.

18. Thus, in the world of appearance, the I which thinks is not, as such, identical with the I which runs.[5] It is therefore tempting to say that Kant rejects a Strawsonian account of persons as objects of experience in favor of a cartesian dualism. But although his account *is* dualistic, it is *not* cartesian. Descartes takes it for granted that "*res cogitans*" is a proper sortal concept, i.e., that we have a positive, indeed adequate, idea of what it is to be a mind. This conviction underlies his argument for a real distinction between mind and body. Kant, on the other hand, denies that we have a positive, let alone adequate, idea of mind as a *sort of being*. There was a time, he tells us, when it seemed to him "so plausible" that "we can form judgments about the nature of a thinking being, and can do so from concepts alone" (A399). But no longer.

19. One important ground he has for saying this emerges when we consider what he means by denying that the categories are innate concepts. Many philosophers who agree with Kant in rejecting such innateness have held, for example, that the category of substance is an *empirical* concept formed by abstraction either from perceived objects or the introspected self. Representational theories of perception undercut the former alternative, suggesting that perception *presupposes*, rather than accounts for, a concept of substance. But do we not directly experience ourselves as substances?

---

[5] Kant, of course, would not deny that the term 'I' might have, in this context, a derivative sense in which it refers to a psychophysical team.

And is not this experience the source of our concept of substance? Such a claim, however, would imply that we experience the mind *in the first instance* as being of a determinate *sort* or *species* of substance, thus as being a "mental substance" or mind, and only subsequently come to see it most generically as *substance*.

20. Kant's revolutionary move was to see the categories as concepts of functional roles in mental activity.[6] Categorial concepts are not, indeed, innate. They *are* formed by abstraction,[7] *not*, however, by reflecting on the self as object, but by reflecting on its conceptual activities. The ability to engage in these activities is, indeed, for Kant, innate; but this does not require that concepts of these activities be innate. Even before entering his Critical period, Kant had come to think of categorial concepts as derived by reflecting on the nature of mental activity. The crystallization of this insight into the Metaphysical Deduction required only a perspicuous classification of the forms of mental activity.

21. The idea that concepts pertaining to thinking are essentially *functional* in character raises the question: What non-functional characterization can be given of the processes which embody these functions? To answer 'They are thoughts' is to move in a circle. Kant's answer is, essentially, that we are not able to give a non-functional characterization. We don't know these processes save as *processes which embody these functions*. A materialist, in some sense of this protean term, might agree with Kant that concepts pertaining to thought are functional in character, but claim that, although *common sense* is unable to give a non-functional characterization of thoughts, theoretical science will ultimately do this in terms of neurophysiology. Kant, of course, denies that scientific theory can answer the question, for he conceives of even sophisticated scientific theory as restricted to appearances construed as above. Hence his *ignorabimus*.[8]

22. To sum up, Kant is claiming that

(1) the I is a being of unknown species which thinks;

---

[6] For an elaboration of this point see the paper referred to in footnote 3 above. See also "Towards a Theory of the Categories," in *Theory and Experience* (Amherst, MA, 1970) [*TTC*, in this volume].

[7] Kant clearly does not reject abstractionism lock, stock and barrel, as do many of his contemporary disciples. The task of assessing the truth contained in traditional abstractionist theories of concept formation is still on the philosophical agenda.

[8] Kant, of course, grants that thought has "content" as well as "form"—but the content consists of concepts, for example, empirical concepts—and these in their turn are "functions". When we think of a shape, e.g., of a triangle, our thought, needless to say is not triangular—it contains the concept of a triangle, itself a rule or function by which the mind can generate representations of triangles (A141; B180). For an elaboration of this point see pp. 639-40 of the paper referred to in footnote 3 [*KTE*, 24-5].

(2) the I doesn't simply "have thoughts": *it thinks*—but in knowing *that* it thinks, and *what* it thinks, we are not knowing what sort of being it is.

Yet,

(3) the I must have a nature—what it is we cannot know, though we *can* know that it is not material substance.

23. Nevertheless, although the I as an object of experience is not a material substance, Kant insists, as pointed out above, that *as noumenon* the I may be the same being as that which appears to us as our bodies. He tells us that

> The transcendental object is equally unknown in respect to inner and outer intuition. (A373)

and suggests the possibility that

> The substance which in relation to outer sense possesses extension is in itself the possessor of thoughts, and that these thoughts can by means of its own inner sense be consciously represented. (A365)

In other words, the being which thinks might, as noumenon, be a Strawsonian person which, in addition to thinking, has the noumenal counterparts of physical attributes. If so, he tells us,

> ...the thesis that only souls (as particular kinds of substances) think would have to be given up; and we should have to fall back on the common expression that men think. ... (A359-60)

According to this hypothesis, a mind would not be an ultimate logical subject, but an aspect of a more fundamental logical subject—the person.
24. Kant goes even further and suggests that the noumenal person might be a composite being. The way is prepared for these possibilities by his critique of the first two paralogisms. He detects in these arguments a common form:

The representation of the I is not *the representation of*
    (a) an aspect of something more basic,
    (b) a composite of parts;

Therefore,

"... *this I or he or it (the thing) which thinks ...*" (I, 81)   409

>   *the I* is not
>   (a) an aspect of something more basic,
>   (b) a composite of parts.⁹

25. The Third Paralogism, that of personality, i.e., of the identity of a person throughout Time, elevates the identity which is implied by the concept of a person as having true and false beliefs (e.g., memory) about *his own* states at various times into the identity of an abiding mental substance. Kant argues, *per contra*, that

> The identity of the consciousness of myself at different times is...only a formal condition of my thoughts and their coherence, and in no way proves the numerical identity of my subject. (A363)

26. Kant, of course, means that it does not prove the numerical identity of the noumenal self. In other words, he suggests the possibility that successive acts of thought might belong together, as acts of the same I, and yet be successive states of different noumenal subjects.

> Despite the logical identity of the 'I', such a change may have occurred in it as does not allow of the retention of its identity and yet we may ascribe to it the same-sounding 'I', which in every different state, even in one involving change of the [thinking] subject, might still retain the thought of this preceding subject and so hand it over to the subsequent subject. (A363)

27. When Kant speaks of "such a change...as does not allow the retention of its identity", he is tacitly contrasting "ontological identity proper"—in this case, the identity of a basic logical subject with respect to its successive states—with the identity appropriate to *entia rationis*—in this case, the identity of a series.¹⁰ He is suggesting that the "logical identity" of the I through Time, which is an analytic implication of the knowledge of oneself as thinking different thoughts at different times, is compatible with the idea that these thoughts are successive states of different ultimate subjects. Compare the materialist who argues that the thoughts which make up the history of an I are states of systems of material particles which are

---

⁹ For an elaboration of this analysis of the logical form Kant finds in the paralogisms see pp. 247 ff. of my essay "Metaphysics and the Concept of a Person," in *The Logical Way of Doing Things*, edited by Karel Lambert (Yale Univ. Press, New Haven, 1969), pp. 219-52 [*MP*, in this volume, 46ff].

¹⁰ The temptation to speak of different kinds of identity is endemic in philosophy. It is clear, in any case, that the term 'identity' is appropriately used in radically different contexts.

constantly losing old and gaining new constituents.[11]

28. Thus, although I do not represent my successive thoughts as successive states of a series of different subjects of attributes, and do not need to do so in order to know my "logical identity" through the period in which these thoughts occur, a being with suitable cognitive powers might know me to be such a series. This insight, however, would not require him to say that my knowledge of myself as logically identical through the period of time in question is an illusion, but only that the logical identity of the I *as I represent it* is not an adequate conceptualization of "the nature of our thinking being".

29. Exposed as a fallacy, the Third Paralogism has the form:

> *The representation of* the successive states of the I is not *the representation of* successive states of a series of different subjects of attributes.
>
> Therefore, *the successive states* of the I are not *successive states of* a series of different subjects of attributes.[12]

30. Now, the most intriguing feature of the situation resulting from Kant's analysis of the Paralogisms is that it opens the way for him to hold (if he were to relax his restrictions on what attributes an object of external perception can have),

(1) that the empirical self—the I which we experience as thinking in time—is an aspect of a perceptible object which, as having physical attributes, is a body (i.e., that the logical subject which, as representing and capable of representing, is a being which thinks *is identical with* the being which, as having material attributes, is the body);

(2) that the empirical I which, in so far forth as it is represented as thinking, is not represented as a composite is nevertheless identical with (i.e., *is*) a composite physical object.

---

[11] The reader should ponder the fascinating footnote which Kant appends to the passage quoted above. Furthermore, the Third Paralogism as a whole should be carefully studied by those who are tempted to think that because the noumenal realm is not in Newtonian Time, it is therefore "unchanging" or "static". Of course, the only concept of change we can render intuitive, according to Kant, is temporal alteration. See also footnote 17 below.

[12] The phrase 'different subjects of attributes' is essential. For, as I pointed out on p. 251 of the essay referred to in footnote 9 [*MP*, in this volume, 54-5], the idea that the I might be a series must not be confused with the idea that it might be a series of 'I's.

"... *this I or he or it (the thing) which thinks* ..." *(I, 81)* 411

For, according to the above analysis, a logical subject which is not *represented as* an aspect of something more basic, *may be* an aspect of something more basic, and a logical subject which is not *represented as* composite may nevertheless *be* composite.

31. As a matter of fact, there are important considerations which push Kant toward a "materialist"—though not "reductively" materialist—interpretation of the phenomenal world. Thus, consider the First Analogy:

> In all change of appearances, substance is permanent. Its quantum in nature is neither increased nor diminished. (B224)[13]

Kant does not speak here of "outer appearances," but "appearances" *tout court*, not of transitory *material* states, but of transitory states *sans phrase*. And the argument which follows is equally general. It seeks to establish that matter is the correlate, in the world of experience, of Time, and that its permanence represents the *permanence* of Time.[14] Time, then, is everlasting.

32. Now if Time were a transcendentally real "container", it might be everlasting, and yet, in principle, be *occupied* for only a finite stretch, a period preceded by empty time and followed by empty time. But although Kant thinks of Time as an individual in which ordinary things come into being, endure, change, and cease to be, he rejects the idea that the existence *of* Time is independent of the existence of things *in* Time. In this sense he is an Aristotelian, holding that Time is *ens rationis* which constitutes the framework in which change is measured with respect to before and after. This Aristotelian theme, however, is combined with the claim (the crux of the Aesthetic) that "before" and "after" themselves cannot be understood apart from Time.[15]

33. Aristotle argued from the everlastingness of Time to the everlastingness of First Matter. Roughly, if portions of First Matter could cease to exist, then all First Matter could cease to exist—but then Time would cease to exist. Time, as everlasting, cannot cease, so First Matter cannot. Kant's argument is essentially the same. This is why it is essential to realize that when Kant uses the term 'substance' in the First Analogy, he is using it in

---

[13] In A: All appearances contain the permanent (substance) as the object itself, and the transitory as its mere determination, that is, as a way in which the object exists. (A182)

[14] Kant *does*, on occasion, speak of time as always changing. When he does so, however, he has in mind what McTaggart calls A-determinations. And while Time is, in this sense, continually changing, it abides, as numerically identical through these changes.

[15] For a discussion of the way in which Kant's treatment of time runs together different strata of temporal concepts see *Science and Metaphysics*, pp. 57-9 [perhaps the reference is ch. II, 14-8].

Aristotle's sense of First Matter. Changeable substances (in the plural) are, for Aristotle, portions of First Matter variously qualified by powers and potentialities ranging from those characteristic of the elements to those characteristic of rational animals.

34. Descartes' *res extensa* is the conceptual heir of Aristotle's First Matter, though, like Kant after him, Descartes denies that powers and acts pertaining to representation can characterize portions of *res extensa* or First Matter.

35. It is instructive, in this context, to note that, contrary to what we might expect, Kant relates his categories of substance and attribute to categorical judgment. He does, indeed, characterize the latter as involving the "relation" of subject to predicate, but whereas we tend to think of the category of substance as peculiarly related to the *singular* subject-predicate judgment, thus judgments of the form

S is P,

(where 'S' is a singular referring expression and 'P' a predicate), which we tend to assimilate to the form

x is f,

Kant explicitly says that in the categorical judgment we consider *two* concepts. Of course, singular referring expressions can be said to stand for "individual concepts". Thus Kant's formulation does not exclude the cases

This S is P
A *certain* S is P.

But, and this is the crucial point, it does *not* exclude the case

All S is P.

And, as is well known, traditional logic tended to view the singular categorical judgment as a special case of the universal.

36. The point at which I am driving is that the concept of substance as that of a subject which is not also a predicate has the *general form* of the categorical judgment as its context. It is the concept of a term, 'S', which stands, indeed, for a *concept*, and thus occurs appropriately in the context

>   All S is P
>   Some S is P
>   This S is P

but *not* appropriately in the predicate position, thus

>   All S' is S
>   Some S' is S.
>   This S' is S.

In one sense 'S' is a predicate, for it, or something like it, is predicable of individuals, but *in the sense of belonging in the predicate position of a categorical judgment*, it is not a predicate.

37. This is exactly the role played by a "stuff" predicate which stands for First Matter in Aristotle's system. Thus, if Fire is First Matter,

>   All (portion(s) of) Fire are P
>   Some (portion(s) of) Fire is P
>   This (portion(s) of) Fire is P

is appropriate, but not

>   All (portion(s) of) S' are fiery
>   Some (portion(s) of) S' is fiery
>   This (portion(s) of) S' is fiery

38. Now *prima facie* it was open to Kant (as it was to Aristotle) to hold that a person is a portion of First Matter which has powers not only on the corporeal level, but also those which pertain to life and mind. As a matter of fact, the explicit argument of the First Analogy *requires* him to do so, for he speaks of substance as "the substratum of all change" (B225), not just of *material* change, and tells us that "all change or coexistence must, in being apprehended, be perceived in this substratum" which is "the substratum of all that is real" (B225). Again: "...all that belongs to existence can be thought of only as a determination of substance..." (B225). The argument is studded with similar passages.

39. This clearly defined line of thought confronts Kant with a dilemma. If all change is a change of (portions of) material substance, then either acts

of representing are states of material substance, or the states of the empirical self are not "changes" nor "alterations", nor "in Time". No other alternative seems to be permitted by the thesis that

> All existence and all change in Time have thus to be viewed as simply a mode of the existence of that which remains and persists. (A183; B227)

40. Suppose Kant had taken a "materialistic" line with respect to the phenomenal world. In doing so he would be construing mental acts as *objects of empirical knowledge* to be states of organized portions of matter. They would either be physical states in the tough sense that they are, in principle, reducible to "primary qualities", or, if he relaxes this requirement, in the broader sense that they belong to the causal order. The first alternative would constitute a "reductive" materialism. It is so radically incompatible with Kant's account of inner experience that there is little point in considering it. The second has more to recommend it, in that it allows for certain objects in the phenomenal world to have the powers of sensory and perceptual consciousness, and of conceptual thinking. These Strawsonian objects, however, would be "appearances" belonging to a deterministic natural order.

41. Instead, however, of opting for a Strawsonian account of the empirical self, Kant opts for a dualistic model. He must therefore explain how alterations which are not states of corporeal substance can nevertheless be located in an objective time order. This he does by arguing that the temporal objectivity of the mental is somehow derivative from, or dependent on, the objective order of material events.[16]

42. In order to understand the dependent status of the temporal objectivity of the empirical self, we must take into account Kant's theory of self knowledge, for the empirical self is the self as known.

43. The first thing to note is that according to Kant introspective knowledge involves an element of passivity. Kant clearly thinks of the self as passive with respect to the representations of *outer* sense. He also thinks that an analogous passivity is involved in what he calls, using Locke's

---

[16] This, of course, is the explicit thesis of the second edition Refutation of Idealism, and somewhat less obviously—because the connection between "objective time order" and "events in Material substance" stands out less clearly—of the first edition Deduction.

dangerous metaphor, "inner sense". Here also the mind is caused[17] to represent something; only this time, the "cause" is one of our own states. Schematically, the noumenal state of thinking *that S is P* causes one to represent *that one is thinking that S is P*. The mind, by being in a certain state, "affects" itself. The "affecting" may involve a certain agency—as when we *seek* to find out what we are thinking. In this sense the mind both "affects" and "is affected by" itself. (Compare the "agency" of *looking* with the passivity involved in *seeing*.) I shall return to this "agency" shortly. But abstracting from it for the moment, we can say that in "inner sense" or, better, "inner perception", one is caused to have representations of the form

I have just (a moment ago) represented such and such.[18]

44. Now we saw that the argument of the First Analogy requires the empirical self to be a portion of corporeal substance endowed with life and thought. But even if the implications of the First Analogy are evaded, the other two analogies require that the states of the empirical self belong to a deterministic system of events, the core of which consists of material events occurring to interacting material substances.

45. I pointed out a moment ago that in inner perception we are *caused* to represent ourselves as in a temporally located state of representing something. But notice that there is another way in which "causation" can come into the picture. In addition to the inner perception of the empirical self being "noumenally" caused, the empirical self as an object of knowledge may be represent*ed* as *passive*, i.e., as in a state which *it is caused to be in* by something other than itself.

---

[17] Notice, of course, that the causation involved is noumenal causation, the concept of which has as its core the purely logical concepts of ground and consequence. While it would obviously be a mistake to identify the concept of noumenal causation with that of the *generic* notion of ground and consequence, for noumenal causation must be a *species* of this relationship, we do not have intuitive content in terms of which to give the *differentia* of this species, as we do in the case of the schematized category of causation applicable to the phenomenal world. Thus we do not have an *adequate*, but at best an *analogical*, concept of noumenal causation. Another example of such causation is the impact of things in themselves on outer sense which Kant calls "*affizieren*".

[18] Notice that the metaphor of "inner sense" should not lead us to think that inner sense gives us "inner sensations". If we take the metaphor too seriously, we are likely to think that what we know in inner perception stands to the noumenal states of the noumenal self, as the colored and shaped objects of outer perception stand to the unknowable attributes of things in themselves. Actually, what we know in the inner perception of our thoughts differs from the corresponding reality only

(1) by being temporal, located in Time;
(2) by being conceived in purely *functional* terms, that is to say, by failing to reveal the contentual character of noumenal thinking.

46. In principle, it would seem, we could be noumenally "caused" to represent the empirical self as *active*, i.e., as in states which it is *not* caused to be in by something other than itself. It is important, therefore, to see that Kant seems to take it for granted that since the states of the empirical self belong to the order of nature, they must be states with respect to which the empirical self is *passive*, states which it is *caused to have*.

47. Now this seems to be a confusion—though one which is by no means limited to Kant. That it is a confusion is shown by the fact that even with respect to purely physical phenomena, the idea that the state of a system is determined by a preceding state of the system *is not the same as* the idea of a state which the system is *caused to have*, i.e., a state with respect to which the system is passive.

48. In the Third Antinomy, Kant speaks of the causality of nature as one in which "the causality of the cause is caused". This phrase occurs a number of times, and is echoed, for example, in the *Fundamental Principles of the Metaphysics of Morals*, where he writes

> Physical necessity is a heteronomy of the efficient causes, for every effect is possible only according to this law, that something else determines the efficient cause to exert its causality. (Abbott edition, p. 65)

The picture is that all natural objects are passive with respect to their states—so that if they cause other things to change, they do so because they have, in their turn, been caused by other things to be in the states by virtue of which they are causes.

49. Yet the fact that a state of a system is a physically necessary consequence of an antecedent state means merely that relative to this antecedent state it could not have been the case that the system did not come to be in its subsequent state. It does not mean that the system was caused to be in its present state by a "foreign cause".[19]

The past is not something with respect to which we are passive.

To be sure, the explanation of why a system is in a certain state may largely lie in what other things have done to it in the past. But the very existence of the concept of a closed system makes it clear that it would be a mistake to suppose that the explanation of the present state of such a system lies

---

[19] Abbott, p. 65.

entirely in "other things".[20]

50. If I am right, Kant, instead of taking it to be a simple consequence of the fact that the empirical self belongs to the order of nature, would have to give some special reason for holding that the self known in inner perception is essentially passive with respect to "foreign causes".

51. It is not, however, difficult to find just such an argument, for once Kant rejects the Strawsonian account of the empirical self, yet continues to think of material substance as the embodiment of objective temporal order, he is committed to the view that the states of the empirical self borrow their temporal objectivity from states of material substance. And the most obvious way of developing such a view is by construing these states of the empirical self as states which it is caused to be in by material substance, thus, for example, perceptual states. Indeed there is a temptation to construe it exclusively in terms of perceptual states.[21]

52. Now it is certainly reasonable to say that a model which contains a core of passivity or being acted upon is appropriate to perceptual representation. Yet what of our knowledge of ourselves as philosophizing, as cooking up plots for novels or reflecting on what to do? Surely even perceptual experience is not purely passive, involving as it does choosing what to look at and deciding what we want to find out. Shall we deny that knowledge of such activity falls within the scope of "inner sense"? It is impossible to find an explicit, let alone a satisfying, answer to these questions in the Kantian corpus.

53. It is simply not true, then, that all self-awareness is awareness of states in which the self is passive and conceived to be passive.[22] There are two lines of thought open to Kant at this point. In the first place he can argue that even if we are not *aware* of these states as passive, they must *be* passive, as belonging to the order of nature. In other words it is philosophical reflection that reveals them to be passive. And when, in this context, the possibilities of neurophysiology are viewed with a speculative eye, the suggestion naturally arises that even such unperceptual activities

---

[20] If it is argued that the explanation of the very existence of natural objects lies in other things which existed before they came into being, it must surely be pointed out:

(a) that the concept of passivity has no application in this context;
(b) that if the natural order is construed in a deterministic way, then the existence of *any* object at *any time* involves conditions of compatibility which limit the existence of other things at other times as much as they limit it.

[21] That this is a strand in Kant's thinking is indicated by his stress on the role of "inner sense" in perceptual experience, and by his puzzling claim that the materials of "inner sense" are provided by "outer sense".

[22] Even granted that our *awareness* of these states is passive.

as philosophizing find their place in the objective time order by their connection with bodily states. And even if, as I have suggested, the immensity of nature does not preclude a relative autonomy of the *body*, could we not conclude, from the necessity of material correlates for all conceptual states of the empirical self, that the mind is passive with respect to the *body*? Is not the phenomenal self an epiphenomenon? A good case can be made for this being Kant's position.

54. Yet it is not difficult to find a second thread in Kant's thought which, though not ultimately inconsistent with the above, points in another direction. For he distinguishes two modes of self awareness, one of which ("inner sense") is a *passive* awareness of states which are *passive*, while the other is an awareness of the self as having a certain "spontaneity", as not merely responding to the impingement of "foreign causes".

55. Now the notion of a self-awareness which is not that of inner sense may strike one as pre-critical and even anti-critical. Yet, once one looks for it one finds it throughout the *Critique*. Perhaps the most striking passage is the following.

> Man, who knows all the rest of nature solely through the senses, knows himself through pure apperception; ...and this, indeed, in acts and inner determinations which he cannot regard as impressions of the senses. (A546; B574)

It might be thought that by 'senses' Kant here means "external sense", and that the passage is compatible with the idea that the "acts and inner determinations" in question are known through inner sense, and are, hence, appearances. Interestingly enough, he explicitly excludes this interpretation, writing

> He is thus to himself, on the one hand phenomenon, and on the other hand, in respect of certain faculties the action of which cannot be ascribed to the receptivity of sensibility, a purely intelligible object. We entitle these latter faculties understanding and reason.

56. This suggests that according to Kant the domain of inner "sense" is mental states in which the mind is passive with respect to "foreign causes". Pure apperception, on the other hand, gives us a non-passive awareness of the mind as active. Indeed, Kant insists again and again that the mind is aware of the "unity" and "spontaneity" of its acts of synthesis. He even characterizes these acts as "successive" in a way which implies that not all

successiveness is the successiveness of objective Newtonian Time.[23]

57. How can these themes be reconciled? If we focus attention on the *Critique of Pure Reason*, and lay aside for the moment questions concerning other forms of "spontaneity" than those involved in constituting phenomenal objects, we can conceive Kant to argue that although we are conscious of ourselves as *spontaneous* in the synthesizing of empirical objects, this spontaneity is still only a *relative* spontaneity, a spontaneity "set in motion" by "foreign causes".

58. The following model may be helpful:

> Consider a computer which embodies a certain logical program, a set of computational dispositions. Even if "turned on" and humming with readiness, it still does nothing unless a problem is "fed in". Furthermore, once this happens, it moves along in accordance with its logical disposition. At certain stages it may "search its memory bank". This search, however, is *itself* the outcome of the initial input and its computational development. And although, with this qualification, it "initiates" the "search", the information it gets is information which, as computer, it is *caused to have*—i.e., more input. Here also it is passive.

59. In other words, from the standpoint of the problems discussed in the *Critique*, even if we take into account an awareness of self which is not that of "inner sense", the spontaneity of which we are conscious is, though not *sheer* passivity, nevertheless *a* passivity in that the inner development is set in motion by a foreign cause and follows a routine. In the awareness of noumenal activities of synthesis we would encounter simply another example of a cause the causality of which is caused. If this were all that the spontaneity of the noumenal self amounted to, then although it would not be a part of the phenomenal nature of outer and inner sense, it would be *like* an object in nature and might be called a noumenal mechanism.

60. Notice that if the domain of pure apperception were limited as above, it would correspond closely to the domain of inner sense. Thus, even if the concepts of inner *experience* and pure apperception did not coincide, the domain of the latter would, roughly speaking, coincide with that of the

---

[23] An elaboration of this theme would take me far afield. Yet it seems to me clear that Kant is committed to the view that we have some conception of a mode of successiveness which characterizes the activity and agency of the noumenal self, and the noumenal realm to which it belongs. This successiveness would be reflected in, but not identical with, the Time of experienced events. For a discussion of this point see my *Science and Metaphysics*, chapter 2, sections 12-8, and the Appendix on inner sense. The considerations advanced in footnote 17 above are relevant to this topic.

former, the self as passive. The distinctive feature of inner *experience* would be its location of these passive states of the self in an objective time order, by virtue of their connection with material process.

61. The question thus arises: Does pure apperception give us access to *another* spontaneity, one which is not, *in the above sense*, relative?

62. Now, at last, I am in a position to return to my text and comment on one of its more interesting features—

> ...this I or he or it (the thing) which thinks... .

One can complain that the list does not include 'she'; but why does it include '*it*'? Does this not suggest once again that the being which thinks is, when we come right down to it, simply a *substratum* of thoughts, and that it is an I by virtue of the fact that the accidents it supports are "thoughts"—"thoughts" which have the "synthetic unity" pertaining to "apperception"?

63. Nothing could be further from the truth. The noumenal subject of thoughts is a *thinker*, not a bare substratum, and we are conscious of it, in pure apperception, as such. But is it, in the full sense of the term, a *person*? For what is a "thing" in the sense relevant to our text? The answer comes out loud and clear:

> That which is not capable of any imputation is called a thing.[24]

Thus Kant is leaving open the possibility that the being which thinks might be something "which is not capable of imputation". It might, in other words, be an *automaton spirituale* or *cogitans*, a thinking mechanism along the lines we have described. According to Kant we are indeed conscious of ourselves as something more than such a thinking mechanism, but might not the *more* be a delusion, a "figment of the brain"?

64. In our text, then, Kant is hinting at the problem of freedom, which, placed on the agenda in the Introduction, first makes its presence felt in the resolution of the Third Antinomy. The argument of the analytic justifies us, Kant believes, in attributing to the noumenal self at least a relative spontaneity; or, to introduce another way of putting it, a relative *autonomy*. Can any other considerations lead us to say more?

65. What is haunting Kant, in this cryptic passage, is the concept of an *automaton spirituale*, a mind which conceptualizes, but only in response to challenges from without, and in ways which, however varied, realize set

---

[24] *The Metaphysic of Morals*, Introduction, Abbott, p. 280.

dispositions. He thinks of the perception of external objects as the paradigm of conceptual activity being called into play. But, as we have seen, he interprets even self knowledge as involving a causal dimension, a conceptual response to inner states, by virtue of which it is not inappropriately called 'inner sense'.

66. He grants that "inner perception" may be prepared for by an activity of searching, a direction of attention in which the mind affects itself,[25] just as perceptual response may occur in a context in which we are looking for something, seeking relevant observations. But why the searching? Why the direction of attention? Relevance to what? Here considerations of purpose enter in, and the first *Critique* simple *abstracts* from the purposive aspects of the conceptualization involved in experiential knowledge.

67. Now it is clear that although the structure of the first *Critique* highlights what I have called the relative spontaneity of the conceptualizing mind, it clearly presupposes a larger context in which the mind is thinking to some purpose. Thus reference to reason in its practical aspect is implicit throughout the *Critique*, but only in the Dialectic, after the constructive argument is over, does it become explicit.

68. I have been developing the idea of a *theoretical automaton spirituale*. But can we not also conceive of a *practical automaton spirituale*? One which, given an input of "practical propositions"—roughly intentions and purposes—would add factual information, select and combine this "mix" according to built-in conceptual procedures, and come up with coherent practical scenarios, alternative courses of action, one or other of which, *ratified* by the appetitive faculty, would become the decided course of action?

69. To use Hempel's metaphor, practical reason, thus conceived, would be a sausage machine. Chunks of purpose meat go in at one end. Purpose sausages come out the other. The "customer" is—not practical reason itself—but the very aspect of the self which brought the raw material to the machine.

70. It is some such picture which Kant has in mind, when he speaks of the heteronomy of the will. A paradigm formulation is given by Hume's challenging (and puzzling) statement that "reason is and ought to be the

---

[25] Which must be contrasted with the passivity in which the mind is affected by itself. The most interesting passage in this connection is the following: "If the faculty of coming to consciousness of oneself is to seek out (to apprehend) that which lies in the mind, it must affect the mind, and only in this way can it give rise to an intuition of itself. The form of this intuition, which exists antecedently in the mind, determines, in the representation of time, the mode in which the manifold is together in the mind, since it then intuits itself not as it would represent itself if immediately self active, but as it is affected by itself, and therefore as it appears to itself, not as it is." (B68-9)

slave of the passions". According to this point of view, reason also in its *practical* role would have only that relative spontaneity which Kant finds in the synthetic activity by which the understanding constitutes the objects of experience.

71. Now it might be argued that although particular desires and aversions constitute a "sausage meat" which comes into the machine from without, there is, in addition, a purpose which is, so to speak, *intrinsic* to the machine, the purpose to promote one's own happiness in the long run. Is not practical reason perhaps *fully autonomous* by virtue of self-love providing a practical *premise* which, unlike particular desires and aversions, does not come in to reason from without?

72. This suggestion has the merit of implying that for practical reason to be *autonomous*, there must be a practical *premise* which is as intrinsic to reason as are its conceptual or "transformational" procedures. For, surely, if all its premises come from without, then it is indeed "set in motion" from without—its "causality" is "caused"; its "spontaneity" relative.

73. Now, it might be objected that reference to "self-love", instead of pointing to an additional and over-arching premise, would simply be another way of describing the fact that practical reason turns out unified practical packages from which the "appetitive faculty" must choose. Would not the choice of one such package be *ipso facto* a choice of how to promote one's happiness in a concrete situation?

74. This move, however, would clearly be mistaken. Self-love clearly provides a practical premise of its own, indeed a "higher order" premise which refers to the satisfactions to be obtained from particular desires and aversions. Notice that

> I shall promote my happiness

is not a "hypothetical imperative". Hypothetical imperatives reflect procedural aspects of practical reason in that they formulate *implications* between purposes, and must be supplemented by practical *premises* to get practical *conclusions*. Indeed, 'I shall promote my happiness' is not even an "assertorial hypothetical imperative", for these have the form

> If I want (as I do) to promote my happiness, I ought to do A.

Self-love does, indeed, put in its appearance as a practical *premise*. And if so, why can we not construe it as "intrinsic" to practical reason and the principle of its autonomy?

75. There seem to be a number of possible answers, each of which can be found in Kant. Thus: *Because* it presupposes the fragmentary premises supplied by particular desires and aversions. They are the source of such determinate content as it can have, and, since practical reason is passive with respect to the latter, the pursuit of one's own happiness in the long run must also be heteronomous. This argument is not, by itself, convincing. But it is easy to see what Kant has in mind. He thinks of the premise which formulates self-love as also implanted in practical reason from without—not, it is true, by partial aspects of man as a natural object, but as corresponding to man as a unified natural whole. In Spinoza's terms, it is the "idea" which is the mental aspect of the *conatus in suo esse perseverare* which constitutes the individual man as a finite mode in *Natura Naturata*.

76. But if self-love does not provide a premise which is intrinsic to practical reason, then, unless we can find another candidate, we are left with the sausage machine, the *automaton spirituale*. We must look elsewhere. Now, what Kant finds is, in outline, a familiar story. The intrinsic practical premise is, in one of the many senses in which he uses this term, the Moral Law. And, if he is right, then one and the same idea defines *both* what it is for a rational being to be autonomous, *and* the moral point of view.

77. Of course, this intrinsic practical premise does not, of itself, by purely conceptual procedures, generate specific practical scenarios. Nevertheless, even if particular circumstances occasion the question, 'What shall I do?', and even though this premise must be supplemented by factual information which satisfies its criteria of relevance, it nevertheless serves as a premise which does not come into reason from without.

78. Kant's conception of this premise is difficult to disentangle from the complicated—indeed tortuous—apparatus in which it is embedded. In particular, it must be disentangled from the higher-order philosophical propositions which describe the criteria which a practical premise must satisfy if it is (a) to constitute the moral point of view; (b) to exhibit practical reason as autonomous. That these criteria are satisfied by one and the same practical proposition is the central burden of the *Critique of Practical Reason*, and its forerunner, the *Fundamental Principles of the Metaphysics of Morals*.

79. The necessarily *generic* character of this premise together with certain less than perspicuous Kantian formulations of the role of universality in moral reasoning have led to the mistaken idea that it is "purely formal", somehow deriving its authority solely from the principle of contradiction.

I shall short-circuit these issues, by formulating it without further ado as follows:

> Let any of us persons do that in each circumstance which promotes our common good.

I shall not attempt to justify the ascription of exactly this premise to Kant. Nor, indeed, shall I embark on the lengthy commentary which would be necessary to show that it satisfies the criteria referred to above. I note simply:

(a) It is logically intersubjective.

(b) It constitutes a purpose which can be said to be implied by the very concept of a community of persons.

(c) If content can be given to the idea of promoting our common good, it implies, together with factual information, general practical propositions of the form

> Let any of us do A, if in C.[26]

(d) If promoting the common good involves as its necessary condition certain *practices*, and, hence, *sanctioned legislation*, it provides a theory of morally justified legislation.[27]

80. I have said that this intrinsic generic practical proposition is a "premise" in practical reasoning. Strictly speaking, this is not correct. For practical reasoning proceeds by working out the *implications* of practical propositions. Since I am not concerned to defend any particular formulation of the above generic practical proposition, I shall, in the argument to follow, express it as follows:

> Let any of us persons do that which satisfies condition α.

---

[26] These practical propositions would be "derivative moral laws" in a first sense of this phrase.
[27] Such legislation would constitute "derivative moral laws" (obligations) in a second sense to be carefully distinguished from those defined in the preceding note—which, indeed, they would presuppose. For an elaboration of this point see the distinction between "principles" and "sanctioned imperatives" in my "Reason and the Art of Living in Plato," in *Phenomenology and Natural Existence: Essays in Honor of Marvin Farber*, State University of New York Press, 1973.

Thus, practical reasoning as such would tell us that this proposition, with relevant information, *implies*

> Let me now do A.

To apprehend this implication is *not* to draw the corresponding inference. *That* would involve "affirming the antecedent", with a result which could be expressed by,

> Let me now do A, *because* let any of us do that which satisfies α.

81. That one in point of fact "affirms the antecedent" is not intrinsic to practical reason, but a matter of free choice. The concept of *autonomy* must not be confused with that of *free choice*. Kant's point is that *if* one affirms the antecedent, one acts from a premise which does not come into practical reason from without, as do other purposes. Thus, according to Kant, we always act either *in the way of autonomy* or *in the way of heteronomy*.

82. Schematically—and over simplifying by treating self-love as *the* alternative to action on principle—practical reasoning, in cool hours, would generate *two* implications:

> I. 'Let any of us do actions which satisfy α' *implies* (with the facts) 'Let me now do A'.
>
> II. 'Let me promote my happiness' *implies* (with the facts) 'Let me now do B'.

An implication from the moral point of view confronts an implication from the "personal" point of view.[28]

83. If, now, I affirm the antecedent of the first implication, I end up with

> Let me now do A, *because* let any of us do actions satisfying α, *although* this implies not promoting my happiness by doing B

which amounts to a long-winded version of choosing to do A, as being what I ought to do.

84. If, on the other hand, I affirm the antecedent of the second implication,

---

[28] It should be remembered that, as indicated above, self-love is simply one special case of the personal point of view, a fact which will be taken into account in a moment.

I end up with

> Let me now do B, *because* let me now promote my happiness, *although* this implies my not doing A, which is subsumable under the principle "let any of us do actions satisfying α"

which amounts to a long-winded version of choosing to do B, as being what will promote my happiness, in spite of the fact that it conflicts with duty.
85. Kant, in other words, argues that unless we can choose to do something for the reason that it is implied by the moral law, then although there would be "free choice" (*Willkuer*)—for it would still be up to us whether we did that which promotes our happiness, or (out of sympathy) that which helps a person in distress, or (out of impulse) that which satisfies a momentary whim, there would be no freedom in the deeper sense which he has been seeking to explicate. For, in practical reasoning limited to such motives, *which* practical premise was affirmed would be determined by "inclination". That practical reason is autonomous means that a choice is possible in which practical reason itself affirms the antecedent. A rational being which had no inclinations (desires and aversions) would always act in accordance with the moral law, and hence in the way of autonomy.[29] A being which has inclinations, but not the possibility of acting for the sake of principle, would always act in the way of heteronomy. It would be, an "it (the thing) which thinks".
86. Kant ends on an agnostic note. We are conscious, in pure apperception, of ourselves as autonomous rational beings, beings which *can* act out of respect for principle. But is not, perhaps, this consciousness an illusion? He claims to know, on philosophical grounds, that as objects of empirical knowledge we are *not* autonomous beings. We cannot, alas, show, on philosophical grounds, that *as noumena* we *are* autonomous. He therefore takes refuge in the claim that, equally, we cannot *know*, on philosophical grounds, that as noumena we are *not* autonomous.
87. At no time has Kant been taken more seriously than today, particularly in the English speaking world. A whole new generation of commentaries is coming into existence. And with good reason. For his views, when translated into contemporary idiom, have invariably been found to contain insights which the "dogmatic rationalism" and the "skeptical empiricism"

---

[29] Whether or not the concept of such a being makes sense hinges on how far it is intended to abstract the concept of reason from the weighing of alternatives, and, hence, from change or process. Kant is as willing as most theologians to make use of "analogy". But, as has often been pointed out, when the granted negative analogy is of a certain character, only the word remains.

of his day—brought up to date—do not provide. If my interpretation of his views on the nature of reason are essentially correct, then they challenge *first* those who take the cartesian line—dare I call them 'rational psychologists'?—to take the scientific image of man seriously. But second, they also challenge "scientific realists", those who are already committed to the scientific image—perhaps they should, as Chisholm has wittily suggested, be called 'rational physicists'—to come up with a concept of nature which not only finds a place for *reason* and *the causality of reason* (tasks which any naturalist will undertake), but also for the *autonomy of reason* and the *reality* of the moral point of view.

88. That Kant is an insightful guide to this problem has been the burden of my remarks. Whether, and to what extent, the details of his solution survive translation into contemporary idiom is, of course, a test of Kantian views. One suspects, however, that, as so often before, it will also be a test of the translators.

BERKELEY AND DESCARTES: REFLECTIONS ON THE THEORY OF IDEAS

Part One

I

1. Descartes appends to his reply to the second set of objections a brief formulation, *more geometrico*, of his argument in the *Meditations* for the existence of God and the distinction between soul and body. Of particular relevance to my topic are certain of the definitions with which this appendix begins:

> I. *Thought* is a word that covers anything that exists in us in such a way that we are immediately conscious of it. Thus all the operations of will, intellect, imagination and of the senses are thoughts. ...
> II. *Idea* is a word by which I understand the form of any thought, that form by the immediate awareness of which I am conscious of that said thought; in such a way that, when understanding what I say, I can express nothing in words, without that very fact making it certain that I possess the idea of what those words signify.
> III. By the objective reality of an idea I mean that in respect of which the thing represented in the idea is an entity insofar as that exists in the idea; ...whatever we perceive as being as it were in the object of our ideas, exists in the ideas themselves objectively.
> IV. To exist formally is the term applied where the same thing exists in the object of an idea in such a manner that the way in which it exists in the object is exactly like what we know of it when aware of it.[1]

2. Of these definitions the most interesting is the third, for to work out its implications is to find oneself at the very center of the Cartesian philosophy. The second is interesting, but also puzzling. It implies that all thoughts, i.e., everything that exists in us in such a way that we are immediately conscious of it, are ideas. But this conflicts with the classification of thoughts in the third *Meditation*, according to which only certain thoughts are properly called 'ideas', namely those which "are, so to speak, images of the things...examples are my thought of a man, or of a chimera, of heaven, of an angel or [even] of God."[2]

3. As examples of thoughts that are not ideas, he gives "willing, fearing. approving, denying." He emphasizes, however, that although a "willing" or an "affection" or a "judging" is not an idea, it must be conjoined with an

---

[1] *The Philosophical Works of Descartes*, trans. E. S. Haldane and G. T. R. Ross. 2. vols. (New York: Dover, 1934), 2:52-53 (hereafter cited as HR).
[2] Ibid., 1:159.

idea, for "I always perceive something as the subject of the action of my mind."³ In other words, one can not will or fear or affirm without a willing or fearing or affirming *something*, and this something is in the mind by virtue of an idea.

4. I shall return in a moment to the problem posed by the definition of the term 'idea' in the appendix to the reply to *Objections* II, but the important thing to note is that it is the narrower account given in the *Meditations* themselves that has the most direct connection with the definition of the 'objective reality of an idea' which follows that definition.

5. The most general theme in Descartes' account of 'ideas' in the narrower sense is that *ideas* represent things—where 'thing' is used in that inclusive sense in which *anything* is a thing. He seems to have taken for granted that the term 'represents' as applied to thoughts is univocal. Thus in explaining what it is for a thought (or modification of the mind) to represent something (and hence to be an idea), he has no hesitation in appealing to one type of paradigm, namely, mental states in which we are *conceiving* of something, e.g., an angel.

6. Now it is obvious that when we are conceiving of an angel, the thought, which is a modification of our mind, is not itself an angel. It is angelic only in the sense that it represents an angel. Again, when we conceive a chimera, we represent something that does not exist. How are these facts to be understood? Descartes offers just two metaphors, only one of which is sufficiently elaborated to be a proto-theory. The simple metaphor is that of an image. After all, the image of a chimera is not itself a chimera, although it is serving to represent it. But, unless the image is a physical image—in which case Descartes is not interested—it has none of the characteristics of what it represents; thus the mental image of a chimera has no shape at all, let alone one that, in some generic way, might resemble that which a chimera would have. For mental images, being modes of thought, simply do not have shape.

7. That is to say that they do not have shape *formally* as, according to the fourth definition, an actual chimera would. Thus, according to the extended system of metaphors that is Descartes' proto-theory of representation, there are two aspects of ideas, i.e., of thoughts that represent:

    a. their character as modifications of the mind
    b. their character as representing what they represent.

---

³ Ibid.

The latter is explained in terms of the metaphor of containment, and the concept of a mode of 'reality' ('objective reality') other than that of actual existence. It is a familiar fact that this concept has a scholastic origin and that the term 'objective reality' connotes 'being as an object of thought' rather than 'what is the case regardless of what we think' as it does today.

8. Anything, whether it actually exists or not, is the objective reality of a thought if it is what the thought is *about*. It, the 'anything' or entity in question, exists 'in' the idea. Thus 'ideas' are those thoughts that 'contain' entities which exist 'objectively' in them.

9. The contrasting term to 'objective reality' is 'formal reality'. Thus we could say that *a man* or, perhaps, the character of being a man has objective reality in our thought of President Nixon, but formal reality in that Nixon actually exists and is a man.

10. Thus when I conceive of a triangle, my thought is not triangular, but 'contains' a triangle objectively. The terminology is flexible. Thus the thought can even be said to *be* triangular, but only 'objectively', for the character of being a triangle is only 'objectively' present in the thought, whereas it is 'formally' present in a triangular material surface.

11. Descartes has little to tell us about the first aspect of those thoughts that represent, i.e., their character as modifications of the mind. One is tempted to say that the only respect in which they differ (apart from occurring in different minds or at different times or in different contexts) is that they 'contain' different entities, i.e., that different entities exist 'in' them 'objectively'. Yet, although the metaphor of containment is to be taken seriously as an essential element in this proto-theory of representation, it should not be given exclusive rights, for metaphors always limp and need to be buttressed, in proto-theories, by other metaphors. Thus we have seen that instead of saying that a thought contains a triangle that has objective existence in it, we can say that the thought is objectively, though not formally, triangular. In this terminology the contrast is between two ways of being triangular, rather than between a material triangle and a triangle that is 'contained' in a thought 'in' which it exists objectively.

12. Thus ideas would differ as modifications of the mind with respect to different characters, even though they had them only 'objectively'. If, now, we return to the definition of 'idea' in the appendix to the reply to *Objections* II, we see that every thought, whether or not it represents (i.e., is an idea in the narrower sense), has a form, i.e., a character by virtue of which it is the sort of thought it is. Thus a volition has the form *volition*, and when we are conscious of a volition we are conscious of it as a

volition, i.e., of its form.

13. Though the volition is not an idea in the narrower sense, in being conscious of it as a volition we do have an idea, in the narrower sense, *of* a volition. We have an idea of what the word 'volition' signifies.

14. On the other hand, when I am conscious of an idea in the narrower sense, e.g., an idea of an angel, I am conscious of it as an idea of an angel, and, hence, of its form, which is the character of being an angel. But whereas the volition has the character of being a volition *formally*, the idea of an angel has the character of being an angel only *objectively*. Of course, we can also say that the form of the idea is *containing an angel as its objective reality*. But then my purpose has only been to show that Descartes' proto-theory enables him to make consistent (if highly metaphorical) sense of the wider definition of 'idea'.

II

15. In the definition of the wider sense of 'idea', Descartes speaks of our consciousness of our thoughts, but does not give an account of this consciousness. We do, however, find such an account in the treatise *The Passions of the Soul*, and it will be useful to consider it briefly, for it will enable some relevant distinctions to be made. In Article XIX ("Of the Perceptions"), he distinguishes between two sorts of perceptions, those "which have the soul as a cause" and those which have "the body [as a cause]".[4]

> Those which have the soul as a cause are the perceptions of our desires, and of all the imaginations or other thoughts which depend on them. For it is certain that we cannot desire anything without perceiving by the same means that we desire it; and, although in regard to our soul it is an action to desire something, we may say that it is also one of its passions to perceive that it desires. Yet because this perception and this will are really one and the same thing, the more noble always supplies the denomination, and thus we are not in the habit of calling it a passion, but only an action.[5]

16. I have quoted this passage at length because it is easily misunderstood, and contains distinctions that are highly relevant to the understanding of other philosophers of this period. The first thing to note is that Descartes thinks it appropriate to limit the term 'action' as applied to mind to volitions and to items that are akin to volitions, thus to desires, which, like volitions, are ascribed to the 'will'. We find in Descartes no distinction

---
[4] Ibid., 1:340.
[5] Ibid., 1:340-41.

between mental *act* and mental *action*, such that it would be appropriate to speak of any (occurrent) state of mind, as a 'mental act', so that merely by virtue of being an *actualization* of a mental capacity it would be an *act* (as contrasted with a *potency*). In the latter sense of 'act' a state could be one in which the mind was passive and still be an act. The concept of a 'passive act' would be a coherent one. Descartes would not *object* to such a distinction. He simply does not use the term 'act' in this purely Aristotelian sense in connection with the mental. And obviously he would not be happy with the concept of a 'passive *action*'.

17. Yet the fundamental theme of the above passage is Aristotelian. For when he says that "this perception and this will are one and the same thing," we must bear in mind the opening paragraph of *The Passions of the Soul*, where he makes the general metaphysical point that

> all which occurs or that happens anew is by the philosophers, generally speaking, termed a passion, in so far as the subject to which it occurs is concerned, and an action in respect to him who causes it to occur. Thus, although the agent and the recipient [patient] are frequently very different, the action and the passion are always one and the same thing, although having different names, because of the two diverse subjects to which they may be related. (Pp. 331-32)

An example of this general metaphysical thesis would be that when fire heats a piece of metal, the actualization of the capacity of the fire to heat metal is 'the same thing' as the actualization of the capacity of the piece of metal to be heated by fire. Thus the fire's heating the metal is the same event as the metal's being heated by the fire. On the other hand, two *changes* involved in this event are *not* identical, namely, the fire becoming cooler and the metal becoming warmer, although these changes are aspects of that one identical event.

18. Thus when Descartes tells us that "the perception and the will are one and the same thing," we must be careful not to conclude that the perception and the will are one and the same mental state *simpliciter*. What is one and the same state is the desire causing itself to be the object of a perception and a perception of the desire being caused by the desire. Being a perception caused by the mental state that is its object is the counterpart of being *heated* by something hot.

19. Those who are inclined to say, and they are legion, with an air of puzzlement that according to Descartes a mental act is identical with the awareness of that act are likely to be misinterpreting this passage.

III

20. It is high time that topics more closely related to perception were adumbrated. The best way to do so is to turn directly to Descartes' theory of sensation. The term *sensation*, as he uses it, includes visual sensation (e.g., a sensation of a certain shade of blue), sensations of the other senses, also bodily sensations (e.g., sensations of warmth) and sensations of pain or pleasure. Sensations are modifications of the mind of which we are immediately conscious, and hence are, according to Descartes' definition, 'thoughts'. But the definition is a bit puzzling, because to say that something is an immediate object of consciousness is to give it a relational or extrinsic characterization, whereas to classify it as a thought looks like an intrinsic characterization. What, we are inclined to ask, does a feeling of pain have intrinsically in common with a mental affirming, or a conceiving of an angel, and what is implied about its intrinsic character by classifying it as a modification of the *mind*? Of course, they share the negative character of not being definable in terms of the attribute of extension, but how much further does that get us?

21. Instead, however, of answering these questions directly, let us ask: Which are sensations more akin to, those thoughts that represent ('ideas') or those thoughts (e.g., volitions) that do not represent, though they are intimately related to those which do?

22. We are immediately pulled in different directions. Thus a sensation or feeling of pain does not *represent* a pain, it *is* a pain. In this respect it resembles an 'action of affirmation'. The latter does not *represent* an affirmation, it *is* an affirmation. The phrases 'of pain' and 'of affirmation' are, in grammatical terms, subjective genitives and serve to classify what is referred to by the terms they modify.

23. Shall we say, then, that sensations belong to that species of thoughts which do not represent, and which therefore are not ideas in the narrower sense? Descartes does not press this question, and no coherent position is implied by the relevant texts. And there is good reason for this lacuna. To be sure, in the *Principles of Philosophy* he writes (part 1, LXXI):

> ... Such sensations were encountered as we called tastes, smells, sound, heat, cold, light, colors, etc., which in truth represent nothing to us outside of our mind, but which vary in accordance with the diversities of the parts and modes in which the body is affected.[6]

---

[6] Ibid., 1:249-50.

But the primary burden of this passage, in the context in which it occurs, is to emphasize the falsity of our childhood belief that material objects or processes resemble our sensations, e.g., that a material thing can resemble a sensation of blue.[7]

24. Yet if a feeling of pain does not *represent* but *is* a pain, this does not mean that it can not legitimately be said to represent *something*. And, indeed, the most plausible candidate is a bodily state, e.g., some aspect of the state of a hammered finger. This state need not be thought of as *resembling* the pain,[8] but nevertheless as being represented by it in accordance with a systematic manner of representation. And if, with Descartes, we construe a sensation of blue on the analogy of a feeling of pain, we might well be inclined to say that although a sensation of blue does not *represent* blue but *is* blue, it nevertheless does represent something, perhaps a certain state of the physical object that is its external cause.

25. And, indeed, Descartes stresses the functional role of pains and other modes of sensation in enabling men to find their way around safely in their environment. As a matter of fact, he stresses the kinship of men with animals in this respect—though the sensory states of animals, of course, as purely mechanical systems are limited to what, in the human case, are the physical correlates of feeling and sensation. The latter faculties were given us, not to illuminate the nature of the world, but to enable us to survive.[9] Pain keeps our hands off hot stoves.

26. But it is one thing to interpret sensations as having, in a *generic* sense, a representative function, and quite another to interpret this function in terms of the categories that are appropriate to conceivings. Yet Descartes implicitly does this by taking the latter as his paradigm of the modifications of the mind that represent. And in the absence of an explicit, if only schematic, account of an alternative variety of representation in the generic sense, the temptation to do so must inevitably be present—and, as we shall see, was clearly present in Leibniz and Spinoza.

27. Descartes himself does refer to sensations on a number of occasions not only as thoughts, but as *confused* thoughts.[10] He connects this character

---

[7] One can imagine Berkeley reading Principle LXX (ibid., 1:249) according to which "we can find no intelligible resemblance between the color which we suppose to exist in objects and what we are conscious of in our senses. ... It is easy to allow ourselves to fall into the error of holding that what we call color in objects is something entirely resembling the color we perceive, and then supposing that we have a clear perception of what we do not perceive at all," nodding his head and saying, "Indeed, only a sensation (perception, idea) can be like a sensation (perception, idea)."

[8] At least as one pyramid resembles another—for the concept of resemblance can be extended to cover all sorts of 'analogies'.

[9] *Principles of Philosophy*, Part II, Principle III (HR. 1:255).

[10] Ibid., Part IV, Principle CXCI (HR. 1:291). *Meditations*: VI (HR. 1: 193).

of being confused with the intimate, indeed 'substantial', tie between the human mind and its body. Thus he writes:

> Nature also teaches me by these sensations of pain, hunger, thirst, etc., that I am not only lodged in my body as a pilot in a vessel, but that I am very closely united to it, and so to speak so intermingled with it that I seem to compose with it one whole. For if that were not the case, when my body is hurt, I, who am merely a thinking thing, should not feel pain, for I should receive this wound by the understanding only, just as the sailor perceives by sight when something is damaged in his vessel; and when my body has neither drink nor food, I should clearly understand the fact without being warned of it by confused feelings of hunger and thirst. For all these sensations of hunger, thirst, pain, etc., are in truth none other than certain confused modes of thought which are produced by the union and apparent intermingling of mind and body.[11]

This characterization of sensations, if taken at its face value, would require that sensations, although confused, belong to the same generic kind as clear and distinct thoughts, and would therefore require that they be analyzable in terms of the contrast between formal and objective reality. I shall return to this topic in a later section and shall limit myself for the moment to pointing out that *sometimes* when Descartes speaks of confusion in the context of sensation, he has in mind that as children, and, in the absence of sound philosophy, as adults, we tend to have confused beliefs about a similarity of sensations to their physical causes. Although, strictly speaking, it is the *beliefs* that are confused, the sensations may be said to be confused because of their role in this confusion.[12]

IV

28. Now it is most important to note that when Descartes speaks of visual sensations, the examples he has in mind are not of the form 'sensation of a blue triangle' or 'sensation of a triangular expanse of blue', but simply 'sensation of blue'. In a perception of a shape we are conscious of or represent the shape, but we do not have a sensation of it. Thus, after the passage quoted in paragraph 23 above, he continues,

> The mind at the same time also perceived magnitudes, figures, movements and the like which were exhibited to it not as sensations, but as things or the modes of things existing, or at least capable of existing, outside thought, although it did not yet observe this distinction between the two.[13]

---

[11] HR. 1:193.
[12] A related point concerning the "material falsity" of "the idea of cold" is made in his *Reply to Objections IV* (HR. 2:106).
[13] HR. 1:250.

29. This difference in status between the color and the shape involved in perceptual experiences generates puzzles which were endemic in seventeenth- and eighteenth-century philosophy, bound up as it is with the distinctions between primary and secondary qualities and between the mental and the physical. It is time we began to take a closer look at some of the conceptual pressures involved.

30. Descartes is clearly committed to the view that when we have a perception of a shape, the shape has only 'objective' existence in the perceptual act or state. The perception has a shape 'objectively' but not 'formally'. One way of symbolizing this would be to introduce a new form of the copula, thus '[is]'. Accordingly we would say, where α is a perceptual act,

α [is] a triangle

whereas, x being a physical surface, we would say

x is a triangle.

If we now ask, "What can be predicted *formally* of α that pertains to its 'objective' triangularity?", we can, of course, be given a true but unilluminating answer, 'The character of being objectively a triangle', or, perhaps,

α is something that [is] a triangle.

The answer is unilluminating because what is desired is a 'formal' predication that is not derivative from an 'objective' predication. The answer

α is a triangle

would, of course, be ruled out by the principle that mental acts cannot be extended.

31. Notice, however, for future reference, that instead of introducing a new mode of predication, '[is]', we could have introduced a new predicate, '[a triangle]', and expressed the proposition that α is objectively a triangle by

α is [a triangle].

In the absence of a longer story, of course, there is no significant difference between these two modes of representation. They both indicate that α has a *special* connection with *ordinary* triangularity. Yet there is one difference worth noting. The second, unlike the first, is designed to give at least a nominal reply to the challenge: Granted that it is differentiated from other acts by occurring in *this* mind at *this* time, must not α actually (i.e., formally) have a character other than that of simply being a perception? And, in particular, must not a perception of a triangle differ in some character that it actually has from a perception of a circle? "Yes," the reply is, "it differs by having the character of being an [a triangle] perception."[14]

32. It is essential to remember that both the special copula and the special predicate of the above symbolic forms are, by virtue of Cartesian presuppositions, tied to the paradigm of conceptual thinking. Thus we would have

α [is] an angel
α is [an angel]

where α is the act in which Jones at a time, t, conceptually represents ('intends') an angel.

33. But might there not be another way in which ordinary physical triangularity might be 'in' a mental state without that state being physically triangular? Is there no *via media* between being physically triangular and being a conceptual representation of a physical triangle? The answer, I shall argue, is, Yes, there is. But the failure of this period to consider, or if considered to elaborate, this alternative had serious consequences for philosophy.

34. Now if Descartes is clearly committed to the view that when we have a perception of a shape, the shape has only 'objective' existence ('intentional inexistence') in the perception, he seems equally committed (though not perhaps as *distinctly*) to the view that when one has a sensation of blue, the sensation is a case of blue *formaliter*. I use this circumlocution rather than speaking of the sensation as blue *formaliter*, since Descartes does not attribute color to visual sensations.

35. One might put this by saying that whereas Descartes might well have been uncomfortable about the statement, where α is a sensation,

---

[14] If the point is pressed, i.e., must not α have a *determinate* character by virtue of which it represents what it does, a problem is posed that will be explored in connection with Berkeley's rejection of abstract general ideas.

α is blue,

he would have been at least as uncomfortable about the claim that blue is in a sensation only as an angel is in a thought of an angel.

36. At this point one might attempt to capture a possible Descartes by introducing either a new copula '{is}' or a new predicate '{blue}' to express this unique presence of blueness in a sensation of blue. But to do so would imply that the actual Descartes was in a position to ask, but simply failed to ask, the question: Why could not a perception be an {a triangle} perception or {be} a triangle? That is, why could it not involve physical triangularity in a way that does not require the perception to be *either* a physical triangle *or* a mere conception of a triangle? It is important to bear in mind that nothing which could reasonably be construed as a form of this question is explicitly raised by Descartes. Yet the question is a useful one to bear in mind when studying the Cartesian tradition.[15]

V

37. Let us return to our main line of thought. We have found Descartes to be committed to the view that blue and triangle *enter* in different ways into perceptual experience. Yet as far as the phenomena are concerned—and it was not left to phenomenologists to point this out—the shape we perceive is the shape of a color expanse, and the color has a shape. Indeed, the shape is there because color contrasts are there. Thus there is enormous pressure to say that the shape and the color have the same 'mode of being'.[16]

38. If we say that the color has formal reality, i.e., is a case of color *formaliter* as a case of pain is a case of pain *formaliter*, then the shape of the color is the shape of a case of color *formaliter*, and must surely be a case of shape *formaliter*. Indeed, if a sensation is a case of color *formaliter*, the shape must surely be the shape of a sensation—though perhaps not itself a sensation. If the color is a modification of the mind, the shape would be a modification of a modification of the mind.

39. Could we expect Descartes to consider for a moment the view that a shape could be even a modification of a modification of the mind, let alone a modification of the mind?

---

[15] Malebranche would be a case in point, but an examination of the nature and motivations of his doctrine that we see all things in God would require the space of another essay.

[16] To be sure, we might want to add that the color is 'matter' and the shape is 'form', but this distinction, important though it is, cuts across the categories with which we are concerned in this paper.

40. If, on the other hand, the shape of which we are conscious is merely the objective reality of a *cogitatio*, i.e., characterizes the latter only 'objectively', then surely the same must be true of the color expanse of which it is the shape!

41. Thus either we pay one price and assimilate the status of the experienced shape to that of the experienced color or we pay another and assimilate the status of the experienced color to that of the experienced shape. Descartes does not resolve this dilemma; indeed, he does not face it. How can this be? Did he think that one and the same modification of the mind could be both a case of blue *formally* and a triangle *objectively*, and, by virtue of this hermaphroditic character, be an experience of a triangular expense of blue? Yet he does, after all, think that a modification of the mind can be both *formally* a case of desire and *objectively* a case of a sloop, and by virtue of these facts be a desiring of a sloop.

42. Or, which is more likely, did he think that the case of blue which has the shape is not the case of blue which is the sensation? He can be interpreted as holding that when we look at a blue and triangular object in standard conditions, the resultant state of the pineal gland causes us to have a *sensation*, α_1, of blue and, at the same time, a *perception*, α_2, of a triangle. We thereupon form an additional cogitatio, α_3, which is the idea of a blue triangle, i.e., an idea of which the objective reality is a blue triangle, thus

α_1 is a case of blue;
α_2 [is] a triangle;
α_3 [is] a blue triangle.

43. But why should the mind connect the blue with the shape? Of course the modification of the pineal gland that, by virtue of its microstructure, causes the sensation of blue is also, in its gross character, triangular. And perhaps this is all that needs to be said.[17]

44. If Descartes had dwelt on this issue, it would have confronted him with the question: Why is it not *evident* that the experience of blue-*cum*-triangle is either constituted by, or derivative from, two radically different kinds of experience, one of which is of blue and the other of which is of a triangle? Descartes holds not only that we can be immediately conscious of

---

[17] Yet one can envisage a position according to which the sensation of blue, *qua* sensation, has a character, not itself triangularity, nor the character of *intending* a triangle, by virtue of which *it*, rather than the state of the pineal gland, is the direct cause of the perception of a triangle. This would naturally develop into the view, adumbrated in paragraph 36 above, that there is an 'analogical' sense of 'triangular' in which the sensation itself might actually *be* triangular.

our sensations but that we can have a *clear* knowledge of them. To be sure, *clear* knowledge need not be *distinct*, and it is the latter which is presupposed by the above challenge. Yet Descartes does tell us that "we have a clear or distinct knowledge of pain, color, and other things of the sort when we consider them simply as sensations or thoughts."[18]

45. Descartes, however, is content to remind us that in ordinary perceptual experience we do not ask these questions. After all, the point of perception is to guide practice rather than to inspire ontology, and in this respect the philosopher's experience does not differ from the child's. Nevertheless, when, as philosophers, we *do* ask these questions, should not the answers be evident? A well-convinced philosophy must be able to account not only for the knowledge that it is true but for the fact that otherwise intelligent philosophers are convinced that it is false. If Descartes had explored with sufficient care the above problems, he would surely have been forced to realize that the categories of his philosophy of mind were arrived at dialectically, rather than by philosophically inspired inspection.

46. There remains the possibility that Descartes simply took for granted that the relation of blue to the sensation of blue is the same as that of triangle to the perception of a triangle. This would mean that blue has merely *objective* existence, even in a sensation of blue. On this alternative the classification of blue as a sensation would amount to the thesis that objective reality is the only kind of reality of which blue is capable.[19] Shape, on the other hand, would also have reality as a modification of material things.

47. Again, on this alternative, the confused belief about blue shared by children and unsophisticated philosophers would be not the belief that 'blue' material things have a property that belongs formally only to sensations, but rather the belief that 'blue' material things have a property that belongs formally to *nothing*, not even sensations, for it is possessed only *objectively* by those *cogitationes* which are sensations of blue. Since the concept of a property that, though not self-contradictory, can be possessed formally by nothing is, to say the least, paradoxical, the point should be made in a way that involves no commitment to the idea that blue is a property or quality or even a modification (for the concept of a modification that cannot be *formally* the modification of anything is equally paradoxical). Fortunately there remains the catch-all category of *nature*. Blue, then, unlike shape, would be a nature that is capable only of objective being,

---

[18] HR. 1:248.
[19] If this position were represented by the slogan 'the *esse* of blue is *sentiri*', the latter would be a cousin of the slogan that 'the *esse* of abstractions is *concipi*', i.e., that abstractions as such have no formal being in extra-mentality.

though it can be confusedly believed to have formal being in the material world.

48. How could such a position be held, even 'implicitly', by a subtle and perceptive mind? How could a philosopher of Descartes' caliber assimilate the status of blue in a sensation of blue (let alone the twinge in a feeling of pain) to the status, say, of the number Two in a mathematician's reasoning? The general clue to such a possibility lies in the absence from Descartes' philosophy of a clear and distinct theory (as opposed to a highly metaphorical proto-theory) of intentionality. This absence made it possible to think that the difference between sensation of blue and conception of Two consists not in a difference between the relation of blue to the sensation and the relation of Two to the conception, but in a difference between the natures *blue* and *Two*.

49. What difference? There is an obvious candidate. A sensation of blue, is always a sensation of a determinate shade of blue, thus $blue_{29}$. Two, on the other hand, is, in some sense of this slippery term, an 'abstraction'. Might not the striking phenomenological difference between a sensing of blue (or even a feeling of a specific kind of twinge!) and a conceiving of Two be the striking difference between the *determinate* nature $blue_{29}$ (or $twinge_{63}$!) and the abstract nature *Two*? Would not this step also illuminate the distinction between *sensing* $blue_{29}$ and *conceiving* generic blue or color as such? Generic blue and color as such are also 'abstractions', and our awareness of them falls on the side of conceiving rather than sensing or imaging.

50. It is a familiar fact that, as hinted above, the term 'abstraction' covers a number of distinctions. Is *Two* abstract in the same way in which *blue* as such is abstract? Is there not perhaps a sense in which $blue_{29}$ is abstract? These questions are lurking in the background and will play their role in the development of Cartesian themes, particularly across the channel. But let us continue to collect before we divide.

51. Notice that the alternative we have been exploring since paragraph 46 above would mitigate the problem of how $blue_{29}$ and triangularity get together in the experience of a $blue_{29}$ triangle. There would be no need to posit a transition from sensing $blue_{29}$, where the sensing is *formally* a case of $blue_{29}$, to conceiving $blue_{29}$, on the ground that this latter alone, as *objectively* a case of $blue_{29}$, would be suited to merge with the perception of a triangle. $Blue_{29}$ would *ab initio* have the same status as the triangular shape. Thus instead of the α_1, α_2, and α_3 of paragraph 43 above, we would need to postulate only one mental act, the perception of a triangular

expanse of blue. We would add, of course, that just as the blue must be a determinate shade of blue, so the shape must be a determinate sort of triangularity.

52. But why, then, distinguish between a *sensation* of color and a *perception* of shape? This distinction would presumably be justified by the fact that shape is a nature which *can* be realized by material things, whereas color is not. This categorial difference would find expression in the presumed fact that shape presents itself to us as a modification of an extended object,[20] whereas color does not so present itself to us, but is (confusedly) believed to be such a modification.

VI

53. I pointed out (above, paragraph 24) that even if a feeling of pain is interpreted as a case of pain *formaliter*, there is nevertheless a sense of 'represent' in which the feeling can be said to represent a bodily state, e.g., that of having a hammered finger. In such a case the feeling is not only a constituent of the seeming to feel one's finger to be hammered, it is also a feeling of a sort that is normally brought about by a hammering of one's finger, but that, in abnormal circumstances (e.g., in the case of a finger amputee), can be brought about by a state of one's animal spirits which is itself normally brought about by such a hammering.

54. As in the case of visual sensation one takes blue to be a feature of a material thing, so in the case of the hammered finger one takes a pain of that kind to be a feature of the finger. Pain-as-feature-of-finger would be the content of a confused belief. As in the case of color, the feeling itself could be said to be confused (in a derivative sense) by virtue of the fact that people have a natural tendency to be confused *about* it. But might there not be a deeper sense in which the feeling is *intrinsically* a confused idea? If, as in the case of color, we were to assimilate the 'in-ness' of pain in the feeling with the 'in-ness' of *Two* in a conceiving, and if we were to assimilate the sense in which pain 'represents' the bodily state with which it is correlated to the sense in which a conceiving 'represents' (i.e., 'intends') that which has objective being in it, we would have the tiglon (or liger) notion of a certain complex bodily state (the bodily correlate or pain) as having objective reality in the feeling. The objective reality of the feeling could be described both as *pain* and as *complex bodily state*.

55. There is, I suppose, a use for the form of words 'pain is really a com-

---

[20] See the passage quoted in paragraph 28 above.

plex bodily state', in which it stands for a coherent idea. But the implications of the above conceptual tangle are paradoxical in the extreme. For it has built into it the notion that the *nature* pain$_{30}$, which is 'in' my feeling, is identical with the *nature* bodily-state$_{53}$ which is also 'in' this feeling. An *identity* of natures is, of course, no mere 'correlation'.

56. Shall we say that *qua* pain$_{30}$ the nature is 'confused', whereas *qua* bodily-state$_{53}$ is not? How do *natures* become confused? One gropes for an answer. One comes up with something like this. Consider a conceiving which is 'of a bachelor', and a conceiving which is 'of an unmarried adult male human'. One is tempted to say that there is a legitimate sense in which the same nature is objectively present in the two conceivings. Yet is there not the following difference? Can we not suppose that in the second case the articulation of the conceiving as mental state, i.e., its form,[21] is (more) adequate to the articulation of the nature that is its objective reality than is true in the first case?

57. Perhaps, in the first instance, a confused (*con-fusa*: fused together) idea is one that stands to a clear and distinct idea as a conceiving of a bachelor stands to a conceiving of an unmarried adult male human. Certainly clarity and distinctness is connected by Cartesians with definability.

58. Now the touch of nutmeg. We elaborate this analogy by drawing the following distinction. An idea is *non-essentially confused*, if it could be replaced, in the mind that has it, by an idea that stands to it as an idea of an unmarried adult male human stands to an idea of a bachelor. If ideas were linguistic entities, we would speak of replacing *definienda* by *definientia*. Let us add this to our analogy.

59. It now occurs to us that since, for humans at least, all definitions must involve a finite number of steps, the above suggestion has as a consequence that a human idea which contains a nature of *infinite* complexity would be *essentially* confused—though its counterpart in the mind of God would, of course, be ideally clear and distinct.

60. Since we must shortly move across the channel, there is no time to do more than throw out some hints as to how bridges might be built from the above analysis to the philosophies of Leibniz and Spinoza.

61. Thus if we add to the above the idea that the nature of an individual must be infinitely complex, since it must distinguish that individual from every other *possible* individual, we would have the Leibnizian thesis that an adequately individuating idea of a given individual must be infinitely complex, so that only God could have a clear and distinct *adequately* indi-

---

[21] In the sense of Definition II quoted in the opening paragraph of this essay.

viduating idea of that individual. We humans could have *adequately* individuating ideas of individuals—but they would be *essentially* confused. Indeed, according to Leibniz, our *petites perceptions* are exactly such essentially confused ideas. On the other hand, humans can have clear and distinct ideas pertaining to individuals, but they would pick them out (successfully, *for practical purposes*) by means of generalities that hold of an infinite number of possible individuals, and hence are not *adequately* individuating ideas. Our *petites perceptions* of Adam are *adequately* individuating but *essentially* confused. Our clear and distinct idea of Adam is really the general idea of *an Adam*, and does not adequately individuate.[22]

62. Again, to point the discussion toward Spinoza, if the nature of any modification of any finite mode involves the nature of every other modification of every other finite mode (the whole face of the universe), then every human idea of that modification which does not pick it out in terms of common notions, but which contains all the content necessary to *understand* exactly *that* modification (why it exists, why it has the features it does) must be *essentially* confused. As in the case of Leibniz, these *essentially* confused ideas are the ideas of sense. The natures that are (objectively) in such confused ideas are the natures that are realized *formaliter* by states of the brain. But these natures essentially involve the natures of all other modifications of all other finite modes. If *every* such nature involves *every other* such nature, are they not all the same? One is tempted to reply that each such nature involves every other such nature 'from a point of view'. But *this* profound kinship between Leibniz and Spinoza must be left unexplored.[23]

Part Two

VII

63. The presence of traditional categories, as reshaped by Descartes, in British philosophy, and it is pervasive, has been less clearly discerned, particularly by British historians and commentators, than in the case of Continental philosophy. I shall have almost nothing to say about Locke, though many of the points I shall make in connection with Berkeley are of equal relevance to Locke's *Essay*. No one would be surprised to find traces

---

[22] The points made in this paragraph are spelled out in my essay, "Meditations Leibnitziennes," *American Philosophical Quarterly* 2 (1965):105-18, (reprinted as chapter 6 in *Philosophical Perspectives* (Springfield, IL.: C. C. Thomas, 1968) [thereafter reprinted in *Philosophical Perspectives: History of Philosophy* (Ridgeview Publishing Co.)].

[23] The essay referred to in the previous note explores certain themes that are common to Leibniz and Spinoza by constructing a fictitious Leibnoza.

of the most divergent frameworks in Locke's amiable syncretism. Berkeley and Hume, on the other hand, seem to be, as they conceived themselves to be, veritable paradigms of radical originality, illuminating the murky philosophical scene like flashes of lightning and capable of being understood apart from carefully articulated traditions (as even that kindred spirit Descartes was not) as though they had sprung from the Modern Spirit like Minerva (as yet un-owled) from the head of Zeus.

64. But before looking in detail at Berkeley's theory of 'Ideas', it is important to take advantage of hindsight and draw some distinctions that are clearly required by an adequate phenomenology of perception, and that were seen as through a glass darkly in seventeenth- and eighteenth-century philosophy. The history of philosophy is appropriately rewritten by each generation, not because they have better historical methods, but because philosophy itself has made available not only finer distinctions but finer distinctions between distinctions. We can understand Plato better than Plato understood himself not primarily because we see things that Plato did not see but because we see more complicated patterns of sameness and difference in the things he saw.

65. Moving, as sooner or later must be done, to the proper (and common)[24] sensibles and constructing the concept of a 'basic' perceptual experience as an analytic tool, let us take as our paradigm an ostensible seeing of an object *over there* that is red and triangular on the facing surface. By an *ostensible* seeing of an object let us understand an experience that would be a seeing of such an object, if it were both true,[25] that there is an object *over there* that is red and triangular on the facing surface, and that the experience had the right causal connections, i.e., the object is appropriately responsible for the occurrence of the experience.

66. As capable of truth, an ostensible seeing belongs to the conceptual order. Appropriately characterized in semantic terms, it is analogous to a linguistic episode. *Not*, however, to a *sentential* occurrence, thus

> There is a cube of pink over there which faces me cornerwise

or

> That, over there, is a cube of pink which faces me cornerwise

---

[24] In this essay I shall so use the expression 'proper sensibles' that shape as well as color is a 'sensible' proper to vision.

[25] It is customary to use the term 'veridical', a fact that reflects the insight, not always fully appreciated, that ostensible seeings do not have explicit propositional form. Since, however, as we shall see, ostensible seeings have propositional correlates, the necessary adjustments are unproblematic.

but, rather,

> That cube of pink over there facing me cornerwise ...

where the dots indicate the place for explicit predication, e.g., 'is made of ice'.

67. One might put this by saying that what is taken by a perceptual taking is an *object*, rather than a *state of affairs*. Yet the 'object' is not *simply* an object as contrasted with a state of affairs, for it implicitly *contains* a state of affairs much as

> That cube of pink over there ...

'implicitly contains'

> That over there is a cube of pink.

68. This portmanteau ability of terms to encapsulate predications is no mere device of economy. For in perceptual contexts, the subject term (which refers to the perceptual object) is not only a subject of predication but also, *as term*, a perceptual *response*. And to refer to an object, it must be not only a *response* but a response to a (correctly or incorrectly) identified object. And it is, of course, the predication contained *in* the subject term that carries the criteria of identification.

69. Failure to appreciate this fact has led to the incoherent notion of a purely demonstrative reference, a pure 'this', everything else falling into an explicitly predicative position, thus:

> *This* is a cube of pink and is over there and faces me cornerwise.

It has also generated the mistaken idea that a perceptual taking is a 'judgment', a believing *that* something is the case. Thus (relaxing, for the moment, our limitation to the proper sensibles), taking there to be a cat on the roof would have the form

> *That* is a cat and it is on the roof

whereas, according to the position sketched above, it actually has the form

That cat on the roof ... .

70. Roughly, what is *taken* is what is packed into the *subject term*. If we regiment the concept of *belief* for perceptual contexts, we should say that perceptual taking is a form of 'occurrent' believing *in* rather than believing *that*. The distinction would be an important one, even if perceptual takings always occurred (as they do not) as *constituents* of believings *that*, e.g.,

That cat on the roof is hunting for birds.

71. Perceptual beliefs have been characterized as examples of 'thinking without question' that something is the case, and as 'snap judgments'. But the psychological distinction between judgments that do or do not answer a prior question, or answer it without a pause for reflection, misses the point, which is that the distinction between what is 'taken for granted' and what is 'up for grabs' in a given statement is embodied in grammatical structure.

That cat on the roof is φ

takes for granted, that is, in one sense of the term, presupposes, that there is a cat on a certain roof and asserts that it is φ. Of course, the statement may have been preceded by the dialogue (or monologue)

What is that over there (in the trees)? A roof.
What is that on the roof? A cat.
What is that cat on that roof doing?. ...

But, of course, it *need* not—in which case it can be said to be an *original* as contrasted with a *derived* presupposition.

72. Perceptual presuppositions or takings can be either original or derived. Observation, i.e., looking with questions in mind, as contrasted with merely happening to look in a certain direction, generates derived presuppositions. But looking with questions in mind itself requires a subject term that 'contains' a predication that is not itself in question, thus,

What is that over there *in the trees*?
A roof.

73. Philosophers have searched for basic perceptual takings. One way of describing them has been to say that they are takings that do not presuppose anything that is vulnerable to certain kinds of challenge.

> That over there in the trees is a roof.
> But are those things over there trees?

The term 'tree' carries with it a rich cluster of implications. Trees are richly endowed with unperceived aspects, thus opposite sides, wooden insides, not to mention capacities, propensities, indeed, a wide variety of causal properties that specify the results of hypothetical transactions with other objects, including perceivers. We see trees, but *of* trees we do not see their opposite sides or their insides or their causal properties. Yet in perceptually taking a *tree*, we are *ipso facto* taking something having an opposite side with *some* kind of bark and branches, an inside of *some* kind of wood, and endowed with *some* form of the causal properties characteristic of trees. Thus the sortal concept involved in the perceptual taking of an object carries with it generic or specific implications concerning *that of the object* which is not perceived.

74. In a limiting case, the sortal is simply *physical object*, and the implications are of the categorial character explored by Kant. In other words, the more we press the question 'But do we see *that* feature of the object?', (a) the more what we see *of* the object tends to be limited to occurrent proper sensibles, and (b) the more the sortal in terms of which the object is identified approximates the concept of an 'object in general'.

75. A 'basic' perceptual taking, then, is a taking that is minimal in two respects: (a) it is minimal in that it is restricted to features that are proper sensibles; (b) it has minimal implications concerning what is not seen *of* the object. It is the first respect that has tended to occupy the center of the stage. Thus the concept of pure occurrent sensible qualities and relations has been thought to define the 'content' of minimal perceptual takings.

76. But, as emphasized above, to eliminate *specific* implications concerning what is not perceived *of* an object need not (and, indeed, cannot) be to eliminate *generic* or *categorial* implications. This, of course, was Kant's brilliant insight. Thus, the perceptual taking

> This now occurring yellow flash over there

where 'flash' does not carry with it the specific sortal 'of lightning', has no *specific* implications concerning future developments, and is minimal in both the above respects. Even so, it implies that *something* has happened *before now* and that *something* will happen *after now*, in places other than *there*. Indeed, if Kant is right, it implies that the flash belongs to a world of changing and interacting things, a spatial-temporal-causal system.

77. In the absence of Kant's insight, the categorial sortal (physical) object (or event), which remains after all the above pruning, is treated as though it were the mere notion of a *something* (I know not what?), or, as I shall put it, an *item*, that has sensible 'qualities'.[26] Thus the idea that perceptual takings can be appropriately *minimal* and yet carry rich categorial commitments was lost to the empiricist tradition.

78. In other words, though it is obvious that a *quality* is always a quality of a thing, a *relation*, a relation between things, and a *manner*, a manner of what a thing does, the temptation to suppose that to minimize the *specific* implications of basic perceptual takings is to minimize their implications *simpliciter* proved well nigh irresistible. After all, *being a quality of a thing* is not itself a perceptible characteristic, nor is *having some causal property or other*, let alone *having the causal properties characteristic of some sort of thing*.

79. With these reflections in mind, let us contrive a minimal perceptual taking, the concept of which will help illuminate the internal structure of Berkeley's 'ideas'. We begin with a reasonably sound example of a minimal perceptual taking, thus

> This red and triangular on the facing side physical object over there....

We then, ostensibly continuing to minimalize in the same manner, cut it down to

> This red and triangular surface perpendicular to my line of sight ...

and continuing to cut, eliminating everything smacking of perspectives in three-dimensional physical space, and of surfaces as surfaces of physical objects,

> This triangular expanse of red ...

---

[26] Even the notion that it 'has' sensible qualities, or even that it *is*, for example, red, was watered down to the notion that it somehow 'consists' of sensible qualities. That this does violence to the very category of *quality* and makes nonsense of *relations* is a familiar story.

which we finally telescope into

> This red and triangular item ...

or

> This red triangle ... .

80. We are now *almost* in a position to take into account a radically different dimension of perceptual taking. Before doing so, however, we must pick up a thread that was laid aside at the beginning of the above analysis. The perceptual taking expressed by

> That cat over there ...

was characterized as a perceptual taking *of a cat*. This classifies the taking by specifying one constituent of its conceptual content, i.e., as

> (demonstrative) *cat*

rather than, for example,

> (demonstrative) *dog*.

The phrase 'of a cat' can be so used, of course, that a perceptual taking can be the taking of a cat, even though no cat is there to be taken. In this sense, 'of a cat' serves to classify a taking without commitment to its success in either its referential or (implicitly) predicative dimensions.

81. Again, the above perceptual taking is, in an obvious sense, a perceptual awareness of something *as a cat*. The 'as a cat' locution simply formulates in the material mode of speech the conceptual-grammatical point that the referring expression

> That cat over there ...

is a transformation, appropriate to perceptual contexts, of an expression in which 'a cat' occurs as an explicitly predicative expression, thus,

> That over there is a cat.

82. The perceptual taking can be a *mis*taking, not only because there is no appropriately located cat, but, more radically (as in the case of hallucination), because there is no object *over there* that might be a cat. If the taking successfully picks out such an object, then, even if the object is not in fact a cat, the taking has a limited referential success. That it can succeed to this limited extent is, in our example, a function of the identifying criteria other than 'cat' that are contained in the referring expression. Thus 'that (object which could be a cat) over there' where 'over there' carries (by virtue of the context) information of the form 'in direction D'.[27]

83. The above is intended to explicate the idea that our contrived taking is an awareness *of something as a red triangle* and, in the case of fully successful reference, an awareness of a red triangle as a red triangle. But can the reference involved in such a minimal perceptual taking fail? Can there fail to be an object? Can the object fail to be a red triangle? These obviously relevant questions must be left at the margin. An attempt to answer them would take us too far into a systematic theory of perception proper, and away from our historical concerns.[28]

VIII

84. I have been constructing a frame of reference in terms of which to account for the idea that basic perceptual experiences are, for example, of something *as a red triangle*, and, indeed, *of a red triangle as a red triangle*. This frame of reference has taken as its point of departure the conceptual character of perceptual takings, i.e., that character by virtue of which a perceptual taking of a red triangle is analogous to a candid tokening, in perceptual contexts, of the referring expression

---

[27] Even if the example were '*this* cat', it could have limited referential success by virtue of the fact that a pure demonstrative on the surface, e.g., 'this' in 'this is a cat', is a transformation of 'this' + [criterion], where the criterion is contextually supplied.

[28] I have argued in an unpublished [later published, *GEC* (92)] paper, "Givenness and Explanatory Coherence," that the referential aspect of a perceptual taking is best construed as a reference to the sensory aspect of the taking. Thus, in terms of our contrived example, the reference of

This red triangle

would be to a sensing of a red triangle. Since the latter is, of course, *not* a red triangle, the reference, thus construed, involves a *miscategorizing*, and can be characterized as a 'successful' reference to the sensing only in a dramatically extended sense of the 'limited success of a reference' explored in paragraph 82 above.

This red triangle.

It must now be noted that a perceptual taking is not an *exclusively* conceptual episode. The point is a crucial one for a full understanding of the problem that we were helping Descartes wrestle with in the first part of this paper.

85. In its conceptual aspect, a minimal perceptual taking is *of a red triangle as such* in a sense analogous to that in which an appropriate tokening of the expression 'this red triangle' is a demonstrative reference to a red triangle as such.[29] To characterize it as an 'ostensible' reference is to classify it functionally as a demonstrative singular term. To characterize it as a reference *to a red triangle as such* is to classify it as including a sortal that plays the same inferential and non-inferential roles as does 'triangle' in our language, which sortal is modified by an adjective which plays the same inferential and non-inferential roles as does 'red' in our language. Thus an appropriate tokening by a Frenchman of

Ce triangle rouge-ci

would also be a demonstrative reference *to a red triangle as a red triangle*.

86. The important point is that the semantic classification of linguistic items is not only functional classification but functional classification that, at its core,[30] is a matter of how the expression functions in inferences. Thus to say that an utterance by Jones of a certain term *refers to a red triangle as such* is to classify the utterance in a way that attributes to a knowledgeable user propensities to say such things as

So, it is not green.
So, it has three sides.

---

[29] Where failure of reference is a possibility, we should gloss 'reference' as 'ostensible reference'.

[30] The following remarks stress what I have called 'same level' inference patterns. The dimension of linguistic functioning that I have called 'language-entry transition'—thus, 'This red triangle' as a response to red and triangular objects in standard conditions—involves the validity of such inference patterns as

Jones candidly uttered "This red triangle is ...," so, *ceteris paribus*, there is a red triangle in front of him.
There is a red triangle in standard conditions in front of Jones' open sightful eyes, so, *ceteris paribus*, he has a propensity to say, "This red triangle is ...".

Etc.[31]

87. Thus, by analogy, the core of the criteria in terms of which we classify a minimal perceptual taking as one of the *of a red triangle as a red triangle kind*[32] is constituted by the inference patterns appropriate to the concepts *red, triangle*, and, last but not least, *this*.

88. I have implied that minimal perceptual takings also have a non-conceptual aspect, the understanding of which is essential to the resolution of Descartes' problem. The modifying clause is the heart of the matter, for that perceptual takings have non-conceptual aspects is vague enough to be non-controversial. Thus it is reasonable to suppose that a taking which is of a red triangle as such has as proximate cause a bodily state that is brought about in standard conditions by the influence of an object that is red and triangular on the facing side, and in nonstandard conditions by other influences that may or may not involve external objects.[33]

89. The crucial step is that in which we think of the immediate cause[34] of the conceptual aspect of a perceptual taking as having an occurrent character that consists in its *somehow* exemplifying the perceptible qualities and relations of physical objects,[35] where the 'somehow' carries with it the rider 'other than by being a conceiving of an item exemplifying such qualities and relations'.

90. For, as I have argued on a number of occasions, the perceptual experience that we have been characterizing as a taking of a red triangle as such and that, therefore, involves a conceiving of a red triangle (indeed, a conceptual reference to a red triangle) also involves the presence of redness and triangularity in a manner other than mere conception. If we say that a

---

[31] That the cluster of inferences by virtue of which an expression refers to a red triangle as such (or a bachelor as such) are open-textured and variable, and need only have a family resemblance from context to context, is the truth contained in Quine's attack on the analytic-synthetic distinction. My central concern over the years in stressing *material* rule of inference has been *not* to deny the point Quine is making—indeed, to a behavioristically oriented anti-Platonist, the denial would be foolish—but rather to insist that inference patterns other than those formulated by logical truths *are essential to meaning and reference*. That these extra-logical inference patterns do not neatly divide into 'explicit' and 'implicit' definitions, and that they trail off into contingent generalizations, are theses that have emotional charge only for those who are still fighting the battle of the Museum.

[32] In general to specify the 'content' of a conceptual episode is to classify it in terms of the inference patterns appropriate to the concepts involved.

[33] This is as far as Smart's topic-neutral approach gets one.

[34] To refer to something as 'the' cause is, of course, to isolate it from propitious circumstances, in this case, for example, the presence (or absence) of a certain mental 'set'.

[35] These qualities and relations are to be construed in what are often called 'naively realistic' terms. Thus physical objects are literally colored in the aesthetically interesting sense of color—as contrasted with merely having causal powers with respect to color experiences, Locke's 'secondary qualities'.

red triangle has being-for-sense in the experience as well as being-as-*conceptum*, we establish direct contact with Descartes' puzzle.

91. But the Cartesian, with his sharp dualism of mind and matter, is disposed to think of the being-for-sense of a case of red as equivalent to a modification of the *mind* being a case of red.[36]

92. If, now, we bear in mind that redness like triangularity is initially tied to the category of physical objects, we could say that for a case of red to have being-for-sense in a state of a perceiver (or of his sensorium) is neither for that state to be red as physical objects are red, nor for it to be red as *conceivings* that intend a case of red are red. The state in question (let us call it s) is properly characterized not by

   s is a case of red

nor by

   s is [a case of red]

but, as adumbrated above in paragraph 36,

   s is {a case of red}, or s is {a red item}

where to be {a red item} is to be a state that has a character *analogous*[37] to the physical redness of a facing surface.

93. Thus s, which we can now call a sensation, can be {a blue item} without being either a case of blue or [a blue item]. If this seems like multiplying distinctions *praeter necessitatem*, the proper reply is that exactly these distinctions are necessary. For it enables us to see that s, which is {a blue item} without being blue, might also be {a triangular item} without being triangular, and yet without being merely [a triangular item], i.e., a triangular item that has being-as-*conceptum*.

94. If the minimal perceptual experience, the conceptual aspect of which was characterized above as a perceptual taking *of a red triangle as a red triangle* and, hence, as of the [this red triangle] kind also has an aspect in which it is of the {a red triangle} kind, i.e., of the {a red and triangular

---

[36] The Cartesian would have been well advised either to think of the 'mind' as consisting of a 'sensorium' as well as a faculty of conceptual thinking, or to stick, at least initially, with the Aristotelian conception of a person as a substance having faculties ranging from 'physical' to 'intellectual', one of which would be the ability to sense.

[37] Thus, for example, a state that is {a uniform case of red} cannot also be {a uniform case of blue}.

item} kind, then color and shape each enter into the experience in the same two ways, and the problem of getting them together would disappear.

95. In other words, what I have so far referred to as *the* explication of the perceptual taking of a red triangle, namely its construal as a believing *in* a red triangle, is but one aspect of a more complex state that also includes a *sensing* of a red triangle, i.e., a state that is of the {a red triangle} kind. It is this more complex state, about the structure of which far more needs to be said than is possible on the present occasion, that is properly described as the state of ostensibly seeing (or seeming to see) a red triangle *as* a red triangle.

96. We are now in a position to comment on the fact that when, in the *Meditations*, Descartes attempts to specify exactly what he has in mind by 'sensation', he writes,

> Finally, I am the same who feels, that is to say, who perceives certain things as by the organs of sense, since in truth I see light, I hear noise, I feel heat. But it will be said that these phenomena are false and that I am dreaming. Let it be so; still it is at least quite certain that it seems to me that I see light, that I hear noise and that I feel heat. That cannot be false; properly speaking it is what in me is called feeling [sentire]; and used in this precise sense that is no other thing than thinking.[38]

97. A number of things should be noted about this passage. (1) It begins the *equation* of sensing with *seeming to see* (*hear*, etc.) which has become endemic in Anglo-American theories of perception. Since *seeming to see* does, indeed, have a conceptual *aspect*, the interpretation of sensing, thus construed, as a mode of 'thinking' is not completely wrongheaded. (2) Descartes does not explicitly include shape in his examples of what is sensed, although it is surely the case that we can seem to see a shape as we can seem to see 'a light'. The pain model (which is lurking near warmth) is still exerting its influence.[39] (3) The passage collapses into one supposedly homogeneous state—a sensation—items that, correctly understood, are distinguishable aspects (one conceptual, a believing *in*; one non-conceptual, the sensation proper) of a seeming to see.

98. Before advancing to Berkeley, we should remind ourselves that, like any other experience, the experience of seeming to see a red triangle as a red triangle does not wear its analysis on its sleeve. The analysis requires a painstaking philosophical dialectic that touches on most of the sensitive issues in ontology and the philosophy of mind. Solutions can be quick and

---

[38] HR, 1:153.
[39] One cannot help but remember, in this connection, Berkeley's confusion between the idea that a feeling of intense heat is a painful feeling, and the idea that it is a feeling of pain.

obvious—arrived at almost by 'scrutiny'—only because one begins with so much inherited dialectic that there is room for only one alternative which is either not absurd or the absurdity of which can be parsed as the paradoxical wisdom of the learned.[40]

99. Berkeley, as is well known, formulates the 'act-object' account of perceiving in the *Three Dialogues between Hylas and Philonous*, only to reject it. His explicit reason for rejecting it is a bad one,[41] turning as it does on an equation of 'act' with 'deed'. He points out that what we *do* in perception is *look*. On looking we see, but in seeing we are passive. We can choose where to look but not what to see.

100. Berkeley's real reason for rejecting the act-object account is to be found in the principle that the *esse* of what is perceived is *percipi*, i.e., to be sensed. The act-object metaphor implies that what is perceived could exist without being perceived, and hence implies, in traditional terms, a real distinction between perceiving and its object. Could there, however, be a perceiving that lacked an object? Is it a contingent fact that perceivings only come into being when there is an appropriate object to which it can be related? Does it even make sense to suppose a perceiving without a something perceived? Perhaps there could be a modification of the mind that had no 'object', but that *would* be a perceiving, *if* there were something appropriately related to it. One thinks: Why not? A seeming to see would be a seeing only if there was something appropriately related to it. Indeed, but is there not a sense in which even a *mere* seeming to see has an 'object'? And is not this sense of 'have an object' the basic sense? In *this* sense there could no more be a perceiving without an 'object', i.e., *something perceived* than there could be a believing without an 'object', i.e., *something believed*. Surely, it is tempting to conclude, there is at most a distinction of reason between perceiving and what strictly speaking is perceived.

101. But what is perceived in this strict or minimal sense is, for example, a red triangle.[42] Hence in this case a red triangle is the 'object' of perception. But, then, there is only a distinction of reason between the perceiving of 'the' red triangle and 'the' red triangle perceived. The situation, however, is symmetrical. There is a red triangle? It is perceived.[43]

102. It surely does not distort the situation too much to say that for Berkeley a perceiving of a red triangle does not have the form

---

[40] Although, like Berkeley, one makes a brave effort to speak with the vulgar.
[41] *A New Theory of Vision and Other Select Philosophical Writings*, ed. by A. D. Lindsay, (London: J. M. Dent, 1938), pp. 226 ff.
[42] For a less minimal sense in which a red triangle can be an object of perception for Berkeley, see below, paragraph 107.
[43] See previous footnote.

(perceiving) R (a red triangle)

but rather

   (of a red triangle) perceiving,

i.e., to interpret him as holding that for a perceiving to be 'of a red triangle' is for it to be a perceiving of a certain sort.

103.   Now a *conceiving* of an angel can occur without the actual existence of a certain angel of which it is the conceiving, or even of any angels at all. To be a conceiving of an angel as such is to be a conceiving of a certain kind, for example, the conceiving that is a constituent of a mental act of the

   [an angel was dancing on the point of a pin one day]

kind.

104.   The same is clearly true where the conceiving of an angel is the conceiving of a specific kind of angel, as in a thought of the kind,

   [a rosy cheeked, blond, blue-eyed angel was dancing on the point of a pin one day].

No matter how specific we make the content of the conceiving, the conceiving can occur without the extra-conceptual existence of the object conceived. And, of course, no matter how specific the content of the conceiving of an angel, the conceiving never becomes an angel.

105.   Now Berkeley clearly insists that that which is perceived is always of an absolutely specific character.[44] Suppose now, two perceptions each of which is *of* something red_{29} and $triangular_{30}$. They are perceptions 'of the same'. Does it follow that there is a 'same something' of which they are perceptions? *Only*, of course, in the sense that they belong to the same kind, i.e., are two perceptions each of which is *of* something red_{29} and $triangular_{30}$.

106.   But is there not another sense in which these two perceptions can be perceptions of the same *thing* (or, for that matter of different *things*)? Of

---

[44] Both with respect to perceptible qualities and, presumably, though the point is for the most part implicit, perceptible relations to other perceived items.

course. If we construe *things* as patterns of actual and obtainable perceivings, two perceivings can, be 'of exactly the same' (i.e., belong to the same *kind*) without being perceptions that are *of the same thing* in the sense of being among its constituents.

107.   It is important, therefore, to see that Berkeley so uses the word 'particular' that to say of a perception that it is of a *particular* triangle is simply to say that its content is, as *we* would put it, completely *determinate*, i.e., to use the more traditional term, completely *specific*. Thus there can in Berkeley's sense be a perception of a particular triangle without there being what we would call a particular triangle, i.e., an individuated triangular item. What corresponds to the latter in Berkeley's ontology is, for example, a triangle on a blackboard—an appropriate pattern of actual and obtainable perceivings, some of which would, of course, *in the internal or classificatory sense* be perceivings of something determinately triangular. It is, of course, such patterns of perceivings that are *individuated*, ultimately by virtue of the individuation of the minds in which they occur.

108.   In short there can be a perception of a particular triangle without there being a particular (i.e., individual) triangle of which the perception is a perception. The perception can, even in the internal sense, be said to be 'of an individual', but only if all implications pertaining to *individuation* have been removed from 'individual', leaving only the consideration that the perception is not of the abstraction triangularity$_{30}$, but of an *item* (a *something*) which is triangular$_{30}$.

109.   The rationale of Berkeley's insistence that perceptions are in the above sense particular (i.e., specific or determinate) can best be grasped by laying aside geometrical examples, and considering that strand of his theory of ideas which directly involves the assimilation of ideas to feelings of pain. A pain simply *is* a feeling of pain. (There was a pain? It was felt.) In the case of shape, we can distinguish between an *individual triangular object* (e.g., the triangle on the blackboard) and an *individual perception of a triangle*. As was noted above, an individual perception of a triangle need not be a perception of (i.e., a constituent of) an individual triangular object. On the other hand, *all there is to the individuality of a pain is the individuality of a feeling of pain.*[45] Thus we can mobilize the classical principle that all individuals are completely specific (most determinate) in character to argue,

---

[45] A twentieth-century Berkeleian might demur by arguing that it does make sense to say, "That is the same pain again," where this does not simply mean the same kind of pain. In this usage the pain would be an individual in the sense in which the triangle on the blackboard is an individual. But to attribute this idea to Berkeley himself would surely be an anachronism.

All individual pains are determinate with respect to pain.
Individual pains are individual feelings of pain.
Therefore, individual feelings of pain are determinate with respect to pain, i.e., are feelings *of* determinate pain.

110. If a case of color[46] is a perception of color as a pain is a feeling of pain, then, by parity of reasoning, a perception of color is always a perception of a determinate color.

111. The assimilation of color to pain would amount, in terms of the distinctions drawn at the beginning of this section, to the equation of

α is an {a red item} perception

with

α is a red item,

an equation he would never have considered in the case of shape. Thus the *direct* use of the above pattern of argument in connection with perceptions of shape would have involved the puzzling premise

a (case of) shape is a perception of shape.

Sensing this, Berkeley relies on the identity in ontological status of the color and the shape in a perception of a shaped color to extend his conclusion to shape by analogy.

112. Of course, Berkeley *could* have recognized that a perception can be *of a red item* without being a red item, i.e., can be an {a red item} perception without being red, and argued from the premise that 'everything which exists is particular' that an individual perception cannot be *of a red item* unless it has some determinate form of the property of being *of a red item*. But then it would remain to be shown why being *of a red$_{29}$ item* is a determinate form of being *of a red item*.

113. As a matter of fact, however, it is built into the explanatory framework of sensations that the structure of determinates and determinables pertaining to the perceptually distinguishable features of physical objects is reflected in the predicates of sensation. Thus the *determinable*

---

[46] I use 'a case of color' instead of 'a color' because the latter normally refers to shades of color.

predicate 'red', which applies to physical objects, has as its counterpart the *determinable* sensation predicate 'of a red item'—in our notation '{a red item}'—just as the *determinate* physical object predicate 'red$_{29}$' has the *determinate* counterpart '{a red$_{29}$ item}'. And as a physical object cannot be red without being some determinate shade of red, e.g., red$_{29}$, so a sensation cannot be {a red item} without being, e.g., {a red$_{29}$ item}.[47]

114.   Thus, even if Berkeley had not confused between

   α is an {a red item} perception
and
   α is a red item,

he could legitimately have argued that α cannot be an {a red item} perception without being *of* a determinately red item, thus an {a red$_{29}$ item} perception.

115.   But the case of shape was crucial. Berkeley clearly would not wish to say that a perception of a triangle is a triangle. Obviously not in the metaphysically interesting sense in which the surfaces of material objects (the "unthinking things" of the "Materialist") might be triangular. Nor, of course, does he think that a perception of a triangle can be a triangle in the sense in which, on his own positive view, the triangle on the blackboard[48] is a triangle. And failing to realize that it could be an {a triangular item} perception without being a triangular item, he, like Descartes, opts for the alternative that it [is] a triangular item, i.e., (equivalently) that it is an [a triangular item] perception. Like Descartes he assimilates the being-for-sense of a triangular item to the being-for-the-understanding of a triangular item.

> ... It may perhaps be objected, that if extension and figure exist only in the mind it follows that the mind is extended and figured, since extension is a mode or attribute which (to speak with the Schools) is predicated of the subject in which it exists. I answer, those qualities are in the mind only as they are perceived by it, that is, not by way of *mode* or *attribute*, but only by way of *idea*; and it no more follows that the soul or mind is extended because extension exists in it alone, than it does that it is red or blue, because these colors are on all hands acknowledged to exist in it, and nowhere else.[49]

---

[47] To use a simpler notation which establishes connection with the widespread (but contrived) usage in which one speaks of 'red sensations'—at the cost of obscuring the logical structure of sensation predicates—it cannot be {red} without being, e.g., {red$_{29}$}.

[48] In a less interesting sense an 'unthinking thing'.

[49] *A Treatise Concerning the Principles of Human Knowledge*, section XLIX. pp. 136-37 (hereafter cited as *Principles*).

116. Yet compared with Berkeley, Descartes was clear about the difference between being for sense and being for the understanding. Berkeley *blithely* puts all ideas, including sensations and images, in the understanding.[50] The inevitable result was to collapse the delicate unity of the being-for-the-understanding of *this red triangle* and the being-for-sense of a red triangle in an ostensible seeing of a red triangle, into the being-for-the-understanding of a determinately red and triangular item as such— without any of the signs of discomfort manifested by Descartes' appeal to naive childhood beliefs, *from childhood*.

IX

117. Now if one is aware of the relevant distinctions, he need find no immediate discomfort in the idea that the *conceptual* aspect of an ostensible seeing *of a red triangle as such* might have a *determinable* content. Why might it not involve generic concepts of *red* and *triangular*, and have as its content *this red and triangular item* without having this content in a *determinate* form, for example, *this red$_{29}$ and triangular$_{30}$ item*? After all, it might be argued, the content of a non-perceptual thought can be simply *an angel dancing on the point of a pin* as contrasted with, for example, *a blue-eyed, etc., seraph waltzing thus-and-so-ly on the point of a pin made of brass, etc.*

118. At this point a venerable ghost returns to haunt us. Must not an individual act of the understanding have a *determinate* character?—a vexing problem in classical philosophies of mind, as unavoidable as it was insoluble. Suppose there to be an act which is a thinking of a triangle, but not of a determinate sort of triangle. Would the act, exactly insofar as it is *of a triangle*, have a determinate character? Surely the character of an act that really exists must be determinate in all respects. Can being *of* something *generic*, thus being an [a triangular item...] be a *specific* feature of the total character of a mental act? If one thinks that the specific features of a mental act, α, must be, so to speak, 'qualities' that are quasi-perceptually discerned by the mind's eye, one will be puzzled. Finding no such specific features, one will be confronted by two alternatives: (a) Hold that acts of the understanding, while having a determinate character *in other respects*, need only, with respect to what they are *of*, have the character of *being of*

---

[50] See, for example, entries 280, 282, 286, 579, 587, and 878 in the *Philosophical Commentaries* in *The Works of George Berkeley*, vol. 1, ed. A. A. Luce and T. E. Jessop (London: Thomas Nelson, 1964).

it. From this point of view

   α [is] a triangle

could be true without, for example,

   α [is] a triangle$_{30}$

being true. Or, using intentional predicates instead of the intentional copula,

   α is an [a triangle] act

could be true even though no attempt was made to construe '[a triangle]' as somehow a determinate predicate, nor to argue that

   α is an [a triangle$_{30}$] act

must also be true, where '[a triangle$_{30}$]' is supposed to be a determinate predicate.[51] (b) Continue to insist, on general metaphysical grounds, that even with respect to what it is of, an act of the understanding *must* have a determinate character, and ostensibly *find* this character in the rich internal structure of minimal perceptual takings, and the imaginings that are their free-floating cousins.

119.   Of these two alternatives, it is fair to say Descartes and, in general, the Platonic tradition adopts the former. Berkeley, on the other hand, clearly opts for the latter. It is important, however, to see that in rejecting abstract general ideas, Berkeley is essentially following in Aristotelian footsteps.

X

120.   How, then, according to Berkeley, do we think of a triangle simply as such, if there is no such thing as a mental state that can be said to be *of a triangle as a triangle* without being *of some specific kind of triangle as of that specific kind*? The first step in the answer is the Aristotelian one that we apprehend the common (generic or specific) in a *phantasm*,

---

[51] We shall shortly see that it does not make sense to suppose that α might be both an [a triangle] act and an [a triangle$_{30}$] act—a fact that is only more neatly disguised by the use of the intentional copula.

i.e., a direct representation of an individual, the content of which is completely specific.[52] This approach, tidily carried out, requires a distinction between two kinds of mental states: (a) phantasms having determinate content; (b) acts of 'noticing', 'considering', and 'making use of' more of less generic features of that content.

121.   According to the type of view we are considering, in order for the understanding to be aware of something *as* generically a triangle, it must begin with a representation of a *determinate* kind of triangle *as a triangle of that determinate kind*, e.g., of a *triangular$_{30}$ item as triangular$_{30}$*. It can then consider the triangular$_{30}$ item in its generic character as triangular. For the contents of phantasms *have* generic features, even though these features cannot occur other than as features of more specific contents.[53]

122.   It is important to note that when Berkeley insists that all ideas are particular, he is *not* insisting that all ideas are 'particulars' in the contemporary sense of the term. He does, of course, think that ideas as modifications of mind are dependent individuals, individuated by the minds that have them, their place in the temporal order, and the sorts to which they belong. But the particularity he primarily has in mind concerns not the *individuation* of an idea but the absolute *determinateness* of its content, i.e., of the sort to which it belongs. Thus two ideas that are of a red$_{29}$ triangle$_{30}$ are in the relevant sense particular, not by virtue of the individuation by which they are two, but by virtue of the fact that their content is determinate. They are both of exactly the same determinate sort by virtue of the fact that each is *of a red$_{29}$ triangle$_{30}$*.

123.   Consider, now, two idea-occurrences, one of a red$_{29}$ triangle$_{30}$, the other of a red$_{29}$ triangle$_{15}$. They are, of course, not of the same determinate sort with respect to shape, but they are of the same generic sort, for each of them is *of* a triangle of *a* determinate sort. Either idea, then, can be the occasion on which one becomes aware of a triangle simply as a triangle. In the first case one begins, so to speak, by being aware of a triangle$_{30}$ as a triangle$_{30}$ and proceeds to 'notice' that generic feature of its content by

---

[52] By speaking of the representation as 'direct,' I mean that it does not have the form of a definite description, e.g., 'the tallest man in London'. It is a representation of a *this-such*, where, according to the Aristotelian, the *such* aspect is not an application of a general concept but the very source of general concepts. This aspect of the Aristotelian tradition is elaborated in chapter one of my *Science and Metaphysics*. It should be noted that Kant's concept of a perceptual intuition belongs directly in this tradition, though with distinctively Kantian variations. The concept of a perceptual taking as a believing *in* also belongs to this tradition. See also my essay "Kant's Transcendental Idealism," in the *Proceedings* of the 1974 Kant Congress held in Ottawa, Canada [*KTI*, in this volume].

[53] Compare the view of moderate realism, according to which individuals *in rerum natura* have generic features, though these features of individuals are not themselves *individuals* and cannot occur save as features of individuals that are completely specific in character.

virtue of which it is *of a triangle*. In the second case the point of departure is different (an awareness of a triangle$_{15}$ as a triangle$_{15}$), but here also the generic feature by virtue of which its content as a triangle-content is 'noticed'.

124. It is at this point that Berkeley makes the move that reveals the hollowness of his strategy. It is not, however, the silly move that is usually attributed to him: i.e., the view that a mental reference to items having a common character, determinable or determinate, consists in a certain 'use' of an item that actually has this character—for example, a determinately triangular item, say an equilateral triangle which item is *somehow* 'mind dependent'—to 'represent' all items that are, in some respect, of the same sort—thus, all equilateral triangles or all isosceles triangles or all triangles or even all shaped items. As has been repeatedly pointed out by Berkeley's critics, such an account would be obviously circular, presupposing an awareness of the item *as* an equilateral triangle, *as* an isosceles triangle, *as* a triangle, *as* having shape and hence, in the relevant sense, an awareness of common characters.

125. The crucial point is that for Berkeley an idea of an equilateral triangle is *not* simply a 'mind dependent' equilateral triangle—though, properly understood, it is that. It is an awareness of an equilateral triangle *as such*, a conflation of an equilateral triangle of which the *esse* is *being sensed* with a conceptual awareness of the form [this equilateral triangle]. Berkeley's problem is not that of constructing an awareness of sorts out of an awareness of 'mind dependent' entities having color and shape. Ideas are *ab initio* awareness of items *as determinately shaped and colored*. His problem was rather that of accounting for our awareness of *generic* sorts without acknowledging mental states that are merely of the generic as such.

126. Thus Berkeley *begins* with the assumption that we can be aware of a triangle$_{30}$ not only *as a triangle$_{30}$* but *as (generically) a triangle*.[54] He then takes it for granted that this provides the key to understanding how we can think of *any item* (or *all items*) of the same sort, determinable or determinate, as the item that is the content of a given idea-occasion. It enables us to understand how, given an idea of a triangle$_{30}$, we can think of all triangles$_{30}$, of all isosceles triangles (supposing triangularity$_{30}$ to be a determinate form of isosceles triangularity), and, even, of all triangles. Berkeley put this, of course, in terms of thinking of all *ideas* of the same sort (as the

---

[54] "... It must be acknowledged, that a man may consider a figure merely as triangular, without attending to the particular qualities of the angles or relations of the sides" (*Principles*, XVI. p. 104).

given idea-occasion),[55] but it must be remembered that the content of an idea is not really distinct from the idea-occasion of which it is the content. Counting contents is counting kinds; counting idea-occasions is counting individuals belonging to a kind. Two idea-occasions can be the same (in kind) without being the same *idea-occasion*.

127. In the example Berkeley offers to illustrate his theory of general ideas,[56] the structure of the argument is obscured. Using as an example of a particular idea, "a black line of an inch in length" drawn by a geometrician, presumably on a piece of paper, the *particularity* of the line, which consists in its *specific* character of being one inch in length (as contrasted, for example, with two inches in length), is not distinguished with the necessary care from its *individuality* as *this* black line, one inch in length, on *this* piece of paper. In his attempt to speak with the vulgar, Berkeley has blurred an essential distinction.

128. Once he returns to the language of the learned, Berkeley makes his point correctly:

> ... Thus, when I demonstrate any propositions concerning triangles, it is to be supposed that I have in view the universal idea of a triangle; which ought not to be understood as if I could frame an idea of a triangle which was neither equilateral, nor scalenon, nor equicrural. But only that the particular triangle I consider whether of this or that sort it matters not, doth equally stand for and represent all rectilinear triangles whatsoever, and is, in that sense, universal.
>
> XVI. *Objection.—Answer.* But here it will be demanded, *how we can know any proposition to be true of all particular triangles, except* we have first seen it *demonstrated of the abstract idea of a triangle* which equally agrees to all? For, because a property may be demonstrated to agree to some one particular triangle, it will not thence follow that it equally belongs to any other triangle, which in all respects is not the same with it. For example, having demonstrated that the three angles of an isosceles rectangular triangle are equal to two right ones, I cannot therefore conclude this affection agrees to all other triangles, which have neither a right angle, nor two equal sides. It seems therefore that to be certain this proposition is universally true, we must either make a particular demonstration for every particular triangle, which is impossible, or once for all demonstrate it of the *abstract idea of a triangle*, in which all the particulars do indifferently partake, and by which they are all equally represented. To which I make answer, that though the idea I have in view whilst I make the demonstration, be, for instance, that of an isosceles rectangular triangle, whose sides are of a determinate length, I may nevertheless be certain it extends to all other rectilinear triangles, of what sort or bigness soever.[57]

---

[55] "... An idea, which considered in itself is particular, becomes general by being made to represent or stand for all other particular ideas of the *same sort*" (Introduction to the *Principles*, XII. p. 100).
[56] Ibid.
[57] Ibid., XV-XVI, pp. 103-4.

It is surely clear that in this passage the term 'particular' means *absolutely specific or determinate*, rather than *individual*, and that when he writes that "[the demonstration] extends to all other rectilinear triangles, of whatever sort or bigness soever," the reference to "all other rectilinear triangles" is *directly* to all other *determinate sorts of triangle*, and only derivatively to all *individual* triangles of these sorts.

129.   The nagging question remains, however: How, on Berkeley's principles, can there be an act of the understanding that has as its content either

> Any (all) idea(s) of a triangle is an (are) idea(s) of an item which has the area = ½ bh

or

> Any (all) triangle(s) has (have) an area = ½ bh?

The point is a simple one. The 'grammatical' subject of such a propositional act is an act-element that corresponds to a *referring* expression of the form 'any φ' (or 'all φs') where 'φ' stands either for the generic character of being an occurrent idea of a triangle or the generic character of being a triangle-content. Is the feature by virtue of which this act-element has such a generic reference a determinate feature? The problem of the determinateness of acts of generic reference has simply been postponed.

130.   It is at this point that one can appreciate Hume's attempt to replace ostensible mental acts that refer to all ideas of the same *generic* sort by associative connections between determinate *ideas* and generic *words*, so that the only acts of the *understanding* involved in the awareness of the generic would be 'particular' idea-occasions, that is, idea-occasions with determinate content. Unfortunately, as should be obvious, the problem of accounting for mental reference to all items that are *generically* of the same sort is but a special case of the more general problem of accounting for mental reference to all φs, no matter how determinate φ may be. To explore the confusions that made it possible for Berkeley and, for that matter, Hume to suppose that they had clarified *this* aspect of the activity of the understanding will be the concluding topic of this essay.

131.   The sophisticated Aristotelians of the late scholastic period, with their keen sense of logical form,[58] were, of course, not unaware of this problem. As a result they were less strident than was Berkeley in what they had to say about those acts of the understanding that ostensibly have a

---

[58] Which soon disappeared, not to be recovered until the Kantian revolution.

merely generic character. They realized that even though, in their opinion, there might be good empiricist reasons for tying generic (not to mention analogical) intellectual references to features of the determinate contents of phantasms-occasions, this tie-in provides by itself no *explication* of the concept of general reference to all items of the same sort, whether generic or specific.

XI

132. A final sharpening of tools. If, as is reasonable, one takes it to be a *part* of the truth about generic or determinable characters that they are exclusive disjunctions of specific or determinate characters,[59] it would follow that one could not be aware of something as having a generic character without being *implicitly* aware of it as having one or other, though not more than one, of the determinate characters that belong to the appropriate family. By 'implicitly aware' I mean, for present purposes, aware as one is aware of a person's being unmarried by virtue of being aware that he is a bachelor.

133. Implicit awareness, of course, should not be construed in quasi-perceptual terms. But to take, as Berkeley did, as one's paradigm for being aware of something *as of a certain character*, the state of seeming to see (or imagining) a triangular item as such, enables the fact that the *non-conceptual* aspect of the state must be of a determinate character to mobilize the above partial truth about generic characters in a way that enriches the confusions involved in the concept of an idea.

134. Thus the fact that a mind in which there occurs a conceptual act, α, with a generic content,

    α is [this triangle]

is 'implicitly aware' of 'the' triangle *as either isosceles or scalene*, in that there is 'available' to that mind a further act that is [that isosceles or scalene triangle ...],[60] is bred to the fact that a sensation or image, s, can't be an {a triangle} state without being an {isosceles triangle} state or an {a scalene triangle} state and, in the last analysis, an {a triangle$_1$} state or an

---

[59] More accurately, that G-ness has the form (S_1 *or* S_2 *or* ... S_n)-ness, where '*or*' stands for exclusive disjunction, and 'G' and 'S_i' represent generic and specific predicates of the same family.
[60] Or, to climb down the ladder of determinates [this triangle$_1$ or triangle$_2$ ... or triangle$_{11}$ or ...].

{a triangle$_2$} state, and so on.[61] The result is the conviction that the awareness of a triangular item as such is always, at least in the first instance, an awareness of a *determinately* triangular item as such. For the fact that in its *sensory* aspect the seeming to see or imagining must be a sensation or image of a determinate triangle, that is, must be, for example, {a triangle$_{30}$}, leads, by a confusion of sensory of-ness with conceptual of-ness, to the conclusion that the seeming to see (or imagining) must be, at least in the first instance, an awareness of a triangle$_{30}$ *as a triangle$_{30}$*, which implies that in its conceptual aspect it is [this triangle$_{30}$].

135.   As I see it, then, one element involved in the mass of confusions that is the Berkeleian theory of ideas is the confusion between an awareness of a disjunction and a disjunction of awarenesses,[62] which leads to the notion that the awareness of a generically triangular item as generically triangular must be an awareness of a triangle of *one* of the disjunction of determinate sorts *as of that determinate sort*. The fact that an awareness of the generic is 'implicitly' an awareness of an exclusive disjunction of specifics, e.g., that the awareness of an item as generically triangular is 'implicitly' an awareness of an item *as either isosceles or scalene*, has been confused with the fact that a sensory state that has a generic sensory character, e.g., is of a triangular item, i.e., is {a triangular item}, must have one (and only one) of the specific characters falling under that genus, i.e., must be *either* {an isosceles triangle} or {a scalene triangle}.

XII

136.   One final ingredient of the witches' brew, certainly not the least interesting one, remains to be isolated. Notice that the *predicates* that apply to sensory states are constructed from expressions that, though they *contain* predicates, are actually *referring* expressions. Thus, the expression 'a triangle,' which occurs as a predicate in

This is a triangle

occurs as an indefinite referring expression in

---

[61] Notice that in classifying the *conceptual* states the 'or' occurs *inside* the brackets, whereas in classifying the *non-conceptual* states it occurs *outside* the braces.

[62] One only needs to take into account the fact that 'and' and 'or' are interchangeable in certain ordinary language contexts to understand the confusion involved in Locke's unhappy (but diagnostic) reference to "...the general idea of a triangle...[which] must be neither oblique nor rectangle, neither equilateral, equicrural, nor scalenon; but all and none of these at once" (*Essay*, IV, 7, 9).

A triangle is on the blackboard

and as a general referring expression in

A triangle is a relatively simple construction.

137.   Now a sensation of a triangle owes its classification as an *of a triangle* sensation—an {a triangle} sensation—to the fact that it is, according to the explanatory framework of sensations, of a kind normally brought about by the presence of *a triangle*, and that the conceptual space of its intrinsic attributes is analogous to that of the attributes of *a triangle*. (Note the indefinite references!)

138.   Furthermore, the conceptual aspect of a seeming to see, e.g., that by virtue of which it is an awareness *of a triangle as a triangle*, is its aspect as a [this triangle] awareness. It is a mental *reference* and though, correctly understood, it is a singular-demonstrative reference, it is not improper, provided one is careful, to characterize it informally as 'a reference to a triangle'. The indefinite article keeps the question 'reference to *which* triangle?' sufficiently at bay to make comfortable, even in this case, the material mode of speech use of the rubric 'reference to ...' to *classify* referential expressions and mental acts, rather than *to make references*.

139.   The phrase 'a triangle' as it occurs in the description of a seeming to see is thus available as a verbal bridge to the idea that the mental state in question *contains* a general reference to triangles. The verbal bridge is indeed a strong one, since both the conceptual and the sensory aspects of the seeming to see (or imagining) are described by the use of the referring expression 'a triangle'.

XIII

140.   With the addition of this final ingredient we can now understand how the confusing of the conceptual and the sensory aspects of a seeming to see generates the following properties of a Berkeleian 'idea'.

(1a) The idea is of a determinately triangular (e.g., triangular$_{30}$) item; it cannot be an {a triangular item} idea without being, e.g., an {a triangular$_{30}$ item} idea.

(1b) The idea is of a triangular$_{30}$ item *as such*; it is a [this triangular$_{30}$ item] idea.

(2a) The idea is of an item that is generically triangular by virtue of being of an item that is triangular in some specific way (e.g., triangular$_{30}$); the idea is an {a triangular item} idea because it is an {a triangular$_{30}$ item} idea.

(2b) The idea is of an item that is generically triangular *as such* by virtue of being of an item that is specifically triangular$_{30}$ as such; the idea is a [this triangular item] idea by virtue of being a [this triangular$_{30}$ item] idea.

Here we can put our finger on a key symptom of the confusion. For while being {a triangular$_{30}$ item} is, indeed, a determinate form of being {a triangular item}, the same is not true at the conceptual level, i.e., using the corresponding bracketed expressions. The latter are, indeed, interestingly related, but nothing that is [a triangular$_{30}$ item] can also be [a triangular item]—any more than a linguistic inscription can be a token of both 'a triangular$_{30}$ item' and 'a triangular item'.

141.   Notice that the confusion involves treating being aware *of a triangular$_{30}$ item as a triangular$_{30}$ item* as a species of being aware *of a triangular item as a triangular item*. For once one sees that this is not the case, one would have to fall back on the thesis that a mind which is aware *of a triangular$_{30}$ item as triangular$_{30}$* is only 'implicitly' aware *of a triangular item as triangular*, i.e., the thesis that a thought about a triangular$_{30}$ item as triangular$_{30}$[63] is appropriately picked up by, for example, a thought about a triangular item as triangular.[64]

142.   It is worth pausing to notice that the distinctions we have been drawing throw light on the internal structure of the Berkeleian (and Aristotelian) theory of geometrical knowledge. Thus, to continue,

(3a) The idea is of an item that is (generically triangular by virtue of being specifically triangular$_{30}$); it is an {a (triangular because triangular$_{30}$) item} idea.[65]

(3b) The idea is of an idea that is (generically triangular by virtue of being specifically triangular$_{30}$) *as being generically triangular because specifically triangular$_{30}$*; it is a [this (triangular because triangular$_{30}$) item] idea.

---

[63] Strictly, a thought of the [*this* triangular$_{30}$ item ...] kind.

[64] Thus, a thought of the [*that* triangular item is ...] kind, where the [*that*] component picks up the reference of the [*this*].

[65] Compare the physical object statement, "This is a (triangular because triangular$_{30}$) item"; it can be generated, by transformation, from "This item is triangular because it is triangular$_{30}$".

At this stage, the confusion injects an awareness of logical connections into ideas. Since, as has been emphasized, Berkeley's confusions are simply a special case of confusions endemic to the Aristotelian tradition, we have put our finger both on the source of the plausibility of theories of geometrical knowledge based on a concept of 'intuitive induction', and on the explanation of Berkeley's conviction that his account of geometrical knowledge was unproblematic.[66] Thus,

> (4a) The idea is of an item that is (equilateral because equiangular); it is an {an (equilateral because equiangular) item} idea.
> (4b) The idea is of an item that is (equilateral because equiangular) *as (equilateral because equiangular)*; it is a [this (equilateral because equiangular) item] idea.

143.   But we have not yet crossed the verbal bridge described at the beginning of this section. It takes us from (1b) above to

> (1c) The idea is a general reference to triangular$_{30}$ items as such; it is an [a (any, all) triangular$_{30}$ item(s) is (are) ...] idea.

and from (2b) to

> (2c) The idea is a general reference to generically triangular items as such; it is an [a (any, all) triangular item(s) is (are) ...] idea.

XIV

144.   To the extent that Berkeley saw, as through a glass darkly, that an awareness of a triangular$_{30}$ item as a triangular$_{30}$ item cannot be identical with an awareness of a triangular$_{30}$ item as triangular, or of a triangular item as triangular, he can be said to construe the latter awarenesses as somehow 'implicit' in the former, to take them as additional *aspects* of one and the same idea, aspects that can be brought to the center of the stage by such 'unproblematic' acts of the understanding as 'noticing', 'comparing' or 'considering'.

145.   It is at this point that the most sympathetic reader will find it

---

[66] Of course, Berkeley denies the 'extra-mental' existence of geometrical objects, but his theory of how we know necessary truths about geometrical objects, whatever their ontological status, is clearly in the Aristotelian tradition.

difficult to contain any longer the following objection: You have gone to great trouble to explain by a dialectical depth-analysis how Berkeley *might* have come to think that ideas themselves *contain* a general reference. But is it not a simple, unblinkable fact that according to Berkeley an idea becomes general *by being used to stand for all ideas of the same sort*? Does this not directly imply a distinction between the idea (which I grant to be an awareness of a φ item as φ) and the *reference* to a (any, all) φ item(s)? Surely it is gratuitous to attribute to Berkeley the view that an idea-occasion that is of a triangular$_{30}$ item as triangular$_{30}$ *contains* a general reference to triangular$_{30}$ items, let alone to triangular items. Surely his view (however confused he may be) is that such an idea-occasion is simply a necessary condition for the occurrence of an *additional* act of the understanding of the form

[an (any, all) item(s) of the same sort as this ...]

where for an item to be of 'the' same sort as *this* is for it to be either of the same *specific* sort, e.g., a triangular$_{30}$ item, or of the same *generic* sort, e.g., a triangular item.

146. Berkeley's point, the objector might add, is simply that although the *referring act* is other than the *idea-occasion*, it is not *really distinct* from the latter, for it could not occur in its absence, as is shown by its demonstrative reference.

147. The force of this objection is weakened when we remember that Berkeley's account of how 'particular' ideas become 'general' is that positive account he offers to replace the rejected doctrine of *abstract* general ideas. Thus it is open to us to reply that Berkeley is thinking of 'particular' ideas, i.e., idea-occasions with *determinate* content (e.g., an idea of a triangle$_{30}$), as not only an awareness of *a triangle$_{30}$ as a triangle$_{30}$*, but as a general reference to *a triangle$_{30}$*. After all, his task, as he saw it, was to explain how we come to be able to think of all items of a *generic* sort. To Berkeley (and to Hume) it is the generic or determinable that poses the problem.

148. It should also be borne in mind that the post-scholastic period was not *that* clear about the distinction between *universality* (the *common*) and *generality* (general reference) on which the above objection turns—nor, for that matter, between a *character* that is most determinate 'in all respects'

and an *individual*.[67]

149. The point can be brought to a focus as follows: To the extent that Berkeley confusedly thinks of ideas as *containing* a general reference to any item of a determinate sort, then no distinct act of the understanding having the logical form of general reference would need to be introduced at this level. To the extent that Berkeley confusedly thinks of an idea of a triangle$_{30}$ as not only an awareness of a triangle$_{30}$ as a triangle$_{30}$, but also as an awareness of a triangle$_{30}$ as a triangle, he can think of acts of noticing, considering, and comparing, as *simply* noticings, considerings and comparings, i.e., as lacking content of the sort possessed by idea-occasions. They would be, so to speak, acts of peering into contents that they cannot have.

150. On the other hand, Berkeley does tell us that 'particular' idea-occasions become general ideas of *generically* characterized items *as such*, by virtue of an act of the understanding that *uses* the idea-occasion to represent all idea-occasions of the same generic sort. He clearly thinks of this use as including the noticing and the considering a generic feature of the content of the idea-occasion. Does it also include a *distinct* (though not, of course, *really* distinct) act of the understanding which has the logical form

Any (all) item(s) of the same generic sort as *this* ...?

Or should we construe the understanding as simply 'disengaging' or 'highlighting' a reference that is 'implicit' in the idea itself? After all, if the idea contains a general reference to any item of a *determinate* sort, does it not enfold a general reference to any item of the relevant *generic* sort? The answer, of course, is a disappointing "yes and no." The most we can say is that, as in the case of the other elements in his confusions, the concept of a distinct act of general reference finds explicit recognition only when the context clearly demands it.

---

[67] Thus in the absence of a clear understanding of the category of individuated substance, there was a constant temptation to construe the idea of an individual as an idea of determinates, $D_1, D_2, D_3, ... D_n$, ... (where D_1 is, for example, *white*, and the idea is the idea of a white individual) assembled by the sheer aggregation of more elements like *white*.

KANT'S TRANSCENDENTAL IDEALISM

I

1. When Kant mobilizes the position which he calls 'transcendental idealism' to resolve the antinomies, he describes it as the doctrine that "everything intuited in space and time, and therefore all objects of any experience possible to us, are nothing but appearances, that is, mere representations which, in the manner in which they are represented, as extended beings or as series of alterations, have no independent existence outside our thoughts." He contrasts this thesis with that of the "realist, in the transcendental meaning of the term" who "treats these modifications of our sensibility as self-subsistent things, that is, treats *mere representations* as things in themselves" (A490-1; B518-9).

2. Since Kant calls his idealism 'transcendental' in order to indicate that it enables him to account for the existence of synthetic *a priori* knowledge concerning objects in space and time, he has, strictly speaking, no use for the term 'transcendental realism', since on his account of synthetic *a priori* knowledge we could have no such knowledge of spatio-temporal objects if they were things in themselves. Nor did realists, as he sees it, claim that their realism accounted for the existence of such knowledge, although at least some of them would have taken realism to be compatible with it.

3. The title of this essay is, of course, overly ambitious. In particular, it seems to promise as much discussion of 'transcendental' as of 'idealism'. My primary concern, however, is with the ontological aspects of Kant's idealism, and only incidentally (and by implication) with epistemological issues concerning synthetic *a priori* knowledge. I note in passing, however, that since the ontological aspects of Kant's idealism concern in large part the ontology of mental states, and since, although epistemology is not psychology, it is mental states which are the proper subjects of epistemic appraisal, Kant's ontology of mental states is directly relevant to his epistemology and, consequently, to his transcendental philosophy.

4. I shall be primarily concerned with the views Kant expresses in the first edition. I am, however, in whole-hearted agreement with his claim that there is a fundamental identity between the views expressed in the two editions. In the *Preface* to the second edition (Bxxxviiff.), he explains the changes he has made as a matter of removing "difficulties and obscurity" which "not, perhaps, without my fault, may have given rise to misunder-

standings," and of omitting or abridging, to make room for new material, "certain passages which, though not indeed essential to the completeness of the whole may yet be missed by many readers as otherwise helpful." He suggests that the "loss [...] can be remedied by consulting the first edition," thus implying that the deleted material coheres with the new material. As regards "the propositions themselves and their proofs," however, he claims that he has "found nothing to alter," a statement which he shortly repeats with even greater force by characterizing the new edition as "altering absolutely nothing in the fundamentals of the propositions put forward or even in their proofs," though he does grant that this [he hopes] more intelligent exposition [...] "here and there departs so far from the previous method of treatment that mere interpolations could not be made to suffice" (Bxlii).

5. It is surely implied by these claims that in Kant's eyes the refutation of idealism which was added in the second edition is not only compatible with the teachings of the first, but is implied by them. I think this is correct. The 'new' refutation simply applies the content of the *Analytic of Principles*, and, in particular, the *Analogies* to the topic of idealism, an application which is present in, though not highlighted by, the first edition refutation. And when Kant explains why he has relocated the refutation in the *Postulates of Empirical Thought*, his reason is a good one rather than, as Bennett characterizes it, a "silly" one.[1] Anyone who studies the fourth Paralogism must feel the awkwardness involved not only in classifying the theses of Rational Psychology in terms of 'relation', 'quality', 'quantity' and 'modality', but, in particular, the treatment of problematic idealism as the modal counterpart of the substantiality, simplicity and personal identity of the soul. The relation of our knowledge of material things to our perceptual experiences is far more at home in a section devoted to the thesis that "that which is bound up with the material conditions of experience, that is, with sensation, is actual." For this bound-up-ness, when one spells it out *does have* an inferential aspect and therefore does lead naturally to the Cartesian problem.

6. I shall not, therefore, discuss the second edition refutation as such, since I hope to convince you that its familiar claims are indeed contained in the first edition, indeed in the first edition refutation itself. For in spite of its 'subjectivist' flavor, the latter contains a reference to and, indeed, a summary of the answer to the question "What is an object of representations?" raised first in the introductory passages of the first edition Transcendental Deduction, answered in highly schematic form, raised again in

---

[1] *Kant's Analytic*, p. 166.

the Second Analogy, and this time given a fleshed-out answer which is repeated in the text of the second edition. And it is Kant's answer to *this* question which is central to the contrast he draws between his idealism and the idealisms he calls 'dogmatic' and 'problematic'.

II

7. In the passage from the *Dialectic* with which I began, transcendental idealism is characterized *directly* as the view that "everything intuited in space and time, and therefore all objects of any experience possible to us, are nothing but appearances, that is mere representations which [...] have no independent existence outside our thoughts." It is characterized *indirectly* by its contrast with realism "in the transcendental sense," according to which these objects are "self-subsistent things," or "things in themselves." In a key footnote which occurs in the fourth Paralogism (A375n) Kant writes

> We must give full credence to this paradoxical but correct proposition that there is nothing in space save what is represented in it. For space is itself nothing but representation, and whatever is in it must therefore be contained in the representation. Nothing whatsoever is in space, save insofar as it is actually represented in it. It is a proposition which must indeed sound strange, that a thing can exist only in the representation of it, but in this case the objection falls, in as much as the things with which we are concerned are not things themselves, but appearances only, that is, representations.

Kant here does not use the contrast between existence 'inside' or 'outside' our 'thoughts', but it is clear that he is treating the relevant sense of 'representation' as equivalent to 'thought', for he has just written that while "something which may be (in the transcendental sense) outside us"—i.e., which exists in itself—"is the cause of our outer intuitions [...] this is not the object of which we are *thinking* in the representations of matter and of corporeal things; for these are merely appearances, that is mere kinds of representation, which can never be met with save in us ..." (A372). It is clear that to 'represent' is here a case of to 'think' and that Kant, who is elaborating the definition he has just given of 'transcendental idealism' as

> the doctrine that appearances are to be regarded as being one and all representations only and not things in themselves (A369)

is introducing in his comments on this definition the formula of the later definition in the *Dialectic* according to which the objects of intuition "have no independent existence outside our thoughts."

8. Intuitions, in the relevant sense, are a species of 'thought' and when Kant says that appearances are "mere kinds of representation," we certainly should not interpret this as meaning that appearances are mental acts of thinking. They are items which exist 'in' our thoughts, i.e., which are, in an appropriate sense, represent*eds* rather than acts of represent*ing*. And when he adds that "appearances are not to be met with save in us" this must, of course, be construed in terms of his distinction between the 'empirical' and the 'transcendental' senses of 'in us' and 'outside us'.

9. Now mental acts which are intuitings are not, of course, *judgings*. But they are nevertheless *thoughts*. In the important classification of representations (*vorstellungen*) which Kant gives in an introductory passage of the *Dialectic* (A319; B376), Kant includes sensations as well as intuitions as representations. A sensation however is a "mere modification of the mind," whereas an intuition (though not a *general* concept) is an "*erkenntnis*" ("*Cognitio*"). Its distinctive feature is that, although, like a general concept, a *cognitio*, it is a singular one and does not refer to an object "mediately by means of a feature which several things may have in common" as do general concepts.

10. Kant holds the interesting and important view (which I have explored elsewhere[2]) that an 'intuition of a manifold', as contrasted with a sheer 'manifold of intuition', is an 'erkenntnis' which presents us, much as does an Aristotelian 'phantasm', a this-such (*tode-ti*), though it is not a judgment of the form '(this) is (such)'.[3] In a paragraph (A79; B105) of the Metaphysical Deduction of the Categories, which can almost be described as the Transcendental Deduction and the Schematism in embryo, Kant tells us, in effect, that intuitions of manifolds contain the very categories which can be found in the general concepts which we apply to these intuitions (and which we have, indeed, by "analytic thinking," derived from them) (A78-9).

> The same function which gives unity to the various representations *in a judgment* also gives unity to the mere synthesis of various representations *in an intuition*; and this unity, in its most general expression, we entitle the pure concept of the understanding. The same understanding through the same operations by which in concepts, by means of analytical unity, it produced the logical form of a judgment, also introduces a transcendental content into its representations, by means of the synthetic unity of the manifold in intuition in general. On this account we are entitled to call

---

[2] *Science and Metaphysics*, chapter I.
[3] One should also bear in mind Ockham's concept of a perceptual intuition, and his claim that God could bring it about that the object intuited not exist.

these representations pure concepts of the understanding, and to regard them as applying *a priori* to objects—a conclusion which general logic is not in a position to establish.

Thus singular judgments which express basic perceptions have the form

(This-such) is *so and so*

and the categories which are implicit in the general concept *so-and-so* can be true of the subject of the judgment, i.e., the object intuited, because the intuition of the *this-such* also contains the categories.

11. It is essential to see that intuition is a species of *thought*, for any sense-datum like approach makes essential features of Kant's theory of knowledge unintelligible, e.g., the *Schematism*. Thus the categories apply to intuitions, because, although the content of *sensations* does not contain the categories, the content of *intuitions* (of manifolds) does. *This* is the point of Kant's problem about homogeneity and of his solution.

III

12. Let us take seriously, then, the thesis that intuitions of manifolds are thoughts. And let us apply to them the ontological categories which the Cartesian tradition, rooted in scholastic tradition had applied to thoughts. An adequate discussion would call for a whole cluster of distinctions in which themes from Husserl, the early Brentano, Meinong, and the later Brentano would be inextricably involved. I shall use a bare minimum of distinctions and resolutely avoid probing into the deeper metaphysical issues involved.

13. Descartes distinguishes between the act and the content aspects of thoughts. The content, of course, 'exists in' the act. And, of course, contents *as contents* exist only 'in' acts. On the other hand, there is a sense in which something which 'exists in' an act can also exist, to use Kant's phrase, 'outside' the act. In Descartes' terminology, that which exists 'in' the act as its 'content' can have 'formal reality' in the world.[4]

14. The concept of 'existence in thought' is, of course, a metaphor. So, of course, is the idea that a thought is *true* if its content 'corresponds' to something actual in the world. In the Cartesian tradition, this account of truth holds both of thoughts of individuals and thoughts of states of affairs.

---

[4] I have avoided Descartes' use of the phrase 'objective reality' in connection with contents, since it has, of course, a quite different meaning in Kant and in contemporary philosophy.

Thus a thought of an individual is true if there 'corresponds' to it an actual individual, i.e., if the individual exists not only 'in the thought' as its content, but in the actual world. Similarly, the thought of a state of affairs is true if there 'corresponds' to it an actual state of affairs, i.e., if the state of affairs which exists in the thought as its content, also exists in the actual world.

15. I have spoken of *actuality* where Descartes speaks of 'formal reality'. In Kant's terminology what Descartes means by 'formal reality', and which Cartesians would equate with actuality, is 'existence in itself' or, to use the latinate term of the *Prolegomena*, existence '*per se*'. Kant clearly accepts the Cartesian contrast between 'existence in thought' and 'existence *per se*'—so much so that he takes it for granted, as did most of his predecessors.[5]

16. One final terminological point: The *content* of the thought of an individual was considered to be, in an important sense, an *object* of the thought. Indeed the thought would have in this sense an object even if nothing in the actual world corresponded to it. Later philosophers drew tidy distinctions between 'immanent objects' and 'transcendent objects', and we are all familiar with the intuitive appeal of these metaphors. Philosophical terminology consists largely of metaphor added to metaphor in the hope that the mixture will crystallize out into clear and distinct categories.

17. For Kant, then, an act of intuiting a manifold is a thinking of a this-such in space and/or time. The this-such is something that exists 'in' the act. The problem with which Kant is dealing can be characterized initially as that of whether individuals in space and/or time also have existence *per se*. Kant's answer, to anticipate, is that these intuited items exist *only* 'in' acts of intuition.[6] That is, no items in space and/or time exists *per se*. He will nevertheless insist that some items which exist in acts of intuition are *actual*. This obviously requires a distinction between *actuality* and *existence per se*, which were conflated by his predecessors.

---

[5] Including the British Empiricists who, in the process of muddling through to important philosophical insights, muddied many classical distinctions.

[6] A more complete discussion of this point would have to comment on those passages in which Kant allows that things in themselves are objects of perceptual intuitions. After all, if the latter contain the pure categories, and if the latter constitute 'the pure concept' of an 'object' ["The pure concept of this transcendental object which...(concept) in all our knowledge is always one and the same" (A109)], then things in themselves would 'correspond' (in the Cartesian sense) to intuitions, though not *qua* intuitions of spatio-temporal items. See A490-1; B518-9 quoted in the first paragraph; see also *Science and Metaphysics*, pp. 42ff.

IV

18. It will be useful to connect Kant's concept of the 'intuition of a manifold' with that strand of contemporary perception theory which operates with fairly traditional concepts of intentionality. A familiar notion is that of a perceptual taking. Perceptual takings are, so to speak, thinkings which are evoked in our minds by our environment or, in limiting cases, by abnormal states of our nervous system. Perceptual takings are usually thought to have propositional form. One takes *this is a cat*. One takes *there is a cat on that mat*. I suggest that what is taken is best expressed by a *referring* expression, thus 'this cat on this mat'. We should think of perceptual takings as providing *subjects* for propositional thought, rather than already having full-fledged propositional form.

19. Again, if we think of a taking as a special case of a *believing*, it is best to think of it as a 'believing in' rather than a 'believing that'. In a perceptual taking one believes in *this cat on this mat*, and may believe, for example, that *this cat on this mat* is a Siamese. Thus construed, perceptual takings are in many respects the counterparts of Kant's 'intuitions of manifolds'. They represent this-suchs; and it is worth noting that although they are *not* explicitly propositional in form, they obviously *contain* propositional form in the sense in which 'that green table is broken' contains 'that table is green'.

V

20. Little needs to be said at this stage of the argument about the 'problematic idealism' Kant attributes to Descartes. Problematic idealism regards the claim that material things and processes exist *per se* as a coherent one, but one which can be established only by an inference from our perceptual states, an inference from effect to cause. Mental states have a privileged position in that they not only can have existence *per se*, but it is known, indeed 'directly' known, that some mental states exist *per se*.

21. Before looking at Kant's refutation of problematic idealism, it is worth pausing to ask: If this is 'problematic' idealism, what might 'dogmatic' idealism be? One would expect it to be the view that material objects in space and time *could not* have existence *per se*, i.e., that there was an absurdity or contradiction in the idea of the existence *per se* of material objects. Berkeley certainly held this position, a fact which might strengthen the temptation to interpret dogmatic idealism along these lines.

22. It is also worth noting that Berkeley did not deny that in a sense we (and *a fortiori* God) can conceive of material objects in space and time, where by the phrase 'material objects' I mean, so to speak, Lockean objects and *not* patterns of actual and counterfactual perceptual experiences.[7] Berkeley can be construed as holding that our actual and counterfactual perceptual experiences are grounded in God's plan to cause us to have those experiences we would have if (a metaphysical counterfactual) there *were* material objects including human bodies with sense organs, and minds and bodies were able to interact. In less theological terms, this can be formulated as the view that what exists *per se* other than our minds is the causal ground of our actual and counterfactual perceptual experiences.

23. To return to the main line of argument, it is only too clear that if we mean by 'dogmatic idealism' with respect to material objects the view that they cannot have existence *per se*, then Kant is a dogmatic idealist of the first water. Indeed, as we have seen, Kant makes dogmatic idealism *in this sense* the very cornerstone of his transcendental idealism.

24. What, then, does Kant mean by dogmatic idealism? And is any such view to be found in Berkeley? It should be clear that the only answer to the first question which satisfies the requirements of the argument to date is that Kant means by dogmatic idealism the view that nothing spatial can be *actual*, where actual does not mean 'exists *per se*'. Indeed Kant's own idealism, while denying that material objects exist *per se*, nevertheless insists that some at least of the spatial objects which exist 'in our thoughts' and, in particular, in our acts and intuitions, or perceptual takings, are, in the critical sense, *actual*.

25. But what of the second question? To what extent is Kant justified in attributing to Berkeley the view which he (Kant) would express by saying that no spatial items are actual?[8] After all, *if,* as is often claimed, Kant in the first edition and on occasion in the second edition construes physical objects in terms of actual and counterfactual perceptual experiences, is he not in essential agreement with Berkeley?[9]

---

[7] I deliberately use this vaguer expression 'perceptual experiences' instead of 'perceptual takings', since one of the essential differences between Kant and Berkeley concerns the analysis of what it is to be a perceptual experience.

[8] Notice that to pinpoint the issue I have retreated from the phrase 'material object' to 'spatial item'.

[9] Notice once again that I deliberately used the vaguer phrase 'perceptual experience', for in the last analysis everything will hinge on how this phrase is interpreted.

VI

26. At this point we must retrace our steps in order to advance. My discussion of Descartes' ontology of mental acts was not only schematic but radically incomplete. For Descartes had *two* paradigms of what it is to be a mental state. Let me begin with the one I have neglected. Sensation is a mental state, though one in which the body is intimately involved, and his paradigm of a sensation is a feeling of pain.[10] To us, the obvious feature of a feeling of pain is that a feeling of pain simply *is* a pain. The existence of a feeling of pain is identical with the existence of a pain. Much more would need to be said to nail this point down,[11] but after all the analytic work has been done, the fact remains that a pain is a kind of feeling. If we put this by saying that a pain is a 'content' or 'object' of feeling, this should be regarded simply as a (misleading) paraphrase of the above. The danger arises from the fact that this usage would tend to assimilate feelings of pain to Descartes' second paradigm, the clear distinct *thought* of an object. It is in connection with the latter that he elaborates the distinctions which were inherited by Kant.

27. It was obvious to Descartes that the mental state of thinking of a cube is not (at least in any ordinary sense of 'is') a cube. Thus, whereas a feeling of pain is a pain, a thinking of a cube is not a cube. Now in his systematic account of sensation, Descartes construes visual sensation on the model of pain. In terms of this paradigm, a sensation of red would be a case of red as a feeling of pain is a case of pain. His construal, however, as Gassendi saw,[12] confronted Descartes with a problem. Surely the colors we experience have shape. But if the colors we experience have shape, then, if they are sensations construed on the model of pain, mental states can have shape. To get experienced color and shape together, Descartes, it seems, must either

  (a) give experienced colors the same status as shapes (deny that either can be a modification of the mind);
  (b) give the shapes of experienced colors the same status as colors (admit that modifications of the mind can have shape, as

---

[10] Another paradigm is to be found in his use of 'sensation' in connection with *seeming to see* in the second meditation. But while there is clearly a close connection between sensing and seeming to see an object, they are not identical, nor does Descartes equate them in his developed philosophy of mind.

[11] I have discussed this topic in "Metaphysics and the Concept of a Person," in *The Logical Way of Doing Things*, edited by Karel Lambert, New Haven, 1969 (reprinted as chapter XI in *Essays in Philosophy and its History* published by Reidel, Dordrecht, Holland, 1974) [*MP*, in this volume].

[12] *Philosophical Works of Descartes*, eds. Haldane and Ross, Dover, 1934. Vol. II, pp. 196-7.

Gassendi thought he should).

28. Descartes gives no clear account of the matter. His official account is that while the sensation of red as such is unextended, the shape we perceive, and which has existence 'in thought', is confusedly believed to be the shape of something which *resembles* the sensation of red. Such beliefs date from early childhood. They are confused, because nothing can be like a sensation of red without being a sensation of red, and hence a modification of the mind.[13] In effect, Descartes gives perceived red the status of *believed in* red, and, by doing so, gives it the existence 'in thought' which the shape also has. This move requires a distinction between the sensed red which we introspect, and which is not extended, and the perceived shaped red, which is a *content* rather than a *modification* of the mind.

29. Now Berkeley, as is well known, also assimilated color to pain. What, then, of shaped colors? When one feels a pain, there is an actual case of pain. When one senses a color, there is an actual case of color. But when the mind senses a triangle of red, is there an actual case of shape? When directly confronted with this question,[14] Berkeley's answer is *no*. The shape exists only 'by way of idea', and it is clear that *here* the operative conception is a Cartesian *cogitatio* of which the shape is a *content* in a sense which does not entail that a mental state has a shape. But though Berkeley gives this answer, he is simply not clear about the status of shapes, and what stands out is his assimilation of the status of shape to that of color and, ultimately, to that of pain.[15]

30. Now if Berkeley had consistently held that perceived shapes are not features of mental states, but have existence only 'in our thoughts' (in the Cartesian sense), he could nevertheless have argued (perhaps on proto-Kantian grounds) that no shapes have existence *per se*. Shapes would not exist 'outside the mind' in what Kant called the transcendental sense. They would exist only 'in' the mind, not as features of its states but as immanent objects. Berkeley, however, because of the slippery slope pain-color-shape, makes the quite different claim that shapes can not exist 'outside the mind' in the sense in which *pains* can not exist outside the mind. Even though he

---

[13] *Principles of Philosophy*, Part I, LXVII-LXX.
[14] *Principles of Human Knowledge*, Part I, section 49 (Fifth Objection).
[15] A more penetrating account would demonstrate that Berkeley initially conceived of all 'perceptions' as in the 'understanding' a move which, by taking thoughts as the paradigm of mental states, constituted exactly that blurring of the distinction between sensibility and understanding—so obviously present in Spinoza, Leibniz and the Wolffians—which Kant was to regard as a key philosophical error.

is not prepared to say in so many words that shapes are essentially features of mental states, he actually commits himself to this position.

31. Thus it is not unfair on Kant's part to attribute to Berkeley the view that the concept of shaped items which are not mental states is an incoherent one, as incoherent as would be the concept of a pain which was not a mental state.

32. Now it is as evident to Kant as it was to Descartes that neither space itself nor any spatial object can be a modification of the mind or of a mental state. Thus, while Kant denies that either space or any spatial object has existence *per se* and argues that the idea that they do is an incoherent one, he *also* argues that the idea of shapes which are not features of mental states is itself a coherent one. Thus, if shapes which are not features of mental states do not exist *per se*, it is not because shapes are essentially features of mental states, but because shapes belong in space, and neither space nor anything in space can exist in itself.

33. We can now begin to appreciate why in Kant's sense of the term Berkeley was a 'dogmatic idealist', and to interpret the following passage:

> Berkeley [...] maintains that space, with all the things of which it is the inseparable condition, is in itself impossible and he therefore regards the things in space as merely imaginary entities. (B274)

Given that Kant is clearly aware that on his own view neither space nor objects in space can exist in themselves, the *gravamen* of the charge against Berkeley must be that the latter's *reason* for holding this is such as to require, as his (Kant's) reasons do not, that "things in space are merely imaginary entities." For, once again, Kant clearly has up his sleeve the view that material things, though they necessarily lack existence *per se*, which was the *traditional* concept of actuality, can in the *critical* sense be actual. On my interpretation Kant would be recognizing that Berkeley's reason for rejecting the existence *per se* of space and spatial objects would be that shape and extension are essentially features of mental states. The concept of spatial items which are not mental states would be a figment of the *philosophical* imagination. They would be radically imaginary, not just imaginary in the empirical sense.

34. Kant obscures the justice of his characterization of Berkeley's position in the remark which follows, in which he claims that

> Dogmatic idealism is unavoidable if space be interpreted as a property that belongs to things in themselves. For in that case, space and everything to which it serves as a condition, is a non-entity. (B274)

Here the direct connection with Berkeley is lost. But that is as it should be, for Kant is merely pointing out that one can arrive at the conclusion that the concept of actual spatial items other than mental states is incoherent by a route other than Berkeley's. For if space is a property which must belong to things in themselves, then, Kant has argued, there can be no such thing. Hence, given the classical interpretation of actuality as existence *per se*, it would follow that the concept of an *actual* spatial object is incoherent. And if the only alternative to holding that space is a property of things in themselves were, as Berkeley thought it was, the view that spatial items are features of mental states, then the concept of actual spatial items which are not features of mental states would *also* be incoherent. We would be faced by a dilemma.

> *Either* space is by nature a thing in itself or a property of things in themselves *or* the spatial items which underlie our concepts of space and spatial items are (features of) mental states (sensations). On either alternative the concept of actual spatial items which are not mental states is incoherent.

Kant has prepared the way for an escape through the horns of this dilemma. He points out that the argument of the *Aesthetic* enables him to avoid the view that space is either a thing in itself or a property of things in themselves without agreeing with Berkeley that the concept of spatial items which are not mental states is incoherent.

35. Yet even after he has established to his own satisfaction that the concept of an *actual* spatial item which is not a mental state is coherent, he still has to make the essential point that the concept of *actuality* does not coincide, as it traditionally did, with that of existence *per se*.

36. I take it to be clear, then, that Kant holds that no spatial item (notice the cautious use of the term 'item' as contrasted with the richer term 'object') is a mental state. It can, however, be argued that in the first edition and on occasion in the second edition Kant held that material *objects* are, to use an anachronistic turn of phrase, logical constructions out of mental states which, though not spatial, are *representations* of spatial *items*—i.e., of which spatial items are the *content* or immanent objects. After all, he *does* write that

> In our system, on the other hand, these external things, namely matter, are in all their configurations and alterations nothing but mere appearances, that is, representations

in us, of the reality of which we are immediately conscious. (A371-2)

I think that this interpretation is a mistake, though it must be confessed that because of his failure to make it clear when he is using 'representation' (and, in particular, 'intuition') in the sense of *act* of representing, and when he is using these terms in the sense of *content* represented, it has some initial plausibility.

37. The crux of the matter as Kant clearly saw is his account of what it is to be an object of acts of representing. He formulates this account schematically in a passage (A104) which prepares the way for the first edition Transcendental Deduction, and develops it in a more full-bodied way in a key passage in the Second Analogy which occurs in both editions.[16]

38. Our primary concern is with *perceptual* acts or takings. But in the first passage referred to above, Kant makes his key point in a way which abstracts, as the passage in the Second Analogy does not, from essential aspects of perceptual takings. Nevertheless, the concept for which Kant is preparing the way is that of *rules for generating perceptual takings*.[17]

39. The term 'rule' is a dangerous one, for it suggests deliberate activity or, at least, activity which would be deliberate if it weren't so *hasty* and, in the ordinary sense, thoughtless. Actually the most useful concept is that of a sequence of acts of representing which can reflectively be classified as conforming to a rule which is (at least in principle) graspable by thought. The rules in question must, according to Kant, be available, if one is to recognize that one's acts of representing belong together as an intelligible sequence.[18]

40. Now it might be thought that by introducing the concept of a rule-governed sequence of perceptual representings, i.e., acts of perceptual taking, I am giving hostages to the view that material objects consist of rule-conforming sequences of perceptual takings. That I am *not* is implied by the fact (which I hope to make clear) that even the most tough-minded transcendental realist grants that veridical perceptual takings have the coherence which Kant is attempting to clarify by the concept of rule-conforming sequences. Roughly, Kant's transcendental realist thinks of the perceiver as deriving these rules by induction from experience, whereas

---

[16] I have in mind the passage (A190; B235) introduced as follows: "...it is a question for deeper inquiry what the word 'object' ought to signify in respect of appearances when these are viewed not in so far as they are (as representations) objects, but only in so far as they stand for an object."

[17] It might be helpful, here, to think of rules for generating sequences of acts of *imagining* which would be the counterparts of perceptual takings, if they had their source in outer sense.

[18] An elaboration of this theme would require an exploration in detail of Kant's conception of the transcendental unity of apperception as a necessary correlate of the intuition of objects.

Kant thinks that induction itself presupposes an antecedent grasp of these rules.

VII

41. We can now turn our attention to Kant's initial explanation of what it is to be an 'object of representations'. He asks us to consider the intuitive representation of a triangle. Here the rich implications of the concept of a perceptual taking are laid aside, for the moment, and we are given an explanation which could concern a construction in pure geometry. For the essential point he wants to make is that while the object of the intuitive representing is indeed a *triangle*, the triangle is not an existent *per se*, and that although the content *triangle* specifies sequences of representing which count as *coming to represent a triangle*, the object of the representing of a triangle is not the sequence of representings which culminate in the representing of the triangle. A triangle is neither a mental act of representing a triangle, not is it a sequence of mental acts each of which represents a part of a triangle.

42. Before turning to the passage in the Second Analogy which is essentially a development of the passage on which I have been commenting but one which does take into account the specific character of perceptual takings, let me elaborate briefly on the triangle example in a way which will make for a smooth and easy transition. After all, Kant's account of 'drawing figures in thought', i.e. in pure intuition, is an idealized version, ascribed to the mind, of drawing figures on paper. Now if we take seriously the three-dimensionality of space, it strikes us that to represent a triangle in space is always to represent it *from a point of view*. Thus, what we represent is

> this equilateral triangle facing me straight-on

or

> this equilateral triangle at such and such an angle to my (metaphorical) line of sight.

43. Now it is by no means an original idea on my part that intuitive representings of figures in three-dimensional space are essentially point-of-viewish. But its importance has been underestimated. For it means that we must distinguish between the figures—which are *not* point-of-viewish—and the total content of the representing of the figure, which *total* content is

point-of-viewish, thus

> equilateral triangle facing me straight on.

Let me repeat. Equilateral triangles are not point-of-viewish, but they are, so to speak, intuited in perspective. The representing has a content which specifies a point of view.

44. Thus, the *object* of a representing of an equilateral triangle from a certain point of view is simply the equilateral triangle. But, according to Kant's position, according to which we 'construct' or 'draw' figures in space, the concept of an equilateral triangle must specify not only a sequence of representations in which we represent one line, then, continuing to represent that line, represent another line at a sixty degree angle, then, continuing to represent these we represent the third side, it must also specify in an intelligible way what it means for two representations to be representations of an equilateral triangle from different points of view, i.e., representations which have the contents

> equilateral triangle face-on
> equilateral triangle at such and such an angle to my 'line of sight'.

45. The notion of representations which have contents of this form obviously builds on pervasive features of perceptual takings. I do not simply perceptually accept a house; the content of my perceptual acceptance is something like

> this house over there facing me left-edge-of-front-wise.

46. The point I am making is simple, but it is so essentially a part of a larger story that I shall have to disguise the torn edges to put it across. When, in the Second Analogy, Kant says (A191; B236) that "the object is *that* in the appearance which contains the condition of this necessary rule of apprehension," he is commenting on the example of a house which he has just introduced:

> ...immediately I unfold the transcendental meaning of my concepts of an object, I realize that the house is not a thing in itself but only an appearance, that is a representation... .(A190-1; B236)

Here it is clear that he means by 'representation' something *represented*, i.e., a content or immanent object of an act of representing.

47. Nevertheless, although he calls the house an appearance, where this clearly does not mean that the house is an act of *representing,* he does say that

> The appearance...is nothing but the sum of these representations (of apprehension)

and it might be thought that Kant is characterizing the house as a sum of *acts* of representing. It is therefore important to note that he characterized the representations in question as "*that which lies in* the successive apprehension." (A191; B236, emphasis mine) This must surely be his way of warning us that 'representation' here means *represented* rather than *representing,* i.e., Kant is relating the content *house* to the *contents* of successive *acts* of apprehension.

48. Kant is answering the question 'In what sense is the house the *object* of successive acts of apprehension?'. His negative answer is that it is not *qua* house in itself. The actuality of the house *qua* object is not its existence *per se*. What is his positive answer? As I see it, he is telling us that the house *qua* object is that aspect of the content of the perceptual takings which explains (together with certain other factors) the belonging together, *as states of the perceiver,* of certain perceptual takings (apprehendings). *But that aspect of the content of these perceptual takings is simply the content house which they share,* thus

> house over there left-front-edgewise to me
> house over there facing me
> left side of house over there facing me
> etc., etc.

49. As in the geometrical example, all the representings are representings of a non-point-of-viewish object—the house—from a point of view, i.e., representings of house-from-a-certain-point-of-view. It is, in this sense, that the house is the sum of the point-of-viewish appearances. But if the total content of a perceptual act is point-of-viewish, it is *because* it is the content of a *perceptual* act. Thus, while the content *house* is not a point-of-viewish content, it explains (together with certain other factors) why such and such perceptual represent*ings* with contents which can be subsumed under the rubric

> house-from-such-and-such-a-point-of-view

take place. Thus, the concept of a house as a perceptible object essentially involves a reference to perceptual acts, i.e., to the perceptual takings of a perceiver.

50. Nevertheless the concept of a house as perceptible object is not the concept of the sequences of perceptual takings (actual and counterfactual) which (together with other factors) it explains. To pull my points together in one sentence,

> The object of a perceptual representing of a house is the non-perspectival content *house*; yet as the sort of item that can be the object of a perceptual representing, it must provide rules for explaining (together with other factors) why such and such sequences of perceptual takings with perspectival contents were necessary.

51. It will have been noticed that I have written in several passages above that the content *house* is the source of rules which explain *together with other factors* why such and such sequences of perceptual takings were necessary. What do I mean by 'other factors'? The answer should be obvious, and peeks out from almost every page of the *Analogies*. *House* by itself can generate no explanation of the occurrence of a sequence of perceptual takings. It is only *house in such and such relations to a perceiver* which can do this. And this, obviously, means to a perceiver's body, and, of course, his sense organs. The essential structure of the content of perceptual takings is not just

> house from a certain geometrical point of view

but, to make a complicated point in a simple way,

> house in front of my *sightful eyes*
> ship in water moving to the left *of my sightful eyes*.

In my argument I have thinned out this mutual involvement of object, circumstances and embodied perceiver into a ghostly 'object from a point of view'. But Kant took seriously the fact that perceivers are embedded in a spatio-temporal system of interacting substances. In other words the doctrine of the double affection of the self, far from being a problematic feature of Kant's critical idealism, is an essential feature of it, and is present in and, indeed, an essential feature of the argument of the Second Analogy.[19]

52. Kant denies that material things and processes exist *per se*, but he holds that in the critical sense they can be *actual* as contents which make an essential contribution to the explanation of the patterns in which perceptual experiences occur. But the deeper thrust of Kant's transcendental idealism is the thesis that the core of the knowable self is the self *as perceiver of material things and events*. And if it is relatively easy to see that the distinction between actual and non-actual material things and events is tied to the concept of an *actual* sequence of perceptual takings, it has (until recently) proved less easy to see that the distinction between actual and non-actual sequences of perceptual takings, i.e., between perceptual takings which are correctly and those which are incorrectly taken to have occurred in one's mental history, is tied to the concept of actual material things and events.

53. Kant saw that the concept of an *object* of perception contains a reference to the perceptual takings which are the criteria for its actuality. He *also* saw that the concept of a perceptual taking, as the taking of an *object*, contains a reference to material things and events which, if actual, would imply its own actuality. The actuality of perceptual takings and the actuality of material things and processes are not logically independent. And since, for Kant, the concept of matter-of-factual truth concerns the agreement of what we represent with what is, *in the critical sense*, actual, rather than, as traditionally, with what exists *per se*, he can pay his respects to what he calls "the nominal definition of truth" while giving it a radically new interpretation.

---

[19] As noted above (paragraph 22) even Berkeley came to see that the intelligibility of the patterns in which perceptual experiences occur involves the concept of embodied perceivers in a material world. However, since he was convinced that material objects could not exist *per se*, he gave them existence in God's Understanding and Providence as essential features of his plan for causing us to have the experiences we do.

THE ROLE OF THE IMAGINATION IN KANT'S THEORY OF EXPERIENCE

Dotterer Lecture
May 12, 1978

I

1. My aim in this paper is to give a sympathetic account of Kant's theory of the role played by what he calls the productive imagination in perceptual experience. My method, however, will not be that of textual exegesis and commentary, but rather that of constructing an ostensibly independent theory which will turn out, it just so happens, to contain the gist of the Kantian scheme. Proceeding in this way will enable me to avoid the tasks involved in coping with Kant's terminology, architectonic and polemical orientation. By concentrating attention on the subject matter itself, this approach will make possible a relatively brief treatment of what would otherwise be a time consuming enterprise.

2. By referring to the theory I am about to construct as 'ostensibly independent', I also mean to imply that although I shall stick reasonably close to what I think to be the truth, I shall not be above warping and slanting the argument to fit the role of a sympathetic interpretation of the *Critique*. The extent to which I succeed in capturing the spirit of Kant's thought must be measured by the degree to which it illuminates the letter of the text.

3. Our access to the external world and to the nature and variety of the objects (in a suitably broad sense) of which it consists is through perception. Phenomenological reflection on the structure of perceptual experience, therefore, should reveal the categories, the most generic kinds or classes, to which these objects belong, as well as the manner in which objects perceived and perceiving subjects come together in the perceptual act.

4. I shall therefore begin my reflections on Kantian themes with a careful account of the relevant features of perceptual (in point of fact, visual) experience. An initial survey will provide a framework of working distinctions which will subsequently be refined. These distinctions, in one form or another, are familiar tools of the philosopher's trade. It is the subsequent refinements that will lead into the arena of controversy.

5. In the first place there is the distinction between the act of seeing and the object seen. Visual experience presents itself as a direct awareness of a complex physical structure. It also presents itself as having a point of

view, as perspectival. Opaque objects present themselves as endowed with facing colored surfaces. I do not mean by this that they present themselves as complex structures of color expanses (visual 'sense data'), but rather that they present themselves as three dimensional physical objects which stand in such and such relations to each other and to the perceiver's body.

6. In the second place, there is the distinction, already alluded to, between the objects perceived and what they are perceived *as*. Thus in veridical perception occurring in optimum circumstances—I shall have nothing to say about illusions, misperceptions or hallucinations—the object is not only, for example, a brick which is red and rectangular on the side facing me, it is seen *as* a brick which is red and rectangular on the facing side. How is this to be understood?

7. Traditionally a distinction was drawn between the visual object and the perceptual judgment *about* the object. The latter was construed as a special kind of occurrent believing. Occurrent acts of belief were, in their turn, construed as propositional in form; as having, so to speak, a syntactical form which parallels or is analogous to the syntactical form of the sentence which would express it in overt speech. Believings, so to speak, occur in Mentalese.

8. This suggested to some philosophers that to see a visual object as a brick with a red and rectangular facing surface consists in *seeing* the brick and *believing* it to be a brick with a red and rectangular facing surface:

This is a brick which has a red and rectangular facing surface

where the *judgment* has a demonstrative component analogous to the linguistic demonstrative, 'this', in the sentence by which it would be expressed.

9. Now I think that there is *something* to the idea that seeing *as* involves an occurrent act of belief, but I also think that the standard account misconstrues the structure of the believing. Notice that the subject term of the judgment was exhibited above as a *bare* demonstrative, a sheer *this*, and that what the object is seen *as* was placed in an explicitly predictive position, thus 'is a brick which has a red and rectangular facing surface'.

10. I submit, on the contrary, that *correctly represented*, a perceptual belief has the quite different form:

This brick with a red and rectangular facing surface.

Notice that this is not a sentence but a complex demonstrative phrase. In other words, I suggest that in such a perceptually grounded judgment as

> This brick with a red and rectangular facing side is too large for the job at hand,

the perceptual belief proper is that tokening of a complex Mentalese demonstrative phrase which is the grammatical subject of the judgment as a whole. This can be rephrased as a distinction between a perceptual *taking* and *what is believed about* what is taken. What is *taken* or, if I may so put it, believed *in* is represented by the complex demonstrative phrase while that which is believed *about* the object is represented by the explicitly predicative phrase which follows. Perceptual takings, thus construed, provide the perceiver with perceptual subject-terms for judgments proper.

11. From this point of view, what the visual object is seen *as* is a matter of the content of the complex demonstrative Mentalese phrase.

II

12. I shall prepare the way for the next major step in the argument by changing my example. Consider the visual perception of a red apple. Apples are red on the outside (have a red skin) but white inside. Other features of apples are relevant, but this will do to begin with. The initial point to be made about the apple is that we see it not only as having a red surface but *as* white inside. This, however, is just the beginning. Notice that the experience contains an actual quantity of red. By 'actual quantity of red' I mean a quantity of red which is not merely *believed to exist* as did the Fountain of Youth for Ponce de Leon. The Fountain of Youth does not actually exist. By contrast, the quantity of red which is a constituent of the visual experience of the apple not only actually exists but is actually or, to use a familiar metaphor, bodily present in the experience.

13. But what of the volume of white apple flesh which the apple is seen *as* containing? Many philosophers would be tempted to say that it is present *in the experience* merely by virtue of being believed in. It has, of course, actual existence as a constituent of the apple, but, they would insist, it is not present in its actuality. Phenomenologists have long insisted that this would be a mistake. As they see it, an actual volume of white is present in the experience in a way which parallels the red. We experience the red *as containing the white*.

14. But if what is experienced is red-containing-white *as* red-containing-white, and if both the red and the white are actualities actually present, how are we to account for the fact that there is a legitimate sense in which we don't *see the inside of the apple*? To be sure, we see the apple *as* white inside, but we don't *see* the whiteness of the inside of the apple.

15. We must add another distinction, this time between *what we see* and *what we see of* what we see. The point is a delicate one to which justice must be done if we are not to be derailed. Thus when I see a closed book, the following are all typically true.

(a) I see the book.
(b) The book has pages inside.
(c) I see the book *as* having pages inside.
(d) I do not see the inside pages.
(e) The book has a back cover.
(f) I see the book *as* having a back cover.
(g) I do not see the back cover.

16. How can a volume of white apple flesh be present *as actuality* in the visual experience if it is not seen? The answer should be obvious. It is present by virtue of being *imagined*. (Notice that to get where we have arrived, much more phenomenology must have been done than is explicitly being done on this occasion. We are drawing on a store of accumulated wisdom.)

17. But notice where this leads us. The *actual* volume of white is experienced as contained in the *actual* volume of red. Yet if the actuality of the white apple flesh consists in it being *imagined*, it must be dependent for its existence on the perceiver; it must, in a sense to be analyzed, be 'in' the perceiver.

18. Before following up this point, it should be noticed that the same is true of the red of the other side of the apple. The apple is seen *as* having a red opposite side. Furthermore, the phenomenologist adds, the red of the opposite side is not merely *believed in*; it is bodily present in the experience. Like the white, not being seen, it is present in the experience by being imagined.

19. Notice that to say that it is present in the experience by virtue of being imagined is not to say that it is *presented as* imagined. The fruits of careful phenomenological description are not to be read from experience by one who runs. Red may present itself *as* red and white present itself *as* white;

but sensations do not present themselves *as* sensations, nor images *as* images. Otherwise philosophy would be far easier than it is.

20. The phenomenologist now asks us to take into account a phenomenon frequently noted, but as frequently misinterpreted. Consider the snow seen on a distant mountain. It looks cool. Do we *see* the whiteness of the snow, but only *believe in* its coolth. Perhaps this is sometimes so; but surely not always. Sometimes actual coolth is present in the experience, as was the *white* inside the apple and the *red* on the opposite side. Once again, we do not *see* the coolth of the snow, but we see the snow *as* cool; and we experience the actual coolth as we experience the actual whiteness of the snow. An actual coolness is bodily present in the experience as is an actual volume of white.

21. Let us combine our results into one example. We see the cool red apple. We see it *as* red on the facing side, *as* red on the opposite side, and *as* containing a volume of cool white apple flesh. We do not see *of* the apple its opposite side, or its inside, or its internal whiteness, or its coolness, or its juiciness. But while these features are not seen, they are not *merely* believed in. These features are present in the object of perception as actualities. They are present by virtue of being imagined.

22. We must introduce a further refinement. We see an apple. We see it *as* an apple. Do we see *of* it its *applehood*? We see a copper penny. We see it *as* a copper penny. Do we see *of* it its consisting-of-copperness? We see a lump of sugar. We see it *as* white and *as* soluble. We see *of* it its whiteness. Do we see *of* it its solubility? The answer to the last question is surely negative, as are the questions concerning applehood and copperness, and for the same reason. Aristotle would put it by saying that we see *of* objects only their occurrent proper and common sensible features. We do not see *of* objects their causal properties, though we see them as having them.

23. To draw the proper consequences of this we must distinguish between imagining and imaging, just as we distinguish between perceiving and sensing. Indeed the distinction to be drawn is essentially the same in both cases. Roughly imagining is an intimate blend of imaging and conceptualization, whereas perceiving is an intimate blend of sensing *and* imaging *and* conceptualization. Thus, imagining a cool juicy red apple (*as* a cool juicy red apple) is a matter of (a) *imaging* a unified structure containing as aspects images of a volume of white, surrounded by red, and of mutually pervading volumes of juiciness and coolth, (b) *conceptualizing* this unified image-structure as a cool juicy red apple. Notice that the proper and common sensible features enter in *both* by virtue of being *actual features* of the

image and by virtue of being items thought of or conceptualized. The applehood enters in only by virtue of being *thought of* (intentional in-existence).[1]
24. On the other hand, seeing a cool juicy red apple (as a cool juicy red apple) is a matter of (a) *sensing-cum-imaging* a unified structure containing as aspects images of a volume of white, a sensed half-apple shaped shell of red, and an image of a volume of juiciness pervaded by a volume of white; (b) *conceptualizing* this unified sense-image structure as a cool juicy red apple. Notice that the proper and common sensible features enter in both by virtue of being actual features of the sense-image structure and by virtue of being items conceptualized and believed in. As before, the applehood enters in only by virtue of being thought of (believed in).

III

25. The upshot of the preceding section is that perceptual consciousness involves the *constructing of sense-image-models of external objects*. This construction is the work of the imagination responding to the stimulation of the retina. From this point on I shall speak of these models as image-models, because although the distinction between vivid and less vivid features of the model is important, it is less important than (and subordinate to) the perspectival feature of the model (its structure as point-of-viewish and as involving containing and contained features).
26. The most significant fact is that the construction is a unified process guided by a combination of sensory input on the one hand and background beliefs, memories and expectations on the other. The complex of abilities included in this process is what Kant calls the 'productive' as contrasted with the 'reproductive' imagination. The former, as we shall see, by virtue of its kinship with both sensibility and understanding unifies into one experiencing the distinctive contributions of these two faculties.
27. Notice once again that although the objects of which we are directly aware in perceptual consciousness are image-models, we are not aware of them *as* image-models. It is by phenomenological reflection (aided by what Quine calls scientific lore) that we arrive at this theoretical interpretation

---

[1] The essential point is that the experience involves the *actual* rather than merely *believed in* existence of the volume of white. The phenomenologist thinks of this volume as an image-volume of white. A tough-minded contemporary might insist that while the *actuality* is a three-dimensional neurophysiological process of the kind correlated with stimulation by white objects, it need not be construed as an image in a more traditional sense. Nothing in the argument of this paper hinges on this controversy. One can think of the neurophysiological process as occasionally generating image-samples of white. On the other hand, when we look, not at an opaque object but, for example, at a pink ice cube, the neurophysiological process involves the actual existence of a volume of sensory pink.

of perceptual consciousness.

28. Notice also that the construction of image-models of objects in the environment goes hand in hand with the construction of an image-model of the perceiver's body, i.e., what is constructed is an image-model of oneself-in-one's environment. The perspectival character of the image-model is one of its most pervasive and distinctive features. It constitutes a compelling reason for the thesis of the transcendental ideality of the image-model world. Image-models are "phenomenal objects". Their *esse* is to be *representatives* or *proxies*. Their *being* is that of being complex patterns of sensory states constructed by the productive imagination.

29. Still more important is the fact that although the image-models are perspectival in character, the objects in terms of which they are conceptualized are not. Thus, *apples* are not perspectival in character. The concept of an apple is not the concept of a perspectival entity. Apples are *seen from* a point of view. Apples are *imagined from* a point of view. A spatial structure is *imagined from* a point of view. Yet the concept of a spatial structure, e.g., a pyramid, is not the concept of a point-of-viewish object. Thus we must distinguish carefully between objects, including oneself, as *conceived* by the productive imagination, on the one hand, and the image-models *constructed* by the productive imagination, on the other.

30. We are now in a position to put the elements of visual perception which we have been distinguishing together.

31. In the first place, the productive imagination is a unique blend of a capacity to form images *in accordance with* a recipe, and a capacity to conceive of objects in a way which *supplies* the relevant recipes. Kant distinguishes between the *concept* of a dog and the *schema* of a dog. The former together with the concept of a *perceiver* capable of changing his relation to his environment implies a family of recipes for constructing image models of *perceiver-confronting-dog*.

32. The best way to illustrate this is by a very simple example, for our perceptual experience does not begin with the perception of dogs and houses. The child does not yet have the resources for such experience. But though the child does not yet have the conceptual framework of dogs, houses, books, etc., he does, according to Kant, have an innate conceptual framework—a proto-theory, so to speak—of spatio-temporal physical objects capable of interacting with each other, objects—and this is the crux of the matter—which are capable of generating visual inputs which vary in systematic ways with their relation to the body of a perceiver.

33. Consider the example of a perceiver who sees a pyramid and is

walking around it, looking at it. The *concept* of a red pyramid standing in various relations to a perceiver entails a *family* of concepts pertaining to sequences of *perspectival* image-models of oneself-confronting-a-pyramid. This family can be called the schema of the concept of a pyramid. ["P.I.": productive imagination.]

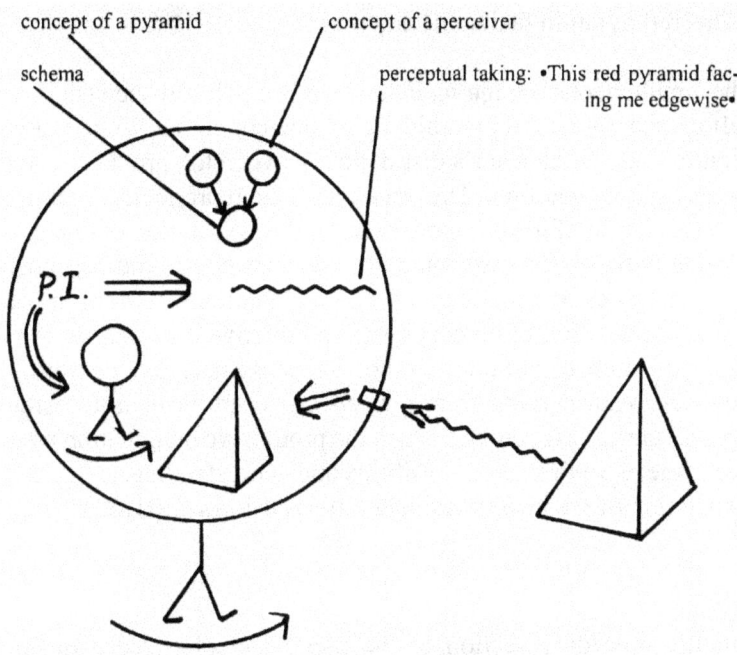

34. Notice that the pyramid schema doesn't follow from the concept of a pyramid *alone*. It follows from the complex concept of *pyramid in such-and-such relations to a perceiver*. This accounts for the fact that whereas the concept of a pyramid is not a point-of-viewish concept, the associated *schemas* concern sequences of perspectival models of a pyramid.

35. It is in terms of these considerations that Kant's distinction[2] between (a) the concept of an object, (b) the schema of the concept and (c) an image of the object, as well as his explication of the distinction between a house

---

[2] A140ff; B179ff. That Kant does not emphasize the role of the concept of the perceivers body and sense organs in determining the rules of the successive apprehension of the manifold of an object (e.g., a house) is, presumably, to be accounted for by the fact that the concept of the perceiving subject and its faculties is a constant factor in the generation of all object-schemata. The source of the difference between different object-schemata is the difference between the object-concepts involved (e.g., *house*, *dog*, etc.). The reader should ponder Kant's examples of the house and the ship in explaining the distinction between subjective and objective succession (A192; B237).

as object and the successive manifold in the apprehension of a house is to be understood. "The object is *that* in the appearance which contains the condition of this necessary rule of apprehension."[3]

36. To sum up, the productive imagination generates both the complex demonstrative conceptualization

This red pyramid facing me edgewise

and the simultaneous[4] *image-model*, which is a point-of-viewish image of oneself confronting a red pyramid facing one edgewise. We are now in a position to understand Kant's distinction between the productive and the reproductive imaginations.[5] The principle of the reproductive imagination is the "association of ideas": more exactly, the association of *objects*. The connection between the associated items is contingent, and dependent on the happenstances of experience. As an association of *objects* it presupposes the constitution of objects by the productive imagination. And the principle of such constitution is not happenstance, but conformity to recipe—schemata derived from concepts. We are also in a position to understand the precise sense in which the productive imagination mediates between "the two extremes, ...sensibility and understanding...," (A124) and is "...an action of the understanding on the sensibility" (B152).

IV

37. In the preceding section of the paper I emphasized a distinction between what we perceive the object *as* and what we perceive *of* the object. I related this distinction to the distinction between the complex demonstrative thought component and the complex-image component of the perceptual experience. I now want to do this in a more systematic way and to relate it to Kant's theory of categories.

38. The basic idea is that what we perceive of the object in visual perception consists of those features which actually belong to the image-model,

---

[3] A191; B236. For a more detailed explication of this Kantian thesis, which plays a central role in the transcendental deduction—most explicitly in the first edition (A104, A120)—see my paper "Kant's Transcendental Idealism," *Proceedings of the International Kant Congress, Ottawa, 1976* [*KTI*, in this volume].

[4] A momentary image-model is, of course, an abstraction from the image-model sequence which realizes the schema for a particular sequence of relations between perceiver and object.

[5] See A120-4. The discussion of the role of the productive imagination in the second edition transcendental deduction is very abstract and emphasizes the self-consciousness involved in the construction and awareness of perceptual representations (but see B138; B150ff). The specifics were left to the *Analytic of Principles*, where the account coincides with the first edition.

i.e., its proper and common sensible qualities and relations. Also its perspectival structure. On the other hand, what we perceive the object *as* is a matter of the conceptual content of the complex demonstrative thought. I pointed out that the sensible features belong in both contexts. Thus the phrase 'cube of pink (from a certain point of view)' refers to both an actual feature of the image-model and (in second intention) a component of the conceptual content of the demonstrative thought. Thus,

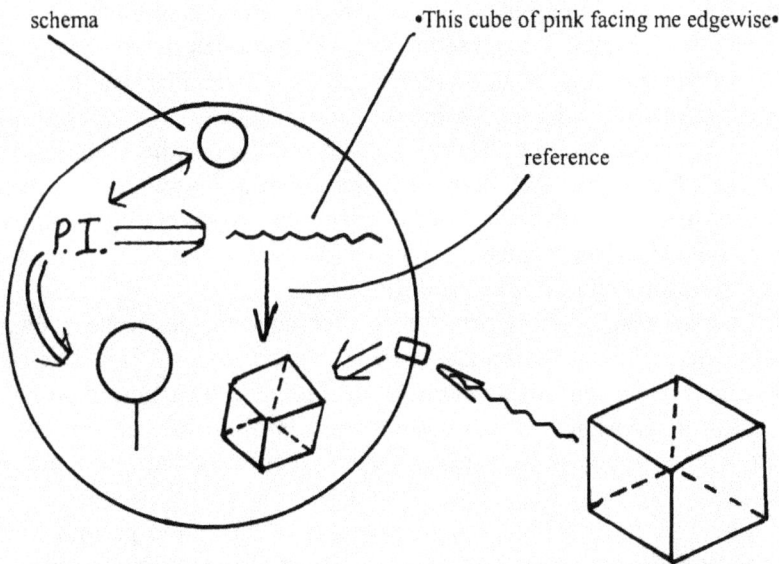

39. Now I emphasized that we do not perceive of the object its *causal properties*. What we see of it are its occurrent sensible feature. This can now be generalized as follows. We do not perceive *of* the object its character as a *substance* having *attributes*, its character as belonging with other substances in a system of interacting substances, its character as conforming to laws of nature. In short, we do not perceive of the object what might be called 'categorial' features. For the image construct does not *have* categorial features. It has an *empirical* structure which we can specify by using words which stand for perceptible qualities and relations. But it does not have logical structure; not-ness, or-ness, all-ness, some-ness are not features of the image-model. They are features of judgment. More generally we can say that the image-model does not have grammatical structure. (It will be remembered that we are construing mental *judgments* as analogous to sentences. A judgment, we said, is, as it were, a *Mentalese* sentence epi-

sode.) And, of course, Kant's categories are grammatical classifications. They classify the grammatical structures and functions of Mentalese.

40. Thus the category of substance-attribute is the structure 'S is P', the form of subject-predicate judgment. The category of causality is the form 'X implies Y'. The category of actuality is the form 'that-p is true'. More accurately, the categories are these forms or functions *specialized* to thought about spatio-temporal object.

41. In the preceding section we were concerned with the distinction between concepts of empirical object and the schemata of these concepts, i.e., the rules for image-model sequences which are determined by the concept of object-in-various-successive-relations-to-perceiver. But Kant also uses the term schema in connection with the categories. The categories do not specify image-models. There is no image of causality as there is an image of a house. Yet they do have in their own way schemata, i.e., rules specified in terms of abstract concepts pertaining to perceptible features of the world. Thus the schema for causality is the concept of uniform sequence throughout all space and time.

42. The Humean concept could be said to have images in an extended sense. Thus a person in a thunderstorm who experiences a finite stretch of lightning-thunder uniformity could be said to have experienced an image of causality. Kant, of course, does not say this, and I introduce it only to show that this new use of 'schema' is not completely foreign to the previous one.

43. The schematized category of causality, then, is the ground-consequence category where the ground (antecedent) concerns the occurrence of one kind of event, K_1, at t and the consequence concerns the occurrence of another kind of event, K_2, at $t + \Delta t$. Since the ground is an event being of kind K_1 it must be true that whenever K_1 occurs, K_2 also occurs.

44. The categories are in first instance simply identical *with* the forms of judgment, a point which must be grasped if traditional puzzles about the metaphysical deduction of the categories are to be avoided. These forms of thought would be involved in thinking about any subject matter from perceptual objects to metaphysics and mathematics.

45. The so-called pure categories are these forms of thought specialized to thought about *objects* (matter-of-factual systems) in general. Such objects need not be spatio-temporal, as are the objects of human experience. The full-blooded categories with which Kant is concerned in the *Critique* are the pure categories, specialized in their turn to thought about spatio-temporal objects. The relation of the forms of thought to the pure

categories is that of genera to species, as is the relation of the pure categories to the schematized categories.

V

46. Let me conclude with some remarks on Kant's concept of an intuition. Consider the statements

> This is a pyramid.
> This pyramid is made of stone.

The first has the explicit grammatical form of a sentence. So does the second. But notice that the grammatical form of a sentence is lurking in the subject of the second sentence. From the standpoint of transformational grammar we would think of it as derived from the deep structure

> This is a pyramid and it is made of stone.

47. One might be tempted to think of 'this' as a pure demonstrative having no other conceptual content than that involved in being a demonstrative. Kant *does* think of an act of intuition as a demonstrative thought, a Mentalese 'this'. However he does not think of this Mentalese demonstrative as a *bare* Mentalese 'this'. An example of an act of intuition would be the Mentalese counterpart of

> This cube facing me edgewise

where this is *not* to be understood as, so to speak, a Mentalese *paraphrase* of

> This is a cube which faces me edgewise.

48. The role of an intuition is a basic and important one. It is the role of bringing a particular object before the mind for its consideration. Thus, though there is a close relationship between

> This cube facing me edgewise ...

and

> This is a cube which faces me edgewise,

the former is an *irreducible* kind of representation. It is a demonstrative representation which has conceptual content and grammatical form. As noted above it contains the form and content of the judgment 'This is a cube'.

49. Thus for Kant intuitions are complex demonstrative thoughts which have implicit grammatical (and hence *categorial*) form.

50. However thin—as in the case of the child—the intuitive representation may be from the standpoint of the empirical concept involved, it nevertheless contains in embryo the concept of a physical object *now*, over *there*, interacting with other objects in a system which includes *me*. It embodies a proto-theory of a world which contains perceivers of objects in that world. (The reader should ponder A127-8.)

51. Kant emphasizes the difference between intuitions on the one hand and sensations and images on the other. He emphasizes that it is intuitions and not sensations or images which contain categorial form. When he speaks of *synthesis* in connection with perception, he has two things in mind:

(1) the construction of image-models;
(2) the formation of intuitive representations (complex demonstratives).

There is also the synthesis which is the formation of the explicit judgment, thus

(3) (This cubical substance) is a piece of ice.

52. Since intuitions *have* categorial form, we can find categorial form *in* them. In this sense we can arrive at categorial concepts by abstraction from experience—but only because experience contains *intuitions* which have categorial form. We cannot abstract the categories from sensations or images.

53. To sum up. Kant's categories are forms and functions of judgment. They are grammatical *summa genera*. From Kant's point of view, Aristotle's theory of categories was a failure because, failing to distinguish between intuition and image-model, his list of categories is haphazard (though guided obscurely by grammatical intuitions), and Aristotle confuses them with generic concepts of entities in the world. There is a legiti-

mate place for a theory of such concepts. But it must be carefully distinguished from the grammar of thought.

SOME REFLECTIONS ON PERCEPTUAL CONSCIOUSNESS

I

1. My aim in this paper is to put together some views on visual perception which I have developed in rather fragmentary form—usually subordinated to other topics—since my first attempt at a synoptic view in "Empiricism and the Philosophy of Mind."[1]

2. I still think that the general strategy of that essay was sound, but its explicit results were so schematic that, in spite of the fact that one of its central themes was a reassessment of the treatment of visual perception by philosophers in the analytic tradition it provides nothing worthy of being called a theory of visual perception. Nevertheless such a theory was obviously hovering in the background, if only as a research program and an attempt to specify certain adequacy conditions which such a theory would have to satisfy.

3. In the allotted time I can scarcely present a full fledged theory of visual perception. I can, however, turn my attention directly to some of the problems with which it deals, instead of subordinating them to other topics, let alone to an attempt to sketch an entire philosophy of mind. The situation will call for a delicate balance of assumptions and arguments, of raising hares and letting sleeping dogs lie.

4. Having thus construed my task, I do not expect my remarks to contain many surprises. Perception theory has been developed by able men, and the alternatives they present can be expected not only to contain a large measure of truth, but to agree in ways which, though not easily noticed because of differences in the larger contexts in which they are embedded, are nevertheless genuine.

5. Furthermore, for longer than I care to remember I have conceived of philosophical analysis (and synthesis) as akin to phenomenology. I would therefore expect this audience to be more sympathetic to what I have to say than many of my colleagues would expect. On the other hand, since I shall be dealing with specifics, I also would expect this sympathy to be laced with disagreement. Indeed some measure of disagreement is exactly what I am hoping for. After all, disagreement presupposes communication.

---

[1] Minnesota Studies in the Philosophy of Science, Vol. 1, edited by Herbert Feigl and Michael Scriven, pp. 253-330; reprinted as Chapter 5 of *Science, Perception and Reality,* London, 1965 [reprinted by Ridgeview Publishing Company, 1991].

II

6. The primary datum to be approached from the standpoint of conceptual analysis (or phenomenology) is that in the standard or paradigm cases we see physical objects from a point of view in physical space; thus, a red brick over there facing me edgewise.

7. Phenomenological reduction begins when we distinguish between the *object* seen (in this case an opaque object) and what we see *of* the object. We see the brick, but *of* the brick we see certain of its surfaces. These surfaces are, in a sense which I shall not attempt to define, dependent particulars. If one is careful, one can call them "parts" or "constituents" of the brick. They, too, we see from a point of view in physical space.

8. It is important that we think of these perceptible constituents as particulars. For what we see *of* an object also includes, as will shortly emerge, certain universals (attributes, relational properties); and universals are in no useful sense constituents of objects.

9. It is customary to distinguish between

    seeing a physical object (e.g., a brick)

and

    seeing *that* the physical object is a brick

or

    seeing *that* the physical object has a red facing surface.

Taking into account the above distinction between what we see (e.g., a brick) and what we see *of* what we see (e.g., a certain part of its surface), one would add a distinction between

    seeing *of* a physical object its facing surface

and

    seeing *that* the facing surface of a physical object is (e.g.) red.

10. Schematically the distinction is between seeing *objects*, thus

    seeing O   (where O is a physical object)

or

    seeing O'   (where O' is a perceptible constituent of O)

and what is often called "propositional seeing", thus

seeing *that* O (or O′) is φ.

11. These distinctions are reflected in traditional accounts of the mental activity involved in visual perception. I shall limit my remarks to those accounts which speak of perceptual *takings*, where takings are construed as occurrent beliefs (in the sense of believ*ings*) which (given ones perceptual set) we are caused to have in visual perceptual situations. In standard conditions the objects seen are in a legitimate sense (by no means easy to analyze) the external causes of takings.

12. Occurrent believings are construed as mental acts, the appropriate expression of which is the tokening of a sentence. Where the sentence is a subject-predicate sentence, we can speak of the subject and the predicate of the corresponding believing. It is commonly held that perceptual takings have subject-predicate form and that the subject constituent is appropriately expressed by a demonstrative. This constituent is itself construed as a demonstrative, not because acts of belief are linguistic, but because they are sufficiently analogous in essential structure and function to the sentence tokens which express them in candid speech, for it to be appropriate to make an analogical use of semantical terminology in describing them.

13. It is often noted that we express at least some of our perceptual experiences by using sentences, the grammatical subject of which is a complex demonstrative phrase, thus

> *This red brick* is larger than that one.

This sentence is obviously related to the compound sentence

> This is a brick and it is red and it is larger than that one.

Those who carefully distinguish between thought and its verbal expression can be tempted to construe the thought which the *first* of these sentences expresses in terms of the structure of the *second* sentence.

14. If this move is made, the result is to construe the subject of the perceptual taking as a bare "this", all characterizing being put in an explicitly predicative position; thus, to return to our original example,

> *This* is a red brick facing me edgewise.

15. The referent of "this" in perceptual contexts is construed as the object which in fact is seen. Thus, if the referent is a certain black bush, the perceiver is said to see the bush. If his taking has the form

> This is a bear

then he is said to take what is in point of fact a bush to be a bear. In our example, which I shall suppose to be a case of veridical perception, the perceiver sees a certain red brick facing him edgewise and sees *that* it is a red brick facing him edgewise, by virtue of the occurrence of a perceptual believing or taking of the form

> This is a red brick facing me edgewise.

16. But this division of visual takings into a subject which is a pure demonstrative and predicative constituent in an explicitly predicative position simply won't do as it stands. To appreciate this, however, we must back up a little.

17. Thus it is not clear, to begin with, that all perceptual takings are to be construed on the model of sentences with demonstrative subjects, though they may (and, perhaps, must) contain a demonstrative component. Thus, on certain occasions one can correctly be said to see that an airplane is flying high overhead without seeing the airplane. Perhaps in such cases the taking has the form

> There is an airplane flying way up there.

On the other hand, a distinction between the *situation* we see, and what we see *of* the situation may convince us of the primacy, in some sense, of the demonstrative analysis. What we see *of* the situation might be, for example, a vapor trail which grows at one end and fades at the other. The vapor trail is an object, and it seems natural to generalize the example and conclude that visual perception always in *some* sense includes the perception of an object,[2] and a taking of the form, to use the above example,

> This is a vapor trail.

---

[2] Of course, the object need not be a physical object in the narrow sense in which the red brick is an example. It might be a flash of lightning.

18. Leaving this issue aside for the moment, it must also be noted that even within the demonstrative model a distinction must be drawn between *what* we see, and what we see it *as*. The point is a familiar and important one, and part of its importance lies in the fact that the pure demonstrative model is incapable of handling it.

19. On the other hand, the complex demonstrative phrase model shows promise. Thus it is not implausible to suggest that one who sees a bush as a bear has a perceptual belief or taking of which the subject constituent is the complex demonstrative

>This large black bear ... .

20. If the believing of which the demonstrative phrase is the subject can be said to be a perceptual believing, perhaps

>This large black bear is moving toward me,

then we might distinguish between

>takings *that*

and
>takings *as*

and suggest that what one sees an object *as* is what belongs in the demonstrative phrase along with "this".

21. Indeed, one might go further and say that, properly speaking, takings simply *are* the complex demonstrative constituents of perceptual beliefs and that the explicitly predicative constituent of the belief is not part of what is *taken*, but simply what is *believed* about what *is* taken.

22. The model for taking, then, would be presupposition in something like Strawson's sense. The concept of occurrent belief could be extended to cover this sense of taking, by distinguishing between believing *that* and believing *in*. A perceptual believing *in* would be illustrated by the subject constituent of the believing expressed by

>*This red brick facing me edgewise* is too large to fit that gap.

23. The complex demonstrative constituent could be construed as a presupposing that the referent of "this" is a red brick facing one edgewise, and

argued that by virtue of this presupposing the referent of "this" is perceptually taken by the perceiver *as* a red brick facing him edgewise.

24. Suppose that the referent of "this" is a brick shaped piece of red modeling clay. Is the occurrence of the taking sufficient to warrant us in saying that the perceiver (Jones) sees a red brick shaped piece of red modeling clay facing him edgewise *as* a red brick facing him edgewise?

25. Clearly part of the problem is to give a clear account of the sense in which the "this" of

> This red brick facing me edgewise ...

can be construed as having a reference which is independent of the predicates which accompany it in the complex demonstrative phrase, so that it makes sense to say that "this" refers to something which is not a red brick. The proper move to make here seems to be the move from the phrase to what it presupposes, put in explicitly propositional form, e.g.,

> This is a red brick,

and determine the referent of "this" in the latter context. One must be careful to do this, however, without construing the perceptual believing expressed by

> This red brick facing me edgewise is too large

as identical with the perceptual believing expressed by

> This is a red brick and it faces me edgewise and is too large.

These considerations will loom larger at a later stage of the argument.

26. If we leave them aside, the question raised above (in paragraph 24) can be put more accurately as follows: Should we say that Jones' *seeing* a certain object *as* a red brick facing him edgewise *consists in* his believing *in* a red brick facing him edgewise, where this believing *in* is visual in the sense that his having this belief is, given his mental set, brought about by the action of that object on his visual apparatus?

III

27. Before tackling this question we must refine our distinction between the object seen and what we see of the object. For what we see of an object includes not just the dependent particulars we call "parts" or "constituents" (e.g., the surface of the brick), it also, as was suggested at the time, includes certain qualities or attributes and relations. That it includes them will be clear enough, though just *how* it includes them will be highly problematic.

28. Consider, for example, my favorite object, this pink ice cube. Its consisting of ice is largely a matter of its causal properties. It cools tea and is melted by fire.

29. We see the pink ice cube and, supposing the conditions of perception to be normal, we see *that* the transparent pink cube is made of ice. We even see the pink ice cube *as* a cube of pink ice. But do we see *of* the pink ice cube the causal properties involved in its being made of ice?

30. Of course, in seeing it *as* a pink ice cube we are seeing it as having the causal properties characteristic of ice. But do we see *of* the object these causal properties? The question is, to be sure, an awkward one. But if we consider certain other questions of a similar form, the answer seems to be *no*.

31. Thus, by contrast, we not only see *that* the ice cube is pink, and see it *as* pink, we see *the very pinkness* of the object; also its very shape—though from a certain point of view.

32. Even more interesting is the fact that in seeing the cube *as* a cube of ice we are seeing it *as* cool. But do we see *of* the cube its coolness? Here we are torn in a familiar manner. On the one hand we want to say that the pinkness and coolness are "phenomenologically speaking" on a par, and are tempted to say that the idea that we don't see its coolness is a matter not of phenomenology, but of scientific theory. On the other hand, when asked point blank whether we see its coolness, we find an affirmative answer intuitively implausible and are tempted to fall back on the idea that its coolness is *believed in,* i.e., that it is *taken as* cool.

33. Obviously we want to say that the ice cube's very coolness is not *merely* believed in, even though its very coolness is not seen. It clearly won't do to say that we feel or imagine a coolness on seeing the cube, what is in question is *its* coolness.

34. But though this topic is of great intrinsic importance, it must be postponed to another occasion, although I believe that the framework I am about to develop—enriched with an account of *synaesthesia*—provides the

key to the answer.

IV

35. Sufficient to the occasion is an analysis of the sense in which we see of the pink ice cube its very pinkness. Here, I believe, sheer phenomenology or conceptual analysis takes us *part of* the way, but finally lets us down. How far does it take us? Only to the point of assuring us that *something, somehow* a cube of pink in physical space is present in the perception other than as merely *believed in*.

36. In traditional terminology, the *somehow* presence of a cube of pink does not consist in its intensional in-existence as the content of a conceptual act. Nor is its character as a cube of pink in physical space facing me edgewise a matter of its actually being a cube of pink in physical space. It is *somehow* a cube of pink in physical space facing me edgewise without *actually being* a cube of pink in physical space facing me edgewise, yet without merely being the content of a *belief in* a cube of pink in physical space facing me edgewise.

37. Seeing *of* the cube its very pinkness and its cubicity (from a point of view) would be analyzed in terms of this *somehow, other than merely believed in* presence of a cube of pink in physical space facing one edgewise in the visual experience.

38. I say "visual experience" because it is time to take into account, at least provisionally, the fact that we can seem to see a cube of pink ice from a point of view in physical space when there is, in point of fact, no cube of pink ice in the neighborhood.

39. We can use the phrase "*ostensible* seeing of a cube of pink ice facing one edgewise *as* a cube of pink ice facing one edgewise" to refer to a visual experience which would be a case of seeing a cube of pink ice facing one edgewise as a cube of pink ice facing one edgewise, if there was such a cube of pink ice and it was (in a sense requiring analysis) causally responsible for the ostensible seeing.

40. Thus the *somehow*, other than as believed in, presence of a cube of pink ice facing one edgewise would be common to what can provisionally be called veridical and non-veridical ostensible seeings of a cube of pink ice facing one edgewise.

41. Now the obvious move is to introduce visual sensations as prototheoretical states of perceivers to *explain* these results of phenomenological or conceptual analysis. Thus the fact that we see (veridical perception) from

a point of view or *merely* ostensibly see (unveridical perception) from a point of view, the very pinkness and cubicity of a cube of pink ice would be explained by postulating the occurrence in the perceiver of a sensation of a cube of pink facing one edgewise. The fact that we don't see its very character of being made of ice would be explained by the exclusion of the proto-theory of the expression "sensation of a cube of ice".

42. It is by the introduction of visual sensations that we transcend phenomenology or conceptual analysis. They are not yielded by phenomenological reduction, but postulated by a proto-(scientific)-theory.

43. A sensation of a cube of pink facing one edgewise is a sensation *of a certain kind*, the kind normally brought about by the action on the visual apparatus of the perceiver by transparent physical cubes of pink (e.g., pink ice) which face the perceiver edgewise from a certain distance.

44. Visual sensations, which are states of the perceiver, are not (for example) *literally* cubes of pink facing the perceiver edgewise. On the other hand it is not *simply false* that they are cubes of pink facing the perceiver edgewise. It is tempting to appeal to the tradition of analogy and say that the pinkness and cubicity of a sensation which belongs to the "of a cube of pink" kind are *analogous* to the pinkness and cubicity of its standard cause.

45. But analogies are useful only if they can be cashed or spelled out. One way of doing this is by saying—as I have said on a number of occasions—

> According to this version of the adverbial theory of sensing, then, sensing a-pink-cube-ly is sensing in a way which is normally brought about by the physical presence to the senses of a pink and cubical object, but which can also be brought about in abnormal circumstances by objects that are neither pink nor cubical, and, finally, according to this form of the adverbial theory, the manners of sensing are analogous to the common and proper sensibles in that they have a common conceptual structure. Thus, the color manners of sensing form a family of incompatibles, where the incompatibilities involved are to be understood in terms of the incompatibilities involved in the family of ordinary physical color attributes. And, correspondingly, the shape manners of sensing would exhibit, as do physical shapes, the abstract structure of a pure geometrical system.[3]

46. I have come to see, however, that we must be able so to formulate the analogy between manners of sensing and perceptual attributes of physical objects, that it is made evident that the analogy preserves in a strict sense the conceptual *content* of predicates pertaining to the perceptible attributes of physical objects, while transposing this content into the radically dif-

---

[3] "The Structure of Knowledge: Perception," the first of a series three Matchette Lectures for 1971 at the University of Texas, published in *Action, Knowledge and Reality*, edited by Hector-Neri Castañeda, Bobbs-Merrill, Indianapolis, 1975, p. 313.

ferent categorial framework to which manners of sensings belong. Just what more (if anything) this would involve than spelling out in greater detail the analogies referred to above, and (perhaps) adding additional dimensions of analogy, I am not able to say. I believe, however, the problem is an important one, and that an adequate answer is necessary to explain the sense in which color concepts preserve their content throughout their migration from the manifest image to the scientific image.

47. In particular, the idea that there is a sense in which conceptual content can be preserved through a change of category seems to me necessary to give meaning to the idea that the *very pinkness and cubicity* of pink ice cubes can be *somehow* present in ostensible seeings of pink ice cubes *as* pink ice cubes.

V

48. It is an essential feature of the sensings postulated by the proto-theory I have been describing that they are not sensing *as*. To sense (a cube of pink)ly is not to sense something *as* a cube of pink, though it is a state postulated by a theory designed to explain what it is to *see* (or seem to see) a cube of pink *as* a cube of pink. Thus, sensing, though it is a *constituent* of seeing something *as* something, is not itself a case of seeing something *as* something.

49. I have distinguished two constituents of an ostensible seeing of a cube of pink ice as a cube of pink ice,[4]

   (1) the taking or believing in, construed on the model of the complex demonstrative phrase

   This cube of pink ice

   (2) the sensing (a cube of pink)ly.

The crucial question concerns how these constituents are related, the kind of togetherness they have.

50. It might be thought that the relation is merely a causal one, i.e., that given a certain perceptual set, the sensing is the *immediate* cause of the taking. If the perceptual set includes the belief that the room is illuminated by pink light, the perceiver might have a perceptual belief in a colorless ice

---

[4] For purpose of simplification, I omit the perspectival element.

cube. In this case he would be conceptualizing a cube of colorless ice, though sensing (a cube of pink)ly.
51. Would we say that he is seeing a cube of pink ice *as* a cube of colorless ice? In any event, he would not be seeing its colorlessness. A necessary condition of seeing its colorlessness is to sense (a cube without color)ly.
52. That the relation between the sensing and the taking is at least in part that of the former (given a certain perceptual set) being the immediate cause of the latter, is, I believe, clear. Might not the relation be even more intimate?
53. To appreciate this possibility, let us ask: What, in a case of veridical perception, is the referent of the demonstrative phrase

> This cube of pink ice ... .

The obvious answer would seem to be a certain cube of pink ice.
54. Suppose that what is in fact there is a cube of colorless ice. Would we say that the reference has failed, i.e., that the demonstrative phrase has no referent? Perhaps we would be willing to say that it does have a referent, namely, the cube of colorless ice, but that the perceiver is taking it to be a cube of pink ice. Would we also say that he sees the referent as a cube of pink ice? We can not say that he sees its very pinkness, but we can say that he ostensibly sees (or seems to see) its very pinkness. A similar move can be made if we suppose that what confronts the perceiver is a cube of glass.
55. But suppose that there is nothing there, i.e., that the perceiver is hallucinating. Would we say that the reference has failed, i.e., that the demonstrative phrase has no referent? Many philosophers would say that the answer is obviously yes. They would argue the previous move to save reference is no longer available for there is nothing *over there in physical space* of which it can be said that the perceiver takes it to be a cube of pink ice. The latter is, indeed, the case ex hypothesi. But is it the end of the matter?
56. What of the possibility that when all of the presuppositions packed into the complex (Mentalese) demonstrative phrase

> This cube of pink ice facing me edgewise ...

have been put into explicitly propositional form, it makes sense to preserve the reference of "this" by construing the referent as the *sensation* of a cube of pink facing one edgewise?
57. This suggestion faces a high hurdle, however, in the fact that if we

construe the process of making the presuppositions embedded in the (Mentalese) demonstrative phrase explicit on the model of moving in the direction of minimal perceptual takings, e.g.,

> This dangerous black bear standing on its hind legs ... .
> This dangerous black bear ... .
> This black bear ... .
> This black object ... .
> •
> •
> •

the minimal takings belonging to such series seem to concern items in physical space, thus, as in our example,

> This cube of pink (over there) facing me edgewise.

The latter seems to require that the referent of "this" must be the sort of thing which *could* be over there facing me edgewise. And it is surely a categorial feature of sensations that they are not over there facing me.

58. Nevertheless the possibility remains that whereas one can properly deny that the perceiver is seeing anything over there in space facing him edgewise, let alone a cube of pink ice, it would be incorrect to deny that he sees anything. After all, the perceiver is not *imagining* something, which is what the denial that he is seeing *anything* would normally imply.

59. Indeed, if we take seriously the idea that the thinning out of perceptual commitment which is implied by phenomenological reduction ends not with

> This cube of pink over there facing me edgewise

but rather with

> This *somehow* (a cube of pink over there facing me edgewise) ...

then the way would be open to save the reference by construing it to be the sensation, for the sensation is indeed that in the experience which is *somehow* a cube of pink over there facing one edgewise.

60. Notice that this move does not require the perceiver to conceptualize

his sensation *as* a sensation.

61. Notice *also* that "somehow" admits as a special case "straightforwardly". Thus while the referent of the most *cautious* perceptual taking can be construed as a sensation, we need not conclude that the referent of all perceptual takings is a sensation. For while it could be argued that the *ultimate* referent is always a sensation, by construing our original complex demonstrative phrase along the lines of phenomenological reduction as

> This *somehow* (a cube of pink facing me edgewise) which is a cube of pink ice facing me edgewise ...

the initial stages of reference saving can proceed without interpreting the referent as a sensation.

ON ACCEPTING FIRST PRINCIPLES

1. My purpose in this essay is to examine the authority of first principles. The first principles I shall discuss may not have the full stature, the all-around primacy usually associated with this term. Indeed some of them would be taken by many to belong to a much lower order, if they are accepted as 'principles' at all. But principles they are, I shall argue, and, in a legitimate sense, 'first'.

2. It is clear that a first principle does not gain its authority by having been derived from premises for the simple reason that, if it did, they and not it would be 'first'. On the other hand, a first principle must have authority. It is as rational beings that we accept them; it is *reasonable* to accept them. But what *kind* of reasonableness might first principles have? And how can they be shown to have it?

3. Now the idea of showing or establishing that it is reasonable to accept a first principle suggests that there is such a thing as reasoning of the following kind

> [premises].
> Therefore, it is reasonable to accept P,

even when there is no corresponding argument

> [premises].
> Therefore, P.

Where there is a good argument of the latter kind, there must be a good argument of the former kind. It is the vice versa that doesn't hold.

4. Let us consider this in more detail. Suppose we have an argument

> P.
> If P, then Q.
> Therefore, Q.

For example: If it is day it is light; it is day; therefore, it is light. Here we have a good argument. In the first place it is logically valid. It is also a good argument in that the premises are true so that, since it is valid, the conclusion must also be true. Furthermore, it is a good argument as it stands. No additional premise needs to be "understood."

5. On the other hand, intimately related to the above is another argument; something like the following:

Q follows logically from P and if P, then Q.
P and if P, then Q are true.
Therefore, it is reasonable to accept Q.

This time there may well be "understood" premises, or at least definitions. But the major premise is powerful, and surely takes us a long way towards the conclusion.

6. The first of the preceding arguments is a good, explicitly valid, argument of which Q is the conclusion. The second argument, though closely related, doesn't have as its conclusion Q by itself, but rather "It is reasonable to accept Q". Nor does its content seem to be quite as explicit. That there *are* good arguments of the second kind is clear. But what is their significance? Should we look them in the face and then walk on? I want to suggest that a careful study of such arguments provides the key to the problem with which we began.

7. Notice, to begin with, that the conclusion of the second argument says something about the conclusion of the first. It pats Q on the back, so to speak, by telling us that it is reasonable to accept it. The conclusion of the first argument, on the other hand, doesn't *say* that it is reasonable to accept Q. It simply says Q, though by preceding it by a "therefore" it *implies*, in some sense, that it is reasonable to accept Q.

8. Now accepting a proposition is, in a broad sense, a *doing*.[1] It is not a physical doing, but rather a mental doing, but it is a doing, none the less, and, like all doings, is something that can be correctly or incorrectly done. It is, so to speak, subject to a kind of ethics or morality, as are all doings. Let us, therefore, consider briefly the general idea of its being reasonable and proper to do something. Perhaps, by turning our attention to the ethics of doing in general, we gain some insight into the ethics of this very special kind of doing which is accepting a proposition.

9. "It is reasonable and proper to do A". What does this mean? Surely something like the following: There is a good and sufficient argument for doing A. What kind of argument? Arguments for doing something are clas-

---

[1] It should be clear that here as elsewhere I have been influenced by Herbert Feigl's fruitful distinction between 'validation' and 'vindication' in his important essay *"De Principiis Non est Disputandum...?"* in *Philosophical Analysis*, ed. Max Black, Ithaca: Cornell University Press, 1950.

sically called 'practical' arguments. So, in effect, we have led to the topic of the practical syllogism. This topic is of great importance not only for ethics but for a theory of action or conduct generally. I have no time on the present occasion even to articulate this topic, let alone touch on the many exciting issues it involves. I shall therefore select a simple paradigm and elaborate it just enough to mobilize your logical and philosophical intuitions for the use to which I am going to put the concept of a practical syllogism.

10. Consider the following piece of reasoning:

> Bringing about E implies doing A.
> I shall bring about E.
> Therefore, I shall do A.

The argument has the ring of validity. Can it be a *good* argument? In our earlier discussion we characterized a good argument as one which is valid and has true premises. In the present case, the major premise is the sort of thing which can be true. But what of "I shall bring about E"? If this were a mere prediction, it, too, could be true. But in the present context it expresses an intention, and it is not clear that intentions are properly characterized as true or false. I shall, for the moment at least, simply dodge this issue and assume that an argument of the above form can be good as well as valid, and that what makes it good (though not necessarily, of course, *morally* good) as opposed to *merely* valid (as a valid argument with a false premise is *merely* valid) is a matter of my actually having the intention to bring about E. There might be a stronger sense of 'good' which requires that I not only intend to bring about E, but that the bringing about of E has some kind of objective or natural claim on me. But whether this might be so, and if so, in what sense, is not my problem on the present occasion.

11. Let me call the conclusion of the above argument—"I shall do A"—its *logical* outcome. But "I shall do A" expresses an intention. Thus, if I am persuaded by the argument, I will acquire the intention to do A. Let me call the acquisition of this intention the *practical* outcome of the argument. Finally, there will be what I call its *terminal* outcome, namely a doing of A.[2] Other things being equal, we do what we intend to do. We may fail, but, unless we change our minds, we try to do what we intend to do.

12. Let us now return to our original example of a logically valid or

---

[2] These distinctions, as well as the framework in which they are used, were developed in my "Induction as Vindication," *Philosophy of Science*, Vol. 31, No. 3, July, 1964.

deductive argument.

(α) P.
if P, then Q.
Therefore, Q.

Clearly, if this argument presents our grounds for accepting Q, then Q is not a first principle, because P, as its ground, would be prior or, so to speak, "more first". Consider, now, the argument which we found to be correlated with it:

(β) Q follows logically from P and if P, then Q.
P and if P, then Q are true.
Therefore, it is reasonable to accept Q.

Argument (β) ends up with a conclusion which surely amounts to the idea that there is a good and sufficient practical argument for accepting Q. In a sense argument schema (β) is the schema of a proof that there is a good and sufficient practical argument for accepting Q. What would that practical argument be?

13. Notice that (β) itself is not a practical argument. It does not have a conclusion of the form 'I shall do A'. We are looking for an argument of the form,

[premises].
Therefore, I shall accept Q.

Argument (β) not only tells us *that* there is such an argument, it tells us *something* about its nature. If we follow its clues, we arrive at something like,

(γ) Accepting the logical implications of true beliefs is conducive to E.
Q is logically implied by P and if P, then Q.
I shall bring about E.
I believe P and if P, then Q.
P and if P, then Q are true.
Therefore, I shall accept Q.

What exactly the end-in-view, E, might be, is by no means easy to spell out. Clearly it is some advantageous epistemic state involving the making explicit of our beliefs so that inconsistent beliefs can be confronted with one another and questions pinpointed for subsequent investigation.

14. However this may be, I shall say nothing more about argument (γ) on the present occasion. My aim has been to highlight the distinctions between three closely related kinds of argument:

(1) the ground floor argument (α) which culminates in the assertion of Q;
(2) the third floor argument (β) which culminates in the assertion that there is a good and sufficient argument for accepting Q;
(3) the second floor argument (γ) which has as its conclusion "I shall accept Q".

15. The above distinctions present a framework in terms of which, I believe, some light can be thrown on the problem of first principles. And the first first principles which I shall examine are the first principles of a scientific theory. Consider the hackneyed example of the kinetic theory of gases developed as a deductive system. One distinguishes between its postulates and the theorems which are derived from them by logical means, thus:

[Postulates].
Therefore, [Theorems].

The theory isn't a mere, or 'uninterpreted', deductive system. Its point is to be so correlated with empirical generalizations that it can be said to explain them. These empirical generalizations are based on observations and experiments, and constitute what many contemporary philosophers of science call 'confirmed law-like statements'. They can, for our present purposes, be called empirical laws. In our present example, these laws pertain to temperature, volume, pressure, etc. as empirical constructs, definable in terms of observable and measurable quantities. The correlation of empirical laws with theorems in the deductive system is made by correlating the empirical concepts which occur in the empirical laws with theoretical expressions defined in terms of the basic vocabulary of the theory. This correlation of the vocabulary of the empirical laws with the vocabulary of the theory was compared by Norman Campbell to a dictionary. The dictionary is such as to correlate each confirmed empirical generalization or law with a theorem in the theory, and no theorem in the theory with an empirical generalization which has been falsified in the laboratory. The theory, if it is a good one, will have 'surplus value' in at least the following sense. There will be indefinitely many theorems which the dictionary 'translates' into empirical law-like statements which have not yet been tested, indeed may not yet have been thought of, or entertained. Thus the theory suggests hypotheses some of which, given the current state of experimental technique, can be put to the test. If they survive, this is a feather in the cap of the theory; if not something in the theory must be modified.

16. But my purpose today is not to discuss in detail the correlation of theoretical structures with experimental laws. The reader who is interested in this topic will find an excellent account in Ernest Nagel's *The Structure of Science*.[3] My aim is rather to call attention to and philosophize about a very simple and obvious point. It is not necessary to support a theory by deriving its postulates or assumptions from other propositions, thus

[prior principles].
Therefore, [postulates of the theory].

If we refer to the postulates of the theory as its first principles, one doesn't, typically, support a theory by deriving its principles from something 'more first'. Yet even without such derivation it is often reasonable to accept a theory. What makes it reasonable? What kind of reasonableness is involved?

17. If we can solve the problem of the reasonableness of accepting theories, we may get some light on the problem of the reasonableness of first principles generally. For, it will be remembered, the problem with which we began was exactly how it could be reasonable to accept first principles in view of the fact that this reasonableness cannot consist in their being derivable by logical means from prior principles.

18. Now the general lines of the move I am going to make are obvious. We accept the first principles of a theory because we accept the theory; and we accept the theory because of what it enables us to *do*. This suggests that the *rationale* of accepting the theory is bound up with practical reasoning. In other words we try to show that there is a good and sufficient practical argument of which the conclusion is 'I (or better, we) shall accept the theory'. We have thus established contact with the considerations advanced

---

[3] Hackett Publishing Co.

above.

19. In other words, we need something like the following:

>   [premises].
>   Therefore, we shall accept the theory.

And our previous discussion suggests that it will be of the form:

>   We shall bring about E.
>   Bringing about E implies accepting theories of such and such a character.
>   T is of this character.
>   Therefore, we shall accept T.

The logical outcome of this practical syllogism would be our intention to accept the theory. The terminal outcome would be the accepting of it.

20. Clearly the above is but the bare bones of an argument. I shall attempt shortly to put some flesh on these bones and, in particular, to discuss (albeit briefly) the character a theory must have in order to be worthy of acceptance. But before I do this, let me call attention to the fact that intimately related to the above is another argument schema of decisive importance for our problem.

21. It will be remembered in the case of the deductive argument

>   P.
>   If P, then Q.
>   Therefore, Q.,

we distinguished between three interestingly related arguments. This time we find only two, because *ex hypothesi* there is no relevant argument which has the first principles of the theory as its conclusion.

22. As we saw, this is exactly the difference between a first principle and derivative principles. In the case of derivative principles there is a relevant deductive argument which ends up with the principle. In the case of a *first* principle, there is no such argument, but there is nevertheless a relevant *practical* argument and a higher order argument which concludes with the assertion that there is such a good and sufficient practical argument. The latter is of the form:

[premises].
Therefore, there is a good and sufficient practical argument of kind K for accepting T.

But what might the premises of this meta-argument be?

23. Before attempting to answer this question, let me call attention to the fact that its conclusion seems to be equivalent to "It is *probable* that T" (where 'T' abbreviates the principles of the theory). It is sometimes denied that the concept of probability has any application to theories. Many theories of probability take as their paradigm a metrical probability which can be manipulated in accordance with the mathematical calculus of probabilities, for example the probability which is relevant to statistical contexts. This I regard as a radical error, which has led to Procrustean theories of probability. I shall argue that the concept of probability, though in a non-metrical and, perhaps, comparative form, legitimately applies to theories and that the way in which it applies illuminates the concept of probability generally. The suggestion is that probability statements are statements asserting the existence of a good and sufficient argument for accepting the proposition which is said to be probable.

24. What would it be to show that there is a good and sufficient argument of a certain kind for accepting a certain proposition. Consider the argument schema

(A_1) We shall bring about E.
Bringing about E implies accepting Ts which are φ.
T_1 is φ.
Therefore, we shall accept T_1.

What would the *probability* argument schema which corresponds to this *practical* argument schema look like? Its conclusion, according to the above, will be: "Therefore there is a good and sufficient argument of a certain kind for accepting T_1" (i.e., according to our analysis, "T_1 is probable").

25. The higher order argument, itself, will look something like this:

(MA_1) A_1 is a good and sufficient argument of kind K.
The conclusion of A_1 is 'We shall accept T_1'.
Therefore there is a good and sufficient argument of kind K for accepting T_1.

But what kind of argument is kind K? It is, in the first place, a practical argument. Furthermore it is an argument of a kind which postulates a certain end E and relates accepting theories of a certain character φ to that end. But what kind of end-in-view might E be? In the essay referred to above,[4] I characterize the property φ and the end-in-view E in the case of the probability of theories as follows:

> φ is the character of being the simplest available framework which generates new testable law-like statements, generates acceptable approximations of empirically confirmed law-like statements, and generates no falsified law-like statements.

26. What, then, is the end-in-view which we might have, so that we would be favorably disposed to accept theories of such a character? It will be remembered that in our discussion of the practical reasoning which has as its outcome the intention to accept the conclusion of a *deductive* argument, we found the end-in-view to be achieving an epistemically advantageous state in which inconsistent beliefs can be explicitly confronted with one another and brought within the scope of systematic investigation. If we suppose that the end-in-view of the latter investigation is the direct ability to produce adequate conceptual pictures of relevant parts of our environment, then epistemic states which contribute to this ability would come within the scope of practical reasoning of the kinds we are considering. How 'good' (fine grained, coarse grained, etc.) a conceptual picture must be to make possible the achieving of specific ends-in-view of a 'practical' character in a narrower sense of this term is a relative matter. A map which is adequate for our purpose may be totally inadequate for another.[5]

27. Thus, the epistemic end-in-view of *unlimited* accuracy and *open-ended* relevance is one which appeals to very few, and, of course, to those to whom it has no appeal it cannot provide a major premise for reasoning which culminates in "Therefore, I shall perform such and such an epistemic

---

[4] Footnote 2.
[5] For an exploration of the connection between factual truth and conceptual picturing see: "Truth and 'Correspondence'" *Journal of Philosophy*, 59, 1962, reprinted as chapter II in *Science, Perception and Reality*, Routledge and Kegan Paul (London, 1963) [reprinted by Ridgeview Publishing Company]; chapters IV and V of *Science and Metaphysics*, Routledge and Kegan Paul (London, 1967) [reprinted by Ridgeview Publishing Company]; and chapter 5 of *Naturalism and Ontology*, Ridgeview Publishing Co. (Atascadero, CA, 1979). For a discussion of the relevance of this connection to the problem of the truth of scientific theories see my "Scientific Realism and Irenic Instrumentalism: A Critique of Nagel and Feyerabend on Theoretical Explanation" in Robert S. Cohen and Marx Wartofsky (eds.) *Boston Studies in the Philosophy of Science* (Vol.II) New York, The Humanities Press.

act".

28. Who, then, has the end-in-view of producing adequate conceptual pictures, and what does having it involve? To one who does have this end-in-view, whatever may be involved in having it, the value of explicit consistency is clear. So, also, is the value of working with theories which, in addition to generating observationally acceptable approximations of established empirical generalizations, provide new empirical hypotheses which can be put to the test, as is the value of modifying or laying aside theories which generate disconfirmed law-like statements. But the upshot of this is that while we have filled in some of the details of the family of arguments pertaining to the accepting of theories by bringing in as proximate end-in-view the having of confirmed empirical law-like statements, thus

> We shall have confirmed law-like statements.
> Accepting theories which are φ is conducive to having confirmed law-like statements.
> T_1 is φ.
> Therefore, we shall accept T_1.

(with which is correlated a higher order argument which has as its conclusion

> Therefore, there is a good and sufficient argument of kind K for accepting T_1.,

i.e., T_1 is probable in the way in which theories are probable), there is a gap between the abstract end-in-view we were discussing a moment ago, and the end-in-view of having confirmed law-like statements.

29. To fill this gap I must develop one more line of thought pertaining to the concept of probability. I argued above that those philosophers who work with this concept and take as their paradigm those probabilities which fit neatly into the mathematical equations of the calculus of probability tend to overlook the real conceptual core of probability. It is characterized by some as a logical relation which holds between an hypothesis and its evidence, but which, unlike implication, does not authorize the *acceptance* of the hypothesis on the basis of the evidence. Thus the rationale of accepting probable hypotheses is left obscure—or it is even denied that there is such a rationale. By others, probability statements are classified with des-

criptive and factual statements about relative frequencies, idealized into statements about the limits of such relative frequencies. Again the connection of such factual statements with the reasonableness of accepting hypotheses concerning a short run to which these ideal frequencies are relevant is left obscure, or even denied.

30. On the approach I have been defending, however, the connection between probability and reasonable acceptance is analytic. Thus, given that a proposition is probable, no additional step need be taken to show that it is reasonable to accept it. To recommend this view, however, I must take into account more than the probability of theories—for the very significance of this phrase is denied by many of those with whom I am taking issue. I want, therefore, to show how this approach can be extended to the probability of empirical generalizations. It is my conviction that once we get a feeling for what probability amounts to in the case of theories, then the classical problem of induction with respect to empirical generalizations turns out to be much more manageable, and many things fall into place which would otherwise remain a tangled mess.

31. Let's suppose therefore that to say of a law-like statement, LL_1, that it is probable means something like this:

> There is a good and sufficient argument of a certain kind for accepting LL_1.

This would itself be the conclusion of an argument of the type represented by (β) in our earlier discussion. And the argument which is asserted to exist will be a practical syllogism of the type represented by (γ).

32. The practical argument in question has the form:

> We shall bring about E.
> Bringing about E involves accepting law-like statements which are ψ.
> LL_1 is ψ.
> Therefore, we shall accept LL_1.

This schema raises the questions,

> What is E?

and

> What is the character, ψ?

To take up the latter question first, it is clear that ψ has something to do with the relation of LL_1 to observation. This relation is a logical relation, R_L. Let us put it by saying that the law-like statement must 'accord' with the observational evidence. To determine what 'according', R_L, might be, we must first come to some conclusion about the form of a law-like statement. And, curiously enough, to do this we must come to some conclusion about the nature of the end-in-view, E.

33. Is it, perhaps, the state of possessing true beliefs about the limit frequency of a quaesitum property, Q, in an infinite reference class, R? In other words, the relative frequency of cases of Q among cases of R "in the long run"? Is it, limiting ourselves for simplicity to non-statistical law-like statements, the state of having true beliefs of the form:

$$(x)(fx \to gx),$$

i.e., (roughly) for all values of 'x', if x is f then x is g? Whichever line we take we run into the difficulty that the end is one we could never know ourselves to have reached, and I submit that any end with reference to which the doing of a certain action is to be justified must be the sort of thing that can be known to be realized.

34. The general point is related to our earlier attempt to distinguish between a *good* practical argument and one which was *merely* valid, i.e., to specify something which would play a role analogous to "having true premises" in the case of good non-practical arguments. There we suggested that it was a matter of the actual existence of the intention to bring about E. But it now appears that the appraisal of a practical argument as good requires that we say not only that the agent had the intention and that he *believed* that the action would realize it, but that it is actually realized. Thus, "Jones' action was justified *because it brought about E*".

35. Instead of the phantom ends considered above I suggest that the end-in-view, E, in the case of the acceptance of law-like statements is the state of being in a position to draw inferences concerning new cases, in a way which explains the observed cases. In other words, our proximate end-in-view is to have a principle of inference which applies in the same way to 'new' and 'old' cases. And the state of having such a principle *is* the sort of thing that we can know that we are in. And to be in this state requires *accepting* principles of inference which conform to this criterion. This *accepting* is what in our terminology is called the *terminal* outcome of a practical syllogism which has as its *logical* outcome or conclusion, "I shall

accept LL_1".

36. Thus, reflection on the proximate end-in-view of inductive reasoning supports the view, which, as we shall see, has independent support, that law-like statements have the form of principles of inference. In the case of non-statistical law-like statements, we can suppose that they have the form (roughly):

From 'x is f', it may be inferred that 'x is g'.

The statistical case is more complex, and its exposition would involve the discussion of still another dimension of probability, that which is represented by the schema

n/m Rs are Q.
This is an R.
Therefore, the probability that this is Q is n/m.

I have discussed this, as well as the above modes of probability, in the essay referred to above[6] and shall omit the topic here.

37. Now new evidence may well lead us to abandon one inference ticket and accept another. But the point is that as long as we have the evidence we do have, and this evidence is that all observed cases of f are g, we know that we have an inference ticket which accords with evidence and applies to the cases we expect to encounter.

38. As I see it, then reflection on the probability of law-like statements reinforces a conception which arises independently in the exploration of problems pertaining to counterfactual conditionals, the intuitive distinction between accidental and non-accidental uniformities and the concept of 'natural necessity'. For this exploration has constantly generated the idea (rejected only because it treads on radical empiricist toes) that law-like statements are inference tickets. Unlike the inference tickets of formal logic, they are empirically based in the sense that they are accepted because it is reasonable to accept them, given the evidence and given our proximate end-in-view.

39. Law-like statements, therefore, are empirically based principles of inference which authorize such inferences as, to use a crude example, 'Lightning now, therefore thunder shortly'. It also authorizes such conditionals as 'If there had been lightning then, there would have been thunder

---

[6] Footnote 2.

shortly' and such statements as 'There was thunder then *because* there had been lightning shortly before' and 'That there was lightning shortly before made it necessary that there be thunder then'.

40. It might well be said, "If the character of being a first principle, as you conceive it, is one which can be possessed by "low-level empirical generalizations", it can scarcely be that which makes First Principles First." I would begin my reply with an aside. The process of theoretical explanation is *in a sense* the process of turning low-level first principles into derivative principles. I would then add that there are many varieties (indeed dimensions) of first principles which play into each others hands in the course of inquiry without losing their firstness. But above all I would point out that our problem was not "What is a first principle?" but "How can it be reasonable to accept a first principle?" and it may well be that the strategy outlined above for dealing with the reasonableness of law-like statements and theories may throw some light on the reasonableness of holding those more exalted First Principles with which philosophy must sooner or later come to grips.

**Sellars' Notes
for**

**The Ernst Cassirer Lectures
(April 16, 18, 19, 1979 at Yale University)**

Kant's Transcendental Metaphysics

1. The Ontological Framework
2. The Epistemological Turn
3. Transcendental Realism?

[The following 9 paragraphs were on two yellow sheets inserted into the Cassirer Lectures folder.]

I. Some Background Considerations

1.   The aim of this slender volume is ambitious indeed. It is nothing less than to delineate in readily intelligible terms the fundamental principles of Kant's metaphysics as presented in the *Critique of Pure Reason*.
2.   The first edition clearly belongs to what Reichenbach called the order of discovery. We see the product as emerging from the dialectical process which gave it birth, and hence as conceptually tied to the historical contingencies of the latter's starting point.
3.   However self-contained and ordered a system may be in an "ideal" formulation, it can be reached by many roads and each turning leaves its traces on the end result. 'The' system is but an abstraction from the many dialogues which embody it and which alone have genuine philosophical existence.
4.   It is no news that to understand the metaphysics of the *Critique*, one must be at home in the climate of ideas shared by Kant with those whose views he took seriously. Of these ideas the most important for the historian to grasp are the most elusive, for they are those whose intelligibility was taken for granted, so that they were rarely submitted to scrutiny.
5.   It is relatively easy for the scholar to get the sense of explicitly drawn distinctions and of concepts whose content is pinned down by explicitly formulated principles. But when concepts and contrasts remain implicit like subterranean forces, a special skill is called for on the part of the historian. Indeed it is exactly here that history of philosophy without philosophy is likely to be blind. For to the extent that one is unaware of the range of conceptual structures which might have been at work, one will be at the mercy of the surface grammar of the argument. And to be aware of this range of possibilities is to have philosophized.

6. Philosophical explanation begins as metaphor. Philosophical theories are generated by propping metaphor against metaphor as in building a house of cards. One hopes that the resulting structure will fuse into an intelligible whole which no longer depends on metaphor for its power to convince.

7. This goal, however, remains elusive, realized most fully in those branches of philosophy which have split off to form separate disciplines. But the closer one gets to the driving force of philosophy as the attempt to grasp the togetherness of things, the more entrenched one finds the role of metaphors and while this role can be disguised by embedding them in an elaborate system of principles and proofs (one thinks of Spinoza and Hegel), they are there to the eye which is not taken in by appearances.

II

8. In the *Critique of Pure Reason*, Kant elaborates a system of categories. How the categories to which he calls attention constitute a system is, for Kant, the essence of the matter. Other philosophers had discerned summa genera of the matters of fact which make up the experienced world. But, as Kant saw it, they had not explained in what their character as categories consists, i.e., the family trait which sets these apart from other abstract concepts.

9. Categories are, of course, classifications. But classifications of what? It clearly wouldn't do to answer 'things' in any ordinary sense of this term. Nor is it illuminating to add, with a wave of the hand, that of this term is to be taken in the broadest of senses—a sense in which, so to speak, *anything* can be a thing.

[Here begins the main body of notes.]

1. The Ontological Framework

A1. Kant's ontological categories: existence "in itself" versus existence for thought. **Existence in itself is** existence independent of thought: what would exist even if (metaphysical counterfactual) there were no thinking; i.e., **an item exists in itself if its existence** is logically independent of there being any thinking of which *it* is the object. **Existence for thought** is existence as an object of thought, i.e., existence of something *represented* by a mind *as so* represented.

(*SM*, ch. II, 3)
3. The importance of the categories Descartes applies to mental acts lies, as I have indicated, in the fact that they can be seen to be less sophisticated counterparts of distinctions which are drawn with more or less rigour in those contemporary philosophies of mind which have been influenced by formal semantics. The distinctions fall into two closely related, indeed complementary sets, one focused on concepts pertaining to truth, the other on concepts pertaining to existence—none of which is surprising, since it would generally be admitted that there is the closest of connections between existence and truth, at least in the case of things and their modifications. The

first set of categories distinguishes between:

(a) a representation *qua* act, i.e., qua represent*ing* or 'operation of the mind';
(b) the character by virtue of which it represents what it represents; and,
(c) where appropriate, the substance or modification of which the represent*ing*, *qua* representing what it represents, is true.

Closely related to the above a contrast between two ways in which things or substances and their modification can exist:

(a) They can exist 'in' mental acts of representing—i.e., they can be, in Descartes' phrase, 'the objective reality of an idea' by which, he tells us, he understands 'the entity or being of the thing represented by the idea, in so far as the entity is in the idea'.
(b) They can, as I shall put it, exist *simpliciter*. In Descartes' terminology, 'the same things are said to be formally in the object of the ideas when they are such as they are conceived'.

(*SM*, ch. II, 5-6)
5. The first set of distinctions is related to the second as follows:

(1) For a thing or modification to exist 'in' a mental act is for the latter to represent it.
(2) A mental act representing a modification is true of a substance which exits *simpliciter* if and only if the modification exists *simpliciter* as a modification of the substance.

I have deliberately put *these* two points in a make-shift way, since more subtle formulations require distinctions—e.g. between objects and states of affairs—which were not part of Descartes' technical apparatus, though, of course, they made their presence felt.
6. We can tie these distinctions in with the 'new way of ideas' by identifying ideas with entities which are capable of existing 'in' representings, as thus capable. If we do so, however, we must take account of the fact that the term is often used (as in the passage quoted above) to stand for represent*ings*, as contrasted with what they represent. If we drop this usage to avoid confusion we can say that 'ideas' in the sense of representables *qua* representables are capable of two interesting relations, the 'in' relation to mental acts, and the 'truth' relation to things and their modifications *qua* existing *simpliciter*.

(*SM*, ch. II, 12-13)
12. The root notion of 'existing in itself' is that of existing *simpliciter* as contrasted with existing *as represented*, i.e. existing 'in' a representing or as 'idea'. Clearly represent*ings* (conceptual or non-conceptual) as well as non-represent*ings* may be represent*ed*. Thus we can distinguish:

(1a) non-representings *qua* existing *simpliciter*;
(1b) representings *qua* existing *simpliciter*;
(2a) represented non-representings *qua* represented;

(2b) represented representings *qua* represented.

13. Let us now introduce the term 'in itself' for anything, representing or not, which exists *simpliciter as* existing *simpliciter*; and let us use the term 'content' for anything, representing or not, which exists 'in' a representing, *qua* so doing. ...

(*KTI*, 13)
13. Descartes distinguishes between the act and the content aspects of thought. The content, of course, 'exists in' the act. And, of course, contents *as contents* exist only 'in' acts. On the other hand, there is a sense in which something which 'exists in' an act can also exist, to use Kant's phrase, 'outside' the act. In Descartes' terminology, that which exists 'in' the act as its 'content' can have 'formal reality' in the world.

A1a. In this sense [the sense of 'existence in itself' discussed above], a Berkeleian mind or spirit is an existence "in itself". If it seems a "thing" in itself, that would be because of the special connotations of the term 'thing'.

A1b. For Berkeley, "ideas" are mind-dependent. Now this might be because they are *modifications of* the mind, acts of representing. Are "ideas" acts of representing? Berkeley would not have called them such because 'act' for him connoted *action* and volition. True actions *are* volitions. But a modification of the mind need not be, in this sense, an "act".

A1c. Are "ideas" *objects* of the mind? Clearly Berkeley thinks of ideas as items with which thinking is concerned. But then they could also be *modifications* of the mind.

A1d. Presumably a modification of the mind doesn't depend for its existence on being noticed, on being an object of concern.

(*BD*, 99-100)
99. Berkeley, as is well known, formulates the 'act-object' account of perceiving in the *Three Dialogues between Hylas and Philonous*, only to reject it. His explicit reason for rejecting it is a bad one, turning as it does on an equation of 'act' with 'deed'. He points out that what we *do* in perception is *look*. On looking we see, but in seeing we are passive. We can choose where to look but not what to see.

100. Berkeley's real reason for rejecting the act-object account is to found in the principle that the *esse* of what is perceived is *percipi*, i.e., to be sensed. The act-object metaphor implies that what is perceived could exist without being perceived, and hence implies, in traditional terms, a real distinction between perceiving and its object.

...

A1e. One theme in Berkeley's conception of an idea is certainly that of its being a modification of the mind:

a feeling of pain is a modification of the mind
a sensation of blue is a modification of the mind

A1f. Thus one theme in Berkeley's esse (of this) is *percipi* is that for a case of blue to exist is for a mind to have a sensation of blue where the phrase 'sensation of blue' is a nominalization of

> senses blue (senses this).

> (*BD*, 102)
> 102. It surely does not distort the situation too much to say that for Berkeley a perceiving of a red triangle does not have form
>
>> (perceiving) R (a red triangle)
>
> but rather
>
>> (of a red triangle) perceiving,
>
> i.e., to interpret him as holding that for a perceiving to be 'of a red triangle' is for it to be a perceiving of a certain sort.

A1g. But there is another theme which gets tangled up with this in Berkeley's system—a *Cartesian-Scholastic* theme: "idea", "representation".

A1h. To uncover this theme let us turn our attention away from sensing and feeling to *thinking*:

> A thought of the sun occurred to Jones.

[The contrast at issue in this and the preceding paragraphs is one Sellars discusses in *KTI*, first, with respect to Descartes, then with respect to Berkeley.]

> (*KTI*, 26)
> 26. ... For Descartes had *two* paradigms of what it is to be a mental state. Let me begin with the one I have neglected. Sensation is a mental state, though one in which the body is intimately involved, and his paradigm of a sensation is a feeling of pain. To us, the obvious feature of a feeling of pain is that a feeling of pain simply *is* a pain. ...a pain is a kind of feeling. If we put this by saying that a pain is a 'content' or 'object' of feeling, this should be regarded simply as a (misleading) paraphrase of the above. The danger arises from the fact that this usage would tend to assimilate feelings of pain to Descartes' second paradigm, the clear distinct *thought* of an object. ...

> (*KTI*, 29)
> 29. Now Berkeley, as is well known, also assimilated color to pain. What then, of shaped colors? When one feels a pain, there is an actual case of pain. When one senses a color, there is an actual case of color. But when the mind senses a triangle of red, is there an actual case of shape? When *directly* confronted with this question, Berkeley's answer is *no*. The shape exists only 'by way of idea,' and it is clear that *here* the operative conception is a Cartesian *cogitatio* of which the shape is a *content* in a sense which does not entail that a mental state has a shape. ...

(*BD*, 115)
115. But the case of shape was crucial. Berkeley clearly would not wish to say that a perception of a triangle is a triangle. ... Like Descartes he assimilates the being-for-sense of a triangular item to the being-for-the-understanding of a triangular item.

> ... It may perhaps be objected, that if extension and figure exist only in the mind it follows that the mind is extended and figured; since extension is a mode or attribute, which (to speak with the Schools) is predicated of the subject in which it exists. I answer, those qualities are in the mind only as they are perceived by it, that is, not by way of *mode* or *attribute*, but only by way of idea; ... [*A Treatise Concerning the Principles of Human Knowledge*, section XLIX]

A2. [Sellars instructs himself to make some comments on the relational construal of thinking, especially with regard to contents. See *KPT*, chs. 3 and 4.]

A3. [This paragraph sets out, in diagrams and with almost no accompanying text, some of the possibilities for thinkings (representings) and contents with respect to the existence (and non-existence) of immanent objects and transcendent objects. Presumably Sellars made some remarks on which of the various possibilities (might) fit Berkeley and which (might) fit Descartes. These diagrams all presupposed some sort of "relational approach", one in which there is a "thinking" and "object thought of". See *KPT*, chs. 3 and 4.]

A4. Pictures and Metaphors. [This paragraph contains a diagram showing, on the relational model, two individuals, Jones and Smith, "thinking of the *same* thing". This figure is entitled "*intersubjectivity*". See *KPT*, ch. 4, sections B and C.]

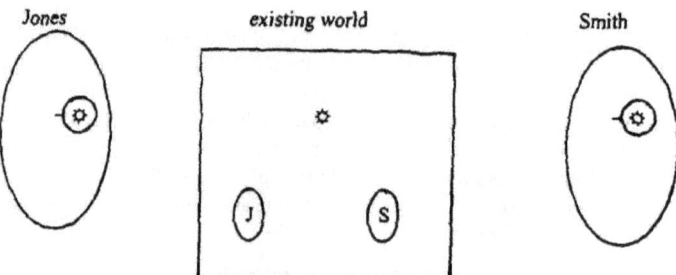

[In the existing world are the sun (✺) and both Jones and Smith who also appear as thinkers, thinking about the sun. Each thought is an act (→) and a content (✺) shown in a circle. The content is shown in the diagram to be the same for both Jones and Smith. Thinkers are shown in figures as ellipses set in an orientation convenient to the figure.]

A5. Intersubjectivity and the non-existing. [Presumably Sellars commented that the figure in **A4** seems, in at least one respect, too simple for the philosophers of the period he is discussing. Sellars introduces items called "thinkables", or, as he will subsequently call them, "representables". Jones and Smith now think of the sun and also think of Pegasus. Thinkables (representables) are indicated by overlining and items in the existing world are indicated by underlining. See *KPT*, ch. 4, section C.]

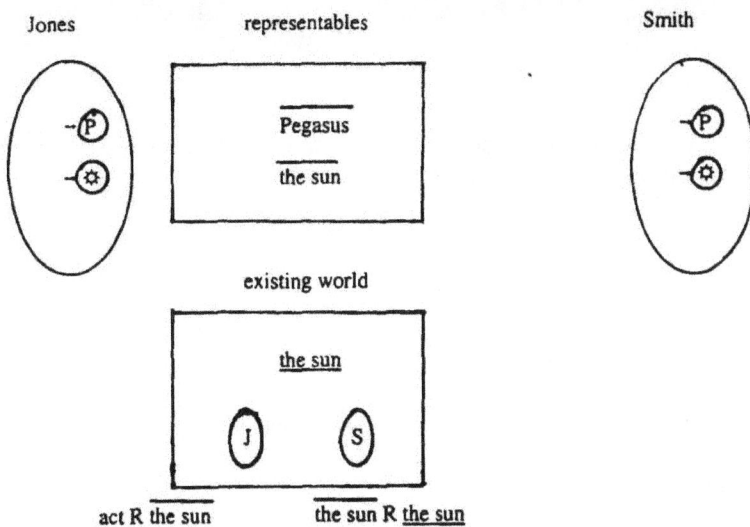

[The acts have a relation to the representables (thinkables) and some representables have a relation to existing items.]

(*KTI*, 14)
14. The concept of 'existence in thought' is, of course, a metaphor. So, of course, is the idea that a thought is *true* if its content 'corresponds' to something actual in the world. In the Cartesian tradition, this account of truth holds both of thoughts of individuals and thoughts of states of affairs. Thus a thought of an individual is true if there 'corresponds' to it an actual individual, i.e. if the individual exists not only 'in the thought' as its content, but in the actual world. Similarly, the thought of a state of affairs is true if there 'corresponds' to it an actual state of affairs, i.e. if the state of affairs which exists in the thought as its content, also exists in the actual world.

(*KTI*, 16)
16. One final terminological point: The *content* of the thought of an individual was considered to be, in an important sense, an *object* of the thought. Indeed the thought would have in this sense an object even if nothing in the actual world corresponded to it. Later philosophers drew tidy distinctions between 'immanent objects' and 'transcendent objects,' and we are all familiar with the intuitive appeal of these metaphors. ...

A6. Notice that we now have a four-fold distinction [The following list was accompanied by a note indicating that Sellars takes the four entries as items that can be associated with Kant's term 'Vorstellung' and its various grammatical compounds]:

  a. representing
  b. content
  c. representable
  d. transcendent object

[Sellars instructs himself to "postpone" any questions about "the ontological status of representables" and its connection with "intersubjectivity". See *KPT*, chs. 4-6.]

A6a. Whatever their intrinsic mode of being, representables have two modes of being *realized* or *actualized*:

  (a) by acts of representing (as the content);
  (b) by objects in the world.

A6b. We have been talking about representings of *things*. We now turn our attention to states of affairs.

A7. Judgeables as representables.

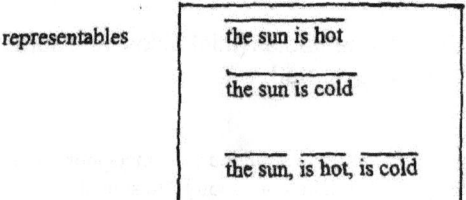

A8. Judgeables also have two modes of being realized or actualized [see **A16ff**]:

  (a) as content (being actually represented);
  (b) as fact.

Existence and truth as predicated of representables:

the sun is hot is true, the sun exists, Pegasus does not exist

A9. From "act-content" to "act-form of act": judgments as mentalese tokens. [With the change to "act-form of act", Sellars changes, though not always, from overlining for contents to quotation marks. Intro, 26-55.]

The Notes for the Cassirer Lectures (CLN, 120)

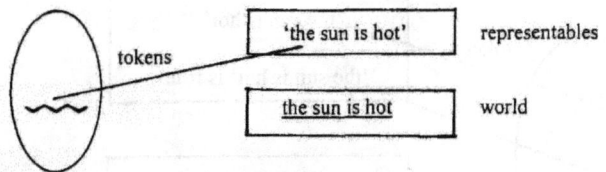

But to be a mentalese sentence is essentially to have a certain meaning.

A10. Judgeables as having syntactical form. [See *SM*, ch. IV, section VIII.]

A11. A judgeable as a unity of representables.

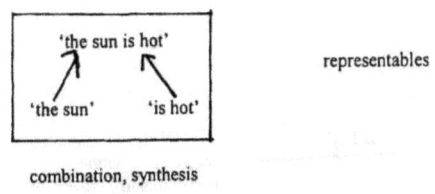

A12. A judging versus a mere concurrence of representings. [See *KPT*, ch. 12.]

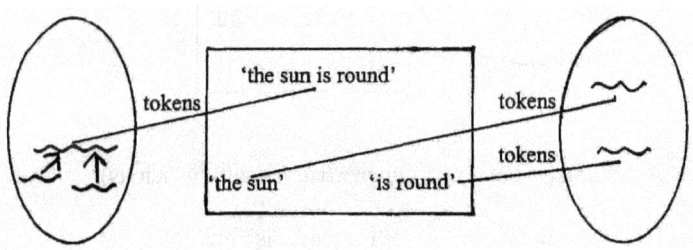

A13. Judgeables and truth. The judgeable 'the sun is hot' is correlated with the judgeable '"the sun is hot' is true'.

542 The Notes for the Cassirer Lectures (CLN, 120)

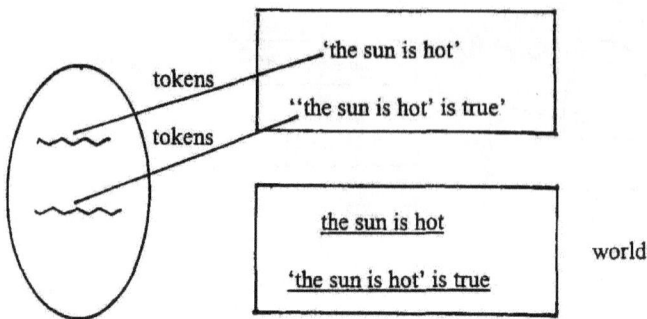

A13b.   Apperception: the judgeable 'the sun is hot' is correlated with the judgeable 'I judge 'the sun is hot''.

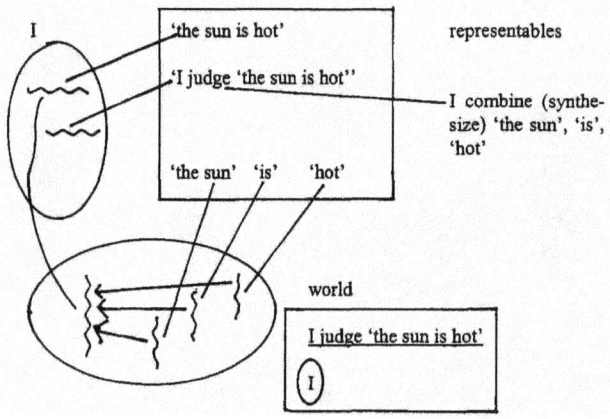

A13c.   A judging is something *apperceivable* (self-conscious).

| I | think
unite
synthesize
combine | 'the sun', 'is', and 'hot' |

I am (potentially) conscious of a unique mode of togetherness of representings.

A judgeable is a unity of *representables*. It is actualized as an apperceptible act of synthesis. The kind of unity a judgeable has can be called an apperceptible unity. What is *apperceived* is not the *judgeable* (type) but an *actual judging* (token).

In this derivative sense a *judgeable* can be called a *unity of apperception*. [See **A20** and **A32d**ff. Intro, 308-20.]

The Notes for the Cassirer Lectures (CLN, 120)   543

A14. The judgeable 'the sun is hot' becomes actually judged (by someone) by virtue of its being tokened by the result of a putting together, in a unique way, of tokenings of 'the sun', 'is', and 'hot'.

A15. We can put this by saying that the form of the *actualization in thought* of the judgeable 'the sun is hot' is:

> an I combining in a unique way representings of the sun and of being hot

or

> an I thinking the sun is hot.

[or, in general,]

> an I thinking S is P.

A15a. This is the correct interpretation of Kant's statement (in the Paralogisms (A341; B399)) to the effect that "...the judgment 'I think' is the *vehicle* of all concepts...and therefore of transcendental concepts, and so is always included in the conceiving of the latter and is itself transcendental."

[Somewhere near here, the second section, **2. The Epistemological Turn**, begins.]

A16. Against this background let us take another look at the other mode of actuality pertaining to the judgeable 'the sun is hot'. This concerned the correlation of this judgeable with the fact that the sun is hot.

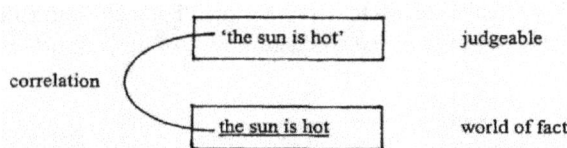

A16a. Now to say that 'the sun is hot' is true is, to put the point in a very abstract way (which is a placeholder for a sound theory), to say that the representables 'the sun' and 'hot' *belong together* in actual representation in a way which *independent of the idiosyncracies of the mental histories of individual minds*, i.e., in a way which, in Kantian terms, is objectively and intersubjectively valid. [See *KPT*, ch. 12.]

A16b. Compare association. To make the point, we must distinguish between a representable, e.g., 'black cat', and

> the presence of the representable in the mental vocabulary of a certain mind (e.g., Jones'),

i.e., Jones' ability to *token the representable*,
i.e., Jones' ability to have representings which are of a black cat.

Let us put this by saying that Jones has the concept of a black cat.

A16c.   Suppose that Jones has the concept of a black cat and also that of bringing bad luck. Suppose that, on a number of occasions, Jones has seen the presence of a black cat followed by a disaster. He may be expected

- (a) to think of disasters when he thinks of a black cat (co-occurrence of thoughts)
- (b) (which is not the same thing) to think

            (the presence of) black cats bring bad luck.

A16d.   In the first case (a), we have a tendency to co-occur (mere) of representings of 'presence of a black cat' and 'bad luck'; in the second case (b), a tendency to judge 'the presence of a black cat brings bad luck'.

A16e.   In both cases, however, we can speak of a *belonging together* with respect to Jones' mind of the representables 'presence of a black cat' and 'bad luck'.

But this belonging together (with respect to Jones) of the representables is *idiosyncratic* and a function of the contingencies of Jones' experience.

A16f.   We can put this by saying that they belong together not *qua* representables but *qua* representables in *Jones'* conceptual vocabulary.

A16g.   We might then contrast this belonging with the belonging together of 'the sun' and 'hot': truth associates the sun with heat.

But how are we to analyze this contrast?

The transcendental realist claims that 'the sun' and 'hot' belong together in the desired objective sense by virtue of the correspondence of the *judgeable* with the *fact*.

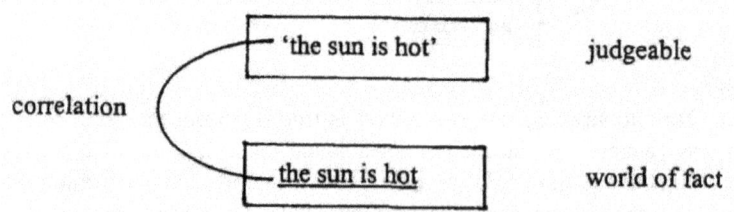

A16h.   The essential feature of this position is that it interprets the *independently real* (the world in itself) as a structure isomorphic to the structure of *true judgeables*.

A16i.   If we think of the system of true judgeables as the true history of the world, then the true system of judge*ables* stands over and against an isomorphic *structure* of *facts* construed as items having logical form (categorial form) and existing independently of thought and mind. If it is *true* that the earth was hot two

The Notes for the Cassirer Lectures (CLN, 120)   545

billion years ago, then there *is* the fact that the earth was hot two billion years ago, and similarly for every true judgeable about the history of the universe.

A16j. Now it is important to bear in mind that Kant does not wish to deny that there is a sense in which the domain of true judgeables

"corresponds"

to things as they are in themselves (independent reality). But he rejects the account of this correspondence as given by the Transcendental Realist.

A16k. The key point is that Kant rejects the idea that reality in itself has

propositional form (judgmental form).

A16l. Reflect on the obvious picture.

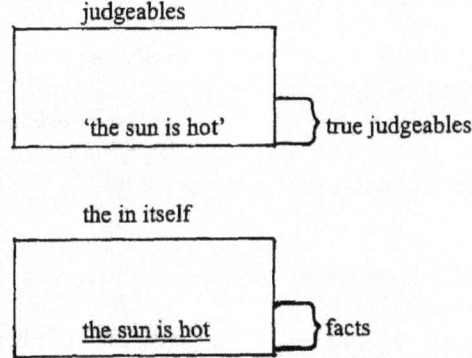

A16m. For Kant the in itself doesn't have propositional form. For Kant, not only do the *logical constants* not represent (cf. Wittgenstein), the subject-predicate form does not represent.

The in itself does have *structure* but not *logical* structure.

A17. What, then, are the fundamental theses of Transcendental Idealism?

1. It *identifies* facts with true judgeables.

2. Judgeables aren't true *because* they correspond to *facts*. If a judgeable is true, it is a *fact*. Though

'the sun is hot' is true ≡ the sun is hot,

to *explain* why 'the sun is hot' is true involves more than the above equivalence. (Cf. $2 + 2 = 4 \equiv 3 + 3 = 6$.)

How the explanation involves the sun and being hot is the problem. The explanation would involve knowing that the sun is hot: 'the sun is hot' is true *because* the sun is hot (knowledge claim) *and* ... ?

3. In that sense of 'object' of knowledge which refers to *what* is known, the objects of knowledge are *true judgeables*, for what is known are *facts* and facts are true judgeables.

A18. For the Transcendental Idealist, the objects of knowledge are *essentially* representable. Their only mode of *actualization*, or realization, is to be *actually represented* (i.e., tokened).

A19. The basic distinction is between *true* and *false judgeables*. [See **KPT**, ch. 12, section E.]

A20. We characterized a judgeable above as a unity of apperception, i.e., as the unity which representables have by virtue of the fact that when actualized in a judging, they are actualized as an apperceptible *combining* of representings which actualizes each of them.

A20a. True judgeables are those the constituents of which are representables the synthesis of which is objectively valid. The synthesizing is not only an apperceptible judging, *all* judgings are either true or false.

I judge 'the sun is hot'

my judging 'the sun is hot' is true
   The apperceptible unity (unity of apperception) of which my judging is a tokening is "objectively (and intersubjectively) valid."

'the sun is hot' is an objectively valid apperceptible unity.

A21. The *objective* unity of apperception is the system of true judgeables, i.e., the judgments the constituents of which *belong together qua* representables, i.e., not by virtue of the happenstances of association.

A22. *Nature* as a system of possible objects of knowledge (true judgeables) is identical with the objective unity of apperception:

nature = the objective unity of apperception.

A22a. Nature is identical with the true world story, the privileged system of judeables (i.e., the true as contrasted with the false). [See **[A36]** and **B13**; Intro, 301-7.]

A22b. In what does this privileged character consist? I.e., *what is empirical truth*? All we have said so far is that

The Notes for the Cassirer Lectures (CLN, 120)

truth is objective and intersubjective belongingness

and

truth does *not* consist in the correspondence of judeables with facts, construed as items which

(a) have *independent* being,
(b) have *propositional form*, and
(c) are representables *per accidens* (transcendent objects of representation).

A22c. What positive account of this privileged status of "true judgeables" can be given?
[A23 is not in the notes; A27 returns to the above question. No doubt the intervening material would have been relocated by Sellars.]
A24. Notice that, on the account I have given, this world story does not have an external subject matter as this is construed by the Transcendental Realist:

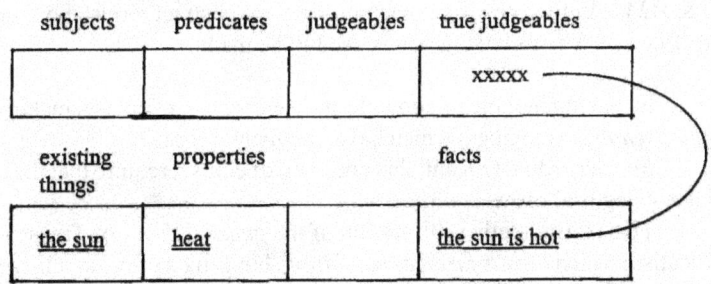

Existing things are individual representables concerning which there is empirical truth. *Properties* are *predicates of judgeables*. Individuals and properties, like the facts of which they are constituents, essentially have logical form.

The supposed transcendent subject matter of the true world story is simply the domain of representables considered with respect to truth. The relation of representables to this domain does not explain truth.

[At this point, the B manuscript parallels, in content, the A manuscript. I have put together the comparable sections.]
A25. & B20. [B manuscript contains two paragraphs marked '20'; this is the second of the two]. Yet there is a legitimate sense in which, from the standpoint of the Transcendental Idealist, the true world story has an independent subject

matter.

> The domain of the *in itself* does not have *logical form*. It has, however, form or structure.

We distinguish between logical form

> e.g., conjunction, negation, quantification, subject-predicate

and "descriptive" form

> e.g., spatial and temporal relations, change of place.

B21. But the term 'descriptive' has connotations of perceptibility and for Kant things in themselves do not have perceptible features.
A25. We might call the latter *non-logical* structure.
A26. & B22. Now Kant thinks of the in itself as having *non-logical structure*. Of course, for reasons which will be examined later, Kant holds that the non-logical structure of the world in itself does not coincide with the non-logical structure of the world as object of empirical knowledge. In particular, the world in itself does not have spatio-temporal structure.
A26a. & B24. Yet we can say something in very abstract terms about this non-logical structure. The following points need to be made.

> In making judgments about the in-itself we are, of course, making use of *representings* (judgings) which have judgmental form.
> *But*, according to Kant, this does not, of course, require that the in-itself have categorial form.
> This is just another illustration of the *general thesis* of Transcendental Idealism which *awaits further elucidation*, but can be provisionally accepted perhaps in a willing suspension of disbelief.

A26b. & B25. *A word about the categories*: Metaphysical Deduction (the form of judgment). The Metaphysical Deduction is regarded as seriously flawed. Kant, it is said, simply fails to "derive" his categories from the forms of judgment.
The crucial point to appreciate here is, to put it bluntly, that the categories *are* the forms of judgment.
A26c. & B26. More delicately put, the categorial concepts,

> substance, attribute, negation, plurality, etc.,

are concepts of the *forms* of judgments (not always form in the sense of syntactical role). **The categories are** concepts of the conceptual powers of a judgeable or of a representable-as-a-constituent-of-a-judgeable by virtue of a subject matter independent feature of the judgeable.

A26c. & B27. Thus if we use the phrase

>Category C applies to x

to mean

>Category C is true of x,

then what C is true of is always a judgeable or a representable as a constituent of a judgeable.

A26c. This is obviously true of negation:

>'the sun is not hot' is the negation of 'the sun is hot'.

A26c. & B28. In scholastic terminology, the subject of categorizing judgments are terms taken in second intention.

>the sun is a substance
>'the sun' is a subject

A26c. & B29. Notice that the categories are not limited to what we would call syntactical features of judgeables:

>it is necessary that every number is either (evenly) divisible or not (evenly) divisible by 4.
>'every number is either (evenly) divisible or not (evenly) divisible by 4' is unconditionally assertable (which involves reference to a judging mind).

>lightning is the cause of thunder
>'there is lightning at t' causally implies 'there is thunder at $t + \Delta t$'.

A26d. & B30. I said "subject matter independent". Obviously we must distinguish between the categories as features common to judgments about any subject matter, e.g., common to empirical, metaphysical, mathematical, theological, ethical judgments, e.g.,

>being a triangle is the ground of having an area equal one-half base times height

>being a case of promise keeping is a ground of being a duty,

from those which are specified as being about individuals in a spatio-temporal world. The latter are the schematized categories.

A26e. & B30. In between the pure-pure categories and the schematized categories are categorial concepts which concern the characteristic features of judgeables specified to a subject matter which consists of individuals (objects of possible experience), but where they are not specified to be *spatio-temporal*, i.e., might be experienced by *non-human* finite minds.

> pure-pure categories—completely subject matter independent;
> pure categories—apply to judgeables and representables which are possible objects of experience, but not necessarily spatio-temporal.

This is really a generalization of the concept of a schematized category:

> schematized categories—categories which apply to judgeables about the spatio-temporal world.

Thus the category of ground-consequence applies to the judgeable

> things in themselves are the ground of the manifold of sense

and that of subject-attribute to

> judgings are attributes of minds.

A26e. & B31. Obviously the judgments which belong to transcendental philosophy (the metaphysics of knowledge) have logical form and categorial concepts are true of and apply to the terms of such judgments.

> But none of this requires, or so Kant argues, that this world of things in themselves and thinking subjects in themselves have categorial form.

Putting it bluntly, only judgeables and constituents of judgeables have categorial form. (Once again, how this thesis is to be understood is perhaps the central problem concerning Transcendental Idealism.)

Once again, only judgeables—whatever their subject matter—have logical form.

A26f. & B32. Just as Transcendental Idealism rejects the "picture"

The Notes for the Cassirer Lectures (CLN, 120)

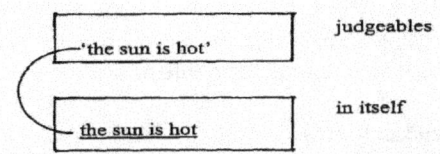

so it rejects the picture

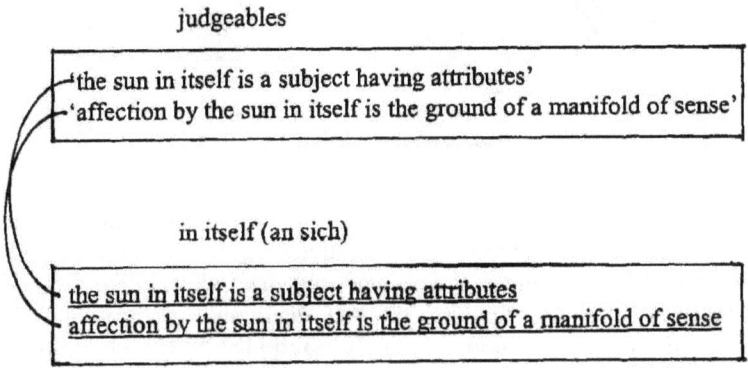

[**26g** through **26j** were renumbered by Sellars as **B33** through **B36**; they appear in the latter part of the B manuscript.]

A27. A first approximation to a solution of what selects the "true" judgeables which make up the true world story.

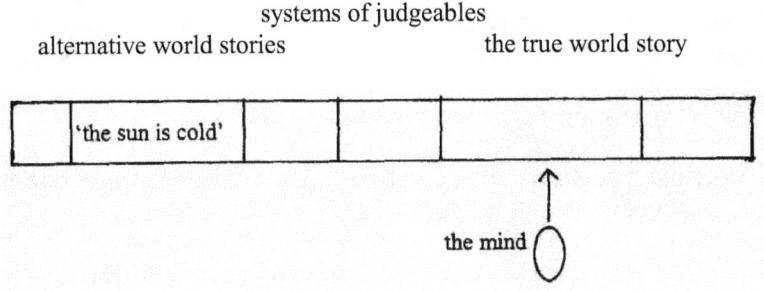

A28. Compare God's selection of a certain possible world to be actual in Leibniz. Consider a Transcendental Realism which holds that the primary constituents of reality as it is *in itself* are *possibilia*, possible *things* and possible *facts*:

existing things are possible things which have the attribute existence; facts are possible facts which have the attribute existence.

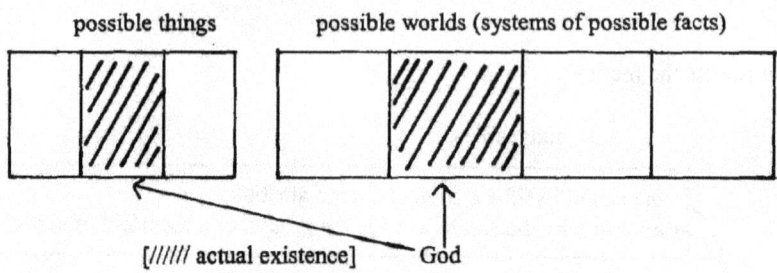

A28a. The fundamental difference would be that in the Leibnizian system, we have a distinctive metaphysical thesis as to how the *in itself* is structured and an account of its constituent properties and relations *independent* of any essential reference to *knowability* (and hence to *judgeables* and *representables*). [Sellars has a reference in the margin to A270/B326.] [See *KPT*, ch. 8 and Appendix, Leibniz.]

Kant's metaphysical account includes an essential reference to knowability: an abstract account of what must be true of the in itself in order for there to be such a thing as truth about nature.

Kant's account is very abstract and **includes** his ontology of *representation* (a *pure theory* of empirical knowability). [See **B34**.]

[Here Sellars has a margin note which reads "The concept of the empirical is not an empirical concept" and which contains a reference to A343/B401 where, in discussing rational psychology, Kant says that the investigation of the empirical in general is a "transcendental inquiry".]

This is the epistemological turn in his metaphysics.

[It seems clear that Sellars intended the third section, **3. Transcendental Realism**, to begin near this point.]

A28b. For Kant the modalities are not features of the in itself. There are true modal judgeables, but they are not true by virtue of corresponding to *independently real* entities having modal features. There is no modal in itself.
A28c. There are modal judgeables. They belong in a package with principles (logical principles, laws of nature).

it is logically possible that there be diangles.
it is geometrically impossible that there be diangles.
it is physically possible that the sun will be cold.

A29. A peek at the problem of the status of representables:

representables
'the sun is hot' 'it is possible that a mind represents 'the sun is hot''

'the sun is hot' is a *judgeable*
it is possible that a mind judges 'the sun is hot'
it is possible that a mind combines, into a judging, representations of a priori categories.

A30. The mode of being of representables is that of its being true that a mind might represent them. Principles of a theory of representables determine what is a representational possibility just as the laws of physics determine what is a physical possibility. [See **B34**.]

A31. Theory of *empirical representation*.

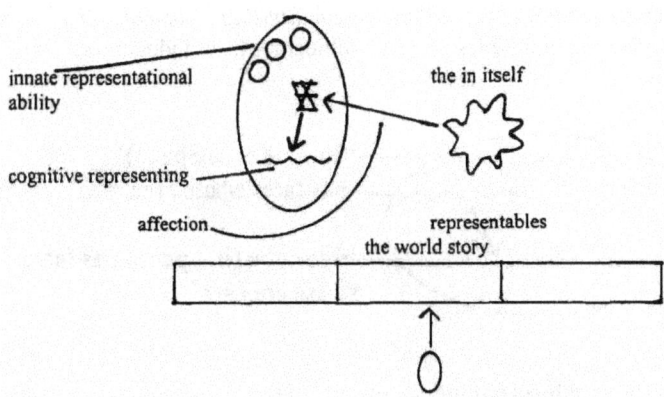

A manifold is a function of laws pertaining to the mind and the action of the in itself on sensibility. *NB*. Things in themselves would conform to laws of their own (B164).

A32. The concept of there being empirical truth requires that of a lawful connection between the character of the affecting in itself and the character of the resulting manifold of outer sense.

A32a. Here we must carefully distinguish between *sensations* and *intuitions*. Sensations are modifications of the mind in the sense in which feelings of pain (pains) are modifications of the mind. They are not *cognitive representings* though they are *objects* of cognitive represent*ings*.

A32b. Intuitions of spatial objects are representations of individual (singular) objects and events in Space and Time. Intuitions are to be contrasted with *both* sensations and judgments. (See Introduction to *Dialectic*, p. 314.) [A320/B376-7.] [Sellars has a margin note which cites A28/B44.] [Intro, Part III, sections A and B.]

A32c. As in the case of judgments where we distinguished between

(a) act of judging,
(b) content of judging,

so we must now distinguish between

(a) an act of intuiting,
(b) the content (or immanent object) of the act of intuiting.

The latter has an essential this-ness (*tode ti*). An Aristotelian this-such needn't be being singled out as a *this*: it is capable of being singled out as a this.

A32d. Just as we distinguish between a representing and a represent*able* which is *actualized* as the content of a representing, so we must distinguish between an intuit*ing* and the *intuitables actualized by an intuiting as its content*.

Notice that the intuitables serve as subject terms in judgeables:

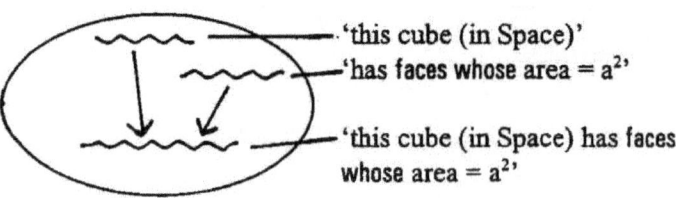

Intuitings serve as subjects of judgments.

Notice that although intuitings are erkenntnisse ('knowledge'), *knowledge proper* only comes into judgments which are synthetic. Contrast

        this-cube is a cube

with

        this cube (in Space) has faces whose area = a^2.

The Notes for the Cassirer Lectures (CLN, 120)

I use pictorial means of representing the *content* of an act of intuiting because Kant relies heavily on the metaphor of *drawing*:

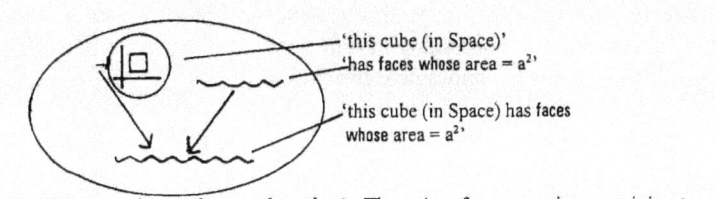

Intuition enters into *judgmental synthesis*. The unity of apperception pertaining to a judgeable:

I combine 'this cube' with 'has faces whose area = a^2'.

But intuition involves another mode of synthesis (and hence of apperception).

[At this point, I commingle paragraphs on the same topic from the A and the B manuscripts. Sellars, however, failed to number paragraphs A33 through A36. I have supplied the numbers. In addition, it is important to remember that Sellars did not plan to repeat himself extensively; only one formulation of any point was meant to stand in the final manuscript.]

[**A33.**] & **B1.**   The judgmental metaphor: example of a triangle.

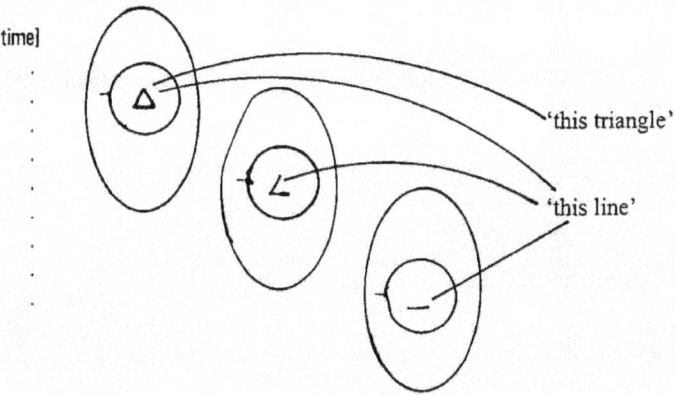

Just as the mode of actualization of a judgeable is a combining of, for example, a representing of 'the sun' and a representing of 'is hot' which is apperceived as

I combine 'the sun' and 'is hot',

the mode of actualization of the intuitable 'this triangle' is actualized by a successive drawing (synthesis, combining) of representings of lines into one representing. **B2.** The mode of actualization of 'this triangle' (in Space) is a successive drawing in thought, a successive combining of representing of lines into one representing. **[A33.]** & **B3.** Thus the ontological form of an

is
> *intuitive* representing of a complex (e.g., a triangle)

> an identical I successively intuiting constituents, continuing to represent them and, as an outcome, representing the complex.

[A34.] It is essential to note that an intuiting is always a representing of something *as* a something.

> an intuiting of a cube [triangle] is an awareness of a cube [triangle] <u>as</u> a cube [triangle].

[A35.] In the sense in which

> I synthesize 'the sun is round'

is the truth about the actualization in thought of the judgeable 'the sun is round', so

> I synthesize 'this triangle'

is the truth about the actualization in a representing of the intuitable 'this cube [triangle] (in Space)'.

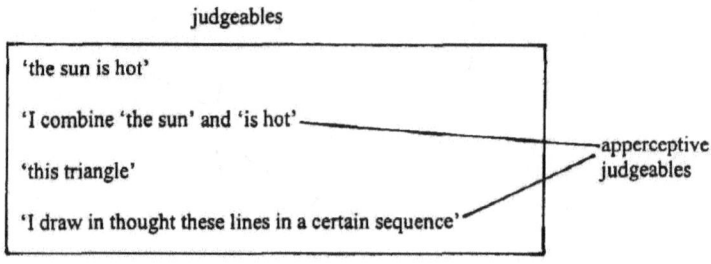

The apperceiving **is:**

The Notes for the Cassirer Lectures (CLN, 120) 557

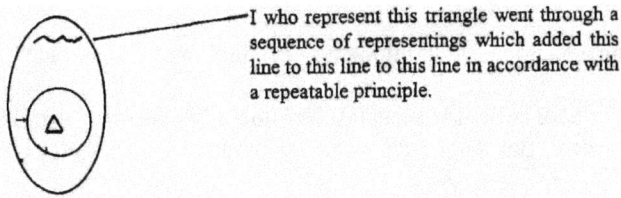

B4. The apperception of this process is the judging that

> I constructed this representation of this complex by following recipe R. I who represent this triangle went through a sequence of representings which added this line to this line to this line in accordance with a repeatable procedure, a recipe.

[A35.] Obviously there is, as a special case of this drawing, the making of still bigger ones out of littler ones:

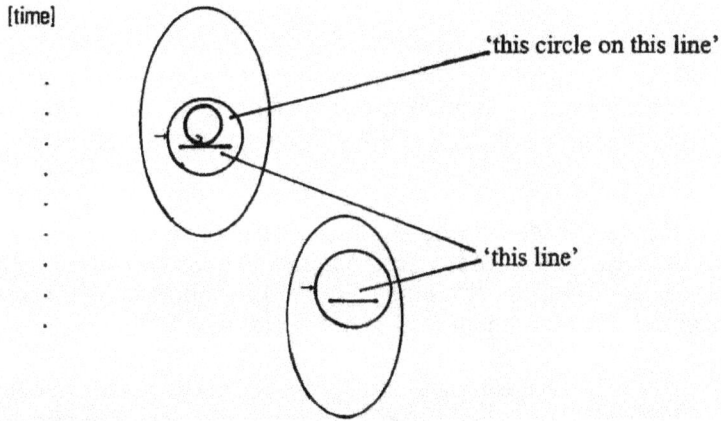

The intuiting of a complex as a complex is *apperceptible* as a sequence of drawings in accordance with a repeatable principle. The abstract formulation of this process is forming one intuition of a manifold from a manifold of intuitions. [Sellars has a margin note which cites B135ff, B143ff, B154-5, and the example of the house at B162.]

B5. The intuition of a complex (as a complex) is apperceptible as

> my constructing in thought of this representing of a complex in accordance with a recipe (rule).

The abstract formulation of this process of construction in intuition is combining a manifold of intuition into the intuition of a manifold.

[A35.] & B6. I have been discussing (as Kant does) the synthesizing of intuitions as in pure geometry. But among the items we intuitively represent are material objects.

Notice that even geometrical intuit*ables* have logical form (pure categories):

this-cube (this is a cube)

The same is true of the intuiting of a *physical cube*: this *physical* cube.

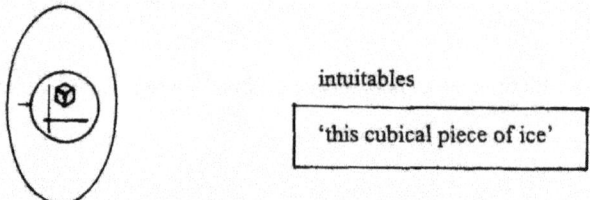

The intuiting of it *as a physical* complex involves all the categories involved in the concept of the physical. **This intuiting requires** synthesis of intuitions into complexes in accordance with rules. [**Sellars has a margin note which cites A156/B195.**]

[B7 and B8 are very sketchy notes which continue the theme that physical objects must be synthesized in accordance with rules; the rules of physical complexes are the "laws of nature". Further comments on this matter are interspersed with other matters in what follows; see A43ff.]

[A36.]   The existence and non-existence of (physical) intuitables can compared with the truth and falsity of judgeables. Just as a true judgeable is one that belongs to the privileged system of judgeables, so an *existing* intuitable is one which belongs to the world construed as the privileged system of intuitable *objects* which are basic perceptible complex objects and basic complexes of objects having perceptible features. Nature is a system of intuitable objects-events belonging together in accordance with rules.

B9. Just as a judgement can be false, an intuitive representing can be *false* in the sense that one represents

this ice cube

and there is no ice cube.

B10.   Just as a true judgeable is one that belongs to the privileged system of judgeables, so an intuitable which *exists* is one which belongs to the privileged system of perceptual objects and events. *Nature* is a system of *perceptual intuitables* belonging together in accordance with the *laws of nature*: this is nature as a 'true' system of intuitables.

A37. The *unity* of intuitables is no more a matter of their being de facto intuited together, than the unity of judgeables is a matter of the subject concept and the predicate concept occurring together in the mind.

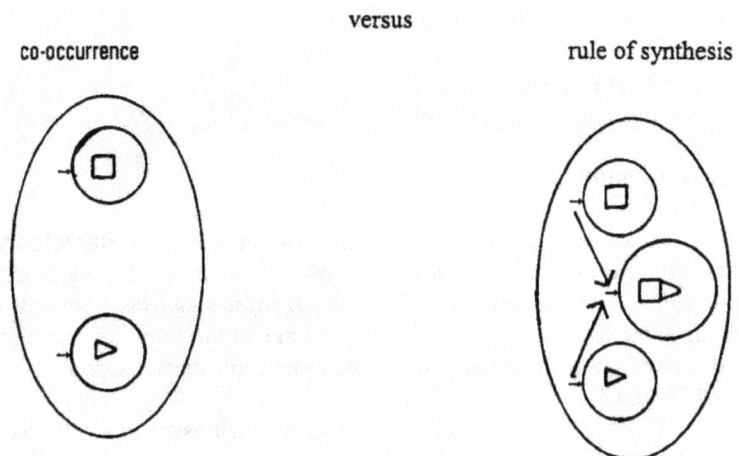

[See **A13c** and compare the figure in **A12**.]

A38. *Furthermore*, the *belonging together* of *existing* complex intuitables is not just a matter of their being synthesized according to a rule, but of their belonging to the one complex synthesizable *individual* which is nature as a system of intuited *objects*.

A39. The belonging together of an event (as *representable*) with a time is a matter of it belonging to a certain region in nature.

A40. Nature is infinite as a system of representa*bles*. Any *actualization* of this system of representables is finite as the content of a representing which is generated by a successive synthesis.

A41. Double affection. [This paragraph contains merely a complicated diagram with no comment by Sellars. In *SM*, ch. II, 22, 23, 52, 53 and especially 57, Sellars makes brief observations on double affection. A more elaborate account occurs in ch. 17 of *KPT*. When Amaral, the editor of *KPT*, directly asked Sellars about double affection, Sellars drew very complicated diagrams and repeated what he says at the end of *KTE* (44-5). The A manuscript has a diagram that resembles ones in *KPT*. In the introduction (paragraph 741), I reproduce part of ch. 17 of *KPT* with a few of Sellars' diagrams.]

A42. The concept of belonging to an objective time order (nature) involves the concept of nature as a deterministic system.

A43. The de facto synthesis of a representation of nature involves an innate framework of specific recipes for constructing sequences of object behaviors:

if object is a K, then if φ's, it ψ's.

Compare: if an object is a triangle, then a = ½ bh

The a priori *available* concepts are:

concepts of geometric shapes;
concepts of (basic) kinds of physical objects.

[Here the A manuscript ends.]

B11. Innate tendencies to represent in terms of basic kinds characterized by certain basic causal properties: what is innate is the *ability* to think in terms of specific kinds and causal properties pertaining to physical objects. If we didn't have these innate tendencies, we couldn't go on from there to formulate more sophisticated classifications in terms of more and more sophisticated causal properties. [Intro, 127-154.]

B12. We must distinguish carefully between what is psychologically necessary in order for us to have *beliefs about* objects and events in nature and what is necessary for truth about nature and the classification of nature.

B13. Nature is a system of *intuitables* and *judgeables* which can be known to be *true*.

B14. Thus we must not only have beliefs about the lawfulness of nature, there must be knowable truth about the laws of nature.

B15. Truth and the objectively and intersubjectively valid belonging together of representables.

B16. A special case (the second analogy): the knowable temporal location of an event requires that it have a cause.

B17. Not only that every event has a cause must be knowable—specific laws must be knowable. Or, *at least* be justified true belief; but Kant seems to think basic laws of nature, Newtonian laws, are *knowable a priori*.

B18. [Sellars has a note to compare Kant's account with] Descartes' theory of science concerning basic *a priori* laws and inductive generalizations. [I discuss part of what Sellars has in mind in Part IV of the introduction; see paragraph 830ff.]

B19. Nature is a system of spatio-temporal representables having categorial structure and involving such representables as existence, possibility-necessity ('because', e.g., '*this because that*').

B20. If *nature* is a system of judgeables (and intuitables) and if categorial features are essentially features of judgeables and judgeables are *realized* only by acts of representing, then there is a clear sense in which we put the categorial features into nature.

[The paragraphs in the B manuscript numbered B20 (the second one) through B32 appeared earlier intermixed with the paragraphs from the A manuscript numbered A25 through A26f. Sellars himself renumbers

A26g through A26f   as   B33 through B36.

So, now, the next paragraphs is B33 (=A26g).]

B33. [26g]   Transcendental philosophy makes use of concepts which are more than empty categories from the list of the pure-pure categories of the Metaphysical Deduction.
B34. [26h]   (Kant's ontology of representation) It makes use of the abstract concepts of, e.g.,

    1. a judging, a judeable, a true judgeable
    2. the affection of a finite mind by an existence in itself
    3. the affection of a finite mind by itself
    4. an act of synthesis
    5. unity of apperception
    6. an act of intuiting, an intuitable
    7. manifold of sense

and many, many others.
B35. [26i]   These concepts are clearly not definable in terms of Kant's pure-pure categories. Nor is, come to think of it, the concept of a category definable in terms of the pure-pure categories, for the concept of a category **requires** that of a judgment and a judgment can't be defined in terms of the categories.
B36. [26j]   Transcendental philosophy needs a battery of concepts which pertain to the pure theory of a finite mind acquiring knowledge of [page 10a in part A has the rest of the sentence] a nature which is intersubjective and non-arbitrary.
[sic] **B36.** I now turn to the sense in which Kant is a Transcendental Realist. He rejects Transcendental Realism as a theory of the status of the spatio-temporal world (nature).

    Nature is a coherent and complete system of represent*ables*.
    Space and Time are forms of intuitables.

B37.   But Kant is a Realist. For him, it is obvious that there is a domain which is not dependent for its being on being represented (or even being representable).

To make an obvious point: if we take seriously the idea of that there is such a thing as a

    being dependent for its being on being thought of

as is, to go back to the beginning,

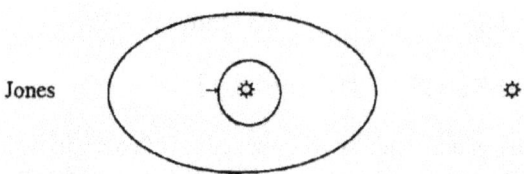

the being of a content of a thought, e.g., the sun *qua* in Jones' understanding, then we must grant that the act in which it has its being as content does not depend for its existence on being the content of an act.

Of course, one can think of a thought of the sun

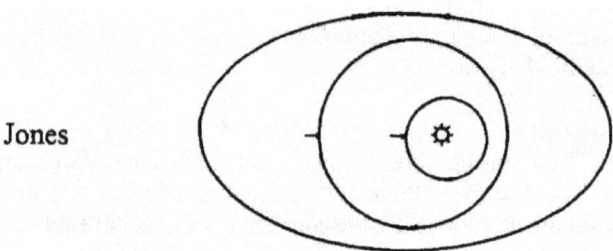

but this act does not depend for its existence on being the content of an act.

B38. What does Kant mean by calling an **investigation** 'transcendental'? The theory of how knowledge is possible is theory of how a finite mind can come to gain knowledge of *a coherent system of* objects. Kant's theory is *realistic* because it includes as an essential ingredient features of the in itself.

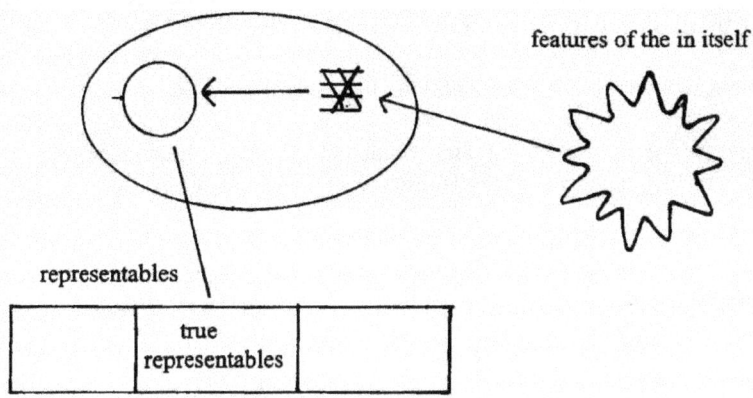

B39. According to Kant, all that we can say, in theoretical metaphysics, about the in itself is what it must be like for there to be a knowable and intersubjective system of representables singled out by

> the notion of the mind (ego)
> and the notion of the non-ego.

B40. Once again, Kant isn't proving that there is knowledge. His strategy is to counter the arguments for the negation by showing that their basic *philosophical categories* are mistaken.

B41. Finally, a question: are the propositions of Transcendental Metaphysics analytic or synthetic? (They are *a priori*.) Kant says that knowledge of principles through concepts only (as opposed to based on *experience*) is always analytic. Kant tells us that philosophical knowledge (Transcendental Metaphysics) is knowledge through concepts only.

> *Philosophical* knowledge is the *knowledge gained by reason from concepts*. (A713/B741)

Therefore, it must be *analytic*.

B42. We can't know the causal principle through the concepts of event and cause.

B43. We need the concept of *"possible experience"*. (See A736-7/B764-5 and A788/B816.) [Intro, 275-293.]

B44. This third lecture has the title

> Transcendental Realism?

I have tried to show that whereas in the sense in which Kant's metaphysics specifies what it is to be a Transcendental Realist,

> Kant is not a Transcendental Realist

whereas in the sense that his Transcendental Idealism, which includes a theory of the in itself, is a feature of his Transcendental Metaphysics,

> he is a Transcendental Realist.

The Philosophical Works of Wilfrid Sellars

This bibliography is the most complete and correct bibliography of Sellars' work as of the date of publication. It contains corrections from Dr. Andrew Chrucky's web site on Sellars: (http://www.ditext.com/sellars/bib-s.html).

Abbreviations: *APQ* for *American Philosophical Quarterly*; *JP* for *The Journal of Philosophy*; *P&PR* for *Philosophy and Phenomenological Research*; *PREV* for *Philosophical Review*; *PSC* for *Philosophy of Science*; *PS* for *Philosophical Studies*; *ROM* for *Review of Metaphysics*.

PPE	1.	"Pure Pragmatics and Epistemology," *PSC* 14 (1947): 181-202. In *PPPW* (112).
ENWW	2.	"Epistemology and the New Way of Words," *JP* 44 (1947): 645-60. In *PPPW* (112).
RNWW	3.	"Realism and the New Way of Words," *P&PR* 8 (1948): 601-34. Reprinted in *Readings in Philosophical Analysis*, edited by Herbert Feigl and Wilfrid Sellars (Appleton-Century-Crofts, 1949). In *PPPW* (112).
CIL	4.	"Concepts as Involving Laws and Inconceivable without Them," *PSC* 15 (1948): 287-315. In *PPPW* (112).
APM	5.	"Aristotelian Philosophies of Mind," in *Philosophy for the Future*, edited by Roy Wood Sellars, V.J. McGill, and Marvin Farber (The Macmillan Co., 1949): 544-70. In *KPT* (117).
LRB	6.	"Language, Rules and Behavior," in *John Dewey: Philosopher of Science and Freedom*, edited by Sidney Hook (The Dial Press, 1949): 289-315. In *PPPW* (112).
LCP	7.	"On the Logic of Complex Particulars," *Mind* 58 (1949): 306-38. In *PPPW* (112).
AD	8.	"Acquaintance and Description Again," *JP* 46 (1949): 496-505.
RC	9.	"Review of Ernest Cassirer, *Language and Myth*," *P&PR* 9 (1948-49): 326-29.
ILE	10.	"The Identity of Linguistic Expressions and the Paradox of Analysis," *PS* 1 (1950): 24-31.
QMSP	11.	"Quotation Marks, Sentences, and Propositions," *P&PR* 10 (1950): 515-25. In *PPPW* (112).
GQ	12.	"Gestalt Qualities and the Paradox of Analysis," *PS* 1 (1950): 92-4.
OM	13.	"Obligation and Motivation," *PS* 2 (1951): 21-25.
RP	14.	"Review of Arthur Pap, *Elements of Analytic Philosophy*," *P&PR* 11 (1950): 104-9.
OMR	15.	"Obligation and Motivation," in *Readings in Ethical Theory*, edited by Wilfrid Sellars and John Hospers (Appleton-Century-Crofts, 1952): 511-17. A revised and expanded version of *OM* (13).
RCA	16.	"Review of C. West Churchman and Russell L. Ackoff, *Methods of Inquiry: An Introduction to Philosophy and Scientific Method*," *P&PR* 11 (1951): 149-50.
CHT	17.	"Comments on Mr. Hempel's Theses," *ROM* 5 (1952): 623-25.
MMB	18.	"Mind, Meaning, and Behavior," *PS* 3 (1952): 83-95.
P	19.	"Particulars," *P&PR* 13 (1952): 184-99. In *SPR* (53).
ITSA	20.	"Is There a Synthetic A Priori?," *PSC* 20 (1953): 121-38. Reprinted in a revised form in *American Philosophers at Work*, edited by Sidney Hook (Criterion Press, 1957); also published in Italy in translation. In *SPR* (53).
SSMB	21.	"A Semantical Solution of the Mind-Body Problem," *Methodos* 5 (1953): 45-82. In *PPPW* (112).
IM	22.	"Inference and Meaning," *Mind* 62 (1953): 313-38. In *PPPW* (112).
PRE	23.	"Presupposing," *PREV* 63 (1954): 197-215. Reprinted in *Essays on Bertrand Russell*, edited by E.D. Klemke (Univ. of Illinois Press, 1970): 173-89.
SRLG	24.	"Some Reflections on Language Games," *PSC* 21 (1954): 204-28. A revised version is in *SPR* (53).

NPD	25.	"A Note on Popper's Argument for Dualism," *Analysis* 15 (1954): 23-4.
PR	26.	"Physical Realism," *P&PR* 15 (1955): 13-32. In *PPME* (102).
PSB	27.	"Putnam on Synonymity and Belief," *Analysis* 15 (1955): 117-20.
VTM	28.	"Vlastos and 'The Third Man'," *PREV* 64 (1955): 405-37. In *PPHP* (101).
IIO	29.	"Imperatives, Intentions, and the Logic of 'Ought'," *Methodos* 8 (1956): 228-68.
CE	30.	"The Concept of Emergence," (with Paul Meehl), in *Minnesota Studies in the Philosophy of Science*, Vol. I, edited by Herbert Feigl and Michael Scriven (University of Minnesota Press, 1956): 239-52.
EPM	31.	"Empiricism and the Philosophy of Mind," (Presented at the University of London in Special Lectures in Philosophy for 1956 under the title "The Myth of the Given: Three Lectures on Empiricism and the Philosophy of Mind"), *ibid.*, 253-329. In *SPR* (53).
LSPO	32.	"Logical Subjects and Physical Objects," *P&PR* 17 (1957): 458-72. Contribution to a symposium with Peter Strawson held at Duke University, November, 1955.
CDCM	33.	"Counterfactuals, Dispositions, and the Causal Modalities," in *Minnesota Studies in the Philosophy of Science*, Vol. II, edited by Herbert Feigl, Michael Scriven, and Grover Maxwell (University of Minnesota Press, 1958): 225-308.
ITM	34.	"Intentionality and the Mental," a symposium by correspondence with Roderick Chisholm, *ibid.*, 507-39. Reprinted in *Intentionality, Mind and Language*, edited by A. Marras (Univ. of Illinois Press, 1972).
SFA	35.	"Substance and Form in Aristotle," *JP* 54 (1957): 688-99. The opening paper in a symposium on Aristotle's conception of form held at the December, 1957 meeting of the American Philosophical Association. In *PPHP* (101).
EAE	36.	"Empiricism and Abstract Entities," in *The Philosophy of Rudolf Carnap (The Library of Living Philosophers)* edited by Paul A. Schilpp (Open Court, 1963): 431-68.
GE	37.	"Grammar and Existence: A Preface to Ontology," *Mind* 69 (1960): 499-533. Two lectures delivered at Yale University, March, 1958. In *SPR* (53). Reprinted in *The Problem of Universals*, edited by C. Landesman (Basic Books, 1971).
TWO	38.	"Time and the World Order," in *Minnesota Studies in the Philosophy of Science*, Vol. III, edited by Herbert Feigl and Grover Maxwell (University of Minnesota Press, 1962): 527-616. A Metaphysical and Epistemological Analysis of Becoming.
IIOR	39.	"Imperatives, Intentions, and the Logic of 'Ought'," in *Morality and the Language of Conduct*, a collection of essays in moral philosophy edited by Hector-Neri Castaneda and George Nakhnikian (Wayne State University Press, 1963): 159-214. A radically revised and enlarged version of *IIO* (29).
BBK	40.	"Being and Being Known," *Proceedings of the American Catholic Philosophical Association* (1960): 28-49. In *SPR* (53).
LT	41.	"The Language of Theories," in *Current Issues in the Philosophy of Science*, edited by Herbert Feigl and Grover Maxwell (Holt, Rinehart, and Winston, 1961): 57-77. In *SPR* (53). Reprinted in *The Problem of Scientific Realism*, edited by E.A. McKinnon (Appleton-Century-Crofts, 1972).
CM	42.	"Comments on Maxwell's "Meaning Postulates in Scientific Theories,"" *ibid.*, 183-92.
PSIM	43.	"Philosophy and the Scientific Image of Man," in *Frontiers of Science and Philosophy*, edited by Robert Colodny (University of Pittsburgh Press, 1962): 35-78. In *SPR* (53).
RMSS	44.	"Raw Materials, Subjects and Substrata," in *The Concept of Matter*, edited by Ernan McMullin (The University of Notre Dame Press, 1963): 259-72 and 276-80; remarks by Sellars on 55-7, 100-1, and 245-7. In *PPHP* (101).
CMM	45.	Comments on McMullin's "Matter as a Principle," *ibid.*, 209-13.
NS	46.	"Naming and Saying," *PSC* 29 (1962): 7-26. In *SPR* (53).
TC	47.	"Truth and Correspondence," *JP* 59 (1962): 29-56. In *SPR* (53).
AE	48.	"Abstract Entities," *ROM* 16 (1963): 627-71. In *PPME* (102).
CAE	49.	"Classes as Abstract Entities and the Russell Paradox," *ROM* 17 (1963): 67-90. Iin *PPME* (101).
PANF	50.	"The Paradox of Analysis: A Neo-Fregean Approach," *Analysis* Supplementary Vol.

		24 (1964): 84-98. In *PPME* (102).
TE	51.	"Theoretical Explanation," in *Philosophy of Science: The Delaware Seminar*, Vol. II (John Wiley, 1963): 61-78. In *PPME* (102).
IRH	52.	"The Intentional Realism of Everett Hall," (in *Commonsense Realism: Critical Essays on the Philosophy of Everett W. Hall*, edited by E. M. Adams) *The Southern Journal of Philosophy* 4 (1966): 103-15. In *PPME* (102).
SPR	53.	*Science, Perception and Reality* (Routledge and Kegan Paul, 1963). Includes items (19), (20), (24), (31), (37), (40), (41), (43), (46), (47), and a hitherto unpublished essay, *PHM*, "Phenomenalism". Re-issued by Ridgeview Publishing Company in 1991.
IV	54.	"Induction as Vindication," *PSC* 31 (1964): 197-231.
NI	55.	"Notes on Intentionality," *JP* 61 (1964): 655-65. Presented in a symposium on intentionality at the 1964 meeting of the American Philosophical Association (Eastern Division). In *PPME* (102). Reprinted in *Intentionality, Mind and Language*, edited by A. Marras (Univ. of Illinois Press, 1972).
IAMB	56.	"The Identity Approach to the Mind-Body Problem," *ROM* 18 (1965): 430-51. Presented at the Boston Colloquium for the Philosophy of Science, April, 1963. In *PPME* (102).
ML	57.	"Meditations Leibnitziennes," *APQ* 2 (1965): 105-18. An expanded version of the opening paper in a symposium on Rationalism at the May, 1958, meeting of the American Philosophical Association. In *PPHP* (101).
SRI	58.	"Scientific Realism or Irenic Instrumentalism: A Critique of Nagel and Feyerabend on Theoretical Explanation," *Boston Studies in the Philosophy of Science*, Vol. II, edited by Robert Cohen and Max Wartofsky (Humanities Press, 1965): 171-204. In *PPME* (102).
TA	59.	"Thought and Action," in *Freedom and Determinism*, edited by Keith Lehrer (Random House, 1966): 105-39.
FD	60.	"Fatalism and Determinism," *ibid.*, 141-74.
RPH	61.	"The Refutation of Phenomenalism: Prolegomena to a Defense of Scientific Realism," in P.K. Feyerabend and G. Maxwell (eds.), *Mind, Matter, and Method* (University of Minnesota Press, 1966).
PP	62.	*Philosophical Perspectives* (Charles C. Thomas, Publisher, 1967; reprinted in two volumes by Ridgeview Publishing Co.). Includes items (26), (28), (35), (44), (48), (49), (50), (51), (52), (55), (56), (57), (58), and *VTMR*, a rejoinder to Gregory Vlastos on the Third Man Argument, and three previously unpublished essays: *SC*, "The Soul as Craftsman" (on Plato's Idea of the Good), *AMI*, "Aristotle's Metaphysics: An Interpretation," and *SE*, "Science and Ethics."
SM	63.	*Science and Metaphysics: Variations on Kantian Themes*, The John Locke Lectures for 1965-66 (Routledge and Kegan Paul, 1967). Re-issued in 1992 by Ridgeview Publishing Company.
PH	64.	"Phenomenalism," in *Intentionality, Minds and Perception*, edited by H-N. Castaneda (Wayne State University Press, 1967): 215-74. An abbreviated version of essay *PHM* (53).
RA	65.	"Reply to Aune," *ibid.*, 286-300.
FCET	66.	*Form and Content in Ethical Theory*, The Lindley Lecture for 1967 (Department of Philosophy, University of Kansas, 1967). In *SM* (63).
KTE	67.	"Some Remarks on Kant's Theory of Experience," *JP* 64 (1967): 633-47. Presented in a symposium on Kant at the 1967 meeting of the American Philosophical Association (Eastern Division).In *KTM* (118).
MP	68.	"Metaphysics and the Concept of a Person," in *The Logical Way of Doing Things*, edited by Karel Lambert (Yale University Press, 1969): 219-52. In *KTM* (118).
SRTT	69.	"Some Reflections on Thoughts and Things," *Nous* 1 (1967): 97-121. Reprinted as Chapter III of *SM* (63).
CDI	70.	"Reflection on Contrary to Duty Imperatives," *Nous* 1 (1967): 303-44.

KSU	71.	"Kant's Views on Sensibility and Understanding," *Monist* 51 (1967): 463-91. Reprinted as Chapter I of *SM* (63). The first of the six John Locke Lectures.
SPB	72.	"Some Problems about Belief," in *Philosophical Logic*, edited by J. W. Davis, D. T. Hockney, and W. K. Wilson (D. Reidel, 1969): 46-65. Reprinted in *Words and Objections: Essays on the Work of W.V. Quine*, edited by D. Davidson and J. Hintikka (D. Reidel, 1969): 186-205.
NDL	73.	"Are There Non-deductive Logics?" in *Essays in Honor of Carl G. Hempel*, edited by Nicholas Rescher et al., Synthese Library (D. Reidel, 1970): 83-103.
LTC	74.	"Language as Thought and as Communication," *P&PR* 29 (1969): 506-27. Reprinted in *Language and Human Nature*, edited by P. Kurtz (Warren H. Green, 1971) with commentary by M. Dufrenne, E. Morot-Sir, J. Margolis, and E.S. Casey.
KBDW	75.	"On Knowing the Better and Doing the Worse," *International Philosophical Quarterly*, 10 (1970): 5-19. The 1969 Suarez Philosophy Lecture delivered at Fordham University. In *KTM* (118).
SSIS	76.	"Science, Sense Impressions, and Sensa: A Reply to Cornman," *ROM* 25 (1971): 391-447.
TTC	77.	"Towards a Theory of the Categories," *Experience and Theory*, edited by L. Foster and J.W. Swanson (University of Massachusetts Press, 1970): 55-78. In *KTM* (118).
AAE	78.	"Actions and Events," *Nous* 7 (1973): 179-202. Contribution to a symposium on the topic at the University of North Carolina, November, 1969.
SK	79.	"The Structure of Knowledge: (1) Perception; (2) Minds; (3) Epistemic Principles," The Matchette Foundation Lectures for 1971 at the University of Texas. Published in *Action, Knowledge and Reality: Studies in Honor of Wilfrid Sellars*, edited by Hector-Neri Castañeda (Bobbs-Merrill, 1975): 295-347.
RAL	80.	"Reason and the Art of Living in Plato," in *Phenomenology and Natural Existence: Essays in Honor of Marvin Farber*, edited by Dale Riepe (The University of New York Press, 1973): 353-77.
I	81.	"...this I or he or it (the thing) which thinks," the presidential address, American Philosophical Association (Eastern Division), for 1970, *Proceedings of the American Philosophical Association* 44 (1972): 5-31. In *KTM* (118).
RD	82.	"Reply to Donagan," an essay on fatalism and determinism (1971). *PS* 27 (1975): 149-84.
OPM	83.	"Ontology and the Philosophy of Mind in Russell," in *Bertrand Russell's Philosophy*, edited by George Nakhnikian (Duckworth, and Barnes and Noble, 1974): 57-100.
RM	84.	"Reply to Marras," *Canadian Journal of Philosophy* 2 (1973): 485-93.
CC	85.	"Conceptual Change," in *Conceptual Change*, edited by P. Maynard and G. Pearce (D. Reidel, 1973): 77-93.
RQ	86.	"Reply to Quine," *Synthese* 26 (1973): 122-45.
AR	87.	"Autobiographical Reflections: (February, 1973)." Published in *Action, Knowledge and Reality*, edited by H.-N. Castañeda (Bobbs-Merrill, 1975): 277-93.
DKMB	88.	"The Double-Knowledge Approach to the Mind-Body Problem," *The New Scholasticism* 45 (1971): 269-89.
MFC	89.	"Meaning as Functional Classification (A Perspective on the Relation of Syntax to Semantics)," (with replies to Daniel Dennett and Hilary Putnam) *Synthese* 27 (1974): 417-37. Reprinted in *Intentionality, Language and Translation*, edited by J.G. Troyer and S.C. Wheeler, III (D. Reidel, 1974). An expanded version of *BEB*, "Belief and the Expression of Belief", in *Language, Belief, and Metaphysics*, edited by H.E. Kiefer and M.K. Munitz (State University of New York Press, 1970): 146-158.
RDP	90.	"Reply to Dennett and Putnam" *Synthese* 27 (1974): 457-446. Reprinted in *Intentionality, Language and Translation*, edited by J.G. Troyer and S.C. Wheeler, III (D. Reidel, 1974).
IAE	91.	"On the Introduction of Abstract Entities," in *Forms of Representation*, Proceedings of the 1972 Philosophy Colloquium of the University of Western Ontario, edited by B. Freed, A. Marras and P. Maynard (North Holland, 1975): 47-74.

GEC	92.	"Givenness and Explanatory Coherence," (presented at a symposium on Foundations of Knowledge at the 1973 meeting of the American Philosophical Association (Eastern Division)). An abbreviated version is in *JP* 70 (1973): 612-24.
SSS	93.	"Seeing, Seeming, and Sensing," in *The Ontological Turn: Studies in the Philosophy of Gustav Bergmann*, ed. by M.S. Gram and E.D. Klemke (University of Iowa Press, 1974): 195-210. The first in a series of three Matchette Lectures (79).
EPH	94.	*Essays in Philosophy and its History* (D. Reidel, 1974). Includes items (36), (49), (51), (54), (67), (68), (72), (73), (74), (75), (77), (78), (80), (81), (84), (85), (86), and (91).
BD	95.	"Berkeley and Descartes: Reflections on the 'New Way of Ideas'" (presented in 1974 in the Program in the History and Philosophy of Theories of Perception at Ohio State University). Published in *Studies in Perception: Interpretations in the History of Philosophy and Science*, edited by Peter K. Machamer and Robert G. Turnbull (Ohio State University Press, 1977): 259-311. In *KTM* (118).
ATS	96.	"The Adverbial Theory of the Objects of Sensation," in *Metaphilosophy* 6, edited by Terrell Bynum (Basil Blackwell, 1975): 144-60.
VR	97.	"Volitions Re-affirmed," *Action Theory*, edited by Myles Brand and Douglas Walton (D. Reidel, 1976): 47-66. Presented at a conference on action theory at Winnipeg, May, 1975.
KTI	98.	"Kant's Transcendental Idealism" (presented at an International Kant Congress at the University of Ottawa). Published in volume 6, *Collections of Philosophy* (1976): 165-181. In *KTM* (118).
SRT	99.	"Is Scientific Realism Tenable?" (presented at a symposium at the 1976 Philosophy of Science Association Meeting in Chicago). Published in volume II, *Proceedings of PSA* (1976): 307-334.
MMM	100.	"Hochberg on Mapping, Meaning, and Metaphysics," in *Midwest Studies in Philosophy II*, edited by Peter French, Theodore Vehling, Jr., and Howard Wettstein (University of Minnesota Press, 1977): 214-24.
PPHP	101.	*Philosophical Perspectives: History of Philosophy* (Ridgeview Publishing Co., 1977). A reprint of Part I of *Philosophical Perspectives* (62). Includes items (28), (35), (44), (57) and *VTMR*, a rejoinder to Gregory Vlastos on the Third Man Argument, *SC*, "The Soul as Craftsman" (on Plato's Idea of the Good), *AMI*, "Aristotle's Metaphysics: An Interpretation," and *SE*, "Science and Ethics."
PPME	102.	*Philosophical Perspectives: Metaphysics and Epistemology* (Ridgeview Publishing Co., 1977). A reprint of Part II of *Philosophical Perspectives* (62). Includes items (26), (48), (49), (50), (51), (52), (55), (56), and (58).
IKTE	103.	"The Role of Imagination in Kant's Theory of Experience," The Dotterer Lecture 1978 in *Categories: A Colloquium*, edited by Henry W. Johnstone, Jr. (Pennsylvania State University): 231-45. In *KTM* (118).
NAO	104.	*Naturalism and Ontology* (Ridgeview Publishing Co., 1980). The John Dewey Lectures for 1973-4. Reprinted with corrections in 1997.
MGEC	105.	"More on Givenness and Explanatory Coherence," in *Justification and Knowledge*, edited by George Pappas (D. Reidel, 1979): 169-182.
SRPC	106.	"Some Reflections on Perceptual Consciousness," in *Selected Studies in Phenomenology and Existential Philosophy*, edited by R. Bruzina and B. Wilshire (1977): 169-185. In *KTM* (118).
ORAV	107.	"On Reasoning About Values," *APQ* 17 (1980): 81-101. One of three Tsanoff Lectures presented at Rice University, October 1978.
SSOP	108.	"Sensa or Sensings: Reflections on the Ontology of Perception," *PS* 41 (Essays in Honor of James Cornman) (1982): 83-111. Presented at a Colloquium at the University of North Carolina, October 1976.
BLM	109.	"Behaviorism, Language and Meaning," *Pacific Philosophical Quarterly* 61 (1980): 3-30.
FMPP	110.	"Foundations for a Metaphysics of Pure Process" (The Carus Lectures) *The Monist* 64

570 The Philosophical Works of Wilfrid Sellars

		(1981): 3-90.
CPCI	111.	"Conditional Promises and Conditional Intentions (Including a Reply to Castañeda)," in *Agent, Language and the Structure of the World: Essays Presented to Hector-Neri Castaneda, With His Replies*, edited by James E. Tomberlin (Hackett Publishing Co., 1983): 195-221.
PPPW	112.	*Pure Pragmatics and Possible Worlds: The Early Essays of Wilfrid Sellars*, edited and introduced by Jeffrey F. Sicha (Ridgeview Publishing Co., 1980). Includes items (1), (2), (3), (4), (6), (7), (11), (21), and (22).
MEV	113.	"Mental Events," *Philosphical Studies* 39 (1981): 325-45. Contributed to a symposium of that title at the 1980 meeting of American Philosophical Association (Western Division).
TTP	114.	"Towards a Theory of Predication," in *How Things Are*, edited by James Bogen and James McGuire (Reidel, 1983): 281-318. Presented at a conference on predication at Pitzer College in April, 1981.
OAFP	115.	"On Accepting First Principles," in *Philosophical Perspectives, 2, Epistemology, 1988*, edited by James E. Tomberlin (Ridgeview Publishing Co., (1988): 301-14. This paper was written in the sixties but first published here. In *KTM* (118).
ME	116.	*The Metaphysics of Epistemology: Lectures by Wilfrid Sellars*, edited by P.V. Amaral (Ridgeview Publishing Co., 1989).
KPT	117.	*Kant and Pre-Kantian Themes: Lectures by Wilfrid Sellars*, edited by P.V. Amaral (Ridgeview Publishing Co., 2002). In addition to Sellars' Kant lectures, this volume includes lectures on Descartes, Locke, Spinoza (with an introduction by the editor), Leibniz, and a reprint of *APM* (5).
KTM	118.	*Kant's Transcendental Metaphysics: Sellars' Cassirer Lectures and Other Essays*, edited and introduced by Jeffrey F. Sicha (Ridgeview Publishing Co., 2002). In addition to Sellars' notes for his Cassirer Lectures (*CLN*), this volume includes items (67), (68), (75), (77), (81), (95), (98), (103), (106), (115) and *OAPK*, Part I of the unpublished essay whose Part II is (67). (This unpublished essay is listed as entry "1970" in *Circulated Papers and Lectures*. It was actually written in 1966 or 1967, but revised in 1970, or perhaps, late 1969.)
OAPK	119.	OAPK is Part I of the unpublished essay whose Part II is (67). Published in *KTM*.
CLN	120.	Sellars' notes for his Cassirer Lectures, published in *KTM*.
WSNDL	121.	Wilfrid Sellars Notre Dame Lectures 1969-1986, edited by P.V. Amaral (Ridgeview Publishing Company, 2015).
SMCN	122.	Notes from Wilfrid Sellars Metaphysics Lectures 1973-1974, edited by P.V. Amaral (Kindle, 2015).

Additional Works by Wilfrid Sellars (compiled by P. V. Amaral)

Philosophical Letters

1961 To Bruce Aune, October 19, 1961.
   Analysis and explanation of minimal actions and theoretical reduction.
   To Sellars from Aune, October 23, 1961.
1961 To Bruce Aune, November 11, 1961.
1964 To Jack Smart, March 9, 1964.
   A discussion of Theoretical Reduction.
   To Sellars from Smart, February 27, 1964.
   To Sellars from Smart, March 14, 1964.
1965 To David Rosenthal, September 3, 1965.
   The origin of the mental in *NI, SRLG* and *IM*.
   To Sellars from Rosenthal, July 6, 1965.
1965 To David Rosenthal, September 8, 1965.

	To Sellars from Rosenthal, October 2, 1965.
	To Sellars from Rosenthal, December 17, 1965.
1966	To David Rosenthal, January 4, 1966.
1967	To Ruth Barcan Marcas, August 21, 1967.
	The relation of modality and metalanguage.
1970	To Gilbert Harman, February 26, 1970.
	On Harman's review of *SM*.
	To Sellars from Harman, March 24, 1970.
1970	To Gilbert Harman, November 20, 1970.
1971	To Annette Baier, November 30, 1971.
	A discussion of *SPB*.
	To Sellars from Baier, November 29, 1971.
1972	To Jay Rosenberg, July 25, 1972.
	To Sellars from Rosenberg, August 29, 1972.
1972	To Jay Rosenberg, September 5, 1972.
	A clarification of *AE* and the classification of events as objects.
	From Rosenberg to Sellars, September 28, 1972.
1972	To Annette Baier, January 12, 1972.
	To Sellars from Baier, February 7, 1972.
1973	To Jay Rosenberg, January 16, 1973.
1974	To Roderick Firth, April 16, 1974.
1974	To Roderick Firth, February 12, 1974.
1974	To Roderick Firth, January 22, 1974.
	The exchange explores the anti-Cartesian account of sensing and its role in perceiving (*EPM*, *SK*).
	To Sellars from Firth, February 22, 1974.
	To Sellars from Firth, February 2, 1974.
	To Sellars from Firth, January 13, 1974.
1975	To Bruce Aune, June 23, 1975.
	On the logic of Ought-to-do's and *CDI*.
1975	To Ausonio Marras, November 26, 1975.
	On the theoretical character of common sense: *EPM*, *EAE* and *ITM*.
1978	To Michael Loux, June 23, 2978 (reprinted in *NAO*).
1978	To Michael Loux, November 6, 1978 (reprinted in *NAO*).
	To Sellars from Loux, October 6, 1978.
1979	To Bruce Aune, April 30, 1979.
	On the concept of dependent implication.
	To Sellars from Aune, May 15, 1979
	To Sellars from Aune, June 9, 1979.
1979	To Judith Thomson, June 6, 1979
	A discussion of *IIO* and *ORAV*.
	To Sellars from Thompson, May 25, 1979.

Circulated Papers and Lectures

1959	"Inferencia y significado," *Separata de la Revista Universidad de San Carlos*, number 50, Guatemala, C. A. ("Inference and Meaning" translated by by Hector-Neri Castañeda).
1964	"Introduction to the Philosophy of Science," Lectures given at the Summer Institute for the History of Philosophy of Science at The American University, Washington, D.C., June, 1964.
1966	"'Ought' and Moral Principles," February 14, 1966.
1967	"Fatalism and Determinism," a revised version of *FD* (60), 1966.
1967	"Belief and the Expression of Belief," circulated on December 31, 1967, and later incorporated into *LTC* (73), 1969.
1968	"Reason and the Art of Living in Plato," printed as *RAL* (79), a paper presented in a conference

held at Ohio State University, April 5, 1968.
1970 "Ontology, the A Priori and Kant," Part one: introduction, 1970.
1971 "Practical Reasoning Again: Notes for a revision of Thought and Action," August, 1971.
1976 "Is Scientific Realism Tenable?," July 30, 1976, a prelimary draft of *SRT* (97), 1976.
1976 "Kant and Pre-Kantian Philosophy," university lectures on *The Critique of Pure Reason* and its historical framework: Descartes, Leibniz, Spinoza and Hume. May-June, 1976. (Now published a *KPT* (117).)
1977 "Symposium on Materialism," transcripts of a discussion on materialism: Wilfrid Sellars, George Pappas, William Lycan and Robert Turnbull.

www.ingramcontent.com/pod-product-compliance
Lightning Source LLC
Chambersburg PA
CBHW071641160426
43195CB00012B/1318